Henry Chadwick

Spalding`s official Base Ball guide

For 1897

Henry Chadwick

Spalding's official Base Ball guide
For 1897

ISBN/EAN: 9783742802408

Manufactured in Europe, USA, Canada, Australia, Japa

Cover: Foto ©Stingray / pixelio.de

Manufactured and distributed by brebook publishing software (www.brebook.com)

Henry Chadwick

Spalding`s official Base Ball guide

ALBERT G. SPALDING.

SPALDING'S
OFFICIAL
BASE BALL GUIDE
FOR 1897

The Official Book of the National League

CONTAINING

The Revised Code of Playing Rules

(As Reported by the Rules Committee of the League and Adopted at the League Meeting at Baltimore, February, 1897)

AND

Full Records of the Various University and College Club Campaigns of 1896

FULL AND COMPLETE RECORDS OF THE PROFESSIONAL CHAMPIONSHIPS OF 1896

INCLUDING THOSE OF THE PENNANT RACES OF THE NATIONAL LEAGUE AND OF THE MINOR LEAGUES OF THE NATIONAL AGREEMENT CLUBS.

ILLUSTRATED WITH PORTRAITS OF ALL THE LEADING BASE BALL TEAMS.

Edited by HENRY CHADWICK

PUBLISHED BY THE
AMERICAN SPORTS PUBLISHING COMPANY
241 BROADWAY, NEW YORK CITY

ENTERED ACCORDING TO ACT OF CONGRESS, IN THE YEAR 1897, BY THE AMERICAN SPORTS PUBLISHING CO., IN THE OFFICE OF THE LIBRARIAN OF CONGRESS AT WASHINGTON.

PREFACE

THE issue of SPALDING'S OFFICIAL BASE BALL GUIDE for 1897 is the twenty-second annual edition of the work, as published under the auspices of the National League. Moreover, it is the sixth issue of the book under the government of the existing major league of the professional clubs of the country, and is the *only authorized book of the League* and the only work containing the official records and statistics, alike of the National League and the minor leagues of the National Agreement compact. A feature of the GUIDE for the past decade has been its interesting chapters of instructions in the scientific points of the game, from the pen of the oldest and most experienced writer known to the national game. Its statistical features, of course, embrace not only the official records of the twelve clubs of the National League, the averages of which are specially compiled by Secretary Young, but also the statistics of all of the prominent minor leagues.

The GUIDE, too, has now become the record and reference book of the college clubs of the country, and this year, as last, it contains the detailed records of the college club campaigns of 1896, as participated in by the clubs of the large universities of the country, as well as by those of the lesser collegiate organizations.

The new rules of the game, as reported to the League meeting of February, 1897, by the new permanent Committee on Rules, is a very important chapter of this year's GUIDE, especially as it is the only *authorized and official* publication of the rules issued, these rules governing every professional organization in the country, besides the college clubs and the other amateur clubs at large.

AMERICAN SPORTS PUBLISHING COMPANY.

INTRODUCTION

THE history of professional ball playing, while dating, in fact, from the period of the advent of the old Cincinnati Red Stockings in 1868, cannot justly be said to have entered upon a permanent existence until 1871, the year of the establishment of the first professional National Association. Even then the basis of its organization was not such as to give it the permanency it reached under the government of the National League, which followed the old Association in 1876. From that period, up to 1892, professionalism in base ball had a varied and trying life of it, inasmuch as it not only had to resist an outside pressure, in the form of efforts to make it subject to pool gambling influences and its kindred abuses, but it had private enemies to contend with in its own ranks, as shown in the players' revolt in 1890. In 1892, however, the reconstruction of the League, which resulted in the establishment of the existing twelve-club major league, led to so marked an improvement in the methods of governing the professional fraternity as to insure it a long lease of useful and popular life ; and the end of the fifth year of the major league's existence finds it more firmly fixed in the favor of the best class of the patrons of the game than ever before. In fact, the experience of the past five years of professional club history proves conclusively that the combination which led to the enlargement of the National League to a twelve-club organization did valuable work in their reconstruction policy, and before the League reaches the end of the period of its original ten years' lease it will have become so thoroughly a fixture, as the best form of government for the whole professional class, as to fully warrant its continuation for another decade at least.

Year by year, since 1892, have League methods been improved in the regulations made for governing the branches of the major organization, known as the "minor leagues" of the professional arena. It has taken five years of patient and persistent work to develop the existing regulations in governing the minor leagues, and while the field is still open for further improvement in the League's governmental methods in this respect, still the existing position of affairs is such as to warrant congratulations on the success the magnates have thus far achieved.

There is one important fact the minor league magnates

should bear well in mind, and that is, that *the National League cannot antagonize minor league interests in any way except at the cost of the welfare of their own league.* The business interests of both the great major league and the minor organizations are identical; the one as the governmental power of the whole professional fraternity, the other as the governed class. It is folly to suppose that the ruling league would ignore their own best business interests by any selfish action looking to the self-aggrandizement of their own individual clubs at the cost of a loss to any minor league. However appearances may lead the minor league people to think that the major organization is unduly regardless of the former's interests, depend upon it that ultimately the best course for the welfare of both will be found to have been taken. The majority of the National League magnates comprises too many men of integrity, judgment, intelligence and experience, not to mention their wealth, not to use their ruling power to the best advantage of the professional clubs of the country at large. It is very certain that but for the existence of the National League, with its present governmental power, the minor leagues could not do a paying business, even if they could live at all.

There is another fact to be considered in connection with professional base ball, and that is, that the fraternity comprise only the minority class of the practical exemplars of our national game. Bad government by the rulers of the professional class, while it necessarily involves financial disaster to the class as a whole, does not affect the popularity of the game at large. Where there are thousands of amateurs in base ball, professionals can only be counted by the hundred. Nevertheless, the methods of government employed by the professional club rulers have a great and influential bearing on the welfare of the game at large, especially in their establishment of the playing rules of base ball; inasmuch as the code of rules of the National League virtually governs the playing of every base ball club in the country, amateur and professional alike, with some few trifling exceptions. In view of this fact, the yearly amendments which experience points out as necessary for further progress towards a perfected code of rules, should be made with the single idea of improving the game, and not merely to advance the special interests of the minority class. This wise course has, thus far, been adhered to; but there is a tendency to make changes at times subservient to professional club interests alone, and this is why great care should be observed by the League magnates in the organization of their Rules Committee each year, by the selection of men as members who will act conservatively in the matter of changing the rules of play.

NATIONAL LEAGUE

THE YEARLY CHAMPIONSHIP CAMPAIGNS

From 1892 to 1896, Inclusive

N. E. YOUNG,
President of the National League.

IN reviewing the championship campaigns of the National League, from the period of the change made in the number of clubs comprising the League from eight to twelve, we shall confine our comments chiefly to the main features of each season's pennant race, as shown by the figures of the victories and defeats credited and charged to each club during each yearly campaign. When the twelve-club aggregation began its inaugural season in 1892, it did so under the new arrangement of dividing the season's pennant race into two series of contests, the first lasting from April to July and the second from July to September. The end of the campaign of the first half of the season left Boston in the lead, with Brooklyn second and Philadelphia third; Cincinnati, Cleveland and Pittsburg completing the first six clubs in the half season race. The close of the second campaign, however, saw Cleveland in the van, with Boston second and Brooklyn third; Pittsburg, Philadelphia and New York following in order, Cincinnati having been driven into the ranks of the second division, while Baltimore was left as the tail-ender in the first half and Washington in the second half. This left the Bostons and Clevelands as contestants for championship honors for the full season of 1892, and as the Bostons won easily in their world's championship series, they carried off the honors for 1892. A noteworthy fact in connection with this closing series of contests was that the scheduled games were not played to a finish, thereby avoiding all possible charges of hippodroming in connection with them. The record of the two campaigns of 1892 is as follows ·

The Divided Season's Record of 1892.

FIRST HALF.

Clubs.	Won.	Lost.	Per cent.	Clubs.	Won.	Lost.	Per cent.
Boston	52	22	.708	Washington	35	41	.461
Brooklyn	51	26	.662	Chicago	31	39	.443
Philadelphia	46	30	.605	St. Louis	31	42	.425
Cincinnati	44	31	.587	New York	31	43	.419
Cleveland	40	33	.548	Louisville	30	47	.390
Pittsburg	37	39	.487	Baltimore	20	55	.267

SECOND HALF.

Clubs.	Won.	Lost.	Per cent.	Clubs.	Won.	Lost.	Per cent.
Cleveland	53	23	.697	Chicago	39	37	.513
Boston	50	26	.658	Cincinnati	38	37	.507
Brooklyn	44	33	.571	Louisville	33	42	.440
Pittsburg	43	34	.558	Baltimore	26	46	.361
Philadelphia	41	36	.532	St. Louis	25	52	.325
New York	40	37	.519	Washington	23	52	.307

THE FULL SEASON'S RECORD.

The full table, showing the victories and defeats scored by each club with every other club in 1892, is appended:

Clubs of 1892.	Boston.	Cleveland.	Brooklyn.	Philadelphia.	Cincinnati.	Pittsburg.	Chicago.	New York.	Louisville.	Washington.	St. Louis.	Baltimore.	Victories.	Per cent. of Victories.
Boston		8	9	6	8	7	10	11	12	11	7	13	102	.680
Cleveland	6		6	10	9	7	9	8	13	6	8	11	93	.624
Brooklyn	5	8		9	6	10	10	7	9	10	9	12	95	.617
Philadelphia	7	4	5		9	8	9	9	10	9	7	10	87	.569
Cincinnati	5	5	8	5		5	7	8	7	10	12	10	82	.547
Pittsburg	6	7	4	6	9		7	10	6	6	10	9	80	.523
Chicago	4	3	4	5	6	7		10	5	12	7	7	70	.479
New York	3	5	7	5	6	4	4		10	9	9	9	71	.470
Louisville	2	1	5	4	6	8	9	4		8	9	8	63	.414
Washington	3	8	4	5	3	8	2	4	6		8	7	58	.384
St. Louis	7	5	5	7	2	4	5	4	5	6		6	56	.373
Baltimore	0	2	2	4	4	5	4	5	6	6	8		46	.313
Defeats	48	56	59	66	68	73	76	80	89	93	94	101	903	

The above table, showing the aggregate of the victories and defeats scored during the entire season, left Boston, Cleveland and Brooklyn as the three leaders, with Philadelphia, Cincinnati and Pittsburg as the other three of the first division clubs; Washington, St. Louis and Baltimore being left as the three tail-enders. Only seven of the twelve clubs that year won more games than they lost. Boston's record of 102 victories out of 150 games, won and lost, was an exceptional one in League pennant race history   While the difference in percentage points in the whole race, between the leading club and the club eighth on the list was but 210 points, the difference between the figures of the leader and tail-ender was 367 points, showing the race, as a whole, was not an evenly contested one.

The Campaign of 1893.
In 1893 the League returned to the old rule of a single season's campaign; not that the divided season of 1892 had proved to be a decided failure, but from the fact that it did not reach the successful point anticipated. In the campaign of 1893, Boston again proved successful; but Cleveland had to be content with third position, as Pittsburg stood a good second to Boston; Philadelphia, New York and Brooklyn being the next three on the list of the first division clubs of the season, leaving St. Louis, Louisville and Washington as the three tail-enders. This year—the first, with Manager Hanlon in control of the Baltimores—the Cincinnatis and Baltimores were tied for the lead in the second division, Cincinnati being entitled to be named first in order, in consequence of their winning their series with Baltimore by 8 games to 4. Here is the record in full:

RECORD OF 1893.

Clubs of 1898.	Boston.	Pittsburg.	Cleveland.	Philadelphia.	New York.	Brooklyn.	Cincinnati.	Baltimore.	Chicago.	St. Louis.	Louisville.	Washington.	Victories.	Per cent. of Victories.
Boston............................		10	7	8	8	8	6	10	8	10	10	7	86	.662
Pittsburg.........................	6		3	5	8	4	9	11	9	9	8	9	81	.628
Cleveland........................	5	9		3	6	7	5	4	8	9	6	11	73	.570
Philadelphia.....................	4	7	9		5	5	9	7	6	4	8	8	72	.558
New York........................	4	4	6	7		6	6	8	5	8	7	7	68	.515
Brooklyn.........................	4	8	5	6	6		4	2	7	8	7	8	65	.508
Cincinnati.......................	6	3	6	1	6	8		8	7	7	6	7	65	.508
Baltimore........................	2	1	8	5	4	10	4		5	9	5	7	60	.462
Chicago..........................	4	3	4	6	7	3	5	7		3	6	9	51	.445
St. Louis.........................	2	3	3	8	4	4	5	3	9		8	8	57	.432
Louisville........................	2	4	3	4	5	5	6	5	4	4		8	50	.400
Washington.....................	5	2	1	4	5	3	4	5	3	4	4		40	.310
Defeats..........................	44	48	55	57	64	63	63	70	71	75	75	89	774	

The difference in "percentage of victories" figures between the leader and tail-ender in the race in 1893 stood at 352 points, though that between the leader and the eighth club on the list was but 200, this fact showing that a third of the clubs were disproportionately weak in the individual strength of their teams, an arrangement in the make-up of the twelve teams always financially costly to the League at large, as it weakens the attractions of the pennant race in the closing part of the season. The close of the second year of the twelve club League's experience proved conclusively that the new arrangement was undoubtedly advantageous to the League clubs and a marked improvement over that of the old organization.

The Campaign of 1894.

The special, after-season series of contests known as the "World's Championship" series had ended in 1892, the Bostons acquiring the title in 1893 by the fact of there being no competition outside of that of the clubs which had contested for pennant race honors. In 1894, however, a new series of extra championship games were introduced, through the liberality of Mr. Temple, of Pittsburg, who presented to the League a valuable silver cup to be competed for each season by the clubs ending first and second in each season's race. This was virtually a reintroduction of the World's Championship series, to the extent that the winner of the cup series became the champion team of the base ball world in consequence of their defeat of the League champions. While a defeat of the pennant race victors in this extra series did not lessen the merit of their winning the championship of the League, it certainly had the effect of dimming the lustre of their original triumph somewhat. In the exciting race of 1894 the tail-end club of 1892 bore off the championship of 1894, a result due to the introduction of greater excellence in team-work play by the winning club, that itself being a consequence of more skilful management of the victorious team ; the Baltimores, in these essentials of success, leading all of the other clubs of the League in 1894.

The pennant race this year proved to be a closely-contested one as far as the first eight clubs in the contest were concerned, the difference in percentage points between the leader and the club eighth on the list being 263, while the figures showing the difference between the leader and the tail-ender reached as high as 418 points. It was this year that the feature of the pennant race became that of the exciting struggle between the champion Baltimores and the New Yorks in the September campaign, it being a tough contest between Managers Hanlon and Ward for the lead up to the very last week of the campaign, and when the Temple Cup series were contested in

October, the four straight victories which gave Ward's team possession of the trophy for the following year showed how narrow the margin of victory was for the Baltimores at the end of the pennant race in September. In fact, it was almost as much a triumph for Messrs. Talcott and Ward as if their team had won the pennant. Here is the full record of the season:

RECORD OF 1894.

CLUBS OF 1894.	Baltimore.	New York.	Boston.	Philadelphia.	Brooklyn.	Cleveland.	Pittsburg.	Chicago.	St. Louis.	Cincinnati.	Washington.	Louisville.	Victories.	Per cent. of Victories.
Baltimore........................		6	4	6	8	9	6	9	10	10	11	10	89	.695
New York.........................	6		6	5	7	9	8	11	7	7	10	12	88	.667
Boston.............................	8	6		6	6	9	8	7	6	8	9	10	83	.629
Philadelphia.....................	4	7	6		7	5	8	5	5	8	8	8	71	.559
Brooklyn..........................	4	5	6	5		6	7	6	8	6	9	8	70	.534
Cleveland........................	3	3	3	7	5		4	10	9	8	8	8	68	.527
Pittsburg..........................	4	4	4	4	5	8		6	6	7	8	9	65	.500
Chicago...........................	3	1	5	7	6	2	6		6	6	7	8	57	.432
St. Louis..........................	2	5	6	7	4	3	6	6		5	6	6	56	.424
Cincinnati........................	2	5	4	2	6	3	5	6	7		7	7	54	.419
Washington.....................	1	2	3	4	3	4	4	5	6	5		8	45	.341
Louisville.........................	2	0	2	3	4	3	3	4	6	5	4		36	.277
Defeats...........................	39	44	49	56	61	61	65	75	76	75	87	94	782	

It will be seen that Baltimore, New York and Boston ended the season of 1894 as the three leaders, followed by Philadelphia, Brooklyn and Cleveland. Between the leader and the six clubs in the race there was but a difference of 168 points in percentage figures, and as the struggle was prolonged to the very last week of the season, the campaign, to this extent, became one of unusual interest and excitement. Moreover, the general working of the governmental system of the twelve-club League at the end of the third year of its existence had proved to be so very satisfactory that the magnates were congratulated on their having " builded better than they knew " when they reconstructed their organization.

The Campaign of 1895. The fourth year of the League's new chapter of history opened quite auspiciously in 1895; Cincinnati, Pittsburg and Chicago alternating as leaders in the race in the early part of the campaign, while Baltimore had to be content with sixth position, Boston being in the second division up to June. From that month, however, a decided change in the relative position of the leaders began to be made; and by July the clubs which were previously in the van were relegated to end places, and Baltimore, Boston and Cleveland went to the front. In August, the race between the first eight clubs in the contest became intensely interesting, the latter part of August seeing the difference between the percentage of the leader and that of the eighth club reduced to 96 points only. In fact, at one time, Cleveland held such an important lead over Baltimore in the race—.611 to .593 in August—that it was thought that the Orioles would eventually lose the pennant. But they rallied in September, resumed their leading position, and finally came in victors for the second time in succession by a lead of 23 points over Cleveland, the latter leading Philadelphia by 61 points, Chicago, Brooklyn and Boston following in order. At the finish, the difference in percentage points between the leader and the club eighth in the race, stood at 161 points, while that between the leader and tail-ender was 402 points. This year, Washington ended in tenth position, after rising from the last ditch, which they occupied in 1893. The marked falling off in the New York club from their splendid record of the previous year was a disagreeable feature of the season for the metropolitan patrons of the game, who were positive, early in the year, that the 1895 team was a sure pennant winner.

Here is the full record of 1895:

RECORD OF 1895.

CLUBS OF 1895.	Baltimore.	Cleveland.	Philadelphia.	Chicago.	Brooklyn.	Boston.	Pittsburg.	Cincinnati.	New York.	Washington.	St. Louis.	Louisville.	Victories.	Per cent. of Victories.
Baltimore		5	8	8	7	10	7	8	9	9	6	10	87	.669
Cleveland	6		7	5	10	6	7	6	7	9	11	10	84	.646
Philadelphia	4	5		6	7	7	8	8	8	8	7	10	78	.595
Chicago	4	6	6		6	5	8	5	4	9	10	9	72	.554
Brooklyn	5	2	5	6		7	7	5	3	5	9	11	71	.542
Boston	2	6	5	7	4		7	5	9	9	9	9	71	.542
Pittsburg	5	5	4	4	5	5		8	8	8	9	10	71	.538
Cincinnati	4	6	4	7	7	7	4		4	8	9	6	66	.508
New York	3	5	3	8	3	4	4	8		8	11	9	66	.504
Washington	3	3	4	2	7	3	4	2	4		5	6	43	.336
St. Louis	6	1	5	2	3	3	3	1	6			6	39	.298
Louisville	1	2	2	3	1	3	2	6	3	6	6		35	.267
Defeats	43	46	53	58	60	60	61	64	65	85	92	96	783	

The Campaign of 1896.

We now come to the record of the past year's campaign of 1896, which in many respects proved to be the least satisfactory, as a whole, of any in the brief annals of the twelve-club League. The season opened in the middle of April with the defeat of the Baltimore, Cleveland, Philadelphia, Cincinnati, New York and Louisville clubs, respectively, by the Brooklyn, St. Louis, Boston, Pittsburg, Washington and Chicago clubs, and by the end of the April campaign—of fifteen days play—the two Pennsylvania clubs of the West and East, viz., Pittsburg and Philadelphia, occupied first and second positions, the Pirates having won 8 out of 10 games, the Phillies 8 out of 11 and the Bostons 7 out of 11, Cincinnati being fourth with 6 victories out of their first 10 games, while Brooklyn and Washington, of the East, and Chicago and St. Louis, of the West, were tied for fifth position, each with a credit of 6 victories out of 11 games, Baltimore ending the first month of the season in ninth position, with the percentage figures of .455 only, while Cleveland was down to tenth place, with .444 only to its credit, with New York wrestling with the tail-enders of Louisville in their joint efforts to keep out of the last ditch, each having lost 10 out of 11 games. This was a mighty unpleasant beginning of the race for the Giants and their ' fans'' and "cranks,'' while Louisville took comfort in the novel companionship they held on April 30, viz., that of their standing equal with the Temple Cup winners of 1894, while just on the edge of the last ditch themselves. Thus ended the first month's campaign of 1896, a result puzzling to the calculators of odds on the pennant races and discouraging to the metropolitan patrons of the game.

During the May campaign Pittsburg and Philadelphia kept well up in the van in the race up to the middle of the month, Pittsburg leading with the percentage figures of .650 to their credit, while Philadelphia was second with .636, Baltimore and Cleveland by this time—May 15—having pulled up to third and fourth positions, respectively; Boston, Chicago and Cincinnati were tied at .591 each for fifth place, while New York and Louisville were still the two tail-enders. The first week in June saw Baltimore, Cleveland and Cincinnati occupying the three leading positions in the race, followed by Boston, Pittsburg and Philadelphia; Washington and Brooklyn being then tied for seventh place, with Chicago, New York, St. Louis and Louisville comprising the four tail-enders. From the first week in June up to the middle of July the champions, with the Clevelands and Cincinnatis, alternated in taking the lead in the race, the remarkable success of the Cincinnatis being a new and most interesting feature. From that time up to August 4 the Cincinnatis remained in the front, they leading Baltimore on July 28 by the percentage figures of .701 to .658 and Cleveland by .701 to .639. This was their best record of the season, and at the time of these figures being recorded Cincinnati stock was at a premium in the Queen City, and the attendance at their park was exceptional, alike in numbers and the character of the club's patrons. On August 19 the Cincinnatis began their last Eastern tour, and, opening with a victory at Boston, they once more took the lead in the race, this time by the percentage figures of .697 to Baltimore's .694 and Cleveland's .622, Chicago, Pittsburg and Boston, respectively, following in order, leaving Brooklyn, Philadelphia, New York, Washington, St. Louis and Louisville as the six tail-enders in the race, Philadelphia having taken seats on a toboggan as far back as the last week in June. That first August victory of the Cincinnatis in Boston was, however, the culmination of their brilliant record of 1896, for, from August 20 to September 1, inclusive, the Reds lost every game they played, and on the latter date their percentage figures had been reduced from .697 to .627. By the middle of September they had lost no less than ninety-odd points in percentage figures within a month and Cleveland had forced them down to third place, and all hopes of a share of Temple Cup prize money had vanished. However, despite this great disappointment, their full record for the season stands out in bright colors in comparison to that of their work in 1895, and it is a record that the Cincinnati rooters can take pride in.

RECORD OF 1896.

Clubs of 1896.	Baltimore.	Cleveland.	Cincinnati.	Boston.	Chicago.	Pittsburg.	New York.	Philadelphia.	Washington.	Brooklyn.	St. Louis.	Louisville.	Victories.	Per cent. of Victories.
Baltimore.........................		3	10	5	7	9	9	12	10	6	9	10	90	.698
Cleveland........................	8		5	7	9	4	7	6	9	7	10	8	80	.625
Cincinnati.......................	2	6		6	6	5	6	8	7	10	12	9	77	.606
Boston...........................	7	5	5		3	7	7	7	7	10	8	8	74	.565
Chicago..........................	4	2	4	9		11	5	4	8	6	9	9	71	.555
Pittsburg.........................	2	8	7	5	1		8	6	6	5	8	10	66	.512
New York........................	3	5	6	5	7	4		3	6	8	9	8	64	.489
Philadelphia.....................	0	6	4	5	8	6	8		8	4	8	5	62	.477
Washington.....................	2	3	4	5	4	6	6	4		8	7	9	58	.443
Brooklyn........................	6	5	2	2	6	6	4	8	4		7	8	58	.443
St. Louis........................	3	2	0	4	3	3	3	3	5	5		9	40	.308
Louisville.......................	2	3	3	4	3	2	4	7	3	4	3		38	.290
Defeats..........................	39	48	50	57	57	63	67	68	73	73	90	93	778	

As late as August, 1896, the New York team stood no higher than ninth place, both Brooklyn and Philadelphia leading the Giants. About that time, however, the president of the club secured the services of Beckley, of Pittsburg, and, through a deal with Washington, he exchanged a battery team, Flynn and Farrell, the latter a first-class coaching catcher, for Washington's captain, Joyce. This deal was beneficial to both clubs, as Manager Schmelz and Captain Tom Brown brought the Washingtons up to ninth position at the close of the season—at which time they were tied with Brooklyn for that place, and were entitled to be named first on the list in consequence of their having beaten Brooklyn in their pennant series by eight games to four—and the New York Giants took a brace and managed to end the season in seventh position, thereby leading the six second division clubs for 1896. It is worthy of note that the Washington team has gained one point in position every year since 1893, in which year they ended as the tail-end club. They finished eleventh in 1894; tenth in 1895, and ninth in 1896.

The Leaders' and Tail-Enders' Record From 1892 to 1896, Inclusive.

1892.

The Three Leaders.	Victories.	Defeats.	Games.	Per cent. of Victories.	The Three Tail-enders.	Victories.	Defeats.	Games.	Per cent. of Victories.
Boston	102	48	150	.680	Washington	58	93	151	.384
Cleveland	93	56	149	.624	St. Louis	56	94	150	.373
Brooklyn	95	59	154	.617	Baltimore	46	101	147	.313

1893.

Boston	86	44	130	.662	St. Louis	57	75	132	.432
Pittsburg	81	48	129	.628	Louisville	50	75	125	.400
Cleveland	73	52	128	.570	Washington	40	89	129	.310

1894.

Baltimore	89	39	128	.695	Cincinnati	54	75	129	.419
New York	88	44	132	.667	Washington	45	87	132	.341
Boston	83	49	132	.629	Louisville	36	94	130	.277

1895.

Baltimore	87	43	130	.669	Washington	43	85	128	.336
Cleveland	84	46	130	.646	St. Louis	39	92	131	.298
Philadelphia	78	53	131	.595	Louisville	35	96	131	.267

1896.

Baltimore	90	39	129	.698	Brooklyn	58	73	131	.443
Cleveland	80	48	128	.625	St. Louis	40	90	130	.308
Cincinnati	77	50	127	.606	Louisville	38	93	131	.290

From the above table it will be seen that during the past five years of League history only eight clubs have been rated among the three leaders in the pennant races, while six clubs have been ranked among the three tail-enders. Here is the summary:

LEADERS.

First Place—Baltimore, three times; Boston, twice.

Second Place—Cleveland, three times; Pittsburg and New York, once each.

Third Place—Boston, Brooklyn, Philadelphia, Cincinnati and Cleveland, once each.

TAIL-ENDERS.

Tenth Place—Washington, twice; St. Louis, Cincinnati and Brooklyn, once each.

Eleventh Place—St. Louis, three times; Louisville and Washington, once each.

Twelfth Place—Louisville, three times; Baltimore and Washington, once each.

Another interesting summary table is appended, by which it will be seen how the twelve clubs stood, relatively, during the past five years as occupants of positions in one or the other of the two divisions of each season's race. Here is the record in question, viz., the five-year records of the two divisions of the pennant race tables:

THE FIRST AND SECOND DIVISION RECORDS.

1892.

First Division Clubs.	Per cent. of Victories.	Second Division Clubs.	Per cent. of Victories.
Boston......................	.680	Chicago.....................	.479
Cleveland...................	.624	New York...................	.470
Brooklyn....................	.617	Louisville...................	.414
Philadelphia................	.569	Washington................	.384
Cincinnati...................	.547	St. Louis....................	.373
Pittsburg....................	.523	Baltimore...................	.318

1893.

Boston......................	.662	Cincinnati	.508
Pittsburg....................	.628	Baltimore...................	.462
Cleveland...................	.570	Chicago.....................	.445
Philadelphia................	.558	St. Louis....................	.432
New York...................	.515	Louisville...................	.400
Brooklyn	.508	Washington................	.310

1894.

First Division Clubs.	Per cent. of Victories.	Second Division Clubs.	Per cent. of Victories.
Baltimore	.695	Pittsburg	.500
New York	.667	Chicago	.432
Boston	.629	St. Louis	.424
Philadelphia	.559	Cincinnati	.419
Brooklyn	.534	Washington	.341
Cleveland	.527	Louisville	.277

1895.

Baltimore	.669	Pittsburg	.538
Cleveland	.646	Cincinnati	.508
Philadelphia	.595	New York	.504
Chicago	.554	Washington	.336
Brooklyn	.542	St. Louis	.298
Boston	.542	Louisville	.267

1896.

Baltimore	.698	New York	.489
Cleveland	.625	Philadelphia	.473
Cincinnati	.606	Washington	.448
Boston	.565	Brooklyn	.443
Chicago	.555	St. Louis	.308
Pittsburg	.512	Louisville	.290

✳ ✳ ✳

Every batsman should be charged with a time at bat whenever he gives a chance to the field for an out, no matter whether the chance is accepted or not. Thus, if a batsman hits a foul ball and the chance for a catch is missed, he should be charged with a time at the bat. He should also be charged with a time at the bat if he hits once or twice at the ball without striking it, for he has then had a fair chance to hit the ball and has failed to make a fair hit, and this should, in every case, constitute a time at the bat.

Where is the pitcher that has not had a bad off-day or two in his box-work and been badly punished by having runs earned from base-hits scored against him? There is not one such in the entire professional arena, and yet if a pitcher has one or two of these off-day experiences unexpectedly up goes a howl about his being "played out," a " back number," etc.

It has been pretty clearly demonstrated by practical experience in box-work that with a pitcher who combines great speed with thorough command of the ball, the best point to play in his position is to *put the ball over the plate*. Curves are worse than useless unless you can command that style of delivery enough to curve the ball over the plate. If you cannot be sure of your curves in this respect, send them in swift and straight over the base. Of course, to be able to control your curves so as to put them over the plate is the very acme of pitching skill, but where is the pitcher who can? The habit of putting the ball over the home plate keeps the batsman on the rack and prevents him from having the time to coolly judge the ball which wild curve pitching affords him. In fact, when every ball comes in over the plate, he has to be ready to bat all the time and it is quite a strain on his nerves.

Pitching – Batting – Fielding – Base Running

MORE skilful, strategic pitching, finer exhibitions of fielding, or a higher degree of excellence in the art of place hitting by batsmen, was never seen in any season's campaign in the annals of the National League than that shown by a majority of the clubs in the League's championship campaign of 1896. The display, too, of the art of base-running was also as prominent as the utter failure of the observance of the balk rule last season would admit of. As a natural consequence, the club which excelled in the science of the game in these essentials of success, bore off the honors of the season. It was shown last year, that while the art of fielding had about reached the point of perfection in base ball, that of batting, though of slow growth, still needed advancement. Though old "rutty" methods of handling the bat still prevail—as illustrated in the habit of "fungo" hitting, viz., that of giving easy chances for catches to the outfielders—there was more of the true art of batting seen at the hands of the leading clubs last season than ever before; the latter being exhibited in "*playing for the side*" in batting; that is, in making every hit tell in forwarding runners around the bases, even at the cost of self-sacrifice in consequent outs. Superiority in all these requirements of a pennant-winning team, undoubtedly gave the championship honors of the season to the ably managed team of the Baltimore club. Their team not only worked together with more unity of effort and did more intelligent base-running than the others, but especially excelled in sending runners forward by their batting; while their field support and battery work was up to the highest mark. They achieved the highest honors won by any club in the League during the past five years in 1896, as they not only won the pennant race for the third year in succession, but also the Temple Cup series; and the latter by four straight victories, thereby defeating one of the only two clubs which won a series from them in the pennant race.

All three of the leading clubs did fine work in the field in the four special departments of the game, Baltimore leading the trio in thorough team-work, especially in batting; Cleveland playing up to a high mark in fielding; while Cincinnati held the best record in base-running; the trio being pretty equal in the pitching department, though, taking the season's work as a whole, the Baltimore pitchers bore off the palm.

The Pitching of 1896.

Gradually, but surely, is the art of pitching receiving more attention each year at the hands of the intelligent minority of the occupants of the pitcher's box; and especially was this fact noticeable during the past season of 1896. For one thing, the class of educated ball players has been considerably increased in the National League arena of late years; and hence more attention is devoted to the work of studying up the theory of the art of pitching, and less to that of the habit of following in the timeworn footsteps of pitching predecessors than of old. Experience shows, more and more each year, that the pitching corps of a club's team is the main dependence for success in winning pennants; though it, of course, needs the important assistance of thorough team-work support in the field, as also at the bat and in base-running, to make the team complete as a whole. Season after season has the fact been plainly realized that mere machine work in the pitcher's box has become less and less effective, as the power of defence, at the hands of skilful batsmen, has increased. In this connection it may be truly said that the days of the mere "cyclone" pitcher—the pitcher whose only strength lies in the intimidating speed of his wild delivery—have been numbered, and that those pitchers are being yearly replaced by skilled strategists in the position, whose "head-work" delivery makes them potent factors in a corps of pennant winners.

The annals of the League do not show a single season in which the art of pitching was as strikingly illustrated on its club grounds as in 1896. The special points of really skilful pitching were more frequently exhibited in the League arena during the past season than ever before. Batsmen were more frequently deceived as to the character of the pitching than hitherto; then, too, that effective point of a well disguised change of pace in delivery was brought into play with more telling effect; in addition to which, greater command of the ball by the pitchers—as shown by the lessened average of bases on balls—was exhibited last year than in any previous season. The curves, too, were used with greater effect, especially the eye-deceiving, slow, "drop" ball, which has never been practised with greater success than in 1896.

The past season's pitching may be said to have been exceptionable in regard, not only to the success of the "colts" on League fields, but also in the number of revived veterans, who, in leaving off all machine work in pitching and taking on new points of play in their positions, have come more into line with the true art of pitching than ever before. With all this march of improvement in box-work shown by a minority of League pitchers in 1896, there still remains some habitual weaknesses in their methods which need reforming, to make the work of the corps complete as a whole; and among these "rutty" ways in box-work is that of the folly of failing to control quick tempers, which was characteristic of the majority of the League pitchers of 1896. A pitcher who lacks control of his temper can never excel in strategic skill. Another striking weakness exhibited by the majority of the League pitchers during the past season was that shown by the stupidity of "kicking" against an umpire's decisions on balls and strikes. This latter habit is so plainly at war with common sense that it is surprising that any intelligent player, who excels in other respects in head-work play, will indulge in it. It certainly offsets much of the good work in pitching accomplished in 1896. It is part and parcel of judicious head-work in pitching to curry favor with the umpire, not to obtain partial decisions, but in order to avoid his being prejudiced against you. Every pitcher who kicks against decisions on balls and strikes makes an opponent of the umpire. Nothing can possibly be gained by kicking, while there is no doubt of the costly nature of the stupid habit. No decision of the kind can be reversed, to begin with, while it goes without saying that the pitcher who insults the umpire by questioning his integrity and judgment—as every "kicker" does—is not going to have any doubtful point decided in his favor.

An important matter for serious consideration at the hands of team managers and captains came into notice in 1896, relative to the amount of box-work a pitcher is capable of enduring each week of a season, and attention was called to the subject by the occurrence of a practical investigation of the condition of a pitcher's arm, which had been overworked in curve-pitching. The case in question was that of a pitcher who, at his death, in October last, willed his diseased arm to a surgeon. The surgeon, on examining the arm, found that certain of the muscles had become so twisted as to form a bunch like a ball just above his forearm, thereby rendering the arm quite useless for ordinary purposes. The question naturally arises, How far can a pitcher go in the exercise of the particular muscles brought into active use in developing the curves in pitching without positive injury to his arm? Old pitchers, of the early period of professional ball playing, have been apt to smile rather derisively at the complaints of modern pitchers of being overworked by going in the box every other day or so, remembering, as the veterans did, how, of old, they were accustomed to pitch day in and day out for an entire season without complaint of overwork. But the veterans forget that in their time, curved pitching was almost unknown; only the muscles required in ordinary straight pitching then being used. In accomplishing the variety of curves used in modern pitching, however, a class of previously unused muscles are brought into play, such as those required to give the rotary motion to the pitched ball so necessary in developing the "in" and "out" curves, the "down shoot" and "rising ball," and the "drop ball" in vogue in modern curve pitching. The knowledge of the costly nature of too much work in curve pitching, develops the fact, that a more numerous corps of pitchers will be required in a team for up-to-date box-work than was necessary in the decade of the seventies.

The Pitching Statistics of 1896.

The only reliable criterion of a pitcher's skill in the box is that based on the average of runs earned off the pitching by base hits, *and by such hits only*. Next to this is the percentage of victories pitched in; and lastly—and the least reliable of any—is that of runs earned by the combination of base hits, stolen bases and the special errors base stealing leads to. As there is no other data for judging the pitching used by the League Secretary than that of the latter combination, we are forced to use that of the percentage of victories pitched in, and this is the data which will be used in the GUIDE until the League scoring rules are so amended as to admit of the correct data of runs earned by base hits only.

The first record of the pitching statistics of 1896 is that of the total percentage of victories credited to the full corps of pitchers of each of the twelve League clubs of 1896; and these will be found in the appended table, which not only gives the percentage of victories of each club for the entire season, but also the percentage figures of each club in the first and second divisions, the latter being an important record in judging the pitching strength of each club. The club corps leading in percentage against the six first division clubs, of course, taking the lead of those who excelled only against the six second division clubs.

Here is the record in question:

THE SEASON'S CLUB PERCENTAGES OF VICTORIES.

Rank.	Percentage with First Division Clubs.	Per cent.	Rank.	Percentage with Second Division Clubs.	Per cent.	Rank.	Percentage of Total Record.	Per cent.
1	Baltimore	.596	1	Baltimore	.778	1	Baltimore	.698
2	Cleveland	.579	2	Cleveland	.727	2	Cleveland	.625
3	Chicago	.536	3	Boston	.653	3	Cincinnati	.606
4	Boston	.458	4	Cincinnati	.642	4	Boston	.565
5	Cincinnati	.446	5	Pittsburg	.614	5	Chicago	.555
6	Philadelphia	.403	6	Washington	.600	6	Pittsburg	.512
7	Pittsburg	.390	7	New York	.576	7	New York	.489
8	Brooklyn	.380	8	Chicago	.569	8	Philadelphia	.477
9	Washington	.338	9	Philadelphia	.559	9	Washington	.443
10	New York	.333	10	Brooklyn	.517	10	Brooklyn	.443
11	Louisville	.239	11	St. Louis	.424	11	St. Louis	.308
12	St. Louis	.211	12	Louisville	.356	12	Louisville	.290

It is a noteworthy fact that the two clubs which stand first and second in the pennant race, also occupy similar positions in the record of the percentage of victories pitched in by their respective pitching corps; and also, that the two clubs last on this latter list, occupy the tail-end positions in the pitching percentages table. In the record, however, showing the relative positions of the twelve clubs in the pitching percentages of the two separate divisions, quite a difference is shown between the percentage figures of clubs against first division clubs, and the figures of the clubs against those of the second division. For instance, it will be seen that Chicago leads Boston in their pitching percentages against the first division clubs, while Boston leads Chicago against those of the second division. Then, too, Cincinnati, which club was third in total pitching percentages, is fifth against first division clubs, while being fourth in the second class. In fact, while it will be seen that the club pitching teams of Chicago, Philadelphia, Brooklyn and Louisville did better box-work against their first division opponents than did those of Boston, Cincinnati, Pittsburg, Washington and St. Louis, yet in the percentages as a whole, almost the reverse was the case. The conclusion from these figures is, that the Chicago pitchers were more effective against the six leaders than against the six tail-enders, as were the Cincinnati, Philadelphia, Brooklyn and Louisville pitchers. Managers of League teams may, perhaps, learn a lesson from these statistics which will guide them in the make-up of their pitching corps for 1897.

The Individual Pitching Percentages of 1896. We now come to the table of the percentage of victories pitched in by the leading pitcher of each club, and appended will be found the full record of the percentage figures of each leading pitcher for the entire season, as also that of the percentages of each in pitching against the six clubs of each division. Only the names of pitchers who pitched in at least ten games, are given.

INDIVIDUAL PITCHING TABLE.

Pitchers.	Clubs.	Victories.	Defeats.	Games.	Per cent. of Victories.	First Div. Percentage.	Second Div. Percentage.
Hoffer	Baltimore	26	7	33	.778	.800	.778
Dwyer	Cincinnati	25	10	35	.714	.579	.875
Griffith	Chicago	23	11	34	.676	.667	.684
Young	Cleveland	29	14	43	.674	.615	.765
Nichols	Boston	30	15	45	.667	.556	.741
Meekin	New York	26	13	39	.667	.682	.647
Orth	Philadelphia	15	9	24	625	.533	.778
Killen	Pittsburg	31	19	50	.620	.542	.692
Mercer	Washington	25	19	44	.568	.500	.650
Daub	Brooklyn	14	11	25	.560	.563	.556
Breitenstein	St. Louis	17	26	43	.395	.273	.524
Frazer	Louisville	13	25	38	.342	.158	.526

The table showing the figures of the victories and defeats pitched in by the leading pitcher of each club against the six clubs of the two divisions, is as follows:

THE DIVISION PITCHING RECORD.

Pitchers.	First Division.				Pitchers.	Second Division.			
	Won.	Lost.	Played.	Per cent.		Won.	Lost.	Played.	Per cent.
Hoffer	12	3	15	.800	Dwyer	14	2	16	.875
Meekin	15	7	22	.682	Hoffer	14	4	18	.778
Griffith	10	5	15	.667	Orth	7	2	9	.778
Young	16	10	26	.615	Young	13	4	17	.765
Dwyer	11	8	19	.579	Nichols	20	7	27	.741
Daub	9	7	16	.563	Killen	18	8	26	.692
Nichols	10	8	18	.556	Griffith	13	6	19	.684
Killen	13	11	24	.542	Mercer	13	7	20	.650
Orth	8	7	15	.533	Meekin	11	6	17	.647
Mercer	12	12	24	.500	Daub	5	4	9	.556
Breitenstein	6	16	22	.273	Frazer	10	9	19	.524
Frazer	3	16	19	.158	Breitenstein	11	10	21	.524

The above table shows the value of each pitcher's box-work to a more important extent than the first table does, as it shows which pitcher took the lead of the others in pitching against the six leading clubs, that being the test record of the best work done in the box during the season. It will be seen, for instance, that while Hoffer led Dwyer considerably in pitching against the six leading clubs, Dwyer bore off the palm in leading against the second-class clubs. The question arises: Why is it that a pitcher who is so effective against the six leaders, falls down in his box-work when facing the six tail-enders? It will be seen, in this respect, what a contrast there was between Meekin's pitching against the leaders and what he did against the second-class clubs. In the former he stood second to Hoffer, with the percentage figures of .682, while against the second-class clubs he stood ninth, with the percentage of .647; Griffith, too, who was third against the leaders, stood seventh against the tail-enders. It will be noticed that the Baltimore pitching corps stood at the head against those of both divisions, while Cleveland stood second against both; Breitenstein and Frazer were the last two tail-end pitchers against both classes; though Frazer did better against the first-class clubs than Breitenstein.

※ ※ ※

It may be justly said that the life of a professional base ball player, during his season's play on the field, is not the hard one some people are apt to imagine. Its dangers are, of course, considerable and cannot be avoided. Injuries to the hands from fielding the ball, to the legs or feet from sliding to bases or collisions are often serious and disable a man for weeks, months and even for a season. The injuries are few, however, compared with the number of games played, and the evolution of the game is such that protections in the shape of masks, breast protectors and heavy gloves keep pace with the demand for safeguards against increasing dangers.

The contrast between old-time salaries in professional base ball of the old-time period and those of the present is very great. The salary list of the only professional club that ever played a season without sustaining a defeat was $9,100, that being the sum paid the Cincinnati Red Stockings in 1869. Ten men constituted the team. George Wright got $1,800, Harry Wright $1,500, Brainard, pitcher, Gould and Waterman, first and third baseman, $800 each; Sweasy, second baseman; Allison, catcher; Leonard and McVey, fielders, $700 each; Hurley, substitute, $600. Contrast these figures with the $30,000 club salary lists of 1895 and 1896. When Mike Kelly, of the Boston team—the $10,000 star—first played ball in the Olympic club, of Paterson, N. J., in 1875, he was well content with the $12 a week salary he then received. In 1887 he received $5,000 for six months' servicre. What a difference in a dozen years.

Anson, in managing his colts' team some years ago, said: "There isn't a man in the Chicago team can be called a good sacrifice hitter, and anybody who can hit the ball at all can become quite proficient as a bunter if he will only spend a little time in practicing. The boys must practice bunting." Just as long as the papers praise record-hitting for home runs just so long will team-work at the bat be neglected. "Fungo" hitting is the weakness of the present time in all of our League teams.

League Club Pitching — Individual Records

BELOW we give not only the full table showing the season's pitching record in percentage of victories pitched in by every pitcher employed by the club during the season, but also a special table showing which pitcher—of those who pitched not less than five games—excelled in each of the two divisions. The names are given in the order of best percentage of victories, except in the instance of where a pitcher has occupied the box in but a single game. For instance, a player may have scored a percentage of 1.000 in a single game with the tail-end team in the race, while another may have pitched in five or six games against the first division clubs, and yet only have scored a percentage of .500; yet the latter's record is really the best of the two, taken as a whole.

Here is the full record of the pitching corps of the Baltimore club for 1896:

THE RECORD OF 1896.

BALTIMORE vs.		Cleveland.	Cincinnati.	Boston.	Chicago.	Pittsburg.	Totals.	New York.	Philadelphia.	Washington.	Brooklyn.	St. Louis.	Louisville.	Totals.	Grand Totals.	Per cent. of Victories.
		First Division.						Second Division.								
Hoffer	Won	1	4	2	2	3	12	2	3	3	1	4	1	14	26	.778
	Lost	0	0	2	1	0	3	0	0	0	3	0	1	4	7	
Corbett	Won	0	0	1	0	0	1	1	0	0	0	0	1	2	3	.750
	Lost	1	0	0	0	0	1	0	0	0	0	0	0	0	1	
Esper	Won	0	0	0	4	4	8	3	3	2	0	1	1	10	14	.787
	Lost	4	0	0	0	0	4	0	0	0	0	1	0	1	5	
Hemming	Won	0	2	1	0	0	3	2	3	1	1	1	4	12	15	.682
	Lost	0	0	0	0	2	2	1	0	0	2	1	1	5	7	
Nops	Won	0	0	0	0	0	0	0	1	0	1	0	0	2	2	.667
	Lost	0	0	0	0	0	0	1	0	0	0	0	0	1	1	
Pond	Won	1	2	1	1	2	7	0	1	2	3	1	1	8	15	.652
	Lost	2	1	2	1	0	6	1	0	1	0	0	0	2	8	
McMahon	Won	0	2	0	3	0	5	1	1	1	0	2	2	7	12	.600
	Lost	1	1	2	1	0	5	0	0	1	1	1	0	3	8	
Clarkson	Won	1	0	0	1	0	2	0	0	1	0	0	0	1	3	.600
	Lost	0	0	1	1	0	2	0	0	0	0	0	0	0	2	

Per cent. of victories—Against Cleveland, .273; Cincinnati, .888; Boston, .417; Chicago, .636; Pittsburg, .818; total, first division clubs, .596. New York, .750; Philadelphia, 1.000; Washington, .888; Brooklyn, .500; St. Louis, 750; Louisville, .888; total, second division clubs, .778. Grand total, .698.

While a pitcher may lead in percentage of victories in the full record, the true test of his ability lies more in his work against the six clubs of the first division; for, in the ranks of the six leaders in the race are gathered the best batsmen, as a rule, though, it is not always batting that gives a club the lead. We have, therefore, prepared a special table, in addition to the above, which latter gives a summary of the division work done by the pitchers of the corps who have pitched in at least five games during the season, and below is the special record in question:

DIVISION RECORD.

PITCHERS.	FIRST DIVISION.				PITCHERS.	SECOND DIVISION.			
	Won.	Lost.	Played.	Per cent.		Won.	Lost.	Played.	Per cent.
Hoffer	12	3	15	.800	Clarkson	1	0	1	1.000
Hemming	3	2	5	.600	Esper	10	1	11	.909
Pond	7	6	13	.538	Pond	8	2	10	.800
McMahon	5	5	10	.500	Hoffer	14	4	18	.778
Esper	4	4	8	.500	Hemming	12	5	17	.706
Clarkson	2	2	4	.500	McMahon	7	3	10	.700

The above tables present a pitching record for the club corps unequalled by that of any other of the twelve clubs, inasmuch as there is not a pitcher of the entire Baltimore corps whose percentage of victories figures is below .600; and there is not another League corps which equals this record. It will be seen that Hoffer not only leads in the full record, but also in the record of the pitching against the first division clubs. Corbett is second in the full record; but he only pitched in four games, while Hoffer pitched in thirty-three games. Moreover, Hoffer had a record of .800 in percentage of victories against the first division teams, while Corbett pitched in but two games against the first division clubs, losing one with Cleveland and winning one with Boston. This young pitcher's success in the Temple Cup series, however, won him his merited notoriety in 1896. It was the even work done by the Baltimore corps of pitchers as a whole, that so materially aided in the club's ultimate success, and not the individual box-work of a noted star pitcher. No one pitcher, or even two, of stellar reputation, can make a winning team; an evenly matched corps is the most effective "battery" force. It will be seen that the club employed eight pitchers during the season, and all reached the percentage figures of .600 and over.

The Cleveland Club's Pitching Record of 1896.

The Cleveland club employed but six pitchers in all in 1896, and two of the six, Chamberlain and Gear, only pitched in three of the club games, and neither won a game. The pitching corps of the club, in fact, consisted of Young, Cuppy, Wilson and Wallace, and this strong quartette made a fine record, not one of them securing a less percentage than .600.

RECORD OF 1896.

CLEVELAND vs.		Baltimore.	Cincinnati.	Boston.	Chicago.	Pittsburg.	Totals.	New York.	Philadelphia.	Washington.	Brooklyn.	St. Louis.	Louisville.	Totals.	Grand Totals.	Per cent. of Victories.
		First Division.						Second Division.								
Young	Won	4	3	5	4	0	16	2	2	2	1	2	4	13	29	.674
	Lost	1	3	1	1	4	10	1	1	0	1	1	0	4	14	
Wilson	Won	0	1	0	2	2	5	1	2	3	2	3	1	12	17	.630
	Lost	1	1	1	0	1	4	1	2	1	0	1	1	6	10	
Cuppy	Won	4	1	1	3	2	11	2	2	2	1	4	3	14	25	.625
	Lost	1	2	3	0	1	7	2	3	2	1	0	0	8	15	
Wallace	Won	0	0	1	0	0	1	2	0	2	3	1	0	8	9	.600
	Lost	0	0	0	1	0	1	1	0	0	3	0	1	5	6	
Chamberlain	Won	0	0	0	0	0	0	0	0	0	0	0	0	0	0	.000
	Lost	0	0	0	0	1	1	0	0	0	0	0	0	0	1	
Gear	Won	0	0	0	0	0	0	0	0	0	0	0	0	0	0	.000
	Lost	0	0	0	0	1	1	0	0	0	0	0	1	1	2	

Per cent. of victories—Against Baltimore, .727; Cincinnati, .455; Boston, .563; Chicago, .818; Pittsburg, .333; total, first division clubs, .519. New York, .583; Philadelphia, .500; Washington, .750; Brooklyn, .583; St. Louis, .855; Louisville, .727; total, second division clubs, .662. Grand total, .625.

Young not only excelled in percentage figures in the full table but also against the first division clubs, Wilson being second in the former table but third against the leading clubs, Cuppy excelling him against the leaders. Both Cuppy and Young were very effective against the Baltimores.

DIVISION RECORD.

PITCHERS.	First Division.				PITCHERS.	Second Division.			
	Won.	Lost.	Played.	Per cent.		Won.	Lost.	Played.	Per cent.
Young	16	10	26	.615	Young	13	4	17	.765
Cuppy	11	7	18	.611	Wilson	12	6	18	.667
Wilson	5	4	9	.556	Cuppy	14	8	22	.636
Wallace	1	1	2	.500	Wallace	8	5	13	.615

Young's best record was made against the Boston team, while Cuppy's best record was against St. Louis; Wallace did his best against Washington batsmen, and Wilson against those of Chicago.

The Cincinnati Club's Pitching Record of 1896. The Cincinnati club's pitching corps of 1896 numbered no less than nine pitchers, of whom but five pitched in five games and over. Dwyer led the corps, not only by the highest percentage figures in the full record but also in both the division records, Frank Foreman being second in the full season's record and Rhines third. In the first division table, however, Rhines led Foreman. Fisher stood fourth in the full record, but he did not pitch in a single victory against the six leaders, Ehret leading all but Dwyer in the first division record. Ehret also was the most effective against the Baltimores. Gear pitched in only one game, a victory, as did Gastright, a defeat. J. Foreman was a failure in the box in 1896 with the Cincinnatis, though he did fairly well with the Pittsburgs. Inks pitched but two games.

Here is the full record:

RECORD OF 1896.

CINCINNATI vs.		Baltimore.	Cleveland.	Boston.	Chicago.	Pittsburg.	Totals.	New York.	Philadelphia.	Washington.	Brooklyn.	St. Louis.	Louisville.	Totals.	Grand Totals.	Per cent. of Victories.
Dwyer	Won	1	2	2	3	3	11	1	2	3	2	4	2	14	25	.714
	Lost	3	1	2	1	1	8	0	1	0	0	0	1	2	10	
F. Foreman	Won	0	2	0	1	0	3	2	2	2	1	1	1	9	12	.667
	Lost	2	0	1	0	2	5	0	0	1	0	0	0	1	6	
Rhines	Won	0	2	1	0	1	4	0	1	0	2	0	3	6	10	.588
	Lost	1	1	0	0	1	3	1	1	1	0	0	1	4	7	
Fisher	Won	0	0	0	0	0	0	1	1	3	3	1	0	9	9	.563
	Lost	1	1	0	2	0	4	2	1	0	0	0	3	7	
Ehret	Won	1	0	3	2	0	6	2	2	1	2	3	2	12	18	.545
	Lost	1	2	2	1	3	9	1	1	2	1	0	1	6	15	
Inks	Won	0	0	0	0	0	0	0	0	0	0	1	0	1	1	.500
	Lost	0	0	0	0	0	0	1	0	0	0	0	0	1	1	
J. Foreman	Won	0	0	0	0	0	0	1	0	0	0	0	0	1	1	.250
	Lost	2	0	0	0	0	2	1	0	0	0	0	0	1	3	
Gear	Won	0	0	0	0	1	1	0	0	0	0	0	0	0	1	1.000
	Lost	0	0	0	0	0	0	0	0	0	0	0	0	0	0	
Gastright	Won	0	0	0	0	0	0	0	0	0	0	0	0	0	0	.000
	Lost	0	0	0	0	0	0	0	0	1	0	0	0	1	1	

Per cent. of victories—Against Baltimore, .167; Cleveland, .545; Boston, .545; Chicago, .600; Pittsburg, .417; total, first division clubs, .446. New York, .500; Philadelphia, .667; Washington, .636; Brooklyn, .833; St. Louis, 1.000; Louisville, .750; total, second division clubs, .732. Grand total, .606.

The highest percentage of victories made by the whole corps against a club was that against the St. Louis team, and the smallest was that made against the Baltimores.

In the record showing which pitchers excelled in the two divisions, Dwyer, while leading in the first division, scored the high percentage figures of .933 in the second. He won every game he pitched in against the batsmen of the New York, Washington, Brooklyn and St. Louis clubs, and in three out of four games each with Chicago and Pittsburg; in fact, only one club got the best of him and that one was Baltimore, his field support being demoralized when facing the Orioles.

Here is the division record:

DIVISION RECORD.

PITCHERS.	FIRST DIVISION.				PITCHERS.	SECOND DIVISION.			
	Won.	Lost.	Played.	Per cent.		Won.	Lost.	Played.	Per cent.
Dwyer	11	8	19	.579	Dwyer	14	2	16	.933
Rhines	4	3	7	.571	F. Foreman	9	1	10	.900
F. Foreman	3	5	8	.375	Fisher	9	3	12	.750
Ehret	6	9	15	.357	Ehret	12	6	18	.667
Fisher	0	4	4	.000	Rhines	6	4	10	.600

Frank Foreman was very effective against the second division clubs.

The Boston Club's Pitching Record of 1896. The Boston club employed eight pitchers in 1896, of whom but one pitched in less than five games, and that one was Yerrick, who lost every game he pitched in. Nichols bore off the palm in the full season's record, with Stivetts second and Klobedanz third. But against the batsmen of the first division clubs Klobedanz led, with Nichols second and Stivetts third. Sullivan was the most effective against the Baltimores, except Nichols. Mains was the only other pitcher who reached the percentage of .500 and over in the full season's record. Nichols was the most successful against the St. Louis batsmen, and the least against those of Chicago. Stivetts led against Brooklyn, but found the Clevelands hard to pitch against. Klobedanz was effective against Cincinnati and Chicago, but the Baltimores troubled him, as did also the New Yorks. Mains won a game with the Clevelands, and Sullivan two with the Baltimores. The others did not win a game against a first division club.

Here is the full season's record:

RECORD OF 1896.

BOSTON vs.		First Division.						Second Division.					Grand Totals.	Per cent. of Victories.
		Baltimore.	Cleveland.	Cincinnati.	Chicago.	Pittsburg.	Totals.	New York.	Philadelphia.	Washington.	Brooklyn.	St. Louis.	Louisville.	Totals.		
Nichols	Won	3	2	2	0	3	10	3	4	3	3	4	3	20	30	.682
	Lost	1	1	2	4	0	8	2	1	1	1	0	1	7	15	
Stivetts	Won	2	0	2	1	2	7	2	1	1	5	2	4	15	22	.629
	Lost	1	3	1	1	1	7	1	1	3	0	1	0	6	13	
Klobedanz	Won	0	1	1	1	1	4	0	0	1	0	1	0	2	6	.600
	Lost	1	1	0	0	1	3	1	0	0	0	0	0	1	4	
Mains	Won	0	1	0	0	0	1	1	0	0	0	0	1	2	3	.600
	Lost	0	0	1	0	0	1	0	0	0	0	0	1	1	2	
Sullivan	Won	2	1	0	1	1	5	0	2	2	1	1	0	6	11	.458
	Lost	0	2	1	3	0	6	1	2	1	1	2	0	7	13	
Lewis	Won	0	0	0	0	0	0	0	0	0	1	0	0	1	1	.200
	Lost	0	0	0	1	1	2	0	0	0	0	1	1	2	4	
Dolan	Won	0	0	0	0	0	0	1	0	0	0	0	0	1	1	.200
	Lost	1	0	0	0	2	3	0	1	0	0	0	0	1	4	
Yerrick	Won	0	0	0	0	0	0	0	0	0	0	0	0	0	0	.000
	Lost	1	0	1	0	0	2	0	0	0	0	0	1	1	3	

Per cent. of victories—Against Baltimore, .583; Cleveland, .417; Cincinnati, .455; Chicago, .250; Pittsburg, .583; total, first division clubs, .458. New York, .583; Philadelphia, .583; Washington, .583; Brooklyn, .833; St. Louis, .667; Louisville, .667; total, second division clubs, .653. Grand total, .565.

It will be seen that but four of the eight pitchers reached a percentage record of .500 and over; that being the average of fair work in the box, all figures below that, of course, showing more defeats than victories. The smallest percentage of victories figures by the whole corps of pitchers was made against the Chicago club, and the highest against the Brooklyn and St. Louis teams. Here is the division record of the season:

DIVISION RECORD.

	First Division.					Second Division.			
Pitchers.	Won.	Lost.	Played.	Per cent.	Pitchers.	Won.	Lost.	Played.	Per cent.
Klobedanz	4	3	7	.571	Nichols	20	7	27	.741
Nichols	10	8	18	.556	Stivetts	15	6	21	.714
Stivetts	7	7	14	.500	Klobedanz	2	1	3	.667
Mains	1	1	2	.500	Mains	2	1	3	.667
Sullivan	5	6	11	.455	Lewis	1	1	2	.500
Lewis	0	2	2	.000	Sullivan	6	7	13	.462
Dolan	0	3	3	.000	Dolan	1	2	3	.333

The Chicago Club's Pitching Record of 1896.

The Chicago club employed but seven pitchers in 1896, and of those who pitched in at least five games but three exceeded average figures, viz., Griffith, Briggs and Friend. Thornton did well, but he only pitched in three games, while Griffith pitched in 34 and Friend in 33, Thornton's figures being .667 for his three games. The latter, however, did not pitch in a single victory against the first division clubs. Griffith, who led in the full record, did not pitch in a single defeat against the Boston, Pittsburg, Brooklyn and Louisville clubs; while Briggs failed to pitch in a single victory against either the Baltimore, New York, Philadelphia or Washington teams. Friend was remarkably effective against the Pittsburgs, he pitching in five victories against them, while he took every game against the Clevelands. It is almost an established fact that there is always one team out of the dozen in which a pitcher is very effective against, or quite the reverse, while doing average work against nearly all of the others. Terry was the least effective of the Chicago's quartette of leading pitchers in 1896, his percentage figures being the lowest of the four in both divisions. Parker and McFarland were both failures, the former pitching in but one victory out of six games, and the latter in three defeats.

RECORD OF 1896.

Chicago vs.		Baltimore.	Cleveland.	Cincinnati.	Pittsburg.	Totals.	New York.	Philadelphia.	Washington.	Brooklyn.	St. Louis.	Louisville.	Totals.	Grand Totals.	Per cent. of Victories.
Griffith	Won	2	1	1	4	2	10	1	2	2	4	1	3	13	23	.676
	Lost	2	2	1	0	0	5	2	1	1	0	2	0	6	11	
Thornton	Won	0	0	0	0	0	0	0	0	0	0	1	1	2	2	.667
	Lost	1	0	0	0	0	1	0	0	0	0	0	0	0	1	
Briggs	Won	0	1	1	1	2	5	0	0	0	1	4	2	7	12	.600
	Lost	1	2	1	1	0	5	0	1	1	0	0	1	3	8	
Friend	Won	1	0	0	2	5	8	2	1	3	0	2	3	11	19	.576
	Lost	1	3	2	0	0	6	3	2	1	1	0	1	8	14	
Terry	Won	1	0	1	2	2	6	2	1	3	1	1	0	8	14	.483
	Lost	2	2	2	1	1	8	1	2	0	3	0	1	7	15	
Parker	Won	0	0	1	0	0	1	0	0	0	0	0	0	0	1	.167
	Lost	0	0	0	1	0	1	1	1	0	1	1	0	4	5	
McFarland	Won	0	0	0	0	0	0	0	0	0	0	0	0	0	0	.000
	Lost	0	0	0	0	0	0	1	1	1	0	0	3	3		

Per cent. of victories—Against Baltimore, .864; Cleveland, .181; Cincinnati, .400; Boston, .750; Pittsburg, .917; total, first division clubs, .586. New York, .417; Philadelphia, .888; Washington, .500; Brooklyn, .667; St. Louis, .750; Louisville, .750; total, second division clubs, .569. Grand total, .555.

DIVISION RECORD.

PITCHERS.	First Division.				PITCHERS.	Second Division.			
	Won.	Lost.	Played.	Per cent.		Won.	Lost.	Played.	Per cent.
Griffith	10	5	15	.667	Briggs	7	3	10	.700
Friend	8	6	14	.571	Griffith	13	6	19	.684
Briggs	5	5	10	.500	Friend	11	8	19	.579
Parker	1	1	2	.500	Terry	8	7	15	.533
Terry	6	8	14	.429	Parker	0	4	4	.000

The Pittsburg Club's Pitching Record of 1896.

The Pittsburg club placed only six pitchers in the box in 1896, five of whom pitched in not less than ten games, Horton being in the box in but two games only, and both were defeats. Out of this corps but two excelled the average in percentage of victories figures, viz., Killen and Hawley, all the others having percentages below .500. Killen was very effective against Cleveland, winning five out of six games, but did little against Chicago; while Hawley did not pitch in a single victory against Baltimore and Chicago. Neither Hughey nor J. Foreman pitched in a single victory against the first division clubs, and Hastings in only one game; the former, however, did well against those of the second division. Here is the season's record in full:

PITTSBURG VS.		First Division.					Second Division.						Grand Totals.	Per cent. of Victories.
		Baltimore.	Cleveland.	Cincinnati.	Boston.	Chicago.	Totals.	New York.	Philadelphia.	Washington.	Brooklyn.	St. Louis.	Louisville.	Totals.		
Killen	Won	2	5	3	2	1	13	4	3	3	2	2	4	18	31	.620
	Lost	2	1	0	4	4	11	1	2	1	1	1	2	8	19	
Hawley	Won	0	3	4	2	0	9	2	2	1	1	3	3	12	21	.500
	Lost	1	2	2	3	3	11	1	4	4	1	0	0	10	21	
Hughey	Won	0	0	0	0	0	0	1	0	1	1	3	0	6	6	.429
	Lost	2	1	1	0	1	5	0	0	1	2	0	0	3	8	
J. Foreman	Won	0	0	0	0	0	0	1	0	0	1	0	1	3	3	.429
	Lost	2	0	1	0	1	4	0	0	0	0	0	0	0	4	
Hastings	Won	0	0	0	1	0	1	0	1	1	0	0	2	4	5	.357
	Lost	2	0	1	0	2	5	2	0	0	2	0	0	4	9	
Horton	Won	0	0	0	0	0	0	0	0	0	0	0	0	0	0	.000
	Lost	0	0	0	0	0	0	0	0	0	2	0	0	2	2	

Per cent. of victories—Against Baltimore, .182; Cleveland, .667; Cincinnati, .583; Boston, .417; Chicago, .085; total, first division clubs, .390. New York, .667; Philadelphia, .500; Washington, .500; Brooklyn, .455; St. Louis, .727; Louisville, .833; total, second division clubs, .614. Grand total, .512.

In pitching against the first division clubs, Killen bore off the palm, Hawley being second. Killen also led against the clubs of the second division, but Hughey did better than Hawley against the last six clubs; Hastings, while not pitching in a single victory against the leaders, reached the average against the second division teams.

Here is the division record of the season:

DIVISION RECORD.

PITCHERS.	FIRST DIVISION.				PITCHERS.	SECOND DIVISION.			
	Won.	Lost.	Played.	Per cent.		Won.	Lost.	Played.	Per cent.
Killen............	13	11	24	.542	Killen............	18	8	26	.692
Hawley..........	9	11	20	.450	Hughey..........	6	8	9	.667
Hastings.........	1	5	6	.167	Hawley..........	12	10	22	.545
Hughey..........	0	5	5	.000	Hastings.........	4	4	8	.500

The New York Club's Pitching Record of 1896. Ten pitchers comprised the New York's "battery" force in 1896, and of the ten who pitched in not less than five games there were but two who reached the average in percentage figures, viz., Meekin and Doheny, Meekin's record being so much superior as to make it an exceptional one for the season. He had the best of it in all six of the first division clubs he pitched against, he pitching in three victories out of his four games with the Baltimores; besides, winning in all three he pitched in against the Cincinnatis, and in three out of four with the Chicagos; his total in percentages against the six first division clubs being .682 to Clarke's .370, Sullivan's .364 and Doheny's .286. Two of the ten pitchers were in the box but once each, both victories against the Washington club, viz., Van Haltren and Gettig; while Reidy, Campfield and Bowers were tried only in a single game each, all defeats. Clarke only pitched in three victories against four of the six leading teams, while he sustained no less than twelve defeats in pitching against the same four clubs, viz., the Baltimores, Clevelands, Cincinnatis and Pittsburgs, and he did not pitch in a single victory against the Philadelphia and Washington teams, with which he lost six games. Doheny also failed in his pitching against the six leading teams, Sullivan excelling him in this respect. With but one pitcher out of ten reaching above the average percentage figures—Meekin, with .667, Doheny just reaching .500—it is not to be wondered at that New York was kept in the second division in the race of 1896.

Here is the record for the full corps for 1896:

RECORD OF 1896.

NEW YORK vs.		Baltimore.	Cleveland.	Cincinnati.	Boston.	Chicago.	Pittsburg.	Totals.	Philadelphia.	Washington.	Brooklyn.	St. Louis.	Louisville.	Totals.	Grand Totals.	Per cent. of Victories.
		First Division.							Second Divis'n							
Meekin	Won	3	2	3	2	3	2	15	1	4	2	1	3	11	26	.667
	Lost	1	2	0	1	1	2	7	2	0	1	2	1	6	13	
Doheny	Won	0	0	1	0	1	0	2	1	0	0	1	3	5	7	.500
	Lost	2	1	1	0	0	1	5	0	1	0	1	0	2	7	
M. Sullivan	Won	0	2	1	0	0	1	4	1	0	4	1	0	6	10	.455
	Lost	2	0	1	2	1	1	7	1	2	1	0	1	5	12	
Clarke	Won	0	1	1	3	3	1	9	0	0	2	4	1	7	16	.372
	Lost	3	3	3	3	2	3	17	4	2	2	0	2	10	27	
Seymour	Won	0	0	0	0	0	0	0	0	0	0	1	1	2	2	.333
	Lost	0	1	0	0	1	1	3	0	1	0	0	0	1	4	
Van Haltren	Won	0	0	0	0	0	0	0	0	0	0	0	0	0	0	1.000
	Lost	0	0	0	0	0	0	0	0	0	0	0	0	0	0	
Gettig	Won	0	0	0	0	0	0	0	1	0	0	0	1	1	1	1.000
	Lost	0	0	0	0	0	0	0	0	0	0	0	0	0	0	
Reidy	Won	0	0	0	0	0	0	0	0	0	0	0	0	0	0	.000
	Lost	0	0	1	0	0	0	1	0	0	0	0	0	0	1	
Campfield	Won	0	0	0	0	0	0	0	0	0	0	0	0	0	0	.000
	Lost	1	0	0	0	0	0	1	0	0	0	0	0	0	1	
Bowers	Won	0	0	0	0	0	0	0	0	0	0	0	0	0	0	.000
	Lost	0	0	0	1	0	0	1	0	0	0	0	0	0	1	

Per cent. of victories—Against Baltimore, .250; Cleveland, .417; Cincinnati, .500; Boston, .417; Chicago, .583; Pittsburg, .333; total, first division clubs, .454. Philadelphia, .273; Washington, .500; Brooklyn, .667; St. Louis, .800; Louisville, .667; total, second division clubs, .576. Grand total, .489.

The highest percentage figures against a club was made against the St. Louis team, and the lowest against that of the Baltimores.

Here is the division record of the season:

DIVISION RECORD.

PITCHERS.	First Division.				PITCHERS.	Second Division.			
	Won.	Lost.	Played.	Per cent.		Won.	Lost.	Played.	Per cent.
Meekin	15	7	22	.682	Doheny	5	2	7	.714
Clarke	9	17	26	.370	Meekin	11	6	17	.647
M. Sullivan	4	7	11	.364	M. Sullivan	6	5	11	.545
Doheny	2	5	7	.286	Clarke	7	10	17	.412

Quinn McMahon Esper Hemming Bowerman Clarke Donnelly
Brodie Hoffer Kelley Hanlon (Mgr.) Robinson Jennings Reitz
Doyle McGraw Keeler Pond

BALTIMORE BASE BALL CLUB, 1896.

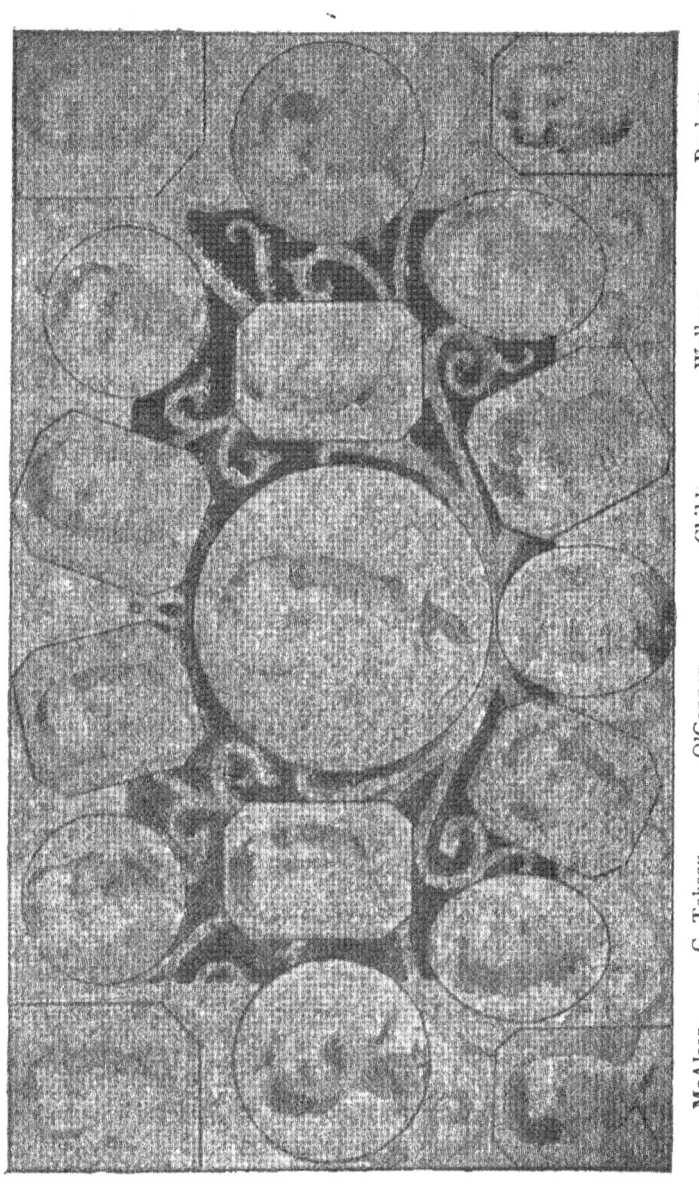

McAleer   G. Tebeau   O'Connor   Childs   Wallace   Burkett
McGarr   McKean   O. Tebeau (Capt.)   Young   Chamberlain
Delehanty   Wilson   Zimmer   Shearon   Blake   Scheible   Cuppy

CLEVELAND BASE BALL CLUB, 1896.

Tenney   Yerrick   Ganzel   Mains   Stivetts   Tucker   Ryan   Harrington
  Lowe   Hamilton   Duffy (Capt.)   Selee (Mgr.)   Collins   Bergen   Bannon
  Long   Sullivan   Dolan   Nichols

BOSTON BASE BALL CLUB, 1896.

Reiley   Friend   Griffith   Parker   Ryan   McBride   Flynn
Briggs   Decker   Lange   Anson   Donahue   Everett   Terry   McFarland
Truby   Dahlen   Kittridge

CHICAGO BASE BALL CLUB, 1896.

Stenzel Hawley Bierbauer Donovan Balliett Merritt Killen Ely
Smith Hughey Mack Beckley Lyons
Hastings Goar Sugden Foreman
PITTSBURG BASE BALL CLUB, 1896.

Copyright, 1896, by Havens.

Farrell Cavelle Stanhope Meekin G. Davis H. Davis Wilson Seymour
Davis (trainer) German Kagey Foster Tiernan Flynn Fuller
Gleason Stafford Pfeffer Van Haltren W. Clark Zearfoss Bowen W. H. Clarke
Mulligan Battam Connaughton

NEW YORK BASE BALL CLUB, 1896.

Hallman Turner Boyle Sullivan Brouthers Thompson Eiler Orth
         Grady   Clements Cross   Nash   Lucid   Carsey
         Hulen   Delehanty   Taylor McGill

The Philadelphia Club's Pitching Record of 1896.

The Philadelphia club led all of the League clubs in the number of pitchers employed. It may be said that in this respect, its multiplicity of pitchers proved to be a weakness that was costly to the team, inasmuch as of the whole dozen of pitchers who pitched in at least five games, there were but four who reached the average in percentage of victories figures, viz., Orth, Gumbert, Taylor and McGill, the latter just reaching the percentage of .500 in the eight games he pitched in. Of the twelve pitchers, five did not pitch in a single victory against the first division clubs, and five even failed to score a victory against the clubs of the second division. In this respect, the pitching corps record of the Phillies in 1896 stands exceptional and on the wrong side of the ledger. Not a single pitcher was able to pitch the team to victory against the Baltimores.

RECORD OF 1896.

PHILADELPHIA VS.		First Division.							Second Divis'n						Grand Totals.	Per cent. of Victories.
		Baltimore.	Cleveland.	Cincinnati.	Boston.	Chicago.	Pittsburg.	Totals.	New York.	Washington.	Brooklyn.	St. Louis.	Louisville.	Totals.		
Orth............	Won	0	1	1	2	2	2	8	0	1	2	3	1	7	15	.625
	Lost	2	2	2	1	0	0	7	0	1	0	0	1	2	9	
Gumbert........	Won	0	1	0	0	0	1	2	1	1	1	0	1	4	6	.600
	Lost	1	0	0	2	0	0	3	0	0	0	1	0	1	4	
Taylor..........	Won	0	2	2	2	4	2	12	4	2	0	0	2	1	9	21	.525
	Lost	4	1	1	2	0	2	10	1	2	4	1	2	10	20	
McGill..........	Won	0	0	0	0	1	0	1	1	0	0	2	0	3	4	.500
	Lost	0	0	1	0	1	1	3	0	0	0	1	1	1	4	
Wheeler.........	Won	0	0	0	0	0	0	0	0	0	1	0	0	1	1	.500
	Lost	1	0	0	0	0	0	1	0	0	0	0	0	0	1	
Carsey..........	Won	0	2	1	1	0	0	4	2	3	0	1	1	7	11	.458
	Lost	1	2	1	0	1	3	8	1	1	2	0	1	5	13	
Lucid...........	Won	0	0	0	0	0	1	1	0	0	0	0	0	0	1	.200
	Lost	2	0	1	0	0	0	3	0	0	0	1	1	2	4	
Keener..........	Won	0	0	0	0	0	0	0	0	1	0	0	1	2	2	.167
	Lost	1	1	1	2	1	0	6	1	0	1	1	1	4	10	
Nops............	Won	0	0	0	0	1	0	1	0	0	0	0	0	0	1	1.000
	Lost	0	0	0	0	0	0	0	0	0	0	0	0	0	0	
Whitrock........	Won	0	0	0	0	0	0	0	0	0	0	0	0	0	0	.000
	Lost	0	0	1	0	0	0	1	0	0	0	0	0	0	1	
Garvin..........	Won	0	0	0	0	0	0	0	0	0	0	0	0	0	0	.000
	Lost	0	0	0	0	1	0	1	0	0	0	0	0	0	1	
Inks............	Won	0	0	0	0	0	0	0	0	0	0	0	0	0	0	.000
	Lost	0	0	0	0	0	0	0	0	0	1	0	0	1	1	

Per cent. of victories—Against Baltimore, .000; Cleveland, .500; Cincinnati, .533; Boston, .417; Chicago, .667; Pittsburg, .500; total, first division clubs, .403. New York, .727; Washington, .667; Brooklyn, .833; St. Louis, .727; Louisville, .417; total, second division clubs, .569. Grand total, .477.

Taylor had the best record in pitching against the six first
division clubs, while Gumbert excelled against the clubs of the
second division. Keener lost all six of the games in which he
pitched against the leaders, and also a majority of those against
second division teams; in fact, Taylor, Orth and Gumbert
were the leading trio of the corps in 1896.
Here is the division record:

DIVISION RECORD.

PITCHERS.	FIRST DIVISION.				PITCHERS.	SECOND DIVISION.			
	Won.	Lost.	Played.	Per cent.		Won.	Lost.	Played.	Per cent.
Taylor	12	10	22	.545	Gumbert	4	1	5	.800
Orth	8	7	15	.533	Orth	7	2	9	.778
Gumbert	2	3	5	.400	Carsey	7	5	12	.583
Carsey	4	8	12	.333	Taylor	9	10	19	.474
Keener	0	6	6	.000	Keener	2	4	6	.333

The highest percentage figures made by the full corps against
any one club were those against the New York and St. Louis
clubs, and the lowest was that against the Baltimores.

The Washington Club's Pitching Record of 1896.

The Washington club's pitching corps
for 1896 comprised ten pitchers, and
of these but four exceeded the average
in percentage figures, viz., Maul, King,
Norton and Mercer; the latter, fourth on the list in the full
record, and second against the first division clubs. Mercer
opened the season brilliantly, he pitching in nine victories out
of the first ten games he pitched in in April and May, after
that he fell off, and during the club's tour West, in July,
he pitched in six defeats out of eight games. He had
better figures against the five Eastern teams than against the
six Western by .591 to .545. Maul had a good record when
he was disabled for the season, he only being able to pitch in
seven games, five of which were victories; his full record shows
a percentage of .714, thereby leading the corps. Against
the first division clubs he was third, but he led against those of
the second division. The veteran, King, was the surprise of
the season. He not only led against the first division clubs,
but he was the only pitcher of the leading quartette who
pitched in a victory against the Baltimores. McJames was very
unsuccessful against the first division clubs, he pitching in no
less than fifteen defeats out of seventeen games; his two victories

being against the Cincinnatis. German was a dead failure throughout, and neither Anderson, Flynn nor Mullarky pitched in a single victory, and Boyd only did fairly well. Norton won three out of the five games he pitched in.

RECORD OF 1896.

WASHINGTON VS.		First Division.						Second Divis'n					Grand Totals.	Per cent. of Victories.
		Baltimore	Cleveland	Cincinnati	Boston	Chicago	Pittsburg	Totals	New York	Philadelphia	Brooklyn	St. Louis	Louisville	Totals		
Maul...........	Won	0	1	0	1	0	0	2	0	0	0	2	1	3	5	.714
	Lost	0	0	1	0	1	0	2	0	0	0	0	0	0	2	
King...........	Won	1	0	0	1	2	1	5	0	0	0	3	2	5	10	.625
	Lost	0	0	0	1	1	0	2	1	3	0	0	0	4	6	
Norton.........	Won	0	0	0	0	0	1	1	1	0	0	1	0	2	3	.600
	Lost	0	1	0	0	0	0	1	0	0	0	1	1	2		
Mercer.........	Won	0	2	2	2	2	4	12	3	2	6	0	2	13	25	.568
	Lost	3	1	2	3	2	1	12	1	1	1	3	1	7	19	
McJames........	Won	0	0	2	0	0	2	2	2	2	1	3	10	12	.364	
	Lost	3	1	2	3	3	3	15	1	1	3	1	0	6	21	
Boyd...........	Won	1	0	0	0	0	0	1	0	0	0	0	0	0	1	.333
	Lost	1	1	0	0	0	0	2	0	0	0	0	0	0	2	
German.........	Won	0	0	0	1	0	0	1	0	0	0	0	1	1	2	.105
	Lost	3	3	2	0	1	2	10	2	2	0	1	2	7	17	
Anderson	Won	0	0	0	0	0	0	0	0	0	0	0	0	0	0	.000
	Lost	0	1	0	0	0	0	1	0	0	0	0	0	0	1	
Flynn..........	Won	0	0	0	0	0	0	0	0	0	0	0	0	0	0	.000
	Lost	0	1	0	0	0	0	1	0	0	0	0	0	0	1	
Mullarky.......	Won	0	0	0	0	0	0	0	0	0	0	0	0	0	0	.000
	Lost	0	0	0	0	0	0	0	1	0	0	0	1	1	1	

Per cent. of victories—Against Baltimore, .167; Cleveland, .250; Cincinnati, .364; Boston, .417; Chicago, .333; Pittsburg, .500; total, first division clubs, .338. New York, .500; Philadelphia, .333; Brooklyn, .667; St. Louis, .583; Louisville, .750; total, second division clubs, .567. Grand total, .443.

Here is the division record:

DIVISION RECORD.

Pitchers.	First Division.				Pitchers.	Second Division.			
	Won	Lost	Played	Per cent.		Won	Lost	Played	Per cent.
King............	5	2	7	.714	Maul...........	3	0	3	1.000
Mercer	12	12	24	.500	Norton.........	2	1	3	.667
Maul...........	2	2	4	.500	Mercer.........	13	7	20	.650
Norton.........	1	1	2	.500	McJames.......	10	6	16	.625
McJames........	2	15	17	.118	King...........	5	4	9	.556
German.........	1	10	11	.091	German........	1	7	8	.125

The Brooklyn Club's Pitching Record of 1896.

The Brooklyn club's pitching corps for 1896 numbered but seven pitchers, and yet but two of the seven exceeded the average in percentage of victories figures, viz., Daub and Payne, Abbey just reaching .500, the average. Kennedy pitched in more defeats than victories against the six first division clubs, and he was still less effective against those of the second division. Daub won all of his games against the Baltimores, and two out of three against the Clevelands, thus winning five out of six games against the two leaders; while Payne lost five out of seven against the same two clubs, and Kennedy three out of five. Harper did not pitch in a single victory against the first division teams, but was successful with nearly all of those of the second division. Stein was the least successful, and Gumbert was allowed to pitch in but one game during the season against the first division clubs, though he did such good work with the Phillies in September. There was no questioning the fact that the club had pitching talent enough in 1896 to have placed the team in the first division, but the utter lack of united effort in the field support given the pitching corps proved very costly, the club's record in 1896 being the poorest for the past ten years.

Here is the full season's record for 1896.

RECORD OF 1896.

Brooklyn vs.		First Division.							Second Divis'n					Grand Totals.	Per cent. of Victories.
		Baltimore.	Cleveland.	Cincinnati.	Boston.	Chicago.	Pittsburg.	Totals.	New York.	Philadelphia.	Washington.	St. Louis.	Louisville.	Totals.		
Daub............	Won	3	2	2	0	1	1	9	0	1	0	2	2	5	14	.560
	Lost	0	1	3	2	1	0	7	0	0	1	2	0	4	11	
Payne............	Won	1	1	0	0	1	1	4	1	3	2	1	1	10	14	.519
	Lost	2	3	1	2	1	0	9	3	1	0	1	4	13		
Abbey............	Won	0	0	0	0	2	2	4	1	1	0	1	2	4	8	.500
	Lost	1	1	0	2	0	1	5	0	1	0	1	0	3	8	
Kennedy.........	Won	1	1	0	2	2	2	8	1	1	1	2	2	7	15	.405
	Lost	2	1	2	2	0	4	11	1	1	3	1	2	11	22	
Harper...........	Won	0	0	0	0	0	0	0	4	1	1	1	1	4	4	.333
	Lost	1	1	2	0	2	0	6	0	0	0	1	2	8		
Stein............	Won	1	1	0	0	0	0	2	1	1	0	0	0	1	3	.300
	Lost	0	0	1	2	2	0	5	0	0	2	0	0	2	7	
Gumbert.........	Won	0	0	0	0	0	0	0	0	0	0	0	0	0	0	.000
	Lost	0	0	1	0	0	0	1	0	1	1	1	0	3	4	

Per cent. of victories—Against Baltimore, .500; Cleveland, .455; Cincinnati, .167; Boston, .167; Chicago, .500; Pittsburg, .545; total, first division clubs, .380. New York, .833; Philadelphia, .667; Washington, .333; St. Louis, .588; Louisville, .667; total, second division clubs, .517. Grand total, .443.

The highest percentage figures made by the full pitching corps of the club against a single club was that against the Philadelphia and Louisville teams, while the lowest figures were those against the Cincinnatis and Bostons. Here is the division record:

DIVISION RECORD.

Pitchers.	First Division.				Pitchers.	Second Division.			
	Won.	Lost.	Played.	Per cent.		Won.	Lost.	Played.	Per cent.
Daub	9	7	16	.563	Payne	10	4	14	.714
Abbey	4	5	9	.444	Daub	5	4	9	.625
Kennedy	8	11	19	.421	Abbey	4	3	7	.571
Payne	4	9	13	.308	Kennedy	7	11	18	.389
Stein	2	5	7	.286	Harper	1	2	3	.333
Harper	2	5	7	.286	Stein	3	7	10	.300

The St. Louis Club's Pitching Record of 1896. But one pitcher of the seven comprising the full pitching corps of the St. Louis club in 1896 reached the average in percentage figures, and he only pitched in two games. Of those who pitched in not less than five games Breitenstein bore off the palm, and yet he pitched in more defeats than victories against both of the division clubs. Breitenstein lost five games out of eight against the Baltimores and Clevelands, as did Hart; Donahue losing five out of six with the same two leaders. Hart was badly punished by the Cincinnatis, he losing all of the five games he pitched in against the Reds. Kissenger was useless against the first division clubs and did very little better against those of the second division. Hill was allowed to pitch in but one game, but that was a victory, while McDougal was a bad tail-ender of the corps. Parrott, while heading the list in percentage figures, only pitching in two games, he winning against Louisville and losing with Cleveland. Breitenstein was very effective against the Louisville batsmen, but he was badly punished by those of Philadelphia, which club's team won 4 games with him in the box against them and did not lose one. The Chicago team also got the best of him by 4 victories against 2 defeats. Breitenstein's percentage of victories figures against the six first division clubs were .273, while against the five second division clubs his figures were .524.

Here is the full season's record for 1896:

RECORD OF 1896.

St. Louis vs.		Baltimore.	Cleveland.	Cincinnati.	Boston.	Chicago.	Pittsburg.	Totals.	New York.	Philadelphia.	Washington.	Brooklyn.	Louisville.	Totals.	Grand Totals.	Per cent. of Victories.
		\multicolumn{6}{c}{First Division.}		\multicolumn{5}{c}{Second Divis'n}			
Parrott	Won	0	0	0	0	0	0	0	0	0	0	0	1	1	1	.500
	Lost	0	1	0	0	0	0	1	0	0	0	0	0	1	1	
Breitenstein	Won	1	2	0	1	1	1	6	1	2	2	2	4	11	17	.395
	Lost	3	2	2	2	4	3	16	3	4	1	2	0	10	26	
Hart	Won	1	0	0	1	2	1	5	2	0	2	2	2	8	13	.335
	Lost	3	2	5	2	3	2	17	1	2	2	2	2	9	26	
Donahue	Won	1	0	0	0	0	1	2	0	1	1	1	1	4	6	.207
	Lost	2	3	2	1	1	3	12	3	1	3	3	1	11	23	
Kissenger	Won	0	0	0	1	•0	0	1	0	0	0	0	1	1	2	.133
	Lost	1	2	3	3	0	0	9	2	1	1	0	0	4	13	
Hill	Won	0	0	0	1	0	0	1	0	0	0	0	0	0	1	1.000
	Lost	0	0	0	0	0	0	0	0	0	0	0	0	0	0	
McDougal	Won	0	0	0	0	0	0	0	0	0	0	0	0	0	0	.000
	Lost	0	0	0	0	1	0	1	0	0	0	0	0	0	1	

Per cent. of victories—Against Baltimore, .250; Cleveland, .167; Cincinnati, .000; Boston, .333; Chicago, .250; Pittsburg, .273; total, first division clubs, .211. New York, .250; Philadelphia, .273; Washington, .417; Brooklyn, .417; Louisville, .750; total, second division clubs, .424. Grand total, .808.

The highest percentage made by the corps against a single club was that against the Louisvilles, the smallest being that against the Cincinnatis. Parrott was only allowed to pitch in two games, one of which was a victory over the Louisvilles. Here is the division record, in which Breitenstein and Hart bore off the palm.

Here is the division record:

DIVISION RECORD.

Pitchers.	\multicolumn{4}{c}{First Division.}	Pitchers.	\multicolumn{4}{c}{Second Division.}
	Won.	Lost.	Played.	Per cent.		Won.	Lost.	Played.	Per cent.
Breitenstein	6	16	22	.273	Breitenstein	11	10	21	.524
Hart	5	17	22	.227	Hart	8	9	17	.471
Donahue	2	12	14	.143	Donahue	4	11	15	.267
Kissenger	1	9	10	.100	Kissenger	1	4	5	.200

The Louisville Club's Pitching Record of 1896.

The worst pitching record of the season was that made by the eleven pitchers used by the Louisville club, not a pitcher of which reached the average in percentage figures, the best average of the corps being only .400, while four of the eleven did not pitch in a single victory. Every pitcher pitched in more defeats than victories.

Here is the corps' record in full for 1896:

RECORD OF 1896.

LOUISVILLE vs.		First Division.						Second Divis'n					Grand Totals.	Per cent. of Victories.
		Baltimore.	Cleveland.	Cincinnati.	Boston.	Chicago.	Pittsburg.	Totals.	New York.	Philadelphia.	Washington.	Brooklyn.	St. Louis.	Totals.	
Weyhing........	Won	0	0	0	0	1	0	1	0	0	0	1	0	1	2	.400
	Lost	0	0	0	1	0	1	2	0	0	0	0	1	1	3	
Herman.........	Won	0	1	1	0	0	0	2	0	0	1	0	0	1	3	.375
	Lost	1	1	0	0	0	1	3	0	1	0	1	0	2	5	
Frazer...........	Won	0	0	0	2	1	0	3	3	2	1	2	2	10	13	.342
	Lost	2	4	4	0	4	2	16	1	3	3	1	1	9	25	
Cunningham....	Won	0	1	1	2	0	1	5	1	0	0	1	0	2	7	.333
	Lost	1	1	2	2	2	0	8	2	0	2	2	0	6	14	
Hill.............	Won	1	1	1	0	1	1	5	0	3	1	0	1	5	10	.256
	Lost	5	2	3	2	2	4	18	3	1	2	2	3	11	29	
McDermott......	Won	1	0	0	0	0	0	1	0	1	0	0	0	1	2	.222
	Lost	0	0	0	1	0	0	1	1	0	1	2	2	6	7	
Smith...........	Won	0	0	0	0	0	0	0	0	1	0	0	0	1	1	.167
	Lost	1	0	0	2	0	0	3	1	0	0	0	1	2	5	
McCreery........	Won	0	0	0	0	0	0	0	0	0	0	0	0	0	0	.000
	Lost	0	0	0	0	1	0	1	0	0	0	0	0	0	1	
Emig............	Won	0	0	0	0	0	0	0	0	0	0	0	0	0	0	.000
	Lost	0	0	0	0	0	0	0	0	1	0	0	1	1	1	
Clausen.........	Won	0	0	0	0	0	0	0	0	0	0	0	0	0	0	.000
	Lost	0	0	0	0	0	1	1	0	0	0	0	0	0	1	
Holmes.........	Won	0	0	0	0	0	0	0	0	0	0	0	0	0	0	.000
	Lost	0	0	0	0	0	1	1	0	0	0	0	1	1	2	

Per cent. of victories—Against Baltimore, .167; Cleveland, .272; Cincinnati, .250; Boston, .333; Chicago, .250; Pittsburg, .167; total, first division clubs, .239. New York, .333; Philadelphia, .583; Washington, .250; Brooklyn, .333; St. Louis, .250; total, second division clubs, .263. Grand total, .290.

The highest percentage figures made by the corps were those made against the Philadelphia team, and the lowest those against the Baltimore and Pittsburg teams. Of those who pitched in five games and over the following is the division record:

DIVISION RECORD.

PITCHERS.	First Division.				PITCHERS.	Second Division.			
	Won.	Lost.	Played.	Per cent.		Won.	Lost.	Played.	Per cent.
McDermott......	1	1	2	.500	Frazer............	10	9	19	.526
Herman..........	2	3	5	.400	Weyhing.........	2	3	5	.400
Cunningham.....	5	8	13	.385	Herman..........	1	2	3	.333
Weyhing.........	1	2	3	.333	Hill.............	5	11	16	.313
Hill.............	5	18	23	.217	Cunningham.....	2	6	8	.250
Frazer............	3	16	19	.158	McDermott.......	2	7	9	.222
Smith............	0	3	3	.000	Smith............	1	5	6	.167

We append a summary table which presents some interesting figures. It is that showing the highest and lowest percentage of victories which each club's corps of pitchers made against a single club. Also the total percentage figures scored against the clubs of the two divisions in the aggregate, together with the figures showing the number of pitchers employed by each club during the season of 1896. Also the number of pitchers in each club who pitched in not less than twenty games, and of those who pitched in not less than ten games; also the number of pitchers who failed to pitch in a single victory and the number who exceeded the average of .500 in percentage of victories during the season:

SUMMARY RECORD.

Clubs.	Highest percentage against a single club.	Lowest percentage against a single club.	Percentage against 1st division clubs.	Percentage against 2d division clubs.	Players who pitched in 20 games and over.	Players who pitched in less than 10 games.	Number of players who failed to pitch in a single victory.	Number of pitchers who exceeded the average of .500.	Number of pitchers employed by each club.
Baltimore......	1.000	.273	.596	.778	4	3	0	8	8
Cleveland.......	.833	.333	.519	.662	3	2	2	4	6
Cincinnati.....	1.000	.167	.446	.732	2	4	1	5	9
Boston..........	.833	.417	.458	.653	3	4	1	4	8
Chicago........	.917	.181	.586	.569	4	3	1	4	7
Pittsburg.......	.833	.085	.390	.614	2	2	1	1	6
New York......	.800	.250	.454	.576	3	6	3	1	10
Philadelphia....	.727	.000	.403	.569	3	7	3	3	12
Washington....	.750	.167	.338	.567	2	6	3	4	10
Brooklyn........	.667	.167	.380	.517	3	1	1	2	7
St. Louis........	.750	.000	.211	.424	3	3	1	0	7
Louisville......	.588	.167	.239	.263	1	8	4	1	11

The foregoing figures present "food for thought" by club managers, as they show up the strong and weak points in the pitching department of the twelve clubs quite plainly in some instances. For instance, the leading club in the race, it will be seen, did not have a player in its pitching corps in 1896 who failed to pitch in at least one victory, while the tail-end club had no less than four. Then, too, while Cleveland—second in the race—employed only six pitchers during the season, the Louisvilles—last in the contest—employed no less than eleven. In fact, while the six clubs of the first division had an aggregate of forty-seven pitchers in their employ the six second division clubs employed no less than fifty-seven pitchers.

It will be seen that while Baltimore stood first in its aggregate of percentage of victories by its pitching corps against the five first division clubs it was the Chicagos who stood second in this respect, not Cleveland, the latter being third. The respective percentages were: Baltimore, .596; Chicago, .536, and Cleveland, 519. Pittsburg, in this record, stood eighth on the list and St. Louis last. Against the second division clubs, while Baltimore led with .778 in percentage of victories pitched in by its club corps, Cincinnati was second with .732 and Cleveland third with .662, Louisville being last with .263, Pittsburg beating Chicago in this respect with .614 to Chicago's .589. In the multiplicity of pitchers employed during the season by each club it will be seen that while the six leaders had enough, the tail-end six had too many for their own good. In the number of pitchers each club had who exceeded the average of .500 in percentage of victories during the entire season, while Baltimore had no less than eight pitchers the Louisvilles had but one, and St. Louis did not have a single pitcher whose percentage figures exceeded .500 and but one who reached that average. It will be seen, too, that while the six leaders had only an aggregate of six pitchers who failed to pitch in a single victory—Baltimore having none and Cleveland two—the six tail-end clubs aggregated no less than fifteen such pitchers, a comparative weakness which tells its own tale. Another thing was that while the first division clubs had no less than an aggregate of twenty-six pitchers who exceeded the average of .500 in percentage figures, the last six clubs of the second division aggregated but eleven such pitchers. This latter account shows the comparative weakness in pitching talent very plainly. One merit of the percentage rule is that it presents contrasts in figures very strikingly, showing how teams excel each other in their pitching departments, though the figures may not present a perfect criterion.

Runs Earned Off the Pitching.

The record of earned runs was established over twenty years ago, and solely for the purpose of having a record from which to judge the ability of the pitcher; and in order to do this we recorded runs as earned which were scored solely by means of base-hits, and not runs earned by means of base-stealing and errors of judgment in fielding. There is a marked difference between runs earned off the pitching solely, and those earned off the pitching and fielding combined, and the rule governing earned runs should be so worded as to confine them to those earned off the pitching alone. For instance, suppose the first batsman in an inning leads off with a safe hit for a single base, and he then steals second and third bases, and is sent home by a long fly ball to the outfield, which, though being caught, enables the runner to get home on the hit. Under the existing scoring rules this is recorded as an earned run, though it has plainly enough not been earned off the pitching alone.

There is another point bearing upon the record of runs legitimately earned off the pitching, and that is, runs scored by base-hits which are made before the fielders have been afforded three chances for outs off the pitching. If the pitcher delivers three balls to the bat, which successively afford three plain chances to put the side out, and the fielders fail to accept such chances, and then base-hits are made off his pitching, no runs can justly be charged to him as earned off his pitching, no matter if home runs are afterwards made; yet the existing code charges him with earned runs if such runs are made chiefly by base-running, unaided by but a single hit or a sacrifice. This is unjust to the pitcher, as the fault lies with the catcher's inability to throw well to base, or to the base-player who fails to properly accept chances to put the runners out.

A Special Pitching Record.

We herewith present a special pitching table which gives the records of the pitchers who have done service in the box for the past three years in the same club. The list includes twenty pitchers who pitched for their respective clubs for three consecutive years from 1894 to 1896, inclusive. We give the names of the pitchers in the order of their club's position in the pennant race of 1896, in each of the two divisions. The record gives the percentage of victories figures of each year, and is as follows:

FIRST DIVISION.

Pitchers.	Club.	Per cent., 1894.	Per cent., 1895.	Per cent., 1896.
McMahon	Baltimore	.758	.714	.600
Esper	Baltimore	.818	.429	.737
Young	Cleveland	.543	.767	.674
Cuppy	Cleveland	.568	.667	.625
Wallace	Cleveland	.500	.519	.600
Dwyer	Cincinnati	.486	.581	.714
Nichols	Boston	.717	.628	.682
Stivetts	Boston	.650	.500	.629
Griffith	Chicago	.645	.641	.676
Killen	Pittsburg	.558	.538	.630

SECOND DIVISION.

Meekin	New York	.783	.593	.667
Clarke	New York	.333	.563	.372
Taylor	Philadelphia	.706	.667	.525
Carsey	Philadelphia	.533	.585	.450
Maul	Washington	.423	.647	.714
Mercer	Washington	.410	.368	.568
Daub	Brooklyn	.406	.500	.560
Kennedy	Brooklyn	.545	.594	.405
Stein	Brooklyn	.650	.536	.300
Breitenstein	St. Louis	.519	.375	.466

Added to the above is a summary table which gives the totals of the victories and defeats pitched in each year by each pitcher, as also his aggregate percentage of victories figures. In this summary the names of the pitchers are given in the order of their total percentage figures for the three years of club service. Here is the summary record:

Pitchers.	Clubs.	1894. W.	1894. L.	1895. W.	1895. L.	1896. W.	1896. L.	Total. W.	Total. L.	Total Per cent.
Griffith	Chicago	20	11	25	14	23	11	68	36	.731
McMahon	Baltimore	25	8	10	4	12	8	47	20	.672
Meekin	New York	36	10	16	11	26	13	78	34	.696
Nichols	Boston	33	12	27	16	30	15	90	43	.677
Young	Cleveland	25	21	33	10	29	14	87	45	.659
Esper	Baltimore	9	2	10	12	14	5	33	19	.635
Taylor	Philadelphia	24	10	26	13	21	20	71	43	.623
Cuppy	Cleveland	21	16	26	13	25	15	72	44	.621
Killen	Pittsburg	14	10	7	6	31	19	52	35	.598
Stivetts	Boston	26	14	16	16	22	13	64	43	.598
Dwyer	Cincinnati	18	19	18	13	25	10	61	42	.592
Wallace	Cleveland	2	2	14	13	15	9	31	24	.564
Stein	Brooklyn	26	14	15	13	3	7	44	34	.564
Maul	Washington	11	15	11	6	5	2	27	23	.540
Carsey	Philadelphia	16	14	24	17	11	13	51	44	.537
Kennedy	Brooklyn	24	20	19	13	15	22	58	55	.513
Daub	Brooklyn	10	15	10	10	14	11	34	36	.486
Breitenstein	St. Louis	27	15	18	30	17	26	62	71	.466
Mercer	Washington	16	23	14	24	25	19	55	66	.455
Clarke	New York	2	4	18	14	16	27	36	45	.444

Louisville had no pitchers who had been with the club three consecutive years up to date.

These two tables present a very interesting statistical record, and the figures tell a plain story as to which player improved or deteriorated in his box-work each year.

It will be seen that Griffith, of Chicago, bears off the palm, not only in having the highest percentage figures, but also in not having a lower percentage of victories in any one year than .641, a record, for the three years, equalled by no other of the twenty pitchers named in the table.

Of those who led each year in percentage figures Esper took the honors in 1894, Young in 1895, and Esper in 1896. The lowest each year were Clarke, in 1894; Mercer, in 1895, and Stein, in 1896. Pitchers Wallace, Dwyer, Maul and Daub improved in their percentage figures from 1894 to 1896, and Pitchers McMahon and Taylor fell off each year.

In 1895 Pitchers Esper, Nichols, Stivetts, Killen, Meekin, Mercer, Stein and Breitenstein went back; while Young, Cuppy, Carsey, Maul and Kennedy each made a forward movement in that year.

In 1896 Wallace, Dwyer, Griffith, Killen, Maul, Mercer, Daub and Breitenstein all led their previous years' records, while McMahon, Young, Cuppy, Taylor, Kennedy, Stein and Clarke all fell off, the latter two especially. The summary gives some interesting figures in the way of the records of the victories won and defeats sustained each year by the twenty pitchers, Griffiths leading in having the best general percentage of victories, with McMahon second and Meekin third, Griffith's figures being the "best on record" in the League in a three years' consecutive record. Clarke was a bad tail-ender.

It will be seen that in aggregate percentage figures 16 pitchers out of the 20 scored above the average of .500.

Of the twelve clubs, two had three pitchers with a three years' consecutive record, four clubs each had two pitchers for the full record, and four had only a single pitcher who has served three years, Louisville having none.

The experience of the past season in connection with the limit of the speed in pitching, as to the point when it ceases to be effective, presents some valuable suggestions which team managers and captains will do well to bear in mind. The season of 1896 was marked by some exhibitions of swift pitching unequaled in the annals of the game, and yet it was not effective in placing the team which held the cyclone pitchers in the lead. If the speed is too great for catchers to handle, even with the protection the defensive paraphernalia at command yields, why then it is worse then useless.

The Batting of 1896

WHILE fielding in base ball has almost reached the point of perfection, the true art of batting in the game is yet but little known among the large majority of professional batsmen ; and there is but slight hope apparently of its advancement until the "masses" of the thousands of patrons of our professional ball fields come to a realizing knowledge of what the art of batting is. The general idea is that the acme of batting is reached when a heavyweight "slugger," by mere shoulder hitting, sends the ball over the heads of the outfielders for a "homer." To such, evidences of scientific play at the bat as are shown in the art of *placing the ball*, of *facing for position at the bat*, of skilfully *tapping* swiftly pitched balls over the heads of infielders and not far enough out for catches by the outfielders, of well-judged *bunting* hits, or of the timely *sacrifice hits*, are practically unknown features of the art of batting. All of these essentials of scientific play in batting come under the head of *team-work at the bat* and constitute the essential of pennant-winning teams in batting known as *playing for the side*, and it differs as much from the *chance hits* method of mere machine work in batting as does the "cyclone" work of a machine pitcher from the skilful "head-work" play of the scientific occupant of the box in the team.

However desirous we might be of commenting intelligently upon the batting of 1896, based upon the data of the official averages of the League for that year, it is impossible to arrive at any reliable conclusion in judging the batting skill of the season from such data, owing to the fact of the entire absence of any figures showing "team-work at the bat ;" that is, batting which tells in sending runners around the bases by base-hits. All there is left to make an estimate of a batsman's skill is the base-hit percentages, which do not tell what the batsmen do in forwarding runners around the bases, and this latter is the only true estimate of team-work at the bat.

What the batting averages should show in order to get at a fair criterion of excellence of the work done at the bat is as follows :

Batsmen.	Field position.	Clubs.	Per cent. of runners forwarded by base hits.	Per cent. of base hits	Per cent. of sacrifice hits.	Per cent. of times struck out.	Per cent. of bases taken on balls.	Average of runs per game.	Per cent. of stolen bases.	Per cent. of fielding.
Burkett	F.	Cleveland		.410						.925
Jennings	S.S.	Baltimore		.397						.925
Delehanty	P.	Philadelphia		.394						

The above short table shows how meagre the data is that the official averages of the League have furnished for years past. It is true that the official averages give the total runs, sacrifice hits and stolen bases, but nothing else bearing upon a batsman's value as a batsman, base-runner and fielder.

Here is a table that we have made up from the official averages which partially shows what the leading ten batsmen did in general play in 1896, the position of each being based on the figures of his percentage of base hits, the only batting criterion the League figures afforded up to 1897. Only players who participated in 100 games and over are included in the appended table:

Batsmen.	Positions.	Clubs.	Games.	Base-hit percentage.	Runs scored.	Sacrifice hits.	Average of stolen bases.	Fielding percentage.
1—Burkett	l.f.	Cleveland	133	.410	159	5	.023	.925
2—Jennings	s.s.	Baltimore	129	.397	125	11	.000	.926
3—Delehanty	l.f.	Philadelphia	122	.394	131	4	.025	.947
4—Keeler	r.f.	Baltimore	127	.392	154	13	.000	.973
5—Kelley	l.f.	Baltimore	130	.370	147	5	.067	.955
6—Stenzel	c.f.	Pittsburg	112	.366	104	6	.050	.928
7—Hamilton	l.f.	Boston	131	.363	153	6	.074	.937
8—Tiernan	r.f.	New York	133	.361	132	5	.026	.964
9—Dahlen	3b.	Chicago	125	.361	153	27	.046	.912
10—E. Smith	l.f.	Pittsburg	120	.358	118	6	.025	.947

By the above figures it will be seen that Burkett excelled in base-hit percentage and in scored runs; but he was ninth in fielding percentages; seventh in sacrifice hits—an important part of team-work in batting—and last in averages of stolen bases; while Dahlen, almost last in base-hit percentages, led in sacrifice hits and was third in total runs. To judge as to what value a batsman—as a batsman—is to a team, one must find out if he excelled in forwarding runners by base-hits or sacrifice hits, for that is where the batting tells in winning games, not in mere base-hit averages alone.

Sacrifice Hits. Sacrifice hitting was not a feature of the batting of 1896. The fact is, this peculiar characteristic of team-work at the bat is not yet generally appreciated, or, in fact, understood. The highest record made by any batsman in sacrifice hitting was that by Hoy, of Cincinnati, and he only made 33 such hits in 121 games. Indeed, out of 186 batsmen only 35 of them scored double figures in their total of sacrifice hits, and 16 did not make a single hit of the kind. The 186 batsmen who played in not less than 15 games during 1896, included 66 who played in 100 games and over, 21 who played in at least 75 games and in less than 100, and 26 who played in at least 50 games and in less than 75, while the remainder numbered 73, who played in less than 50 games and in more than 14. The three leaders in sacrifice hits were Hoy, with 33; Ely, with 28, and Dahlen, with 27, a total of 88 such hits in 372 games, a very small average indeed. No less than 140 of the players on the list failed to exceed single figures in their totals of sacrifice hits; so it will be plainly seen that such hitting was not frequently indulged in during the past season.

LEADERS OF EACH CLUB IN SACRIFICE HITS, 1896.

Batsmen.	Clubs.	Games.	Total Sacrifice Hits.	Total Runs Scored.	Total Bases Stolen.	Base Hit Average.
Hoy	Cincinnati	121	33	120	53	.296
Ely	Pittsburg	126	28	64	18	.287
Dahlen	Chicago	125	27	137	59	.362
Tenney	Boston	88	21	65	18	.342
Donnelly	Baltimore	104	20	64	39	.330
McAleer	Cleveland	116	18	70	26	.288
Hallman	Philadelphia	120	18	83	16	.318
Miller	Louisville	125	18	91	75	.318
Shindle	Brooklyn	131	18	74	26	.281
Cooley	St. Louis	104	14	91	23	.301
T. Brown	Washington	113	14	87	34	.299
Gleason	New York	133	10	78	44	.292

We noticed that in the comments of scribes on the game during the last winter interregnum, some of them advocated the doing away with sacrifice hitting in the rules. This is simply out of the question. Sacrifice hitting can no more be prevented than hitting foul balls can. It is part and parcel of the game. What can be done is either to give a premium for such hitting, by not including a sacrifice hit as a time at the bat, or removing that reward.

The official batting averages sent in by Secretary Young give further information in regard to the batting done by the twelve League clubs in 1896.

Base Running Statistics

SOME first-class base-running was exhibited by a minority of the players of the leading clubs in 1896, but the season's record did not equal, as a whole, that of previous years, especially in the case of the high record of 1893. The main obstacle to successful base-running was the dead failure on the part of the staff of League umpires to carry out the spirit and intent of the balk rule. In this they were, in a measure, excusable from the fact that that wretched "box," which the rules allowed to be used, gave a latitude to balking which the umpires were unable to prevent; inasmuch as the pitcher had too much freedom of movement allowed him in throwing to bases, and especially in regard to his making feints to throw, in doing which he stepped out of what should be his box boundaries.

Base-running in base ball has come to be as much of an art as strategic pitching, and it is certainly a very important element of success in a game. Your club team may contain one of the best "battery" pairs in the League and also have a fine supporting force in the field, but without the strong point of excellence in base-running it will lack a third of its required strength for winning pennants. The following record of base stealing of 1896 shows a list of but 50 base-runners who exceeded a record of 25 stolen bases for the entire season out of over 200 players. It is comparatively a poor record, especially in view of the fact that but one base-runner reached a record of 100 stolen bases, and not one succeeded in making an average of 1 stolen base to a game.

The Boston team, under Nash, Duffy and McCarthy in 1893, used to play this base-running point: The man on first makes a bluff attempt to steal second, but runs back to first. By this it becomes known whether the second baseman or the shortstop is going to cover second for the throw from the catcher. Then the batsman gets a signal from the man on first that he is going to steal on a certain pitched ball. The moment he starts for second the batsman just pushes the ball for the place occupied only a moment before by the infielder who has gone to cover second base. That is, if the second baseman covers the bag the batter places the ball slowly to right field; if it is the shortstop, the ball is placed to left field. Of course, it takes a skilful batter to do this, but they had such hitters on the Boston nine that year. Now, when that ball is hit to the outfield, the man who has already started to steal second just keeps right on to third, while the batsman is safe at first.

Here is the record, including the total runs made by each of the base-stealers, as also their batting and fielding averages:

Rank.	Base Runners.	Club.	Games.	Runs.	Stolen bases.	Per cent. of stolen bases.	Base hit averages.	Fielding averages.
1	Lange, fielder........	Chicago............	123	114	100	.081	.333	.928
2	Hamilton, fielder.....	Boston.............	131	153	93	.071	.363	.937
3	Ewing, first base.....	Cincinnati.........	67	41	47	.070	.282	.981
4	Kelley, fielder........	Baltimore..........	130	147	90	.069	.370	.955
5	Miller, fielder......	Cincinnati.........	125	91	75	.060	.318	.907
	Doyle, first base....	Baltimore.........	118	115	71	.060	.345	.973
6	Keeler, fielder........	Baltimore..........	127	154	73	.057	.392	.973
7	Jennings, shortstop...	Baltimore..........	129	125	73	.056	.397	.926
8	Stenzel, fielder........	Pittsburg...........	112	104	59	.052	.366	.928
9	Dahlen, shortstop.....	Chicago............	125	153	60	.047	.361	.912
10	Burke, fielder......	Cincinnati.........	122	120	57	.045	.342	.934
	McPhee, second base	Cincinnati.........	116	81	58	.045	.299	.982
11	Hoy, fielder..........	Cincinnati.........	121	120	53	.043	.296	.949
12	Everett, third base...	Chicago............	131	130	55	.041	.333	.908
13	Selbach, fielder.......	Washington........	121	100	49	.040	.316	.951
14	Anderson, first base	Brooklyn..........	104	69	40	.038	.314	.982
	Donovan, fielder....	Pittsburg..........	129	110	50	.038	.316	.947
15	Joyce, third base....	Wash'ton and N.Y.	129	125	49	.037	.323	.892
	Donnelly, third base	Baltimore..........	104	69	39	.037	.330	.902
16	Geo. Davis, shortstop.	New York..........	124	98	49	.036	.315	.936
17	Dowd, fielder........	St. Louis...........	125	93	53	.033	.266	.960
	Gleason, second base	New York.........	133	78	47	.033	.292	.927
18	Long, shortstop.....	Boston.............	119	108	40	.033	.334	.906
	Van Haltren, fielder.	New York..........	133	138	43	.032	.353	.942
	Duffy, fielder.......	Boston.............	131	93	45	.032	.302	.957
19	Delehanty.........	Philadelphia.......	122	131	37	.030	.394	.947
	T. Brown, fielder...	Washington........	113	87	34	.030	.299	.939
20	Davis, first base.....	Pittsburg..........	107	68	33	.030	.234	.965
	Irwin, third base....	Cincinnati.........	127	76	33	.029	.295	.932
	McCreary, fielder..	Louisville..........	110	87	32	.029	.351	.904
21	Jones, fielder.........	Brooklyn..........	102	82	29	.028	.353	.918
22	Decker, first base ..	Chicago............	106	68	29	.027	.281	.976
	Dexter	Louisville..........	98	64	27	.027	.284	.888
	Lush, pitcher.......	Washington........	91	71	25	.027	.245	.882
23	Ryan	Chicago............	127	83	35	.026	.312	.921
	Anson, first base...	Chicago............	106	72	28	.026	.335	.982
	Tiernan, fielder ...	New York..........	133	132	35	.026	.361	.964
24	E. Smith, fielder...	Pittsburg..........	120	118	32	.025	.358	.947
	F. Clark, fielder....	Louisville..........	131	93	32	.025	.327	.904
25	Burkett.............	Cleveland..........	133	159	32	.024	.410	.925
26	M. Cross, shortstop...	St. Louis...........	124	64	38	.023	.264	.891
	Brodie.............	Baltimore..........	132	90	30	.022	.294	.971
	Demontreville, s. s.	Washington........	130	93	29	.022	.349	.892
27	Cartwright, fielder.	Washington........	131	78	29	.022	.274	.977
	Griffin, fielder......	Brooklyn..........	122	102	27	.022	.315	.961
	McAleer............	Cleveland..........	116	70	26	.022	.288	.951
28	Shindle, third base...	Brooklyn	131	74	26	.019	.281	.918

Club Records of Stolen Bases.

The following records present a comparison of the work done in base-stealing by the twelve League clubs from 1892 to 1896, inclusive. The record gives the totals of the players of each club who stole bases.

RECORD OF 1892.

Clubs.	Total Stolen Bases.	Total Players.	Clubs.	Total Stolen Bases.	Total Players.
1—Brooklyn	475	16	7—Cleveland	232	14
2—New York	375	18	8—Chicago	231	14
3—Boston	351	15	9—Philadelphia	226	16
4—Cincinnati	347	22	10—Baltimore	218	20
5—Washington	316	22	11—St. Louis	187	19
6—Louisville	237	18	12—Pittsburg	183	16

Total stolen bases, 3,378; total players, 210.

RECORD OF 1893.

Clubs.	Total Stolen Bases.	Total Players.	Clubs.	Total Stolen Bases.	Total Players.
1—New York	433	17	7—Boston	247	14
2—Baltimore	331	20	8—Cincinnati	220	18
3—Brooklyn	264	15	9—Pittsburg	200	18
4—St. Louis	257	18	10—Louisville	187	16
5—Cleveland	256	14	11—Philadelphia	184	15
6—Chicago	255	15	12—Washington	168	15

Total stolen bases, 3,002; total players, 194.

RECORD OF 1894.

Clubs.	Total Stolen Bases.	Total Players.	Clubs.	Total Stolen Bases.	Total Players.
1—New York	346	15	7—Washington	267	17
2—Baltimore	328	17	8—Boston	243	15
3—Chicago	320	16	9—Louisville	226	22
4—Brooklyn	303	17	10—Cleveland	219	17
5—Philadelphia	281	17	11—Cincinnati	219	16
6—Pittsburg	271	17	12—St. Louis	154	16

Total stolen bases, 3,177; total players, 202.

RECORD OF 1895.

Clubs.	Total Stolen Bases.	Total Players.	Clubs.	Total Stolen Bases.	Total Players.
1—Baltimore	373	20	7—Pittsburg	243	14
2—Cincinnati	297	18	8—Brooklyn	230	17
3—New York	295	18	9—Cleveland	228	15
4—Chicago	275	13	10—Boston	218	13
5—Washington	268	16	11—St. Louis	172	17
6—Philadelphia	262	17	12—Louisville	118	23

Total stolen bases, 2,979; total players, 201.

RECORD OF 1896.

Clubs.	Total Stolen Bases.	Total Players.	Clubs.	Total Stolen Bases.	Total Players.
1—Baltimore	444	13	7—Pittsburg	248	12
2—Cincinnati	371	15	8—Brooklyn	230	14
3—Chicago	365	14	9—St. Louis	218	15
4—Washington	293	15	10—Louisville	192	15
5—Boston	258	14	11—Cleveland	169	14
6—New York	251	14	12—Philadelphia	168	14

Total stolen bases, 3,263; total players, 169.

It will be seen that four of the six first division clubs of 1896 excelled in base-stealing, and but for the weakness of Cleveland in this respect that club would have given the champions a very close race. Philadelphia was the tail-ender in base-stealing in 1896. They thought that the strong point in pennant-winning was to excel in "slugging for homers," whereas it is the weakest; *team-work at the bat* and *base-stealing* being the main essentials, provided no glaring weakness is shown in the "*battery*" *force* and the *field support*.

Those who failed to steal a single base during the season of 1896 were Cunningham and Johnson, of Louisville; Carsey and Taylor, of Philadelphia; Killen, Hughey and Mack, of Pittsburg; Esper, of Baltimore; Cuppy, of Cleveland; Sullivan, of Boston; Dad Clarke, of New York; Rhines, of Cincinnati; King, of Washington; Abbey, of Brooklyn; Briggs, of Chicago, and Nilands, of St. Louis, all but two being pitchers.

Here is a portion of an article I wrote in the early eighties on base-running which will be instructive to players for 1897:

"There is a great difference between reaching first base and running the other bases. You may earn your first base, or you may reach it by an error or have it given you on balls; but after getting the base in question it depends largely on your own efforts whether you get further ahead or not. To the careless looker-on at a match it seems a comparatively easy thing to run bases; but it is something that requires more head-work to excel in than the large majority of players possess. To know when to start and when to stop, to avoid hesitancy and vacillation, are as important essentials as fast running and pluck and nerve. There are so many things to look out for and so little time to judge when to start and to stop, and so much quick perception of chances, that it comes to be quite an art to excel in base-running. How many first-class fielders in catching and throwing balls and in fast running are there, who in base-running are as easily trapped as are novices by keen-sighted, strategic pitchers and catchers. They are slow in perception and when they act, do it by jerks, as it were, in which case they are just as likely to be put out as to make a base. They start—when they do go—either too late or too soon, and are either touched before reaching second base or are caught napping at first before they can get off for the second. There are plenty of points peculiar to good, sharp base-running, which hundreds of professional ball players are apparently ignorant of, or if they know them, they practically cannot play them from lack of the requisite mental powers. Your good base-runner necessarily must be quick-witted and sharp to see favorable openings for stealing a base, as well as prompt to act at a moment's notice. In base-running the great rule is: "The man who hesitates is lost." It requires pretty sharp sight on the part of a base-runner on first base to take in at a glance the positions of the catcher and the second baseman in playing the point of a throw to second so as to know what to do when he reaches the base—whether to duck in under the reach of a high-thrown ball or to leave the line to avoid a short-thrown ball—which obliges the base player to swing his arm round in front of the line—and to be prepared to continue on to third on a muff or an overthrow. Ordinary players lack the head-work power to accomplish all this in base-running and hence the majority are poor base-runners. Some very fast runners show up in poor form as base-runners from the lack of this very essential of head-work. They possess the speed of foot, but do not have the quick perception or the promptness in action which are necessary to make their fast running available."

The Fielding of 1896

THERE are two classes of fielders in the ranks of the professional base ball fraternity, both of which make themselves prominent during each season's campaigns, but in different ways. The first-class fielders are known by their earnest method of doing their work in their field positions, while those of the second class are mere machine players, as a rule—men who only do their field work perfunctorily, they being careless and, too often, negligent and indifferent in their ways, even when they get their pay regularly. The former class go for a ball with their minds bent on making the play, even at the risk of a chargeable error, while the latter avoid all risks they can which involve the chance of a misplay. The former class are the team-workers of the club, the latter mere record players, who seek to avoid an increase in their error-column figures, even if it involves poor support of the battery force in the field. It is needless to state that the leading class of players are sadly in the minority and they decidedly were so in 1896. It is a noticeable fact that most of the earnest team-workers in the field are to be found among the ambitious "colts" of the professionals. Now and then one sees a few veterans who go into their field duties heart and soul, and who play ball for all it is worth, and with a degree of earnest effort which frequently masters difficulties in the field which the indifferent veteran does not trouble himself about Then, too, there is another class of fielders who are apt to weaken their general play by fits of the sulks, occasioned by some just criticism of their play which they have been amenable to. These sulky players are a hard lot to get along with when they indulge in these ugly moods. Generally, this latter class belong to the hot-tempered players in the ranks, fellows who are constantly allowing nerve and judgment to be ruined by their ill temper. Such fielders can no more "play for the side" or do regular team-work in the field than they can fly.

A great essential of success in fielding, as in all other of the departments of the game, is this endeavoring, on the part of the fielder, to always *play for the side;* that is, to use his most earnest efforts to aid his club to win, no matter at what cost to his individual record. In selecting fielders for their teams managers should bear in mind this important fact and not trust to a player's fielding averages or to the partial reports of a player's special admirers.

Fielding Statistics of 1896.

Some very fine catching behind the bat marked the fielding of 1896, and that, too, in the face of a fire of very difficult pitching to back up. In regard to the most work done behind the bat in 1896 McGuire, of the Washingtons, held the lead with a total record of 95 games as catcher; Zimmer, of the Clevelands, being second, with 89, and McFarland, of St. Louis, with 80.

In fielding percentages as catchers Ganzel led the Bostons, with .968 to his credit ; Vaughn, the Cincinnatis, with .951 ; Boyle, the Philadelphias, with .950 ; Sugden, the Pittsburgs, with .939 ; Kittredge, the Chicagos, with .932 ; Zimmer, the Clevelands, with .925 ; Robinson, the Baltimores, with .919 ; McFarland, the St. Louis, with .919 ; McGuire, the Washingtons, with .912 ; Grim, the Brooklyns, with .907 ; Farrell, the New Yorks, with .899, and George Miller, the Louisvilles, with .894—a very fine high average record in catching.

Vaughn led all the catchers in having the fewest passed balls charged to him, Boyle being second in this respect and Ganzel third, all these catching in not less than twenty-five games.

In first base play Lajoie had but 5 errors charged to him in 39 games, Anson but 7 in 96 games—a splendid record for the sturdy veteran—and Lachance but 13 in 89 games.

In second base play McPhee had only 13 errors charged to him in 116 games, while in third base play Cross had but 13 in 63 games.

In the short field play, Jennings, who led all in team-work play in the position, had 68 errors charged to him in 129 games, but he covered a large space and went for everything in sight, despite of the chances for errors. Cross did good work in this position as well as at third base for the Phillies, though Dolan, of Louisville, led all in percentage figures.

In right field play Keeler had a wonderful record, only 7 errors in 127 games, while Griffin led at centre field with but 13 errors in 119 games, and Kelly, of Baltimore, led at left field with but 13 errors in 130 games.

The outfielding in 1896 was of a high order, no less than 40 outfielders out of 51, who played in 15 games and over, excelling the high fielding percentage figures of .900, while out of 89 infielders no less than 60 exceeded the .900 standard. The tail-enders of the infield positions in 1896 were Davis, of Pittsburg, first base ; Joyce, of Washington, second base ; Harrington, of Boston, third base, and Shannon, of Louisville, shortstop. The lowest record in the outfield was that of Holmes, of Louisville, who did not exceed .793.

The Monthly Campaigns of 1896

NO record of the championship season of each year gives a better idea of the progress made by each club in the pennant race than that of each monthly campaign of the season, from April to September, inclusive. It is an interesting record from first to last, and shows the ups and downs of each club's team in the race very plainly.

APRIL RECORD.

First Division Clubs.	Victories.	Defeats.	Played.	Per cent. of Victories.	Second Division Clubs.	Victories.	Defeats.	Played.	Per cent. of Victories.
Pittsburg........	8	2	10	.800	St. Louis........	6	5	11	.545
Philadelphia.....	8	3	11	.727	Chicago.........	6	5	11	.545
Boston...........	7	4	11	.636	Baltimore	5	6	11	.455
Cincinnati.......	6	4	10	.600	Cleveland.......	4	5	9	.444
Washington......	6	5	11	.545	New York.......	1	10	11	.090
Brooklyn.........	6	5	11	.545	Louisville...	1	10	21	.090

These tables include each separate month's victories and defeats scored by each of the twelve clubs, the names of the clubs being given in the order of most victories credited.

To this table is added that of the pennant race record as it stood at the end of each month of the championship season ; this latter record showing, in addition, the relative positions in the two divisions occupied by each of the twelve clubs.

The above record for April, of course, includes the pennant race record also, up to April 30. It will be readily seen that the two Pennsylvania clubs of Pittsburg and Philadelphia took a commanding lead at the start, while Boston and Cincinnati also showed up well among the leaders ; but the next four clubs were tied for fifth position in the race on April 30, their names being placed in the record in the order of their precedence over each other in winning the series of the month ; thus Washington, having won their series with Brooklyn, thereby led Brooklyn to that extent, as did St. Louis lead Chicago. Baltimore and Cleveland opened badly in April, while New York vied with Louisville for the occupancy of the last ditch.

The May Record. Cleveland again took the lead for the month of May, leaving Baltimore second and Cincinnati third, Pittsburg having lost ground, as did Boston, Brooklyn, Washington and Philadelphia; Cincinnati, on the other hand, gained a point in May, while New York did well. Baltimore also began championship work for the season, and with Cleveland close at hand, they soon showed who the leaders were likely to be in the race.

MAY RECORD.

First Division Clubs.	Victories.	Defeats.	Games.	Per cent. of Victories.	Second Division Clubs.	Victories.	Defeats.	Games.	Per cent. of Victories.
Cleveland	16	6	22	.727	Chicago	12	14	26	.462
Baltimore	17	7	24	.708	Pittsburg	10	12	22	.455
Cincinnati	16	10	26	.615	Washington	10	13	23	.435
Philadelphia	15	11	26	.577	Brooklyn	10	13	23	.435
Boston	13	10	23	.565	Louisville	7	18	25	.280
New York	13	11	24	.542	St. Louis	5	19	24	.268

The pennant race record on May 31, of course, left the clubs occupying somewhat different relative positions in the two divisions to what the monthly table gave them, as will be seen by the appended table.

PENNANT RACE RECORD ON MAY 30.

First Division Clubs.	Victories.	Defeats.	Played.	Per cent. of Victories.	Second Division Clubs.	Victories.	Defeats.	Played.	Per cent. of Victories.
Cleveland	20	11	31	.645	Chicago	18	19	37	.486
Baltimore	22	13	35	.629	Washington	16	18	34	.471
Cincinnati	22	14	36	.611	Brooklyn	16	18	34	.471
Philadelphia	22	14	36	.611	New York	14	21	35	.400
Boston	20	14	34	.588	St. Louis	11	24	35	.314
Pittsburg	18	14	32	.563	Louisville	8	27	35	.229

The June Record. Cincinnati did better than Cleveland in June by 10 percentage points in the monthly record, but not in the pennant race able. Baltimore pulled up in both records. Philadelphia fell off badly this month, while Boston did better than in May.

Here is the June record of victories and defeats. Seven of the twelve clubs, it will be seen, won more games than they lost this month.

THE JUNE RECORD, 1896.

First Division Clubs.	Victories.	Defeats.	Played.	Per cent. of Victories.	Second Division Clubs.	Victories.	Defeats.	Played.	Per cent. of Victories.
Baltimore........	15	6	21	.714	Chicago..........	14	12	26	.538
Cincinnati........	18	8	26	.692	Pittsburg.........	12	13	25	.480
Cleveland........	15	7	22	.682	New York........	10	12	22	.455
Boston...........	14	8	22	.636	Philadelphia......	8	15	23	.348
Washington......	11	8	19	.579	St. Louis.........	4	20	24	.167
Brooklyn.........	13	11	24	.542	Louisville........	3	17	20	.150

In the pennant race record of June 30, Pittsburg got in the first division in place of Brooklyn, while Philadelphia still continued to lose ground. Here is the race record as it stood on June 30:

PENNANT RACE RECORD ON JUNE 30.

First Division Clubs.	Victories.	Defeats.	Games.	Per cent. of Victories.	Second Division Clubs.	Victories.	Defeats.	Games.	Per cent. of Victories.
Baltimore........	37	19	56	.661	Chicago..........	32	31	63	.508
Cleveland........	35	18	53	.660	Philadelphia.....	30	29	59	.508
Cincinnati........	40	22	62	.645	Brooklyn.........	29	29	58	.500
Boston...........	34	22	56	.607	New York........	24	33	57	.421
Pittsburg.........	30	27	57	.526	St. Louis.........	15	44	59	.254
Washington......	27	26	53	.509	Louisville........	11	44	55	.200

The July Record. Cincinnati did what was thought to be a winning business in July, leading all the clubs in that hot summer campaign, as the club's figures of 21 victories out of 28 games show. Chicago was the next successful team in that month, and Baltimore was third, Cleveland falling off badly as did Boston, Philadelphia, Brooklyn and Washington, the latter team losing 21 games out of 28 in July, and Brooklyn 17 out of 26. Louisville improved considerably. Here is the record for the month:

RECORD FOR JULY.

First Division Clubs.	Victories.	Defeats.	Games.	Per cent. of Victories.	Second Division Clubs.	Victories.	Defeats.	Games.	Per cent. of Victories.
Cincinnati	21	7	28	.750	New York	10	16	26	.385
Chicago	20	7	27	.741	Louisville	10	16	26	.385
Baltimore	18	8	26	.692	Boston	10	17	27	.370
Cleveland	20	12	32	.625	Philadelphia	9	16	25	.360
Pittsburg	16	12	28	.571	Brooklyn	9	17	26	.346
St. Louis	12	14	26	.462	Washington	8	21	29	.276

The pennant race figures changed the above relative position of the clubs considerably, as will be seen by the appended table. It was in this month that the Cincinnati team was looked upon as a sure participant in the Temple Cup games, but they failed to realize expectations.

PENNANT RACE RECORD OF JULY 31.

First Division Clubs.	Victories.	Defeats.	Games.	Per cent. of Victories.	Second Division Clubs.	Victories.	Defeats.	Games.	Per cent. of Victories.
Cincinnati	61	20	81	.678	Philadelphia	39	45	84	.464
Baltimore	55	27	92	.671	Brooklyn	38	46	84	.452
Cleveland	55	30	85	.647	Washington	34	46	80	.425
Chicago	52	38	90	.578	New York	34	49	83	.410
Pittsburg	46	39	85	.541	St. Louis	27	58	85	.318
Boston	44	39	83	.536	Louisville	21	60	81	.259

Record For August. Next to Baltimore the New York team were the most successful in the August campaign, while Washington and Cincinnati both fell off badly.

RECORD FOR AUGUST.

First Division Clubs.	Victories.	Defeats.	Games.	Per cent. of Victories.	Second Division Clubs.	Victories.	Defeats.	Games.	Per cent. of Victories.
Baltimore	19	8	26	.731	Chicago	12	10	22	.545
New York	18	10	28	.643	Cleveland	10	12	22	.455
Boston	15	10	25	.600	Cincinnati	8	11	19	.421
Brooklyn	14	10	24	.583	Washington	9	18	27	.333
Pittsburg	13	10	23	.565	St. Louis	7	16	23	.304
Philadelphia	15	12	27	.556	Louisville	6	18	24	.250

BASE BALL GUIDE. 59

The pennant race record on August 31 changed the relative positions of the clubs from the above order materially. By this time Baltimore had virtually won the pennant, and the only question of interest in the race as to the three leaders was in regard to Cincinnati's and Cleveland's chances for playing in the Temple Cup series. The next point of interest was as to which of the three clubs leading the second division would obtain seventh place. This point the September campaign had to decide. Here is the pennant race record for August:

PENNANT RACE RECORD ON AUGUST 31.

First Division Clubs.	Victories.	Defeats.	Games.	Per cent. of Victories.	Second Division Clubs.	Victories.	Defeats.	Games.	Per cent. of Victories.
Baltimore	74	34	108	.685	Philadelphia	53	57	110	.482
Cincinnati	69	40	109	.633	Brooklyn	52	56	108	.481
Cleveland	65	42	107	.607	New York	52	59	111	.468
Chicago	64	48	112	.571	Washington	43	64	107	.402
Boston	59	49	108	.546	St. Louis	34	74	108	.315
Pittsburg	59	49	108	.546	Louisville	27	79	106	.255

The September Record. Before September was half over two points had been decided: first, that Cleveland and Cincinnati would play with Baltimore in the Temple Cup series, and that the New York club would lead the second division clubs. After this, but little interest was manifested in the closing month of the contest. The September record ended as follows:

SEPTEMBER RECORD.

First Division Clubs.	Victories.	Defeats.	Games.	Per cent. of Victories.	Second Division Clubs.	Victories.	Defeats.	Games.	Per cent. of Victories.
Baltimore	16	5	21	.762	Philadelphia	9	11	20	.450
Cleveland	15	6	21	.714	Louisville	11	14	25	.440
Boston	15	8	23	.652	Chicago	7	9	16	.438
Washington	15	8	23	.652	Pittsburg	7	14	21	.333
New York	12	8	20	.600	St. Louis	6	16	22	.273
Cincinnati	9	10	19	.474	Brooklyn	6	17	23	.261

A feature of the September campaign was the battles made by Washington and New York. Washington lost ground in August, but both clubs pulled up in September. Cincinnati managed to retain third place in the race, though losing more games in September than they won, as did seven of the twelve clubs. Brooklyn did wretchedly in September, losing more games than any other club, viz.: 17 out of 23 won and lost. Louisville battled well, but could not escape the last ditch. Here is the pennant race record for the last month of the campaign:

THE PENNANT RACE RECORD ON SEPTEMBER 30.

First Division Clubs.	Victories.	Defeats.	Games.	Per cent. of Victories.	Second Division Clubs.	Victories.	Defeats.	Games.	Per cent. of Victories.
Baltimore........	90	39	129	.698	New York........	64	67	131	.489
Cleveland........	80	48	128	.625	Philadelphia.....	62	68	130	.477
Cincinnati.......	77	50	127	.606	Washington......	58	73	131	.443
Boston...........	74	57	131	.565	Brooklyn........	58	73	131	.443
Chicago..........	71	57	128	.555	St. Louis........	40	90	130	.308
Pittsburg........	66	63	129	.512	Louisville.......	38	93	131	.290

Though the Washington club was tied in percentage victories with the Brooklyns, we give the Senators the lead in the record, as they are entitled to it on the basis of winning their series with Brooklyn by 8 games to 4. The names of the clubs are given in the order of their final pennant race record. The full monthly record for the whole season is as follows:

THE FULL SIX MONTHS' RECORD OF 1896.

Clubs.	April.		May.		June.		July.		Aug.		Sept.		Total.	
	W.	L.	W.	L.	W.	L.	W.	L.	W.	L.	W.	L.	W.	L.
Baltimore............	5	6	17	7	15	6	18	8	19	7	16	5	90	39
Cleveland............	4	5	16	6	15	7	20	12	10	12	15	6	80	48
Cincinnati...........	6	4	16	10	18	8	21	7	8	11	9	10	77	50
Boston...............	7	4	13	10	14	8	10	17	15	10	15	8	74	57
Chicago..............	6	5	12	14	14	12	20	7	12	10	7	9	71	57
Pittsburg............	8	2	10	12	12	13	16	12	13	10	7	14	66	63
New York............	1	10	13	11	10	12	10	16	18	10	12	8	64	67
Philadelphia.........	8	3	15	11	8	15	9	16	13	12	9	11	62	68
Washington..........	6	5	10	13	11	8	8	21	9	18	15	8	58	73
Brooklyn.............	6	5	10	13	18	11	9	17	14	10	6	17	58	73
St. Louis.............	6	5	5	19	4	20	12	14	7	16	6	16	40	90
Louisville............	1	10	7	18	3	17	10	16	6	18	11	14	38	93
Totals...............	64	64	144	144	137	137	163	163	144	144	128	128	778	778

The Individual Club Records of 1896

IN making up the tables of the individual club records of the contests in the championship arena for 1896 we present two tables for each club, one to record the victories, defeats, games played, drawn games and the percentage of victories figures with each club played with, as also those of the clubs of the two divisions separately, as well as the grand total figures ; the second table giving the figures of the series won, lost, tied and unfinished, together with the "Chicago" victories and defeats with each club, the number of games won and lost by a single run, the single and double figure scores in victories and defeats and the victories and defeats scored by each club with each opposing team on the home fields, as well as on fields abroad. These two tables combine all the essential points in an individual club's season's record.

The Champions of 1896. The Baltimore club, in 1896, achieved the high honor of making the record of three successive pennant race triumphs, viz., those of 1894, 1895 and 1896. The only other clubs which have scored such a record in National League history, were the Chicagos, in 1880, 1881 and 1882, and the Bostons in 1891, 1892 and 1893. In the old Professional Association's annals, from 1871 to 1875, inclusive, the Boston Red Stockings, under Harry Wright, won the pennant four years in succession, but Managers Anson, Selee and Hanlon have yet to equal this four-times-winner record. In the annals of the old American Association, too, the St. Louis club won that Association's pennant four times in succession, viz., in 1885, 1886, 1887 and 1888. Manager Hanlon has an advantage over the veterans Anson and Selee, in regard to the chances for a four-times-winner record ; inasmuch as he has but to win the pennant of 1897 to achieve the honor, and to lead both Anson and Selee in League annals, and also to equal the late Harry Wright's record ; while the others have to begin over again and build up a new record. That Hanlon and his team of 1897 will strive their best to do so goes without saying, while there is not the least doubt that eleven other League clubs will equally try their best to prevent him. This struggle by the Baltimores of 1897 for the four-times-winner record in League history, will unquestionably be a great feature of the coming year's campaign. Next to that will come the fight for second position in the race in order to take part in the Temple Cup series of 1897.

The Baltimores' Campaign of 1896. The Baltimores opened the first month of the championship campaign of 1896 with more defeats than victories, their April record being 5 victories to 6 defeats; but in May they got down to pennant-winning work, and though closely pushed by both Cincinnati and Cleveland, they managed to keep well up in the van, their May record being 17 victories to but 7 defeats, while in June their figures were respectively 15 to 6, and in July, 18 to 8. In August they made their best record, 19 to 7, and they finished up with 16 to 5 in September.

In the race of 1896 the Cleveland team was found to be the Baltimores' most difficult opponents to win games from, and yet in the Temple Cup series the latter won with four straight victories to their credit. Next to the Clevelands, the Bostons did the best against the champions and—of the first division clubs—Cincinnati the poorest, this latter team, with the Louisville, Washington and Philadelphia teams, only winning 6 games out of the 48 the three played with the champions, the Phillies being "Chicagoed" by 12 to 0 in their series of twelve games with the Baltimores. The champions had but three drawn games in their season's record, viz., their 5 to 5 ten innings game, and 11 to 11 eight innings game with the Chicagos and their 4 to 4 game with the Clevelands. Their highest percentage of victory figures during the season was with the Phillies, viz., 1.000, and their lowest with the Clevelands, .273. The champions won 8 of their 11 series, lost 2 and drew 1. They played 129 games of their quota of 132, 3 being drawn. Here is the above record in full:

BALTIMORE VS.	FIRST DIVISION.						SECOND DIVISION.						Grand Totals.
	Cleveland.	Boston.	Chicago.	Pittsburg.	Cincinnati.	Totals.	Brooklyn.	New York.	St. Louis.	Louisville.	Washington.	Philadelphia.	Totals.
Victories..................	3	5	7	9	10	34	6	9	9	10	10	12	56	90
Defeats....................	8	7	4	2	2	23	6	3	3	2	2	0	16	39
Played.....................	11	12	11	11	12	57	12	12	12	12	12	12	72	129
Drawn.....................	1	0	2	0	0	3	0	0	0	0	0	0	0	3

Per cent. of victories.—Against Cleveland, .273; Boston, .417; Chicago, .636; Pittsburg, .818; Cincinnati, .833; total, first division clubs, .596. Brooklyn, .500; New York, .750; St. Louis, .750; Louisville, .833; Washington, .833; Philadelphia, 1.000; total, second division clubs, .778. Grand total, .698.

BASE BALL GUIDE. 63

The second table, giving the other statistics of their full season's record, is appended. By this second table it will be seen that of the 129 victories and defeats combined, they won 52 victories by single figure scores and only 38 by double figures; while they lost 27 games by single figures and only 12 by double figures, leaving their totals at 79 single figure games to 50 marked by double figure scores. A notable record was that of their victories at home and abroad, they winning no less than 43 abroad against 47 at home, the best record of the kind of the season.

THE BALTIMORE CLUB'S RECORD FOR 1896.

BALTIMORE vs.	First Division.					Second Division.						Grand Totals.
	Cleveland.	Cincinnati.	Boston.	Chicago.	Pittsburg.	Totals.	New York.	Philadelphia.	Washington.	Brooklyn.	St. Louis.	Louisville.	Totals.	
Series won......................	0	1	0	1	1	3	1	1	1	0	1	1	5	8
Series lost......................	1	0	1	0	0	2	0	0	0	0	0	0	0	2
Series tied......................	0	0	0	0	0	0	0	0	0	1	0	0	1	1
Series unfinished...............	1	0	0	1	1	3	0	0	0	0	0	0	0	3
"Chicago" victories............	0	0	0	0	2	2	1	0	2	1	2	1	7	9
"Chicago" defeats.............	2	1	2	0	1	6	0	0	0	1	0	1	2	8
Won by one run.................	0	2	1	2	3	8	2	2	2	0	0	1	7	15
Lost by one run.................	1	0	3	1	0	5	0	0	0	1	1	2	4	9
Single figure victories.........	1	7	3	4	6	21	5	8	5	3	6	4	31	52
Single figure defeats...........	3	2	5	2	1	13	2	0	2	5	3	2	14	27
Double figure victories	2	3	2	3	3	13	4	4	5	3	3	6	25	38
Double figure defeats..........	5	0	2	2	1	10	1	0	0	1	0	0	2	12
Victories at home..............	1	6	2	3	5	17	6	6	4	4	4	6	30	47
Defeats at home................	4	0	1	2	1	8	0	0	1	3	2	0	6	14
Victories abroad................	2	4	3	4	4	17	3	6	6	2	5	4	26	43
Defeats abroad..................	4	2	6	2	1	15	3	0	1	3	1	2	10	25

The difference in percentage points at the close of the April campaign between the leading Pittsburg team and the tail-ender of Louisville was no less than .710, showing a very uneven race.

The Clevelands' Campaign of 1896.

The Cleveland team opened their campaign of 1896 very unpromisingly in April, as they only won 4 out of the 9 games they played that month, and ended their first month's work as occupants of tenth place in the race; but in May they rallied in fine style, they winning no less than 16 of the 22 games played in May, and at the end of the month they led in the race with the percentage figures of .645, Baltimore being second with .629 and Cincinnati third with .611, New York, St. Louis and Louisville being the tailenders. In June the Clevelands were headed by the Baltimores, with the percentage figures of .661 to .660 on June 30 ; Cincinnati being third, with .645. In July the Clevelands were forced to return to third position in the race, the percentage figures on July 31 showing Cincinnati to be in the van with .678 to their credit, Baltimore being second with .671 and Cleveland a poor third with but .647. In August both Cleveland and Cincinnati lost more games than they won, the former winning but 10 out of 22 games, while Cincinnati only won 8 out of 19. Baltimore still kept in the van, however, and on August 31 the champions led with .685 to their credit to Cincinnati's .633 and Cleveland's .607, and the Spiders' chances for taking part in the Temple Cup series at that time were not promising. But the September campaign settled this latter question very satisfactorily to the Clevelands, as they rallied well, while the Cincinnatis fell off badly. Before the last month of the season began it had become a foregone conclusion that the Baltimores would make a three-times-winner record for 1896, and the only question of interest in the race at this time was the struggle between Cincinnati and Cleveland for second place. The former had kept so bravely in the race up to the middle of August that their chances for playing in the cup series had become very favorable. But their bad tumble in September put an end to that ; and when the last month's campaign ended the Clevelands had secured second place in the race, with the privilege of playing in the Temple Cup series. Here is the record of their victories, defeats, games played and drawn games for the full season, together with their percentage of victories as scored against each of their eleven adversaries in the pennant race of 1896 :

CLEVELAND VS.	First Division.						Second Division.						Grand Totals.
	Pittsburg.	Cincinnati.	Boston.	Baltimore.	Chicago.	Totals.	Philadelphia.	New York.	Brooklyn.	Louisville.	Washington.	St. Louis.	Totals.	
Victories	4	5	7	8	9	33	6	7	7	8	9	10	47	80
Defeats	8	6	5	3	2	24	6	5	5	3	3	2	24	48
Played	12	11	12	11	11	57	12	12	12	11	12	12	71	128
Drawn	1	0	1	1	1	4	0	0	0	2	1	0	3	7

Per cent. of victories—Against Pittsburg, .333; Cincinnati, .455; Boston, .583; Baltimore, .727; Chicago, .818; totals, first division clubs, .579. Philadelphia, .500; New York, .583; Brooklyn, .583; Louisville, .727; Washington, .750; St. Louis, .833; totals, second division clubs, .662. Grand totals, .625.

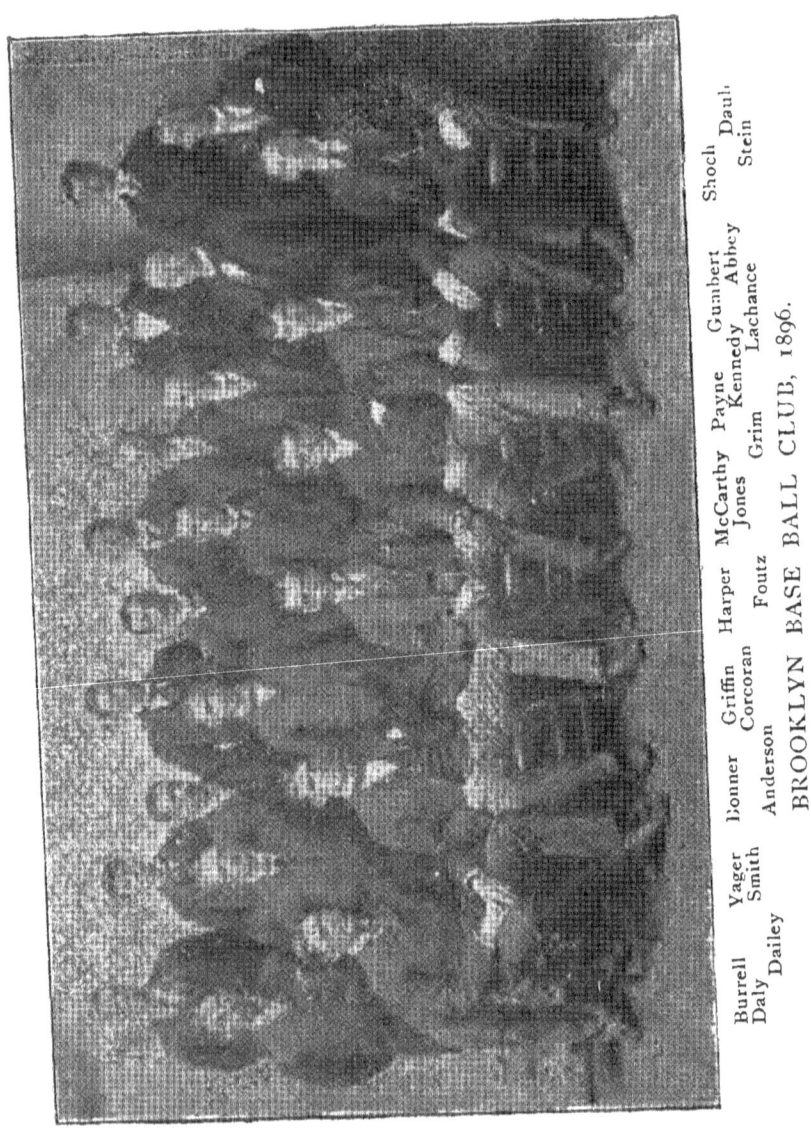

Burrell Yager   Bonner   Griffin   Harper   McCarthy Payne   Gumbert   Shoch   Daub
Daly   Smith   Corcoran   Jones   Kennedy Abbey   Stein
Dailey   Anderson   Foutz   Grim   Lachance

BROOKLYN BASE BALL CLUB, 1896.

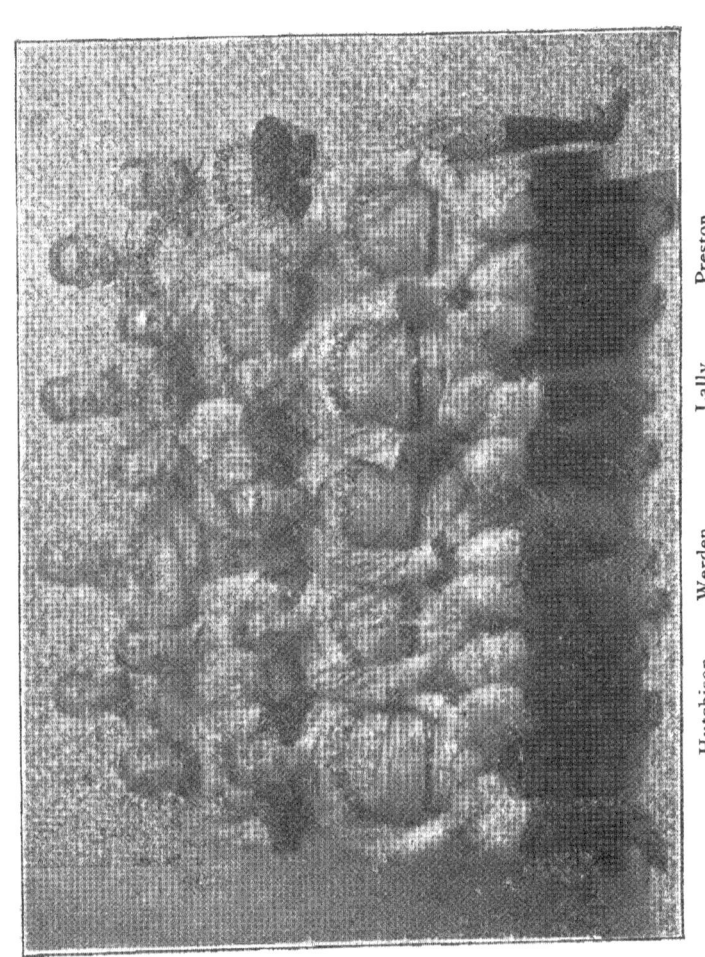

Tiggemeier Hutchison Werden Lally Preston Moran
Pickett Parker Conners Schriver
Ball Wilmot Kuehne Baker
THE CHAMPION MINNEAPOLIS BASE BALL CLUB, 1896.

Ladd Geier Lajoie Marston (Mgr.) Kennedy Lyons Rupert
       Reilly McDermott   Klobedanz Fitzpatrick
FALL RIVER BASE BALL CLUB, 1896.

Hausman   Carl   Phelan   Gonding   Bowman
 Drinkwater Smith   Knox   Powell   Dowie
THE CHAMPION NEW ORLEANS CLUB OF THE SOUTHERN LEAGUE.

Vetters Ferguson Kihm Cook Cecil
Beck Coyle Stroebel (Mgr.) Kelb Smith
     Keenan Arthur Hartman

TOLEDO BASE BALL CLUB. 1896.

Figgemier Purvis McCradie Letcher Preston
Sonier Frick (Pres.) Traffley (Mgr.) Burrell
Hickey Andrews Lohman (Capt.) McKibben Mohler

DES MOINES BASE BALL CLUB, 1896.

Wayave   Jayne   Elliott (Mgr.)   Smith
Easton   Gunster   Earle   Bradley (Capt.)   Wilson   Altman   Wheeler
Titus   Ward   Sankey

PRINCETON COLLEGE BASE'BALL TEAM, 1896.

Jerrems Twombley Simmons Thorn Letton Greenway De Saulles Smith
Keator Quinby (Capt.) Trudeau Barlett
Hazen

YALE UNIVERSITY BASE BALL TEAM, 1896.

It will be seen that the smallest percentage of victories figures against the first division clubs was made in their series with the Baltimores and their highest figures with the Chicagos. With the second division clubs their lowest figures were with the Phillies and their highest with St. Louis. Their percentage figures with the five first division clubs was .579 and with the six second division clubs .662, while their combined figures for the whole season against the eleven clubs was .625. The Clevelands had more drawn games during the season than any other of the twelve clubs.

The table showing the series record, the "Chicago" games, the games won and lost by a single run, the single and double figure score games and the games played at home and abroad for the entire season, is appended. By this it will be seen that the Clevelands won 8 of their 11 series of games, they losing to Pittsburg club, while they won their series with Baltimore, Boston and Chicago, of the first division clubs, and all but one with those of the second division. They were beaten 6 games out of their 11 with Cincinnati and were tied with Philadelphia, 6 to 6.

They had a good record of victories abroad, scoring next to Baltimore in this respect. They also excelled the Baltimores in their proportion of single figure games to those of double figures. Here is their full record of the second table figures:

CLEVELAND vs	FIRST DIVISION.					SECOND DIVISION.						
	Baltimore.	Cincinnati.	Boston.	Chicago.	Pittsburg.	Totals.	New York.	Philadelphia.	Washington.	Brooklyn.	St. Louis.	Louisville.	Totals.	Grand Totals.
Series won................	1	0	1	1	0	3	1	0	1	1	1	1	5	8
Series lost.................	0	1	0	0	1	2	0	0	0	0	0	0	0	2
Series tied.................	0	0	0	0	0	0	0	1	0	0	0	0	1	1
Series unfinished.........	1	1	0	1	0	3	0	0	0	0	0	1	1	4
"Chicago" victories.......	2	0	0	1	0	1	0	1	3	0	0	2	6	7
"Chicago" defeats.........	0	0	0	0	2	2	0	0	0	0	0	0	0	2
Won by one run...........	1	2	1	0	1	5	1	1	0	1	3	3	9	14
Lost by one run...........	0	2	0	1	0	3	2	1	1	2	0	0	6	9
Single figure victories....	3	3	4	6	8	19	4	4	5	5	8	6	32	51
Single figure defeats.....	1	5	3	2	7	18	5	1	3	3	2	1	15	33
Double figure victories...	5	2	3	3	1	14	3	2	4	2	2	2	15	29
Double figure defeats....	2	1	2	0	1	6	0	5	0	2	0	2	9	15
Victories at home........	4	4	3	4	2	17	4	3	5	4	6	4	26	43
Defeats at home..........	2	1	2	1	3	9	2	3	1	2	0	2	10	19
Victories abroad..........	4	2	3	5	2	16	3	3	4	3	4	4	21	37
Defeats abroad...........	1	5	3	1	5	15	3	3	2	3	2	1	14	29

The Cincinnatis' Campaign of 1896.

The Cincinnati club, under Manager Ewing, passed through the most successful championship campaign in 1896 known in the annals of the club since they won the American Association's first pennant race in 1882. From the time the team closed its April campaign in 1896 to the close of that season the team was never out of the first division class in the race. The Cincinnatis took up their position in the van on the 19th of May, with the percentage figures of .654 to Cleveland's .652 and Boston's .640, Baltimore being fifth on that date; and they remained at the head until May 28, after which they alternated with Cleveland between second and third positions right through the season. They occupied first place in the race, with a few days' exception, from July 11 up to August 4 and stood in second place until September 2, when they lost ground badly and finally had to allow the Clevelands to pair the Baltimores in the Temple Cup series. The cause of the sudden downfall in September has never been fully explained, but we think over-confidence in the team's ultimate success had a great deal to do with it. Confidence in a team is a great aid to success, as a rule, but it can be carried to an extreme, and when it is there are apt to be sudden failures as a result. The success of the club, even though it failed to reach the goal or even a share in the Temple Cup prizes was sufficient, however, to make its season of 1896 an exceptional one, especially in the financial profits it yielded.

The first table of the campaign records of 1896 shows that the Cincinnatis' only failure in their 11 series was with the Baltimores. With all the other first division clubs they had a close fight and they defeated all the second division clubs except New York, whom they tied. Here is the record:

CINCINNATI VS.	Baltimore.	Pittsburg.	Cleveland.	Boston.	Chicago.	Totals.	New York.	Washington.	Philadelphia.	Louisville.	Brooklyn.	St. Louis.	Totals.	Grand Totals.
Victories...	2	5	6	6	6	25	6	7	8	9	10	12	52	77
Defeats...	10	7	5	5	4	31	6	4	4	3	2	0	19	50
Played...	12	12	11	11	10	56	12	11	12	12	12	12	71	127
Drawn...	0	0	0	0	1	1	0	0	0	0	0	0	0	1

Per cent. of victories—Against Baltimore, .167; Pittsburg, .417; Cleveland, .545; Boston, .545; Chicago, .600; total, first division clubs, .446. New York, .500; Washington, .636; Philadelphia, .667; Louisville, .750; Brooklyn, .833; St. Louis, 1.000; totals, second division clubs, .732. Grand total, .606.

The Cincinnatis, though they only won 5 series of games of the season's 11, lost but 2, viz., with Baltimore and Pittsburg. They had 3 unfinished series with first division clubs and one with those of the second division clubs. The Reds led all the clubs in "Chicagoing" opponents, and were only "Chicagoed" once. They lost more games by a single run than they won, and they took the lead in single figure games. They played their best on their home field, and lost more games on fields abroad than either Baltimore or Cleveland or any first division club. Here is the second table record by the club for 1896:

CINCINNATI VS.	First Division						Second Division						
	Baltimore.	Cleveland.	Boston.	Chicago.	Pittsburg.	Totals.	New York.	Philadelphia.	Washington.	Brooklyn.	St. Louis.	Louisville.	Totals.	Grand Totals.
Series won............	0	0	0	0	0	0	0	1	1	1	1	1	5	5
Series lost............	1	0	0	0	1	2	0	0	0	0	0	0	0	2
Series tied............	0	0	0	0	0	0	1	0	0	0	0	0	0	1
Series unfinished......	0	1	1	1	0	3	0	0	1	0	0	0	1	4
"Chicago" victories...	1	0	1	1	2	5	2	1	0	2	1	1	7	12
"Chicago" defeats....	0	0	0	1	0	1	0	0	0	0	0	0	0	1
Won by one run.......	0	2	1	0	0	3	1	1	0	2	2	2	8	11
Lost by one run.......	2	2	1	0	2	7	0	1	1	0	0	3	5	12
Single figure victories.	2	5	5	5	3	20	6	5	2	7	9	6	35	55
Single figure defeats...	7	3	3	4	6	23	3	4	4	1	0	3	15	38
Double figure victories.	0	1	1	1	2	5	0	3	5	3	3	3	17	22
Double figure defeats..	3	2	2	0	1	8	3	0	0	1	0	0	4	12
Victories at home.....	2	5	4	3	2	16	4	6	5	6	8	6	35	51
Defeats at home.......	4	2	1	1	4	12	2	0	1	0	0	0	3	15
Victories abroad.......	0	1	2	3	3	9	2	2	2	4	4	3	17	26
Defeats abroad........	6	3	4	3	3	19	4	4	3	2	0	3	16	35

The Bostons' Campaign of 1896.

The Boston team disappointed the expectations of its admirers in 1896. It opened the season among the second division teams, and was low as eighth position the last week in April. The team pulled up in May, but it was no higher than fifth place on May 31. In June the team improved its position somewhat, but lost ground in July, it being down to sixth place on July 23, and remained there until the last of August. Then the team rallied, and finally worked up to fourth position by the close of the campaign. The Boston team found the Chicagos the hardest team to whip, as they only won 3 games out of the 12 played with Anson's Colts, one game being drawn. They had no difficulty defeating the Baltimores and Pittsburgs, but lost their series with the Cincinnatis and Chicagos. They won every series with the second division clubs, beating Brooklyn no less than 10 games out of 12. Here is the first table record:

BOSTON vs.	FIRST DIVISION.						SECOND DIVISION.						Grand Totals.
	Chicago.	Cincinnati.	Cleveland.	Baltimore.	Pittsburg.	Totals.	Philadelphia.	New York.	Washington.	St. Louis.	Louisville.	Brooklyn.	Totals.	
Victories	3	5	5	7	7	27	7	7	7	8	8	10	47	74
Defeats	9	7	6	5	5	32	5	5	5	4	4	2	25	57
Played	12	11	12	12	12	59	12	12	12	12	12	12	72	131
Drawn	1	1	0	0	0	2	0	0	0	0	0	0	0	2

Per cent. of victories.—Against Chicago, .250; Cleveland, .417; Cincinnati, .455; Baltimore, .583; Pittsburg, .583; totals, .458. Against Philadelphia, .583; New York, .583; Washington, .583; St. Louis, .667; Louisville, .667; Brooklyn, .833; totals, .653. Grand total, .565.

In the second table record it will be seen that the Bostons won 8 of the series with the other 11 clubs, they losing to Cleveland and Chicago only, their series with Cincinnati being unfinished, 5 to 6 in the Cincinnatis' favor. A feature of their record was their two "Chicago" victories over the Baltimore champions. They were well up with the leaders in single figure games, but they won a third more victories on home fields than on those abroad. Appended is the record of the second table:

BOSTON vs.	FIRST DIVISION.						SECOND DIVISION.						Grand Totals.
	Baltimore.	Cleveland.	Cincinnati.	Chicago.	Pittsburg.	Totals.	New York.	Philadelphia.	Washington.	Brooklyn.	St. Louis.	Louisville.	Totals.	
Series won	1	0	0	0	1	2	1	1	1	1	1	1	6	8
Series lost	0	1	0	1	0	2	0	0	0	0	0	0	0	2
Series tied	0	0	0	0	0	0	0	0	0	0	0	0	0	0
Series unfinished	0	0	1	0	0	1	0	0	0	0	0	0	0	1
"Chicago" victories	2	0	0	0	0	2	1	0	1	0	0	2	4	6
"Chicago" defeats	0	0	1	0	1	2	0	0	0	1	0	1	3	3
Won by one run	3	0	1	0	3	7	0	1	2	4	1	0	8	15
Lost by one run	1	1	1	2	0	5	2	0	2	1	1	0	6	11
Single figure victories	5	3	3	3	5	19	6	5	6	10	3	1	31	50
Single figure defeats	3	4	5	5	4	21	3	3	3	2	2	2	15	36
Double figure victories	2	2	2	0	2	8	1	2	1	0	5	7	16	24
Double figure defeats	2	3	1	4	1	11	2	2	2	0	2	2	10	21
Victories at home	6	3	4	2	3	18	4	5	4	5	5	4	27	45
Defeats at home	3	2	2	4	3	15	2	1	3	1	1	2	10	25
Victories abroad	1	2	1	0	4	8	3	2	4	5	3	4	21	29
Defeats abroad	2	4	4	5	2	17	3	4	2	1	3	2	15	32

BASE BALL GUIDE.   69

The Chicagos' Campaign of 1896.

The Chicagos did better against the first division clubs in 1896 than the Bostons did, but the former lost ground against those of the second division clubs, two of the latter clubs winning their series against the Chicagos. The Colts found their toughest opponents in the Cleveland team, while with the Pittsburgs they had an easy task, as the Pirates only won 1 game out of the 12 they played with Anson's team. The latter also got the best of the Bostons, but lost to all three of the leaders, as they did to New York and Philadelphia. With Brooklyn they had a tie series, while they won easily against Washington, St. Louis and Louisville. Their poorest percentage figures were with the Clevelands, .182, while their highest figures were .917 with the Pittsburgs. Against the five first division clubs their percentage figures was .536, while with those of the second division they were but .569. Their combined total figures for the season were .555. Their first table record for 1896 is given herewith:

Chicago vs.	First Division.						Second Division.						Grand Totals.
	Cleveland.	Baltimore.	Cincinnati.	Boston.	Pittsburg.	Totals.	Philadelphia.	New York.	Brooklyn.	Washington.	Louisville.	St. Louis.	Totals.	
Victories..................	2	4	4	9	11	30	4	5	6	8	9	9	41	71
Defeats	9	7	6	3	1	26	8	7	6	4	3	3	31	57
Played.....................	11	11	10	12	12	56	12	12	12	12	12	12	72	128
Drawn	1	2	1	0	0	4	0	0	0	0	0	0	0	4

Per cent. of victories—Against Cleveland, .182; Baltimore, .364; Cincinnati, .400; Boston, .750; Pittsburg, .917; total, first division clubs, .536. Philadelphia, .333; New York, .417; Brooklyn, .500; Washington, .667; Louisville, .750; St. Louis, .750; total, second division clubs, .569. Grand total, .555.

The Chicago Colts won but 5 of their 11 series, despite of the fact of their leading all but the two leaders in percentage of victories against first division clubs. They did not do much in "Chicagoing" opposing teams, as they lost more games that way than they won. They did well in single figure games, but were far more successful on their home field than in games abroad, by 42 to 29. They won 4 more games than they lost by one run, the figures being 16 to 12, respectively. Their second table record for 1896 is given on the following page:

CHICAGO VS.	First Division.						Second Division.							Grand Totals.
	Baltimore.	Cleveland.	Cincinnati.	Boston.	Pittsburg.	Totals.	New York.	Philadelphia.	Washington.	Brooklyn.	St. Louis.	Louisville.	Totals.	
Series won	0	0	0	1	1	2	0	0	1	0	1	1	3	5
Series lost	1	1	0	0	0	2	1	1	0	0	0	0	2	4
Series tied	0	0	0	0	0	0	0	0	0	1	0	0	1	1
Series unfinished	0	0	1	0	0	1	0	0	0	0	0	0	0	1
"Chicago" victories	0	0	1	0	1	2	0	0	0	0	0	0	0	2
"Chicago" defeats	0	1	1	0	0	2	1	0	1	1	0	0	3	5
Won by one run	1	1	0	2	1	5	1	1	3	2	2	2	11	16
Lost by one run	2	2	0	1	2	7	0	1	1	0	0	3	5	12
Single figure victories	2	2	4	5	8	21	2	3	4	3	7	7	26	47
Single figure defeats	4	6	5	3	0	18	5	3	3	6	2	3	22	40
Double figure victories	2	0	0	4	3	9	3	1	4	3	2	2	15	24
Double figure defeats	3	3	1	0	1	8	2	5	1	0	1	0	9	17
Victories at home	2	1	3	5	5	16	4	3	5	3	6	5	26	42
Defeats at home	4	5	3	1	1	14	2	3	1	3	0	1	10	24
Victories abroad	2	1	1	4	6	14	1	1	3	3	3	4	15	29
Defeats abroad	3	4	3	2	1	13	5	5	3	3	3	2	21	34

The Pittsburgs' Campaign of 1896.

The Pittsburg team in 1896 could do nothing against Anson's Colts, while they had a comparatively easy task in winning against the New York team, but the latter defeated the Chicagos without much difficulty. The Pirates, however, got the best of Cleveland and Cincinnati in their series together and also against New York, but it was close fighting for them against Philadelphia, Washington and Brooklyn, while they easily polished off the two tail-enders, St. Louis and Louisville. The first table record for 1896:

PITTSBURG VS.	First Division.						Second Division.							Grand Totals.
	Chicago.	Baltimore.	Boston.	Cincinnati.	Cleveland.	Totals.	Brooklyn.	Philadelphia.	Washington.	New York.	St. Louis.	Louisville.	Totals.	
Victories	1	2	5	7	8	23	5	6	6	8	8	10	43	66
Defeats	11	9	7	5	4	36	6	6	4	3	2	2	27	63
Played	12	11	12	12	12	59	11	12	12	12	11	12	70	129
Drawn	0	0	0	0	1	1	1	0	0	0	0	1		2

Per cent. of victories—Against Chicago, .083; Baltimore, .182; Boston, .417; Cincinnati, .545; Cleveland, .667; total, first division clubs, .390. Brooklyn, .455; Philadelphia, .500; Washington, .500; New York, .667; St. Louis, .727; Louisville, .833; total, second division clubs, .614. Grand total, .512.

The figures of their second table record shows that while they won but 5 of their 11 series they lost but 2, 2 being tied. In "Chicago" games they won more than they lost. They did well, too, in single figure games, and almost won as many games on fields abroad as they did on their home grounds. Here is the second table record for 1896:

PITTSBURG vs.	\multicolumn{5}{c	}{First Division.}	\multicolumn{6}{c	}{Second Division.}	Grand Totals.
	Baltimore.	Cleveland.	Cincinnati.	Boston.	Chicago.	Totals.	New York.	Philadelphia.	Washington.	Brooklyn.	St. Louis.	Louisville.	Totals.	
Series won..................	0	1	1	0	0	2	1	0	0	0	1	1	3	5
Series lost..................	1	0	0	0	1	2	0	0	0	0	0	0	0	2
Series tied..................	0	0	0	0	0	0	0	1	1	0	0	0	2	2
Series unfinished............	1	0	0	0	0	1	0	0	0	1	1	0	2	3
"Chicago" victories.........	1	2	0	1	0	4	0	0	1	1	1	1	4	8
"Chicago" defeats...........	2	0	2	0	1	5	0	0	0	0	0	0	0	5
Won by one run.............	0	0	2	0	0	2	2	2	1	1	1	4	11	13
Lost by one run.............	3	1	0	3	1	8	1	2	0	0	0	1	4	12
Single figure victories.......	1	7	6	4	0	18	5	4	2	4	8	6	29	47
Single figure defeats........	6	3	8	5	8	25	2	5	3	3	2	2	17	42
Double figure victories......	1	1	1	1	1	5	3	2	4	1	0	4	14	19
Double figure defeats.......	3	1	2	2	3	11	2	1	3	3	1	0	10	21
Victories at home...........	1	5	3	2	0	11	4	4	4	3	4	5	24	35
Defeats at home............	4	2	3	4	6	19	2	2	2	3	1	2	12	31
Victories abroad............	1	3	4	3	1	12	4	2	2	2	4	5	19	31
Defeats abroad.............	5	2	2	3	5	17	2	4	4	3	2	0	15	32

The New Yorks' Campaign of 1896.

The New York team of 1896 made a poorer record as a whole than that of 1895, inasmuch as they won 5 series that year, while in 1896 they only won 4. Moreover, their total percentage figures in 1895 were .504, while in 1896 they only reached .489. With the first division clubs in 1895 they won but 26 games and lost 47. With the same class of clubs in 1896 they won 30 and lost 42. So, in this one respect, they did better last year than in 1895 and this last result was due to a rally made in September, when they braced up and secured seventh position at the finish, after closing the August campaign in ninth place in the race. Their poorest record in 1896 was made with the Baltimore club, and they did but little better with the Phillies, their best record being made with the St. Louis team. The only first division clubs they won a series from in 1896 was with the Chicagos, they tieing in their series with Cincinnati and losing their series with Baltimore, Pittsburg, Boston and Cleveland. As to the second division clubs they lost to Philadelphia, tied with the Washingtons and won with Brooklyn, Louisville and St. Louis. Here is the first table record for 1896:

| | \multicolumn{7}{c|}{First Division.} | \multicolumn{5}{c|}{Second Divis'n} | |
New York vs.	Baltimore.	Pittsburg.	Boston.	Cleveland.	Cincinnati.	Chicago.	Totals.	Philadelphia.	Washington.	Brooklyn.	Louisville.	St. Louis.	Totals.	Grand Totals.
Victories	3	4	5	5	6	7	30	3	6	8	8	9	34	64
Defeats	9	8	7	7	6	5	42	8	6	4	4	3	25	67
Played	12	12	12	12	12	12	72	11	12	12	12	12	59	131
Drawn	0	0	0	0	0	0	0	0	0	0	1	1	2	2

Per cent. of victories—Against Baltimore, .250; Pittsburg, .333; Boston, .417; Cleveland, .417; Cincinnati, .500; Chicago, .583; total, first division clubs, .417. Philadelphia, .273; Washington, .500; Brooklyn, .667; Louisville, .667; St. Louis, .750; total, second division clubs, .576. Grand total, .489.

The second table's record shows that the New York team in 1896 lost 5 series, of which 4 were with the first division clubs. They had but 1 "Chicago" score victory to their credit against 4 "Chicago" defeats. They lost more games by single figure scores than they won, as they did double figure score games, and they won 39 games in their home field to 25 on fields abroad. They were badly whipped on the latter field by 42 to 25. Here is the second table:

| | \multicolumn{7}{c|}{First Division.} | \multicolumn{5}{c|}{Second Divis'n} | |
New York vs.	Baltimore.	Cleveland.	Cincinnati.	Boston.	Chicago.	Pittsburg.	Totals.	Philadelphia.	Washington.	Brooklyn.	St. Louis.	Louisville.	Totals.	Grand Totals.
Series won	0	0	0	0	1	0	1	0	0	1	1	1	3	4
Series lost	1	1	0	1	0	1	4	1	0	0	0	0	1	5
Series tied	0	0	1	0	0	0	1	0	1	0	0	0	1	2
Series unfinished	0	0	0	0	0	0	0	1	0	0	0	0	1	1
"Chicago" victories	0	0	0	0	1	0	1	0	0	0	0	0	0	1
"Chicago" defeats	1	0	2	1	0	0	4	0	0	0	0	0	0	4
Won by one run	0	2	0	2	0	1	5	0	3	1	0	1	5	10
Lost by one run	2	1	1	0	1	2	7	1	1	2	0	0	4	11
Single figure victories	2	5	3	3	5	2	20	1	5	7	4	5	22	42
Single figure defeats	5	4	6	6	2	5	28	2	4	4	3	2	15	43
Double figure victories	1	0	3	2	2	2	10	2	1	1	5	3	12	22
Double figure defeats	4	3	0	1	3	3	14	6	1	1	0	2	10	24
Victories at home	3	3	4	3	5	2	20	1	4	5	5	4	19	39
Defeats at home	3	3	2	3	1	4	16	4	1	0	2	2	9	25
Victories abroad	0	2	2	2	2	2	10	2	2	3	4	4	15	25
Defeats abroad	6	4	4	4	4	4	26	4	5	4	1	2	16	42

The Philadelphias' Campaign of 1896.

The Philadelphia team in 1896 opened the season's campaign with a rush, they occupying second place in the race, with the percentage figures of .696 to Baltimore's .619 and Cleveland's .600, on May 14. Then, however, their brilliant dash, like the rise of the rocket, was followed by the falling of the stick, inasmuch as on May 24 they had gone down to seventh place in the race, with the percentage figures of .517 only to their credit. Against but one of the first division clubs did they win a series and they not only sustained a "Chicago" defeat in their series with the Baltimores—losing 12 games to 0—but they allowed the tail-end Louisville club to win their series against them by 7 games out of the 12. Their lowest percentage figures were 3 blanks against the champions and their highest .727, against the St. Louis Browns. They, however, tied in their series with Cleveland and Pittsburg and got the best of Anson's Colts, besides winning their series with New York, Washington and St. Louis. Against the six first division clubs their percentage figures were .403, while against those of the second division they were .569, their total figures being .477 only. Here is their first table record for 1896:

PHILADELPHIA VS.	First Division.							Second Divis'n					Grand Totals.
	Baltimore.	Cincinnati.	Boston.	Cleveland.	Pittsburg.	Chicago.	Totals.	Brooklyn.	Louisville.	Washington.	New York.	St. Louis.	Totals.	
Victories	0	4	5	6	6	8	29	4	5	8	8	8	33	62
Defeats	12	8	7	6	6	4	43	8	7	4	3	3	25	68
Played	12	12	12	12	12	12	72	12	12	12	11	11	58	130
Drawn	0	0	0	0	0	0	0	0	0	1	0	0	1	1

Per cent. of victories—Against Baltimore, .000; Cincinnati, .333; Boston, .411; Cleveland, .500; Pittsburg, .500; Chicago, .667; total, first division clubs, 403. Brooklyn, .333; Louisville, .417; Washington, .667; New York, .727; St. Louis, .727; total, second division clubs, .569. Grand total, .477.

In their second table record it will be seen that the Phillies won 4 series and lost 5. They played but 5 games marked by "Chicago" scores, of which they won 3. Singularly enough, they won as many games by a single run as they lost, and did fairly well in single figure games. But they won 42 games on their home field to but 20 on fields abroad. Here is their second table record in full:

PHILADELPHIA VS.	Baltimore	Cleveland	Cincinnati	Boston	Chicago	Pittsburg	Totals	New York	Washington	Brooklyn	St. Louis	Louisville	Totals	Grand Totals
Series won	0	0	0	0	1	0	1	1	1	0	1	0	3	4
Series lost	1	0	1	1	0	0	3	0	0	1	0	1	2	5
Series tied	0	1	0	0	0	0	1	0	0	0	0	0	0	1
Series unfinished	0	0	0	0	0	0	0	1	0	0	1	0	2	2
"Chicago" victories	0	0	0	0	0	0	0	0	2	0	0	1	3	3
"Chicago" defeats	0	1	1	0	0	0	2	0	0	0	0	0	0	2
Won by one run	0	1	1	0	2	2	6	1	2	1	1	3	8	14
Lost by one run	2	1	1	1	1	2	8	0	1	3	2	0	6	14
Single figure victories	0	1	4	3	3	5	16	2	4	2	6	3	17	33
Single figure defeats	8	4	6	5	3	4	30	1	2	4	2	4	13	43
Double figure victories	0	5	0	2	5	1	13	6	4	2	2	2	16	29
Double figure defeats	4	2	2	2	1	2	13	2	2	4	1	3	12	25
Victories at home	0	3	4	3	5	4	20	4	5	3	5	5	22	42
Defeats at home	6	3	2	2	1	2	16	2	1	4	2	2	11	27
Victories abroad	0	3	0	1	3	2	9	4	3	1	3	0	11	20
Defeats abroad	6	3	6	5	3	4	27	1	3	4	1	5	14	41

The Washingtons' Campaign of 1896.

The Washington club had a varied experience during their campaign of 1896. They opened rather promisingly by keeping among the first division clubs up to the 5th of May, but then they began to fall off, gradually but surely, their poor record out West proving very costly in August, as on the 8th of that month they were away down to tenth place. Later on in August, however, they rallied and finished the season tied in percentage figures with the Brooklyns, whom they defeated in their series together by 8 games to 4. Here is their record:

WASHINGTON VS.	Baltimore	Cleveland	Chicago	Cincinnati	Boston	Pittsburg	Totals	Philadelphia	New York	St. Louis	Brooklyn	Louisville	Totals	Grand Totals
Victories	2	3	4	5	6	4	24	4	6	7	8	9	34	58
Defeats	10	9	8	7	7	6	47	8	6	5	4	3	26	73
Played	12	12	12	11	12	12	71	12	12	12	12	12	60	131
Drawn	0	1	0	0	0	0	1	0	0	0	1	0	1	2

Per cent. of victories—Against Baltimore, .167; Cleveland, .250; Chicago, .333; Cincinnati, .364; Boston, .417; Pittsburg, .500; total, first division clubs, .338. Philadelphia, .333; New York, .500; St. Louis, .583; Brooklyn, .667; Louisville, .750; total, second division clubs, .567. Grand total, .443.

The Washington second table record shows that all their series victories were won against the second division clubs, and of these they won 3, viz., with the Brooklyn, St. Louis and Louisville clubs. They managed to tie with the Pittsburgs and lost with all the other first division clubs, as they did with the Phillies, of the second class. In the "Chicago" games record, they were "shut out" 10 times out of 12 such games. They lost 16 games, however, by one run and did very well in the single figure game record. But they were far more successful on their home field than on those abroad. The full second table record is appended :

WASHINGTON VS.	First Division.						Second Divis'n					Grand Totals.
	Baltimore.	Cleveland.	Cincinnati.	Boston.	Chicago.	Pittsburg.	Totals.	New York.	Philadelphia.	Brooklyn.	St. Louis.	Louisville.	Totals.	
Series won.....................	0	0	0	0	0	0	0	0	0	1	1	1	3	3
Series lost......................	1	1	1	1	1	0	5	0	1	0	0	0	1	6
Series tied.....................	0	0	0	0	0	1	1	1	0	0	0	0	1	2
Series unfinished.................	0	0	1	0	0	0	1	0	0	0	0	0	0	1
"Chicago" victories...........	0	0	0	0	1	0	1	0	0	1	0	0	1	2
"Chicago" defeats.............	2	3	0	1	0	1	7	0	2	1	0	0	3	10
Won by one run.................	0	1	1	2	3	0	7	1	1	1	0	2	5	12
Lost by one run.................	2	0	0	2	3	1	8	3	2	0	2	1	8	16
Single figure victories...........	2	3	4	3	3	3	18	4	2	6	3	4	19	37
Single figure defeats.............	5	5	2	6	4	3	25	5	4	2	5	3	19	44
Double figure victories..........	0	0	0	2	1	3	6	2	2	2	4	5	15	21
Double figure defeats............	5	4	5	1	4	3	22	1	4	2	0	0	7	29
Victories at home................	1	2	3	2	3	4	15	5	3	5	5	5	23	38
Defeats at home.................	6	4	2	3	3	2	20	2	3	2	1	1	9	29
Victories abroad.................	1	1	1	3	1	2	9	1	1	3	2	4	11	20
Defeats abroad..................	4	5	5	4	5	4	27	4	5	2	4	2	17	44

The Brooklyns' Campaign of 1896.

No club in the League in 1896 disappointed its local patrons so much as did the Brooklyns. This team began the season very promisingly at Baltimore by defeating the champions in the first two games at their opening series, but they offset the good start by losing 2 out of 3 at Washington, and the same score was made at Philadelphia. Then they lost 2 out of 3 with the Washingtons at Brooklyn, and did the same thing with the visiting Chicagos the next week, following it up with a similar result with the Clevelands. So, after tieing for first place with 4 other clubs on April 20, by May 7 they had fallen down to ninth position in the race. Two months later, or on July 7, they stood in the same position. After that they made matters worse by allowing the New Yorkers—occupants of tenth place at the same date—to win their series from them by 8 games to 4, this capping the climax of the team's poor work in 1896, in the opinion of the local cranks. In August the team rallied a little and got to the head of the second division, but they failed to get into the first class again, and finally had to be content with tieing in the campaign series with the Washingtons, after the latter had beaten them in the series by 8 to 4. They tied in their series with the Baltimore and Pittsburg clubs; had the best of it in their unfinished series with the Chicagos by 6 games to 5, and won with Philadelphia, St. Louis and Louisville, and had a close fight with Cleveland. But Boston and Cincinnati knocked them out badly—10 games to 2 each—and New York and Washington scored heavily against them. Their lowest percentage figures were .167, with Cincinnati and Boston, and their highest were with the Phillies and the Louisvilles, .667 each; while their percentage against the six first division clubs reached but .380, and against the second division, .517, their total figures being .443. Here is their first table record for 1896:

BROOKLYN VS.	FIRST DIVISION.							SECOND DIVIS'N						Grand Totals.
	Cincinnati.	Boston.	Cleveland.	Pittsburg.	Baltimore.	Chicago.	Totals.	New York.	Washington.	St. Louis.	Philadelphia.	Louisville.	Totals.	
Victories..................	2	2	5	6	6	6	27	4	4	7	8	8	31	58
Defeats....................	10	10	7	6	6	5	44	8	8	5	4	4	29	73
Played....................	12	12	12	12	12	11	71	12	12	12	12	12	60	131
Drawn.....................	0	0	0	0	1	0	0	1	0	1	0	0	0	1	2

Per cent. of victories—Against Cincinnati, .167; Boston, .167; Cleveland, .417; Pittsburg, .500; Baltimore, .500; Chicago, .545; total, first division clubs, .380. New York, .333; Washington, .333; St. Louis, .583; Philadelphia, .667; Louisville, .667; total, second division clubs, .517. Grand total, .443.

The club's second table record is appended, by which it will be seen that the Brooklyns won but 3 series and lost 5, 2 being tied and 1 unfinished. In victories in "Chicago" games they lost more than they won by 5 to 3. In games won and lost by a single run they stood even. In single figure victories they did finely, as they scored 43 such games to but 15 by double figure scores. They lost ground, however, by a record of 45 defeats on fields abroad to but 36 victories on their home ground. Here is their second table record in full for 1896:

BASE BALL GUIDE. 77

BROOKLYN VS.	First Division.						Second Divis'n					Grand Totals.
	Baltimore.	Cleveland.	Cincinnati.	Boston.	Pittsburg.	Totals.	New York.	Philadelphia.	Washington.	St. Louis.	Louisville.	Totals.	
Series won........................	0	0	0	0	0	0	0	0	1	0	1	1	3	3
Series lost........................	0	1	1	1	0	0	3	1	0	1	0	0	2	5
Series tied........................	1	0	0	0	1	0	2	0	0	0	0	0	0	2
Series unfinished................	0	0	0	0	0	1	1	0	0	0	0	0	0	1
"Chicago" victories.............	1	0	0	0	1	0	2	0	0	1	0	0	1	3
"Chicago" defeats...............	1	0	2	0	0	1	4	0	0	1	0	0	1	5
Won by one run.................	1	2	0	1	3	0	7	2	3	0	1	3	9	16
Lost by one run.................	0	1	2	4	2	1	10	1	1	1	1	2	6	16
Single figure victories..........	5	3	1	2	6	3	20	4	4	2	6	7	23	43
Single figure defeats............	3	5	7	10	3	4	32	7	2	6	5	2	22	54
Double figure victories.........	1	2	1	0	0	3	7	0	4	2	1	1	8	15
Double figure defeats...........	3	2	3	0	3	1	12	1	2	2	0	2	7	19
Victories at home................	3	3	2	1	3	3	15	4	4	2	5	6	21	36
Defeats at home.................	2	3	4	5	3	2	19	3	1	3	1	1	9	28
Victories abroad.................	3	2	0	1	3	3	12	0	4	2	2	2	10	22
Defeats abroad..................	4	4	6	5	3	3	25	5	3	5	4	3	20	45

The St. Louis' Campaign of 1896.

The St. Louis club was fortunate enough to occupy a position in the first division on April 21, when their percentage figures stood at .600, but this was the highest standpoint they reached in the race. They were in company with the New York and Louisville clubs as the three tail-enders during May, June and July and even in August. But on the 4th of that month the New Yorkers took Washington's place and the St. Louis team thereafter occupied their old stamping-ground of eleventh place in the race and remained there to the finish.

The St. Louis team were shut out in their series with Cincinnati in 1896 by 12 to 0 and came near being similarly treated by Cleveland, and they were badly whipped by Baltimore, Chicago, Pittsburg, Philadelphia and Boston. They made a close fight with Brooklyn and Washington and got the best of Louisville, the only series they won, as they lost no less than 10. They drew three blanks in their percentage with Cincinnati and had .750 in their series with Louisville, their total percentage being .308 only. Here is the first table record for 1896:

St. Louis vs.	First Division.							Second Divis'n					Grand Totals.
	Cincinnati.	Cleveland.	Baltimore.	Chicago.	Pittsburg.	Boston.	Totals.	New York.	Philadelphia.	Washington.	Brooklyn.	Louisville.	Totals.	
Victories	0	2	3	3	3	4	15	3	3	5	5	9	25	40
Defeats	12	10	9	9	8	8	56	9	8	7	7	3	34	90
Played	12	12	12	12	11	12	71	12	11	12	12	12	59	130
Drawn	0	0	0	0	0	0	0	1	0	0	0	0	1	1

Per cent. of victories—Against Cincinnati, .000; Cleveland, .167; Baltimore, .250; Chicago, .250; Pittsburg, .273; Boston, .333; total, first division clubs, .309. New York, 250; Philadelphia, 273; Washington, .417; Brooklyn, .417; Louisville, 750; total, second division clubs, .424. Grand total, .308.

This second table record shows that the Browns "Chicagoed" opposing teams but once, while they similarly lost 5 games. They lost more games by a single run than they won. They were credited, however, with playing no less than 94 single figure games, next to the best record of the kind of the season. But they were poor players on fields abroad, as they won only 13 games off their own field against 55 defeats. Here is the club's second table record for 1896:

St. Louis vs.	First Division.							Second Divis'n					Grand Totals.
	Baltimore.	Cleveland.	Cincinnati.	Boston.	Chicago.	Pittsburg.	Totals.	New York.	Philadelphia.	Washington.	Brooklyn.	Louisville.	Totals.	
Series won	0	0	0	0	0	0	0	0	0	0	1	1	1	
Series lost	1	1	1	1	1	1	6	1	1	1	1	0	4	10
Series tied	0	0	0	0	0	0	0	0	0	0	0	0	0	0
Series unfinished	0	0	0	0	0	1	1	0	1	0	0	0	1	2
"Chicago" victories	0	0	0	1	0	0	1	0	0	0	0	0	1	1
"Chicago" defeats	2	0	1	0	0	1	4	0	0	0	0	1	1	5
Won by one run	1	0	0	1	1	0	3	0	2	2	1	2	7	10
Lost by one run	0	3	2	1	2	1	9	0	2	0	1	0	3	12
Single figure victories	3	2	0	2	2	2	11	3	2	5	5	6	21	32
Single figure defeats	6	8	9	3	7	8	41	4	6	3	6	2	21	62
Double figure victories	0	0	0	2	1	1	4	0	1	0	0	3	4	8
Double figure defeats	3	2	3	5	2	0	15	5	2	4	1	1	13	28
Victories at home	1	2	0	3	3	2	11	1	1	4	4	6	16	27
Defeats at home	5	4	4	3	3	4	23	4	3	2	2	0	11	34
Victories abroad	2	0	0	1	0	1	4	2	2	1	1	3	9	13
Defeats abroad	4	6	8	5	6	4	33	5	5	5	4	3	22	55

The Louisvilles' Campaign of 1896.

We now come to the last of the twelve clubs in the pennant race cf 1896, and the tail-end club had the credit of tieing the champions, the Cincinnatis, the Bostons, and the New Yorks one day in April, when each of these clubs had to be content with the percentage figures of .333 only. After that the team settled down to their old position in the last ditch, leaving St. Louis on the ragged edge, as it were, The Colonels managed to get the best of the Phillies, but it was the only series they won, as all the remaining series were won by their opponents, Their smallest percentage figures .161, were scored in their series with Baltimore and Pittsburg; and their highest with the Philadelphias by .583. With the six first division clubs the percentage figures were but .250, and with the second-class clubs only .350; their total being .290.

Here is their first table record for 1896, showing their victories, defeats and drawn games in the championship contest:

LOUISVILLE VS.	FIRST DIVISION.							SECOND DIVIS'N					Grand Totals.
	Baltimore.	Pittsburg.	Cincinnati.	Chicago.	Cleveland.	Boston.	Totals.	Washington.	St. Louis.	New York.	Brooklyn.	Philadelphia.	Totals.	
Victories	2	2	3	3	3	4	17	3	3	4	4	7	21	38
Defeats	10	10	9	9	8	8	54	9	9	8	8	5	39	93
Played	12	12	12	12	11	12	71	12	12	12	12	12	60	131
Drawn	0	0	0	0	1	0	1	0	0	0	0	1	1	2

Per cent. of victories—Against Baltimore, .167; Pittsburg, .167; Cincinnati, .250; Chicago, .250; Cleveland, .273; Boston, .333; total, first division clubs, .230. Washington, .250; St. Louis, .250; New York, .333; Brooklyn, .333; Philadelphia, .583; total, second division clubs, .350. Grand total, .290.

Their second record shows 10 series lost to a single series won, they pairing off with the St. Louis in this respect. They were "Chicagoed" eight times out of their 10 shut-out games. They lost no less than 23 games by a single run, and did not figure very well in single figure games. They also lost double the number of games on fields abroad to what they did on their home field, winning only 13 games away from home, and had 12 more defeats than victories on their home grounds. The second table record, showing just what they did during 1896, is given in full on the following page:

LOUISVILLE VS.	First Division.							Second Divis'n					Grand Totals.
	Baltimore.	Cleveland.	Cincinnati.	Boston.	Chicago.	Pittsburg.	Totals.	New York.	Philadelphia.	Washington.	Brooklyn.	St Louis.	Totals.	
Series won....................	0	0	0	0	0	0	0	0	1	0	0	0	1	1
Series lost....................	1	1	1	1	1	1	6	1	0	1	1	1	4	10
Series tied....................	0	0	0	0	0	0	0	0	0	0	0	0	0	0
Series unfinished.............	0	1	0	0	0	0	1	0	0	0	0	0	0	1
"Chicago" victories...........	1	0	0	0	0	1	0	0	0	0	0	1	1	2
"Chicago" defeats.............	1	2	1	2	0	1	7	0	1	0	0	0	1	8
Won by one run................	2	0	3	0	2	1	8	0	0	1	2	0	3	11
Lost by one run................	1	3	2	0	2	4	12	1	3	2	3	2	11	23
Single figure victories........	2	1	3	2	3	2	13	2	4	3	2	2	13	26
Single figure defeats..........	4	6	6	1	7	6	30	5	3	4	7	6	25	55
Double figure victories.......	0	2	0	2	0	0	4	2	3	0	2	1	8	12
Double figure defeats.........	6	2	3	7	2	4	24	3	2	5	1	3	14	38
Victories at home..............	2	1	3	2	2	0	10	2	5	2	3	3	15	25
Defeats at home...............	4	4	3	4	4	5	24	4	0	4	2	3	13	37
Victories abroad...............	0	2	0	2	1	2	7	2	2	1	1	0	6	13
Defeats abroad................	6	4	6	4	5	5	30	4	5	5	6	6	26	56

The following is a summary of the record of games marked by single and double figure scores during 1896:

SINGLE AND DOUBLE FIGURE GAMES.	Single Figure Victories.	Double Figure Victories.	Total Games.	Single Figure Defeats.	Double Figure Defeats.	Total Games.	Total Single Figure Games.	Total Double Figure Games.	Grand Total Games.
Baltimore......................	52	38	90	27	12	39	79	50	129
Cleveland.....................	51	29	80	33	15	48	84	44	128
Cincinnati.....................	55	22	77	38	12	50	91	34	125
Boston........................	50	24	74	36	21	57	86	45	131
Chicago.......................	47	24	71	40	17	57	87	41	128
Pittsburg......................	47	19	66	42	21	63	89	40	129
New York......................	42	22	64	43	24	67	85	46	131
Philadelphia...................	33	29	62	43	25	68	76	54	129
Washington....................	37	21	58	44	29	73	81	50	131
Brooklyn......................	43	15	58	54	19	73	97	34	131
St. Louis......................	32	8	40	62	28	90	94	36	130
Louisville.....................	26	12	38	55	38	93	81	50	130

It will be seen that Brooklyn leads in playing the most games marked by single figure scores, St. Louis being second and Cincinnati third. In double figure scores, Philadelphia takes the lead, followed by Baltimore and Washington.

The appended table shows the percentage figures of each of

the twelve clubs, as they stood at the end of each month of the League campaign from April to May:

	April.	May.	June.	July.	August.	September.	Total per cent. for the Season.
Baltimore	.455	.629	.661	.671	.685	.698	.698
Cleveland	.444	.645	.660	.647	.607	.625	.625
Cincinnati	.600	.611	.645	.678	.633	.606	.606
Boston	.686	.588	.607	.530	.546	.565	.565
Chicago	.545	.486	.508	.578	.571	.555	.555
Pittsburg	.800	.506	.526	.541	.546	.512	.512
New York	.090	.400	.421	.410	.468	.489	.489
Philadelphia	.727	.611	.508	.464	.482	.477	.477
Washington	.545	.471	.509	.425	.402	.443	.443
Brooklyn	.545	.471	.500	.452	.481	.443	.443
St. Louis	.515	.314	.254	.318	.315	.308	.308
Louisville	.090	.229	.200	.259	.255	.290	.290

The above record shows very plainly the progress made by each club during each month of the campaign, the percentages at the end of the month showing where the club had improved or fallen off in its play. It will be seen that the first three in the race on the 30th day of April were Pittsburg with .800, Philadelphia with .727 and Boston with .686; the three tail-enders being Cleveland with .490, and New York and Louisville with only .090 each. By the end of May it will be seen that quite a material change had taken place in the relative positions of the twelve clubs in the race. Baltimore, Cleveland and Cincinnati having attained the first three places, leaving New York, St. Louis and Louisville as the three tail-enders. The same relative positions were occupied by the same six clubs at the end of the June campaign, all of the other clubs having lost ground between April and June. At the end of July Cincinnati stood in the van, with Baltimore leading Cleveland by a single point for second place, the same three clubs as before being tail-enders. Chicago and Pittsburg pulled up closer to the leaders in July, but not so the other four. At the end of the August campaign Baltimore had pulled up to first place, and Cleveland had replaced Cincinnati in second position. New York rallied this month, and Washington took the Giants' place as heading the three tail-enders. Boston also pulled up ahead of Chicago. Then came the finale of the campaign, with Cincinnati still among the three leaders, despite all their losses on their last Eastern trip, while Brooklyn was sent to keep company with the three tail-enders, Washington having beaten them out by 8 games to 4 in their full series.

Interesting League Data.

The "Chicago" Games of 1896. There were a great many games in the championship contests of 1896 which were marked by "shut-outs" or "Chicago" scores, that is, scores in which the defeated nine failed to score a single run. The Cincinnati Club was credited with playing the largest number of this class of contests which resulted in victories, and Washington, with those in which they were charged with most defeats. In the summary score, showing the percentage of "Chicago" victories, the relative positions of the clubs are as follows:

Clubs.	Victories.	Defeats.	Per cent. of Victories.	Clubs.	Victories.	Defeats.	Per cent. of Victories.
Cincinnati	11	1	.917	Brooklyn	3	5	.375
Cleveland	9	2	.800	Chicago	2	5	.286
Boston	6	3	.667	New York	1	4	.200
Pittsburg	8	5	.615	St. Louis	1	4	.200
Philadelphia	3	2	.600	Washington	2	10	.167
Baltimore	9	8	.529	Louisville	1	8	.111

The record in full is appended:

"CHICAGO" GAMES FOR 1896.

Date.	Contesting Clubs.	Where Played.	Pitchers.	Score.
April 23	Boston vs. Baltimore	Baltimore	Nichols...Clarkson	7-0
" 28	Pittsburg vs. Cleveland	Pittsburg	Hawley......Cuppy	2-0
May 2	Pittsburg vs. Louisville	Louisville	Killen.....Weyhing	14-0
" 5	Baltimore vs. Pittsburg	Pittsburg	Pond.........Killen	8-0
" 6	Cincinnati vs. Boston	Cincinnati	Rhines.......Mains	6-0
" 8	Boston vs. Louisville	Louisville	Stivetts......Smith	7-0
" 19	New York vs. Chicago	Chicago	Clarke.......Friend	7-0
" 20	Cincinnati vs. Philadelphia	Cincinnati	Rhines........Orth	4-0
" 21	Louisville vs. Baltimore	Louisville	McD'rm'tt.H'mm'g	1-0
" 24	Cincinnati vs. Louisville	Cincinnati	Rhines.......Frazer	6-0
" 27	Baltimore vs. St. Louis	Baltimore	Hoffer. Breitenstein	9-0

"CHICAGO" GAMES FOR 1896—*Continued*.

Date.		Contesting Clubs.	Where Played.	Pitchers.	Score.
June	4	Cincinnati vs. Brooklyn....	Brooklyn...	Ehret.........Stein	6-0
"	6	Cincinnati vs. Brooklyn....	Brooklyn...	Fisher........Daub	13-0
"	8	Pittsburg vs. Brooklyn.....	Brooklyn...	Killen.....Kennedy	9-0
"	9	St. Louis vs. Boston........	Boston.....	Breitenstein.S'lliv'n	5-0
"	10	Baltimore vs. Louisville....	Baltimore...	Hemming .....Hall	9-0
"	16	Baltimore vs. Brooklyn.....	Brooklyn...	Hemming....Abbey	4-0
"	19	Pittsburg vs. St. Louis......	Pittsburg...	Killen.........Hart	6-0
July	3	Baltimore vs. New York....	New York..	Hoffer..M. Sullivan	6-0
"	5	Cincinnati vs. St. Louis....	Cincinnati..	Fisher....Kissenger	7-0
"	8	Pittsburg vs. Washington..	Pittsburg...	Hawley.....Mercer	19-0
"	9	Cleveland vs. Baltimore....	Cleveland...	Young........Pond	7-0
"	10	Cleveland vs. Baltimore....	Cleveland...	Cuppy........Esper	12-0
"	14	Pittsburg vs. Boston........	Pittsburg...	Hawley...... Lewis	7-0
"	16	Cincinnati vs. Baltimore....	Cincinnati..	Dwyer...McMahon	5-0
"	19	Cleveland vs. Louisville....	Louisville..	Young.........Hill	7-0
"	21	Cleveland vs. Washington..	Cleveland..	Wilson......Mercer	2-0
"	21	Cleveland vs. Washington..	Cleveland..	Wallace...McJames	7-0
"	21	Pittsburg vs. Baltimore. ...	Pittsburg...	Killen......Hemming	4-0
"	21	Baltimore vs. Pittsburg.....	Pittsburg...	Esper......Hastings	6-0
"	21	Cincinnati vs. New York...	Cincinnati..	Dwyer..M. Sullivan	4-0
"	23	Cleveland vs. Philadelphia...	Cleveland..	Young...... Keever	2-0
"	29	Brooklyn vs. Washington...	Brooklyn...	Payne......Mercer	5-0
Aug.	1	Baltimore vs. Washington..	Baltimore...	Hoffer...... Mercer	7-0
"	3	Baltimore vs. Washington..	Baltimore...	Hemming.McJames	7-0
"	6	Boston vs. Washington.....	Boston.....	Nichols...McJames	1-0
"	11	Chicago vs. Cincinnati	Chicago....	Terry....... Dwyer	6-0
"	12	Brooklyn vs. Baltimore.....	Brooklyn...	Payne....... Hoffer	3-0
"	12	Philadelphia vs. Washington	Phil'delphia	Taylor......Mercer	9-0
"	13	Cincinnati vs. Chicago......	Chicago....	Ehret........Briggs	7-0
"	14	Boston vs. New York.......	Boston.....	Nichols.....Clarke	4-0
"	14	Philadelphia vs. Washington	Phil'delphia	Gumbert....German	14-0
"	15	Pittsburg vs. Cleveland	Pittsburg...	Killen.........Gear	6-0
"	19	Philadelphia vs. Louisville..	Phil'delphia	Carsey......Frazer	15-0
"	20	Cleveland vs. Washington..	Washington	Young......Norton	2-0
"	21	Baltimore vs. St. Louis......	Baltimore..	Pond.....Kissenger	7-0
"	24	Brooklyn vs. Chicago	Brooklyn...	Kennedy.....Terry	1-0
"	29	Boston vs. Louisville.......	Boston.....	Stivetts..Cunn'gh'm	16-0
"	31	Washington vs. Chicago....	Washington	Mercer......Friend‡	1-1
Sept.	2	Cincinnati vs. New York...	New York..	J. Foreman.Clar':e*	4-0
"	10	Chicago vs. Pittsburg.......	Pittsburg...	Friend..... Hawley	2-0
"	14	Washington vs. Brooklyn...	Washington	Mercer......Payne	7-0
"	14	Cleveland vs. Chicago......	Cleveland...	Young......Friend	2-0
"	16	Cincinnati vs. Pittsburg....	Pittsburg...	Rhines.H'st'gs(Am)	11-0
"	16	Cincinnati vs. Pittsburg....	Pittsburg...	Dwyer......Hawley†	4-0
"	17	Boston vs. Baltimore.......	Boston......	Sullivan......Hoffer	2-0
"	23	Cleveland vs. Louisville....	Cleveland...	Wallace......Frazer	2-0

* Seven innings.   † Eight innings.   ‡ Eleven innings.

It is a fact not generally realized that the batsman, as he stands in the box, waiting for balls to cross the plate, occupies a position which renders it impossible for him to judge balls or strikes correctly. His view of the ball is an angular one, and in nine cases out of ten balls which "cut the corners" look to him as going clear of the plate.

Extra Innings Games of 1896.

The most noteworthy of the extra innings games played in 1896 were the 1 to 0 eleven innings contest at Washington, on August 31; the 2 to 1 game at Pittsburg, on September 11, and the 3 to 2 twelve innings match at Chicago, on July 1. Here is the record in full:

Date.	Contesting Clubs.	Where Played.	Pitchers.	Innings.	Score.
May 2	Boston vs. Baltimore........	Boston.....	Stivetts....Hoffer	10	10-9
" 4	Baltimore vs. Pittsburg.....	Pittsburg...	Esper ....Hawley	11	5-4
" 9	Baltimore vs. Cincinnati....	Cincinnati.,	Hoffer ....Rhines	10	6-5
" 12	New York vs. Pittsburg....	Pittsburg...	Meekin ...Hawley	10	8-7
" 13	Boston vs. Chicago.........	Chicago....	Stivetts ...Terry*	10	4-4
" 14	Baltimore vs. Chicago......	Chicago....	Pond......Parker	10	5-5
" 19	Pittsburg vs. Brooklyn.....	Pittsburg...	Hughey.Kennedy	10	6-5
" 24	Chicago vs. Washington....	Chicago....	Friend....German	10	4-3
" 29	Cleveland vs. Boston.......	Boston.....	Wilson ....Cuppy	12	7-7
June 3	Cleveland vs. Washington..	Washington	Young ....Mercer	10	3-3
" 8	Cleveland vs. Philadelphia..	Phil'delphia	Young ....Taylor	10	8-7
" 18	Brooklyn vs. New York....	Brooklyn...	Kennedy .Meekin	10	4-3
" 20	Pittsburg vs. St. Louis.....	Pittsburg...	J.F'rem'n H'g'h'y	11	7-4
July 3	Brooklyn vs. Boston........	Brooklyn...	Kennedy.Sullivan	11	8-7
" 4	Baltimore vs. New York....	N. Y. (A.M.)	Esper......Clarke	10	11-10
" 5	Chicago vs. Louisville......	Chicago....	Friend........Hill	10	7-6
" 11	Chicago vs. New York......	Chicago....	Friend....Meekin	12	3-2
" 13	St. Louis vs. Washington...	St. Louis...	Hart....McJames	12	5-4
" 16	Philadelphia vs. Pittsburg..	Pittsburg...	Gumbert...Killen	10	5-3
" 22	Cincinnati vs. New York ...	Cincinnati...	F, For'm'n.Clarke	10	9-8
" 22	Chicago vs. Boston.........	Chicago....	Griffith ...Nichols	11	10-9
" 22	Louisville vs. Brooklyn....	Louisvile,..	Cun'gham.Ken'dy	13	11-8
" 25	Philadelphia vs. Cleveland.	Clevl'd(A.M)	Taylor.....Wilson	10	10-9
Aug. 4	Pittsburg vs. Louisville.....	Louisville..	Keller........Hill	10	9-5
" 4	New York vs. Washington..	New York..	Meekin...German	10	6-5
" 7	Pittsburg vs. Cleveland.....	Cleveland..	Killen.....Cuppy	11	3-3
" 11	Louisville vs. Cleveland....	Cleveland..	Frazer.....Young	11	3-3
" 17	Cleveland vs. Pittsburg	Pittsburg...	Cuppy....Hawley	10	6-2
" 31	Washington vs. Chicago....	Washington	Mercer....Friend	11	1-0
Sept. 1	Philadelphia vs. Cincinnati.	Phil'delphia	Orth......Dwyer	11	9-6
" 12	New York vs. Boston.......	New York..	Clark..Klobedanz	10	9-8
" 12	Cleveland vs. St. Louis.....	Cleveland...	Cuppy..Kissenger	10	3-2
" 21	Pittsburg vs. Louisville	Pittsburg...	Hawley..Herman	11	2-1

* Forfeited, 0–0.

Record of Drawn Games of 1896.

There were several notable drawn games in 1896, among them the two games in which Cleveland participated in at Boston, on May 29 and July 29; at Cleveland, on August 7 and 11, and at Washington, on June 3. Here is the full record:

Date.	Contesting Clubs.	Where Played.	Pitchers.	Innings.	Score.
May 14	Baltimore vs. Chicago	Chicago	Pond......Parker	10	5-5
" 29	Cleveland vs. Boston	Boston	Cuppy....Nichols	12	7-7
June 3	Cleveland vs. Washington	Washington	Young.....Mercer	10	3-3
" 26	Cleveland vs. Louisville	Louisville	Cuppy ......Hill	9	4-4
July 6	New York vs. St. Louis	St. Louis	Sullivan.Donohue	8	6-6
" 29	Cleveland vs. Boston	Boston	Cuppy......Mains	12	7-7
" 30	Washington vs. Brooklyn	Brooklyn	McJames..Abbey	9	4-4
Aug. 7	Pittsburg vs. Cleveland	Cleveland	Keller.....Cuppy	11	3-3
" 11	Louisville vs. Cleveland	Cleveland	Frazer.....Young	11	3-3
" 12	Cincinnati vs. Chicago	Chicago	F.For'man.G'ffith	8	3-3
" 21	Pittsburg vs. Brooklyn	Brooklyn	Hawley....Payne	9	2-2
" 24	Louisville vs. New York	New York	H'rm'n.M.S'lliv'n	6	4-4
" 25	Cleveland vs. Baltimore	Baltimore	Cuppy......Pond	9	4-4
Sept. 4	Chicago vs. Baltimore	Baltimore	Friend ....Hoffer	8	11-11
" 15	Chicago vs. Cleveland	Cleveland	Briggs....Wallace	9	6-6

A Twenty-one Years' Record.

As a matter of reference we append a table which shows the victories and defeats, games played and the percentage of victories of each pennant-winning club in the National League from 1876 to 1896, inclusive; also the number of championship games played each year, and the name of the manager of each winning club:

Year.	Pennant Winners.	Won.	Lost.	Played.	Per cent. of Victories.	Grand Total Games Played Each Year	Managers.	No. of Clubs Playing.
1876	Chicago	52	14	66	.788	257	Spalding	8
1877	Boston	31	17	48	.646	120	Harry Wright	6
1878	Boston	41	19	60	.680	180	Harry Wright	8
1879	Providence	55	23	78	.705	288	George Wright	8
1880	Chicago	67	17	84	.798	332	Anson	8
1881	Chicago	56	28	84	.667	334	Anson	8
1882	Chicago	55	29	84	.655	334	Anson	8
1883	Boston	63	35	98	.643	390	Morrill	8
1884	Providence	84	28	112	.750	447	Bancroft	8
1885	Chicago	87	25	112	.776	442	Anson	8
1886	Chicago	90	34	124	.725	480	Anson	8
1887	Detroit	79	45	124	.637	492	Watkins	8
1888	New York	84	47	131	.641	532	Mutrie	8
1889	New York	83	43	126	.659	518	Mutrie	8
1890	Brooklyn	86	43	129	.667	531	McGunnigle	8
1891	Boston	87	51	138	.630	545	Selee	12
1892	Boston	102	48	150	.680	918	Selee	12
1893	Boston	86	43	129	.667	774	Selee	12
1894	Baltimore	89	39	128	.695	782	Hanlon	12
1895	Baltimore	87	43	130	.669	788	Hanlon	12
1896	Baltimore	90	39	129	.698	778	Hanlon	12

A summary of the above table shows that Chicago, Boston and Baltimore are to be credited with having won the League pennant three consecutive years. The order of most pennants won in the twenty-one years of the annals of the National League is as follows:

Chicago won in 1876, 1880, 1881, 1882, 1885 and 1886—six years.

Boston won in 1877, 1878, 1883, 1891, 1892 and 1893—six years.

Baltimore won in 1894, 1895 and 1896—three years.

Providence won in 1879 and 1884—two years.

New York won in 1888 and 1889—two years.

Detroit won in 1887—one year.

Brooklyn won in 1890—one year.

The highest percentage of victories figures scored in the twenty-one years' races was that in 1880 by the Chicago club, .798, and the lowest that of 1891, by the Bostons, .630. The largest number of games played in any one season was 150—102 won, 48 lost—by the Boston club in 1892, when the double season's record was made. The smallest number played, too, was by the Bostons in 1878, when they won the pennant with a record of 31 victories to 17 defeats; total, 48 games; only six clubs playing in the League contest of that year. In the whole twenty-one years' of pennant races, but seven different clubs bore off the honors.

First Division Clubs From 1892 to 1896.

A new element of attraction for ambitious aspirants for League honors has opened up in the League arena since the introduction of the Temple Cup series, and it is that of the desire to close the season as one of the first division clubs, if the goal of the championship fails to be reached, or if the next best point in the race—that of sharing in the financial prizes of the Temple Cup games—is lost. Whatever disappointment may be experienced by a team in not winning one or the other of the first three positions in the pennant race, there is quite a degree of satisfaction in being able to escape being left among the last six clubs at the close of the season's campaign. There is a consolation prize, too, even for the second-class clubs, and that is in a club's team standing at the head of the second division clubs on October 1—the New York Giants finding quite a degree of comfort in it in 1896. In fact, there are now but three places in the pennant race which all of the clubs feel bad about occupying, and they are those of the three tail-enders. Thus far in the annals of the reconstructed League the clubs which have occupied first division places at the end of a championship campaign, from 1892 to 1896, inclusive, are as follows:

1892—Boston, first; Cleveland, second; Brooklyn, third; Philadelphia, fourth; Cincinnati, fifth; Pittsburg, sixth.

*1893—Boston, first; Pittsburg, second; Cleveland, third; Philadelphia, fourth; New York, fifth; Brooklyn, sixth.

1894—Baltimore, first; New York, second; Boston, third; Philadelphia, fourth; Brooklyn, fifth; Cleveland, sixth.

1895—Baltimore, first; Cleveland, second; Philadelphia, third; Chicago, fourth; Brooklyn, fifth; Boston, sixth.

1896—Baltimore, first; Cleveland, second; Cincinnati, third; Boston, fourth; Chicago, fifth; Pittsburg, sixth.

It will be seen that during the past five years of League pennant race history, with twelve clubs each season striving for championship honors, that only five of the Eastern clubs and four of the Western have occupied places in any one year of the five in the first division of the pennant race contestants. Boston and Baltimore have monopolized first place; Cleveland, Pittsburg and New York second position; Brooklyn, Boston, Philadelphia, Cleveland and Cincinnati third place; Philadelphia, Boston and Chicago, fourth position; Brooklyn, New York, Chicago and Cincinnati, fifth place, and Boston, Brooklyn, Cleveland and Pittsburg, sixth position. Boston has been in the first division five years; Cleveland, four years; Brooklyn, three years; Pittsburg, three years; New York, two years, and Cincinnati two years. There are only three clubs of the twelve which have not yet closed any season of the five outside of the second division, and these three have been either in the last ditch or on the ragged edge of it.

New York vs. Brooklyn Series.

A feature of the League season each year in the great metropolis, since the Brooklyn club entered the National League, has been the battle between the New York and Brooklyn clubs for the championship of the metropolitan district. Sometimes these contests were decided by the League pennant race figures between them, while some seasons extra series were played. The two clubs had lively skirmishes in their exhibition games series at the close of the championship season, in

1887 and 1888, in which Brooklyn had rather the best of it, but it was not until 1889—when the Brooklyn club won the American Association pennant—that the two clubs entered upon a scheduled series of games together for the metropolitan championship, and in this initial series New York won by 6 games to 3 in the extra series of 9 games. In 1890 Brooklyn took the lead by 6 to 4 in the extra series of 10 games played; but in 1891 New York went to the front with a record of 11 games to 8 in the series. Then came the reconstructed League in 1892, and in the two half seasons of that year the two clubs were tied 7 to 7, the Brooklyns leading in the first half by 4 to 3 and the New Yorks in the second by the same figures. In 1893 the score was a tie in the pennant race record at the end of the season, 6 games to 6, and to settle the question of superiority an extra series was played, in which New York was successful by 11 games to 8. New York also won in 1894 by 7 games to 5; but in 1895 Brooklyn bore off the palm by 9 games to 3 in the pennant race record. Last year New York turned the tables and won by 8 games to 4 in the race series. In the whole series together from 1889 to 1896, inclusive:

Year.	Contesting Clubs.	Won.	Lost.	Per cent.	Year.	Contesting Clubs.	Won.	Lost.	Per cent.
1889	New York vs. Br'klyn	6	3	.667	1893	Br'klyn vs. New York	6	6	.500
1890	Br'klyn vs. New York	6	4	.600	1894	New York vs. Br'klyn	7	5	.583
1891	New York vs. Br'klyn	11	8	.579	1895	Br'klyn vs. New York	9	3	.750
1892	Brooklyn vs. N. Y.	4	3	.571	1896	New York vs. Br'klyn	8	4	.667
	N. Y. vs. Brooklyn	4	3	.571					

Total victories—New York, 52; Brooklyn, 48. Highest percentage of victories in a single season—Brooklyn, .750. Lowest percentage of figures in a single season—New York, .250.

That splendid outfielder of the Washington team of 1896, Al Selbach, says. "A player who doesn't use tobacco in any form will retain his keenness of vision longer than one who uses the weed, and will prove a steadier and more consistant batter. Tobacco affects the nerves, and as the eye is a bunch of nerves, it stands to reason that the sight is impaired by the use of the weed. I have heard players complain that they were in tough luck as regards their batting, and I found in nine cases out of ten the cause was tobacco."

Base ball has been introduced in South Africa, and promises to be a leading feature of sport in that new and sport-loving country. In Johannesburg and several other towns teams, have been organized, and the interest taken in the game has been very encouraging to the organizers of the clubs.

Baltimore – Chicago – Boston.

Full Pennant Race Records of the Champions and the Two Senior Clubs of the League.

The Champion Baltimore Club's Full Race Record.

The brilliant success of the Baltimore club in completing a record, in 1896, of winning the National League championship pennant three consecutive years, is worthy of special comment, as it fully illustrates the value of good team management in a club. From 1882—the year of the organizing of the old American Association—up to the period of its secession from the National Agreement ranks in 1891, the Baltimore club was the occupant of the "last ditch" in the American Association's pennant races for no less than four years, viz., in 1882, 1883, 1885 and 1886. In 1884, when twelve clubs were in the Association race of that year, the highest the Baltimore club reached was sixth position. In 1888, 1889 and 1890 the club got no higher than fifth place in the three races of those years; while the nearest it could get to first place during the decade of the eighties was in 1887, when it ended in third place, being led by St. Louis and Cincinnati.

In 1892 Van Haltren was appointed manager, and that year the Baltimores again occupied their old position in the pennant race—the last ditch. Late in the season of 1892 the management of the club was given to Hanlon, but too late to affect the position of the club in the race. In 1893 he began to strengthen the team, and in 1894, when he became president of the club and had entire control of the team, the club won its first pennant race. It will be remembered that in 1891 the Baltimores had a close race with the Cincinnatis, the Bostons being the leader that year; but when the Cincinnatis were transferred to Milwaukee in 1891 the Reds fell down badly, and Baltimore took third place in the race of that year. In 1893 they began low down in the race record, but they finally pulled up among the six leaders, beating out Brooklyn in the race by 10 games to 2, as well as St. Louis, Louisville and Cleveland; but they were so badly beaten by Boston—2 games to 10—and by

Pittsburg—1 game to 11—that they finished in eighth place only. This was their last season as a second division club, however, as since then they have led all opponents in the annual pennant races of the League. The following record shows the club's victories, defeats, percentage of victories, position in each year's pennant race, and the number of clubs which competed each year, alike in the old American Association and in the existing National League:

THE BALTIMORE CLUB'S FIFTEEN YEARS' RECORD.

Year.	Won.	Lost.	Per cent.	Race Position.	Number of Clubs.	Manager.
1882	19	54	.260	Last	6	Barnie.
1883	28	68	.292	Last	8	Barnie.
1884	63	43	.594	Sixth	12	Barnie.
1885	41	66	.377	Last	8	Barnie.
1886	48	83	.366	Last	8	Barnie.
1887	77	58	.570	Third	8	Barnie.
1888	57	80	.423	Fifth	8	Barnie.
1889	70	65	.518	Fifth	8	Barnie.
1890	15	19	.441	Fifth	8	Barnie.
1891	71	64	.526	Third	8	Barnie.
1892	46	101	.313	Last	12	Van Haltren.
1893	26	46	.361	Tenth	12	Hanlon.
1894	89	39	.695	First	12	Hanlon.
1895	87	43	.669	First	12	Hanlon.
1896	90	39	.698	First	12	Hanlon.

The Chicago Club's Quarter of a Century Race Record—From 1870 to 1896.

The League club next in seniority to the veteran Boston club in League history is the Chicago club, which was first organized in 1870, specially to defeat the then champion Red Stocking team, of Cincinnati. That was before the professional National Association was organized, however, and does not count in the appended record. The old amateur Excelsior club, of Chicago, had, prior to that year, been the representative club of the Lake City; but when the Cincinnati Reds became the world's champions in 1869, and remained so up to June, 1870, the Chicago cranks determined to raise a professional team to win the year's series—best two games out of three—from their Cincinnati rivals, and they did it, as the appended record shows:

Date.	Contesting Clubs.	Where Played.	Pitchers.	Score.
Sept. 7, 1870.	Chicago vs. Cincinnati	Cincinnati	Pinkham-Brainard	10- 6
Oct. 18, 1870.	Chicago vs. Cincinnati	Chicago	Pinkham-Brainard	16-13

There was no need of a third game. The nine of Chicago for that year was Pinkham, pitcher; Mort King, catcher; McAtee, first base; Jimmy Wood, second base and captain; Myerle, third base; Hodes, shortstop; Tracey, left field; Cuthbert, centre field, and Flynn, right field. That was the first professional nine the club ever placed in the field, and it included players from the old Eckford, Athletic and Haymaker nines, of Brooklyn, Philadelphia and Troy.

The Chicago club joined the newly organized "National Professional Association of Base Ball Players" in 1871, and under Foley's management they came in third in the first regular pennant race known to professional base ball history. Only twenty-five legal championship games were played by the club in 1871. The nine of that year was nearly the same as that of 1870, except that Zettlein, of Brooklyn, pitched, Pinkham playing second base; Duffy playing at shortstop, Simmons at right field and Foley as substitute, Hodes catching. The latter and Duffy are dead. The great fire at Chicago stopped ball playing for the next two years as far as placing a representative professional nine was concerned; but, in 1874, Jimmy Wood was placed in charge of the reconstructed Chicago team, and they entered the field that year with Zettlein and Fergy Malone as their battery, Jas. Devlin, Wood and Myerle on the bases, Dave Force—the noted "killer" of hard hit ground balls—at short field, and with Cuthbert, Tracey and Glenn in the outfield; Pinkham and Hines being substitutes.

This team, however, only reached fifth place in the pennant race of that year. In 1875 the Chicago team was a very mixed set of players, and under Rob Ferguson did not do better than end in sixth place in that season's race, their team comprising Zettlein and Hastings as the battery; Glenn, Peters and Warren on the bases; Keerl at short field, with Hines, Dick Higham and Devlin in the outfield. Higham afterwards being expelled for dishonesty as umpire—the only one on record—and Jim Devlin for selling games, Bielaski being the new substitute.

The Chicago club's League history, of course, began in 1876, and the club made an auspicious opening by winning the League pennant, its champion team comprising A. G. Spalding and Jas. White as the battery; McVey, Barnes and Anson on the bases; Peters, shortstop, and Glenn, Hines and Addy in the outfield. Spalding was captain and manager of the champions of the Centennial year of 1876, and that was the culmination of his notable and honorable career on the ball field, as afterwards he established his sporting goods house and permanently retired from active service in the field. Then began Anson's twenty years' career as the Chicago club's captain and manager. He started in 1877 with his team as champions, but they only reached fifth place in the race of that year. After that he gradually pulled them up to first position in 1880, when the Chicagos began their three-times-pennant-winners' record of 1880, 1881 and 1882. After that they lost ground, and in 1884 reached fourth place. Then they rallied, and in 1885 and 1886 won the pennant each year. From 1886 they alternated between second and third positions in the annual races, and in the year of the players' revolt they stood second again. Then they took seats on the toboggan in 1892, and got down to seventh place that year, and in 1893 made the "worst on record" count, as they ended in ninth place that year. Then Anson began raising a colts' team, and he has been raising it ever since, until in 1896 he had pulled up from ninth place in 1893 to fifth position in 1896, and for 1897 his call is, "We'll win the flag this year sure, and I'm betting on it, boys." Here is the full twenty-five years' record of the Chicago club, from 1871 to 1896, deducting 1872 and 1873:

Year.	Victories.	Defeats.	Per cent.	Race Position.	Number of Clubs.	Manager.
1871	16	9	.640	Third	8	Foley.
1872	..	..	....	....	..	
1873	..	..	....	....	..	
1874	19	30	.612	Fifth	8	Wood.
1875	30	37	.448	Sixth	10	Ferguson.
1876	52	14	.788	First	8	Spalding.
1877	18	30	.375	Fifth	6	Anson.
1878	30	30	.500	Fourth	6	Anson.
1879	44	32	.579	Third	8	Anson.
1880	67	17	.798	First	8	Anson.
1881	56	28	.667	First	8	Anson.
1882	55	29	.655	First	8	Anson.
1883	59	39	.602	Second	8	Anson.
1884	62	50	.554	Fourth	8	Anson.
1885	87	25	.776	First	8	Anson.
1886	90	34	.725	First	8	Anson.
1887	71	50	.587	Third	8	Anson.
1888	77	58	.578	Second	8	Anson.
1889	67	65	.508	Third	8	Anson.
1890	83	53	.610	Second	8	Anson.
1891	82	53	.607	Second	8	Anson.
1892	70	76	.479	Seventh	12	Anson.
1893	51	71	.445	Ninth	12	Anson.
1894	57	75	.432	Eighth	12	Anson.
1895	57	50	.533	Seventh	12	Anson.
1896	71	57	.555	Fifth	12	Anson.

The Boston Club's Full Race Record of Twenty-six Consecutive Years.

The only professional club known to League annals which has played in each year's championship campaign, from the inauguration of the old Professional National Association in 1871 to the closing League year of 1896, is the Boston club, which holds the "best on record" of continual service in the championship campaigns of the past twenty-six years of professional club history. Next in order comes the Chicago club, with a record of twenty-four years of pennant-racing in the regular professional campaigns, though they also played professionally in 1869 and 1870, making twenty-six years in all. But these two years were of irregular play, without any authorized championships to contest for. From 1871 to 1896, however, the Chicagos only played in twenty-four championship campaigns, and therefore the Boston club bears off the palm, as the Chicagos did not play in 1872 and 1873. Moreover, the Boston club leads all others in pennant-winnings in the professional arena, as they hold the record of winning a total of *ten pennant races*, four of which were won in consecutive years; they being successful from 1872 to 1875, inclusive; also again in 1877 and 1878; in 1883, and in 1891, 1892 and 1893. In all those twenty-six years the club has had but five team managers, viz., the late veteran Harry Wright for 11 years, from 1871 to to 1881, inclusive; John Morrill for 6 years, from 1882 to to 1887, inclusive; Mike Kelly and James Hart for 1 year each during 1888 and 1889, and Selee from 1890 to 1896, inclusive. Under Harry Wright the club won 6 pennant races; under Morrill 1; under Selee 3, and under Kelly and Hart none, though Hart took them to second place in 1889. The highest percentage of victories in winning any pennant race was in 1875, when they won with .899 to their credit, this being the highest percentage in any pennant race known in the annals of professional ball-playing. In 1872 they won by .830 and in 1874 by .825. The club stood in first position 10 times, in second place 4 times, in third place once; fourth position 5 times, in fifth 3 times and in sixth 3 times. They ended fourth once under Harry Wright, and second twice with him, the sixth twice, the other years being pennant victories in his record. They were second once under Morrill, fourth twice and fifth twice, and won one pennant. They were from first to sixth under Selee, second under Hart and fourth under Kelly. The lowest percentage figures scored in a pennant race was .410 in 1885 under Morrill. The Boston club held the best on record of most victories in a championship season of any League club, viz., 102 in 1892, when the double season occurred.

THE BOSTON CLUB'S TWENTY-SIX YEARS' RECORD.

Year.	Won.	Lost.	Per cent.	Race Position.	Number of Clubs.	Manager.
1871	22	10	.688	Second..............	8	Harry Wright.
1872	39	8	.830	First................	10	Harry Wright.
1873	43	16	.729	First................	8	Harry Wright.
1874	52	18	.825	First................	8	Harry Wright.
1875	71	8	.899	First................	8	Harry Wright.
1876	52	14	.788	Fourth..............	8	Harry Wright.
1877	31	17	.648	First................	6	Harry Wright.
1878	41	19	.707	First................	6	Harry Wright.
1879	49	29	.628	Second..............	8	Harry Wright.
1880	40	44	.474	Sixth...............	8	Harry Wright.
1881	38	45	.458	Sixth...............	8	Harry Wright.
1882	45	39	.536	Fourth..............	8	Morrill.
1883	63	35	.643	First................	8	Morrill.
1884	73	38	.658	Second..............	8	Morrill.
1885	46	66	.410	Fifth...............	8	Morrill.
1886	56	61	.478	Fifth...............	8	Morrill.
1887	61	60	.502	Fourth..............	8	Morrill.
1888	70	64	.522	Fourth..............	8	Kelly.
1889	83	45	.648	Second..............	8	Hart.
1890	76	57	.571	Fifth...............	8	Selee.
1891	87	51	.630	First................	8	Selee.
1892	102	48	.680	First................	12	Selee.
1893	86	43	.667	First................	12	Selee.
1894	83	49	.629	Third...............	12	Selee.
1895	87	43	.669	Sixth...............	12	Selee.
1896	90	39	.698	Fourth..............	12	Selee.

A noteworthy fact in connection with the new appointment of the members of the Rules Committee of 1896 is that thoroughly practical men were selected. In the first place its chairman, President Hart, of the Chicago club, comes into the committee as a representative team manager, thereby representing that class of officials on the committee. Then in the persons of the next two members we have the veteran infielder, President Reach, of the Philadelphia club, and President Hanlon, of the Baltimore club, as a veteran outfielder. Here, therefore, are an ex-team manager and two ex-professional players comprising the personnel of the Rules Committee of 1897. In addition, by virtue of his membership of the committee ex-officio, we have in President Young not only the amateur player class represented, but also the veteran umpire class.

Feet-first sliding should be legislated out of the game. It is dangerous at all times, and sometimes results in valuable players being disabled and kept out of the game for weeks at a time. Some infielders are so intimidated by the sight of steel spikes after they have been the victims of them once or twice, that they do not go after the base runner for fear of being injured.

Official League Statistics

THE following are the official averages of the League season of 1896, as prepared by President Young. A careful perusal of the tables shows that the figures, in several instances, differ from those published last fall. In one case the records published in the dailies last November, gave Holliday a credit of fifty-seven stolen bases, whereas he only stole a single base, according to the official figures. The amended scoring rules for 1897, will, at least, lead to improved data for earned runs and the pitching records, but the door is still open for further improved revision.

BATTING RECORD
Of Players Who Have Taken Part in Fifteen or More Championship Games—Season of 1896.

Rank.	Name.	Club.	Games.	At Bat.	Runs.	1st Bases.	Per cent.	T. B.	S. H.	S. B.
1	Burkett.........	Cleveland................	133	585	159	240	.410	308	5	32
2	Jennings.........	Baltimore................	129	523	125	208	.397	251	11	73
3	Delehanty.......	Philadelphia.............	122	505	131	199	.394	313	4	37
4	Keeler...........	Baltimore................	127	546	154	214	.392	265	13	73
5	Kelly............	Baltimore................	130	516	147	191	.370	282	5	90
6	Stenzel..........	Pittsburg................	112	467	104	171	.366	229	6	59
7	Hamilton........	Boston...................	131	523	153	190	.363	238	6	93
8	Clements........	Philadelphia.............	50	182	34	66	.362	93	6	2
9	Tiernan..........	New York................	133	526	132	190	.361	265	5	35
	Dahlen..........	Chicago.................	125	476	153	190	.361	268	27	60
10	E. E. Smith.....	Pittsburg................	120	475	118	170	.358	229	6	32
11	McGraw.........	Baltimore................	19	73	19	26	.356	31	0	18
12	Robinson........	Baltimore................	66	243	43	86	.354	113	4	11
	Van Haltren..	New York................	133	564	138	199	.353	269	4	43
13	Jones...........	Brooklyn................	102	399	82	141	.353	175	6	29
	Stivetts........	Boston..................	59	221	44	78	.353	110	4	5
14	McCreary.......	Louisville...............	110	441	87	155	.351	236	9	32
15	Demontreville..	Washington..............	130	523	93	183	.349	240	16	29
16	Childs..........	Cleveland................	132	502	109	175	.348	222	13	21
17	Holliday........	Cincinnati...............	22	75	15	26	.346	31	1	1
18	Doyle...........	Baltimore................	118	487	115	168	.345	204	9	71
19	Burke...........	Cincinnati...............	122	520	120	178	.342	232	9	57
	Tenny..........	Boston..................	86	345	65	118	.342	141	21	18
20	McKean........	Cleveland................	133	567	100	190	.335	257	12	13
	Anson..........	Chicago.................	106	402	72	135	.335	263	5	28
21	Long............	Boston..................	119	508	108	170	.334	225	12	40
	Everett........	Chicago.................	131	573	130	191	.333	241	7	55
22	Lange..........	Chicago.................	123	469	114	156	.333	219	6	100
	Grady.........	Philadelphia...........	62	234	48	78	.333	107	0	11

SPALDING'S OFFICIAL

BATTING RECORDS—*Continued.*

Rank	Name	Club	Games	At Bat	Runs	1st Bases	Per cent	T.B.	S.H.	S.B.
23	Donnelly....	Baltimore...............	104	396	69	131	.330	152	20	30
	Brouthers...	Philadelphia.............	57	218	41	72	.330	96	1	8
24	Lajoie.......	Philadelphia.............	39	174	37	57	.328	94	2	6
25	Clark........	Louisville...............	131	517	93	169	.327	242	7	32
26	McGuire......	Washington..............	95	381	59	124	.325	162	6	11
27	Joyce........	Wash'gton and New York.	129	477	125	154	.323	243	2	49
28	Lowe.........	Boston...................	78	309	59	99	.320	118	6	14
29	Miller.......	Cincinnati...............	125	503	91	160	.318	251	18	75
	Hallman......	Philadelphia.............	120	472	83	150	.318	180	18	17
30	Donovan.....	Pittsburg................	129	569	110	180	.316	215	5	50
	Selbach......	Washington..............	121	477	100	151	.316	205	8	49
	Davis........	New York................	124	495	98	155	.315	216	6	49
31	Griffin......	Brooklyn.................	122	492	102	155	.315	207	6	27
	McGann......	Boston...................	42	168	24	53	.315	78	0	2
	Kissengen...	St. Louis................	22	73	7	23	.315	27	2	1
32	Anderson.....	Brooklyn.................	104	429	69	135	.314	200	1	40
33	Ryan.........	Chicago..................	127	490	83	153	.312	209	10	35
34	Burrell......	Brooklyn.................	58	205	19	63	.307	82	4	1
35	Lyons........	Pittsburg................	116	438	77	134	.306	182	11	13
36	Thompson.....	Philadelphia.............	119	517	103	158	.305	229	3	11
37	Tucker.......	Boston...................	122	474	74	144	.304	178	8	4
	Young........	Cleveland................	48	181	33	54	.304	80	2	1
38	W. Clark....	New York................	65	241	38	73	.303	90	2	6
	Pickering...	Louisville...............	45	165	28	50	.303	68	1	15
39	Duffy........	Boston...................	131	533	93	161	.302	213	20	45
40	Cooley.......	St. Louis and Philadelphia.	104	458	91	138	.301	165	14	23
	Hoffer.......	Baltimore................	35	126	23	38	.301	52	3	10
41	Collins......	Boston...................	83	303	52	91	.300	122	8	10
	O'Connor.....	Cleveland................	60	243	38	73	.300	86	7	16
42	Corcoran.....	Brooklyn.................	132	527	64	158	.299	196	12	18
	McPhee.......	Cincinnati...............	116	434	81	130	.299	177	8	53
	Brown........	Washington..............	113	432	87	129	.299	159	14	34
	Farrell......	New York and Wash'gton.	82	308	38	92	.298	117	12	7
43	Sugden.......	Pittsburg................	77	295	39	88	.298	103	13	5
	Peitz........	Cincinnati...............	67	208	35	62	.298	92	6	8
44	Vaughn.......	Cincinnati...............	113	435	71	129	.297	174	7	10
45	Hoy..........	Cincinnati...............	121	449	120	133	.296	190	33	53
	Merritt......	Pittsburg................	70	260	24	77	.296	93	10	3
46	Irwin........	Cincinnati...............	127	481	76	142	.295	179	10	33
	O'Brien......	Louisville and Wash'gton.	118	458	62	134	.295	174	8	10
47	Brodie.......	Baltimore................	132	516	99	152	.294	192	3	30
48	Meekin.......	New York................	40	140	27	41	.293	63	0	1
49	Gleason......	New York................	133	540	78	158	.292	197	10	47
50	Clark........	Baltimore................	77	303	48	88	.290	122	8	7
51	Parrott......	St. Louis................	118	475	53	137	.288	166	14	13
	McAleer.....	Cleveland................	116	454	70	131	.288	156	18	26
	Boyle........	Philadelphia.............	39	149	18	43	.288	52	2	3
	Smith........	Washington..............	34	125	21	36	.288	47	4	9
52	Ely..........	Pittsburg................	126	524	84	150	.287	193	28	19
53	Dexter.......	Louisville...............	98	394	64	112	.284	150	2	27
54	Reitz........	Baltimore................	119	459	75	130	.283	165	12	23
55	Connor.......	St. Louis................	126	485	68	137	.282	187	0	14
	Smith........	Cincinnati...............	119	457	64	129	.282	187	7	21

Cozzens   Little (Mgr.)   T. Stevenson   Haughton   Paine   Rand
Chandler   Burgess
Scannell   Clarkson   Dean (Capt.)   R. H. Stevenson
THE HARVARD COLLEGE BASE BALL TEAM, 1896

Hoefer   Wunder   Allen   McKeehan   Jackson   Voigt
Wilhelm   Holloway   Darte   Blakcley Grey   Tracy   Johnson
                    Cantlin   Middleton
UNIVERSITY OF PENNSYLVANIA BASE BALL TEAM, 1896.

Steere   Lang   Casey   Rodman   Gammons   Robinson   Sedgwick
Watson (Asst. Mgr.) Lander   Brady   Fultz (Capt.)   Summersgill   Matteson Mgr.
   T. Dunne   Phillips   J. Dunne
BROWN UNIVERSITY BASE BALL CLUB. 1896.

Davis Root (Mgr.) Corey Whitney (Asst. Mgr.) Goodrich
Heffernan Bradley Street Lewis (Capt.) Dewey Doughty
Drysdale Ashton Ross

WILLIAMS COLLEGE BASE BALL TEAM, 1896.

McIntyre McLaughlin Mahoney   Tracey   Lambert
   Flemming.   Harley O'Brien   McCarthy   Maloncy
          Dugan   Reardon   Lamb

Gaffney Sockalexis Cavanaugh (Mgr.) Kelly Finn (Sec.)
W. J. Fox Pappalau Powers (Capt.) Maroney W. H. Fox McTigue
Garvey Lavin Curley

HOLY CROSS COLLEGE BASE BALL TEAM.

Jones H. T. Clarke Adkinson Stagg Nichols Brown
       M. G. Clarke Winston   Abells (Capt.) Sawyer Sweet
                              Herschberger

UNIVERSITY OF CHICAGO BASE BALL CLUB, 1896.

BASE BALL GUIDE.

BATTING RECORDS—*Continued.*

Rank	Name	Club	Games	At Bat	Runs	1st Bases	Per cent	T.B.	S.H.	S.B.
55	Ewing	Cincinnati	67	266	41	75	.282	107	4	47
	Stafford	New York	59	230	28	65	.282	71	2	15
56	Shindle	Brooklyn	131	519	74	146	.281	195	18	26
	Decker	Chicago	106	423	68	119	.281	176	8	29
57	Lachance	Brooklyn	89	349	60	98	.280	146	8	19
	Daly	Brooklyn	64	225	43	63	.280	95	0	24
58	Shoch	Brooklyn	76	251	36	70	.278	88	7	12
	King	Washington	16	54	8	15	.278	19	3	0
	Sullivan	Philadelphia and St. Louis	98	400	70	111	.277	132	7	17
59	Bierbauer	Pittsburg	57	249	30	69	.277	90	2	6
	Cuppy	Cleveland	41	137	29	38	.277	48	4	0
60	Holmes	Louisville	37	134	23	37	.276	44	4	11
61	Cartwright	Washington	131	496	78	136	.274	169	6	29
62	Zimmer	Cleveland	89	329	49	90	.273	125	5	8
	Miller	Louisville	84	322	54	88	.273	114	3	17
63	Tebeau	Cleveland	132	546	53	148	.271	183	14	18
64	Grim	Brooklyn	80	284	32	76	.269	95	10	7
	Beckley	Pittsburg and New York	99	395	79	106	.268	167	10	19
65	Hulen	Philadelphia	85	336	87	90	.268	121	9	22
	Douglas	St. Louis	79	298	43	80	.268	89	5	14
	Breitenstein	St. Louis	48	164	21	44	.268	50	7	7
	Bergen	Boston	62	239	42	64	.267	86	4	7
66	Flynn	Chicago	29	105	14	28	.267	34	3	13
	Cunningham	Louisville	24	86	11	23	.267	35	1	0
	Dowd	St. Louis	125	522	93	139	.266	179	11	58
67	McGarr	Cleveland	111	455	68	122	.266	148	9	17
	Griffith	Chicago	36	135	22	35	.266	50	2	2
68	Cross	St. Louis	124	431	64	114	.264	140	12	38
	Rogers	Wash'gton and Louisville	112	447	60	118	.264	152	3	17
69	Ganzel	Boston	44	179	29	47	.262	52	5	2
	Wilson	Cleveland	29	99	18	26	.262	32	2	1
	Cross	Philadelphia	106	409	62	107	.261	140	14	10
70	Hemming	Baltimore	25	88	15	23	.261	34	2	3
	Foreman	Cincinnati	22	65	9	17	.261	19	5	1
71	Terry	Chicago	28	100	14	26	.260	34	3	4
72	Myers	St. Louis	122	458	48	117	.258	138	8	10
73	Connaughton	New York	83	315	48	81	.257	95	5	20
74	Bannon	Boston	87	343	53	88	.256	107	8	15
75	Abbey	Washington	75	294	46	75	.255	99	10	17
76	McCarthy	Brooklyn	101	378	62	96	.254	121	9	23
	Dwyer	Cincinnati	38	110	17	28	.254	41	3	2
77	Mercer	Washington	43	146	19	37	.253	39	2	7
78	Turner	St. Louis	59	234	43	59	.252	76	1	7
79	Crooks	Wash'gton and Louisville	61	207	40	52	.251	75	5	11
	Murphy	St. Louis	48	175	12	44	.251	51	6	1
80	Quinn	St. Louis and Baltimore	68	273	40	68	.249	78	8	17
81	Mertes	Philadelphia	35	141	20	35	.248	45	4	19
	Hassamaer	Louisville	26	97	6	24	.248	85	0	2
82	McCauley	Washington	21	81	14	20	.247	28	3	3
83	Lush	Washington	91	347	71	85	.245	120	5	25
84	Pond	Baltimore	24	78	10	19	.243	22	5	1
85	Blake	Cleveland	102	379	66	92	.242	113	9	9
	Nash	Philadelphia	64	23	29	56	.242	75	4	4

BATTING RECORDS—*Continued.*

Rank.	Name.	Club.	Games.	At Bat.	Runs.	1st Bases.	Per cent.	T.B.	S.H.	S.B.
86	{ Truby.......	Chicago and Pittsburg.....	35	141	13	34	.241	46	1	6
	{ Fisher.......	Cincinnati...................	20	58	10	14	.241	18	4	1
87	{ Pfeffer......	New York and Chicago.....	99	375	46	90	.240	126	3	23
	{ Friend......	Chicago.....................	33	125	12	30	.240	38	4	3
88	{ McFarland.	St. Louis....................	80	289	47	69	.239	84	10	11
	{ Padden......	Pittsburg....................	60	217	32	52	.239	78	4	8
89	Orth..........	Philadelphia................	22	84	12	20	.238	32	0	2
90	Killen.........	Pittsburg....................	48	166	27	38	.235	59	3	0
91	{ Davis.......	Pittsburg and New York...	107	401	68	94	.234	150	9	33
	{ Hawley.....	Pittsburg....................	44	162	19	38	.234	56	3	1
92	Johnson......	Louisville...................	24	86	10	20	.232	24	2	0
93	Wallace......	Cleveland...................	33	130	17	30	.231	45	4	1
94	{ Clingman...	Louisville...................	120	426	58	98	.230	118	4	22
	{ Wilson......	New York...................	69	252	33	58	.230	60	10	8
95	Daub..........	Brooklyn....................	27	83	9	19	.229	24	0	1
96	Warner........	Louisville and New York...	49	163	18	37	.227	42	8	6
97	Donohue......	Chicago.....................	54	190	27	43	.226	56	4	11
98	German.......	Washington.................	24	71	12	16	.225	17	0	2
99	{ Kittridge....	Chicago.....................	61	215	17	48	.223	58	5	9
	{ Sullivan.....	Boston......................	24	85	9	19	.223	25	2	0
100	{ Carsey......	Philadelphia................	23	81	13	18	.222	20	3	0
	{ Hughey.....	Pittsburg....................	21	63	4	14	.222	15	0	0
101	Cassidy.......	Louisville...................	48	181	16	40	.221	44	3	6
102	Zearfoss.......	New York...................	16	59	5	13	.220	14	0	1
103	{ McCormick..	Chicago.....................	45	169	22	37	.219	43	3	10
	{ Dolan.......	Louisville...................	44	164	14	36	.219	48	1	7
104	Payne.........	Brooklyn....................	32	96	5	21	.218	28	4	1
105	{ Gray........	Cincinnati...................	35	116	13	25	.216	30	6	6
	{ Sullivan.....	New York...................	23	74	9	16	.216	17	2	1
106	Delehanty.....	Cleveland...................	16	57	10	12	.210	16	1	3
107	W. H. Clarke.	New York...................	40	143	11	30	.209	33	1	0
108	Mack.........	Pittsburg....................	30	116	7	24	.207	29	1	0
109	{ Harrington..	Boston......................	53	197	26	40	.203	52	3	1
	{ Hill........	Louisville...................	36	118	11	24	.203	25	4	1
110	Ehret.........	Cincinnati...................	31	100	10	20	.200	26	5	3
111	McFarland....	Louisville...................	25	106	10	21	.198	28	1	5
112	Kennedy......	Brooklyn....................	37	122	12	24	.197	26	4	2
113	{ Hart........	St. Louis....................	46	163	9	32	.196	38	4	8
	{ Rhines......	Cincinnati...................	17	51	4	10	.196	11	1	0
114	Taylor........	Philadelphia................	44	156	11	30	.192	34	8	0
115	Nichols.......	Boston......................	43	132	22	25	.189	36	9	2
116	Esper.........	Baltimore...................	19	66	7	12	.181	17	1	0
117	Fuller.........	New York...................	17	72	10	13	.180	13	0	2
118	{ Abbey......	Brooklyn....................	19	63	7	11	.174	16	4	0
	{ Shearon.....	Cleveland...................	15	63	7	11	.174	13	0	3
119	McJames......	Washington.................	34	115	10	19	.165	20	3	1
120	Eustace.......	Louisville...................	25	98	17	16	.163	24	1	4
121	Nilands.......	St. Louis....................	18	68	3	11	.162	13	1	0
122	Shannon......	Louisville...................	31	118	15	19	.161	25	4	3
123	Donahue......	St. Louis....................	33	108	5	17	.157	18	3	1
124	Frazer........	Louisville...................	43	144	10	21	.146	25	0	2
125	Briggs.........	Chicago.....................	22	75	5	10	.133	14	0	0
126	McMahon.....	Baltimore...................	21	71	5	9	.126	12	0	1

BASE BALL GUIDE.

FIELDING RECORD, 1896.

FIRST BASEMEN.

Rank.	Name.	Club.	Games.	Put Outs.	Assists.	Errors.	Total Chances.	Per cent.
1	Lajoie...............	Philadelphia...............	39	360	11	3	374	.992
2	{ Tebeau............	Cleveland................	122	1341	79	19	1439	.987
	{ Lachance...........	Brooklyn.................	89	953	40	13	1006	.987
3	{ Connor............	St. Louis.................	126	1223	86	17	1326	.985
	{ Tucker.............	Boston...................	122	1213	73	19	1305	.985
4	Beckley............	Pittsburg and New York..	95	941	51	16	1008	.984
5	{ W. Clarke..........	New York.................	65	634	27	12	673	.983
	{ Brouthers..........	Philadelphia.............	57	570	23	10	603	.983
6	{ Anson............	Chicago..................	96	886	53	17	956	.982
	{ Vaughn............	Cincinnati...............	56	586	33	11	630	.982
	{ Anderson..........	Brooklyn.................	38	420	20	8	448	.982
	{ Ewing.............	Cincinnati...............	67	669	49	14	732	.981
7	{ Cassidy............	Louisville................	38	345	17	7	369	.981
	{ Mack..............	Pittsburg.................	25	240	18	5	263	.981
8	Cartwright..........	Washington..............	131	1248	72	30	1350	.977
9	Decker.............	Chicago..................	36	349	24	9	382	.976
10	Doyle..............	Baltimore.................	118	1157	43	33	1233	.973
11	{ Rogers............	Louisville and W'shington	60	590	37	20	647	.969
	{ Delehanty.........	Philadelphia.............	21	213	11	7	231	.969
12	Hassamaer..........	Louisville................	26	256	28	10	294	.966
13	Davis..............	Pittsburg and New York..	58	553	27	19	599	.965

SECOND BASEMEN.

1	McPhee.............	Cincinnati................	116	299	358	12	669	.982
2	Lowe................	Boston....................	73	188	284	16	488	.967
3	Bierbauer............	Pittsburg.................	97	138	204	12	354	.966
4	Quinn...............	St. Louis and Baltimore..	54	110	196	12	318	.962
5	Shoch...............	Brooklyn.................	63	109	181	13	303	.957
6	Reitz................	Baltimore	116	251	324	26	601	.956
7	Hallman.............	Philadelphia	120	312	354	35	701	.950
8	Johnson.............	Louisville................	24	58	63	7	128	.945
9	Pfeffer..............	New York and Chicago...	99	239	316	33	588	.944
10	O'Brien.............	Louisville and W'hington	118	281	364	41	686	.940
11	Childs..............	Cleveland................	132	369	496	57	922	.938
12	Truby...............	Chicago and Pittsburg...	35	96	97	13	206	.937
13	Gleason.............	New York................	130	331	392	57	780	.927
14	Padden..............	Pittsburg.................	60	176	147	25	348	.922
15	Daly................	Brooklyn.................	64	175	186	31	392	.921
16	Miller...............	Louisville................	21	32	49	7	88	.920
17	Crooks..............	W'hington and Louisville	55	168	165	30	363	.917
18	Dowd...............	St. Louis.................	77	182	219	37	438	.915
19	McGann	Boston...................	42	87	109	22	218	.899
20	Joyce...............	W'hington and New York	32	83	79	21	183	.885

THIRD BASEMEN.

1	Cross................	Philadelphia..............	63	89	135	13	237	.945
2	Irwin................	Cincinnati................	127	191	260	33	484	.932
3	{ McGarr............	Cleveland................	111	132	213	29	374	.922
	{ G. Davis...........	New York................	73	115	169	24	308	.922
4	Nash................	Philadelphia..............	64	88	153	21	262	.919

THIRD BASEMEN—Continued.

Rank	Name	Club	Games	Put Outs	Assists	Errors	Total Chances	Per cent
5	{ Shindle	Brooklyn	131	143	261	36	440	.918
	{ Clingman	Louisville	120	193	278	42	513	.918
6	Collins	Boston	78	135	208	32	375	.915
7	Everett	Chicago	99	151	183	34	368	.908
8	Donnelly	Baltimore	104	140	218	39	397	.902
9	Joyce	Washingt'n and New York	97	129	210	41	380	.892
10	Lyons	Pittsburg	116	167	200	46	413	.886
11	Rogers	Louisville and W'hington	32	28	72	14	114	.877
12	Myers	St. Louis	122	169	238	58	465	.874
13	Smith	Washington	34	32	77	17	126	.865
14	McCormick	Chicago	35	34	77	21	132	.840
15	Farrell	New York and Washingt'n	21	23	29	10	62	.838
16	McGraw	Baltimore	18	22	38	12	72	.833
17	Delehanty	Cleveland	16	18	31	10	59	.830
18	Harrington	Boston	48	55	95	35	185	.810

SHORTSTOPS.

Rank	Name	Club	Games	Put Outs	Assists	Errors	Total Chances	Per cent
1	Dolan	Louisville	44	99	157	16	272	.941
2	Cross	Philadelphia	36	84	131	14	229	.939
3	G. Davis	New York	45	109	143	17	269	.936
4	Connaughton	New York	53	92	198	22	312	.929
5	{ Jennings	Baltimore	129	380	476	68	924	.926
	{ Smith	Cincinnati	119	206	412	49	667	.926
6	Ely	Pittsburg	126	254	430	57	741	.923
7	Corcoran	Brooklyn	132	321	477	68	866	.921
8	McKean	Cleveland	133	220	398	58	676	.914
9	Dahlen	Chicago	125	315	463	75	853	.912
10	Long	Boston	119	312	416	75	803	.906
11	Demontreville	Washington	130	300	475	92	869	.892
12	Cross	St. Louis	124	296	395	84	775	.891
13	Hulen	Philadelphia	73	153	202	47	402	.883
14	Fuller	New York	17	41	65	15	121	.876
15	Eustace	Louisville	22	46	68	24	138	.826
16	Shannon	Louisville	29	60	76	30	166	.819

OUTFIELDERS.

Rank	Name	Club	Games	Put Outs	Assists	Errors	Total Chances	Per cent
1	Keeler	Baltimore	127	229	22	7	258	.973
2	Brodie	Baltimore	132	321	20	10	351	.971
3	Thompson	Philadelphia	119	235	28	8	271	.970
4	Tiernan	New York	133	211	6	8	225	.964
5	{ Griffin	Brooklyn	122	315	7	13	335	.961
	{ Parrott	St. Louis	112	278	21	12	311	.961
6	Dowd	St. Louis	48	116	4	5	125	.960
7	Sullivan	Philadelphia and St. Louis	90	176	9	8	193	.958
8	Duffy	Boston	120	250	17	12	279	.957
9	Kelley	Baltimore	130	278	22	13	313	.955
10	{ Selbach	Washington	121	298	14	16	328	.951
	{ McAleer	Cleveland	116	275	19	15	309	.951
11	Hoy	Cincinnati	121	307	14	17	338	.949
12	{ Donovan	Pittsburg	129	222	30	14	266	.947
	{ E. E. Smith	Pittsburg	120	297	11	17	325	.947
	{ Delehanty	Philadelphia	100	269	16	16	301	.947

OUTFIELDERS—Continued.

Rank	Name	Club	Games	Put Outs	Assists	Errors	Total Chances	Per cent.
13	Blake	Cleveland	102	185	17	12	214	.944
14	Van Haltren	New York	132	271	24	18	313	.942
15	Brown	Washington	118	256	8	17	281	.939
16	Hamilton	Boston	131	278	8	19	305	.937
16	Tenney	Boston	60	81	9	6	96	.937
17	Turner	St. Louis and Philadelphia	59	81	8	6	95	.936
18	Burke	Cincinnati	122	287	14	21	322	.934
19	Douglas	St. Louis	74	110	13	9	132	.932
20	Lange	Chicago	122	311	13	25	349	.928
20	Stenzel	Pittsburg	112	245	13	20	278	.928
20	Anderson	Brooklyn	66	118	12	10	140	.928
21	Cooley	St. Louis and Philadelphia	104	222	28	20	270	.926
22	Burkett	Cleveland	133	271	15	23	309	.925
22	McCarthy	Brooklyn	101	179	20	16	215	.925
23	Ryan	Chicago	127	207	26	20	253	.921
24	Holliday	Cincinnati	15	33	1	3	37	.919
25	Jones	Brooklyn	102	171	9	16	196	.918
26	Bannon	Boston	74	131	13	13	157	.917
27	Decker	Chicago	70	132	10	13	155	.916
28	Pickering	Louisville	45	97	8	10	115	.913
29	Davis	Pittsburg and New York	49	99	4	10	113	.911
30	Miller	Cincinnati	125	203	21	23	247	.907
31	Clark	Louisville	131	276	17	31	324	.904
31	McCreary	Louisville	110	174	24	21	219	.904
32	Everett	Chicago	32	57	3	7	67	.895
33	Connaughton	New York	30	45	4	6	55	.891
34	Stafford	New York	52	79	10	11	100	.890
34	Flynn	Chicago	29	66	7	9	82	.890
35	Dexter	Louisville	44	87	9	12	108	.888
36	McFarland	Louisville	24	46	7	7	60	.883
37	Lush	Washington	89	136	22	21	179	.882
38	Abbey	Washington	75	105	10	16	131	.878
39	Mertes	Philadelphia	35	83	3	13	99	.868
40	Shearon	Cleveland	15	19	0	4	23	.826
41	Holmes	Louisville	33	43	7	13	63	.793

CATCHERS' RECORDS.

Rank	Name	Club	Games Played	Put Outs	Assists	Errors	Passed Balls	Total Chances	Percentage Accepted
1	Ganzel	Boston	40	138	47	2	5	192	.968
2	Vaughn	Cincinnati	57	156	57	9	2	224	.951
3	Boyle	Philadelphia	28	75	21	2	3	101	.950
4	Sugden	Pittsburg	65	258	68	15	6	347	.939
5	Peitz	Cincinnati	67	197	46	7	10	260	.934
6	Kittridge	Chicago	61	253	63	16	7	339	.932

CATCHERS'S RECORDS—*Continued.*

Rank	Name	Club	Games Played.	Put Outs.	Assists.	Errors.	Passed Balls.	Total Chances.	Percentage Accepted.
7	Clements	Philadelphia	50	147	50	7	8	212	.929
8	O'Connor	Cleveland	37	107	31	6	5	149	.928
9	Zimmer	Cleveland	89	339	80	11	23	453	.925
10	Merritt	Pittsburg	60	238	78	19	8	343	.921
11	McFarland	St. Louis	80	274	123	16	19	432	.919
11	Robinson	Baltimore	66	260	46	14	13	333	.919
12	McGuire	Washington	95	350	86	31	11	478	.912
13	Grim	Brooklyn	76	240	84	23	10	357	.907
14	Clark	Baltimore	64	197	51	14	12	274	.905
14	Grady	Philadelphia	56	166	64	13	11	254	.905
15	Farrell	New York and W'hington	51	158	57	13	11	239	.899
16	Burrell	Brooklyn	58	172	46	19	6	243	.897
17	Donohue	Chicago	54	241	56	21	14	332	.894
17	Miller	Louisville	46	137	49	16	6	208	.894
18	Wilson	New York	67	260	73	14	26	373	.892
18	Murphy	St. Louis	48	176	49	19	8	252	.892
19	Warner	Louisville and New York	48	193	55	20	12	280	.885
19	Tenney	Boston	26	100	31	10	7	148	.885
20	Zearfoss	New York	16	53	14	6	3	76	.881
21	Bergen	Boston	62	209	70	24	16	319	.874
22	Dexter	Louisville	54	177	61	23	16	277	.859
23	McCauley	Washington	21	72	25	8	9	114	.851

PITCHERS' RECORDS IN ALPHABETICAL ORDER.

Name	Club	Games Played.	Per cent. of Victories.*	Av. Runs Scored Per Game.	Av. Runs Earned Per Game.	Per cent. of Base Hits off Pitcher.	Bases Given on Called Balls.	No. Struck Out.	Per cent. Fielding Chances Accepted.
Abbey	Brooklyn	19	.444	7.28	4.66	.303	45	37	.888
Breitenstein	St. Louis	42	.425	5.60	3.02	.277	110	106	.946
Briggs	Chicago	22	.571	5.81	2.27	.266	105	83	.829
Carsey	Philadelphia	22	.500	7.58	3.37	.335	73	24	.853
Clarke	New York	40	.425	5.66	3.10	.282	54	60	.826
Cuppy	Cleveland	40	.658	4.45	2.52	.286	74	81	.836
Cunningham	Louisville	23	.261	6.91	2.78	.305	71	34	.863
Daub	Brooklyn	27	.481	4.72	3.20	.266	60	48	.851
Donohue	St. Louis	33	.250	7.19	3.39	.318	92	64	.887
Dwyer	Cincinnati	33	.727	4.16	2.25	.288	69	58	.891
Ehret	Cincinnati	31	.613	4.24	2.51	.281	73	60	.882
Esper	Baltimore	19	.789	4.79	2.73	.276	38	18	.875
Fisher	Cincinnati	20	.474	6.05	3.28	.313	35	20	.865
Foreman	Cincinnati	22	.696	4.85	2.80	.260	51	29	.892

*Exclusive of tie games.

PITCHERS' RECORDS—Continued.

Name.	Club.	Games Played.	Per cent. of Victories.*	Av. Runs Scored Per Game.	Av. Runs Earned Per Game.	Per cent. of Base Hits off Pitcher.	Bases Given on Called Balls.	No. Struck Out.	Per cent. Fielding Chances Accepted.
Frazer	Louisville	41	.250	6.85	2.60	.277	154	91	.717
Friend	Chicago	32	.613	6.09	2.36	.267	137	84	.840
German	Washington	21	.053	8.42	4.68	.336	59	17	.819
Griffith	Chicago	36	.628	5.25	2.41	.286	69	82	.891
Hart	St. Louis	40	.300	6.82	3.42	.295	126	61	.885
Hemming	Baltimore	25	.563	4.91	2.83	.297	43	31	.891
Hawley	Pittsburg	44	.535	4.60	2.23	.259	155	136	.865
Hughey	Pittsburg	21	.389	6.47	3.68	.302	55	37	.788
Hoffer	Baltimore	35	.823	3.85	1.83	.266	92	94	.878
Hill	Louisville	36	.270	5.58	1.97	.275	157	108	.856
Kennedy	Brooklyn	37	.500	4.79	2.69	.261	123	76	.856
Killen	Pittsburg	48	.638	4.91	2.85	.270	107	132	.898
King	Washington	16	.625	6.12	2.87	.284	35	30	.827
Kissengen	St. Louis	19	.125	8.23	3.88	.351	37	19	.852
Meekin	New York	40	.675	5.02	2.42	.279	112	107	.773
Mercer	Washington	42	.619	6.20	3.02	.300	108	96	.834
McJames	Washington	34	.394	6.08	2.63	.275	139	103	.692
McMahon	Baltimore	20	.619	4.70	2.25	.268	48	33	.850
Nichols	Boston	45	.666	4.55	2.13	.267	93	95	.972
Orth	Philadelphia	22	.636	5.87	3.74	.302	45	21	.902
Payne	Brooklyn	31	.464	4.21	2.32	.295	64	33	.929
Pond	Baltimore	24	.714	5.04	2.87	.261	51	76	.806
Rhines	Cincinnati	17	.529	3.53	1.59	.224	43	32	.759
Stivetts	Boston	39	.615	5.41	2.92	.260	90	64	.905
Sullivan	Boston	23	.478	5.43	2.65	.279	56	27	.854
Sullivan	New York	23	.348	5.88	2.44	.270	67	49	.818
Taylor	Philadelphia	44	.536	6.70	3.30	.307	96	84	.902
Terry	Chicago	28	.464	5.53	2.53	.294	86	73	.887
Wallace	Cleveland	15	.666	4.47	2.20	.278	43	44	.681
Wilson	Cleveland	29	.577	4.84	2.22	.289	80	53	.742
Young	Cleveland	47	.644	4.28	2.50	.282	64	137	.860

* Exclusive of tie games.

A great deal is said about the special attraction of this and that leading sport of the day. Each kind has its votaries who think no other sport equals their favorite. But if any one can present to us a sport or pastime, a race or a contest, which can in all its essentials of stirring excitement, displays of manly courage, nerve and endurance, and its unwearying scenes of skilful play and alternations of success equal our national game of ball, we should like to see it.

A glance at the crude code of base ball rules in vogue during the year the first national base ball association was organized, in 1857, reveals very plainly the great improvement which has since been made. And season after season has the game been improved by the adoption of amendments each year until a degree of excellence in the playing code has been reached almost approaching a perfected code. The great point to be aimed at in the annual revision of the playing code of rules is to equalize the powers of the attack and defense as much as possible, and also to make as few radical changes in the rules as the desire to improve the game admits of.

The Minor League Arena

THE season's history of the Minor Leagues in 1896 afforded more proof than ever before of the important fact that the government of the great major league, under the compact of the National Agreement, is the corner-stone in the building up of their permanent prosperity. It is the work of years of practical experience only to bring to bear with good effect legislation calculated to protect minor league organizations from abuses and errors, which would otherwise soon end their existence as paying business associations. What the minor leagues require to aid the League in making their several organizations permanent and profitable, is for them to stand by the rules laid out for their individual government; and prominent among these is the rule of a salary list for each league suited to the capital of the individual clubs comprising the league, and the imposition of an effective penalty for every violation of the salary rule limit. Each year's experience of the practical working of the League government of the minor leagues only goes to show more and more its many decided advantages in promoting the business welfare of the minor leagues in particular, and the financial interests of the professional clubs at large.

At the Western League meeting held in the fall of 1896 one of the most important matters brought out was the unanimous feeling in favor of materially reducing salaries. Other Western Leagues have started, seemingly thrived, then dropped off, all on account of broken pledges in the salary business. Cities of the size of those in the present circuit, in which the jumps are long, cannot pay big money for players and make anything out of it. The old Western League, which graduated Hutchison and other stars in 1888, finally succumbed on account of the pay rolls. Of course, the depressed interest in the game after the Brotherhood year had something to do with this, but in 1891 the League again went up, the salaries being unreasonably high.

The present league started out to set an example, and the limit was placed at $1,800 a month. Several of the clubs kept inside of the limit, but one or two overstepped. In 1895 nearly all went beyond, and last year the limit was raised to $2,000. This would be all right if it were observed, but it is said that not a club was as low as $2,000, which is $10,000 on the five-month contract. The two clubs winning the first and second made less money than some of the others, and the feeling now is that *all must pull together* in order that the franchises make any money.

A majority of the minor leagues in 1896 fell by the wayside ; that is, they failed to have all their clubs finish the season's schedule of games, some clubs of their circuits disbanding in July and others in August. This result was partly due to poor club management, but the financial condition of the country also had a good deal to do with it. The fact should be remembered by minor league magnates, in this regard, that election years, and especially the one year in four of a presidential campaign, is always a bad base ball season when compared with other years. Last year has been no exception to the rule, and probably there never will be one. Another matter which affects not only minor league clubs, but all professional clubs, is the failure to enforce the use of that great element of success in winning pennants, *playing for the side ;* in other words, the failure to train up nines to do team-work in every department of the game, without which there is no possibility of success.

The Eastern League

THE season of 1896 was the fourth which the Eastern League ended successfully under the able government of President P. T. Powers, and for the second time the Providence club's team came in victors in the pennant race, the Providence club having won the pennant in 1894 with the percentage figures of .696, and in 1896 with .607. The Providence team did not show special strength until the latter part of the season, when they rallied with telling effect, though closely followed by Buffalo, the former winning 10 games to Buffalo's 8, besides winning in the final after-season Steinert Cup match. The Toronto team was a strong one, but was handicapped by the League's demand upon its players, and wound up in fourth place. Syracuse started out with bright hopes and an expensive team, but finally declined and finished a poor fifth. The champion Springfields of 1895 were so much weakened by the drafts of the National League that it was several months before the team could be brought up to Eastern League standard, and by that time it was too late to secure a respectable position, so the once great team had to be content with sixth place. As usual in this well-conducted League, the campaign progressed smoothly, the only interruption to the usual and regular course of events being the short-lived transfer of the Toronto team to Albany and the re-transfer to Toronto. The full record is as follows:

THE RECORD BY SERIES.

Club.	Providence.	Buffalo.	Rochester.	Toronto.	Syracuse.	Springfield.	Wilkesbarre.	Scranton.	Victories.	Per cent. of Victories.
Providence.........		10	8	11	12	14	9	7	71	.602
Buffalo.............	8		9	9	10	9	12	13	70	.589
Rochester..........	9	11		6	10	9	13	10	68	.540
Toronto............	5	8	9		8	9	11	9	59	.509
Syracuse...........	7	5	11	10		9	6	11	59	.488
Springfield.........	3	9	10	9	7		7	9	54	.458
Wilkesbarre........	7	7	5	5	10	7		8	49	.426
Scranton...........	8	8	6	7	5	7	8		44	.396
Defeats............	47	58	58	57	62	64	66	67	474	

BASE BALL GUIDE.

BATTING AVERAGE.

Player and Club.	Games.	Runs.	Stolen Bases.	Per cent. of Base Hits.	Player and Club.	Games.	Runs.	Stolen Bases.	Per cent. of Base Hits.
Lezotte,Wilkesbar'e	113	94	13	.404	Stricker, Springfield	23	26	6	.292
Brouthers, Sp'gfield	51	42	9	.400	W. Johnson, Roch..	129	103	17	.292
Goeckle, Wilkesb'e.	22	19	9	.393	Dixon, Providence.	95	71	28	.289
Knight, Providence.	119	112	21	.376	Horton, Toronto....	15	10	8	.286
Harley, Springfield.	68	61	16	.357	Sweeney, Spri'gfield	33	33	8	.286
Beard, Rochester...	127	105	20	.355	Mulvey, Rochester.	113	83	20	.282
Betts, Wilkesbarre.	112	86	22	.353	Padden, Toronto...	60	58	18	.281
Wise, Buffalo......	78	76	18	.352	Zahner, Syracuse...	20	4	0	.281
Canavan, Pr'viden'e	119	121	64	.350	Clymer, Buffalo....	121	121	46	.280
Daly, Rochester....	115	100	12	.349	Lynch, Spr. & Roch.	92	93	39	.277
Scheffler, Spri'gfield	121	121	50	.346	Coogan,Spr.& Prov.	82	54	15	.277
Rafferty, Scranton.	24	14	1	.341	H. Smith, Buffalo..	67	41	8	.277
Bonner, Wilkesbarre	106	82	5	.337	C. Smith,Wilkesb're	113	60	10	.276
Massey, Scranton..	40	19	9	.337	Lutenburg,Toronto.	108	64	16	.275
Stahl, Buffalo......	122	129	34	.337	Staley, Toronto....	24	10	4	.272
Drauby, Providence	112	97	9	.334	Reilly, Syr.& Spring	89	57	23	.271
O.Smith,Syr. & Spr.	81	81	23	.333	Whitehill, Syracuse	36	7	1	.269
Meaney, Scranton..	106	91	13	.332	Moran, Toronto....	37	10	0	.268
Casey, Toronto.....	96	83	37	.329	Yerrick,Wilkesb'rre	17	10	0	.268
P. Eagan, Scranton.	103	92	30	.329	Truby, Toronto....	38	22	3	.266
Dooley, Rochester..	126	95	15	.328	Gruber, Spr. & Buff.	41	28	1	.266
Bannon, Syracuse..	54	46	25	.328	Fuller, Springfield..	75	66	47	.265
Gilbert, Springfield.	111	95	34	.325	McPartlin, Toronto.	24	9	1	.263
J. Smith, Toronto..	110	79	37	.323	Griffin, Scranton...	40	22	5	.263
Field, Buffalo......	123	109	18	.322	Keenan, Wilkesb're.	43	21	8	.262
Freeman, Toronto..	114	84	25	.322	Delaney, Syracuse..	49	23	3	.261
Wadsworth, Buffalo	39	18	1	.321	Moss, Scran. & Syr.	115	59	19	.260
D.Shannon, Roch...	79	62	11	.319	Luckey,Wilkesb'rre	33	16	4	.259
Lyons, Providence.	118	106	49	.317	Ryan, Syracuse....	91	48	11	.259
Ward, Scran. & Tor.	104	83	27	.316	Boyd, Rochester...	128	72	18	.258
Murray, Providence	114	99	75	.314	Lewee, Buffalo.....	92	59	9	.258
Greminger, Buffalo.	93	58	11	.314	Leahy, Springfield..	104	71	59	.256
Easton,Spr.& Roch.	32	14	5	.308	Ritchey, Buffalo...	102	68	11	.256
Wright, Toronto....	88	71	37	.307	Knorr, Providence.	15	7	0	.250
Urquhart, Buffalo..	85	54	9	.306	Dolan, Providence.	23	11	5	.250
Diggins, Wilk'sbar'e	78	40	4	.306	Wente,Wilkesbarre.	61	33	5	.250
W. Egan, Syracuse.	107	117	54	.305	Hutchinson, Scran..	78	60	11	.247
Shearon, Syracuse..	98	62	19	.305	Colcolough, Wilkes.	26	14	3	.247
Goodeno'gh,Buffalo	115	83	31	.303	Delehanty,Toronto.	98	86	40	.247
Leighton,Spri'gfield	23	13	14	.302	Willis, Syracuse....	17	7	1	.245
Maguire, Scranton..	109	63	11	.301	Dowse,Roch.& Tor.	50	25	8	.244
Cooney, Providence	110	83	28	.300	Raymond, Syracuse	29	15	5	.244
Lytle, Wilkesbarre.	110	97	36	.300	Dunn, Toronto.....	27	15	5	.242
Gunson,Spr.& Scr'n	63	18	2	.300	Gillon,Roch.&Scr'n	26	12	0	.239
Bassett, Providence.	119	109	29	.300	Latham, Scranton..	44	45	39	.239
Minnehan, Syracuse	112	79	16	.299	McDonald, Spring..	23	9	1	.239
Garry, Syracuse....	110	75	19	.298	Lovett,Roch.&Scr'n	24	10	0	.239
J. J. O'Brien, Scran.	79	65	10	.298	Horner, Scranton...	18	8	0	.237
Bottenus, Rochest'r	126	118	24	.297	Earl, Wilkesbarre..	93	51	16	.236
T. O'Brien, Toronto	108	73	10	.296	Harri'gton,Syr'cuse	30	18	4	.236
Carey, Syracuse....	123	74	11	.293	Berger, Scranton...	50	24	7	.233

SPALDING'S OFFICIAL.

BATTING AVERAGES—Continued.

Player and Club.	Games.	Runs.	Stolen Bases.	Per cent. of Base Hits.	Player and Club.	Games.	Runs.	Stolen Bases.	Per cent. of Base Hits.
McFarlan, Roch'r..	42	23	1	.232	Hess, Syracuse.....	44	24	3	.209
Wagner, Toronto...	20	11	5	.231	Friel, Providence...	29	15	2	.206
Mason, Syracuse...	48	18	2	.225	Dineen, Toronto...	27	8	1	.200
W. Shannon, Spring	29	20	0	.223	Keister, Scranton..	26	12	4	.200
Flack, Scranton....	18	11	2	.221	Gannon, Buffalo...,	35	19	11	.198
Gray, Buffalo......	23	14	1	.218	Herndon, Buff.&Ro.	36	18	3	.173
Outcalt, Scranton..	21	10	1	.215	Callihan, Rochester	21	5	2	.169
McMahon, Wilkes..	107	62	8	.214	T. Johnson, Scran..	37	9	0	.163
Rudderham, Prov..	25	11	2	.213	Hodson, Providence	43	15	3	.158
Herman, Rochester.	16	6	0	.212	Coughlin, Springfi'd	43	14	5	.149
Brown, Scranton...	30	13	0	.211					

FIELDING AVERAGES.

CATCHERS.

Player and Club.	Games.	Percentage.	Player and Club.	Games.	Percentage.
Diggins, Wilkesbarre.....	62	.965	Urquhart, Buffalo........	59	.928
Gunson, Springfield......	61	.949	Wente, Wilkesbarre......	58	.925
Dixon, Providence.......	91	.948	Dowse, Toronto & Roch..	26	.916
H. E. Smith, Buffalo.....	67	.944	Hess, Syracuse...........	44	.904
Berger, Scranton.........	49	.943	Leahy, Springfield.......	58	.900
Ryan, Syracuse..........	61	.942	Rafferty, Scranton........	23	.895
Casey, Toronto...........	66	.986	Coogan, Spring. & Prov..	46	.891
Boyd, Rochester.........	126	.984	Zahner, Syracuse.........	19	.880

PITCHERS.

Player and Club.	Games.	Percentage.	Player and Club.	Games.	Percentage.
Colcolough, Wilkesbarre..	26	1.000	Wadsworth, Buffalo	39	.933
Whitehill, Syracuse......	36	.983	Rudderham, Providence.	25	.932
Gray, Buffalo............	23	.983	Gruber, Spring. & Buffalo.	25	.925
Callihan, Rochester......	19	.977	Keenan, Wilkesbarre.....	42	.920
T. Johnson, Scranton....	34	.973	Knorr, Providence........	15	.905
Gillon, Scranton & Roch.	24	.969	Herndon, Buffalo & Roch	36	.903
Easton, Spring. & Roch..	24	.969	Staley, Toronto..........	24	.900
Dineen, Toronto.........	27	.966	Brown, Scranton.........	30	.899
McPartlin, Tor. & Spring.	24	.964	Hodson, Providence......	43	.898
Herman, Rochester.......	16	.955	Mason, Syracuse........	48	.898
Dunne, Toronto..........	27	.954	Dolan, Providence.......	16	.889
Delaney, Syracuse.......	43	.954	McFarlin, Rochester.....	42	.888
Lovett, Roch. & Scranton.	25	.953	Yerrick, Wilkesbarre.....	17	.822
Gannon, Buffalo..........	35	.952	Friel, Providence.........	18	.821
Coughlin, Springfield....	42	.946	Moran, Toronto.........	24	.804
Outcalt, Scranton........	18	.935	Luckey, Wilkesbarre.....	22	.804
Willis, Syracuse..........	17	.933			

FIRST BASEMEN.

Player and Club.	Games.	Percentage.	Player and Club.	Games.	Percentage.
Goeckle, Wilkesbarre	22	.991	Lutenburg, Toronto	108	.976
Dooley, Rochester	126	.991	Coogan, Spring. & Prov.	17	.973
Carey, Syracuse	123	.988	Massey Scranton	40	.972
Field, Buffalo	123	.980	Earl, Wilkesbarre	87	.967
Drauby, Providence	112	.979	Gilbert, Springfield	23	.964
Hutchinson, Scranton	36	.979	Ward, Scran. & Toronto.	14	.953
Brouthers, Springfield	51	.977	Gruber, Spring. & Buffalo.	14	.895

SECOND BASEMEN.

Player and Club.	Games.	Percentage.	Player and Club.	Games.	Percentage.
Clymer, Buffalo	13	.957	Bonner, Wilkesbarre	106	.914
McDonald, Springfield	23	.955	Padden, Toronto	60	.904
Lewee, Buffalo	32	.955	D. Shannon, Rochester	77	.903
W. Eagan, Syracuse	107	.945	Gilbert, Springfield	29	.896
Canavan, Providence	119	.941	Lynch, Spring. & Roch	39	.893
Dowse, Toronto & Roch.	18	.931	Keister, Scranton	17	.889
Truby, Toronto	31	.927	Hutchinson, Scranton	15	.885
Wise, Buffalo	78	.924	Stricker, Springfield	23	.885
Ward, Toronto & Scran	83	.918			

THIRD BASEMEN.

Player and Club.	Games.	Percentage.	Player and Club.	Games.	Percentage.
Lewee, Buffalo	19	.963	Minnehan, Syracuse	73	.891
Mulvey, Rochester	113	.938	C. A. Smith, Wilkesbarre	113	.889
Harrington, Syracuse	16	.924	Gilbert, Springfield	61	.887
Bassett, Providence	119	.922	Greminger, Buffalo	93	.876
Reilly, Syrac'e & Spring.	89	.900	John Smith, Toronto	110	.876
Maguire, Scranton	4	.893	Latham, Scranton	44	.873

SHORTSTOPS.

Player and Club.	Games.	Percentage.	Player and Club.	Games.	Percentage.
Cooney, Providence	110	.946	Wagner, Toronto	20	.891
Beard, Rochester	127	.929	Maguire, Scranton	63	.889
McMahon, Wilkesbarre	107	.915	Delehanty, Toronto	83	.883
Ritchey, Buffalo	89	.912	Lewee, Buffalo	37	.878
Moss, Scran. & Syracuse.	115	.906	Raymond, Syracuse	27	.875
Fuller, Springfield	75	.896	W. Shannon, Springfield.	17	.825
Lynch, Spring. & Roch	31	.895			

OUTFIELDERS.

Player and Club.	Games.	Percentage.	Player and Club.	Games.	Percentage.
Minnehan, Syracuse	49	.953	T. O'Brien, Toronto	108	.923
Clymer, Buffalo	108	.951	Murray, Providence	114	.922
Bottenus, Rochester	125	.947	Daly, Rochester	115	.919
Lezotte, Wilkesbarre	113	.946	Scheffler, Springfield	121	.919
W. Johnson, Rochester	129	.938	Meaney, Scranton	106	.913
Bannon, Syracuse	54	.938	Lyons, Providence	118	.908
Stahl, Buffalo	122	.937	Sweeney, Springfield	33	.905
Leighton, Springfield	23	.937	O. Smith, Syra. & Spring.	81	.902
Wright, Toronto	88	.934	Freeman, Toronto	114	.902
Knight, Providence	119	.934	Ryan, Syracuse	18	.898
Shearon, Syracuse	68	.933	Lytle, Wilkesbarre	110	.894
Harley, Springfield	68	.933	P. Eagan, Scranton	103	.887
Betts, Wilkesbarre	105	.932	Leahy, Springfield	37	.885
Garry, Syracuse	110	.928	Casey, Toronto	18	.882
Goodenough, Buffalo	115	.925	Lynch, Springfi'd & Roch	22	.871
J. J. O'Brien, Scranton	65	.925	Urquhart, Buffalo	14	.865
Griffin, Scranton	40	.924	Flack, Scranton	13	.857

The Western League

THE Western League finished its season in excellent shape, Minneapolis winning the championship by a good margin. The next four clubs all made a percentage of over .500, the contest between Indianapolis and Detroit for second position being very close, a difference of 11 points only separating them. Glasscock, of Manager Comiskey's St. Paul team, carried off the batting honors, he participating in 135 out of the 136 games played by the club. The records in full are as follows:

CLUB STANDING.

Rank.	Club.	Minneapolis.	Indianapolis.	Detroit.	St. Paul.	Kansas City.	Milwaukee.	Columbus.	Grand Rapids.	Won.	Lost.	Per cent.
1	Minneapolis..........		9	15	12	12	15	12	14	89	47	.654
2	Indianapolis..........	8		9	7	11	14	15	14	78	54	.591
3	Detroit...............	5	11		10	14	11	16	13	80	58	.580
4	St. Paul..............	8	12	8		8	12	10	15	73	63	.537
5	Kansas City..........	7	5	6	12		11	15	13	69	66	.511
6	Milwaukee...........	5	6	9	8	9		13	12	62	78	.443
7	Columbus	8	5	4	10	5	7		13	52	88	.371
8	Grand Rapids........	6	6	7	4	7	8	7		45	94	.324

CLUB BATTING.

Rank.	Club.	Games.	Runs.	Per cent.
1	St. Paul.............	136	1251	.339
2	Minneapolis	136	1080	.321
3	Kansas City.........	135	983	.305
4	Indianapolis........	132	897	.300
5	{ Milwaukee.......	140	960	.298
	{ Detroit...........	138	1087	.298
6	Columbus...........	140	896	.296
7	Grand Rapids......	139	791	.284

CLUB FIELDING.

Rank.	Club.	Games.	Per cent.
1	Kansas City.,............	135	.933
2	Minneapolis..............	136	.931
3	{ Grand Rapids..........	139	.930
	{ Indianapolis............	132	.930
4	St. Paul..................	136	.929
5	Detroit...................	138	.927
6	{ Milwaukee.............	140	.925
	{ Columbus..............	140	.925

BASE BALL GUIDE. III

BATTING AVERAGES.

Rank.	Player.	Club.	Games.	Runs.	Per cent.
1	Glasscock...............	St. Paul........................	135	172	.431
2	Welch...................	Kansas City....................	14	6	.405
3	{ Wolverton...............	Columbus.......................	10	9	.385
	{ Hewitt.................	Grand Rapids...................	12	3	.385
4	Wilmot...................	Minneapolis....................	123	146	.384
5	George...................	St. Paul.......................	138	159	.383
6	Mazena...................	Milwaukee......................	38	30	.380
7	Werden...................	Minneapolis....................	140	145	.377
8	Kling....................	Kansas City....................	54	33	.374
9	Letcher..................	Grand Rapids...................	24	21	.367
10	Schriver................	Minneapolis...................	137	120	.366
	{ McCarthy...............	Indianapolis...................	133	127	.361
11	{ Butler................	Columbus.......................	126	131	.361
	{ Phillips..............	Indianapolis...................	30	16	.361
12	Weaver..................	Milwaukee......................	144	114	.357
13	Anderson................	Minneapolis....................	17	13	.356
14	Mullane.................	St. Paul.......................	69	53	.353
15	Mertes..................	St. Paul.......................	49	62	.347
16	Pickett.................	St. Paul, Minneapolis..........	121	113	.346
	{ Dungan................	Detroit........................	140	137	.345
17	{ Spies.................	St. Paul.......................	122	97	.345
	{ McBride...............	Grand Rapids...................	90	84	.345
18	Nicol...................	Milwaukee......................	127	154	.340
19	Shugart.................	St. Paul.......................	116	117	.339
20	Nicholl.................	Kansas City....................	68	57	.338
21	Knoll...................	Detroit........................	65	70	.336
22	McVicker................	Kansas City....................	51	40	.332
23	Stratton................	St. Paul.......................	64	52	.331
24	{ Gillen................	Detroit........................	139	109	.330
	{ Carney................	Grand Rapids...................	134	82	.330
	{ Lally.................	Minneapolis....................	139	153	.329
25	{ Hassamaer.............	Columbus, Grand Rapids.........	58	41	.329
	{ Sharp.................	Columbus.......................	113	85	.329
26	{ Campau................	Kansas City....................	88	83	.325
	{ Gettinger.............	Grand Rapids...................	83	58	.325
	{ Stafford..............	Milwaukee......................	137	108	.324
27	{ Lake..................	Kansas City....................	114	90	.324
	{ Roat..................	Indianapolis...................	50	50	.324
28	{ Burns.................	St. Paul.......................	114	112	.323
	{ Callahan..............	Kansas City....................	74	53	.323
29	{ O'Rourke..............	St. Paul.......................	129	156	.321
	{ Nyce..................	Kansas City....................	121	105	.321
	{ Cantillon.............	Columbus.......................	111	81	.321
30	{ Trost.................	Detroit........................	69	45	.320
	{ Kehoe.................	Columbus.......................	19	10	.320
	{ Klusman...............	Kansas City....................	136	105	.319
31	{ Stewart...............	Indianapolis...................	135	115	.319
	{ Genins................	Grand Rapids, Columbus.........	124	106	.319
32	Frank...................	Minneapolis, Columbus..........	130	115	.318
33	{ Browning..............	Columbus.......................	26	15	.317
	{ McCormick.............	Indianapolis...................	12	7	.317
34	{ Wood..................	Indianapolis...................	71	49	.316
	{ Preston...............	Minneapolis....................	60	60	.316
	{ Corcoran..............	Detroit........................	38	23	.314
35	{ McCauley..............	Detroit........................	13	6	.314
	{ Pears.................	Detroit, Columbus..............	10	5	.314
36	Connor..................	Minneapolis....................	116	131	.312

BATTING AVERAGES—*Continued.*

Rank.	Player.	Club.	Games.	Runs.	Per cent.
37	Niles	Grand Rapids	14	10	.309
38	{ Glenalvin	Milwaukee	78	59	.308
	{ Donovan	Grand Rapids	35	16	.308
39	{ Hartman	Milwaukee	126	124	.307
	{ McHale	Milwaukee	44	37	.307
40	Hollingsworth	St. Paul	43	36	.303
41	{ Menefee	Kansas City	136	114	.302
	{ Stallings	Detroit	91	83	.302
42	Buckley	Indianapolis	90	52	.301
43	{ Motz	Indianapolis	134	117	.300
	{ Carney	Minneapolis, Kansas City	39	14	.300
44	Strauss	Minneapolis, Columbus	92	61	.299
45	Burnett	Detroit	134	159	.297
46	{ Smink	Grand Rapids	77	44	.295
	{ McGreevy	Columbus	55	21	.295
47	{ Davis	Indianapolis	28	12	.294
	{ Briggs	Grand Rapids	10	5	.294
48	Speer	Milwaukee	134	71	.293
49	Hogriever	Indianapolis	137	133	.292
	{ Taylor	Milwaukee	131	70	.291
50	{ Parrott	Grand Rapids, Columbus	121	60	.291
	{ Wilson	Columbus	120	82	.291
51	Hatfield	Kansas City	138	113	.289
52	{ Nicholson	Detroit	129	144	.286
	{ Whistler	Detroit	128	99	.286
53	{ Scheibeck	Indianapolis	113	76	.285
	{ Camp	Grand Rapids	98	62	.285
54	Fricken	St. Paul	22	11	.284
55	{ Mills	Grand Rapids	94	65	.282
	{ White	Milwaukee	45	32	.282
56	Healy	Minneapolis	16	7	.279
	{ Gilks	Grand Rapids	121	71	.276
57	{ Twineham	Detroit	94	63	.276
	{ Hernon	Columbus	44	20	.276
	{ McFarland	Grand Rapids	44	22	.276
58	Kraus	St. Paul	86	62	.275
59	Kuehne	Minneapolis	135	79	.271
60	{ Ball	Minneapolis	120	89	.269
	{ Twitchell	Milwaukee, St. Paul	104	72	.269
61	{ Gayle	Detroit	35	22	.267
	{ Fisher	Detroit	10	4	.267
62	Jones	Milwaukee	24	12	.266
63	Wolters	Grand Rapids	51	25	.265
64	Luther	Grand Rapids	10	4	.263
65	Barnes	Milwaukee	48	18	.262
66	Shannon	Indianapolis	72	36	.261
67	{ Daniels	Kansas City, Columbus	38	20	.260
	{ Blandford	Kansas City	34	27	.260
68	Callopy	Columbus	22	12	.256
69	Viox	Kansas City	13	17	.255
	{ Hogan	Indianapolis	120	63	.252
70	{ Manning	Kansas City	61	41	.252
	{ Baker	Milwaukee, Minneapolis	42	34	.252
	{ Davis	Grand Rapids	15	5	.250
71	{ Moran	Minneapolis	12	4	.250
	{ Eiteljorg	Grand Rapids	11	4	.250
72	Latham	Columbus	58	56	.248
73	Williams	Indianapolis	10	6	.242

BATTING AVERAGES—*Continued.*

Rank.	Player.	Club.	Games.	Runs.	Per cent.
74	Hutchinson	Minneapolis	53	26	.241
75	Egan	Detroit	36	19	.239
76	Barnett	Kansas City	84	23	.238
77	Campbell	Columbus	45	29	.237
77	Bevis	Kansas City	22	9	.237
78	Esterquest	Indianapolis	15	12	.235
79	Slagle	Grand Rapids	14	7	.234
80	Wetterer	Milwaukee	80	19	.232
80	Morrissey	Columbus	14	11	.232
81	Hines	Kansas City, Detroit	132	123	.231
82	Phyle	St. Paul	28	10	.227
82	Figgemier	Minneapolis	17	7	.227
	Fifield	Detroit	69	44	.219
83	Lowney	Grand Rapids	29	17	.219
	Johnston	St. Paul	12	5	.219
84	Damman	Indianapolis	47	19	.216
85	Thomas	Detroit	20	7	.214
85	Goar	Grand Rapids	13	7	.214
	Rettger	Milwaukee	49	32	.205
86	Jones	Columbus	40	16	.205
	Monroe	Indianapolis	14	7	.205
87	Hodge	Grand Rapids	56	23	.204
88	Wheelock	Columbus, Grand Rapids	100	75	.202
89	Denzer	St. Paul	50	22	.200
89	Mohler	Grand Rapids	15	11	.200
90	Boswell	Columbus	42	15	.196
91	McCormack	Columbus	71	42	.194
92	Cross	Indianapolis	36	11	.183
93	Parker	Grand Rapids, Minneapolis	37	14	.177
94	Nonamaker	Milwaukee	12	2	.167

FIELDING AVERAGES—FIRST BASEMEN.

Rank.	Player and Club.	Games.	Per cent.	Rank.	Player and Club.	Games.	Per cent.
1	Carney, Grand Rapids	184	.989	7	Whistler, Detroit	128	.977
1	Mullane, St. Paul	15	.989	8	Stafford, Milwaukee	137	.976
2	Wilson, Columbus	17	.987	9	Hassamaer, Col., G. R.	21	.972
3	Glasscock, St. Paul	127	.986	10	Campbell, Columbus	29	.966
4	Klusman, Kansas City	136	.980	11	Cantillon, Columbus	16	.964
4	Morrissey, Columbus	14	.980	12	Strauss, Minn. & Col	30	.959
5	Werden, Minneapolis	140	.979	13	Burnett, Detroit	10	.952
6	Motz, Indianapolis	184	.978				

SECOND BASEMEN.

Rank.	Player and Club.	Games.	Per cent.	Rank.	Player and Club.	Games.	Per cent.
1	Hassamaer, Col., G. R.	17	.957	8	Stewart, Indianapolis	193	.927
2	Cantillon, Columbus	30	.955	8	Connor, Minneapolis	103	.927
3	Hollingsworth, St. Paul	15	.942	9	Taylor, Milwaukee	66	.926
4	Pickett, St. Paul, Minn.	120	.937	10	Menefee, Kansas City	55	.919
5	Kraus, St. Paul	17	.936	11	Glenalvin, Milwaukee	77	.914
6	Nicholson, Detroit	129	.931	12	Sharp, Columbus	112	.907
6	Manning, Kansas City	59	.931	13	Nyce, Kansas City	15	.903
7	Mohler, Grand Rapids	13	.928	14	Mills, Grand Rapids	94	.900

THIRD BASEMEN.

Rank.	Player and Club.	Games.	Per cent.	Rank.	Player and Club.	Games.	Per cent.
1	Hatfield, Kansas City...	132	.917	8	Camp, Grand Rapids..	75	.879
2	McCormack, Columbus..	70	.908		Parrott, G. R., Col.....	30	.879
3	Hartman, Milwaukee....	126	.904	9	Niles, Grand Rapids...	14	.875
4	O'Rourke, St. Paul......	129	.898	10	Latham, Columbus......	58	.873
5	Gillen, Detroit..........	139	.887	11	Esterquest, Indianapolis.	15	.816
6	Kuehne, Minneapolis....	135	.885	12	McCormick, Indianapolis	12	.744
7	Sheibeck, Minneapolis...	87	.882	13	Callopy, Columbus......	13	.714

SHORTSTOPS.

Rank.	Player and Club.	Games.	Per cent.	Rank.	Player and Club.	Games.	Per cent.
1	Sheibeck, Indianapolis..	26	.932	10	Lowney, Grand Rapids..	26	.874
2	Genins, G. R., Col.......	28	.928	11	Hollingsworth, St. Paul.	25	.865
3	Parrott, G. R., Columbus	89	.908	12	Viox, Kansas City.......	13	.861
4	Taylor, Milwaukee......	65	.904	13	Shugart, St. Paul.......	116	.844
5	Shannon, Indianapolis...	63	.903		Roat, Indianapolis	43	.844
6	Wheelock, Col., G. R...	100	.900		Corcoran, Detroit.....	38	.837
7	Ball, Minneapolis........	120	.896	14	Strauss, Minn., Col....	10	.837
8	Nyce, Kansas City....	97	.889		Mazena, Milwaukee...	25	.837
	Connor, Minneapolis..	12	.889	15	Burnett, Detroit........	20	.814
9	Hines, Kansas City, Det.	61	.888	17	McHale, Milwaukee....	15	.809
10	Wetterer, Milwaukee....	39	.874	17	Menefee, Kansas City...	11	.803

OUTFIELDERS.

Rank.	Player and Club.	Games.	Per cent.	Rank.	Player and Club.	Games.	Per cent.
1	McHale, Milwaukee.....	21	.983	18	Preston, Minneapolis....	50	.918
2	Kraus, St. Paul.........	41	.968	19	Nicholl, Kan. City....	68	.909
3	McGreevy, Columbus...	19	.967		Trost, Detroit..........	19	.909
4	McCarthy, Indianapolis.	133	.966		Donovan, G'd Rapids.	14	.909
5	Hines, Kansas City.....	69	.962	20	Butler, Columbus.....	126	.905
6	White, Milwaukee.......	48	.954		Stallings, Detroit.....	91	.905
7	Burns, St. Paul.........	114	.943	21	Callahan, Kansas City..	32	.904
8	Gilks, Grand Rapids....	107	.937	22	George, St. Paul......	138	.901
9	Nicol, Milwaukee.....	127	.935		Hogan, Indianapolis..	120	.901
	McBride, Grand Rap's	90	.935	23	Wilmot, Minneapolis....	123	.900
	Genins, G. R., Col's...	86	.935	24	Burnett, Detroit........	96	.898
10	Lally, Minneapolis....	138	.933	25	Frank, Milwaukee, Col..	130	.897
	McVicker, Kan. City..	51	.933	26	Stratton, St. Paul.......	64	.891
11	Strauss, Mil., Columbus.	137	.932	27	Menefee, Kansas City...	70	.888
12	Dungan, Detroit........	140	.931	28	Campau, G'd Rapids....	15	.880
13	Weaver, Milwaukee...	143	.929	29	Browning, Columbus....	25	.875
	Letcher, Grand Rapids	29	.929	30	Mertes, St. Paul........	43	.873
14	Knoll, Detroit..........	65	.928	31	Kling, Kansas City.....	33	.854
15	Hogriever, Indianap's.	137	.927	32	Twitchell, Min., St. Paul	94	.850
	Campau, Kansas City.	88	.927	33	McFarland, G'd Rapids.	16	.840
16	Gettinger, G'd Rapids...	83	.923	34	Hernon, Columbus......	44	.827
17	Cantillon, Columbus.....	65	.921				

CATCHERS.

Rank.	Player and Club.	Games.	Per cent.	Rank.	Player and Club.	Games.	Per cent.
1	Twineham, Detroit......	91	.973	8	Buckley, Indianapolis...	84	.959
2	Kraus, St. Paul..........	17	.968	9	Smink, Grand Rapids...	73	.954
3	Spies, St. Paul..........	122	.966	10	Hodge, Grand Rapids...	56	.951
4	Schriver, Minneapolis.	137	.963	11	Wilson, Columbus......	101	.942
	Kehoe, Columbus.....	18	.963	12	Wood, Indianapolis....	64	.989
5	Speer, Milwaukee.......	134	.962	13	Trost, Detroit..........	49	.926
6	Lake, Kansas City......	102	.959	14	Blandford, Kansas City.	34	.904
7	Welch, Kansas City.....	14	.958	15	Campbell, Columbus	14	.902

The Western Association

The following are the official batting and fielding averages of the players of the Western Association of 1896 who played in ten games and over, as sent in by Mr. Frank Lauder. Mr. Lauder says: "These averages were computed from the official scores, turned over to me by President T. J. Hickey, of St. Joseph, whose business engagements prevented him from giving them attention, and are accurate and complete in every detail."

BATTING AVERAGES.

Rank.	Players.	Games Played.	Runs Scored.	Sacrifice Hits.	Stolen Bases.	Per cent. of Base Hits.	Rank.	Players.	Games Played.	Runs Scored.	Sacrifice Hits.	Stolen Bases.	Per cent. of Base Hits.
1	McFarland	47	56	3	26	.367	21	{ Carruthers	52	45	4	23	.291
2	Kreig	82	79	5	15	.350		{ Richter	65	49	3	16	.291
3	McQuaid	28	25	0	6	.347	22	Sommers	66	61	8	29	.289
4	Purvis	69	58	3	9	.331	23	{ Huff	40	28	2	6	.287
5	La Rocque	80	79	4	28	.330		{ Cole	25	23	1	6	.287
6	Schaub	71	59	3	16	.329	24	Lohman	64	51	6	19	.286
7	J. White	68	68	2	38	.328	25	Hollingsworth	53	38	3	23	.285
8	{ Preston	62	66	4	28	.326	26	Bartson	15	10	2	2	.283
	{ McHale	62	63	8	28	.326	27	Ross	70	59	9	26	.281
9	{ McKibben	72	82	1	31	.324		{ Ferguson	77	64	5	18	.280
	{ Hines	26	23	3	18	.324	28	{ Gilmore	36	43	2	15	.280
10	Jackson	11	9	0	1	.318		{ Barnes	68	49	6	9	.280
11	{ Armstrong	80	52	2	28	.313	29	Van Buren	76	52	9	24	.277
	{ Letcher	71	88	5	30	.313	30	Baer	76	78	3	48	.275
	{ Raymond	76	64	3	18	.313	31	Phillips	68	64	13	20	.274
12	Underwood	35	19	1	3	.312	32	{ Flaherty	54	43	3	13	.271
13	Dillon	81	60	4	11	.308		{ Marcum	68	44	18	10	.271
14	Farrell	66	50	7	24	.307	33	{ O'Connell	78	44	6	19	.270
15	Ebright	48	26	6	13	.304		{ Francis	67	32	4	26	.270
16	Molesworth	30	13	0	0	.300	34	Delaney	14	11	1	5	.269
17	McVicker	71	63	7	15	.299	35	Schoeller	34	28	2	8	.268
18	{ Mohler	72	66	17	47	.296	36	Sullivan	68	38	3	14	.267
	{ Conners	52	51	5	29	.296	37	Devenney	68	44	3	22	.265
	{ Woodside	10	4	0	0	.296	38	{ Kimmerer	60	49	9	19	.264
19	Griffith	18	14	0	0	.295		{ Wilbur	28	15	2	6	.264
20	{ Esterquest	82	52	0	26	.293	39	Zahner	72	45	5	17	.262
	{ Collins	64	39	1	9	.293	40	Seisler	65	47	1	15	.261
	{ Tighe	80	56	0	15	.293	41	Dugdale	41	17	0	8	.257

BATTING AVERAGES—Continued.

Rank.	Player.	Games Played.	Runs Scored.	Sacrifice Hits.	Stolen Bases.	Per cent. of Base Hits	Rank.	Player.	Games Played.	Runs Scored.	Sacrifice Hits.	Stolen Bases.	Per cent. of Base Hits.
42	Cull............	19	8	3	1	.256	58	{ Snyder.........	82	47	5	7	.230
43	Hickey..........	67	37	10	24	.255		{ Reynolds.......	24	10	6	9	.230
44	Eagan...........	27	17	2	7	.254	59	Parker..........	60	34	4	16	.229
45	Long............	67	59	4	24	.253	60	Burke...........	71	35	4	14	.228
46	Reidy...........	36	16	3	8	.252	61	Mahaffy.........	56	29	1	3	.226
47	McCreadie.......	68	47	2	14	.251	62	Driscoll.........	11	4	2	3	.225
48	{ Warner.........	81	52	8	31	.250	63	Smith...........	36	23	4	3	.224
	{ Ulrich..........	65	70	4	13	.250	64	{ Johnson.........	50	24	0	13	.222
	{ Colborn.........	29	18	2	2	.250		{ Dolan...........	21	15	1	3	.222
	{ Horton..........	26	15	3	7	.250	65	Thomas..........	20	10	1	1	.216
49	{ Donovan........	72	43	10	15	.249	66	Figgemeier......	22	11	3	1	.210
	{ Fisher..........	66	58	5	22	.249	67	Holland.........	81	46	10	15	.208
50	Risley...........	43	20	6	26	.248	68	Breen...........	16	11	1	5	.206
51	Ward............	59	41	4	27	.247	69	Visner..........	33	25	2	2	.203
52	Grover...........	16	9	1	3	.245	70	Grim............	27	18	1	7	.198
53	{ Nulton..........	32	18	5	8	.243	71	Lothrop.........	30	14	5	0	.196
	{ Hansen..........	34	26	0	6	.243	72	Hill.............	76	55	4	22	.194
54	{ Heller..........	69	51	18	7	.242	73	Klopf...........	15	7	0	6	.192
	{ Andrews.........	34	29	4	9	.242	74	Carish..........	30	18	3	2	.183
55	{ O'Connor........	80	69	6	37	.239	75	Burgett.........	15	6	0	1	.176
	{ R. White........	75	50	4	19	.239	76	Mauck...........	24	10	4	1	.173
	{ Newman.........	67	55	5	31	.239	77	McMillan........	17	18	2	12	.161
	{ Jones...........	13	3	8	1	.239	78	Sonie...........	26	11	1	2	.160
56	Slagle...........	38	18	2	4	.235	79	Diamond.........	26	4	2	2	.119
57	{ Quinn...........	68	40	5	6	.234	80	Nichols.........	23	10	2	2	.109
	{ Sanders.........	48	28	3	6	.234	81	Gregory.........	19	6	2	5	.100

FIRST BASEMEN.

Rank.	Name and Club.	Games.	Per cent.	Rank.	Name and Club.	Games.	Per cent.
1	Jones, St. Joe............	12	1.000	7	Marcum, Cedar Rapids..	62	.968
2	Krieg, Rockford..........	82	.981	8	{ Carruthers, Burlington	49	.959
3	Purvis, Des Moines......	69	.980		{ Tighe, Dubuque.......	80	.959
4	Haller, St. Joe and Peoria	66	.979	9	Hines, Burlington......	26	.948
5	Collins, Peoria...........	49	.970	10	Parker, St. Joe.........	14	.928
6	Sommers, Quincy........	66	.969				

SECOND BASEMEN.

1	Eagan, Burlington.......	10	.942		Kimmerer, Cedar Rapids	32	.918
2	Mahaffy, Burlington.....	10	.937	8	Mohler, Des Moines.....	72	.916
3	La Rocque, Dubuque....	80	.934	9	McHale, St. Joe.........	27	.910
4	Fisher, Peoria...........	66	.922	10	Schoeller, Burlington....	24	.909
5	O'Connell, Quincy.......	70	.920	11	Cull, Burlington.........	19	.893
6	Rose, St. Joe............	24	.919	12	Ebright, Cedar Rapids..	25	.857
7	Warner, Rockford.......	81	.918	13	Driscoll, St. Joe.........	11	.836

THIRD BASEMEN.

Rank.	Name and Club.	Games.	Per cent.	Rank.	Name and Club.	Games.	Per cent.
1	Esterquest, Burlington	82	.939	8	Ulrich, Quincy	22	.858
2	Klopf, Dubuque	15	.920	9	Delaney, Quincy	13	.857
3	Hill, Cedar Rapids	68	.916	10	Nulton, Burlington	32	.854
4	Raymond, Dubuque	52	.885	11	Schaub, Peoria	71	.848
5	J. White, Burlington	14	.878	12	Hickey, Des Moines	67	.818
6	Flaherty, Rock., Quincy	54	.866	13	Eagan, Burlington	17	.815
7	Ferguson, Rockford	62	.860				

SHORTSTOPS.

1	Hollingsworth, Burl'gton	53	.904	7	{ Holland, Rockford	81	.852
2	Ebright, Cedar Rapids	23	.883		{ Burke, Peoria	40	.852
3	J. White, Burlington	14	.876	8	Richter, Burling., Quincy	10	.850
4	Ulrich, Quincy	43	.872	9	McCredie, Des Moines	64	.827
5	Raymond, Dubuque	24	.871	10	Risley, Cedar Rapids	10	.820
6	{ Deveney, Quincy, Dub.	68	.865	11	Francis, Peoria, St. Joe	65	.818
	{ Ross, St. Joe	45	.865	12	Reynolds, Quincy, C. R.	23	.808

OUTFIELDERS.

1	Johnson, St. Joe	25	.963	18	Wilbur, Burlington	23	.904
2	Sowders, Peoria	22	.959	19	Barnes, Cedar Rapids	65	.901
3	McFarland, Quincy	47	.955	20	R. White, Burlington	75	.900
4	Conners, Peoria	52	.949	21	Seisler, Peoria	36	.895
5	{ Van Buren, Cedar Rapids	76	.944	22	McHale, St. Joe	35	.887
	{ Ferguson, Rockford	15	.944	23	Gilmore, Peoria	34	.885
6	Newman, Dub., Rockford	67	.943	24	Dillon, Rockford	75	.884
7	Cole, Peoria	25	.942	25	Baer, Dubuque	76	.876
8	{ Richter, Bur., Quincy	48	.941	26	O'Connor, Rockford	80	.872
	{ Kimmerer, Cedar Rapids	14	.941	27	McQuaid, Dubuque	26	.869
9	{ Visner, Dubuque	33	.938	28	{ Parker, St. Joe	12	.857
10	J. White, Burlington	31	.937		{ Graver, Dubuque	10	.857
11	McKibben, Des Moines	72	.929	29	Armstrong, Burlington	47	.850
12	McMillan, Quincy	17	.925	30	Underwood, Rockford	10	.846
13	McVicker, St. Joe	71	.921	31	Preston, Des Moines	62	.841
14	{ Long, Dubuque	61	.920	32	Ward, St. Joe	25	.830
	{ Donovan, Cedar Rapids	60	.920	33	Jackson, Burlington	11	.785
15	Letcher, Des Moines	71	.912	34	Mahaffy, Burlington	13	.761
16	Phillips, Quincy	68	.911	35	Hanson, Burlington	12	.652
17	Burke, Peoria	31	.906				

CATCHERS.

1	Snyder, Rockford	82	.920	7	Lohman, Des Moines	63	.885
2	Armstrong, Burlington	23	.916	8	Traffley, Des Moines	13	.882
3	{ Armstrong, Burlington	31	.900	9	Zahner, Dubuque	72	.874
	{ Dugdale, Peoria	41	.900	10	Grim, Burlington	26	.862
4	Seisler, Peoria	25	.898	11	Ward, St. Joe	33	.821
5	Quinn, Quincy	68	.897	12	Donovan, Cedar Rapids	12	.816
6	Sullivan, Cedar Rapids	62	.889	13	Parker, St. Joe	34	.793

New England League

MR. J. C. MORSE, the efficient secretary of the New England League, sends us the season's statistics of the League for 1896.

He says: "The close of the season of 1896 in the New England League brings to the front a new list of leaders in batting and fielding. The interest shown in the players and records of this League is manifest the country over, and a correct statement of the batters and fielders for the season is of value."

In commenting on the batting Mr. Morse says:

"Napoleon Lajoie, of Woonsocket, R. I., now of the Phillies, leads in batting, with the grand average of .429, something remarkable, aside from the fact that the average itself is a tremendous one for any league, as it is what is termed Lajoie's 'first season out.'

"Perhaps the cleanest hitting was done by John Smith, of the Pawtucket team. His work is noted for hard, safe line batting. Breckenridge, of Brockton, is third. He went above the heavy batting limit, which is .300 or over, and put together .406.

"Twelve of the 17 batters at the end of the list are pitchers, and good ones at that, so too much is not expected of them. The averages in batting and fielding are given only of those who played in at least 20 games.

"About 180 players participated in New England League games in 1896, but only an even 100 take rank in these tables. The remainder were not in at least 20 games, or fell short of playing requirements.

"In fielding, the highest average for catchers is won by Dan Burke, of the New Bedfords, a Whitman, Mass., boy, with the fine average of .982.

"Breckenridge leads the first basemen with .988. Ed. Slater had the most total chances, and made the fine record of .977.

"The second basemen are led by Doe with .955 and 105 games, although 'Snap' Lang, of Brockton, has had 217 more chances, and, with an average of .933, is the real leader.

"Magoon, of Portland and Brockton, has made one of the finest records in years at third base, and leads in that position with .922."

The full records are given on following pages.

NEW ENGLAND LEAGUE RECORD OF 1896.

Club.	Fall River.	Bangor.	Brockton.	New Bedford.	Pawtucket.	Augusta.	Portland.	Lewiston.	Victories.	Per cent. of Victories.
Fall River		6	11	11	11	11	11	7	68	.636
Bangor	6		13	5	8	11	11	9	63	.618
Brockton	6	5		9	13	11	11	8	63	.594
New Bedford	11	8	5		10	9	6	8	57	.543
Pawtucket	4	9	5	8		13	10	6	55	.505
Augusta	4	4	5	5	5		4	8	35	.340
Portland†	3	3	2	7	3	7		7	32	.356
Lewiston*	5	4	2	3	4	6	5		29	.354
Defeats	39	39	43	48	54	68	58	53	402	

* Disbanded Aug. 14. † Disbanded Aug. 22.

INDIVIDUAL BATTING AVERAGES.

Rank.	Name.	Club.	Games.	Runs.	Per cent.
1	Lajoie	Fall River	80	94	.429
2	Smith	Pawtucket	88	105	.407
3	Breckenridge	Brockton	99	84	.406
4	Geier	Fall River	77	85	.381
5	Hannivan	Pawtucket	83	89	.380
6	Walters	New Bedford	91	113	.374
7	Waldron	Pawtucket	107	136	.373
8	Weihl	New Bedford	106	82	.360
9	Woddige	New Bedford	106	86	.357
9	Klobedanz	Fall River	51	45	.357
10	Beaumont	Pawtucket	108	91	.352
11	Yeager	Pawtucket	99	117	.351
12	Shea	Lewiston	82	69	.350
13	O'Brien	Bangor	94	85	.348
14	Hernon	New Bedford	31	29	.346
15	News	Pawtucket	107	83	.343
15	Henry	Bangor	96	94	.343
16	Mains	Bangor	28	16	.340
17	Nadeau	Brockton	106	110	.336
18	Wheeler	Bangor	46	35	.333
19	Sheehan	Lewiston	45	37	.332
20	Hayes	Bangor	40	25	.331
21	Ladd	Fall River	106	103	.329
21	Duncan	Portland	87	63	.329
22	Lippert	Lewiston, Fall River	104	115	.326
22	Kennedy	Fall River	74	58	.326
23	Shay	Brockton	76	57	.325
24	Whiting	Pawtucket	97	117	.324

BATTING AVERAGES—*Continued.*

Rank.	Name.	Clubs.	Games.	Runs.	Per cent.
25	Williams................	Lewiston, Fall River.........	44	26	.321
26	Sharrott	Bangor......................	100	113	.317
	Cavanaugh...............	Portland, Bangor............	94	66	.317
	Ropert..................	Fall River..................	90	74	.317
27	Pickett.................	Augusta.....................	97	66	.314
	Hill....................	Portland....................	31	21	.314
	O'Rourke................	Portland....................	57	37	.310
28	Flanangan...............	Lewiston....................	41	24	.310
	Stackhouse..............	Brockton....................	22	12	.310
29	Lyons...................	Fall River..................	106	86	.303
	Simon...................	Bangor......................	98	103	.303
30	Birmingham..............	New Bedford.................	106	77	.302
	M. Kelly................	Augusta.....................	104	67	.301
31	Johnson.................	Augusta.....................	96	67	.301
	Musser..................	Portland....................	62	40	.301
32	Doe.....................	New Bedford.................	105	96	.299
	Pettee..................	Lewiston....................	31	15	.299
33	J. Kelly................	Augusta.....................	31	19	.298
34	Butler..................	Augusta.....................	90	72	.295
35	Coughlin................	Pawtucket...................	96	68	.294
	Woods...................	Portland....................	70	47	.294
36	Day.....................	New Bedford.................	21	13	.292
37	Radford.................	Bangor......................	102	116	.290
38	Leighton................	Portland....................	83	72	.289
39	Fitzmaurice.............	Lewiston, Fall River........	103	83	.285
	Slater..................	Lewiston, Fall River........	98	81	.285
40	R. Moore................	Bangor......................	102	63	.284
41	Doherty.................	Augusta.....................	103	65	.279
42	McKenzie................	Brockton....................	101	72	.278
43	Wise....................	Brockton....................	98	77	.277
44	McDougall...............	Brockton....................	41	22	.276
45	Miller..................	Lewiston....................	81	52	.275
	Shannon.................	Brockton....................	47	35	.275
46	Braun...................	New Bedford.................	68	45	.272
47	Barton..................	Pawtucket...................	28	27	.270
48	Reilly..................	Fall River..................	107	90	.268
	Magoon	Portland, Brockton..........	102	81	.268
49	Willis..................	Brockton....................	24	14	.267
50	Steere..................	New Bedford.................	106	104	.264
51	Murphy..................	New Bedford.................	97	92	.263
	Buelow..................	Brockton....................	44	24	.263
52	Fitzpatrick.............	Fall River, Portland........	42	28	.261
53	Connor..................	Augusta.....................	102	64	.258
	McKenna.................	Brockton....................	53	43	.258
	Killeen.................	Portland....................	44	26	.258
54	Bean....................	Augusta	103	91	.257
55	Flack...................	Lewiston, Augusta...........	72	23	.256
56	Roach...................	Bangor......................	81	50	.249
	Stevick.................	Brockton, Pawtucket.........	39	17	.249
57	Rhoades.................	Pawtucket...................	28	16	.248
58	Sullivan................	Brockton....................	60	33	.247
59	Herr....................	Pawtucket...................	23	12	.243
60	McDermott...............	Fall River..................	91	59	.241
61	G. Moore................	Bangor......................	46	25	.240

BATTING AVERAGES—Continued.

Rank.	Name.	Club.	Games.	Runs.	Per cent.
62	Lang	Brockton	106	69	.237
	Clare	Augusta	21	10	.237
63	Korwan	Brockton	40	20	.236
	Burke	New Bedford	24	8	.236
64	Weithoff	Bangor	25	15	.232
65	Kilfedder	Augusta, Portland	33	12	.230
66	Messitt	Lewiston	75	41	.226
67	Stevens	Fall River	30	19	.223
68	Braham	Bangor	23	9	.214
69	Chestnut	Lewiston, Portland	46	19	.210
70	Goodheart	Lewiston	30	22	.203
71	Newell	Augusta	41	8	.202
72	Dilworth	Augusta	25	3	.173
73	Moynahan	New Bedford	32	15	.171
74	Magee	Brockton	36	10	.166
75	Morse	Lewiston	41	18	.156
76	Lincoln	Fall River, New Bedf'd, Por'd	25	8	.154
77	Weeks	Augusta	33	8	.124

INDIVIDUAL FIELDING AVERAGES—CATCHERS.

Rank.	Name.	Club.	Put Outs.	Per cent.
1	Burke	New Bedford	87	.982
2	Duncan	Portland	362	.963
3	Messitt	Lewiston	306	.966
4	Roach	Bangor	339	.960
5	Shea	Brockton	323	.952
6	Hayes	Bangor	173	.947
7	Yeager	Pawtucket	412	.945
8	Murphy	New Bedford	398	.944
9	Rupert	Fall River	340	.939
10	Butler	Augusta	327	.918
11	Buelow	Brockton	142	.885

FIRST BASEMEN.

1	Breckenridge	Brockton	1072	.988
2	O'Brien	Bangor	906	.987
3	Beaumont	Pawtucket	1124	.982
4	Kennedy	Fall River	743	.980
5	Slater	Portl'd, Lew'n, F. River	1129	.977
	Flanagan	Lewiston	408	.977
6	M. Kelly	Augusta	1032	.974
7	Goodhart	Lewiston	295	.969
8	Birmingham	New Bedford	1031	.966

SECOND BASEMEN.

Rank.	Name.	Club.	Put Outs.	Per cent.
1	Doe...............	New Bedford.............	228	.955
2	R. Moore...........	Bangor....................	251	.935
3	Lang	Brockton..................	282	.933
4	McDermott..........	Fall River.................	189	.932
5	Johnson............	Augusta...................	226	.927
6	Pettee..............	Lewiston..................	69	.917
7	{ News.............	Pawtucket.................	216	.916
	{ Chestnut..........	Lewiston, Portland.........	103	.916
8	Musser.............	Portland..................	144	.911

THIRD BASEMEN.

1	Magoon............	Portland, Brockton..........	198	.922
2	Coughlin...........	Pawtucket.................	137	.895
3	Shea...............	Lewiston..................	113	.893
4	Lyons..............	Fall River.................	155	.887
5	Doherty............	Augusta...................	238	.871
6	{ Weddige..........	New Bedford..............	146	.861
	{ Cavanaugh........	Portland, Bangor...........	154	.861
7	Shannon...........	Brockton..................	80	.860
8	G. Moore...........	Bangor....................	60	.835
9	Stackhouse.........	Brockton..................	25	.786

SHORTSTOPS.

1	Steere.............	New Bedford.............	222	.988
2	Radford............	Bangor....................	237	.899
3	Mackenzie.........	Brockton..................	172	.892
4	Reilly...............	Fall River.................	204	.888
5	Hannivan..........	Pawtucket.................	181	.876
6	Miller..............	Lewiston..................	174	.874
7	Bean...............	Augusta...................	216	.863
8	Stevick.............	Brockton, Pawtucket.......	72	.843
9	Kilfeder............	Augusta, Portland.........	56	.839

OUTFIELDERS.

1	{ Simon............	Bangor....................	220	.954
	{ Woods............	Portland..................	214	.954
2	Wise...............	Brockton..................	220	.943
3	{ Smith.............	Pawtucket.................	132	.931
	{ Lajoie............	Fall River.................	280	.931
4	Sharrott...........	Bangor....................	157	.926
5	Walters............	New Bedford..............	226	.925
6	Fitzmaurice........	Lewiston, Fall River.......	274	.922
7	Connor.............	Augusta...................	231	.921
8	Ladd...............	Fall River.................	247	.911
9	Nadeau............	Brockton..................	188	.907
10	Pickett............	Augusta...................	206	.898
11	Henry.............	Bangor....................	189	.897
12	Sullivan...........	Brockton..................	122	.896
13	Geier..............	Fall River.................	139	.894
14	Flack..............	Lewiston, Augusta.........	151	.892

FIELDERS—*Continued.*

Rank.	Name.	Club.	Put Outs.	Assists.	Errors.	Total Chances.	Per cent.
15	Waldron	Pawtucket	209	21	29	259	.888
	Weihl	New Bedford	204	26	30	260	.888
16	J. Kelly	Augusta	53	17	10	80	.887
17	Whiting	Pawtucket	211	40	34	285	.881
18	Barton	Pawtucket	66	21	13	100	.879
19	Sheehan	Lewiston	46	4	7	57	.878
20	Leighton	Portland	159	13	26	198	.869
21	Hernon	New Bedford	44	7	9	60	.866
22	Hill	Portland	66	2	12	80	.862
23	Lippert	Lewiston, Fall River	148	21	33	202	.837
24	Willis	Brockton	49	3	12	64	.814
25	O'Rourke	Portland	70	6	21	97	.784

PITCHERS.

	Name.	Club.	Put Outs.	Assists.	Errors.	Total Chances.	Per cent.
1	Herr	Pawtucket	4	34	1	39	.976
2	Stevens	Fall River	21	43	2	66	.971
3	Monahan	New Bedford	14	41	2	57	.965
4	Mains	Bangor	64	33	5	102	.951
5	Wheeler	Bangor	20	101	7	128	.946
6	Braham	Bangor	14	49	4	67	.944
7	Day	New Bedford	11	48	4	63	.937
8	Williams	Lewiston, Fall River	38	75	8	121	.934
	Clare	Augusta	20	22	3	45	.934
9	McKenna	Brockton	23	109	10	142	.930
10	Morse	Lewiston	12	66	6	84	.929
11	Klobedanz	Fall River	78	76	12	166	.928
12	Fitzpatrick	Fall River, Portland	66	71	12	119	.920
13	Weithoff	Bangor	1	33	3	37	.919
14	Braun	New Bedford	45	98	13	156	.917
15	Korwan	Brockton	16	85	10	111	.910
16	Lincoln	Fall R'r, N. Bed'd, P't.	9	58	7	74	.906
17	Dilworth	Augusta	5	37	5	47	.894
18	Killen	Portland	41	53	12	106	.887
19	Rhodes	Pawtucket	2	35	5	42	.883
20	Magee	Brockton	16	71	12	99	.879
21	Newell	Augusta	21	56	11	88	.875
22	McDougall	Portland	25	92	18	135	.867
23	Weeks	Augusta	10	53	12	75	.841

The players who made high averages in less than 20 games and more than 10 were: Standish, pitcher, Fall River, 12 games, batting .436, fielding .956; Counihan, catcher, Portland, 13 games, batting .393, fielding .863; Wilder, pitcher, Pawtucket, 13 games, batting .373, fielding .961; Sharp, catcher, New Bedford, 18 games, batting .355, fielding .933; Hart, catcher, Augusta, 12 games, batting .298, fielding .979; Donovan, catcher, Portland, 11 games, batting .261, fielding .848; Coyle, manager, Augusta, 13 games, batting .251, fielding .911.

The Southern Association

THE official averages of the Southern Association for the season of 1896, as compiled by John M. Foster, scorer of the New Orleans club, from statistics in the office of President Henry Powers, are given below. New Orleans won the championship and led the clubs in both batting and fielding, although Montgomery was a very close second in both departments.

Gibson was the nominal leader in batting, but he only played in 12 games. Knowles and Katz are tied for second position, they playing in 73 and 66 games, respectively. Powell did best in base stealing, having 60 to his credit in a total of 102 games.

RESULT OF THE RACE.

Club.	New Orleans.	Montgomery.	Atlanta.	Mobile.	Birmingham.	Columbus.	Won.	Per cent.
New Orleans.........		15	7	13	11	22	68	.686
Montgomery.........	12		9	13	13	13	60	.625
Atlanta..............	6	6		8	7	9	36	.500
Mobile..............	6	9	6		6	12	39	.410
Birmingham.........	3	2	5	9		7	26	.388
Columbus...........	4	4	9	13	4		34	.350
Lost.................	31	36	36	56	41	63		

CLUB BATTING.

Club.	Runs.	Sacrifice Hits.	Stolen Bases.	Per cent.
New Orleans.......	654	43	335	.294
Montgomery.......	672	42	225	.292
Atlanta............	445	26	131	.281
Mobile.............	555	59	140	.276
Birmingham.......	387	48	120	.272
Columbus..........	536	34	145	.268

CLUB FIELDING.

Club.	Per cent.
New Orleans.....................	.934
Montgomery.....................	.930
Atlanta..........................	.918
Columbus.......................	.915
Birmingham.....................	.913
Mobile..........................	.906

BATTING AVERAGES.

Rank.	Player.	Games.	Runs.	Sacrifice Hits.	Stolen Bases.	Per cent.	Rank.	Player.	Games.	Runs.	Sacrifice Hits.	Stolen Bases.	Per cent.
1	Gibson	12	5	1	0	.367	37	Norton	53	31	0	11	.265
2	Knowles	73	67	0	25	.358	38	Wright	48	26	0	0	.264
	Katz	66	46	2	11	.358		Hines	29	17	1	2	.264
3	Deady	97	80	1	30	.350	39	Hall	102	50	2	22	.261
4	Huston	98	87	5	36	.346		Hunt	22	14	2	10	.261
5	Ryan	69	36	4	10	.340	40	Casey	59	27	0	8	.260
6	Fields	73	54	4	20	.332		Folk	18	2	0	0	.260
7	Pabst	97	92	5	24	.328	41	Dobbs	80	60	11	12	.258
8	Davis	43	37	3	16	.325	42	Walker	28	15	1	6	.257
9	Powell	102	94	10	60	.318	43	O'Connell	26	15	4	2	.254
10	Wiley	71	47	2	26	.314	44	McFadden	82	42	2	10	.251
11	Hess	59	50	1	10	.310		Van Dyke	70	60	2	15	.250
	Phillips	14	5	0	1	.310		McGinnis	26	13	1	1	.250
12	Shea	42	29	1	5	.309	45	Adams	22	12	2	1	.250
13	Peeples	91	60	5	25	.308		Wagner	33	28	3	6	.250
	Kehoe	85	70	5	18	.308		Bates	13	1	0	0	.250
14	Fisher	95	78	8	25	.307	46	Smith	42	24	2	5	.248
	Mangan	72	54	7	20	.307	47	Carl	32	10	3	2	.247
15	Fuller	48	37	2	6	.306	48	Hughes	11	0	0	0	.242
16	Walsh	37	35	1	15	.305	49	Sechrist	21	10	0	0	.239
17	Houseman	102	87	2	50	.302		Turner	18	6	1	4	.239
	Wood	39	26	2	2	.302	50	Buschman	59	33	3	10	.237
	Knox	102	82	3	46	.300		Rappold	44	24	0	6	.237
18	Dowie	102	57	6	35	.300	51	Beecher	39	17	2	7	.234
	Phelan	62	26	2	12	.300	52	Paynter	86	42	10	5	.233
19	Roach	16	5	0	0	.298	53	Gonding	108	57	2	25	.230
20	Dillard	78	50	4	8	.296	54	Kellum	27	14	1	2	.229
21	Meara	68	65	3	31	.295	55	Grim	37	15	0	0	.222
22	Daniels	53	21	2	6	.293	56	Sparks	36	25	0	2	.221
23	Carroll	102	72	6	35	.292		Broderick	25	12	1	0	.221
24	Gorman	97	75	7	20	.291	57	Gorton	68	47	10	30	.220
25	Vork	74	59	6	42	.290	58	Lamont	31	9	0	2	.216
26	Wittrock	32	13	1	1	.288	59	Bailey	39	17	3	2	.213
27	Wiseman	97	83	4	2	.287	60	Kirton	16	10	1	7	.211
28	Bowman	103	66	0	40	.285	61	Leighton	11	6	1	1	.200
	Holahan	10	4	1	0	.285	62	Williamson	30	12	0	0	.195
29	Stewart	21	8	0	1	.284	63	Fricken	32	12	3	5	.194
30	Godar	90	62	6	25	.282	64	Linderman	15	4	0	1	.192
	Kling	21	13	0	4	.282	65	Cross	16	8	1	1	.173
31	Callahan	68	42	6	20	.281		Miller	21	4	0	2	.173
32	Schmidt	56	30	0	7	.280	66	Murray	16	9	0	1	.168
33	Grifford	90	58	7	30	.278	67	Hahn	17	4	0	0	.156
34	Pedroes	100	77	3	20	.270	68	McDonald	14	7	0	0	.150
	Lohbeck	59	17	4	0	.270	69	Petty	19	7	1	2	.138
35	Trainor	36	35	1	6	.268	70	Sheehan	29	2	1	0	.138
36	McDade	67	81	3	10	.267	71	Flournoy	13	5	3	3	.089

FIELDING AVERAGES—CATCHERS.

Name and Club.	Per cent.	Name and Club.	Per cent.
Gonding, New Orleans	.953	Lohbeck, Mobile	.892
Hess, Columbus	.947	Rappold, Birmingham	.882
Fields, Atlanta	.930	Wiley, Montgomery	.874
King, Mobile, Columbus	.910	Wright, Mobile, Columbus	.817
Kehoe, Montgomery	.894		

FIRST BASEMEN.

Name and Club.	Per cent.	Name and Club.	Per cent.
Gibson, Columbus	.984	McFadden, Columbus	.963
Bowman, New Orleans	.980	Ryan, Birmingham	.963
Pabst, Montgomery	.978	Casey, Mobile, Columbus	.961
Knowles, Atlanta	.972	Oliver, Mobile	.935
Stewart, Mobile	.966	Hines, Mobile	.831

SECOND BASEMEN.

Name and Club.	Per cent.	Name and Club.	Per cent.
Phelan, Col's, New Orleans	.940	Shea, Atlanta	.909
Leighton, Birmingham	.933	Knox, New Orleans	.903
Payntor, Mobile	.929	O'Connell, Columbus	.890
Hess, Columbus	.920	Trainor, Birmingham	.888
Mangan, Montgomery	.913	McKenzie, Birmingham	.860
Callahan, Atlanta	.911		

THIRD BASEMEN.

Name and Club.	Per cent.	Name and Club.	Per cent.
Dowie, New Orleans	.906	Carroll, Columbus	.855
Gorman, Montgomery	.900	McDade, Atlanta	.855
Godar, Mobile, Birmingham	.868	Buschman, Mobile	.834

SHORTSTOPS.

Name and Club.	Per cent.	Name and Club.	Per cent.
Peeples, Montgomery	.932	Hall, Columbus	.880
Murray, Atlanta	.920	Holahan, Birmingham	.857
Houseman, New Orleans	.906	Beecher, Birmingham	.844
Fuller, Birmingham	.890	Huston, New Orleans	.805
Gifford, Mobile, Atl'ta, Col's.	.888	Phillips, Atlanta	.773
Fisher, Mobile	.882		

OUTFIELDERS.

Name and Club.	Per cent.	Name and Club.	Per cent.
Miller, Columbus	.975	Wiley, Montgomery	.918
Huston, New Orleans	.961	York, New Orleans	.913
Powell, New Orleans	.953	Wood, Atlanta	.905
Phelan, Columbus, N. Orle's.	.946	Deady, Montgomery	.902
Gorton, Birmingham	.946	Kirton, Mobile	.900
Flournoy, Columbus	.944	Katz, Birmingham	.896
Walsh, Birmingham	.942	Dillard, Mont., Mobile	.896
Van Dyke, Atlanta, Mont.	.933	Gifford, Mobile, Atl'a, Col's.	.890
Dobbs, Mobile	.929	Folk, Columbus	.870
Pedros, Columbus	.928	Wagner, Atlanta	.855
Meara, Montgomery	.926	Davis, Mobile	.854
Houseman, New Orleans	.925	Turner, Atlanta	.848
Wiseman, Mobile	.923	Broderick, Columbus	.830

The Texas League

STANDING OF THE CLUBS.

Club.	Won.	Lost.	Per cent.	Club.	Won.	Lost.	Per cent.
Galveston	17	14	.548	Houston	15	16	.484
Austin	15	15	.500	San Antonio	14	16	.448

BATTING AVERAGES.

Rank.	Player.	Club.	Games.	Runs.	Stolen Bases.	Safe Hits.	Per cent.
1	O'Connor	Denison, San Antonio	114	113	68	39	.401
2	Keefe	Fort Worth, San Antonio	81	73	34	23	.393
3	Weikart	Austin	129	117	26	17	.376
4	Slagle	Houston	131	171	86	14	.367
5	Elsey	San Antonio	124	109	44	18	.364
6	Swor	Dallas	13	1	..	..	.363
7	Land	Denison	60	59	14	6	.360
8	Weber	Denison, San Antonio	101	104	59	44	.359
8	Kling	Houston	51	47	18	4	.359
9	Heydon	Austin	122	100	23	7	.357
10	Shaffer	Houston	131	154	86	5	.355
11	Miller	San Antonio	118	87	26	14	.354
12	Huston	Galveston	24	22	4	2	.352
13	McAllister	Fort Worth	76	80	37	12	.351
14	Nance	Fort Worth, Galveston	127	116	33	12	.350
14	Isaacs	Fort Worth	54	41	5	..	.350
15	Robinson	Dallas	75	71	14	1	.345
16	Countryman	Sherman	14	12	2	2	.340
17	Hoffman	Austin	111	103	37	15	.337
18	Hoover	Galveston	129	100	33	7	.335
19	Nie	Austin, Paris	92	82	37	8	.334
19	Blackburn	Austin	66	64	27	9	.334
20	Bailey	Sherman, Austin	125	92	37	15	.333
21	Earle	Dallas	35	36	23	6	.331
22	Brott	Galveston	118	110	50	3	.329
23	Jacobs	Houston	131	109	36	5	.328
24	Quigg	Denison	39	32	10	4	.326
25	Lynch	Sherman, Denison	91	90	46	17	.325
26	Griffin	San Antonio	122	118	47	28	.324
26	Oswald	Sherman, Denison	92	95	30	14	.324
26	Gates	Galveston	26	24	11	..	.324
27	Steinfelt	Fort Worth, Galveston	124	114	29	11	.320
28	Cull	San Antonio	12	7	2	1	.319
29	Kohnle	Denison	87	106	24	4	.318
30	Clarke	Denison, San Antonio	120	112	53	28	.316
31	Becker	Houston	132	95	53	8	.311
31	Valdois	Denison	53	33	18	6	.311
31	R. Roach	Denison	27	18	16	2	.311

BATTING AVERAGES.—Continued.

Rank	Player	Club	Games	Runs	Stolen Bases	Safe Hits	Per cent.
32	Laurence	San Antonio	111	87	54	26	.310
33	Kemmer	Galveston	59	43	13	1	.308
34	Cote	Houston	125	100	64	5	.304
34	Stanley	Fort Worth, San Antonio	118	76	21	19	.304
34	Badger	Galveston, Austin	87	63	39	5	.304
35	Colliflower	Austin	45	37	10	4	.299
36	Nevin	San Antonio	44	31	5	6	.297
37	Callihan	Denison, Sherman	31	22	11		.292
38	Weckbecker	Galveston	111	91	36	6	.291
38	Gear	Fort Worth	77	65	13	9	.291
38	Chamberlain	Sherman, Austin	40	30	11	5	.291
39	Reagan	Dallas	20	15	8	1	.289
40	Herbert	San Antonio	68	42	10	4	.288
41	Reed	Houston	127	96	32	9	.287
42	Bulger	Sherman, San Antonio	89	49	15	10	.286
43	Crotty	San Antonio, Austin	58	51	23	8	.284
44	Blakey	Galveston	49	51	22	2	.283
45	Rankin	Houston	65	30	11	5	.282
46	Van Dresser	Sherman, Paris	77	56	33	14	.281
47	Jantzen	Sherman, Paris	93	79	13	8	.280
48	McKeever	San Antonio	29	38	14	9	.279
49	Myers	Fort Worth	97	79	21	7	.278
50	Pritchard	Dallas	75	54	7	7	.276
51	Kleeman	San Antonio	100	105	33	9	.275
52	Gonding	Galveston	11	4	0	1	.275
53	Kohlkoff	Dallas	66	61	15	7	.273
54	Page	Galveston	68	42	12	6	.272
55	Sage	Sherman, Denison	87	64	33	19	.271
56	Burns	Austin	119	124	47	6	.270
56	Dawkins	Austin	31	20	6	2	.270
57	Belt	Galveston	116	84	38	10	.268
57	McCormick	Houston	37	16	3	1	.268
58	Burris	Galveston	70	52	31	7	.267
58	Zeis	Sherman, Paris	60	45	16	13	.267
58	McGowan	Houston, Dallas	40	27	12	2	.267
59	Chard	Austin	55	16	4	7	.265
59	Thompson	Fort Worth	19	19	14	1	.265
60	Menefee	Sherman, Austin	59	47	4	6	.263
61	Swearingen	Galveston, Paris	84	54	29	7	.260
62	Wolever	Fort Worth	97	76	26	9	.258
62	Ashenback	Dallas	71	44	29	4	.258
63	Mackey	San Antonio, Austin	82	43	27	7	.257
63	Mulkey	Denison, Paris	32	17	3		.257
64	Fabian	Dallas	72	51	18	3	.256
64	Bastian	Dallas	54	43	14	9	.256
65	Wellner	Austin	69	32	5	3	.255
65	Creeley	Denison	35	26	6	6	.255
66	Otten	San Antonio	34	16	7	7	.254
67	Elberfeld	Dallas	38	24	11	1	.252
68	Cole	Galveston	49	26	8	4	.251
69	York	Galveston	10	4	3		.250
70	Cathey	Paris	43	37	9	2	.249
70	Lemons	Dallas	26	15	8	2	.249
71	Kiernan	San Antonio	68	41	9	11	.244
71	Parvin	San Antonio	42	13	7	5	.244

Hollister   Bloomingston Shields Miller   McKenzie Dean McKinney
   Sexton   Holmes   Condon   Watkins   Heard
Kinmond   Lowney   Scott
UNIVERSITY OF MICHIGAN BASE BALL CLUB, 1896.

Stansbury　　Sharp　　Taylor　　Harris　　Wight　　Watson (Mgr.)
　Strohn　　Freeman　Young　McLaine (Capt.)　Thompson　Jeffs
STANFORD UNIVERSITY BASE BALL TEAM, 1896.

B. B. JOHNSON,
President Western League.
P. T. POWERS,
Pres., Sec. and Treas. Eastern League.

E. G. BARROW,
President Atlantic League.

G. A. Van Derbeck, President Detroit Club.
A. J. Leimgruber, President Rochester Club.
David P. Burns, President Mobile Club.
Chas. Comiskey, President St. Paul Club.
Tommie Dowd, Manager St. Louis Club.

NICHOLS, Pitcher, Boston.
JESSE BURKETT, Leading Batter, Cleveland.
JOS. DOLAN, Shortstop, Louisville.
NAPOLEON LAJOIE, First Base, Philadelphia.

THE LEADING PLAYERS OF THE LEAGUE FOR 1896.

WM. KEELER,
Outfielder, Baltimore.
JOHN A. McPHEE,
Second Base, Cincinnati.

LAVE CROSS,
Third Base, Philadelphia.
CHAS. GANZEL,
Catcher, Boston.

THE LEADING PLAYERS OF THE LEAGUE FOR 1896.

GEO. STALLINGS,
Mgr. Philadelphia Club.
P. J. DONOVAN,
Mgr. Pittsburg Club.
OLIVER TEBEAU,
Mgr. Cleveland Club.
WM. JOYCE,
Capt. and Mgr. New York Club.
FOUR PROMINENT LEAGUE MANAGERS.

BATTING AVERAGES.—Continued.

Rank.	Player.	Club.	Games.	Runs.	Stolen Bases.	Safe Hits.	Per cent.
72	Bammert	Fort Worth, Galveston	124	113	39	7	.241
73	Dwyer	San Antonio	14	11	..	1	.239
74	Steinhoff	Denison	16	7	2	..	.235
75	Balsz	Houston	17	9	2	2	.231
76	D. Spencer	Paris, Austin	47	34	23	3	.230
76	Leeson	Houston	27	21	5	..	.230
76	Payne	Paris	25	15	2	2	.230
76	Gray	Dallas	18	5	1	1	.230
77	Stapleton	Fort Worth, Houston	17	6	3	1	.225
78	Herold	Paris	13	9	3	..	.224
79	Graney	Dallas	28	14	1	..	.222
80	Watkins	Galveston	42	18	9	3	.220
80	Peeples	Houston	15	5	3	1	.220
81	Staples	Austin Dallas	26	4	4	3	.219
82	J Roach	Houston	47	19	2	1	.214
83	Douglas	San Antonio	46	29	5	4	.209
84	McCoy	Galveston	17	5	1	..	.202
85	Ward	Dallas	48	22	6	3	.199
86	Conover	Dallas	23	5	1	2	.198
87	Simpkins	Dallas	43	13	3	3	.189
87	Hardy	Galveston	36	16	5	1	.189
88	Zeigler	Austin	18	6	1	..	.182
89	Donahue	Austin	16	4	1	1	.174
89	W. Spencer	Denison, Paris	11	7	1	2	.174
90	Crowell	Paris, Austin	26	11	4	3	.167
91	Hughes	Denison	36	13	4	5	.164
92	Minnehan	Dallas	18	6	4	..	.162
93	Martz	Denison	10	1	..	2	.131

FIELDING AVERAGES—FIRST BASEMEN.

Rank.	Player and Club.	Games.	Per cent.	Rank.	Player and Club.	Games.	Per cent.
1	Weckbecker, Galvest'n.	27	.984	7	Shaffer, Houston	131	.972
2	Jantzen, Sher., Paris	83	.980	7	Elsey, San Antonio	82	.972
3	Weikart, Austin	129	.975	9	Belt, Galveston	16	.969
3	Myers, Fort Worth	100	.975	10	Nie, Austin, Paris	17	.944
4	O'Connor, Den., S. A.	114	.973	11	Douglas, San Antonio	25	.930
4	Pritchard, Dallas	75	.973				

SECOND BASEMEN.

Rank	Player and Club	Games	Pct	Rank	Player and Club	Games	Pct
1	Steinfelt, F. W., Gal.	124	.931	10	Graney, Dallas	20	.901
2	Lynch, Sher., Denison	91	.928	11	Page, Galveston	27	.900
3	Swearingen, Gal., Paris	60	.925	12	Steinhoff, Denison	16	.895
4	Reed, Houston	132	.921	13	Belt, Galveston	11	.893
5	Kiernan, San Antonio	68	.915	14	Crotty, S. A., Austin	53	.892
5	Clark, Denison, S. A.	34	.915	15	Lemons, Dallas	10	.875
7	Hoffman, Austin	26	.911	16	Kahlkoff, Dallas	20	.871
8	Bastian, Dallas	12	.908	17	Elsey, San Antonio	16	.867
9	Weber, Denison, S. A.	18	.904				

THIRD BASEMEN.

Rank.	Player and Club.	Games.	Per cent.	Rank.	Player and Club.	Games.	Per cent.
1	Blakey, Galveston	10	.909	10	Jacobs, Houston	131	.851
2	Clark, Denison, S. A.	55	.903	11	Kleeman, San Antonio	92	.848
3	Simpkins, Dallas	31	.901	12	Van Dresser, Sher., Paris	32	.841
4	Dawkins, Austin	31	.900	13	Wolever, Fort Worth	98	.826
5	Hoover, Galveston	119	.870	14	Blackburn, Austin	16	.825
6	Oswald, Sher., Denison	47	.869	15	Cull, San Antonio	11	.774
7	Hoffman, Austin	52	.867	16	Zeigler, Austin	12	.750
8	Elberfeld, Dallas	38	.866	17	Valdois, Denison	35	.746
9	Donahue, Austin	16	.857				

SHORTSTOPS.

Rank	Player and Club	Games	Per cent	Rank	Player and Club	Games	Per cent
1	Bammert, F. W., Gal.	124	.921	12	Hoover, Galveston	10	.857
1	Bastain, Dallas	42	.921	13	Simpkins, Dallas	12	.855
3	D. Spencer, Den., Austin	47	.903	14	Oswald, Sher., Denison	45	.833
4	Griffin, San Antonio	122	.901	15	Belt, Galveston	26	.824
5	Stapleton. F.W., Hous'n	17	.900	16	Reagan, Dallas	20	.818
6	Blakey, Galveston	39	.889	17	Brott, Galveston	16	.811
7	Peeples, Houston	15	.885	18	Swearingen, Gal., Paris	10	.807
8	Kling, Houston	16	.875	19	Creeley, Denison	35	.805
9	Rankin, Houston	37	.873	20	Clark, Denison, S. A.	31	.797
10	Burns, Austin	119	.864	21	Hoffman, Austin	22	.725
11	Van Dresser, Sher., Paris	45	.863				

OUTFIELDERS.

Rank	Player and Club	Games	Per cent	Rank	Player and Club	Games	Per cent
1	Watkins, Galveston	42	.975	30	Bulger, San Antonio	89	.885
2	Huston, Galveston	16	.970	30	Menofee, Sher., Aus'n	58	.885
3	Robinson, Dallas	75	.969	32	Kling, Houston	28	.882
4	Payne, Paris	12	.960	32	Valdois, Denison	18	.882
5	Cole, Galveston	49	.948		Fabian, Dallas	72	.880
6	Miller, San Antonio	60	.941	34	Rankin, Houston	28	.880
7	Gear, Fort Worth	45	.940	34	Weckbecker, Galvest'n	14	.880
8	Brott, Galveston	80	.934		McCoy, Galveston	11	.880
9	Nance, F.W., Galvest'n	125	.933	38	Kahlkoff, Dallas	29	.875
9	Weber, Denison, S. A.	52	.933	39	Lemons, Dallas	10	.865
11	Hoffman, Austin	12	.930	40	Nie, Austin, Paris	29	.859
12	Keefe, Fort Worth, S. A.	63	.929	41	Colliflower, Austin	31	.853
13	Cathey, Paris	43	.928	42	Quigg, Denison	12	.846
14	Zeis, Sher., Paris	60	.926	43	McKeever, San Antonio	29	.844
15	Lawrence, San Antonio	111	.922	44	McGowan, Hous., Dal.	40	.840
16	Burris, Galveston	25	.921	44	Gates, Galveston	26	.840
17	Slagle, Houston	131	.918		Thompson, Fort Worth	19	.840
18	Kohnle, Denison	87	.916	47	Chard, Austin	28	.833
19	Becker, Houston	132	.909	47	Douglas, San Antonio	21	.833
19	McAllister, Fort Wo'th	41	.909	49	R. Roach, Denison	27	.817
19	Blackburn, Austin	30	.909	50	Swearingen, Gal.. Paris	14	.810
22	Bailey, Sher., Austin	123	.905	51	Chamberlain, Sher., Aus.	14	.809
22	Elsey, San Antonio	26	.905	52	Ward, Dallas	24	.808
24	Page, Galveston	27	.903	53	Badger, Gal., Austin	80	.806
25	Belt, Galveston	19	.902	54	York, Galveston	10	.800
26	Ashenback, Dallas	71	.901	55	Isaacs, Fort Worth	23	.798
26	Herbert, San Antonio	39	.901	56	Wellner, Austin	28	.789
28	Land, Denison	36	.900	57	Heydon, Austin	15	.742
29	Mackey, S. A., Austin	79	.898				

PITCHERS.

Rank	Player and Club	Games	Per cent	Rank	Player and Club	Games	Per cent
1	Weber, Denison, S. A.	31	.979	17	Countryman, Sherman..	14	.921
2	Gear, Fort Worth.	23	.977	18	J. Roach, Houston....	46	.918
3	McAllister, Fort Worth.	18	.968		Chamberlain, Sher. Aus	26	.918
4	Page, Galveston	14	.956	20	Conover, Dallas	23	.914
5	Callahan, Sher., Denison	31	.955	21	Parvin, San Antonio....	42	.911
6	Staples, Austin, Dallas..	17	.952	22	Brott, Galveston	12	.909
7	Keefe, Fort Worth, S. A.	18	.950	23	Leeson, Houston	21	.901
8	Hardy, Galveston	32	.943	24	McCormick, Houston....	37	.895
9	Quigg, Denison	23	.940	25	Nevin, San Antonio	38	.889
	Colliflower, Austin	14	.940	26	Isaacs, Fort Worth	31	.881
	Dwyer, San Antonio..	11	.940	27	Balsz, Houston	17	.868
12	Crowell, Paris, Austin..	26	.937	28	Herbert, San Antonio...	29	.850
13	Blackburn, Austin	19	.930	29	Burris, Galveston	49	.841
14	Mulkey, Denison, Paris	32	.926	30	Chard, Austin	23	.831
15	Wellner, Austin	41	.923	31	Minnehan, Dallas	17	.822
	W. Spencer, D'n., Paris	13	.923				

CATCHERS.

1	Otten, San Antonio	33	.983	9	Gonding, Galveston	11	.926
2	Stanley, Fort W., S. A	118	.981	10	Weckbecker, Galveston.	70	.920
3	Belt, Galveston	48	.974	11	Miller, San Antonio	53	.921
4	Sage, Sher., Denison	87	.970	12	Hughes, Denison	36	.919
5	Cote, Houston	126	.969	13	Jantzen, Sher., Paris....	10	.913
6	Heydon, Austin	107	.949	14	Land, Denison	23	.909
7	Nie, Austin, Paris	56	.948	15	Earle, Dallas	32	.891
8	Kahlkoff, Dallas	27	.932	16	Ward, Dallas	24	.810

CLUB BATTING. CLUB FIELDING.

Rank	Clubs	Games	Runs	Per cent	Rank	Clubs	Games	Per cent
1	San Antonio	126	838	.311	1	Fort Worth	100	.927
2	Houston	132	704	.291	2	San Antonio	126	.919
	Fort Worth	100	757	.291	3	Paris	94	.911
3	Austin	130	908	.285	4	Denison	95	.900
4	Denison	95	684	.280	5	Houston	132	.894
5	Galveston	129	847	.278	6	Austin	130	.892
	Paris	94	576	.278	7	Galveston	124	.882
6	Dallas	90	479	.261	8	Dallas	90	.879

The Atlantic League

THE Atlantic League's first pennant race had a rather unpleasant ending, according to all accounts, inasmuch as the title to first place was disputed by Newark, Hartford and Paterson. In other respects it was an exciting race between three of the six clubs which finished the season. The figures show that the Hartfords beat Newark 15 games to 14, and Paterson 19 games to 11. The Hartford team, under Barnie's skilful leadership, deserves credit for its fine finish, as it had to work its way up by successive stages from the bottom, and had the misfortune to finish its campaign away from home. Paterson finished third, right on the heels of the first and second clubs. The Wilmington team was outclassed from the start, and finished a poor fifth. The New Haven and Metropolitan teams started the season in this league, but the former team dropped out on July 13, and on the same date the Metropolitan club was expelled from the League. Their places were taken by the Lancaster and Athletic teams. The former took up New Haven's record and the Athletics accepted the Mets' record, but we have kept their records separate from the handicaps imposed upon them and give only their actual performance. The Athletic and Metropolitan combined records would give the former 50 victories and 65 defeats, a percentage of .435. The combined Lancaster-New Haven record would be 46 victories, 65 defeats and percentage of .414. The record:

Club.	Newark.	Hartford.	Paterson.	Lancaster.	Wilmington.	Athletic.	Metropolitan.	New Haven.	Victories.	Per cent. of Victories.
Newark		14	11	7	22	11	10	5	82	.573
Hartford	15		19	7	11	9	3	9	78	.566
Paterson	16	10		7	18	5	9	9	74	.552
Lancaster	7	4	4		7	4	0	0	28	.483
Wilmington	12	10	11	2		8	8	7	58	.423
Athletic	4	0	7	5	11		0	0	27	.422
Metropolitan*	4	9	5	0	4	0		8	30	.484
New Haven*	3	9	3	0	4	0	2		21	.362
Defeats	61	56	60	30	79	37	32	38	393	

*Lancaster and Athletic admitted in place of New Haven and Metropolitan July 13.

BATTING AVERAGES.

Rank.	Name.	Club.	Games.	Runs.	S.B.	Per cent.
1	Clark...................	Metropolitan.............	24	37	13	.495
2	Newell....................	Wilmington..............	118	147	72	.416
3	Burns....	Newark...................	111	118	51	.395
4	Wright...................	Newark..................	119	163	45	.385
5	Bannon...................	Metropolitan.............	56	71	47	.358
6	Milligan.........	Athletic	19	14	1	.355
7	Wagner......'..............	Paterson.................	109	106	43	.348
8	Laroque...................	Lancaster................	17	15	4	.347
9	Zearfoss	Metropolitan.............	25	20	3	.344
10	J. Rothfuss...............	Newark..................	123	147	87	.332
11	Elton	Paterson.................	79	55	6	.326
	J. Mills..................	New Haven, Newark.....	42	23	6	.326
12	Leidy....	Lancaster................	43	32	8	.324
13	Vickery....................	Hartford.................	67	38	28	.323
14	Thornton..................	New Haven, Hartford.....	107	80	51	.321
15	Stuart...................	Newark..................	24	24	10	.320
	Irwin....................	Metropolitan.............	49	39	20	.320
16	Bristow	Paterson, Newark.........	53	48	16	.317
17	Gallagher	Wilmington..............	97	105	50	.316
18	Lever ....,.	Athletic.................	63	58	9	.309
19	Daly.....................	Newark..................	114	91	38	.306
	Henry.........	Lancaster................	39	34	6	.306
	O'Hagan.................	Newark, New Haven.....	122	141	74	.306
	Heckman.................	Metropolitan	47	37	27	.306
20	Hamburg.................	Lancaster................	33	19	7	.304
21	Seybold..................	Lancaster................	43	27	11	.301
	Cavelle...	Metropolitan, Hartford...	113	113	77	.301
22	Lehane...................	Hartford.................	32	14	6	.300
23	Gilman..................	New Haven, Newark......	120	104	45	.299
	Drew....................	Wilmington..............	47	37	19	.299
24	Eustace.............	Hartford.................	58	42	34	.298
25	Heine.....................	Newark..................	77	73	55	.295
26	Heidrick.............. ...	Paterson.................	124	103	37	.294
27	Justice...................	Newark..................	22	13	16	.293
	McVey..................	Athletic..................	63	54	20	.293
28	Killacky...................	Paterson.................	114	95	6	.292
29	Seymour.	Metropolitan.............	34	22	11	.290
30	Hayward..................	Metropolitan, Paterson....	67	48	25	.286
31	Mertes....................	Wilmington, Athletic....	23	20	6	.284
32	Pettit	Hartford................ .	99	76	50	.282
	Cogan........	Paterson................	63	33	7	.282
33	A. Smith.................	Hartford.................	86	57	36	.281
34	Battam...................	Metropolitan, Paterson....	73	50	35	.279
	Gunshannon........	Hartford.........	52	39	22	.279
	Cargo....................	Wilmington..............	17	11	1	.279
35	Kinsella..................	Wilmington..............	76	54	22	.276
36	Touhey.....	Paterson, Wilmington.....	68	31	8	.275
	Ellis........	Athletic..................	22	15	3	.275
37	Welsh...................	Wilmington............ ..	17	15	6	.273

BATTING AVERAGES—Continued.

Rank	Name	Club	Games	Runs	Stolen Bases	Per cent.
38	Foster	Metropolitan	59	56	40	.272
39	Schaub	Athletic	46	32	5	.271
40	Buttermore	Lancaster	42	46	14	.269
41	Montgomery	Wilmington	111	69	39	.267
41	Fuller	Athletic, Wilmington	42	31	9	.267
41	Houle	Hartford	69	52	34	.267
42	McIntyre	Wilmington	122	88	41	.263
42	Boyle	Hartford, New Haven	120	84	33	.263
43	McDonald	Hartford	61	50	22	.262
44	Fitch	Paterson	78	53	22	.261
45	Roth	Lancaster	31	12	6	.259
46	Armour	Paterson	120	109	52	.258
47	Fox	Athletic	41	34	13	.257
48	Torreyson	Paterson, Newark, Met'n	53	61	35	.256
48	Cain	Athletic	23	8	1	.256
48	G. Smith	Paterson	112	96	22	.256
49	Graham	Hartford	63	41	8	.255
50	Bottenus	Hartford	116	84	48	.254
51	Childs	Athletic	65	37	9	.252
52	Spratt	Wilmington	114	79	51	.250
52	Taylor	Paterson	61	43	7	.250
52	Hassemer	Newark	20	19	6	.250
52	Scharf	Hartford	60	41	21	.250
52	Whitehill	Newark	22	11	2	.250
53	Mack	Hartford	92	64	32	.249
54	Divinney	Wilmington	24	16	8	.247
55	Stouch	Paterson, Lancaster, Ath	43	23	6	.245
56	A. Moran	Athletic	65	54	19	.242
57	Bastian	Paterson	45	35	8	.240
57	Berryhill	Wilmington	69	42	10	.240
57	J. McQuaid	Lancaster	28	4	1	.240
58	Osbourn	Hartford	17	9	1	.239
59	Smink	Paterson	17	7	3	.235
60	Amole	Wilmington	81	29	12	.228
60	Ames	Athletic	22	6	0	.228
61	Seeds	Hartford	28	14	3	.226
62	Weisbecker	Wilmington, Newark	67	48	35	.220
63	Cauliflower	New Haven	20	8	0	.217
64	Viau	Paterson	16	10	2	.214
65	Scherer	New Haven	43	17	4	.213
66	L. Smith	New Haven, Newark	62	40	14	.211
67	Bowen	Hartford, Metropolitan	43	16	2	.206
68	Standish	Metropolitan	21	12	3	.205
69	Anderson	Wilmington	22	7	0	.203
69	Hodge	New Haven, Newark	73	47	12	.203
70	A. Rothfuss	Newark	111	62	20	.199
71	C. Mackey	Hartford	19	9	9	.197
71	Yeager	Lancaster	23	11	3	.197
72	Wise	Wilmington	33	17	13	.196
72	Cohen	Metropolitan	28	19	11	.196
73	McCafferty	Wilmington, Paterson	24	12	3	.194

BASE BALL GUIDE. 135

BATTING AVERAGES—*Continued*.

Rank.	Name.	Club.	Games.	Runs.	Stolen Bases.	Per cent.
74	J. Nops.................	Wilmington.............	51	23	3	.185
75	{ Keefe..................	New Haven.............	24	13	7	.179
	{ Ruhland...............	Hartford...............	26	11	7	.179
	{ Westlake..............	Lancaster..............	21	4	1	.179
76	Setley.................	Newark.................	27	11	1	.174
77	McMackin..............	Paterson...............	46	16	4	.172
78	Garvin................	New Haven, Newark...	34	16	2	.165
79	Mackey................	New Haven, Newark...	34	12	2	.162
80	Gray..................	Paterson, Wilmington..	22	11	3	.158
81	Gannon................	New Haven.............	15	4	2	.137
82	Fry...................	New Haven, Newark...	49	20	7	.136
83	Lloyd.................	Newark.................	22	6	2	.123
84	Clements..............	Hartford...............	15	5	1	.075

FIELDING AVERAGES—CATCHERS.

Name and Club.	Games.	Per cent.	Name and Club.	Games.	Per cent.
Smink, Paterson..........	17	.985	A. Rothfuss, Newark......	105	.941
Zearfoss, Metropolitan.....	23	.982	Welsh, Wilmington........	17	.941
Hodge, Newark, N. H.....	72	.966	Bottenus, Hartford........	87	.936
Kinsella, Wilmington......	58	.966	Killacky, Paterson.........	46	.934
Wise, Wilmington.........	29	.966	Fox, Athletic.............	28	.933
Elton, Paterson............	71	.962	Milligan, Athletic.........	15	.900
Roth, Lancaster...........	31	.956	Schaub, Athletic..........	28	.896
A. Smith, Hartford........	84	.955	Foster, Metropolitan......	39	.886
Westlake, Lancaster.......	18	.954			

FIRST BASEMEN.

Name and Club.	Games.	Per cent.	Name and Club.	Games.	Per cent.
Clark, Metropolitan........	24	.987	Bottenus, Hartford........	81	.962
Touhey, Paterson, Wil'n...	50	.973	Hamburg, Lancaster......	32	.959
J. Rothfuss, Newark.......	108	.973	Berryhill, Wilmington.....	64	.958
Lehane, Hartford.........	32	.972	Kinsella, Wilmington ..	18	.958
Irwin, Metropolitan........	29	.971	Thornton, Hartford, N. H..	106	.958
Fuller, Athletic............	42	.968	Killacky, Paterson.........	15	.949
Wagner, Paterson.........	78	.968	Mertes, Wilmington, Ath'c.	23	.932
Burns, Newark............	16	.966			

SECOND BASEMEN.

Name and Club.	Games.	Per cent.	Name and Club.	Games.	Per cent.
Childs, Athletic...........	65	.937	Laroque, Lancaster.......	17	.888
Stouch, Athletic, Pat., Lan.	27	.935	Boyle, Hartford...........	50	.878
Heine, Newark............	22	.931	Irwin, Metropolitan.......	20	.874
McIntyre, Wilmington.....	119	.924	Tor'ys'n, Pat., New., Met..	29	.848
G. Smith, Paterson........	68	.914	Hassamer, Newark........	15	.848
Gilman, N. H., Newark....	120	.913	Justice, Newark..........	19	.813
Mack, Hartford...........	70	.904	Cohen, Metropolitan......	15	.788

THIRD BASEMEN.

Name and Club.	Games.	Per cent.	Name and Club.	Games.	Per cent.
Eustace, Hartford	58	.915	G. Smith, Paterson	22	.873
Henry, Lancaster	39	.913	Wagner, Paterson	19	.866
Newell, Wilmington	118	.888	Pettit, Hartford	48	.832
O'Hagan, N. H., Newark	18	.882	Boyle, Hartford	65	.819
Battam, Paterson, Metro'n.	73	.879	Graham, Athletic	58	.817
Daly, Newark	114	.878	Taylor, Paterson	52	.814

SHORTSTOPS.

Bastian, Paterson	45	.918	McDonald, Hartford	61	.862
J. McQuaid, Lancaster	28	.895	Stuart, Newark	24	.856
Heine, Newark	55	.888	Ruhland, Hartford	17	.852
L. Smith, Newark, N. H	57	.878	Scharf, Hartford	49	.839
Ellis, Athletic	22	.871	Heckman, Metropolitan	45	.814
Fitch, Paterson	75	.871	Devinney, Wilmington	16	.806
Gallagher, Wilmington	96	.870			

OUTFIELDERS.

Leidy, Lancaster	43	.971	Cavelle, Hartford, Met	113	.916
Heidrick, Paterson	124	.954	Moran, Athletic	65	.913
O'Hagan, N. H., Newark	79	.953	Bottenus, Hartford	46	.903
Spratt, Wilmington	97	.951	Buttermore, Lancaster	41	.901
Weisbecker, Wil'n Newark.	67	.947	Gunshannon, Hartford	52	.891
McVey, Athletic	63	.945	Drew, Wilmington	46	.891
Pettit, Hartford	50	.942	Scherer, New Haven	43	.880
Wright, Newark	119	.941	Lever, Paterson	63	.879
Burns, Newark	95	.939	Armor, Paterson	126	.878
Hayward, Paterson	34	.933	Mills, Newark, N. Haven	28	.875
Houle, Hartford	69	.932	Tor'ys's, Pat., New., Met	21	.852
Bristow, Paterson, Newark.	37	.931	Montgomery, Wilmington	111	.834
Bannon, Metropolitan	56	.922	Cogan, Paterson	15	.828
Gannon, New Haven	15	.920	Cauliflower, New Haven	30	.811
Killacky, Paterson	49	.920	Amole, Wilmington	28	.809
Mack, Hartford	22	.919	Seymour, Metropolitan	25	.769
Seybold, Lancaster	31	.918			

PITCHERS.

Ames, Athletic	22	1000	McMackin, Paterson	46	.906
Yeager, Lancaster	15	1000	Seeds, Hartford	20	.903
Bristow, Pat., Newark	16	.978	Bowen, Met., Hartford	39	.900
Mackey, N. H., Newark	33	.957	Cogan, Paterson	48	.898
Gray, Paterson	16	.945	Whitehill, Newark	19	.894
Garvin, N. H., Newark	33	.931	G. Smith, Paterson	16	.875
Setley, Newark	25	.927	Amole, Wilmington	51	.867
Nops, Wilmington	42	.925	McCafferty, Paterson, Wil.	23	.864
Vickery, Hartford	56	.922	Keefe, New Haven	23	.860
Fry, N. H., Newark	52	.921	Lloyd, Newark	21	.824
Cain, Athletic	23	.917			

The Virginia State League

THE Virginia State League began the season with six clubs, composed of Lynchburg, Norfolk, Richmond, Roanoke, Portsmouth and Petersburg. The season was not as good as the preceding year in some respects, due, no doubt, in a great measure to the excitement of the Presidential campaign, which was also felt in other sections of the country. The Roanoke and Lynchburg clubs did not finish the season, the former disbanding on August 20 and the latter on August 22. Norfolk headed the clubs with a percentage of .597, having 40 victories and 27 defeats. Richmond was second in the list with a percentage of .581; also leading in sacrifice hits and stolen bases. The batting, as a rule, was heavier; over 30 per cent. of the players batted over .300, which is considered high. In pitching, McFarland, of Lynchburg, won the greatest percentage of games, while Mullarkey had the greatest number of strike-outs, and Tannchill, who stood second in percentage, has the exceptionally low record of giving less than one base on balls to a game pitched. The full pitching record will be found on page 147.

The standing of the clubs at the close of the season was as follows:

VIRGINIA LEAGUE RECORD FOR 1896.

Club.	Lynchburg.	Norfolk.	Richmond.	Roanoke.	Portsmouth.	Petersburg.	Victories.	Per cent. of Victories.
†Lynchburg		5	4	6	5	4	24	.615
Norfolk	4		8	2	16	10	40	.597
Richmond	3	7		6	5	15	36	.581
*Roanoke	2	3	2		7	8	22	.550
Portsmouth	1	10	7	2		11	31	.477
Petersburg	5	2	5	2	1		15	.238
Defeats	15	27	26	18	34	48	168	

* Roanoke disbanded August 20.   † Lynchburg disbanded August 22.

BASE RUNNING FOR SEASON.

Club.	S. H.	S. B.	Club.	S. H.	S. B.
Richmond	183	568	Petersburg	37	197
Norfolk	59	320	Lynchburg	107	323
Portsmouth	63	255	Roanoke	49	248

TOTAL BATTING FOR SEASON.

Player and Club.	Games.	Runs.	Per cent.	Player and Club.	Games.	Runs.	Per cent.
Tate, Roanoke	86	78	.392	Grove, Lynchburg	105	76	.281
Kelly, Petersburg	121	109	.368	McGinnis, Roanoke	16	13	.278
McGann, Lynchburg	86	90	.346	Sanford, Richmond	69	45	.277
Turner, Nor. & Lynch.	75	58	.345	McCann, Petersburg	16	10	.274
McGann, Roanoke	42	34	.345	Fleming, Pe. & Ro	90	72	.273
Marr, Po. & Rich	116	106	.341	Mullarkey, Richmond	41	17	.271
Stephenson, Nor. & Pe.	89	69	.336	Goodheart, Petersburg	22	6	.271
C. McFarland, Norfolk	121	121	.335	Woodruff, Richmond	14	10	.269
Gilroy, Norfolk	50	45	.333	Stultz, Lynchburg	25	11	.269
Dolan, Lynchburg	96	90	.333	Burke, Portsmouth	124	70	.268
Brodie, Petersburg	56	36	.333	Lynch, Roanoke	55	42	.262
Little, Lynchburg	105	72	.330	Raffert, Petersburg	23	17	.262
Armstrong, Norfolk	108	107	.329	Wilson, Rich. & Peters.	34	18	.261
Reiman, Portsmouth	108	75	.328	Tutt, Petersburg	17	3	.261
Langsford, Norfolk	47	35	.325	Williams, Roanoke	97	75	.260
Wrigley, Roanoke	106	91	.322	Groves, Richmond	112	66	.258
Pender, Richmond	126	95	.321	Breen, Lynchburg	102	80	.255
Pickering, Lynchburg	98	94	.321	A. McFarland, Norfolk	73	52	.254
Tannahill, Richmond	57	45	.318	Smith, Lynchburg	103	72	.254
Bradley, Pe. & R	98	65	.317	Davis, Norfolk	71	58	.250
Fields, Norfolk	52	33	.317	Kimball, Roanoke	44	17	.248
Cleve, Norfolk	72	76	.316	Brandt, Portsmouth	48	19	.248
Leahy, Lynchburg	106	94	.312	Cheseboro, Roanoke	22	10	.247
Werrick, Portsmouth	27	18	.309	Heilman, Portsmouth	69	35	.246
Gochenaur, Portsmouth	29	23	.309	Sherrer, Roanoke	10	22	.243
Boylan, Lynchburg	26	14	.309	Mulligan, Petersburg	16	7	.242
Sholta, Richmond	94	67	.305	Leach, Norfolk	31	15	.237
Wells, Richmond	67	40	.305	Ramp, Norfolk	104	54	.234
Dundon, Norfolk	119	89	.303	Hall, Portsmouth	89	49	.234
Wentz, Norfolk	102	82	.303	Hallman, Portsmouth	98	55	.233
Stocksdale, Rich. & Nor.	41	30	.300	Viox, Richmond	41	26	.233
Boyd, Portsmouth	44	34	.299	Gilpatrick, Richmond	16	8	.226
Katz, Portsmouth	59	37	.299	Leach, Petersburg	36	17	.225
Rollins, Portsmouth	100	67	.298	Allison, Petersburg	12	3	.225
Sheckard, Portsmouth	20	17	.296	Kitson, Petersburg	29	14	.221
Norcom, Petersburg	21	15	.296	Berte, Richmond	128	76	.219
Hill, Roanoke	73	52	.295	Kain, Richmond	128	98	.214
McFarlan, Lynchburg	83	25	.295	Ryan, Portsmouth	21	6	.208
Kane, Petersburg	52	36	.290	Coons, Roanoke	46	16	.191
Boland, Richmond	101	55	.289	Lemon, Nor. & Po	28	18	.189
Fear, Lynchburg	76	55	.288	Zimmerman, Richmond	33	13	.183
Rothermel, Norfolk	35	18	.287	Lampe, Portsmouth	17	6	.166
Foster, Richmond	51	52	.286	Quarles, Petersburg	21	8	.164
Cockman, Roanoke	78	57	.285	Evans, Lynchburg	15	3	.161
Armstrong, Lynchburg	27	2	.282	Vetter, Petersburg	40	7	.159
Schabel, Lynchburg	79	61	.282	Pfanmiller, Norfolk	45	29	.140

FIELDING AVERAGES—RICHMOND CLUB.

Barley, pitcher	1.000	Boland, catcher	.955
Clausen, pitcher	1.000	Foster, c., c. f., 3d base	.945
Woodruff, pitcher	1.000	Berte, shortstop	.932
Wells, 1st base	.982	Kain, l. f., 3d base	.924
Pender, 1st, 2d, 3d base	.975	Sanford, left field	.923
Tannehill, pitcher	.972	Sholta, 2d base	.918
Mullarkey, pitcher	.969	Viox, 3d base	.913
Groves, centre field	.964	Marr, right field	.895
Turner, first base	.964		

NORFOLK CLUB.

Leach, pitcher	1.000	Gilroy, pitcher, 2d base, ss	.939
Clauson, pitcher	1.000	Stocksdale, pitcher, right field	.939
Pfanmiller, pitcher, r. f	.974	Fields, catcher	.937
Sechrist, pitcher	.966	C. McFarland, left field	.931
Armstrong, 1st base, catcher	.951	A. McFarland, left field	.927
Cleve, right field	.949	Rothermel, shortstop	.888
Davis, 2d base, 3d base, ss	.949	Lamont, shortstop	.831
Wentz, 2d base	.941	Ramp, third base	.825

PETERSBURG CLUB.

Kitson, pitcher	1.000	Fleming right field	.921
Vetter, catcher	.962	Goodheart, 3d base, catcher	.917
Kimball, pitcher, 1st base	.961	Stephenson, left field	.916
Toft, catcher	.940	Dundon, shortstop, 2d base	.912
McCann, pitcher, 1st base	.940	Leach, 3d base	.892
Hallman, left field	.938	Reiman, 1st base	.888
Bradley, centre field	.936	Quarles, pitcher	.882
Stocksdale, pitcher, 1st base	.933	Breen, 3d base, 2d base	.873
Allison, 2d base	.929	Rothermel, shortstop	.866
Norcomb, pitcher, r. f	.925	Sholta, 2d base	.820
Kelley, 1st base, ss., r. f	.923		

PORTSMOUTH CLUB.

Hallman, left field	1.000	Chandler, pitcher	.941
Stultz, pitcher	1.000	Hall, shortstop, 2d base	.935
Brandt, pitcher	.991	Hargrove, centre field	.931
Rollins, catcher	.971	Stephenson, left field	.920
Wilson, catcher	.962	Katz, right field	.928
Ryan, 1st base	.960	Burke, 3d base	.926
Reiman, 1st base, 2d base, c	.953	Sheckard, left field	.915
Gochenaur, 2d base	.949	Werrick, 2d base, shortstop	.903
Boyd, p., 1st b., 2d b., r. f	.947	Lampe, pitcher	.800
Marr, right field	.946	Lamont, shortstop	.700

ROANOKE CLUB.

Hulse, pitcher	1.000	Lynch, catcher, 3d base	.934
Brummer, pitcher	1.000	McGinnis, right field	.929
Tate, 1st base	.979	Williams, catcher	.917
Sherrer, left field	.970	Kimball, pitcher	.917
Hill, right field	.962	Cockman, 3d base	.912
Coons, pitcher	.945	Wrigley, shortstop	.900
McGann, 2d base	.943	Fleming, centre field	.852

LYNCHBURG CLUB.

Boylan, pitcher	1.000	Leahy, shortstop	.926
Pickering, left field	.986	Dolan, 3d base	.921
Little, 1st base	.973	Smith, centre field	.913
Brown, pitcher	.959	Breen, 2d base	.906
Stultz, pitcher	.949	McGann, 2d base	.876
Schabel, catcher	.944	Turner, right fielder	.864
Grove, right field	.944	Fear, centre field, right field	.849
McFarlan, pitcher	.941		

The Inter-State League

BATTING AVERAGES.

Player and Club.	Games.	Runs.	Per cent.	Player and Club.	Games.	Runs.	Per cent.
Rinehart, Washington	47	43	.471	Esterquest, Fort Wayne	14	11	.311
Flick, Youngstown	31	34	.438	Gallagher, Wheeling	42	39	.305
Curran, Washington	40	36	.435	J. S. Ganzel, Saginaw	53	31	.305
B. Whitehill, New Castle	6	1	.417	McHoverter, Wheeling	26	21	.304
Johnson, Wheeling	6	2	.400	Fitch, Youngstown	6	4	.304
Phillips, Fort Wayne	12	6	.400	Clifford, Toledo	48	43	.301
Shaw, Wheeling	26	21	.394	Beck, Toledo	52	45	.301
Criger, Fort Wayne	61	74	.388	Curtis, Jackson	45	41	.300
Irwin, New Castle	8	4	.381	Kuhn, Washington	52	39	.297
Welch, Fort Wayne	5	9	.381	Powell, Toledo	18	11	.295
Martin, Washington	47	62	.375	King, Fort Wayne	35	26	.292
Grey, Fort Wayne	61	68	.374	Bates, Washington	28	7	.291
Ritz, Washington	45	44	.364	Troy, Washington	16	15	.290
Hardesty, Jackson-Wash.	44	40	.360	Early, Saginaw	5	8	.286
Cargo, Washington	23	13	.358	Summer, Ft. W.-Saginaw.	49	46	.285
Tebeau, Fort Wayne	58	68	.355	Fisher, Fort Wayne	12	16	.283
J. Ganzel, New Castle	88	82	.349	Knell, Fort Wayne	37	35	.283
O'Meara, Fort Wayne	39	39	.347	W. Sowders, N. C.-W.-Sag.	55	46	.282
Rickert, Ft. Wayne-Wash.	51	48	.347	McGinnis, Toledo	48	39	.282
G. Ganzel, New Castle	31	15	.345	Violet, Wheeling	33	41	.280
Thorpe, Saginaw	22	24	.341	Baker, Wheeling	14	8	.279
Myers, Jackson	41	39	.340	McKeown, Washington	39	24	.278
Hazen, Youngstown	43	40	.339	Coughlin, Jackson	41	34	.278
Vetters, Toledo	52	37	.338	Daniels, New Castle	45	29	.275
J. Sowders, N. C.-Wash.	39	27	.335	Davis, Wheeling	19	17	.274
Griffin, Washington	43	33	.333	Briggs, Washington	12	8	.273
M. Whitehill, New Castle	41	34	.333	Beadle, Washington	14	9	.273
Hickman, New Castle	8	4	.333	Mitchell, Washington	29	12	.273
Steen, Youngstown	52	45	.330	Snyder, Saginaw	41	35	.273
Winters, Youngstown	42	22	.329	Hoffmeister, Youngstown	30	24	.273
Gilboy, New Castle	86	81	.327	Schroeder, New Castle	11	10	.272
Wagner, Wheeling	33	50	.326	Ardner, Youngstown	32	15	.270
McGuirk, Jackson	39	33	.322	Miles, Toledo-Saginaw	54	56	.270
McLaughlin, Wheeling	7	6	.321	Hemphill, Saginaw	54	35	.268
Brown, Saginaw	5	3	.319	Allen, Saginaw	16	7	.268
St. Mary, Saginaw	10	3	.317	Thurston, Fort Wayne	45	30	.268
Cecil, Toledo	25	27	.317	Lavelle, New Castle	30	19	.267
Rooney, Youngstown	8	6	.316	Whaley, Wheeling	36	29	.267
Boyle, New Castle, Y.	42	46	.312	Kihm, Toledo	9	6	.266
Corcoran, Jackson	43	26	.312	Kelb, Toledo	19	12	.266
McKevitt, Saginaw	53	47	.311	Arthur, Toledo	48	30	.264

BATTING AVERAGES—*Continued.*

Player and Club.	Games.	Runs.	Per cent.	Player and Club.	Games.	Runs.	Per cent.
Northwang, Sag.-N. C.	14	8	.260	Riley, Washington	17	10	.234
Smith, Saginaw	7	3	.259	Engle, Jackson	15	10	.234
Swayne, Ft. W.-N. C.	21	10	.256	Dinsmore, Washington	16	6	.229
Donovan, Youngs,-N. C.	59	31	.255	Spade, Youngstown	17	5	.229
Brodie, Youngstown	36	16	.255	Miller, Jackson	17	6	.226
Babb, Wheeling-Ft. W.	17	8	.253	Cogswell, Saginaw	9	4	.222
Garvey, Wheeling	14	12	.250	Diesel, Jackson	45	35	.222
Mertch, Wheeling	10	6	.250	Ferry, Saginaw	13	7	.222
McGowan, Toledo	42	30	.250	Jordan, Youngstown	11	9	.214
Smith, Toledo	9	5	.250	Derrick, Jackson	17	11	.212
Russell, Sag.-Youngstown	11	6	.250	Berry, Youngstown	61	39	.212
Flaherty, Jackson	6	3	.250	Cooke, Toledo	9	1	.206
Lynch, Fort Wayne	47	37	.246	Grey, Saginaw	9	6	.200
Doneghy, Washington	32	23	.243	Keenan, Toledo	24	12	.187
Carrick, Fort Wayne	21	19	.241	Hartman, Toledo	9	2	.173
O'Brien, Toledo	16	11	.239	Coyle, Toledo	7	2	.125
Darrah, Wheeling	37	25	.237				

FIELDING AVERAGES—CATCHERS.

Player and Club.	Games.	Per cent.	Player and Club.	Games.	Per cent.
Myers, Jackson	41	.970	G. Ganzel, New Castle	31	.938
Brown, Saginaw	5	.966	Bates, Washington	28	.937
Davis, Wheeling	19	.964	Spanger, Saginaw	6	.937
Grey, Saginaw	9	.958	Donovan, New Castle	34	.932
Zinran, Youngstown	61	.952	Criger, Fort Wayne	61	.930
Briggs, Washington	12	.949	Arthur, Toledo	48	.929
Shaw, Wheeling	31	.947	Mitchell, Washington	29	.922
Northwang, N. Cas.-Sag.	14	.943	Lavelle, New Castle	30	.915
O'Meara, Fort Wayne	39	.940	Hurd, Saginaw	9	.914

FIRST BASEMEN.

Player and Club.	Games.	Per cent.	Player and Club.	Games.	Per cent.
J. Ganzel, New Castle	88	.985	Clifford, Toledo	43	.964
Kihm, Toledo	9	.981	McHoverter, Wheeling	26	.963
McGuirk, Johnson	39	.979	T. Ganzel, Saginaw	53	.963
Winters, Youngstown	42	.977	O'Brien, Toledo	16	.927
Tebeau, Fort Wayne	58	.970	McKeown, Washington	39	.921
Case, Youngstown	5	.964			

SECOND BASEMEN.

Player and Club.	Games.	Per cent.	Player and Club.	Games.	Per cent.
Fisher, Fort Wayne	12	.965	Ardner, Youngstown	32	.902
Kuhn, Washington	52	.930	Hartman, Toledo	9	.900
Donovan, Youngstown	59	.927	Boyle, New Castle	42	.899
Darrah, Washington	37	.914	Miles, Toledo-Saginaw	54	.898
Thurston, Fort Wayne-Wash	45	.909	Hardesty, Jack.-Washington	44	.881
Babb, Wash.-Fort Wayne	17	.907	Fitch, Youngstown	6	.714
Beck, Toledo	52	.906	Early, Saginaw	5	.667
Whitehill, New Castle	41	.903			

SPALDING'S OFFICIAL

THIRD BASEMEN.

Player and Club	Games	Per cent	Player and Club	Games	Per cent
Heller, Saginaw	9	.919	Thorpe, Saginaw	22	.883
Cecil, Toledo	25	.916	Corcoran, Jackson	45	.883
Lynch, Fort Wayne	47	.902	Sullivan, New Castle	88	.878
McGowan, Toledo	42	.895	Wagner, Wheeling	33	.863
Curran, Washington	40	.885	Hoffmeister, Youngstown	30	.846
Cargo, Washington	23	.884			

SHORTSTOPS.

Player and Club	Games	Per cent	Player and Club	Games	Per cent
Esterquest, Fort Wayne	14	.951	Sowders, New Castle-Wash.	55	.858
Diesel, Jackson	45	.936	King, Fort Wayne	35	.830
Ritz, Washington	45	.928	Berry, Youngstown	61	.821
Cooke, Toledo	9	.916	Whaley, Wheeling	36	.819
Farrell, New Castle	88	.907	Rodey, Youngstown	8	.800
Doneghy, Washington	32	.883	Snyder, Saginaw	41	.800
Stoup, Saginaw	35	.874			

OUTFIELDERS.

Player and Club	Games	Per cent	Player and Club	Games	Per cent
Smith, Toledo	9	1.000	Hemphill, Saginaw	54	.862
Provins, New Castle	15	1.000	Grey, Fort Wayne	61	.854
Daniels, New Castle	45	.958	Summer, Saginaw	49	.846
Somers, Youngstown	30	.945	Thomas, Youngstown	10	.844
Vetters, Toledo	52	.941	Griffin, Washington	43	.844
Fraynes, Jackson	18	.933	Phillips, Fort Wayne	12	.842
Steen, Youngstown	52	.916	Gallagher, Wheeling	42	.838
Blake, Fort Wayne	8	.900	Cooper, Youngstown	17	.836
Rinehart, Washington	47	.900	Martin, Washington	47	.835
McKevitt, Saginaw	53	.806	Flick, Youngstown	81	.826
Gilbow, New Castle	86	.892	Coughlin, Jackson	41	.816
McGinnis, Toledo	43	.892	J. Sowders, N. C.-Wash.	39	.787
Curtis, Jackson	45	.881	St. Mary, Saginaw	10	.750
Hazen, Youngstown	43	.875	Kane, Fort Wayne	15	.714
Mertch, Wheeling	10	.867	Clark, New Castle	9	.690
Rickert, Fort Wayne and W.	51	.866	Troy, Washington	16	.667
Violet, Wheeling	33	.863			

PITCHERS.

Player and Club	Games	Per cent	Player and Club	Games	Per cent
Crosby, New Castle	7	1.000	Brown, New Castle	27	.905
Barnes, Youngstown	9	1.000	Spade, Youngstown	17	.904
Terry, Saginaw	13	.980	Swain, Fort Wayne	21	.900
Baker, Wheeling	13	.976	Irwin, New Castle	8	.900
Engle, Jackson	15	.958	Allen, Saginaw	16	.897
Jordan, Youngstown	11	.951	Kelb, Toledo	19	.885
Martin, Toledo	11	.950	Beadle, Washington	14	.875
Hewitt, New Castle	15	.948	B. Whitehill, New Castle	6	.875
Powell, Fort Wayne	13	.938	Johnson, Wheeling	6	.846
Rutherford, Saginaw	17	.936	Cogswell, Saginaw	9	.846
Knell, Fort Wayne	37	.925	Hickman, New Castle	8	.840
Carrick, Fort Wayne	21	.924	Brodie, Youngstown	36	.821
Keenan, Toledo	24	.922	Stevens, Youngstown	7	.800
Dinsmore, Washington	16	.918	Coyle, Toledo	7	.800
Derrick, Jackson	17	.915	Flaherty, Jack.-Youngstown	6	.800
Garvey, Wheeling	14	.913	Riley, Washington	17	.750

Base Ball in Canada

THE records of the Canadian base ball campaign of 1896 show that base ball in the Dominion still continues to share popularity with the old English game of cricket there, as also with the Canadian national game of lacrosse, each being distinct field sports. Cricket being a field game for the leisure class, lacrosse a pedestrians' game suitable only for swift runners, while base ball is the game par exellence for the colleges and schools of the country, and requires no time stolen from study hours for training purposes, as track athletics, foot ball and running do, and affords every opening necessary for manly character, both mental and physical.

We are glad to note another successful season for the home league, which comprises four Canadian clubs, which play for the Canadian championship. There should be at least six clubs in the league, with Toronto and Montreal as two of them. The championship campaign of the Canadian clubs of 1896 resulted in the three-times-winners of the pennant, the noted Maple Leafs, of Guelph, the senior base ball organization of Canada, if we remember correctly. Their most successful rivals were the Hamilton club, and next to them that of London. The Galt club made a plucky effort to complete the season, but unfortunately were unable to keep up the pace, and had to retire before the close of the season. The Guelph team made a red-hot finish, as they won seven of the last eight games of the campaign.

The following is the correct standing of the different clubs, with games won and lost, and their percentage:

Club.	Won.	Lost.	Per cent.	Club.	Won.	Lost.	Per cent.
Guelph	24	12	.667	London	14	18	.413
Hamilton	16	18	.470	*Galt	10	16	.386

* Disbanded.

It will be seen by the above that Guelph had a comparatively easy time winning.

The shortstops and third basemen are given under one head, on account of the way several players alternated between the two positions. Pfeiffer's average includes all positions, as does Delaney's.

The averages given the pitchers are for their work in all positions. Hoffner and Malott, of Hamilton, are first and second among the regular outfielders.

INDIVIDUAL BATTING.

Rank	Player and Club	A.B.	Hits	Per cent.	Rank	Player and Club	A.B.	Hits	Per cent.
1	Morrison, Hamilton	122	53	.434	20	J. Cockman, Guelph	66	17	.258
2	Baker, Hamilton	144	61	.424	21	Sullivan, Guelph	39	10	256
3	Crall, Galt	105	38	.362	22	McGinnis, G't-Hamilt'n	96	24	250
4	Plummer, London	36	13	.361	23	Phillips, Hamilton	53	13	.245
5	Sippi, London	134	46	.343	24	Reid, Galt	83	20	.241
6	Dr. Wood, London	124	42	.339	25	Dean, Hamilton	140	35	.286
						Pfenninger, Hamilt'n	140	33	.236
7	Lyons, Galt	102	34	.333	26	Handley, Guelph	51	12	.235
	T. Cockman, Galt	87	29	.333	27	Delaney, Guel'h-Lon'n.	124	29	.234
	Collins, Galt	63	21	.333	28	McIlroy, Guelph	151	35	.232
	Jennings, Galt	54	18	.333	29	Gallagher, Guelph	53	12	.226
8	Snyder, London	144	46	.319		Fischer, London	31	7	.226
9	Malott, Hamilton	85	27	.318	30	Hoffner, Hamilton	108	24	.222
10	Ripley, Hamilton	41	13	.317	31	Jones, Galt	60	13	.217
11	Humphrey, G't-London	143	44	.308	32	Congalton, Guelph	130	28	.215
12	Lauer, Guelph	154	47	.305	33	Moore, Hamilton	24	5	.208
13	McDonald, G't-London	145	44	.303	34	Roberts, Guelph	125	24	.192
14	Pfeiffer, Hamilton	93	28	.301		Clark, Galt	26	5	.192
15	Dark, Guelph	155	45	.290	35	Stoneman, Hamilton	47	9	.191
	Hutchinson, London	62	18	.290	36	Carney, Guelph	55	10	.182
16	Hynd, London	117	32	.274	37	Tierney, London	28	5	.179
	Mertsch, London	84	23	.274	38	Hewer, Guelph	91	16	.176
17	Sheere, London	26	7	.269	39	Powers, London	77	13	.169
18	McCracken, Guelph	57	15	.263	40	A. Wood, London	45	6	.133
19	Strowger, Guelph	142	37	.261	41	MacGemwell, Hamilt'n	27	2	.074
20	Bradford, Guelph	98	24	.258					

FIELDING AVERAGES—FIRST BASEMEN.

Player and Club	Games.	Chances.	Errors.	Per cent.	Player and Club	Games.	Chances.	Errors.	Per cent.
Morrison, Hamilton	30	289	4	.986	Dr. Wood, London	29	305	18	.941
Lauer, Guelph	35	406	19	.953	Crall, Galt	25	260	20	.923

SECOND BASEMEN.

Hewer, Guelph	23	129	13	.899	Sippi, London	31	217	30	.862
Sullivan, Guelph	11	56	6	.893	Collins, Galt	17	101	14	.861
Dean, Hamilton	33	232	26	.888					

SHORTSTOPS AND THIRD BASEMEN.

J. Cockman, Guelph	16	92	9	.902	Jones, Galt	13	89	17	.809
Strowger, London	32	187	30	.839	Delaney, Gu'ph-Lond'n	29	185	26	807
Pfeiffer, Hamilton	27	119	20	.832	McElroy, Guelph	35	152	32	.789
Phillips, Hamilton	15	70	13	.814	Jennings, Galt	13	89	17	.775
Pfenninger, Hamilton	33	148	28	.811	Tierney, London	6	37	10	.780

OUTFIELDERS.

Player and Club.	Games.	Chances.	Errors.	Per cent.	Player and Club.	Games.	Chances.	Errors.	Per cent.
Hoffner, Hamilton	27	58	5	.914	McDonald, G'lph-Ham.	32	60	9	.850
Malott, Hamilton	22	95	9	.905	Humphrey, G'lph-Lon.	33	80	14	.850
Congalton, Guelph	31	68	7	.897	Stoneman, Hamilton	13	24	4	.838
Lyons, Galt	15	38	5	.869	T. Cockman, Galt	19	66	12	.818
Dark, Guelph	35	98	13	.867	Mertsch, London	22	44	9	.795
McCracken, Guelph	15	44	6	.864	Hutchinson, London	13	22	5	.773
Hynd, London	29	65	9	.862	Ripley, Hamilton	11	18	5	.722
Handley, Guelph	15	27	4	.852	Snyder, London	16	58	17	.707

PITCHERS.

Bradford, Guelph	26	63	4	.937	Plummer, London	9	37	4	.892
Gallagher, Guelph	14	54	4	.926	Moore, Hamilton	8	23	4	.826
Carney, Guelph	17	39	3	.923	MacGemwell, Hamilt'n	9	21	4	.810
A. Wood, London	18	40	4	.900	Clark, Galt	8	26	5	.808
McGinnis, Galt-Ham'n.	25	76	8	.895	Sheere, London	9	12	3	.750

CATCHERS.

Baker, Hamilton	33	209	9	.957	Powers, London	19	130	12	.908
Lyons, Galt	10	42	2	.952	Snyder, London	16	108	12	.890
Roberts, Guelph	35	192	13	.932	Reid, Galt	22	151	19	.874

TEAM BATTING AVERAGES.

Club.	A. B.	Hits.	Per cent.	Club.	A. B.	Hits.	Per cent.
Galt	901	287	.289	London	1203	324	.269
Hamilton	1227	348	.284	Guelph	1294	317	.245

TEAM FIELDING AVERAGES.

Club.	Chan's.	Errors.	Per cent.	Club.	Chan's.	Errors.	Per cent.
Guelph	1503	152	.899	Galt	1422	189	.867
Hamilton	1408	143	.898	London	1128	163	.855

The "best on record" in Canadian base ball history up to date was the match played at Hamilton, Ont., between the Canadian League teams of Hamilton and Galt, on June 23, 1894, a game which yet remains to be surpassed in the annals of Canadian matches.

The following is the game by innings:

	1	2	3	4	5	6	7	8	9	10	11	12	Runs.	Hits.	Errors.
Galt	0	0	0	0	0	0	0	0	0	0	0—		0	8	2
Hamilton	0	0	0	0	0	0	0	0	0	0	0—		0	4	3

Batteries—Burnett and Cockman for Galt, and Moran and Schraeder for Hamilton.

Minor League Pitching Records

New England League.

Rank	Player and Club	Won	Lost	Per cent	Rank	Player and Club	Won	Lost	Per cent
1	Klobedanz, Fall River..	26	6	.813	16	{ Newell, Augusta......	14	14	.500
2	Mains, Bangor..........	14	4	.778		{ Gilder, Bangor, Pawt..	3	3	.500
3	Stevens, Fall River......	12	5	.706	17	Herr, Pawtucket........	9	10	.474
4	{ Wheeler, Bangor......	21	9	.700	18	Lincoln, F. R., Pawt'k't	11	13	.458
	{ Knorr, New Bedford..	7	3	.700	19	Fitzpatrick, Fall River...	4	5	.444
5	{ Braham, Bangor......	14	7	.667	20	{ Standish, Fall River...	3	4	.429
	{ Rhodes, Pawtucket...	12	6	.667		{ Morse, Lewiston......	14	19	.429
6	Weithoff, Bangor........	14	8	.636	21	Yerkes, Pawtucket......	4	6	.400
7	Bristow.................	5	3	.625	22	Killen, Portland........	11	17	.393
8	Braun, New Bedford....	23	14	.622	23	McDougal, Portland....	12	20	.375
9	Moynihan, New Bedford	13	8	.619	24	Horner, Bangor, Pawt'k't	5	9	.357
10	Korwan, Brockton......	23	15	.605	25	{ Dilworth, Augusta.....	8	16	.333
11	Magee, Brockton........	19	14	.576		{ Woods, Portland......	5	10	.333
12	McKenna, Brockton	19	15	.559		{ Kelly, Pawtucket......	5	10	.333
13	{ Day, New Bedford....	10	8	.556	26	Weeks, Augusta.........	11	23	.324
	{ Wilder, Pawtucket....	5	4	.556	27	Hollowell, F. R. N. B...	1	9	.100
14	Leach, Pawtucket	6	5	.545	28	Forrest, Lewiston	1	12	.077
15	Williams, Lewiston......	14	13	.519					

Texas League.

Rank	Player and Club	Won	Lost	Per cent	Rank	Player and Club	Won	Lost	Per cent
1	Gear, Fort Worth........	24	5	.828	14	Wellner, Austin.........	20	21	.488
2	McAllister, Fort Worth.	13	5	.722	15	Callahan, Sher.-Den.....	15	16	.484
3	Keefe, F. W.-S. A.......	13	5	.722	16	Conover, Dallas.........	11	12	.478
4	Isaacs, Fort Worth	21	10	.677	17	Blackburn, Aust.-Dallas	9	10	.474
5	Roach, Houston........	29	17	.630	18	Balsz, Houston..........	8	9	.471
6	Hardy, Galveston.......	20	12	.625	19	Weber, Den.-San Anton.	14	17	.461
7	McCormick, Houston...	23	14	.622	20	Parvin, San Antonio....	19	23	.452
8	Leeson, Houston........	12	9	.571	21	Nevin, San Antonio.....	16	22	.441
9	Burris, Galveston.......	24	20	.545	22	Chard, Austin	10	13	.436
10	Chamberlain, Sher.-Aust	14	12	.538	23	Countryman, Sherman..	5	9	.357
11	Herbert, San Antonio...	15	14	.517	24	Mulkey, Den.-Paris.....	11	21	.344
12	Quigg, Denison	12	11	.522	25	W. Spencer, Den.-Paris.	4	9	.308
13	{ Crowell, Paris-Austin.	13	13	.500	26	{ Staples, Austin-Dallas.	5	12	.294
	{ Page, Galveston.......	7	7	.500		{ Minnehan, Dallas.....	5	12	.294
	{ Colliflower, Austin....	7	7	.500	27	Dwyer, San Antonio....	3	8	.273
	{ Brott, Galveston......	6	6	.500					

Southern Association.

Rank	Player and Club	Won	Lost	Per cent.	Rank	Player and Club	Won	Lost	Per cent.
1	Bates, Columbus	11	3	.786	8	Norton, Atlanta	17	10	.630
2	Callahan, Atlanta	7	2	.778	9	Bailey, Montgomery	19	13	.594
3	McGinnis, N. Orleans	17	7	.708	10	Sheehan, Montgomery	14	12	.538
4	Kellum, Montgomery	19	8	.704	11	Whitrock, Mobile	8	7	.533
5	Carl, New Orleans	19	9	.679	12	Roach, Mobile	6	6	.500
6	Smith, New Orleans	22	12	.647		Adams, Birmingham	4	4	.500
7	Hahn, Mobile	9	5	.643					

Virginia State League.

Pitcher	Games	Per cent.	Pitcher	Games	Per cent.
McFarlan	28	.757	Kagey	10	.500
Tannehill	39	.692	Norcom	25	.480
Stocksdale	24	.667	Quarles	21	.476
Boylan	23	.652	Willis	11	.454
Boyd	22	.636	Coons	31	.451
Brandt	46	.623	Chesebro	18	.444
Stultz	21	.591	Leach	29	.414
Gilpatrick	14	.571	Lampe	17	.412
Pfanmiller	35	.543	Kitson	28	.333
Gilroy	33	.522	Evans	15	.333
Kimball	32	.500	Chandler	10	.300
Mullarkey	36	.500	Armstrong	21	.190

The National League's Testimonial to the Editor of the League Guide.

WASHINGTON, D. C., November 17, 1896.

Henry Chadwick, Esq.:

DEAR MR. CHADWICK—Republics may be ungrateful, but the representative men of our great American game can prove by their many kind and manly acts that they are truly as great as the manly and honorable sport of which they are the recognized champions. At our annual meeting Mr. Byrne offered a motion that, in view of your long service in advancing the best interests of the game with your ready and able pen, and for such services as you may hereafter be able to render the Playing Rules Committee, of which Mr. Hart is chairman, that the treasurer be authorized and directed to pay you a salary of fifty ($50) dollars per month during the balance of your natural life. It is hardly necessary for me to add that I heartily supported Mr. Byrne's motion, and it goes without saying that it was unanimously adopted. I can only add that it was a well merited recognition of your long and faithful service as a champion and advocate of clean, honest base ball, and express the hope that a kind Providence will grant me the pleasure of sending you a monthly check for many long years to come.

Sincerely yours,

(Signed) N. E. YOUNG, President, etc.

The College Arena

NEVER before in the annals of base ball in the colleges and schools of the country has our national game flourished as it did in 1896. So much is public attention called to professional base ball in its season each year, that the advance movement made in the game among the great majority class of the base ball fraternity is almost lost sight of. But while the growth of the game in popularity has been greatly aided by the excellent work done by the National League of professional clubs—especially in regard to the preservation of its character for honest work in all its departments—it is to the colleges and schools of the country at large that the national game must look for its permanent existence; as it is on the college element of the great amateur majority of base ball players that its main support depends.

It is in the West that the game has mostly advanced in favor in the colleges within the past two or three years, and this progress has been largely due to the efforts of that leading college club of the West, the Chicago University Base Ball Club, the team of which, from early April to July of 1896, did such excellent work in advancing base ball interests among the colleges of the Western States. And much of this good work was accomplished through the persistent energy and excellent management of that noted Yale veteran, Mr. A. Alonzo Stagg, the very able director of the department of physical culture in the Chicago University. The worthy President of the University, Mr. William R. Harper, too, by the aid and countenance he has given to rational sports and pastimes in the educational curriculum of the institution, and especially to that game of games in field sports, base ball, has also done valuable service to the cause of physical education in our colleges, thereby promoting the advancement of the position of his University to the high place of Harvard, Yale and Princeton in the great educational institutions of America.

University of Chicago Record. We are indebted to Director Stagg for a full record of the games of the past season's campaign of the University team, which is given on the opposite page.

Date.	Contesting Clubs.	Where Played.	Pitchers.	Score.
April 11	University of Illinois	Champaign..	H. Clarke..........	9-6
" 14	Illinois Cycling Club......	Chicago.....	Nichols†...........	18-6
" 15	Whitings..................	Chicago.....	Brown *...........	19-3
" 16	Lake Forest University....	Chicago.....	G. Clarke †.........	27-3
" 19	Whitings..................	Chicago.....	H. Clarke ‡.........	4-5
" 21	Rush Medical College.....	Chicago.....	Nichols.............	8-5
" 24	Blackburn University.....	Chicago.....	Brown..............	12-9
" 25	Whitings..................	Chicago.....	H. Clarke..........	6-8
" 29	University of Illinois......	Chicago.....	Nichols	10-4
May 1	Chicago (National League).	Chicago.....	H. Clarke..........	2-7
" 2	Northwestern University..	Evanston....	Brown..............	28-5
" 4	Illinois Wesleyan Univ'y..	Chicago.....	Nichols-Clarke *....	22-3
" 7	Rush Medical College.....	Chicago.....	Nichols-Clarke.....	8-4
" 9	University of Michigan....	Chicago	H. Clarke....:.....	7-3
" 11	Detroit (Western League).	Chicago.....	H. Clarke	3-15
" 13	University of Michigan....	Chicago.....	Nichols	0-6
" 16	University of Indiana......	Chicago.....	H. Clarke..........	14-9
" 18	Grinnell College...........	Chicago.....	Brown..............	9-1
" 20	University of Michigan....	Ann Arbor..	H. Clarke..........	2-9
" 22	Cornell University........	Ithaca.......	Nichols.............	8-2
" 23	Orange Athletic Club.....	Orange......	Brown..............	3-6
" 25	University of Pennsylvania	Phila........	H. Clarke..........	15-10
" 27	Yale University............	New Haven..	Nichols-H. Clarke..	5-31
" 28	Harvard University.......	Cambridge...	Brown..............	7-10
June 4	University of Michigan....	Ann Arbor..	Nichols.............	7-3
" 11	University of Michigan....	Ann Arbor..	Nichols.............	10-5
" 13	University of Wisconsin...	Madison.....	Brown..............	9-5
" 27	Brown University.........	Chicago.....	Nichols.............	1-0
" 30	Brown University.........	Chicago.....	H. Clarke..........	3-13
July 2	Brown University.........	Chicago.....	Nichols.............	5-6

* Seven innings. † Eight innings. ‡ Ten innings.

The above table was not sent in in its proper form, as it lacks the names of the opposing club's pitchers.

In sending us records of victories and defeats the formula should be as follows :

Date.	Contesting Clubs.	Where Played.	Pitchers.	In'gs.	Score.
June 27	U. of Chicago vs. Brown U.	Chicago.	Nichols.Su'mersgill	9	1-0

The following is the pitching record for the season :

Pitcher.	Victories.	Defeats.	Per cent. of Victories.	Pitcher.	Victories.	Defeats.	Per cent. of Victories.
G. Clarke........	1	0	1.000	Brown.........	3	5	.625
Nichols.	9	8	.750	H. Clarke.......	6	4	.400

Princeton, Yale and Harvard.

There was really only a dual contest for university championship honors between Harvard, Yale and Princeton in 1896, as Harvard and Yale did not play, and Princeton alone tackled the other two of the university teams.

The college season, in which the three university clubs played in 1896, began at Princeton on May 9, on which occasion the record was as follows:

Date.   Contesting Clubs.   Where Played.   Pitchers.   Score.
May 9.....Princeton vs. Harvard.....Princeton.....Easton—Paine......17-9

By way of offset, the same day Yale's freshmen team beat the Princeton's freshmen at New Haven by 22 to 8, Hecker pitching for Yale against Guerin. The next game of the series also took place at Princeton, when the Yale nine visited Princeton, and they, too, were taken into camp in walk-over form by the Princetons, as will be seen by the appended record:

Date.   Contesting Clubs.   Where Played.   Pitchers.   Score.
May 16......Princeton vs. Yale.......Princeton...Easton—Trudeau....18-0

Easton struck out no less than 16 of the Yale batsmen in this game. Trudeau's support by the Yale fielders, too, was wretched. Yale met Princeton again on May 23, but this time it was at New Haven, and the home team defeated the visitors by the appended score:

Date.   Contesting Clubs.   Where Played.   Pitchers.   Score.
May 23......Yale vs. Princeton......New Haven..Greenway—Easton....7-5

The Princetons played their return game with Harvard at Cambridge on May 30, and it proved to be the exceptional contest of the whole series, as 16 innings had to be played before victory was achieved, and then Princeton won by the appended score:

Date.   Contesting Clubs.   Where Played.   Pitchers.   Score.
May 30....Princeton vs. Harvard.....Cambridge....Wilson—Paine.......8-6

The June campaign of the series began at Princeton on June 6, when the Yale nine visited Princeton, and they had to return home without a single run to their credit in the game, as will be seen by the appended score:

Date.   Contesting Clubs.   Where Played.   Pitchers.   Score.
June 6......Princeton vs. Yale.......Princeton...Wilson—Greenway....5-0

Harvard visited Princeton again on June 10, and this time they returned home victorious, as the appended record shows:

Date.   Contesting Clubs.   Where Played.   Pitchers.   Score.
June 10.. .Harvard vs. Princeton.....Princeton.....Paine—Wilson.......8-5

On June 13 Yale and Princeton played in New York, and Yale won, as the following record shows :

Date. Contesting Clubs. Where Played. Pitchers. Score.
June 13......Yale vs. Princeton.......New York...Greenway—Wilson....8-4

The next game of the series was played at Cambridge on June 18, on which occasion Princeton won the test game of their series with Harvard, as will be seen by the record :

Date. Contesting Clubs. Where Played. Pitchers. Score.
June 18....Princeton vs. Harvard....Cambridge....Wilson—Paine......4-2

The last game of the campaign was played at New Haven on June 23, and it proved to be a closely contested match, Princeton winning by a single run after an 11-inning contest.

Date. Contesting Clubs. Where Played. Pitchers. Score.
June 23......Princeton vs. Yale.. ...New Haven,.Wilson—Greenway....4-3

Here is the full record of the nine games played in 1896 :

CLUB.	Princeton.	Yale.	Harvard.	Victories.	Per cent. of Victories.
Princeton		3	3	6	.667
Yale	2		0	2	.400
Harvard	1	0		1	.250
Defeats	3	3	3	9	

The following are the scores in full of the nine championship contests played between the "big three" of the Eastern universities in 1896 :

GAME OF MAY 9, AT PRINCETON.

PRINCETON.	R.	1B.	P.O.	A.	E.	HARVARD.	R.	1B.	P.O.	A	E.
Ward, s. s	1	2	2	5	2	Dean, 2b	2	2	2	1	0
Easton, p	1	1	0	1	0	Scannell, c	2	0	7	1	1
Altman, r. f	1	2	0	0	0	Burgess, r. f	2	3	2	0	0
Kelly, 1b	0	1	10	0	1	Clarkson, l. f	0	1	2	0	0
Bradley, c. f	2	2	4	2	0	R. Stevenson, 3b	0	1	5	2	1
Smith, c	2	1	4	1	0	Haughton, p., c. f	0	0	2	1	0
Wilson, l. f	2	1	1	0	0	Paine, p., c. f	1	0	0	1	2
Gunster, 3b	4	4	2	1	1	T. Stevenson, 1b	1	0	6	0	0
Wheeler, 2b	4	2	2	0	1	Vincent, s. s	1	0	1	1	4
Titus, c	0	1	1	0	0						
Totals	17	17	26	10	5	Totals	9	7	27	7	8

Princeton.....................0 3 6 4 0 1 2 0 1—17
Harvard ....1 0 0 0 0 0 6 0 2— 9

Earned runs—Princeton, 8; Harvard, 5. Stolen bases—Smith (2), Wilson, Wheeler, Dean, Burgess (2), Vincent. Struck out—By Easton, 6; by Paine, 2; by Haughton, 3. First base on balls—Off Easton, 6; off Paine, 6; off Haughton, 2. Double plays—Bradley and Wheeler, Ward and Kelly. Passed ball—Scannell. Wild pitches—Easton (2), Paine. Umpire— Mr. Campbell. Time of game—2:30.

GAME OF MAY 16, AT PRINCETON.

PRINCETON.	R.	1B.	P.O.	A.	E.	YALE.	R.	1B.	P.O.	A.	E.
Ward, s. s.	1	2	3	2	1	Quinby, 3b	0	0	1	4	1
Easton, p.	1	1	0	1	0	Keator, r. f.	0	1	1	0	0
Altman, r. f.	1	0	0	0	0	Greenway, l. f.	0	0	2	0	1
Kelly, 1b.	2	2	11	1	1	Letton, 1b.	0	1	12	0	0
Bradley, c. f.	3	2	0	0	0	De Saulles, s. s.	0	0	0	1	2
Smith, c.	1	1	2	0	0	Hazen, 2b	0	0	1	3	0
Wilson, l. f.	0	0	0	0	0	Jerrems, c. f.	0	0	5	1	0
Titus, c., l. f.	2	2	10	4	0	Trudeau, p.	0	0	1	1	1
Gunster, 3b.	1	2	0	1	0	Bartlett, c.	0	0	1	0	1
Wheeler, 2b.	1	1	1	2	0	Twombly, c.	0	0	3	1	3
Totals	13	13	27	11	2	Totals	0	2	27	11	9

Princeton.................. 5 0 5 0 0 3 0 0 0—13
Yale....................... 0 0 0 0 0 0 0 0 0— 0

Earned runs—Princeton, 5. Stolen bases—Ward, Altman (2), Bradley (2), Smith, Titus (2), Gunster, Kelly (2). Sacrifice hits—Gunster, Easton, Wilson. First base on balls—Off Trudeau, 4. Struck out—By Easton, 10; by Trudeau, 5. Double play—Jerrems and Letton. Hit by pitcher—Keator. Passed ball—Bartlett. Wild pitch—Trudeau. Umpire—Mr. Harkins. Time of game—2:05.

GAME OF MAY 23, AT NEW HAVEN.

YALE.	R.	1B.	P.O.	A.	E.	PRINCETON.	R.	1B.	P.O.	A.	E.
Quinby, s. s.	0	1	1	6	3	Ward, s. s.	0	0	2	3	1
Murphy, c.	0	1	14	4	0	Easton, p.	0	2	0	2	0
Keator, 2b.	1	1	2	0	1	Altman, r. f.	0	1	1	0	0
Greenway, l. f., p.	1	0	0	0	0	Kelly, 1b.	1	1	12	0	1
Letton, 1b.	1	2	8	0	0	Bradley, c. f.	2	1	1	0	0
De Saulles, 2b.	1	0	2	0	0	Smith, c	1	0	8	1	0
Smith, 3b.	1	1	0	1	0	Titus, l. f.	1	1	2	2	0
Jerrems, c. f.	1	1	0	0	0	Gunster, 3b.	0	1	1	3	2
Trudeau, l. f., p.	1	2	0	2	0	Wheeler, 2b.	0	0	0	3	1
Totals	7	9	27	13	4	Totals	5	7	27	14	5

Yale....................... 3 0 0 2 1 1 0 0 0—7
Princeton.................. 0 1 0 4 0 0 0 0 0—5

Earned runs—Yale, 3; Princeton, 2. Two-base hit—Letton. Three-base hit—Titus. Stolen bases—Yale, 5; Princeton, 4. First base on balls—By Easton, 3; by Trudeau, 2. Hit by pitcher—Ward, De Saulles. Struck out—By Trudeau, 3; by Greenway, 6; by Easton, 7. Wild pitches—Greenway, Easton. Umpire—Mr. Campbell. Time of game—2:45.

GAME OF MAY 30, AT CAMBRIDGE.

PRINCETON.	R.	1B.	P.O.	A.	E.	HARVARD.	R.	1B.	P.O.	A.	E.
Suter, l. f.	1	0	0	0	0	Dean, 2b.	0	1	7	4	0
Wheeler, l. f.	1	2	4	0	0	Scannell, c.	1	2	11	2	0
Easton, p., c. f.	3	3	2	0	2	Burgess, r. f.	1	1	2	0	0
Bradley, 1b.	0	3	24	1	1	Clarkson, c. f.	1	2	5	1	1
Titus, c.	0	1	9	3	1	Haughton, 1b.	2	3	16	1	0
Gunster, 3b.	0	0	2	8	2	Rand, l. f.	1	0	5	0	0
Altman, r. f.	0	2	3	1	0	Stevenson, 3b.	0	2	2	4	0
Smith, 2b.	0	2	2	6	1	Paine, p.	0	2	0	3	2
Wilson, c. f., p.	1	3	0	3	0	Chandler, s. s.	0	2	0	3	1
Ward, s. s.	2	1	2	8	0						
Totals	8	17	48	30	7	Totals	6	15	48	18	4

Princeton.............. 0 0 0 0 4 0 0 1 0 0 0 0 0 1 0 2—8
Harvard............... 5 0 0 0 0 0 0 0 0 0 0 0 0 1 0 0—6

Earned runs—Harvard, 2; Princeton, 5. Sacrifice hits—Dean (2), Titus. Stolen bases—Smith, Bradley, Easton, Rand, Stevenson, Haughton, Chandler. First base on balls—Rand, Paine, Scannell, Clarkson, Gunster, Altman. Struck out—Scannell (2), Rand (2), Paine, Suter (2), Smith (3), Easton, Altman. Double plays—Gunster, Bradley and Titus (2). Wild pitches—Easton (2); Paine (2). Hit by pitched ball—Burgess. Time of game—3:20. Umpire—Mr. O'Rourke.

GAME OF JUNE 6, AT PRINCETON.

PRINCETON.	R.	1B.	P.O.	A.	E.	YALE.	R.	1B.	P.O.	A.	E.
Ward, s.s.	0	0	1	3	0	Keator, r. f.	0	0	1	0	0
Easton, l. f.	1	0	2	1	0	Murphy, c.	0	0	14	1	0
Bradley, c. f.	2	1	3	0	0	Greenway, p.	0	2	0	1	1
Kelly, 1b.	0	2	9	0	0	Letton, 1b.	0	0	4	0	0
Gunster, 3b.	0	0	1	3	0	Quinby, s. s.	0	1	1	0	1
Altman, r. f.	0	1	0	0	0	De Saulles, 2b.	0	0	0	3	0
Smith, c.	0	1	9	3	1	Smith, 3b.	0	0	1	3	0
Wilson, p.	1	1	0	1	1	Jerrems, c. f.	0	0	5	0	0
Sankey, 2b.	1	0	2	1	0	Trudeau, l. f.	0	0	1	0	0
Totals	5	6	27	12	2	Totals	0	3	27	8	2

Princeton.................... 2 2 0 0 1 0 0 0 0—5
Yale........................ 0 0 0 0 0 0 0 0 0—0

Earned runs—Princeton, 2. Stolen bases—Gunster, Smith (2), Sankey (2), Bradley, Kelly, De Saulles, Keator. Double play—Easton and Gunster. First base on balls—Off Wilson, 7; off Greenway, 4. Struck out—By Wilson, 8; by Greenway, 12. Hit by pitcher—Gunster. Wild pitch—Wilson. Umpire—Mr. Campbell. Time of game—2:30.

GAME OF JUNE 10, AT PRINCETON.

HARVARD.	R.	1B.	P.O.	A.	E.	PRINCETON.	R.	1B.	P.O.	A.	E.
Dean, 2b.	1	2	2	2	1	Sankey, 2b.	1	1	2	1	1
Scannell, c.	1	0	6	2	0	Easton, l. f., p.	1	0	1	0	0
Burgess, r. f.	3	1	2	0	0	Bradley, c. f.	0	0	1	0	0
Clarkson, c. f.	1	2	3	0	0	Kelly, c.	0	0	10	0	2
Haughton, 1b.	0	1	6	0	0	Gunster, 3b.	0	1	2	2	0
Rand, l. f.	0	1	4	0	0	Altman, r. f.	0	1	1	0	0
Stevenson, 3b.	1	0	0	2	2	Smith, c.	1	0	6	1	0
Paine, p.	0	0	1	1	0	Wilson, p.	0	1	0	2	0
Chandler, s. s.	1	1	2	1	0	Ward, s. s.	2	0	1	5	3
Totals	8	8	*26	8	3	Totals	5	4	24	11	6

* Smith out; hit by batted ball.

Harvard......................... 0 1 1 0 0 3 3 x—8
Princeton....................... 0 0 2 2 0 1 0 0—5

Earned runs—Harvard, 5; Princeton, 2. Three base hit—Rand. Two base hits—Gunster, Altman. Stolen bases—Burgess, Clarkson, Dean, Sankey (3), Ward (2), Smith, Bradley. Base on balls—Off Paine, 7; off Wilson, 1; off Easton, 3. Struck out—By Paine, 5; by Wilson, 1; by Easton, 3. Hit by pitcher—Burgess (2), Smith, Sankey. Passed ball—Smith. Wild pitch—Paine. Time of game—2:00. Umpire—Mr. Betts.

GAME OF JUNE 13, AT MANHATTAN FIELD, N. Y.

YALE.	R.	1B.	P.O.	A.	E.	PRINCETON.	R.	1B.	P.O.	A.	E.
Keator, r. f.	1	1	1	0	0	Sankey, 2b	0	0	4	1	1
Quinby, s. s.	1	0	1	4	1	Easton, l. f., p.	1	1	0	1	0
Greenway, p.	0	2	0	1	0	Bradley, 1b., c. f.	1	0	12	0	2
Letton, 1b.	1	0	5	0	0	Titus, c. f.	0	1	3	1	1
De Saulles, 2b.	3	2	2	0	0	Kelly, 1b	0	0	0	0	0
Smith, 3b.	1	2	4	3	1	Gunster, 3b.	0	1	3	2	2
Jerrems, c. f.	0	1	4	0	0	Altman, r. f.	1	1	0	0	0
Trudeau, l. f.	0	0	3	0	0	Smith, c.	1	1	5	2	0
Murphy, c.	1	1	7	2	1	Wilson, p.	0	0	0	4	0
						Ward, s. s.	0	1	0	4	1
Totals	8	9	27	10	3	Wheeler*	0	0	0	0	0
						Totals	4	6	27	15	7

* Batted for Sankey in the ninth inning.

Yale .... 0 0 0 1 0 2 0 5 0—8
Princeton .... 1 2 0 0 0 0 0 1 0—4

Earned runs—Yale, 2; Princeton, 1. Two-base hits—Keator, Greenway, Smith (Yale) (2), Altman, Smith (Princeton). Stolen bases—Letton, De Saulles, Smith (Yale), Easton Bradley, Smith (Princeton). First base on errors—Yale, 7; Princeton, 2. First base on balls—Off Greenway, 4; off Wilson, 3. Struck out—By Greenway, 6; by Wilson, 5. Hit by pitcher—By Wilson, 1. Left on bases—Yale, 9; Princeton, 6. Passed balls—Smith, 2; Murphy, 1. Time of game—2:15. Umpire—Mr. Betts.

GAME OF JUNE 18, AT CAMBRIDGE.

PRINCETON.	R.	1B.	P.O.	A.	E.	HARVARD.	R.	1B.	P.O.	A.	E.
Bradley, c. f.	1	0	2	0	0	Dean, 2b	1	0	2	3	1
Easton, l. f.	1	1	0	0	1	Scannell, c.	1	2	0	1	0
Kelly, 1b	0	0	14	0	0	Burgess, r. f.	0	0	2	0	0
Titus, c.	1	1	5	0	0	Clarkson, c. f.	0	3	1	0	0
Altman, r. f.	0	0	1	0	0	Haughton, 1b.	0	1	16	0	0
Wilson, p.	1	1	0	3	0	Rand, l. f.	0	0	4	0	0
Smith, 2b.	0	1	4	6	0	Stevenson, 3b.	0	1	3	3	0
Gunster, 3b.	0	0	2	1	0	Paine, p.	0	1	0	4	2
Ward, s. s.	0	1	2	5	0	Chandler, s. s.	0	1	0	6	1
Totals	4	5	30	15	1	Totals	2	8	30	16	5

Princeton .... 2 0 0 0 0 0 0 0 2—4
Harvard .... 1 0 0 0 0 0 1 0 0—2

Earned run—Harvard. Two-base hits—Scannell, Wilson. Three-base hit—Smith. Struck out—By Wilson, 4; by Paine, 3. Passed balls—Scannell, 2. Wild pitch—Paine. Double plays—Ward and Kelly; Ward, Smith and Kelly; Gunster, Smith and Kelly. Umpire—Mr. O'Rourke. Time of game—2:05.

GAME OF JUNE 23, AT NEW HAVEN.

PRINCETON.	R.	1B.	P.O.	A.	E.	YALE.	R.	1B.	P.O.	A.	E.
Bradley, c. f.	1	2	4	0	0	Keator, r. f.	1	1	2	0	0
Easton, l. f.	1	1	2	0	0	De Saulles, 2b.	0	0	6	1	0
Kelly, 1b.	0	2	10	1	0	Greenway, p.	1	1	1	1	0
Titus, c.	0	1	5	0	0	Letton, 1b.	0	3	8	2	2
Altman, r. f.	0	1	1	0	0	F. Smith, 3b.	0	0	1	2	1
Wilson, p.	0	0	3	2	0	Murphy, c.	0	0	7	4	1
Smith, 2b	1	0	2	2	1	Jerrems, c. f.	0	0	2	0	0
Gunster, 3b.	0	0	3	5	1	Trudeau, l. f.	1	2	2	0	1
Ward, s. s.	1	0	2	4	0	Bartlett, s. s.	0	1	3	1	1
Totals	4	7	*32	14	2	Totals	3	8	†32	11	6

* Letton out for interference.   † Winning run scored with two out.

Princeton............ 0   0 2 0 0 1 0 0 0 0   1—4
Yale................. 2   0 0 0 0 0 1 0 0 0   0—3
    Earned runs—Yale, 2 ; Princeton, 1. Three base hits -Trudeau (2).
Stolen bases—Letton, Easton, Bartlett, Titus, Keator, Kelly, Smith.
Base on balls—Off Greenway, 6; off Wilson, 3. Hit by pitcher—Titus,
Smith, Easton, Greenway, De Saulles. Struck out—By Greenway, 5 ; by
Wilson, 2. Wild pitch—Wilson. Time of game—3:00. Umpire—Mr. Keefe.

The summary record of the three clubs, showing the victories
and defeats with the prominent college clubs, is as follows:

PRINCETON.

Record of 1896.	Princeton.	Yale.	Harvard.	Brown.	Univ'y of Pa.	U. of Chicago.	U. of Virginia.	U. of Vermont.	Cornell.	Wesleyan.	Georgetown.	Lafayette.	Lehigh.	Hobart.	Williams.	Amherst.	Dartmouth.
Victories..........	.	3	3	0	0	0	1	0	1	0	1	2	1	1	0	0	0
Defeats...........	.	2	1	0	0	0	1	0	1	0	0	0	0	0	0	0	0

YALE.

| Victories........ | 2 | . | 0 | 0 | 0 | 1 | 2 | 1 | 0 | 2 | 1 | 1 | 0 | 0 | 0 | 2 | 0 |
| Defeats.......... | 3 | . | 0 | 3 | 0 | 0 | 0 | 0 | 0 | 1 | 0 | 0 | 0 | 0 | 2 | 0 | 0 |

HARVARD.

| Victories........ | 1 | 0 | . | 2 | 3 | 0 | 0 | 0 | 2 | 0 | 0 | 0 | 0 | 0 | 0 | 1 | 1 | 1 |
| Defeats.......... | 3 | 0 | . | 2 | 0 | 0 | 0 | 0 | 0 | 0 | 0 | 0 | 0 | 0 | 0 | 1 | 1 | 2 |

The Princeton Record for 1896.

The Princeton team played in thirty regular matches during their spring and early summer campaign of 1896, of which nine games were with Yale and Harvard, and in these contests they won 6 and lost 3. They did not have a game with either the University of Pennsylvania or Brown; and they only came out even, game and game, with Cornell and the University of Virginia. They defeated Georgetown in one game, won two from Lafayette and won one each from Wesleyan and Hobart College. Among the defeats they sustained were two from Yale, and one each from the University of Virginia and Cornell ; also with the Orange Athletic Club and the Oritani Field Club. Their professional games were all lost, Boston beating them by 13 to 4, New York by 4 to 1 and Richmond by 11 to 5. They shut out Yale by 13 to 0 and 5 to 0, Cornell by 22 to 0, Dickinson College by 25 to 0, and were "Chicagoed" by the Oritanis by 5 to 0. They also won games with the Manhattan College nine, the State College of Pennsylvania, Lawrenceville nine, Washington and Lee University, Rutgers College and the University of North Carolina. Here is the record:

PRINCETON RECORD FOR 1896.

Date.	Contesting Clubs.	Where Played.	Pitchers.	Score.
Mar. 28	Princeton vs. Rutgers......	Princeton....	Wilson........Poole	23-2
April 1	Princeton vs. Hobart.......	Princeton....	Wilson......Hooker	23-4
" 3	Princeton vs. U. of Va......	Charlot'sv'le	Easton....McGuire	5-4
" 4	Princeton vs. W. & Lee U..	Lynchburg..	....	18-1
" 6	Princeton vs. U. of N. C....	Greensboro..	...............‡	10-8
" 7	Princeton vs. Georgetown..	Washington.	Easton.....Tracey†	11-5
" 8	Richmond vs. Princeton....	Richmond...	...............*	4-1
" 10	Boston vs. Princeton........	Princeton....	Stivetts............	13-4
" 11	New York vs. Princeton....	New York...	Seymour.....Easton	11-10
" 15	Princeton vs. Lafayette.....	Easton......	Easton......Altman	8-1
" 18	Princeton vs. Pa. State Col..	Easton......	Easton......Nesbitt	18-5
" 22	Princeton vs. Dickinson....	Princeton....	Wilson....Williams	25-0
" 25	Princeton vs. Orange A.C..	Orange......	Easton...Westervelt	17-5
" 27	Princeton vs. Lawrenceville.	Princeton....	Altman.....Arratt*	16-1
" 29	Princeton vs. Lehigh.......	Princeton....	...............‡	19-1
May 2	Cornell vs. Princeton	Ithaca.......	Young......Wilson§	12-10
" 2	Princeton (Fresh.) vs. St. P.	Garden City.	Guerin.........Hall	8-3
" 5	Princeton vs. Lawrenceville.	Princeton....	Easton.Cadwallader	15-1
" 6	Princeton vs. Manhattan...	New York...	Easton.....Driscoll	13-5
" 9	Princeton vs. Harvard......	Princeton....	Easton...Haughton	17-9
" 9	Yale vs. Princeton (Fresh.).	New Haven.	P. Hecker...Guerin	22-8
" 13	Princeton vs. Lafayette....	Easton......	Wilson...Driesbach	9-8
" 16	Princeton vs. Yale.........	Princeton....	Easton ....Trudeau	13-0
" 20	U. of Va. vs. Princeton.....	Princeton....	Lockett......Wilson	10-6
" 23	Yale vs. Princeton..........	New Haven.	Greenway...Easton	7-5
" 27	Princeton vs. Cornell	Princeton....	Altman.......Young	22-0
" 30	Princeton vs. Harvard.....	Cambridge..	Wilson......Paine¶	8-6
June 3	Orange A. C. vs. Princeton.	Orange......	Priest........Easton	10-8
" 6	Princeton vs. Yale..........	Princeton....	Wilson...Greenway	5-0
" 10	Harvard vs. Princeton......	Princeton....	Paine........Wilson	8-5
" 13	Yale vs. Princeton..........	New York...	Greenway...Wilson	8-4
" 18	Princeton vs. Harvard......	Cambridge..	Wilson ......Paine§	4-2
" 20	Oritani Field vs. Princeton .	Hack'nsack.	Murphy.....Easton	5-0
" 23	Princeton vs. Yale..........	New Haven.	Wilson..Greenway‖	4-3

* Five innings.   † Six innings.   ‡ Seven innings.   § Ten innings.
‖ Eleven innings.   ¶ Sixteen innings.

BATTING AVERAGES.   FIELDING AVERAGES.

Player.	Runs.	S.B.	Per cent.	Player.	Put Outs.	Assists.	Errors.	Per cent.
Bradley.................	46	28	.397	Bradley, c. f., 1b........	87	9	5	.950
Easton..................	36	11	.353	Altman, r. f., p.........	33	17	3	.943
Altman.................	36	14	.336	Titus, c., l. f., c. f......	124	36	10	.941
Sankey.................	14	9	.320	Kelly, 1b...............	244	6	16	.939
Kelly...................	34	19	.312	Smith, c., 2b., 1b.......	138	42	12	.939
Titus...................	32	11	.293	Easton, l. f., c. f., p.....	33	28	6	.910
Gunster................	36	13	.286	Wilson, p., l. f., c. f.....	20	36	6	.903
Smith..................	26	22	.279	Ward, s. s..............	41	94	16	.894
Wilson.................	25	12	.278	Gunster, 3b............	39	51	11	.891
Ward...................	43	25	.250	Wheeler, s. s., 2b., l. f..	13	17	5	.857
Wheeler................	8	1	.250	Sankey, 2b., c. f........	16	7	9	.786
Jayne..................	3	1	.142	Jayne, p., r. f..........	2	5	2	.777

The following are the batting and fielding averages of the Princeton players of 1896 who took part in the regular championship contests of the season:

BATTING AVERAGES.

FIELDING AVERAGES.

Player.	Runs.	S. B.	Per cent.	Player.	Put Outs.	Assists.	Errors.	Per cent.
Titus......	4	3	.308	Bradley, c. f., 1b........	50	3	2	.963
Wheeler....	6	1	.294	Titus, c., l. f., c. f......	33	10	2	.955
Wilson	5	1	.290	Smith, 2b., c............	46	21	4	.943
Bradley.....	12	9	.285	Kelly, 1b................	75	1	5	.941
Easton......	10	5	.257	Easton, p., l. f..........	8	7	1	.937
Gunster.....	5	3	.225	Wilson, p., l. f..........	4	16	2	.909
Altman......	3	2	.225	Altman, r. f.............	8	1	1	.900
Kelly.......	3	5	.200	Ward, s. s..............	15	42	7	.890
Smith.......	7	9	.200	Wheeler, 2b., l. f........	7	6	2	.866
Ward.......	7	6	.175	Sankey, 2b..............	8	3	2	.856
Sankey......	2	4	.143	Gunster, 3b.............	15	23	7	.944

The Yale Record for 1896.

The Yale nine of 1896 began outdoor practice as early as March 22, and the Law School team played two games at Washington in March with the nines of the Columbian University and the Catholic University, of that city, both of which they won. Yale University's first game, however, was with the Johns Hopkins nine at Baltimore, and their campaign lasted from that date to June 23. Their Southern trip in April resulted in victories at Charlottesville, Old Point Comfort and Newport News. Their victories over strong college nines included two with Princeton, two with the University of Virginia, two with the Wesleyans, two with Amherst, and one each with the University of Chicago and the University of Vermont, and Georgetown and Lafayette Colleges. Also with the Oritani Field Club, the Andover nine, against their graduates' nine, and the Johns Hopkins nine. They were defeated three times by Princeton, three times by Brown, twice by Williams College and once each by the Orange Athletics and the Wesleyans. In their games with professional teams, the New Yorks "Chicagoed" the Yales by 4 to 0, and Princeton by 13 to 0 and 5 to 0; while Yale "shutout" the Amhersts by 13 to 0. Their best game was the eleven-inning contest at New Haven on June 23, when Princeton won by a single run, 4 to 3. Here is the team's full record for 1896:

Date.	Contesting Clubs.	Where Played.	Pitchers.	Score.
Mar. 31	Johns Hopkins vs. Yale....	Baltimore...	Herrick..Buck'gh'm	13-5
April 3	Yale vs. Hampton..........	Old Pt. C'ft.,	Smith..............	32-5
" 4	Yale vs. U. of Virginia......	Charlot'sv'le	Greenway..Lockitt*	11-4
" 6	Yale vs. U. of N. C.........	Greensboro..	Smith..............	8-4
" 7	Yale vs. U. of N. C.........	Greensboro..	Trudeau...McGuire	8-7
" 8	Yale vs. Georgetown........	N'port News	Trudeau	16-12
" 11	Yale vs. Wesleyan..........	New Haven..	Smith.......Tyrrell	11-7
" 14	New York vs. Yale..........	New York...	Seymour..Greenway	4-0
" 18	Williams vs. Yale...........	New Haven	Lewis......Trudeau	5-4
" 25	Brown vs. Yale.............	New Haven.	Sum'erg'l.Greenw'y	9-6
" 28	Yale vs. Amherst............	New Haven.	Trudeau......Tyler	13-0
" 28	Yale (F.) vs. Amherst (F.) .	Amherst.....	....	17-1
May 1	Yale vs. Andover............	Andover	Thorne....Goodwin	5-3
" 1	Yale Con. vs. U. of N.Y....	Geneva......	....	6-3
" 2	Brown vs. Yale.............	Providence..	Brady......Trudeau	6-1
" 6	Yale vs. Lafayette..........	New Haven.	Trudeau..Driesbach	11-3
" 9	Orange A. C. vs. Yale......	Orange......	West'vlt..Greenway	11-9
" 9	Yale (F.) vs. Princeton (F.)..	New Haven.	F. Hecker...Guerin	22-8
" 11	Yale vs. Wesleyan..........	Middletown..	Trudeau.....Tyrrell	8-4
" 13	Yale vs. Graduates..........	New Haven.	Trudeau.....Carter	15-3
" 16	Princeton vs. Yale..........	Princeton....	Easton.....Trudeau	18-0
" 20	Yale vs. Oritani	New Haven.	Greenway..Murphy	6-2
" 23	Yale vs. Princeton..........	New Haven.	Greenway...Easton	7-5
" 27	Yale vs. U. of Chicago......	New Haven.	Trudeau....Nichols	31-5
" 30	Brown vs. Yale.............	Providence..	Brady....Greenway	6-4
June 3	Yale vs. U. of Vermont.....	New Haven.	Trudeau.....Miner	19-7
" 6	Princeton vs. Yale..........	Princeton....	Wilson...Greenway	5-0
" 13	Yale vs. Princeton..........	New York...	Greenway...Wilson	8-4
" 17	Yale vs. Amherst...........	Amherst.....	Hecker....Johnston	4-2
" 18	Williams vs. Yale...........	Williamst'n..	Lewis......Trudeau	11-1
" 23	Princeton vs. Yale..........	New Haven.	Wilson..Greenway†	4-3

* Eight innings. † Eleven innings.

BATTING AVERAGES.

Player.	Per cent.
Greenway, pitcher..............	.424
De Saulles, second base.........	.329
Letton, first base...............	.305
Keator, right field..............	.296
Quinby, shortstop..............	.290
Trudeau, left field..............	.286
Bartlett, substitute.............	.265
Smith, third base...............	.255
Hazen, substitute..............	.222
Thorne, substitute..............	.222
Twombly, substitute............	.218
Jerrems, centre field	.216
Murphy, catcher................	.190
McCandloss, substitute.........	.178

FIELDING AVERAGES.

Player.	Per cent.
Letton, first base................	.982
Murphy, catcher................	.970
Trudeau, left field..............	.942
Twombly, substitute............	.926
Thorne, substitute..............	.926
Jerrems, centre field............	.919
De Saulles, second base.........	.898
McCandloss, substitute.........	.868
Greenway, pitcher..............	.865
Smith, third base...............	.852
Keator, right field..............	.833
Hazen, substitute...............	.828
Bartlett, substitute.............	.823
Quinby, shortstop	.797

The Harvard Record for 1896.

The Harvard team held its first field day on March 25, when their freshmen's nine opened the season with the Boston Latin School on April 12, and the campaign continued from that date until June 23, when their last match game was played.

Date.	Contesting Clubs.	Where Played.	Pitchers.	Score.
April 12	Harvard (F.) vs. Boston L.S.	Cambridge..	....	13-9
" 13	Morrills (Prof.) vs. Harvard	Cambridge..	....	14-10
" 16	Harvard vs. Tufts..........	Cambridge..	Haughton...Curran	18-6
" 18	Brockton vs. Harvard......	Brockton....	McGee ..... Paine†	5-4
" 20	Harvard vs. Newton A. A..	Boston......	....‡	5-3
" 21	Harvard vs. Bangor........	Cambridge..	Haughton..........*	15-1
" 23	Harvard vs. Pawtucket.....	Cambridge..	Paine. .... Rhodes	15-8
" 25	Harvard vs. Dartmouth....	Hanover ...	Paine.......Tabor†	4-2
" 28	Dartmouth vs. Harvard....	Cambridge..	Crolius .....Cozzens	13-4
" 29	Dartmouth vs. Harvard....	Cambridge..	Tabor ....Paine	7-6
May 2	Williams vs. Harvard.......	Williamst'n..	Lewis....Haughton	2-1
" 5	Brown vs. Harvard.........	Cambridge..	Summersgill..Paine	9-7
" 9	Princeton vs. Harvard.....	Princeton....	Easton ....Paine	17-9
" 11	Harvard vs. Amherst.......	Cambridge..	Paine......Johnson	8-3
" 13	Harvard vs. Williams......	Cambridge..	Haughton....Lewis	10-9
" 16	Harvard vs. Cornell.......	Ithaca.......	Paine.......Young	13-6
" 18	Newton A. A. vs. Harvard..	Cambridge..	Dowd....Haughton	7-2
" 20	Harvard vs. Brown.........	Cambridge..	Paine..Summersgill	6-1
" 23	Harvard vs. Univ. of Pa....	Philadelphia	Paine....O'Donnell	8-3
" 27	Amherst vs. Harvard.......	Amherst	Boyden,......Paine	9-5
" 28	Harvard vs. U. of Chicago.	Cambridge..	Haughton ... Brown	10-7
" 30	Princeton vs. Harvard......	Cambridge..	Wilson...... Paine‖	8-6
June 1	Newton A. A. vs. Harvard.	Cambridge..	....	15-7
" 3	Harvard vs. Brown.........	Providence..	Paine.........Brady	6-1
" 6	Harvard vs. Univ. of Pa...	Cambridge..	Paine ......Wunder	11-3
" 10	Harvard vs. Princeton.. ...	Princeton.,..	Paine....... .Wilson	8-5
" 13	Harvard vs. Cornell........	Cambridge..	Haughton....Young	10-3
" 15	Brown vs. Harvard........	Cambridge..	Summersgill..Paine	4-0
" 18	Princeton vs. Harvard.....	Cambridge..	Wilson ......Paine†	4-2
" 23	Harvard vs. Univ. of Pa...	Cambridge..	Paine ...... Ritchie	2-0

* Five innings. † Seven innings. ‡ Ten innings. § Twelve innings.
‖ Sixteen innings.

BATTING AVERAGES.

Player.	Runs.	S. H.	S. B.	Per cent.
Dean, second base	32	6	20	....
Scannell, catcher	25	7	6	....
Burgess, right field	27	5	24	....
Clarkson, shortstop, c. f.	15	3	2	....
Haughton, c. f., p., 1b...	25	3	5	....
Rand, left field	22	2	18	.188
R. Stevenson, third base	16	2	12	.229
Paine, c. f., p., 1b	28	2	7	.193
Chandler, shortstop.....	13	0	2	.260
T. Stevenson, first base.	11	2	9	.248

FIELDING AVERAGES.

Player.	Put Outs.	Assists.	Errors.	Per cent.
Dean, second base.....	70	82	16	....
Scannell, catcher.......	178	28	8	....
Burgess, right field....	31	5	8	.818
Clarkson, s. s., c. f....	34	18	7	.870
Haughton, c. f., p., 1b..	141	38	7	....
Rand, left field........	48	2	1	....
R. Stevenson, 3d base..	41	60	24	.808
Paine, c. f., p., 1b......	48	68	13	.895
Chandler, shortstop....	25	30	16	.776
T. Stevenson, 1st base..	149	4	8	....

New England Intercollegiate Base Ball Association. The most successful of all the college leagues of the country for the past ten years has undoubtedly been that of the New England Intercollegiate Association, composed of Amherst, Dartmouth and Williams. It has been admirably governed and managed throughout, and in a manner well calculated to promote the welfare and interests of collegiate base ball in particular and of college athletics in general.

We give below Article 4, of the Constitution of the New England Intercollegiate Association of 1896, as a sample of the rules which should govern college base ball associations desirous of preserving strict amateur playing in their athletic ranks. The first article of the constitution, on the objects of the association, is as follows:

SECTION 3. The object of this Association shall be the promotion of pure college athletics on the "diamond," the "gridiron" and the "track."

In other words, alike on the base ball and foot ball fields and in general athletic games. Its fourth article is appended:

QUALIFICATIONS FOR ELIGIBILITY.

SECTION 1. The eligibility of all participants in championship games shall be subject to the following rules:

Any student of good and regular standing in college shall be eligible to participate in championship contests with the following exceptions:

1. No student shall represent his college for more than four years.

2. No student who has ever been registered as a member of any other college or university shall be eligible until he has been in attendance as a registered student for three full, consecutive terms.

3. No "special" or "partial course" student shall be eligible until he has been in attendance as a registered student for three full consecutive terms.

No "special" whomsoever shall be eligible unless he is taking at least twelve hours per week of prescribed study.

A "special" or "partial student" is hereby defined as one who is not pursuing a regular course for a degree. Whether according to the above definition a student is or is not a "special" or "partial student" shall be decided by the President of the college at which he is in attendance. This decision shall be final.

Louis Heuermann, President Texas Association.
T. J. Hickey, President Western Association.
Henry Powers, President Southern Association.

T. C. Griffin, Manager Scranton Club.
E. Hanlon, President Baltimore Club.
G. F. Kuntzsch, President Syracuse Club.
Dan Shannon, Manager Rochester Club.

A. A. Irwin, Pres. Toronto Club.   W. H. Draper, Pres. Providence Club.
L. J. Powers,   E. F. Bogert,
Pres. Springfield Club.   Pres. Wilkesbarre Club.
James Franklin, President Buffalo Club.
J. H. Buckley, Pres. Rochester Club.   W. G. Parke, Pres. Scranton Club.

J. W. REED,
Capt. Ohio State University.
I. C. KAREL,
University of Wisconsin.
WILLIAM JOHN FULTON,
Capt. Illinois Base Ball Team.

CHARLES WITTER,
Northwestern University.
LAWRENCE KNESS,
University of Kansas.
OTIS H. MACLAY,
Northwestern University.

4. No post-graduate, no member of any graduate school, nor member of the Dartmouth Medical School, shall be eligible.

5. No man who is induced to enter or to remain in college for the purpose of participating in athletics by payment of any part of his expenses, by anyone whomsoever, shall be eligible.

6. No man who is a professional according to the A. A. U. rules shall be eligible.

The Intercollegiate Championship Records of 1896.

Williams College again had the honor of carrying off the championship pennant of the Intercollegiate Association in 1896 as their club team did in 1895. The 'championship campaign opened at Amherst on May 6, on which occasion the home team defeated the visitors from Williamstown by 3 to 2, only after a closely-contested match, both Gregory and Lewis doing effective box-work. The record is as follows:

Date.	Contesting Clubs.	Where Played.	Pitchers.	Score.
May 6	Amherst vs. Williams	Amherst	Gregory......Lewis	3-2
" 15	Dartmouth vs. Amherst	Hanover	Tabor......Boyden	7-2
" 16	Amherst vs. Dartmouth	Hanover	Johnston....Crolius	9-5
" 22	Williams vs. Dartmouth	Will'mstown	Lewis........Tabor	15-7
" 23	Williams vs. Dartmouth	Will'mstown	Lewis.......Crolius	11-2
" 30	Williams vs. Amherst	Will'mstown	Lewis......Johnston	10-9
June 5	Williams vs. Dartmouth	Hanover	Lewis.......Crolius	15-2
" 6	Dartmouth vs. Williams	Hanover	Conway......Lewis	7-5
" 12	Amherst vs. Dartmouth	Amherst	Boyden....Conway	3-2
" 13	Amherst vs. Dartmouth	Amherst	Johnston...Conway	14-3
" 20	Williams vs. Amherst	Will'mstown	Lewis......Gregory	7-3
" 22	Williams vs. Amherst	Amherst	Lewis.....Johnston	5-3

RECORD OF 1896.

Club.	Williams.	Amherst.	Dartmouth.	Victories.	Per cent. of Victories.
Williams		3	3	6	.750
Amherst	1		3	4	.500
Dartmouth	1	1	-	2	.250
Defeats	2	4	6	12	

Outside of the championship series, the games played by the three colleges were as follows:

THE WILLIAMS COLLEGE RECORD.

Date.	Contesting Clubs.	Where Played.	Pitchers.	Score.
April 17	Wesleyan vs. Williams	Middletown.	Beeman......Lewis	3-2
" 18	Williams vs. Yale	New Haven.	Lewis....Trudeau	5-4
" 22	Williams vs. Holyoke A. A.	Williamst'n.	Lewis........Smith	29-12
" 25	Holy Cross vs. Williams	Worcester..	Pappalau....Corey	8-4
May 2	Williams vs. Harvard	Williamst'n.	Lewis....Haughton	2-1
" 13	Harvard vs. Williams	Cambridge...	Haughton....Lewis	10-9
" 16	Holy Cross vs. Williams	Williamst'n.	Pappalau....Lewis	12-1
" 27	Cuban Giants vs. Williams..	Williamst'n.	Miller......Corey	15-8
June 3	Williams vs. Trinity	Williamst'n.	Lewis...Coggeshall	9-4
" 10	Williams vs. Laureates	Williamst'n.	Lewis......Corliss	16-1
" 18	Williams vs. Yale	Williamst'n.	Lewis....Trudeau	11-1

THE AMHERST COLLEGE RECORD.

Date.	Contesting Clubs.	Where Played.	Pitchers.	Score.
April 22	Wesleyan vs. Amherst	Middletown.	Tyrrell...Boyden*	10-9
" 28	Yale vs. Amherst	New Haven.	Trudeau.....Tyler	13-0
" 29	Amherst vs. Wesleyan	Amherst....	Boyden....Tyrrell	5-2
May 2	Holy Cross vs. Amherst	Amherst....	Pappalau.Johnston	9-5
" 9	Amherst vs. Trinity	Hartford....	Boyden.Coggeshall	20-2
" 11	Harvard vs. Amherst	Cambridge..	Paine....Johnston	8-3
" 13	Amherst vs. Techs, of Wor'r.	Amherst....	Chase.....Knowles	14-7
" 20	Amherst vs. Tufts	Amherst....	Johnston...Curran	2-1
" 26	Cuban Giants vs. Amherst	Amherst....	Miller.....Boyden*	7-6
" 27	Amherst vs. Harvard	Amherst....	Johnston.....Paine	9-5
June 2	University of Vt.vs. Amherst	Amherst....	Dinsmore...Boyden	2-1
" 6	Orange A. C. vs. Amherst	Orange......	Westervelt.Johns'n	18-9
" 17	Yale vs. Amherst	Amherst....	Hecker...Johnston	4-2

* Ten innings.

THE DARTMOUTH COLLEGE RECORD.

Date.	Contesting Clubs.	Where Played.	Pitchers.	Score.
April 25	Harvard vs. Dartmouth	Hanover....	Paine.......Tabor	4-2
" 27	Dartmouth vs. Tufts	Medford....	Conway....Curran	7-5
" 28	Dartmouth vs. Harvard	Cambridge..	Crolius......Paine	13-4
" 29	Dartmouth vs. Harvard	Cambridge..	Tabor......Cozzens	7-6
" 30	Brown vs. Dartmouth	Providence..	Sum'rsgill..Conway	6-0
May 1	Wesleyan vs. Dartmouth	Middletown.	Tyrrell....Crolius	14-1
" 2	Dartmouth vs. Trinity	Hartford....	Tabor...Coggeshall	14-6
" 5	Dartmouth vs. Bowdoin	Hanover....	Tabor......Dodge	9-5
" 6	Bowdoin vs. Dartmouth	Hanover....	Sibley.....Conway	9-8
" 8	U. of Vermont vs. Dartmouth	Burlington..	Miner.......Tabor	5-4
" 9	U. of Vermont vs. Dartmouth	Burlington..	Dinsmore..Crolius	5-4
" 12	Dartmouth vs. Tufts	Hanover....	Tabor......Curran	12-11
" 13	Dartmouth vs. Tufts	Hanover....	Conway....Russell	28-18
" 19	U. of Vermont vs. Dartmouth	Hanover....	Dinsmore....Tabor	15-8
" 20	Dartmouth vs. U. of Vermont	Hanover....	Conway.....Miner	15-7
" 30	Holy Cross vs. Dartmouth	Worcester..	Pappalau..Conway	10-5
June 1	Brown vs. Dartmouth	Hanover....	Mellor......Patey	32-4
" 2	Dartmouth vs. Trinity	Hanover....	Conway.....Grover	15-12

BASE BALL GUIDE.   163

VERMONT UNIVERSITY RECORD FOR 1896.

Date.	Contesting Clubs.	Where Played.	Pitchers.	Score.
April 29	U. of Vermont vs. Union....	Sch'nectady	Miner ...... Stumpf	12-5
" 30	U. of Vermont vs. Cornell..	Ithaca......	Dinsmore......Blair	8-7
May 1	Hobart Col. vs. U. of Vt....	Geneva......	Miner...... Hooker	6-3
" 2	U. of Vt. vs. West Point....	West Point.	Dinsmore......Lott	9-8
" 8	U. of Vt. vs. Dartmouth....	Burlington..	Miner........Tabor	5-4
" 9	U. of Vt. vs. Dartmouth....	Burlington.	Dinsmore...Crolius	5-4
" 12	U. of Vermont vs. Bates....	Burlington..	Miner......Slattery	7-6
" 13	Bates vs. U. of Vermont....	Burlington.	Dinsmore.Berrym'n	8-5
" 15	U. of Vermont vs. Tufts....	Burlington.	Miner.......Curran	5-3
" 16	U. of Vermont vs. Tufts....	Burlington.	Dinsmore....Curran	9-6
" 19	U. of Vt. vs. Dartmouth....	Hanover ...	Dinsmore ....Tabor	15-8
" 20	Dartmouth vs. U. of Vt....	Hanover,...	Miner......Conway	15-7
" 22	Wesleyan vs. U. of Vt.....	Burlington.	Miner.......Tyrrell	5-2
" 23	Wesleyan vs. U. of Vt......	Burlington..	Dinsmore...Tyrrell	10-5
" 27	U. of Vermont vs. Colby....	Burlington.	Dinsmore.Patterson	12-2
June 2	U. of Vt. vs. Amherst......	Amherst....	Dinsmore ...Boyden	2-1
" 3	Yale vs. U. of Vermont.....	New Haven	Miner......Trudeau	19-7
" 4	Wesleyan vs. U. of Vt......	Middletown	Dinsmore.T'wnsend	8-5
" •5	Brown vs. U. of Vermont...	Providence.	Dinsmore......Miller	16-4
" 6	Holy Cross vs. U. of Vt....	Worcester..	Miner.....Pappalau	17-1
" 17	U. of Vt. vs. Cuban X G'ts..	Burlington.	Dinsmore....Selden	9-2

UNIVERSITY OF PENNSYLVANIA RECORD, 1896.

Date.	Contesting Clubs.	Where Played.	Pitchers.	Score.
April 4	U. of P. vs. Hobart College.	Philadelphia	Wunder....Voorhis	18-16
" 15	U. of P. vs. Wash. and Jeff.	Philadelphia	....	17-3
" 15	Ineligibles vs. Bridgeton In.	Philadelphia	....................*	10-8
" 18	U. of P. vs. Lehigh	Philadelphia	....	19-1
" 20	U. of P. vs. Pa. State Col...	Philadelphia	....	17-6
" 22	U. of P. vs. Trinity	Philadelphia	Darte... Coggeshall	10-5
" 23	Freshmen vs. Germantown.	Philadelphia	Thatcher McCarthy	6-2
" 27	Brown vs. U. of P..........	Philadelphia	Brady......Wunder	15-7
" 29	U. of P. vs. Lafayette......	Philadelphia	Wunder ....Sigman	11-7
May 2	U. of P. vs. Georgetown....	Philadelphia	O'Donnell Mahoney	13-12
" 6	U of P. vs. Cornell	Ithaca.......	Wunder .....Young	10-9
" 9	U. of P. vs. Cornell	Philadelphia	O'Donnell ...Young	11-6
" 13	U. of P. vs Lehigh	Bethlehem .	Cantler.W. Gannon	13-8
" 23	Harvard vs. U. of P........	Philadelphia	Paine.... O'Donnell	8-3
" 25	Chicago Uni. vs. U. of P...	Philadelphia	Clark....O'Donnell	15-10
" 30	U. of P. vs. Cornell	Ithaca......	Wunder ...... Blair	20-9
" 30	U. of P. Fresh.vs.Har.Fresh	Philadelphia	....	9-5
June 2	U. of P. vs. Cornell	Philadelphia	....	11-2
" 6	Harvard vs. U. of P........	Cambridge..	....	11-8
" 10	Lehigh vs. U. of P.........	Philadelphia	W. Gannon.Ritchie	7-6
" 16	U. of P. vs. Lafayette......	Easton......	....	4-1
" 23	Harvard vs. U. of P........	Cambridge..	Paine.......Ritchie	2-0

* 11 innings.

Brown University's Record of 1896.

The Brown University, of Providence, R. I., made a very creditable record in 1896, they winning no less than 19 games out of 24 played with the prominent college clubs of the Eastern Atlantic States, and with the Chicago University 9 out West. They defeated Yale in 3 straight games and won 2 out of 4 with Harvard.

THE BROWN UNIVERSITY RECORD OF 1896.

Date.	Contesting Clubs.	Where Played.	Pitchers.	Score.
April 15	Brown vs. Exeter			24-1
" 18	Providence vs. Brown	Providence	Hods'n.S'mmersgill	7-4
" 20	Brown vs. Holy Cross	Worcester		7-6
" 25	Brown vs. Yale	New Haven	S'mmersgill.G'nw'y	9-6
" 27	Brown vs. University of Pa.	Philadelphia	Brady......Wunder	15-7
" 30	Brown vs. Dartmouth	Providence	S'mmersgill.C'nw'y	6-0
May 2	Brown vs. Yale	Providence	Brady.....Trudeau	6-1
" 5	Brown vs. Harvard	Cambridge	Summersgill..Paine	9-7
" 6	Brown vs. Wesleyan	Providence		16-13
" 9	Brown vs. Tufts	Providence	Mellor......Curran	11-0
" 13	Brown vs. Wesleyan	Middletown	Summersgill.Terrell	5-3
" 16	Brown vs Providence A. A.	Providence		8-3
" 19	Holy Cross vs. Brown	Providence	Cronin......Setter	4-1
" 20	Harvard vs. Brown	Cambridge	Paine..Summersgill	6-1
" 23	Brown vs. Holy Cross	Worcester	Brady.....Pappalau	5-4
" 25	Brown vs. Brown of '99	Providence	Graves.........Ives	21-7
" 27	Brown vs. Georgetown	Providence	Brady......Mahoney	13-6
" 28	Brown vs. Holy Cross	Providence	S'mmersgill..P'pp'n	16-5
" 30	Brown vs. Yale	Providence	Brady....Greenway	6-4
June 1	Brown vs. Dartmouth	Hanover		32-4
" 3	Harvard vs. Brown	Providence	Paine........Brady	6-1
" 5	Brown vs. University of Vt.			16-4
" 8	Brown vs. Providence A. A.	Providence		10-4
" 15	Brown vs. Harvard	Cambridge	Summersgill..Paine	4-0
" 17	Brown vs. Holy Cross	Providence	Brady....Maroney	3-0
" 27	Chicago Univ'sity vs. Brown	Chicago		1-0
" 30	Brown vs. Chicago Univ'sity	Chicago		13-6
July 3	Brown vs. Chicago Univ'sity	Chicago	T. Dunne...Nichols	6-5

BATTING AVERAGES.

Player	Games.	Runs.	Per cent.	Player.	Games.	Runs.	Per cent.
Lauder	23	22	.380	Gammons	22	16	.191
Robinson	23	38	.354	Brady	17	5	.186
Fultz	23	33	.323	J. Dunne	19	11	.174
Phillips	23	36	.303	Sedgwick	11	6	.150
Mellor	8	3	.262	Lang	5	3	.117
Rodman	23	18	.244	T. Dunne	1	0	.000
Summersgill	15	10	.191				

FIELDING AVERAGES.

Player.	Games.	Per cent.	Player.	Games.	Per cent.
Rodman, 1b	23	.980	Gammons, l. f.	22	.895
J. Dunne, c	19	.952	Phillips, s. s., 2b	23	.890
Brady, p	11	.947	Fultz, 2b., s. s	23	.873
Lang, c	5	.947	Sedgwick, c. f	11	.833
Lauder, 3b	23	.921	Robinson, r. f	23	.805
Mellor, p	4	.916	Mellor, c. f	4	.750
Brady, c. f	5	.909	Summersgill, c. f	6	.700
Summersgill, p	9	.899	T. Dunne, p	1	.000

U. of Virginia's Record of 1896. The University of Virginia's averages sent us are so mixed up in regard to positions occupied by the majority of the players of the team that it is difficult to tell what their home position figures were.

VICTORIES.

Date.	Contesting Clubs.	Where Played.	Pitchers.	Score.
April 2	Virginia vs. Lehigh	Charl'tt'sv'e	Lockett......Givin	25-3
" 8	Virginia vs. Johns Hopkins	Charl'tt'sv'e	Lockett.....Herrick	15-8
" 23	Virginia vs. Trinity	Charl'tt'sv'e	McGuire.Cogg'shall	6-4
" 30	Virginia vs. St. Johns	Charl'tt'sv'e	Lockett....Hilleary	18-12
May 5	Virginia vs. St. Albans	Charl'tt'sv'e	McGuire....Collier	4-3
" 11	Virginia vs. Cornell	Charl'tt'sv'e	McGuire.....Miller	6-5
" 20	Virginia vs. Princeton	Princeton...	Lockett......Wilson	10-6

DEFEATS.

Date.	Contesting Clubs.	Where Played.	Pitchers.	Score.
April 3	Princeton vs. Virginia	Charl'tts'v'e	Easton....McGuire	5-4
" 4	Yale vs. Virginia	Charl'tt'sv'e	Trudeau....Lockett	12-4
" 6	Yale vs. Virginia	Ly'hb'rg,Va	Greenway.McGuire	8-7
" 13	Hobart vs. Virginia	Charl'tt'sv'e	Vorhis.....Lockett	7-4
" 14	Hobart vs. Virginia	Charl'tt'sv'e	Vorhis.....McGuire	3-2
" 25	U. of N. C. vs. Virginia	Danville, Va	Pearsall....Lockett	14-6
May 15	Georgetown vs. Virginia	Washington.	Mahoney...Lockett	31-11
" 16	Georgetown vs. Virginia	Washington.	Mahoney..McGuire	7-0
" 18	U. of Pa. vs. Virginia	Philadelphia	Wunder....McGuire	8-2
" 19	Lehigh vs. Virginia	Bethlehem..	Gannon ....Lockett	10-6

Holy Cross College Records of 1896

The Holy Cross College team, of Worcester, was very successful in 1896. They had games with a dozen college club teams and only lost to one, and that one was the Brown University team. The record sent us was not made out in correct form, as it did not place the victorious clubs first or give the names of the pitchers on each side in the recorded games. The individual averages of the team are as follows:

BATTING AVERAGES.

Player.	Games.	Runs.	Per cent.
Sockalexis	26	38	.444
Powers	25	39	.350
McTigue	27	31	.336
W. H. Fox	24	21	.330
Curley	26	39	.319
W. J. Fox	27	19	.288
Maroney	23	20	.286
Lavin	26	29	.273
Gaffney	10	10	.265
Garvey	13	12	.263
Kelly	13	6	.212
Pappalau	19	13	.190

FIELDING AVERAGES.

Player.	Put Out.	Assist.	Errors.	Per cent.
Maroney	17	26	1	.977
Powers	165	29	7	.965
McTigue	233	4	14	.948
Garvey	14	3	1	.944
Kelly	35	9	3	.936
Curley	64	69	12	.925
Pappalau	2	28	3	.909
W. H. Fox	52	64	12	.906
Lavin	29	17	5	.902
Sockalexis	55	9	8	.888
W. J. Fox	28	55	13	.865
Gaffney	10	2	6	.666

RECORD OF THE LAFAYETTE TEAM, 1896.

Contesting Clubs.	Where Played.	Pitchers.	Score.
Georgetown U. vs. Lafayette	Washington	Sigman	6-4
U. of N. Carolina vs. Lafayette	Chapel Hill	Clarke	18-9
Lafayette vs. Columbia Univ.	Washington	Dreisbach	18-13
Lafayette vs. Rutgers	Easton	Sigman	9-8
Princeton vs. Lafayette	Princeton	Dreisbach	8-1
Lafayette vs. West Point	West Point	Sigman	2-1
Triple City League vs. Lafayette	Easton	Sigman	10-8
Lafayette vs. Lehigh	Easton	Dreisbach	27-6
Lafayette vs. Fordham	Fordham	Sigman	10-5
Lafayette vs. Annapolis	Annapolis	Dreisbach	13-7
Triple City League vs. Lafayette	Easton	Dreisbach	12-7
Univ. of Pa. vs. Lafayette	Philadelphia	Sigman	11-7
Orange vs. Lafayette	Orange	Clarke	26-6
Yale vs. Lafayette	New Haven	Dreisbach	11-3
Lafayette vs. Lehigh	Rittersville	Dreisback-Sigman	21-6
Princeton vs. Lafayette	Easton	Sigman	9-8
Oritani Field Club vs. Lafayette	Hackensack	Dreisbach	4-1
Triple City League vs. Lafayette	Easton	Dreisbach	8-4
Lafayette vs. Lehigh	Easton	Sigman	5-4
Univ. of Pa. vs Lafayette	Easton	Sigman	4-1

BASE BALL GUIDE. 167

UNIVERSITY OF MICHIGAN RECORD FOR 1896.

Date.	Contesting Clubs.	Where Played.	Pitchers.	Score.
April 4	Michigan vs. M. A. C......	Ann Arbor..	....	18-6
" 8	Michigan vs. Albion.........	Ann Arbor..	....	25-4
" 13	Michigan vs. Toledo........	Toledo......	....	11-5
" 14	Michigan vs. Ohio S. U....	Columbus...	....	18-6
" 15	Michigan vs. Wittenberg...	Springfield..	....	13-10
" 16	Indianapolis vs. Michigan..	Indianapolis	....	18-11
" 17	Michigan vs. Indiana U....	Bloomingt'n	....	9-0
" 18	Michigan vs. Uni. of Ill....	Champaign.	....	5-3
May 2	Michigan vs. Oberlin.......	Ann Arbor..	....	13-1
" 7	Michigan vs. Ohio S. U.....	Ann Arbor.	....	14-7
" 9	Chicago vs. Michigan......	Chicago.....	....	7-3
" 11	Michigan vs. Wisconsin...	Madison.....	....	7-3
" 13	Michigan vs. Chicago......	Chicago.....	....	6-0
" 16	Michigan vs. Wisconsin....	Ann Arbor..	....	7-2
" 20	Michigan vs. Chicago......	Ann Arbor..	....	9-2
" 23	Michigan vs. Oak Park.....	Oak Park...	....	9-0
" 25	Michigan vs. Illinois.......	Oak Park...	....	20-3
June 4	Chicago vs. Michigan......	Oak Park...	....	7-4
" 6	Michigan vs. Toronto......	Oak Park...	....	13-8
" 10	Michigan vs. Detroit.......	Oak Park...	....	11-11
" 11	Chicago vs. Michigan......	Oak Park...	....	10-5
" 13	Michigan vs. Oberlin.......	Oberlin.....	....	9-8

CORNELL RECORD FOR 1896.

Date.	Competing Clubs.	Where Played.	Pitchers.	Score.
April 15	Buffalo (E. L.) vs. Cornell..	Ithaca......	Gaffney..... Young	7-4
" 16	Buffalo vs. Cornell.........	Ithaca......	Roach......Preison	17-2
" 18	Cornell vs. Rochester Univ.	Ithaca.....	Young.....Martens	19-1
" 21	Cornell vs. Hobart..........	Ithaca......	Young......Hooker	7-2
" 22	Syracuse (E. L.) vs. Cornell	Ithaca......	Delaney.......Blair	20-5
" 23	Syracuse (E. L.) vs. Cornell	Ithaca......	Jordon...... Young	21-5
" 30	U. of Vermont vs. Cornell..	Ithaca......	Dinsmore...Young	8-7
May 2	Princeton vs. Cornell.......	Ithaca......	Wilson...... Young	12-10
" 6	Pennsylvania vs. Cornell...	Ithaca......	Wunder.....Young	10-9
" 9	Pennsylvania vs. Cornell...	Phil'delph'a	O'Donnell...Young	11-6
" 11	U. of Virginia vs. Cornell..	Charlottsv'e	McGuire.....Miller	6-5
" 12	Georgetown vs. Cornell....	Washington	Mahoney.....Blair	11-1
" 16	Harvard vs. Cornell.........	Ithaca......	Paine....... Young	15-6
" 18	Cornell vs. U. of Wisconsin.	Ithaca......	Blair....... Runkel	8-7
" 22	U. of Chicago vs. Cornell..	Ithaca......	Michallas...Young	3-2
" 25	Manhattan Col. vs. Cornell.	New York..	Driscoll.......Blair	6-1
" 27	Princeton vs. Cornell.......	Princeton..	Actman.....Young	22-0
" 30	Pennsylvania vs. Cornell...	Ithaca......	Wunder ......Blair	26-9
June 2	Pennsylvania vs. Cornell...	Phil'delph a	O'Donnell...Young	10-2
" 3	Georgetown vs. Cornell.....	Scranton....	Mahoney....Young	8-5
" 6	Oberlin vs. Cornell..........	Ithaca......	Young......Vorhis	6-5
" 13	Harvard vs. Cornell.........	Cambridge..	Houghton...Young	11-2
" 18	Cornell vs. Graduates......	Ithaca......	Young........Smith	4-2

The Model College Game of 1896. The finest exhibition of college club ball playing seen in 1896, and the "best on record" between two college teams, was the contest between the Princeton and Harvard nines, which took place on Holmes Field at Cambridge on May 30, 1896. No less than sixteen innings had to be played before the victory was won; Princeton finally winning by two runs, scored in the sixteenth inning. Harvard led off with a score of 5 to 0 in the very first inning, and at once the triumph of the home team in the match was regarded as a foregone conclusion. In this inning Easton was in the box for Princeton against Paine. Afterwards Wilson went in to pitch for Princeton, and successive blanks for Harvard was the result of the change. In the fifth inning the visitors "got onto Paine's curves" to the tune of 4 runs, and then began one of the most noteworthy uphill fights known in the annals of the two clubs. In the eighth inning the visitors added a single to their score and tied the game amidst intense excitement, the ninth inning ending with the score at 5 to 5, with both pitchers doing fine work in the box and receiving excellent support in the field. Neither side scored again until the fourteenth inning, when each added a single to their scores. Then came the sixteenth inning, and Princeton rallied at the bat and got in two runs, and finally came in victors after a splendid uphill contest occupying over three hours.

The official score of the match is as follows:

PRINCETON.	R.	1B.	PO.	A.	E.	HARVARD.	R.	1B.	PO.	A.	E.
Suter, l. f.	1	0	0	0	0	Dean, 2b.	0	1	7	4	0
Wheeler, l. f.	1	2	4	0	0	Scannell, c.	1	2	11	2	0
Easton, p., c. f	3	3	2	0	2	Burgess, r. f.	1	1	2	0	0
Bradley, 1b	0	3	24	1	1	Clarkson, c. f.	1	2	5	1	1
Titus, c.	0	1	9	3	1	Haughton, 1b.	2	3	16	1	0
Gunster, 3b.	0	0	2	8	2	Rand, l. f.	1	0	5	0	0
Altman, r. f.	0	2	3	1	0	Stevenson, 3b.	0	2	2	4	0
Smith, 2b.	0	2	2	6	1	Paine, p.	0	2	0	3	2
Wilson, c. f., p.	1	3	0	3	0	Chandler, s. s.	0	2	0	3	1
Ward, s. s.	2	1	2	8	0						
Totals	8	17	48	30	7		6	15	48	18	4

Princeton............ 0 0 0 4 0 0 1 0 0 0 0 0 1 0 2—8
Harvard .... 5 0 0 0 0 0 0 0 0 0 0 0 0 1 0 0—6

Runs earned—Princeton, 5; Harvard, 2. Base hits—Princeton, 17; Harvard, 15. Sacrifice hits—Princeton, 1; Harvard, 2. Stolen bases—Princeton, 3; Harvard, 4. Base on balls—Princeton, 2; Harvard, 4. Struck out—Princeton, 7; Harvard, 5. Wild pitches—Princeton, 2; Harvard, 2. Hit batsman—Princeton, 1; Harvard, 0. Double plays—Gunster, Bradley and Titus (2). Umpire—Mr. O'Rourke. Time—3:20.

THE TEMPLE CUP AND MINOR LEAGUE PRIZE SERIES OF GAMES.

The third season of the Temple Cup series of games ended in 1896 with the success of the Baltimore team, and it proved to be a special triumph for that club, inasmuch as they not only won the League pennant for the third successive year, but they capped the climax of their three-times-winner record in the pennant race with four successive victories over their old rivals of Cleveland in the Cup series, it being their first victory of the kind, as they lost the Cup games both in 1894 and 1895.

The record from 1894 to 1896, inclusive, is as follows:

SERIES OF 1894.

Date.	Contesting Clubs.	Where Played.	Pitchers.	Score.
Oct. 4	New York vs. Baltimore....	Baltimore..	Rusie.........Esper	4-1
" 5	New York vs. Baltimore....	Baltimore..	Meekin.....Gleason	9-6
" 6	New York vs. Baltimore....	Baltimore..	Rusie'....Hemming	4-1
" 8	New York vs. Baltimore....	New York..	Meekin.....Hawke	16-4

SERIES OF 1895.

Oct. 2	Cleveland vs. Baltimore....	Cleveland..	Young...McMahon	5-4
" 3	Cleveland vs. Baltimore....	Cleveland..	Cuppy......Hoffer	7-2
" 5	Cleveland vs. Baltimore....	Cleveland..	Young...McMahon	7-1
" 7	Baltimore vs. Cleveland....	Baltimore..	Esper........Cuppy	5-0
" 8	Cleveland vs. Baltimore....	Baltimore..	Young.......Hoffer	5-2

SERIES OF 1896.

Oct. 2	Baltimore vs. Cleveland....	Baltimore..	Hoffer.......Young	7-1
" 3	Baltimore vs. Cleveland....	Baltimore..	Corbett....Wallace	7-2
" 5	Baltimore vs. Cleveland....	Baltimore..	Hoffer......Cuppy	6-2
" 8	Baltimore vs. Cleveland...	Cleveland..	Corbett......Cuppy	5-0

In the Temple Cup series in 1894 each New York player pocketed $768.10, and each Baltimore player $360. In 1895 $528.33 went to each Cleveland player, and $352.22 to each Baltimore player. In 1896 the Baltimore players only realized $2,500, or about $200 per man, while the Clevelands got but $1,700, or $117 per man.

Manager Hanlon, in commenting on the series of 1896, said:

"The man who talks about hippodroming in base ball or in this series is a fool, and such started the stories that floated about when the Baltimore team defeated Philadelphia 12 straight. It cost the Quaker management at least $20,000 for that to happen to them, and does anybody think that Reach and Rogers are in base ball for the health of the Baltimore team at the cost to them of a small fortune?"

THE MINOR LEAGUE PRIZES.

Besides the Temple Cup series of after-season championship games, in which clubs first and second in the pennant races play an extra series of games for players' prize money and valuable cups, may be named the handsome cup donated by the Detroit "Free Press," which was competed for in October, 1896, by the two leading clubs in the Western League pennant race; the Steinert Cup, which brought the two leaders of the Eastern League race together, and the Soby Cup series, for which the Hartford and Paterson clubs competed after their contest for the championship of the Atlantic League.

Detroit Free Press Cup Series.

Date.	Contesting Clubs.	Where Played.	Pitchers.	Score.
Sept. 24	Indianapolis vs. Minneapolis	Indianapolis	Fisher......Parker	9-7
" 25	Indianapolis vs. Minneapolis	Indianapolis	Dammon.Figgemier	17-9
" 26	Minneapolis vs. Indianapolis	Indianapolis	Hutchison W.Davis	6-3
" 29	Minneapolis vs. Indianapolis	Minneapolis.	Parker....Dammon	7-6
" 30	Minneapolis vs. Indianapolis	Minneapolis.	Hutchison ...Fisher	4-0
Oct. 1	Minneapolis vs. Indianapolis	Minneapolis.	Parker....Dammon	13-11

The Steinert Cup Series.

Date.	Contesting Clubs.	Where Played.	Pitchers.	Score.
Sept. 17	Providence vs. Buffalo	Buffalo	Dolan........Gray	4-1
" 20	Providence vs. Buffalo	Buffalo	Hodson.......Gray	17-13
" 21	Buffalo vs. Providence	Buffalo	Gannon.Rudderh'm	7-5
" 23	Providence vs. Buffalo	Providence..	Dolan........Gray	16-7
" 24	Buffalo vs. Providence	Providence..	Hodson....Gannon	8-2
" 26	Providence vs. Buffalo	Providence..	Dolan......Gannon	11-4

The Soby Cup Series.

Date.	Contesting Clubs.	Where Played.	Pitchers.	Score.
Sept. 24	Hartford vs. Paterson	Hartford....	Frye.....McMackin	13-3
" 25	Paterson vs. Hartford	Hartford..	Cogan.......Bowen	1-1
" 26	Paterson vs. Hartford	Hartford....	Smith..........Frye	6-2
" 26	Hartford vs. Paterson	Hartford....	Vickery.McCafferty	9-4
" 30	Paterson vs. Hartford	Paterson....	Smith......Vickery	8-7
Oct. 1	Paterson vs. Hartford	Paterson....	Cogan.........Frye	6-2
" 3	Paterson vs. Hartford	Paterson....	Smith ....Bowen	4-3

CARDINAL GIBBONS ENDORSES BASE BALL

Last September the Baltimore team visited St. Charles College at Ellicott City, Md., where, in the presence of Cardinal Gibbons, Bishop Curtis, of Wilmington, Del., the faculty of the college and a number of visiting Catholic priests from Washington and Baltimore, they gave an exhibition of professional ball playing. The feature of the occasion was the comments on the game made by the Cardinal at the dinner given to the players in the college refectory, of which the following paragraphs are worthy of special note as being a valuable endorsement of the merits of professional base ball as exhibited by the most expert exemplars of the game known to the National League in 1896. The Cardinal said:

> "I am not what you might call a crank, but I am surrounded (referring to a number of clergy seated at the same table with him) by several excellent critics of the game, some of them even being well enough versed in the pastime to lay claim to the title of authorities. From them I have learned the merits of Baltimore's base ball players, and, without hesitation, say that these young men, who have obtained such prominence in their chosen profession, are worthy of the praise bestowed upon them, and both the State and city can well afford to be as proud of their achievements as they themselves no doubt are.
>
> "Let me say," he continued, "that I favor base ball as an amusement for the greatest pleasure-loving people in the world. It is necessary that there should be popular amusements, and in consequence it is wise that the most generally patronized of these amusements should be innocent, since, were the opposite the case, the opportunity of committing sins of greater or less degree would be too openly set before the public. Base ball is a clean sport. It is an innocent amusement. Never have I heard that the games were being used as vehicles for gambling, the most insidious of vices, and this one fact alone raises it above the level of the average sporting event. It is a healthy sport, and since the people of the country generally demand some sporting event for their amusement, I would single this out as the one best to be patronized, and heartily approve of it as a popular pastime."

The Cardinal's words were listened to with the closest attention by the players and the clergymen, who had remained in the room after the body of students had filed out. He finished in silence, but his words had made a deep impression on his hearers, and especially upon the players, not one of whom could find words sufficient to thank him for the glowing eulogy of the national game that he had delivered. The Cardinal displayed the greatest interest in the game, toward which he had been looking forward for some time, and which was arranged especially for him at his invitation. The curving of the pitched ball attracted his attention at the outset, and he spent some time in investigating the phenomenon from behind the wire screen. No detail of the game escaped his watchful eye.

HARRY WRIGHT DAY.

Monday, April 13, 1896, was the day appointed by the National League for the playing of games for the benefit of the fund to be devoted to the construction of a monument to the late veteran, Harry Wright, and there were no less than sixteen exhibition games played that day for the purpose, of which five of the Eastern clubs of the League and four of the Western clubs participated, the others being minor league clubs. Philadelphia had the largest crowd at any of the matches, viz., 3,500. Cincinnati had 1,462, the opening of a new race course there that day interfering with the attendance. Baltimore had about 1,500, Washington 800, New York 700, Louisville 500 and Boston 500. Brooklyn, in the East, and Chicago, Cleveland, St. Louis and Pittsburg, in the West, played no games that day.

THE CINCINNATI GAME.

The exhibition game on Harry Wright day was made noteworthy by a gathering of old-timers of the Cincinnati Reds of 1882, the year the club won the American Association pennant. The appended score of the match is as follows:

CLUB OF '96.	R.	1B.	P.O.	A.	E.	TEAM OF '82.	R.	1B.	P.O.	A.	E.
Holliday, l. f.	1	1	3	0	0	J. White, l. f., p.	0	1	0	4	2
Burke, c. f.	3	1	3	0	0	McPhee, 2b.	0	0	3	5	0
Gray, 2b.	0	3	5	5	1	Carpenter, 3b.	0	0	1	2	1
Ewing, 1b.	0	1	4	1	1	Reilly, r. f., 1b.	1	2	10	0	0
Vaughn, 1b.	0	0	4	0	0	Fulmer, s. s.	1	2	0	2	1
Miller, r. f.	0	0	1	0	0	Somers, c. f.	1	1	2	1	0
Smith, s. s.	0	1	1	3	0	Snyder, c.	0	2	4	6	0
Irwin, 3b.	0	2	3	5	0	Gould, 1b., r. f.	0	1	3	0	3
Peitz, c.	1	0	1	0	0	W. White, p.	0	0	0	2	0
Dwyer, p.	2	2	2	1	0	Shoup, l. f.	0	0	0	0	0
Totals	7	11	27	15	2	Total	3	9	*23	22	7

*Peitz out for running out of line.

Club of '96	1	4	0	2	0	0	0	0	x—7
Team of '82	0	0	0	1	0	2	0	0	0—3

Earned runs—Team of '82, 3. Two-base hits—Ewing, Snyder. Bases on balls—Off Dwyer, 1. Struck out—Ewing, Miller (2), Shoup. Double plays—Smith, Gray and Ewing; Irwin, Gray and Vaughn. Wild pitch—W. White. Hit by pitched ball—Snyder. Time of game—1:20. Umpires—Messrs. Draper, Brockway and Bocke. Official scorer—Henry Chadwick.

The club hospitably entertained the visiting players the same night at the Gibson House. Among the special guests of the club on this occasion was Mr. Henry Chadwick, of Brooklyn, who acted as official scorer for the veterans in the match. The brothers, James and Will White, came from Buffalo to attend the game, and Charley Fulmer from Philadelphia. The only veteran of the old Red Stockings of 1869 in the match was Charley Gould.

THE GAME AT ROCKFORD, ILL.

The occasion of the Harry Wright game at Rockford, Ill., on April 13, 1896, was a base ball event the citizens of the town will long remember with pleasure. The meeting was arranged by Mr. A. G. Spalding and a number of old-time Rockford cranks of the decade of the '60s, prominent among whom was Mr. H. H. Waldo, a veteran player over 70 years of age, who acted as umpire.

All parts of the State were represented at the game. Chicago sent a train load, and a special train at that. Freeport sent a similar delegation, and it seemed that every town and hamlet contributed to the grand conclave of cranks. Business was suspended in the town for the day, and every building was gaily decorated. Reception committees met every train and looked after the guests. A monster parade with all the notables in line preceded the game. The veterans were given a guard of honor, and were greeted with the wildest kind of enthusiasm all along the line of march. Unfortunately, the first inning of the game had only been finished, with a score in favor of Spalding's side by 4 to 0, when rain drove every one to shelter, and as it continued further play ended. Hugh Nicol had charge of the contest, and A. G. Spalding and that other veteran, George Wright, selected sides. Here is a list of the players:

A. G. Spalding, George Wright, Roscoe C. Barnes, Dan O'Leary, George E. King, Al Barker, H. N. Starr, H. S. Warner, Frank Trumbull, Fred Cone, Dent Sawyer, Garrett Stires, E. C. Dunn, M. H. Golden, W. B. Osborne, Royal Buckman, Wallace Lightheart, Bob Addy, Leo Cheney, H. W. Price, Scott Hastings, C. A. Works, W. S. Stearns, J. G. Hitchcock and George Bird.

The game was played under the rules of 1869. A banquet ended the day's proceedings.

Other games were played in towns throughout the country, but the whole proceeds did not reach $4,000.

The facts of the history of sports and pastimes in this country show very plainly that in the revision of the rules of play in every game introduced in America within the past quarter of a century through the medium of our system of governing games by National Association action—a system almost unknown to English sports prior to the last decade—the evolution of each particular field game up to the point of a perfected code of playing rules, has been advanced to a degree which never could have been reached under the old English system.

CORRECT DIAGRAM OF A BALL FIELD.

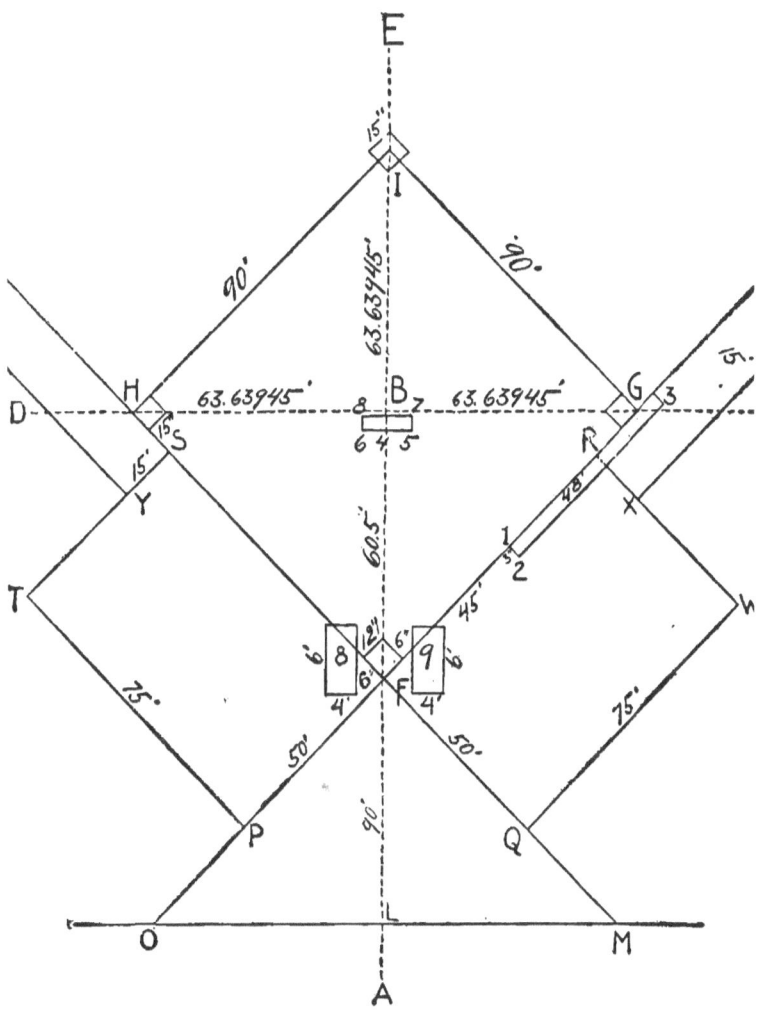

NOTE.—For Specifications See Rules From No. 2 to No. 12.

OF PROFESSIONAL BASE BALL CLUBS

As Adopted by the National League and American Association of Professional Base Ball Clubs.

Alterations and additions to the rules are indicated by *Italics*.

RULE I.—THE BALL GROUND.

The Ground must be an inclosed field, sufficient in size to enable each player to play in his position as required by these rules.

RULE II.

To lay off the lines governing the positions and the play of the game known as *Base Ball*, proceed as follows:

From a point, A, within the grounds, project a right line out into the field, and at a point, B, 154 feet from point A, lay off lines B C and B D at right angles to the line A B; then, with B as centre and 63.63945 feet as radius, describe arcs cutting the lines B A at F and B C at G, B D at H and B E at I. Draw lines F G, G E, E H and H F, and said lines will be the containing lines of the Diamond or Infield.

RULE III.—THE CATCHER'S LINES.

With F as centre and 90 feet radius, an arc cutting line F A at L, and draw lines L M and L O at right angles to F A; and continue same out from F A not less than 90 feet.

RULE IV.—THE FOUL LINE.

From the intersection point, F, continue the straight lines F G and F H until they intersect with the lines L M and L O, and then from the points G and H in the opposite direction until they reach the boundary lines of the grounds.

RULE V.—THE PLAYERS' LINES.

With F as centre and 50 feet radius, describe arcs cutting lines F O and F M at P and Q; then, with F as centre again and 75 feet radius, describe arcs cutting F G and F H at R and S; then from the points P, Q, R and S draw lines at right angles to the lines F O, F M, F G and F H, and continue same until they intersect at the points T and W.

Rule VI.—The Captain and Coacher's Line.

With R and S as centres and 15 feet radius, describe arcs cutting lines R W and S T at X and Y, and from the points X and Y draw lines parallel with lines F H and F G, and continue same out to the boundary lines of the ground.

Rule VII.—The Three Foot Line.

With F as centre and 45 feet radius, describe an arc cutting line F G at 1, and from 1 out to the distance of 3 feet draw a line at right angles to F G, and marked point 2; then from point 2, draw a line parallel with the line F G to a point 3 feet beyond the point G, and marked 3; then from the point 3 draw a line at right angles to line 2, 3, back to and intersecting with line F G, and from thence back along line G F to point 1.

Rule VIII.—The Pitcher's Plate.

With point F as centre and 60.5 feet as radius, describe an arc cutting the line F B at a point 4, and draw a line 5, 6, passing through point 4 and extending 12 inches on either side of line F B; then with line 5, 6, as a side, describe a parallelogram 24 inches by 6 inches.

Rule IX.—The Bases.

Within the angle F, describe a square the sides of which shall be 12 inches, two of its sides lying upon the lines F G and F H, and within the angles G and H describe squares the sides of which shall be 15 inches, the two outer sides of said square lying upon the lines F G and G I and F H and H I, and at the angle E describe a square whose sides shall be 15 inches and so described that its sides shall be parallel with G I and I H and its centre immediately over the angular point E.

Rule X.—The Batsman's Line.

On either side of the line A F B describe two parallelograms 6 feet long and 4 feet wide (marked 8 and 9), their length being parallel with the line A F B, their distance apart being 6 inches added to each end of the length of the diagonal of the square within the angle F, and the centre of their length being upon said diagonal.

Rule XI.

The Home Base at F and the Pitcher's Plate at 4 must be of whitened rubber and so fixed in the ground as to be even with the surface.

Rule XII.

The First Base at G, the Second Base at E, and the Third Base at H must be of white canvas bags, filled with soft material and securely fastened in their positions described in Rule 9.

PLAYING RULES. 177

RULE XIII.

The lines described in Rules 3, 4, 5, 6, 7 and 10 must be marked with lime, chalk or other suitable material, so as to be distinctly seen by the umpire.

Note.—For a simple way to lay off a ball field see addenda to playing rules on page 198.

RULE XIV.—THE BALL.*

SECTION 1. Must not weigh less than five nor more than five and one-quarter ounces avoirdupois, and it must measure not less than nine nor more than nine and one-quarter inches in circumference. The Spalding League Ball, or the Reach American Association Ball, must be used in all games played under these rules.

SEC. 2. For each championship game two regulation balls shall be furnished by the home club to the umpire for use. When the ball in play is batted to foul ground and out of sight of the umpire, the other ball shall be immediately brought into play. As often as one of the two in use shall be lost a new one must be substituted, so that the umpire shall at all times after the game begins, have two balls in his possession and ready for use. The moment the umpire delivers an alternate ball to the pitcher, it comes into play, and shall not be exchanged until it, in turn, passes out of sight to foul ground. At no time shall the ball be intentionally discolored by rubbing it with the soil or otherwise. *In the event of a new ball being intentionally discolored, or otherwise injured by a player, the umpire shall, upon appeal from the captain of the opposite side, forthwith demand the return of that ball, and shall substitute another new ball and impose a fine of* $5.00 *upon the offending player.*

SEC. 3. In all games the balls played with shall be furnished by the home club, and the last ball in play shall become the property of the winning club. Each ball to be used in championship games shall be examined, measured and weighed by the Secretary of the League, inclosed in a paper box, and sealed with the seal of the Secretary, which seal shall not be broken, except by the umpire, in the presence of the captains of the two contesting nines after play has been called.

The home club shall have, at least, a dozen regulation balls on the field ready for use on the call of the umpire during each championship game.

---

*The Spalding League Ball has been adopted by the National League for the past twenty years, and is used in all League contests.

For junior clubs (clubs composed of boys under 16 years of age) we recommend them to use the Spalding Boys' League Ball, and that games played by junior clubs with this ball will count as legal games the same as if played with the Official League Ball.

SEC. 4. Should the ball become cut or ripped so as to expose the interior, or in any way so injured as to be, in the opinion of the umpire, unfit for fair use, he shall, upon appeal by either captain, at once put the alternate ball into play and call for a new ball.

RULE XV.—THE BAT.

Must be entirely of hard wood, except that the handle may be wound with twine or a granulated substance supplied, not to exceed eighteen inches from the end.

It must be round, and it must not exceed two and three-quarter inches in diameter in the thickest part, nor exceed forty-two inches in length.

RULE XVI.—THE PLAYERS AND THEIR POSITIONS.

The players of each club in a game shall be nine in number, one of whom shall act as captain, and in no case shall less than nine men be allowed to play on each side.

RULE XVII.

The players' positions shall be such as may be assigned them by their captain, except, that the pitcher *while in the act of delivering the ball to the bat*, must take the position as defined in Rules 8 and 29.

RULE XVIII.

Players in uniform shall not be permitted to occupy seats, or to stand among the spectators.

RULE XIX.

SECTION 1. Every club shall adopt uniforms for its players, but no player shall attach anything to the sole or heel of his shoes other than the ordinary base ball shoe plate.

SEC. 2. The catcher and first baseman are permitted to wear a glove or mitt of any size, shape or weight. All other players are restricted to the use of a glove or mitt weighing not over ten ounces, and measuring in circumference, around the palm of the hand, not over fourteen inches.

RULE XX.—PLAYERS' BENCHES.

SECTION 1. The players' benches must be furnished by the home club and placed upon a portion of the ground outside of and not nearer than 25 feet to the players' lines. One such bench must be for the exclusive use of the visiting club, and one for the exclusive use of the home club. All players of the side at the bat must be seated on their bench, except such as are legally assigned to coach base-runners, and also the batsman when called to the bat by the umpire, and, under no circumstances, shall the umpire permit any person, except the club president, managers and players in uniform to occupy seats on the benches.

PLAYING RULES. 179

SEC. 2. *To enforce this rule the captain of the opposite side may call the attention of the umpire to a violation, whereupon the umpire shall immediately order such player or players to be seated. If the order is not obeyed within one minute the offending player or players shall be debarred from further participation in the game, and shall be obliged to leave the playing field forthwith.*

RULE XXI.—THE GAME.

SECTION 1. Every championship game must be commenced not later than two hours before sunset.

SEC. 2. A game shall consist of nine innings to each contesting nine, except that

(*a*.) If the side first at bat scores less runs in nine innings than the other side has scored in eight innings, the game shall then terminate.

(*b*.) If the side last at bat in the ninth innings scores the winning run before the third man is out, the game shall terminate.

RULE XXII.—A TIE GAME.

If the score be a tie at the end of the nine innings, play shall be continued until one side has scored more runs than the other in an equal number of innings, provided, that the side last at bat scores the winning run before the third man is out, the game shall terminate.

RULE XXIII.—A DRAWN GAME.

A drawn game shall be declared by the umpire when he terminates a game on account of darkness or rain, after five equal innings have been played, if the score at the time is equal on the last even innings played; except when the side that went second to bat is then at the bat, and has scored the same number of runs as the other side, in which case the umpire shall declare the game drawn without regard to the score of the last equal innings.

RULE XXIV.—A CALLED GAME.

If the umpire calls "Game" on account of darkness or rain at any time after five innings have been completed, the score shall be that of the last equal innings played, except, that the side second at bat shall have scored one or more runs than the side first at bat, in which case the score of the game shall be the total number of runs made.

RULE XXV.—A FORFEITED GAME.

A forfeited game shall be declared by the umpire in favor of the club not in fault, at the request of such club, in the following cases:

SECTION 1. If the nine of a club fail to appear upon the field, or being upon the field, fail to begin the game within five minutes after the umpire has called "Play" at the hour appointed for the beginning of the game, unless such delay in appearing, or in commencing the game, be unavoidable.

SEC. 2. If, after the game has begun, one side refuses or fails to continue playing, unless such game has been suspended or terminated by the umpire.

SEC. 3. If, after play has been suspended by the umpire, one side fails to resume playing within one minute after the umpire has called "Play."

SEC. 4. If a team resorts to dilatory movements to delay the game.

SEC. 5. If, in the opinion of the umpire, any one of the rules of the games is wilfully violated.

SEC. 6. If, after ordering the removal of a player, as authorized by Rules XX. and LX., said order is not obeyed within one minute.

SEC. 7. In case the umpire declares a game forfeited, he shall transmit a written notice thereof to the president of the League within twenty-four hours thereafter. *However, a failure on the part of the umpire to so notify the president shall not affect his decision declaring the game forfeited.*

RULE XXVI.—NO GAME.

"No game" shall be declared by the umpire if he shall terminate play on account of rain or darkness before five innings on each side are completed. Except in a case when the game is called, and the club second at bat shall have more runs at the end of its fourth innings than the club first at bat has made in its five innings, in such case the umpire shall award the game to the club having made the greatest number of runs, and it shall be a legal game and be so counted in the championship record.

RULE XXVII.—SUBSTITUTES.

SECTION 1. In every championship game each side shall be required to have present on the field, in uniform, *a sufficient number of substitute players to carry out the provision which requires that not less than nine players shall occupy the field in any innings of a game.*

SEC. 2. Any such player may be substituted at any time by either club, but a player thereby retired shall not thereafter participate in the game.

SEC. 3. The base-runner shall not have a substitute run for him except by the consent of the captains of the contesting teams.

RULE XXVIII.—CHOICE OF INNINGS—CONDITION OF GROUND.

The choice of innings shall be given to the captain of the home club, who shall also be the sole judge of the fitness of the ground for beginning a game after rain, but, after play has been called by the umpire, he alone shall be the judge as to the fitness of the ground for resuming play after the game has been suspended on account of rain.

RULE XXIX.—THE PITCHER'S POSITION.

The pitcher shall take his position facing the batsman with both feet square on the ground, and in front of the pitcher's plate; but in the act of delivering the ball to the bat, one foot must be in contact with the pitcher's plate, defined in Rule 8. He shall not raise either foot, unless in the act of delivering the ball to the bat, nor make more than one step in such delivery.

When the pitcher feigns to throw the ball to a base he must resume the above position and pause momentarily before delivering the ball to the bat.

If the pitcher fails to comply with the requirements of this rule the umpire must call "A balk."

RULE XXX.—A FAIRLY DELIVERED BALL.

A Fairly Delivered Ball to the bat is a ball pitched or thrown to the bat by the pitcher while standing in his position and facing the batsman, the ball so delivered to pass over any portion of the home base not lower than the batsman's knee nor higher than his shoulder.

RULE XXXI.—AN UNFAIRLY DELIVERED BALL.

An Unfairly Delivered Ball is a ball delivered by the pitcher, as in Rule 30, except that the ball does not pass over any portion of the home base, or does pass over the home base, above the batsman's shoulder or below the knee.

RULE XXXII.—BALKING.

A Balk shall be:

SECTION 1. Any motion made by the pitcher to deliver the ball to the bat without delivering it.

SEC. 2. Any delivery of the ball to the bat while his (pivot) foot is not in contact with the pitcher's plate, as defined in Rule 29.

SEC. 3. Any motion in delivering the ball to the bat by the pitcher while not in the position defined in Rule 29.

SEC. 4. The holding of the ball by the pitcher so long as, *in the opinion of the umpire*, to delay the game unnecessarily.

SEC. 5. *Standing in position to pitch without having the ball in his possession, except in the case of a "block-ball," as provided by Rule 35, section 2.*

RULE XXXIII.—DEAD BALLS.

A Dead Ball is a ball delivered to the bat by the pitcher that touches any part of the batsman's person or clothing while standing in his position without being struck at, or that touches any part of the umpire's person or clothing while he is standing on foul ground without first passing the catcher.

RULE XXXIV.

In case of a foul strike, foul hit ball not legally caught out, dead ball, or base-runner put out for being struck by a fair-hit ball, the ball shall not be considered in play until it is held by the pitcher standing in his position and the umpire shall have called play.

RULE XXXV.—BLOCK BALLS.

SECTION 1. A Block is a batted or thrown ball that is touched, stopped or handled by any person not engaged in the game.

SEC. 2. Whenever a block occurs the umpire shall declare it and the base-runners may run the bases without being put out until the ball has been returned to and held by the pitcher standing in his position.

SEC. 3. In the case of a block, if the person not engaged in the game should retain possession of the ball, or throw or kick it beyond the reach of the fielders, the umpire should call "Time" and require each base-runner to stop at the last base touched by him until the ball be returned to the pitcher standing in his position and the umpire shall have called "Play."

RULE XXXVI.—THE BATSMAN'S POSITION—ORDER OF BATTING.

The batsmen must take their positions within the batsman's lines, as defined in Rule 10, in the order in which they are named in the batting order, which batting order must be submitted by the captains of the opposing teams to the umpire before the game, and this batting order must be followed except in the case of a substitute player, in which case the substitute must take the place of the original player in the batting order. After the first inning the first striker in each inning shall be the batsman whose name follows that of the last man who has completed his turn—time at bat—in the preceding inning.

Rule XXXVII.

SECTION 1. When their side goes to the bat the players must immediately return to the players' bench, as defined in Rule 20, and remain there until the side is put out, *except when called to the bat or they become substitute base-runners* ; provided, that the captain *or one player* only, except that if two or more base-runners are occupying the bases then the captain and one player, or two players, may occupy the space between the player's lines and the captain's lines to coach base-runners.

SEC. 2. No player of the side "at bat," except when batsman, shall occupy any portion of the space within the catcher's lines, as defined in Rule 3. The triangular space behind the home base is reserved for the exclusive use of umpire, catcher and batsman, and the umpire must prohibit any player of the side "at bat" from crossing the same at any time while the ball is in the hands of, or passing between, the pitcher and catcher, while standing in their positions.

SEC. 3. The players of the side "at bat" must occupy the portion of the field allotted them, but must speedily vacate any portion thereof that may be in the way of the ball, or any fielder attempting to catch or field it.

Rule XXXVIII.—The Batting Rules.

SECTION 1. A Fair Hit is a ball batted by the batsman—*while he is standing within the lines of his position—that first touches "fair" ground, or the person of a player, or the umpire, while standing on fair ground, and then settles on fair ground before passing the line of first or third base.*

SEC. 2. *A Foul Hit is a similarly batted ball that first touches "foul" ground, or the person of a player, or the umpire, while standing on "foul" ground.*

SEC. 3. *Should such "fair hit" ball bound or roll to foul ground, before passing the line of first or third base, and settle on foul ground, it shall be declared by the umpire a foul ball.*

SEC. 4. *Should such "foul hit" ball bound or roll to fair ground and settle there before passing the line of first or third base, it shall be declared by the umpire a "fair ball."*

Rule XXXIX.

A foul tip is a ball batted by the batsman while standing within the lines of his position that goes foul sharp from the bat to the catcher's hands.

Rule XL.

A bunt hit is a ball delivered by the pitcher to the batsman who, while standing within the lines of his position, makes a deliberate attempt to hit the ball so slowly within the in-

field that it cannot be fielded in time to retire the batsman. *If such a "bunt hit" goes to foul ground a strike shall be called by the umpire.*

RULE XLI.—BALLS BATTED OUTSIDE THE GROUNDS.

When a batted ball passes outside the grounds, the umpire shall decide it Fair should it disappear within, or Foul should it disappear outside of the range of the foul lines, and Rule 38 is to be construed accordingly.

RULE XLII.

A fair batted ball that goes over the fence shall entitle the batsman to a home run, except, that should it go over the fence at a less distance than two hundred and thirty-five (235) feet from the home base, when he shall be entitled to two bases only, and a distinctive line shall be marked on the fence at this point.

RULE XLIII.—STRIKES.

A Strike is:

SECTION 1. A ball struck at by the batsman without its touching his bat; or,

SEC. 2. A fair ball legally delivered by the pitcher, but not struck at by the batsman.

SEC. 3. Any obvious attempt to make a foul hit.

SEC. 4. *Any intentional effort to hit the ball to foul ground, also in the case of a "bunt hit," which sends the ball to foul ground, either directly, or by bounding or rolling from fair ground to foul ground, and which settles on foul ground.*

SEC. 5. A ball struck at, if the ball touches any part of the batsman's person.

SEC. 6. A ball tipped by the batsman, and caught by the catcher, *within ten feet from home base.*

RULE XLIV.

A Foul Strike is a ball batted by the batsman when any part of his person is upon ground outside the lines of the batsman's position.

RULE XLV.—THE BATSMAN IS OUT.

The Batsman is Out:

SECTION 1. If he fails to take his position at the bat in his order of batting, unless the error be discovered and the proper batsman takes his position before a time "at bat" *is* recorded; and, in such case, the balls and strikes called must be counted in the time "at bat" of the proper batsman, and only the proper batsman shall be declared out; *provided*, this rule shall not take effect unless the out is declared before the ball is delivered to the succeeding batsman, and no runs shall be scored, or bases run, and, *furthermore, no other batsman than the one who batted out of order shall be declared out on the error.*

SEC. 2. If he fails to take his position within one minute after the umpire has called for the batsman.

SEC. 3. If he makes a foul hit other than a foul tip, as defined in Rule 39, and the ball be momentarily held by a fielder before touching the ground ; provided, it be not caught in a fielder's hat or cap, or touched by some object other than a fielder before being caught.

SEC. 4. If he makes a foul strike.

SEC. 5. If he attempts to hinder the catcher from fielding or throwing the ball by stepping outside the lines of his position, or otherwise obstructing or interfering with the player.

SEC. 6. If, while the first base be occupied by a base-runner, three strikes be called on him by the umpire, except when two men are already out.

SEC. 7. If, after two strikes have been called, the batsman obviously attempts to make a foul hit, as in Rule 43, section 3.

SEC. 8. If, while attempting a third strike, the ball touches any part of the batsman's person, in which case base-runners occupying bases shall return as prescribed in Rule 49, section 5.

SEC. 9. If he hits a fly ball that can be handled by an infielder while first and second bases are occupied, or first, second and third with only one out. In such case the umpire shall, as soon as the ball is hit, declare infield or outfield hit.

SEC. 10. If the third strike is called in accordance with section 4, Rule 43.

SEC. 11. *The moment a batsman is declared out by the umpire, he (the umpire) shall call for the batsman next in order to leave his seat on the bench and take his position at the bat, and such player of the batting side shall not leave his seat on the bench until so called to bat, except as provided by Rule 37, section 1, and Rule 52.*

BASE-RUNNING RULES.

RULE XLVI.—WHEN THE BATSMAN BECOMES A BASE-RUNNER.

The Batsman becomes a Base-Runner :

SECTION 1. Instantly after he makes a fair hit.

SEC. 2. Instantly after four balls have been called by the umpire.

SEC. 3. Instantly after three strikes have been *declared* by the umpire.

SEC. 4. If, while he be a batsman, without making any attempt to strike *at the ball*, his person or clothing be hit by a ball from the pitcher ; unless, *in the opinion of the umpire, he plainly avoids making any effort to get out of the way of the ball from the pitcher, and thereby permits himself to be so hit.*

SEC. 5. Instantly after an illegal delivery of a ball by the pitcher.

RULE XLVII.—BASES TO BE TOUCHED.

The base-runner must touch each base in regular order, viz., first, second, third and home bases, and when obliged to return (except on a foul hit) must retouch the base or bases in reverse order. He shall only be considered as holding a base after touching it, and shall then be entitled to hold such base until he has legally touched the next base in order or has been legally forced to vacate it for a succeeding base-runner. *However, no base-runner shall score a run to count in the game until the base-runner preceding him in the batting list (provided there has been such a base-runner who has not been put out in that inning) shall have first touched home base without being put out.*

RULE XLVIII.—ENTITLED TO BASES.

The base-runner shall be entitled, without being put out, to take the base in the following cases:

SECTION 1. If, while he was batsman, the umpire called four balls.

SEC. 2. If the umpire awards a succeeding batsman a base on four balls, or for being hit with a pitched ball, or in case of an illegal delivery—as in Rule 46, section 5—and the base-runner is thereby forced to vacate the base held by him.

SEC. 3. If the umpire calls a "Balk."

SEC. 4. If a ball, delivered by the pitcher, pass the catcher, and touch the umpire, or any fence or building within ninety feet of the home base.

SEC. 5. If, upon a fair hit, the ball strikes the person or clothing of the umpire on fair ground.

SEC. 6. If he be prevented from making a base by the obstruction of an adversary, *unless the latter be a fielder having the ball in his hand ready to meet the base-runner.*

SEC. 7. If the fielder stop or catch a batted ball with his hat or any part of his uniform *except his gloved hand.*

RULE XLIX.—RETURNING TO BASES.

The base-runner shall return to his base, and shall be entitled to so return without being put out:

SECTION 1. If the umpire declares a foul tip (as defined in Rule 39), or any other foul hit not legally caught by a fielder.

SEC. 2. If the umpire declares a foul strike.

SEC. 3. If the umpire declares a dead ball, unless it be also the fourth unfair ball and he be thereby forced to take the next base, as provided in Rule 48, section 2.

Sec. 4. If the person or clothing of the umpire interferes with the catcher, or he is struck by a ball thrown by the catcher to intercept a base-runner.

Sec. 5. The base-runner shall return to his base if, while attempting a strike, the ball touches any part of the batsman's person.

Rule L.—When Base-Runners Are Out.

The Base-Runner is Out:

Section 1. If, after three strikes have been declared against him while batsman and the catcher fail to catch the third strike ball, he plainly attempts to hinder the catcher from fielding the ball.

Sec. 2. If, having made a fair hit while batsman, such fair hit ball be momentarily held by a fielder before touching the ground, or any object other than a fielder ; Provided, it be not caught in a fielder's hat or cap.

Sec. 3. If, when the umpire has declared three strikes on him while batsman, the third strike ball be momentarily held by a fielder before touching the ground; Provided, it be not caught in a fielder's hat or cap, or touch some object other than a fielder before being caught.

Sec. 4. If, after three strikes, or a fair hit, he be touched with the ball in the hand of a fielder before he shall have touched first base.

Sec. 5. If, after three strikes or a fair hit, the ball be securely held by a fielder while touching first base with any part of his person before such base-runner touches first base.

Sec. 6. If, in running the last half of the distance from home base to first base, while the ball is being fielded to first base, he runs outside the three-foot lines, as defined in Rule 7, unless to avoid a fielder attempting to field a batted ball.

Sec. 7. If, in running from first to second base, from second to third base, or from third to home base, he runs more than three feet from a direct line between such bases to avoid being touched by the ball in the hands of a fielder; but in case a fielder be occupying the base-runner's proper path in attempting to field a batted ball, then the base-runner shall run out of the path, and behind said fielder, and shall not be declared out for so doing.

Sec. 8. If he fails to avoid a fielder attempting to field a batted ball, in the manner described in sections 6 and 7 of this rule, or if he, in any way, obstructs a fielder attempting to field a batted ball, or intentionally interferes with a thrown ball;

PROVIDED, that if two or more fielders attempt to field a batted ball, and the base-runner comes in contact with one or more of them, the umpire shall determine which fielder is entitled to the benefit of this rule, and shall not decide the base-runner out for coming in contact with any other fielder.

SEC. 9. If, at any time while the ball is in play, he be touched by the ball in the hands of a fielder, unless some part of his person is touching a base he is entitled to occupy; PROVIDED, the ball be held by the fielder after touching him; but (exception as to first base), in running to first base, he may over-run said base, without being put out for being off said base, after first touching it, provided he returns at once and retouches the base, after which he may be put out as at any other base. If, in over-running first base, he also attempts to run to second base, or after passing the base he turns to his left from the foul line, he shall forfeit such exemption from being put out.

SEC. 10. If, when a fair or foul hit ball (other than a foul tip as referred to in Rule 39) is legally caught by a fielder, such ball is legally held by a fielder on the base occupied by the base-runner when such ball was struck (or the base-runner be touched with the ball in the hands of a fielder), before he retouches said base after such fair or foul hit ball was so caught; PROVIDED, that the base-runner shall not be out, in such case, if, after the ball was legally caught as above, it be delivered to the bat by the pitcher before the fielder holds it on said base, or touches the base-runner with it; but if the base-runner in attempting to reach a base, detaches it before being touched or forced out, he shall be declared safe.

SEC. 11. If, when a batsman becomes a base-runner, the first base, or the first and second bases, or the first, second and third bases, be occupied, any base-runner so occupying a base shall cease to be entitled to hold it, until any following base-runner is put out, and may be put out at the next base, or by being touched by the ball in the hands of a fielder in the same manner as in running to first base at any time before any following base-runner is put out.

SEC. 12. If a fair hit ball strike him before touching the fielder, and, in such case, no base shall be run unless forced by the batsman becoming a base-runner, and no run shall be scored or any other base-runner put out.

SEC. 13. If, when running to a base, or forced to return to a base, he fail to touch the intervening base, or bases, if any, in the order prescribed in Rule 47, he may be put out at the base he fails to touch, or being touched by the ball in the hands of the fielder in the same manner as in running to first base; PROVIDED, that the base-runner shall not be out in such case if the ball be delivered to the bat by the pitcher before the fielder holds it on said base, or touches the base-runner with it.

SEC. 14. If, when the umpire calls "Play," after any suspension of a game, he fails to return to and touch the base he occupied when "Time" was called before touching the next base; PROVIDED, the base-runner shall not be out, in such case, if the ball be delivered to the bat by the pitcher before the fielder holds it on said base or touches the base-runner with it.

RULE LI.—WHEN BATSMAN OR BASE-RUNNER IS OUT.

The umpire shall declare the batsman or base-runner out, without waiting for an appeal for such decision, in all cases where such player is put out in accordance with these rules, except as provided in Rule L., sections 10 and 14.

RULE LII.—COACHING RULES.

The *Coacher* shall be restricted to coaching the base-runner only, and shall not be allowed to address any remarks except to the base-runner, and then only in words of necessary direction; and shall not use language which will in any manner, refer to, or reflect, upon a player of the opposing club, the umpire or the spectators, and not more than *one* coacher, who may be *a* player participating in the game, *or* any other player under contract to it, in the uniform of either club, shall be allowed at any one time, except, that if base-runners are occupying two or more of the bases, then the captain and one player, or two players in the uniform of either club, may occupy the space between the players' lines and the captains' lines to coach base-runners. To enforce the above the captain of the opposite side may call the attention of the umpire to the offence, and, upon a repetition of the same, the offending player shall be debarred from further participation in the game, and shall leave the playing-field forthwith.

RULE LIII.—THE SCORING OF RUNS.

One run shall be scored every time a base-runner, after having legally touched the first three bases, shall touch the home base before three men are put out. (Exception.) If the third man is forced out, or is put out before reaching first base, a run shall not be scored.

THE UMPIRE.

Note.—See "Advice to Umpires" in addenda to the playing rules on page 197.

RULE LIV. The umpire shall not be changed during the progress of a game, except for reason of illness or injury.

Rule LV.—His Powers and Jurisdiction.

Section 1. The umpire is master of the field from the commencement to the termination of the game, and is entitled to the respect of the spectators, and any person offering any insult or indignity to him must be promptly ejected from the grounds.

Sec. 2. He must be addressed by the players as "Mr. Umpire;" and he must compel the players to observe the provisions of all the playing rules, and he is hereby *vested* with authority to order any player, *captain or manager*, to do, or omit to do, any act that he may deem necessary to give force and effect to any and all such provisions.

Rule LVI.—Special Duties.

The umpire's duties shall be as follows:

The Sole Judge of Play.

Section 1. The umpire is the sole and absolute judge of play. In no instance shall any person, except the captains of the competing teams, be allowed to address him or question his decisions, and they (*the captains*) can only question him *as to the legal* interpretation of the rules; *and they shall not be permitted to leave their proper positions in so doing unless permitted by the umpire. The proper positions are: The Coacher's box for the captain for the side which is at bat, and his regular fielding position for the captain in the field.* No manager or any other official of either club shall be permitted to go on the field or address the umpire, under a penalty of a forfeiture of a game.

Must Learn Ground Rules.

Sec. 2. Before the commencement of a game the umpire shall see that the rules governing all the materials of the game are strictly observed. He shall ask the captain of the home club whether there are any special ground rules to be enforced, and if there are he shall see that they are duly enforced, provided they do not conflict with any of these rules.

Must Prevent All Unnecessary Delays.

Sec. 3. The umpire must keep the contesting nines playing constantly from the commencement of the game to its termination, allowing such delays only as are rendered unavoidable by accident, injury or rain. He must, until the completion of the game require the players of each side to promptly take their positions in the field as soon as the third man is put out, and must require the first striker of the opposite side to be in his position at the bat as soon as the fielders are in their places.

CALLING BALLS AND STRIKES.

SEC. 4. The umpire shall count and call every "unfair ball" delivered by the pitcher, and every "dead ball," if also an unfair ball, as a "ball,' and he shall count and call every "strike." Neither a "ball" nor a "strike" shall be counted or called until the ball has passed the home base. He shall also declare every "dead ball," "block," "foul hit," "foul strike" and "balk," "infield" or "outfield hit," as prescribed in Rule 45, section 9.

RULE LVII.—CALLING "PLAY" AND "TIME."

The umpire must call "play" promptly at the hour designated by the home club, and, on the call of "play," the game must immediately begin. When he calls "time" play shall be suspended until he calls "play" again, and during the interim no player shall be put out, base be run, or run be scored. The umpire shall suspend play only for an accident to himself or a player (but in case of accident to a fielder, "time" shall not be called until the ball be returned to and held by the pitcher, standing in his position); or, in case rain falls so heavily that the spectators are compelled by the severity of the storm to seek shelter, in which case he shall note the time of suspension, and should such rain continue to fall thirty minutes thereafter he shall terminate the game; or to enforce order in case of annoyance from spectators.

RULE LVIII.

The umpire is only allowed by the rules to call "time" in case of an accident to himself or a player; a "block," as referred to in Rule 35, section 3; or in case of rain, as defined in Rule 57.

RULE LIX.—REMOVAL OF PLAYERS FROM THE GAME.

The umpire shall remove from the game and the field any player guilty of indecent or vulgar language or conduct, and in addition thereto *he shall be required to assess a fine of* $25 *against the player so removed.*

RULE LX.—FINING CAPTAIN OR COACHER.

SECTION 1. The umpire is directed, *and instructed*, to impose a fine of not less than $5, nor more than $10, during the progress of a game, as follows: For the captain, coacher, or any player of the contesting teams failing to remain within the bounds of his position as defined in the rules. This, however, shall not deprive the captain of either team from appealing to the umpire upon a question involving a *legal* interpretation of the rules, as prescribed in Rule 56, section 1.

Disciplining for Disobedience of Orders.

SEC. 2. For the disobedience by a player of any order of the umpire, or any violation of these rules.

SEC. 3. If a player is guilty of a second violation of this rule the umpire shall impose a fine of $25, and, in his discretion, order the player from the game and the field. For a third offence the umpire must positively order the player from the field, and forthwith notify the captain of the team to which the player belongs that, during the continuance of the game, he will impose no further fines, but instantly remove any player guilty of a violation of any of these rules.

Ordering Players from the Field.

SEC. 4. When an umpire orders a player from the game he shall also insist upon the player's removal from the field, and suspend play until this order is obeyed.

Notification of Fines.

SEC. 5. Immediately upon notification by the umpire that a fine has been imposed upon any manager, captain or player, the Secretary shall forthwith notify the person so fined and also the club of which he is a member, and, in the event of the failure of the person so fined to pay to the Secretary the amount of said fine within five days of notice, he shall be debarred from participation in any championship game until such fine is paid.

Must Not Address Spectators.

SEC. 6. *The umpire shall not address the spectators at any time, except in case of necessary explanation of misunderstood decisions or points of play.*

The Reversal of Decisions.

SEC. 7. *No decision, rendered by the umpire, shall be reversed by him in which the question of an error of judgment is alone involved.*

On Illegal Decisions.

SEC. 8. *Should the umpire render any decision based on an illegal interpretation of any rule of the game, the same shall be reversed on the appeal of either of the two captains, but not otherwise.*

RULE LXI.—Field Rules.

No club shall allow open betting or pool-selling upon its ground, nor in any building owned or occupied by it.

RULE LXII.

No person shall be allowed upon any part of the field during

McVey　Leonard　Spalding　H. Wright　White　Shaffer　Barnes
O'Rourke　　　　G. Wright　　　　Hall　　　　Beals

THE BOSTON CHAMPIONS OF THE EARLY '70S.

the progress of a game in addition to the players in uniform, the manager of each side and the umpire, except such officers of the law as may be present in uniform, and such officials of the home club as may be necessary to preserve the peace.

RULE LXIII.

No manager, captain or player shall address the spectators during the progress of the game, except in case of necessary explanation.

RULE LXIV.

Every club shall furnish sufficient police force upon its own grounds to preserve order, and, in the event of a crowd entering the field during the progress of a game, and interfering with the play in any manner, the visiting club may refuse to play further until the field be cleared. If the ground be not cleared within fifteen minutes thereafter, the visiting club may claim, and shall be entitled to the game, by a score of nine runs to none (no matter what number of innings has been played).

RULE LXV.—GENERAL DEFINITIONS.

"Play" is the order of the umpire to begin the game, or to resume play after its suspension.

RULE LXVI.

"Time" is the order of the umpire to suspend play. Such suspension must not extend beyond the day of the game.

RULE LXVII.

"Game" is the announcement by the umpire that the game is terminated.

RULE LXVIII.

An "Inning" is the term at bat of the nine players representing a club in a game, and is completed when three of such players have been put out, as provided in these rules.

RULE LXIX.

A "Time at Bat" is the term at bat of a batsman. It begins when he takes his position and continues until he is put out or becomes a base-runner; except when, because of being hit by a pitched ball, or in case of an illegal delivery by the pitcher, or in case of a sacrifice hit purposely made to the infield which, not being a base-hit, advances a base-runner without resulting in a put-out, except to the batsman, as in Rule 45.

RULE LXX.

"Legal" or "Legally" signifies as required by these rules.

SCORING.

RULE LXXI.

In order to promote uniformity in scoring championship games the following instructions, suggestions and definitions are made for the benefit of scorers, and they are required to make all scores in accordance therewith.

BATTING.

SECTION 1. The first item in the tabulated score, after the player's name and position, shall be the number of times he has been at bat during the game. The time or times when the player has been sent to base by being hit by a pitched ball, by the pitcher's illegal delivery or by a base on balls, *or has made a sacrifice hit which was manifestly intentional*, shall not be included in this column.

SEC. 2. In the second column should be set down the runs made by each player.

SEC. 3.' In the third column should be placed the first-base hits made by each player. A base-hit should be scored in the following cases:

When the ball from the bat strikes the ground within the foul lines and out of reach of the fielders.

When a hit ball is partially or wholly stopped by a fielder in motion, but such player cannot recover himself in time to handle the ball before the striker reaches first base.

When a hit ball is hit so sharply to an infielder that he cannot handle it in time to put out the batsman. In case of doubt over this class of hits, score a base-hit and exempt the fielder from the charge of an error.

When a ball is hit so slowly towards a fielder that he cannot handle it in time to put out the batsman.

That in all cases where a base-runner is retired by being hit by a batted ball, the batsman should be credited with a base-hit.

When a batted ball hits the person or clothing of the umpire, as defined in Rule 48, section 5.

SEC. 4. In the fourth column shall be placed the sacrifice hits, which shall be credited to the batsman who, when no one is out or when but one man is out, advances a runner a base by a *bunt hit*, which results in putting out the batsman, or would so result if the ball were handled without error.

FIELDING.

SEC. 5. The number of opponents put out by each player shall be set down in the fifth column. Where a batsman is given out by the umpire for a foul strike, or where the batsman fails to bat in proper order, the put-out shall be scored to the catcher.

SEC. 6. The number of times the player assists shall be set down in the sixth column. An assist should be given to each player who handles the ball in assisting a run-out or other play of the kind.

An assist should be given to a player who makes a play in time to put a runner out, even if the player who could complete the play fails through no fault of the player assisting.

And generally an assist should be given to each player who handles or assists in any manner in handling the ball from the time it leaves the bat until it reaches the player who makes the put-out, or in case of a thrown ball, to each player who throws or handles it cleanly and in such a way that a put-out results, or would result if no error were made by the receiver.

ERRORS.

SEC. 7. An error shall be given in the seventh column for each misplay which allows the striker or base-runner to make one or more bases when perfect play would have insured his being put out, except that "wild pitches," "bases on balls," bases on the batsman being struck by a "pitched ball," or in case of illegal pitched balls, balks and passed balls, shall not be included in said column. In scoring errors of batted balls see Section 3 of this rule.

SEC. 8. Stolen bases shall be scored as follows:

Any attempt to steal a base must go to the credit of the base-runner, whether the ball is thrown wild or muffed by the fielder, but any manifest error is to be charged to the fielder making the same. If the base-runner advances another base he shall not be credited with a stolen base, and the fielder allowing the advancement is also to be charged with an error. If the base-runner makes a start and a battery error is made the runner secures the credit of a stolen base, and the battery error is scored against the player making it. Should a base-runner over-run a base and then be put out he shall receive the credit for a stolen base.

EARNED RUNS.

SEC. 9. An earned run shall be scored every time the player reaches the home base *by the aid of base-hits only* before chances have been offered to retire the side.

RULE LXXII.—THE SUMMARY.

The summary shall contain:

SECTION 1. The number of earned runs made *off each pitcher*.

SEC. 2. The number of two-base hits made by each player.
SEC. 3. The number of three-base hits made by each player.
SEC. 4. The number of home runs made by each player.
SEC. 5. The number of bases stolen by each player.
SEC. 6. The number of double and triple plays made by each side and the names of the players assisting in the same.
SEC. 7. The number of men given bases on called balls by each pitcher *and the names of the players who were thus given bases.*
SEC. 8. The number of men given bases from being hit by pitched balls *by each pitcher and the names of the players who are thus given bases.*
SEC. 9. The number of men struck out *by each pitcher and the names of the players struck out.*
SEC. 10. The number of passed balls by each catcher.
SEC. 11. The number of wild pitches by each pitcher.
SEC. 12. *The number of base-runners left on bases by each side.*
SEC. 13. *The number of innings each pitcher played.*
SEC. 14. *The number of base-hits made off each pitcher.*
SEC. 15. *The number of bases on balls given by each pitcher.*
SEC. 16. *The number of batsmen hit by each pitcher.*
SEC. 17. *The number of batsmen struck out by each pitcher.*
SEC. 18. *The number of base-runners of each side who reached first base by fielding errors.*
SEC. 19. *The time it took to play the game.*
SEC. 20. *The condition of the weather.*
SEC. 21. *The condition of the playing field.*
SEC. 22. *The name of the umpire.*

ADVICE TO UMPIRES.

You are the absolute master of the field from the beginning to the termination of a game. You are by these rules given full authority to order any player, captain or manager to do or omit to do any act which you may deem necessary to maintain your dignity and compel respect from players and spectators. (Rule 55.)

The rules are created to be enforced to the letter. If they are poor rules the fault is not yours. If they are disobeyed you are to blame.

Before "play" is called satisfy yourself that the field is correctly laid off with lines, bases and plates in proper places, and that the material supplied for the game are as required by the rules. (Rule 56., section 2.)

Notify each captain that the rules will be enforced exactly as they are written, and that for each violation the prescribed penalty will follow. Do not in any case temporize with a rule breaker.

Make all decisions as you see them. Never attempt to "even up" after having made a mistake.

Be strict in what may seem to be trivial matters, thereby "nipping in the bud" trouble before it fully develops.

Specially observe Rules 20 and 37, which require players to occupy their respective benches; also section 6 of Rule 25, which specifies that a player ordered from the field shall go within one minute from the time you order his removal from the game.

Do not allow a player (not even a captain, to leave his position, which is the bench or coacher's box, for the captain whose side is at bat, or the regular fielding position of the captain whose side is not at bat) to argue with you. The captain only is allowed to appeal to you (and he only from his proper position) on a legal misinterpretation of the rules. If he claims that you have erred, it is proper that the spectators should know what the claim is. (Rule 60, section 1.)

Coachers have heretofore been a disturbing element to the umpire. Rules 52 and 60 provide just what his and what your duties are. These rules are mandatory, not discretionary. If you allow them to be violated you become the chief culprit and do not properly perform the duties of your position. Bear in mind that you are not responsible for the creation of the rules or the penalties prescribed by them.

The umpire who enforces the rules, maintains his dignity and compels respect, gives the fullest satisfaction to both teams and to the spectators.

Compel respect from all and your task will be an easy one.

A SIMPLE WAY FOR LAYING OFF A BALL FIELD.

Lay a tape line from centre of backstop out into the field 217 feet 3½ inches to second base. At 90 feet from backstop place home plate, with the tape-line dividing it diagonally. Between 150 feet 6 inches and 150 feet 10 inches from the backstop place the pitcher's plate, with the tape-line dividing it at the centre; 153 feet 7¾ inches from backstop drive a stake. At right angles to the tape-line, and 63 feet 7¾ inches from the stake and 90 feet from both home plate and second base, place first base on one side and third base on the other. This done remove the stake. Lay lines connecting the bases thus laid, forming the diamond, extending the lines from home base and first base and home base and third base in each direction to the fence, thus forming the foul lines and the catcher's position. Parallel with these lines and 50 feet away lay the player's lines, extending from intersection with lines already laid 75 feet. From this point lay lines at right angles to lines just described, extending to the base lines. At right angles to these and parallel the base lines, 15 feet distant, lay the coacher's lines, extending, say, 30 feet towards the outfield. Parallel with and 3 feet distant from the base line from home base to first base lay a line beginning 45 feet from home plate and extending just past first base.

On each side of home plate, parallel with line from centre of backstop to second base and 6 inches distant from home plate, lay lines 6 feet long, running three feet each way from a line through the centre of home plate, also lay other lines parallel with and 4 feet distant from the ones just described. Form these into parallelograms 4 feet by 6 feet in dimension, thus forming the batsman's position.

Observe Rules 11, 12 and 13.

INDEX TO RULES AND REGULATIONS.

	Sec.	Rule.
The Ground..		1
The Field..		2
Catcher's Lines..		3
Foul Lines...		4
Players' Lines...		5
The Captain and Coacher's Line................................		6
Three-foot Line...		7
Pitcher's Plate...		8
The Bases...		9
The Batsman's Line..		10
The Home Base...		11
First, Second and Third Bases.................................		12
Lines Must be Marked..		13
The Ball..		14
Weight and Size...	(1)	14
Number of Balls Furnished.................................	(2)	14
Fining Player for Discoloring New Ball....................	(2)	14
Furnished by Home Club....................................	(3)	14
Replaced if Injured.......................................	(4)	14
The Bat...		15
Material of...	(1)	15
Shape of..	(2)	15

THE PLAYERS AND THEIR POSITIONS.

	Sec.	Rule.
Number of Players in the Game.................................		16
Players' Positions..		17
Players not to Sit with Spectators............................		18
Club Uniforms...	(1)	19
Gloves..	(2)	19
Players' Benches..	(1)	20
Players Debarred from Game for Not Occupying Benches...........	(2)	20

THE GAME.

	Sec.	Rule.
Time of Championship Game.....................................	(1)	21
Number of Innings...	(2)	21
Termination of Game...	(a)	21
The Winning Run...	(b)	21
A Tie Game..		22
A Drawn Game..		23
A Called Game...		24
A Forfeited Game..		25
Failure of the Nine to Appear.............................	(1)	25
Refusal of One Side to Play...............................	(2)	25
Failure to Resume Playing.................................	(3)	25
If a Team Resorts to Dilatory Practice....................	(4)	25

INDEX TO RULES AND REGULATIONS.

	SEC.	RULE
Wilful Violation	(5)	25
Disobeying Order to Remove Player	(6)	25
Written Notice to President	(7)	25
No Game		26
Substitutes		27
Sufficient Number of Substitute Players	(1)	27
When Player May Be Substituted	(2)	27
Base-Runner	(3)	27
Choice of Innings—Condition of Ground		28
The Pitcher's Position		29
Delivery of the Ball—Fair Ball		30
Unfair Ball		31
Balking		32
Motion to Deceive	(1)	32
Foot Not in Contact with Pitcher's Plate	(2)	32
Pitcher Outside of Lines	(3)	32
Delay by Holding Ball	(4)	32
Standing in Position to Pitch Without Having Ball	(5)	32
A Dead Ball		33
A Foul Strike		34
Block Balls		35
Stopped by Person Not in Game	(1)	35
Ball Returned	(2)	35
Base-Runner Must Stop	(3)	35
The Batsman's Position—Order of Batting		36
Where Players Must Remain	(1)	37
Space Reserved for Umpire	(2)	37
Space Allotted Players "At Bat"	(3)	37
Batting Rules—Fair Hit		38
Foul Hit	(2)	38
Fair Hit Which Rolls to Foul Ground	(3)	38
Foul Hit Which Rolls to Fair Ground	(4)	38
A Foul Tip		39
A Bunt Hit		40
Balls Batted Outside the Grounds		41
A Fair Batted Ball Over the Fence		42
Strikes		43
Ball Struck at by Batsman	(1)	43
Fair Ball, Delivered by Pitcher	(2)	43
Attempt to Make Foul Hit	(3)	43
Intentional Effort to Hit Ball to Foul Ground	(4)	43
Foul Hit While Attempting a Bunt Hit	(4)	43
Ball Struck at after Touching Batsman's Person	(5)	43
Ball Tipped by Batsman	(6)	44
A Foul Strike		45
The Batsman is Out		45
Failing to Take Position at Bat in Order	(1)	45
Failure to Take Position within One Minute after being Called	(2)	45
If he Makes a Foul Hit	(3)	45
If he Makes a Foul Strike	(4)	45
Attempt to Hinder Catcher	(5)	45
Three Strikes Called by Umpire	(6)	45
Attempt to Make a Foul Hit after Two Strikes have been Called	(7)	45
If Ball Hits Him While Making Third Strike	(8)	45
If He Hits a Fly Ball that can Be Handled by Infielder while Bases are Occupied with only One Out	(9)	45
If Third Strike Is Called	(10)	45
Batsman Must Not Leave Bench Until Called by Umpire	(11)	45

BASE-RUNNING RULES.

	Sec.	Rule.
The Batsman Becomes a Base-Runner		46
After a Fair Hit	(1)	46
After Four Balls are Called	(2)	46
After Three Strikes are Declared	(3)	46
If Hit by Ball While at Bat	(4)	46
After Illegal Delivery of Ball	(5)	46
Bases to be Touched		47
Base-Runner Shall Not Pass Another Base-Runner to Reach Home Base		47
Entitled to Bases		48
If Umpire Calls Four Balls	(1)	48
If Umpire Awards Succeeding Batsman Base	(2)	48
If Umpire Calls Balk	(3)	48
If Pitched Ball by Pitcher Passes Catcher	(4)	48
Ball Strikes Umpire	(5)	48
Prevented from Making Base	(6)	48
Fielder Stops Ball with Any Part of His Dress	(7)	48
Returning to Bases		49
If Foul Tip	(1)	49
If Foul Strike	(2)	49
If Dead Ball	(3)	49
If Person of Umpire Interferes with Catcher	(4)	49
If the Ball Touches the Batsman's Person	(5)	49
Base-Runner Out		50
Attempt to Hinder Catcher from Fielding Ball	(1)	50
If Fielder Hold Fair Hit Ball	(2)	50
Third Strike Ball Held by Fielder	(3)	50
Touched with Ball After Three Strikes	(4)	50
Touching First Base	(5)	50
Running from Home Base to First Base	(6)	50
Running from First to Second Base	(7)	50
Failure to Avoid Fielder	(8)	50
Touched by Ball While In Play	(9)	50
Fair or Foul Hit Caught by Fielder	(10)	50
Batsman Becomes a Base-Runner	(11)	50
Touched by Hit Ball Before Touching Fielder	(12)	50
Running to Base	(13)	50
Umpire Calls Play	(14)	50
When Batsman or Base-Runner Is Out		51
Coaching Rules		52
Scoring of Runs		53

THE UMPIRE.

The Umpire Shall Not Be Changed		54
Master of the Field	(1)	55
Must Compel Observance of Playing Rules	(2)	55
Special Duties		56
Is Sole Judge of Play	(1)	56
Must Compel Players to Remain in Proper Positions	(1)	56
Not Permit Manager or Club Officer to Address Him	(1)	56
Must Learn Ground Rules	(2)	56
Must Prevent Unnecessary Delays	(3)	56
Must Count and Call Balls and Strikes	(4)	56
Umpire Must Call Play		57
Umpire Allowed to Call Time		58
Removal of Players from Game		59

	Sec.	Rule.
Umpire Is Empowered and Instructed to Inflict Fines..............		60
Disciplining for Disobedience of Orders....................	(2)	60
Ordering Players from the Field...........................	(4)	60
Notification of Fines......................................	(5)	60
Must Not Address Spectators..............................	(6)	60
The Reversal of Decisions................................	(7)	60
Illegal Decisions...	(8)	60

FIELD RULES.

	Rule
No Club Shall Allow Open Betting...............................	61
Who Shall Be Allowed on the Field..............................	62
Spectators Shall Not Be Addressed..............................	63
Every Club Shall Furnish Police Force..........................	64

GENERAL DEFINITIONS.

	Sec.	Rule
Play..		65
Time..		66
Game..		67
An Inning...		68
A Time at Bat...		69
Legal...		70
Scoring...		71
Batting..	(1)	71
Runs Made..	(2)	71
Base Hits..	(3)	71
Sacrifice Hits...	(4)	71
Fielding...	(5)	71
Assists..	(6)	71
Errors...	(7)	71
Stolen Bases...	(8)	71
Earned Runs..	(9)	71
The Summary..		72
Number of Earned Runs Made Off Each Pitcher............	(1)	72
Number of Two-Base Hits................................	(2)	72
Number of Three-Base Hits..............................	(3)	72
Number of Home Runs....................................	(4)	72
Number of Bases Stolen.................................	(5)	72
Number of Double and Triple Plays......................	(6)	72
Bases on Called Balls..................................	(7)	72
Bases from Being Hit...................................	(8)	72
Men Struck Out...	(9)	72
Passed Balls...	(10)	72
Wild Pitches...	(11)	72
Left on Bases..	(12)	72
Number of Innings by Each Pitcher......................	(13)	72
Number of Base-Hits Off Each Pitcher...................	(14)	72
Number of Bases on Balls by Each Pitcher...............	(15)	72
Number of Batsmen Hit by Each Pitcher..................	(16)	72
Number of Batsmen Struck Out by Each Pitcher...........	(17)	72
Number of Base-Runners Reached First Base by Errors...	(18)	72
Time of Game...	(19)	72
Condition of Weather...................................	(20)	72
Condition of Playing Field.............................	(21)	72
Name of Umpire...	(22)	72

OFFICE OF PRESIDENT

...ATIONAL LEAGUE AND AMERICAN ASSOCIATION
OF
PROFESSIONAL BASE BALL CLUBS.

N. E. YOUNG, PRESIDENT

Washington, DC Dec. 28, 1891.

I take special pleasure in bearing testimony to the superior quality of the "Spalding League Ball." It has been in constant use by the National League for the past fifteen (15) years, and has been unanimously adopted by the new National League and American Association of Professional B. B. Clubs for the coming five years. During the long time that it has been in exclusive use by League Clubs, scarcely a word of complaint as to its quality has been received from Club officials, manager or player. I have no hesitation in recommending it as the perfection of a League Ball.

N. E. Young

NATIONAL LEAGUE AND AMERICAN ASSOCIATION SCHEDULE.
SEASON OF 1897.

CLUBS.	In Boston.	In Brooklyn.	In New York	In Philadel'a	In Baltimore	In Wash'ton.	In Pittsburg.	In Cleveland	In Cincinn'ti	In L'uisv'e	In Chicago	In St Louis
Boston...	....	June 21, 22, 23 Sept. 29, 30 Oct. 2	July 1, 2, 3 Aug. 12, 13, 14	Apr. 26, 27, 28 July 5, 5, 6	Apr. 22, 23, 24 Sept. 24, 25, 27	Apr. 29, 30 May 1 July 31 Aug. 2, 3	May 10, 11, 12 July 15, 16, 17	May 13, 14, 15 July 12, 13, 14	May 27, 28, 29 July 19, 20, 21	May 24, 25, 26 July 22, 23, 24	May 17, 18, 19 July 8, 9, 10	May 20, 21, 22 July 26, 27, 28
Brooklyn.	June 28, 29, 30 Sept. 20, 21, 22	....	May 6, 8 July 5, 5, 30 Sept. 11	Apr. 29, 30 May 1 July 1, 2, 3	Apr. 26, 27, 28 Aug. 16, 17, 18	Apr. 22, 23, 24 Aug. 12, 13, 14	May 27, 28, 29 July 19, 20, 21	May 10, 11, 12 July 15, 17, 18	May 23, 24, 25 July 22, 24, 25	May 20, 21, 22 July 26, 27, 28	May 13, 15, 16 July 11, 12, 13	May 17, 18, 19 July 8, 9, 10
New York	Aug. 9, 10, 11 Sept. 16, 17, 18	May 7 July 6, 31 Aug. 2 Sept. 13, 14	....	Apr. 22, 23, 24 Aug. 5, 6, 7	Apr. 29, 30 May 1 June 21, 22, 23	May 3, 4, 5 June 24, 25, 26	May 17, 18, 19 July 8, 9, 10	May 20, 21, 22 July 26, 27, 28	May 13, 14, 15 July 12, 13, 14	May 10, 11, 12 July 15, 16, 17	May 24, 25, 26 July 22, 23, 24	May 27, 28, 29 July 19, 20, 21
Philadelphia.	Apr. 19 May 3, 4 Sept. 11, 13, 14	June 24, 25, 26 Sept. 24, 25, 27	Aug. 16, 17, 18 Sept. 29, 30 Oct. 2	....	July 31 Aug. 2, 3 Sept. 16, 17, 18	June 21, 22, 23 Aug. 9, 10, 11	May 20, 21, 22 July 26, 27, 28	May 24, 25, 26 July 22, 23, 24	May 17, 18, 19 July 8, 9, 10	May 13, 14, 15 July 12, 13, 14	May 27, 28, 29 July 19, 20, 21	May 10, 11, 12 July 15, 16, 17
Baltimore	June 24, 25, 26 Aug. 5, 6, 7	May 3, 4, 5 Aug. 9, 10, 11	June 28, 29, 30 Sept. 20, 21, 22	May 6, 7, 8 Aug. 12, 13, 14	....	May 10, 11, 12 July 30 Aug. 28, 29, 30	May 24, 25, 26 July 22, 23, 24	May 23, 28, 29 July 19, 20, 25	May 20, 21, 22 July 4, 5, 5	May 17, 18, 19 July 8, 9, 10	May 30, 31 July 15, 17, 18	May 14, 15, 16 July 11, 12, 13
Washington.	May 6, 7, 8 Aug. 16, 17, 18	Aug. 4, 6, 7 Sept. 16, 17, 18	Apr. 26, 27, 28 Sept. 24, 25, 27	June 28, 29, 30 Sept. 20, 21, 22	July 1, 2, 27 Sept. 29, 30 Oct. 2	....	May 13, 14, 15 July 12, 13, 14	May 16, 17, 18 July 8, 10, 11	May 30, 31 July 15, 17, 18	May 27, 28, 29 July 19, 20, 21	May 20, 22, 23 July 4, 5, 5	May 24, 25, 26 July 22, 24, 25

CLUBS.	In Boston.	In Brooklyn.	In New York.	In Philadel'a	In Baltimore.	In Wash'ton.	In Pittsburg.	In Cleveland.	In Cincinn'ti	In L'uisv'e	In Chicago	In St Louis
Pitts-burg.	June 5, 7, 8 Aug. 19, 20, 21	June 9, 10, 11 Aug. 23, 24, 25	May 31,31 June 1 Sept. 8, 9, 10	June 2, 3, 4 Aug. 26, 27, 28	June 16, 17, 18 Sept. 4, 6, 6	June 12, 14, 15 Aug. 31 Sept. 1, 2	....	June 28, 29, 30 Aug. 10, 11, 12	Apr. 29,30 May 1 Aug. 2, 3, 4	Apr. 26, 27,28 Sept. 13, 14, 15	July 1, 2, 3 July 29, 30, 31	Apr. 22, 23, 24 Aug. 5, 6, 7
Cleveland	June 2, 3, 4 Aug. 26, 27, 28	May 31,31 June 1 Aug. 31 Sept. 1, 2	June 16, 17, 19 Aug. 23, 24, 25	June 12, 14, 15 Sept. 4, 4, 6	June 9, 10, 11 Aug. 19, 20, 21	June 5, 7, 8 Sept. 8, 9, 10	July 5, 5, 6 Sept. 30 Oct. 1, 2	....	Apr. 26, 27, 28 July 30, 31 Aug. 1	Apr. 22, 24, 25 Aug. 2, 3, 4	June 24, 26, 27 Aug. 5, 7, 8	Apr. 29 May 1, 2 Sept. 12, 13, 14
Cincin-nati.	June 12, 14, 15 Sept. 4, 6, 6	June 16, 17, 19 Sept. 8, 9, 10	June 9, 10, 11 Aug. 31 Sept. 1, 2	June 5, 7, 8 Aug. 19, 20, 21	June 2, 3, 4 Aug. 26, 27, 28	Aug. 23, 24, 25 Sept. 11, 13, 14	May 6, 7, 8 Sept. 21, 22, 23	May 3, 4, 5 Sept. 16, 17, 18	....	....	May 9, 10, 11 July 26, 27, 28	June 28, 29, 30 Sept. 25, 26, 27
Louisville	June 9, 10, 11 Aug. 23, 24, 25	June 5, 7, 8 Aug. 26, 27, 28	June 2, 3, 4 Aug. 19, 20, 21	May 31,31 June 1 Aug. 31 Sept. 1, 2	June 12, 14, 15 Sept. 8, 9, 10	June 16, 17, 18 Sept. 4, 6, 6	May 3, 4, 5 Aug. 14,16 Sept. 11	June 20, 21, 22 Sept. 25, 26, 27	May 16 June 26, 27 July 11 Aug. 7, 8	....	June 28, 29, 30 July 25 Se. 18, 19	May 22, 23 J'ly 30, 31 Aug. 1 S'p 21,22
Chicago..	June 16, 17, 19 Aug. 31 Sept. 1, 2	June 12, 14, 15 Sept. 4, 6, 6	June 5, 7, 8 Aug. 26, 27, 28	June 9, 10, 11 Sept. 8, 9, 10	Aug. 23, 24, 25 Sept. 11, 13, 14	June 2, 3, 4 Aug. 19, 20, 21	June 21, 22, 23 Sept. 25, 27, 28	May 6, 7, 8 Sept. 21, 22, 23	Apr. 22, 24, 25 Aug. 14, 15, 16	Apr. 29 May 1, 2 Aug. 10, 11, 12	....	Apr. 26, 27, 28 Sept. 30 Oct. 2, 3
St. Louis.	May 31,31 June 1 Sept. 8, 9, 10	June 2, 3, 4 Aug. 19, 20, 21	June 12, 14, 15 Sept. 4, 6, 6	June 16, 17, 19 Aug. 23, 24, 25	June 5, 7, 8 Aug. 31 Sept. 1, 2	June 9, 10, 11 Aug. 26, 27, 28	June 24, 25, 26 Sept. 16, 17, 18	July 3, 4 Aug. 14, 15, 16	June 21, 22, 23 Aug. 10,11 Sept. 19	May 6, 8, 9 July 5, 5, 18	May 3, 4, 5 Aug. 2, 3, 4	....

SPALDING'S Trade-Mark Base Balls.

The Spalding League Ball, adopted by the National League and American Association of Professional Base Ball Clubs. Warranted to last a full game without ripping or losing its elasticity or shape.

		EACH.
No. 1.	The Spalding Official League Ball....	$1.50
No. 1B.	The Spalding Official Boys' League Ball, for Junior Clubs.............	1.00
No. 0.	"Double Seam" Ball, double stitched and warranted to last a full game..	1.50
No. 00.	Wright and Ditson's League Ball, regulation size and weight and warranted to last a full game..........	1.00
No. 2.	"Professional" Ball, regulation size and weight, warranted a first-class ball...............................	1.00
No. 2B.	"Boys' Professional," same as No. 2, in boys' size.....................	.50
No. 3.	"Amateur" Ball, regulation size, horsehide cover...................	.75
No. 5.	"King of the Diamond," regulation size and well made...............	.50
No. 7.	"Boys' Favorite," regulation size, horsehide cover...................	.25
No. 7B.	"League Junior," slightly under regulation size, horsehide cover....	.25
No. 11.	"Bouncer," a very lively and high bounding ball.....................	.25
No. 6.	"Victor" Ball, regulation size.......	.20
No. 14.	"Boys' Amateur" Ball, little under regulation size....................	.15
(All of the above in separate box and sealed.)		
No. 8.	"Eureka" Ball, nearly regulation size.	.10
No. 9B.	"Boys' Lively" Ball, high bounder..	.10
No. 13.	"Rocket" Ball, the best made.......	.05
No. 15.	"Dandy" Ball, two-piece cover......	.05
No. 16.	"Boss" Ball, four-piece cover.......	.05

A. G. SPALDING & BROS.,
New York.   Chicago.   Philadelphia.   Washington.

Spalding's Trade-Mark Bats.

 League Model, made of finest selected timber, oil finish, and in three approved models, A, B, and C. Each bat in separate bag; lngths, 33, 34, 35 and 36 inches. Highest Quality......................Each, **$1.00**
Boys' Model, same quality and finish, in three patterns, A, B and C; lengths, 30 and 32 inches...............................Each, **$1.00**

No. 3/0.

No. **3/0.** Spalding's Black End Wagon Tongue Ash Bat, League quality. Handle roughened by our patented process for better grip. Each, **$1.00**

No. **OX.** Spalding's Black End "Axletree" Bat, finest straight grained ash, improved models......................................Each, **50c.**

No. 2X.

No. **2X.** Spalding's Black End "Antique" Finish Bat, extra quality ash..Each, **25c.**
No. **4.** Spalding's Black End Willow Bat, highly finished and polished and the strongest light wood bat made...................Each, **50c.**

Spalding's Trade-Mark Boys' Bats.

No. **OXB.** Spalding's Black End Boys' Axletree Bat, extra quality ash; lengths, 30 and 32 inches.........................Each, **25c.**
No. **56.** Spalding's Black End Youths' Maple Bat, stained and polished, gilt stripes; lengths, 23 to 32 inches................Each, **10c.**
No. **53.** Spalding's Black End Youths' Maple Bat, polished, and gilt stripes; lengths, 28 to 32 inches........................Each, **10c.**
No. **54.** Spalding's Black End Boys' Maple Bat, plain finish and black stripes; lengths, 26 and 28 inches........................Each, **5c.**

Complete Catalogue Free.

A. G. Spalding & Bros.,

New York.   Chicago.   Philadelphia.   Washington.

Spalding's Masks.

Black Enameled Sun Protecting Mask.
Patented.

No. 4/0.

This is not only the "Highest Quality" Mask made by us, but has also our patent sunshade, which is formed by a piece of molded leather securely fastened to top, forming a perfect shade to the eye without obstructing the view or materially increasing the weight of the mask. Made of best soft annealed steel wire, extra heavy and black enameled, thus further preventing the reflection of light. The mask throughout is constructed of the very best material and has been highly endorsed by the leading catchers..Each, **$5.00**

Spalding's Black Enameled Masks.

No. 3/0. Our Patent Neck Protecting Mask has an extension at bottom giving absolute protection to the neck, without interfering in the least with the movements of the head. The wire is of best annealed steel, is extra heavy and covered with black enamel to prevent the reflection of light. The padding is filled with goat hair and faced with finest imported dogskin, which, being impervious to perspiration, always remains soft and pleasant to the face......Each, **$3.50**

No. 3/0.

No. 2/0. Special League Mask, made of extra heavy and best soft annealed stee. wire, black enameled, the padding filled with goat hair and covered with finest imported dogskin......................Each, **$3.00**

No. OX. Regulation League Mask, made of heavy soft annealed steel wire, black enameled, the padding well stuffed and faced with specially tanned horsehide. Warranted first-class and reliable in every particular.
Each, **$2.50**

No. 0X.

Regulation League Masks.

No. O. This mask is of same style and quality as our No. 0X mask, except that the soft annealed steel wire is bright finished. The padding is well stuffed and faced with specially tanned horsehide, Each, **$2.00**

Spalding's Amateur Masks.

No. A. Spalding's Amateur Mask, made in same size and general style as our League masks, but of lighter soft annealed steel wire, well padded, strongly constructed and warranted perfectly safe...Each, **$1.50**

No. O.

No. B. Spalding's Amateur Boys' Mask, made in same style and quality as No. A mask, only smaller in size, for boys..Each, **$1.00**

No. C. Spalding's Youths' Masks, heavy wire and well padded, without head or chin piece.......Each, **75c.**

No. D. Spalding's Youths' Masks, light wire and padded, without head or chin piece.....Each, **50c.**

No. E. Spalding's Boys' Masks, light wire and padded, without head or chin piece.................Each, **25c.**

No. C.

A. G. SPALDING & BROS.,
New York.　　Chicago.　　Philadelphia.　　Washington.

Spalding's Catchers' Mits.

All of our Mits are furnished for either the Right or Left Hand. The Left Hand Mit always sent unless otherwise ordered. **No Throwing Glove** furnished with any of our Mits.

No. 7/0.

No. 7/0. Baseman's Mit This Mit bearing the Trade Mark of our "Highest Quality" goods is sufficient guarantee that it is the most perfect glove in all its details that our past experience enables us to produce. The leather is of the finest quality specially tanned for that purpose, the padding and workmanship of the very best, and the additional feature of lace back make it—as we intend it shall be—the "PERFECTION" of Catchers' Mits. Made in Rights and Lefts............................Each, **$7.50**

The "**Morrill**" Mit is after the design of the well-known ball player, John Morrill, and has become very popular. It is made throughout of finest quality drab buckskin, is very heavily padded with the softest felt, and thumb laced to palm to prevent ripping. An extremely easy-fitting mit. Made in Rights and Lefts. Not laced back................Each, **$6.00**

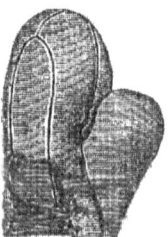

The "Morrill."

No. 5/0. Spalding's League Mit is made throughout of specially tanned and selected buckskin, making it an extra strong and durable mit, at the same time being very soft and pliable. It has our patent Lace Back and heavily padded. Made in Rights and Lefts. Each, **$5.00**

No. O. The Spalding Mit, face, sides and fingerpiece are made of velvet tanned deerskin, and the back of selected asbestos buck, making an exceedingly easy-fitting and durable mit. It has our patent Lace Back and well padded. Made in Rights and Lefts......Each, **$3.00**

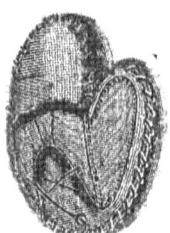

No. OX.

No. OX. Spalding's "Decker Patent" Mit is made exactly the same as our No. 0 Mit, soft tanned deerskin, with the addition of a heavy piece of sole leather on back for extra protection to the hand and fingers, as shown in cut. It has as well the patent Lace Back, and is extremely well padded. Made in Rights and Lefts............................Each, **$3.50**

No. A. Spalding's Amateur Mit is made of extra quality asbestos buck, perspiration proof and extremely tough and durable. It has our patent Lace Back, reinforced at thumb and well made and padded Made in Rights and Lefts. Each, **$2.00**

No. 3.

No. 3. The Spalding Practice Mit, the face and finger-piece of our Practice Mit are made of light brown tanned leather, the edge strip and back of ecru tanned leather. It has our patent Lace Back, reinforced at thumb and substantially padded. Made in Rights and Lefts...........................Each, **$1.00**

COMPLETE CATALOGUE FREE.

A. G. Spalding & Bros. NEW YORK CHICAGO PHILADELPHIA WASHINGTON

Good Sport

IN KANSAS
PRAIRIE CHICKENS, quails, jack-rabbits and ducks abound. The Arkansas Valley and its tributaries afford most satisfactory hunting grounds.

IN COLORADO
HERE the fishing rod should be unpacked. Enough trout to keep your rod and line busy may be found in hundreds of mountain streams, while away from the railroad larger game exists.

IN INDIAN TERRITORY
WILD TURKEYS, prairie chickens, quails and deer are the favorite game in Oklahoma and Indian Territory. A party of three to ten, with guide, will find great sport thirty miles or so from railroad lines.

IN TEXAS
ANYWHERE on the Gulf Coast several days can be enjoyably spent angling for the deep-sea fish that swarm the Gulf waters. Wild fowl are also prevalent in the marshes.

IN NEW MEXICO
UP in the mountains are clear streams where the possible catch of trout may exceed your biggest story—which is saying a good deal. Enough wild game in the wooded wilderness to satisfy the most ardent hunter.

Address W. J. BLACK, G. P. A., A., T. & S. F. Ry., Topeka, Kan., or C. A. HIGGINS, A. G. P. A., Chicago, for detailed information respecting any one or more of the above localities.

All Along the Santa Fe Route

Spalding's Boys' Catchers' Mits.

No. 2.

No. **OXB.** Spalding's "Decker Patent" Boys' League Mit, face, edge strip and finger-piece made of velvet tanned deerskin, very soft and perspiration proof. The heavy piece of sole leather on back affords extra protection to hand and fingers. It has the patent Lace Back and is extra well padded. Made in Rights and Lefts..Each, **$2.00**

No. **2.** Spalding's Boys' Mit, face and finger-piece of mit made of drab tanned buckskin, the back of lighter and the edge strip of darker tanned leather, It has our patent Lace Back, well padded and finished and reinforced at thumb. Made in Rights and Lefts, and little larger in size than our regular Boys' Mits........................Each, **$1.50**

No. 5.

No. **4.** Spalding's Boys' Mit, front and finger-piece of this mit are made of light brown tanned suede leather, with light leather trimmings It is extremely well padded and nicely finished throughout. Made in Rights and Lefts.......Each, **50c.**

No. **5.** Spalding's Boys' Mit, front and back made of ecru tanned leather, the edge strip of lighter tanned leather. Well made throughout, heavily padded and superior to any Boys' Mit ever offered at the price...........................Each, **25c.**

Spalding's Basemen's Mit.

No. BX.

No. **BX.** 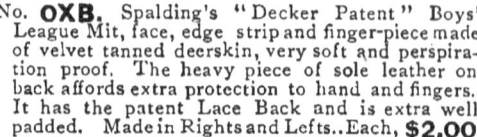 Basemen's Mit, made of fine selected and specially tanned calfskin, extremely well made throughout, and padded to meet the special requirements of a Baseman's Mit. It adapts itself nicely to the conformation of the hand without undue straining, and the addition of our patent Lace Back and "Highest Quality" Trade Mark is a sufficient guarantee of its quality and merits. Made in Rights and Lefts. Each, **$4.00**

Spalding's Basemen's and Infielders' Mits.

No. **3X.**  Mit, made of the very best and softest light tanned buckskin; the thumb and at wrist is extra well padded with the highest quality felt, making it a very safe and easy-fitting mit, combined with strength and durability. The mit throughout is of the best workmanship, as indicated by our "Highest Quality" Trade Mark. Made in Rights and Lefts...**$3.00**

No. 3X.

COMPLETE CATALOGUE FREE.

A. G. Spalding & Bros.
NEW YORK
CHICAGO
PHILADELPHIA
WASHINGTON

Chicago, Milwaukee and St. Paul Railway.

Electric Lighted and Steam Heated Vestibuled Trains between Chicago, Milwaukee, St. Paul and Minneapolis, daily.

Through Parlor Cars on Day Trains, between Chicago, St. Paul and Minneapolis.

Electric Lighted and Steam Heated Vestibuled Trains, between Chicago and Omaha and Sioux City, daily.

Eight fast trains each way daily, between Chicago and Milwaukee.

Solid trains between Chicago and principal points in Northern Wisconsin and the Peninsula of Michigan.

Through Trains with Palace Sleeping Cars, Free Chair Cars and Coaches between Chicago and points in Iowa, Minnesota, Southern and Central Dakota.

The Finest Dining Cars in the World.

The Best Sleeping Cars. Electric Reading Lamps in Berths.

The Best and Latest Type of Private Compartment Cars, Free Reclining Chair Cars and Buffet Library Smoking Cars.

6,150 Miles of Road in Illinois, Wisconsin, Northern Michigan, Iowa, Minnesota, Missouri, South and North Dakota.

Everything First-Class. First-Class People patronize First-Class Lines.

Ticket Agents everywhere sell tickets over the Chicago, Milwaukee & St. Paul Railway, or address GEO. H. HEAFFORD, General Passenger Agent, Chicago, Ill.

Spalding's Basemen's and Infielders' Mits.

No. 4X.

No. 4X. Spalding's Basemen's and Infielders' Mit is made throughout of velvet tanned deerskin and edges morocco bound. It is well padded with fine felt and carefully sewed and finished. Made in Rights and Lefts.....................Each, **$2.00**

No. 5X. Spalding's Basemen's and Infielders' Mit, made of good quality suede leather, extra well padded and constructed throughout in a most substantial manner; an exceedingly good mit at a popular price. Made in Rights and Lefts..........**$1.00**

Boys' Basemen's and Infielders' Mits.

No. 6X.

No. 6X. Spalding's Boys' Basemen's Mit is made throughout of a good quality leather. It is well padded and makes a good and substantial mit for boys. Made in Rights and Lefts.....Each, **50c.**

Infielders' Glove.

No. 2X.

Infielders' Glove is made throughout of specially tanned buckskin, lined and correctly padded with finest felt. It fits the hand perfectly and our Trade Mark "Highest Quality" is a guarantee that the glove is perfect in all its details. Made in Rights and Lefts...........................Each, **$3.00**

Infielders' Gloves.

No. 2X.

No. X. Spalding's Infielders' Glove, made of selected leather, best felt padding and carefully put together. Made in Rights and Lefts. **$1.50**

No. 15. Spalding's Men's Infielders' Glove, all leather; a substantial glove at a popular price. Each, **$1.00**

No. 16. Spalding's Men's Infielders' Glove, all leather..............................Each, **50c.**

Boys' Infielders' Glove.

No. 13. Spalding's Boys' Infielders' Glove, selected leather, felt padded, quality and style as our No. X, in boys' sizes....................Each, **$1.00**

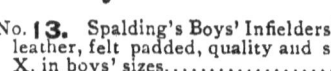

No. X.

Pitchers' Toe Plates.

Worn on toe of shoe and made for left or right foot. A valuable assistant in pitching.

No. **A.** Aluminum Toe Plate...........Each, **50c.**
No. **B.** Brass Toe Plate.............. " **25c.**

COMPLETE CATALOGUE FREE.

A. G. Spalding & Bros. New York
Chicago
Philadelphia
Washington

THROUGH SLEEPER TO WASHINGTON AND BALTIMORE

I SEE YOU'RE BACK

From a trip over the

MONON ROUTE

Solid vestibuled trains Daily, heated by steam, illuminated by Pintsch light,

BETWEEN

**CHICAGO
INDIANAPOLIS
CINCINNATI
LOUISVILLE**
And the SOUTH.

Only line to

West Baden and French Lick Springs

The Carlsbad of America.

W. H. McDoel,
V. P. and Gen. Mgr.

Frank J. Reed,
Gen. Pass. Agt.

CITY TICKET OFFICE,
232 CLARK STREET, CHICAGO.

Spalding's Inflated Body Protector.

No. 0.

We are now the sole manufacturers of the Gray Patent Protectors, the only practical device for the protection of catchers and umpires. They are made of the best rubber, inflated with air, light and pliable, and do not interfere with the movements of the wearer under any conditions. When not in use the air may be let out and the Protector rolled in a very small space. We have added this season a Boys' Protector to the line, which is equal in quality to the other styles, only smaller in size.

		EACH.
No. 0.	League Catchers' Protector	$10.00
No. 1.	Amateur " "	6.00
No. 2.	Boys' " "	5.00

Spalding's Special League Shoe Plates.

Patented.

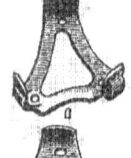

Our Special League Plates are made of the finest tempered steel and the strength increased almost fourfold without increasing weight by our patent reinforced brace, which is formed as shown in cut by splitting the metal at each corner and depressing the centre, thus forming a brace at each side.

No. 0. Spalding's Special Hand Forged Steel Toe Plates..$0.50 PAIR.

No. 2-0. Spalding's Special Hand Forged Steel Heel Plates... .50
Per dozen pairs, $5.00

Professional Shoe Plates.

No. 1. Spalding's Professional Toe Plates, best quality steel.......................... .25

No. 1H. Spalding's Professional Heel Plates, best quality steel............................. .25
Per dozen pairs, $2.50

Amateur Shoe Plates.

No. 2. Spalding's Amateur Shoe Plates, fine steel..................................... .10
Per dozen pairs, $1.00

Pitchers' Toe Plates.

Worn on toe of shoe and made for left or right foot. A valuable assistant in pitching.

No. A. Aluminum Toe Plate..........Each, 50c.
No. B. Brass Toe Plate.............. " 25c.

——— COMPLETE CATALOGUE FREE.———

A. G. Spalding & Bros.,
New York.   Chicago.   Philadelphia.   Washington.

Try the "ALTON'S" NEW LINE
—BETWEEN—
CHICAGO and PEORIA.

JAMES CHARLTON, General Passenger and Ticket Agent, Chicago, Illinois.

Base Ball Caps.

Chicago, College, Boston and University styles.

Chicago Style.

Boston Style.

	EACH.
No. **0** quality, best flannel	**$1.00**
No. **1** quality, lighter flannel	**.75**
No. **2** quality, good flannel	**.65**
No. **3** quality, ordinary flannel	**.50**
No. **4** quality, light flannel	**.40**

Chicago Style, made in 0, 1st, 2d and 3d qualities.
College Style, made in all qualities.
Boston Style, made in 0, 1st, 2d and 3d qualities.
University Style, made in 0 and 1st qualities only.

Base Ball Belts.

Worsted Web Belts.
In all colors.

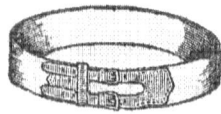
No. 3/0.

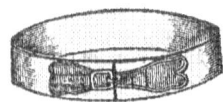
No. 2.

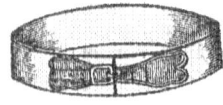
No. 47.

No. **3/0.** Special League Belt, Worsted Web, 2½ inches wide, leather lined, large nickel-plated buckle..........Each, **75c.**

No. **2/0.** League Belt, Worsted Web, 2½ inches wide, large nickel-plated buckle, Each, **50c.**

No. **2.** Worsted Web Belt, 2½ inches wide, double strap, leather covered buckles, Each, **50c.**

No. **47.** Worsted Web Belt, 2½ inches wide, single strap, leather covered buckle, Each, **50c.**

Cotton Web Belts.

Colors: Red, Navy, White, Maroon and Stripes.

No. **23.** Cotton Web Belt, 2½ inches wide, double strap, nickel buckles, Each, **25c.**

No. 23.

No. **4.** Cotton Web Belt, 2⅜ inches, leather mounted, single strap and buckle, Each, **15c.**

Complete Catalogue Free.

A. G. Spalding & Bros.,

New York.   Chicago.   Philadelphia.   Washington.

WRIGHT & DITSON

Makers of the

New Pim

...and...

Famous Campbell Rackets

✦✦✦

Send for our
Complete
Illustrated
Catalogue

Manufacturers of
Fine Lawn Tennis and Golf Goods

WRIGHT &
DITSON'S
Championship
····Ball····

Adopted by the United States Lawn Tennis Association, Intercollegiate Lawn Tennis Association, Southern Lawn Tennis Association, Canadian Lawn Tennis Association, and other Associations of the United States and Canada.

Offices and Salesrooms, 344 Washington St., Boston, Mass.
FACTORY, WAKEFIELD, MASS.

SPALDING'S BASES—Three Bases to a Set.

No. **0.**	League Club Bases, extra quality canvas and quilted, straps and spikes. complete	SET. $7.50
No. **1.**	Canvas Bases, good quality canvas, not quilted, straps and spikes, complete	5.00
No. **2.**	Canvas Bases, ordinary quality, with straps and spikes, complete	4.00

Home Plates are not included in above sets.

Spalding's Home Plates. EACH.

No. **1.**	Rubber Home Plate, complete	$7.50
No. **2.**	Marble Home Plate, best quality	2.00

Spalding's Pitcher's Box Plates.

Made in accordance with National League regulations and of extra quality white rubber. Complete with pins. EACH.

No. **3.** Spalding's Pitcher's Box Plates........$5.00

Spalding's Club Bags.

No. 2. EACH.

No. **0.**	League Club Bag, sole leather, for 18 bats	$15.00
No. **1.**	Canvas Club Bag, leather ends, for 24 bats	5.00
No. **2.**	Canvas Club Bag, leather ends, for 12 bats	4.00

Individual Bags.

No. 02. EACH.

No. **01.**	Sole Leather Bag, for two bats	$4.00
No. **02.**	Heavy Canvas Bag, Leather reinforce at both ends	1.50
No. **03.**	Cavvas Bag, Leather reinforce at one end	1.00

Athletes' Uniform Bag.

For carrying Base Ball and other Uniforms. Made to roll, and will not wrinkle or soil same. Separate compartment for shoes.

No. **1.**	Canvas	Each, $2.50
No. **2.**	Fine Bag Leather	" 5.00

Complete Catalogue Free.

A. G. Spalding & Bros.,

New York.   Chicago.   Philadelphia.   Washington.

Champion Jas. J. Corbett...
USED THE
"CORBETT"
(Trade Mark)

Manufactured by
A. J. REACH CO.,
Tulip and Palmer Sts.,
Philadelphia, Pa.

Boxing Gloves

...In his Fight with **MITCHELL** At Jacksonville, Fla., Jan. 25, 1894.

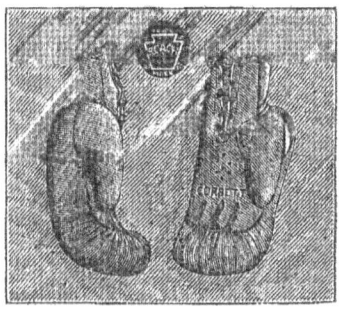

The REACH Trade Mark is on the Wrist of Every Glove.

An Exact Duplicate
of the Gloves used by CORBETT will be sent upon receipt of price.

Per Set, $7.50

If you cannot get them in your city, address

A. J. Reach Co.,

Tulip and Palmer Streets,   **PHILADELPHIA, PA.**

Spalding's Base Ball Uniforms.

COMPLETE.

Including Shirt, Padded Pants, Cap, Belt and Stockings.

No. 0.	*Spalding* Uniform	$14.75
No. 1.	"University" Uniform	11.25
No. 2.	"Interscholastic" Uniform	9.00
No. 3.	"Club Special" Uniform	6.25
No. 4.	"Amateur Special" Uniform	4.50

Our line of flannels for Base Ball Uniforms consists of the best qualities in their respective grades and the most desirable colors for Base Ball Uniforms. Each grade is kept up to the highest point of excellence and quality improved wherever possible every season. Owing to the heavy weight flannels used in our Nos. 0 and 1 Uniforms, we have found it desirable, after many years of experience, to use a little lighter weight material for the shirts; this makes them more comfortable, much cooler, and wear just as well as the heavier weight. If, however, you prefer the heavier goods for the shirts, they will be supplied at same price, but only when *specially ordered*.

Spalding's Base Ball Shirts.

In Lace or Button Front. EACH.

No. 0.	*Spalding* Shirt, any style	$5.50
No. 1.	The "University" Shirt, any style	4.50
No. 2.	"Interscholastic" Shirt, any style	3.75
No. 3.	"Club Special" Shirt, any style	2.50
No. 4.	"Amateur Special" Shirt, any style	1.85

Price includes Lettering on Shirts.

Spalding's Base Ball Pants.

In Tape or Elastic Bottom. All Padded. PAIR.

No. 0.	*Spalding* Pants	$6.00
No. 1.	"University" Pants	4.50
No. 2.	"Interscholastic" Pants	3.50
No. 3.	"Club Special" Pants	2.50
No. 4.	"Amateur Special" Pants	1.75

COMPLETE CATALOGUE FREE.

A. G. Spalding & Bros.,

New York.   Chicago.   Philadelphia.   Washington.

PHYSICIAN'S IDEAL SADDLE

"A perfect saddle for either man or woman is one that will maintain the body in an easy and proper position. It must be a surface large enough to receive the tuberosities, so that the weight comes on the gluteal muscles. It should have, like an army saddle, a hole in the centre, to relieve any injurious pressure; this will prevent urethritis, prostatitis, prostatic abscess and cistitis. The saddle should allow pedaling without needless friction. The rider should have a firm yet elastic seat."

SUCH IS THE

Christy Anatomical Saddle

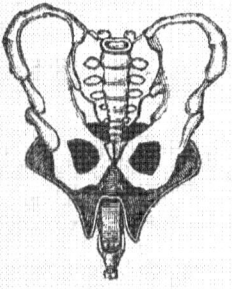 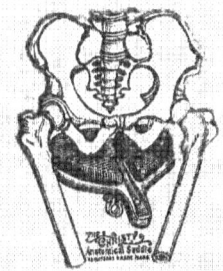

Pelvis as it rests on ordinary saddle.   *Pelvis as it rests on Christy Saddle.*

RIDERS—When ordering your 1897 Bicycle, insist that it be fitted with the **Christy**, and no dealer will lose a sale on account of your preference.

AGENTS—Bicycles fitted with **Christy Saddles** are good sellers—because riders are now educated on the saddle question. Insist, when placing your order, that your '97 wheels come fitted with **Christy Saddles.**

Manufacturers and dealers are notified that the **Christy Saddle** is fully protected by mechanical and design patents, and infringers will be prosecuted.

Booklet, "Bicycle Saddles: From a Physician's Standpoint," Sent Free.

NEW YORK   CHICAGO   **A. G. Spalding & Bros.**   PHILADELPHIA   WASHINGTON

Spalding's Elastic Bandages.

Shoulder.

Shoulder Cap Bandage.

In ordering, give circumference around arm and chest separately.

No. 1.   Cotton thread.........Each, **$3.50**
No. 1A. Silk thread .... "   **5.00**

Elbow Bandage.

Elbow.

In ordering, give circumference above and below elbow, and state whether intended for light or strong pressure.

No. 2.   Cotton thread.........Each, **$1.50**
No. 2A. Silk thread .... "   **2.00**

Fore Arm Bandage.

Fore Arm.

In ordering, give circumference below elbow and just above wrist, and state if light or strong pressure is desired.

No. 3.   Cotton thread.........Each, **$1.50**
No. 3A. Silk thread .... "   **2.00**

Knee Cap Bandage.

Knee.

In ordering, give circumference below knee, at knee, and just above knee, and state if light or strong pressure is desired.

No. 4,   Cotton thread.........Each, **$1.50**
No. 4A. Silk thread .... "   **2.00**

Ankle Bandage.

Ankle.

In ordering, give circumference around ankle and over instep, and state if light or strong pressure is desired.

No. 5.   Cotton thread.........Each, **$1.50**
No. 5A. Silk thread .... "   **2.00**

Wrist Bandage.

Wrist.

In ordering, give circumference around smallest part of wrist, and state whether for light or strong pressure.

No. 6.   Cotton thread.........Each, **$0.75**
No. 6A. Silk thread .... "   **1.00**

A. G. SPALDING & BROS.,
New York.   Chicago.   Philadelphia.   Washington.

Supporters and Bandages.

Spalding's Improved Morton Supporters.

Morton Supporter.

Made of Canton flannel, lace front. Each supporter in separate box.
No. 1. Improved Morton....Each, 35c.
No. 2. Elastic on sides and back, " 50c.

Spalding's Elastic Bandages.

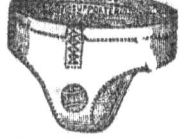

Elastic Bandage.

This bandage is light, porous and easily applied. The pressure can be applied wherever necessary and quickly secured by inserting end under last fold.
No. 25. Width 2½ inches, 5 yards long (stretched) ....Each, 75c.
No. 30. Width 3 inches, 5 yards long (stretched)................Each, $1.00

Leather Wrist Supporter.

Leather Wrist Supporter.

A perfect support and protection to the wrist. Invaluable to base ball, tennis and cricket players, or in any game where the strain is on the wrist.
No. 100. In Domestic Grain Leather— Tan Orange or Black.......Each, 25c.
No. 200. In Imported Grain, " 50c.

The Hackey Ankle Supporter.

Patented May 24, 1887.
A. G. SPALDING & BROS., Sole Licensees.

Relieves pain immediately, cures a sprain in a short time, and prevents turning of the ankle. Made of fine, soft leather, and is worn over stocking, lacing very tight in centre, loose at top and bottom. The shoe usually worn can be used.

Hackey Ankle Supporter. No. H. Hackey Supporter..Pair, $1.25

The Spalding Suspensories.

EACH.
No. 70. Non-elastic bands, knitted sack......$0.25
No. 71. Non-elastic waist bands, full elastic buttock band, knitted sack .... .50
No. 72. Elastic bands, fine English knitted sack... .75
No. 73½. Elastic bands, all silk sack, warranted not to chafe...................................... 1.00
No. 75. Elastic bands, fine Swiss bolting silk sack, satin top piece... 1.25
No. 76. Silk elastic bands, finest Swiss bolting silk sack, satin trimmings.... .... 2.00

Old Point Comfort Suspensories.

EACH.
No. 2. Elastic bands, adjusting buckles, lisle thread sack.....$1.00
No. 3. Elastic bands, adjusting buckles, satin trimmings, fine knitted silk sack.. 1.50
No. 4. Silk elastic bands, adjusting buckles, satin trimmings, fine knitted silk sack... 2.00

A. G. SPALDING & BROS.,

New York. Chicago. Philadelphia. Washington.

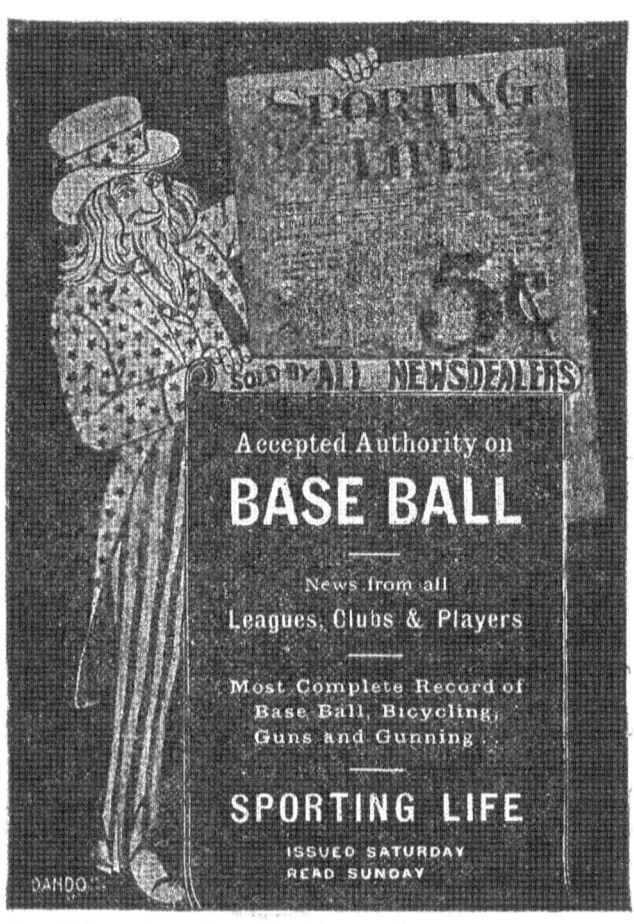

Send for Free Sample Copy of

Sporting Life

P. O. Box 948.   PHILADELPHIA, P_a

SUBSCRIPTION RATES:

One Year,	$2.00
Six Months,	1.25
Single Copies,	.05

A. H. SPINK, Editor.   C. C. SPINK, Business Manager.

...The...
Sporting News

THE BASE BALL PAPER OF THE WORLD. ♣ ♣ ♣ ♣

INVALUABLE to players, indispensable to managers, and intensely interesting to enthusiasts in all parts of the country. Its columns teem with live news of the game, collected by a carefully selected corps of over **500 Correspondents,** and attractively presented. All professional leagues and associations receive due recognition. Departments containing contributions direct from the **Magnates, Managers** and **Players** of the game enliven THE SPORTING NEWS during the off season. The standard of excellence is so well maintained at all times that there is never a dull issue, and the casual reader invariably becomes a regular subscriber.

SUBSCRIPTION PRICE:
One year, $2.00; Six months, $1.00; Single copies, 5 cts.

Sample copies mailed free on application. Send in your address on a postal card and receive a copy by return mail.

The Sporting News
Broadway and Olive St.   ST. LOUIS, MO.

Spalding's..... Home Library

Published Monthly and devoted to all Games and Pastimes of Interest to the Home Circle. . . .

PER COPY, 10 CENTS.

No. 1. CHESS	No. 7. BILLIARDS	No. 15. REVERSI
No. 2. WHIST	No. 8. ECARTE	No. 16. PIQUET
No. 3. DOMINOES and DICE	No. 9. CHECKERS	No. 17. GO-BANG
No. 4. POKER	No. 10. BEZIQUE	No. 18. GAMES OF PATIENCE
No. 5. BACKGAMMON	No. 11. POOL	No. 19. CHILDREN'S GAMES
No. 6. EUCHRE.	No. 12. PINOCHLE	No. 20. CRIBBAGE.
	No. 13. LOTO	
	No. 14. HEARTS	

BOOKS EVERY BOY SHOULD READ.

BASE BALL, by Walter Camp. Specially adapted for colleges and preparatory schools. Interesting chapters are devoted to the batter, catcher, pitcher, basemen, shortstop, outfielders; also chapters on batting and base-running. Fully illustrated.

Price, 10c., postpaid.

PRACTICAL BALL PLAYING, by Arthur A. Irwin. Containing interesting chapters on individual and team batting; essentials of a good batsman, position, bunting, fielding, etc.; with instructive hints to the pitcher, catcher, basemen, shortstop and fielders. Fully illustrated.

Price, 10c., postpaid.

AMERICAN SPORTS PUBLISHING CO.,
241 BROADWAY, NEW YORK.

SPALDING'S BASE BALL SCORE BOOKS.

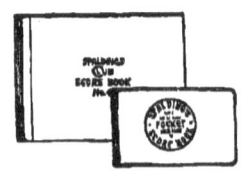

	CLUB SIZES				EACH
No. 4.	Board Cover,	30	games	....	$1.00
No. 5.	Cloth	"	60	"	.... 1.75
No. 6.	"	"	90	"	.... 2.50
No. 7.	"	"	120	"	.... 3.00
	POCKET SIZES				
No. 1.	Paper Cover,	7	games	....	.10
No. 2.	Board	"	22	"	.25
No. 3.	"	"	46	"	.... .50

Score Cards, per doz., 25c.

A. G. SPALDING & BROS.,
NEW YORK.   CHICAGO.   PHILADELPHIA.   WASHINGTON.

GEO. BARNARD & CO.

Brooklyn
Chicago

INCORPORATED

Chicago Office and Salesroom ∞ 199 Madison Street
New York Office and Salesroom ∞ 401 Broadway

Manufacturers of . . . .

Athletic and Sportsmen's Wear

Brooklyn Factory, 6th Ave. and Pacific St.

BASE BALL UNIFORMS

We are the leading manufacturers of the following lines of goods : . . . .

Geo. Barnard & Co.
BROOKLYN
CHICAGO...

Ladies' and Gentlemen's Belts
Athletic Shoes of every kind
Uniforms for Bicycling and all other Sports
Caps for Bicycle and Athletic Purposes.
Sportsmen's Wear for Shooting, Fishing, Etc.
Gun Cases in Canvas and Leather
Leggins in Canvas and Leather
Cartridge Belts and Pistol Holsters.

KNITTED GOODS=Full Fashioned
    Sweaters
    Worsted Jerseys
    Worsted Knee Pants
    Worsted Full Tights
    Worsted Racing Suits
    Worsted Bathing Suits.

WHICH 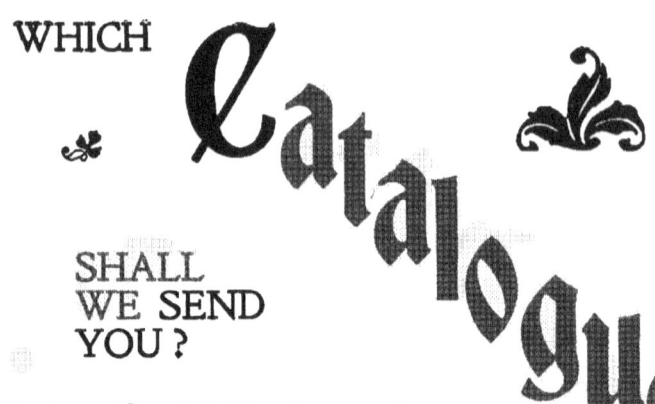 SHALL WE SEND YOU?

We issue Special Catalogues for the various departments mentioned below, and shall be pleased to mail copies free to any address. If a dealer, ask for Trade prices.

SPRING AND SUMMER SPORTS
FALL AND WINTER SPORTS
THE SPALDING BICYCLE
BICYCLE SUNDRIES
ST. LAWRENCE RIVER BOATS
HUNTING EQUIPMENTS
GYMNASIUM APPARATUS

A. G. SPALDING & BROS.

NEW YORK
CHICAGO
PHILADELPHIA
WASHINGTON

SPALDING'S
BASE BALL SHOE

No. 2/0.

Our "Highest Quality" Base Ball Shoe is hand-made through out, and of specially selected kangaroo leather. Extreme c will be taken in their general construction, and no pains o pense will be spared in making this shoe not only of the highest in quality but a perfect shoe in every detail. The plate made exclusively for this shoe, are of the finest hand-forge steel, and firmly riveted to heel and sole.

No. **2/0.**   Per Pair, **$7.50.**

SPRINTING...
Same quality as our No. 2/0 shoe, but built on our famous running shoe last. Weigh about 18 ounces to the pair, and made with extra care throughout.

No. **30 S.**   Per Pair, **$10.00.**

CLUB SPECIAL...
Made of carefully selected satin calfskin, machine s very substantially constructed and a first-class shoe in particular. Steel plates riveted to heel and sole.

No. **33.**   Per Pair, **$5.00.**

AMATEUR SPECIAL...
Made of good quality calfskin, machine sewed. able and durable shoe, and one we can specially recom Plates riveted to heel and sole.

No. **35.**   Per Pair, **$3.00.**

COMPLETE CATALOGUE FREE.

A. G. SPALDING & BROS.,

New York.   Chicago.   Philadelphia.   Washington.

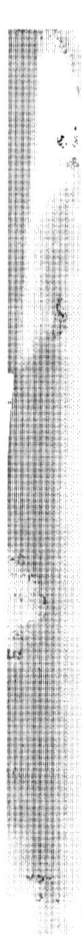

ITS NAME IS ITS GUARANTEE.

The name stands for the Highest Grade in Athletic Goods throughout the world, and now stands for
THE HIGHEST-GRADE BICYCLE MADE.

The Spalding Chainless

has passed the experimental stage, and we present it to the trade as an unqualified success, and the essence of perfection in this type of machine. It is handsome in design, and possesses many points of mechanical detail which simplify its construction and will appeal strongly to the mechanical man.

The Spalding W...

is in design and appearance entirely new machine although embracing many of the mechanical features which have done much to make the Spalding pre-eminent. It is without doubt the best chain bicycle we have produced and in ... nd ... lence leaves nothing to be desired.

A. G. SPALDING & BROS.

NEW YORK.
CHICAGO.
PHILADELPHIA.

Factory, CHICOPEE, MASS.

ALBERT G. SPALDING

SPALDING'S OFFICIAL BASE BALL GUIDE

....1898....

THE OFFICIAL BOOK OF THE NATIONAL LEAGUE

Full and Complete Records of the National and Minor League Professional Championships of 1897.

❧❧❧

THE OFFICIAL CODE OF PLAYING RULES FOR 1898

Historical Chapters, Records of the old Cincinnati Club of 1869, Reference Records, etc.

❧❧❧

FULL RECORDS OF THE VARIOUS UNIVERSITY AND COLLEGE CLUB CAMPAIGNS OF 1897

Illustrated with Portraits of all the Leading Base Ball Teams.

❧❧❧

Edited by HENRY CHADWICK
For Publication by the ❧❧❧❧❧
AMERICAN SPORTS PUBLISHING COMPANY

241 Broadway, New York City
Copyright, 1898❧❧❧❧❧❧❧❧

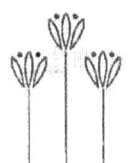 # Preface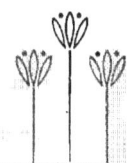

WE CAN point with justifiable pride to the twenty-third annual edition of SPALDING'S OFFICIAL BASE BALL GUIDE as the most complete work of the kind ever issued, as it is not only the largest book of statistics yet published under the auspices of the National League, but the most complete in its chapters of instructive comment on the game; the most valuable in its reference statistics and the most interesting in its historical records of past base ball history. The introductory chapters giving the records of the old Cincinnati club champions of 1869 makes this issue especially valuable. The complete record of all the pennant races in the old professional Association and National League arena from 1871 to 1897, inclusive, is valuable as a reference chapter. Added to this are not only the full statistics of the League season of 1897, but also special articles on the latest scientific points of play developed in the professional arena, together with editorial comments on the leading events of the past season—now regarded as one of the interesting features of the book—and the scores of the model games of 1897, etc. In addition to which is the new code of rules which went into effect in April, 1898, and the editorial explanatory appendix, revised by President Young of the League; the whole making the GUIDE the model base ball manual of the period, the book being of special value, alike to the amateur class of the base ball fraternity as to the class of professional exemplars of the game, the whole edited by Mr. Henry Chadwick, who has had editorial charge of the work for the past sixteen years.

AMERICAN SPORTS PUBLISHING COMPANY,
241 BROADWAY, NEW YORK CITY.

Introduction

IN VIEW of the fact that SPALDING's LEAGUE GUIDE has become not only the record book of the National League for each year, but also a highly interesting and instructive manual of the national game, it follows that its pages should be replete with information on every branch of base ball; and to such an extent as to make it a *vade mecum* for every ball player throughout the land, whether old or young, amateur or professional. To a certain extent, too, it should be a book of reference for the game, not only in regard to important annual records, but especially as an authority in interpreting the rules of play, and in giving instruction through articles on special points of play developed in the past season's experience on the field.

In the pages of former yearly editions of the GUIDE various chapters have appeared of a historical character, bearing upon prominent events which occurred during the most important eras in the annals of the professional class fraternity; but in no instance has a more interesting or instructive chapter on this subject been published than that contained in the GUIDE of 1898, headed "*The Rise and Progress of Professional Base Ball*," which is the most prominent feature of the twenty-third annual edition of the NATIONAL LEAGUE GUIDE, covering, as the chapter in question does, the championship pennant records, not only of the past twenty-one years of League history, but also the annual campaigns of the old National Professional Association, which existed during the early years of the decade of 1870. To this valuable reference chapter, too, is to be added a record of the brilliant work done in 1869 by the old Cincinnati Red Stockings, the first salaried team of ball players that ever entered the base ball arena. This portion of the chapter of professional history is so reminiscent in its character as to make it specially interesting to veterans of the ball field.

Of course, the GUIDE would not be in line with its previous reputation as "a model manual of the game" and an important book of record of the past season's doings on the field, if it did not contain a complete review of the work of the past year's championship campaign and also comments on the conclusions drawn from the season's experience on the field. Neither would it be a truthful chronicler of the season's events if it overlooked the existing evils of professionalism, which lax methods of team management have developed within the last few years. These latter need serious criticism as much as the good deeds of the players deserve commendation, and it is the province of SPALDING'S GUIDE, under its old editorship, to administer both, without fear or favor.

The story of the progress of the National League from its organization in 1876 up to the period of its reconstruction in 1892, presents a chapter of base ball history of the deepest interest; inasmuch as it is descriptive of the evolution of professional base ball, through the wrecking era of pool gambling—which ordeal it had to withstand during the decade of the '70s—to that harbor of safety the "National Agreement," in which it was anchored in 1889. The League's successful resistance to the greed of the "star" players of the fraternity in 1890, and its signal victory in its fight with the old American Association in 1891, closed its checkered career up to the time of its final establishment on the plane of true business principles in 1892. It was during this long period of its history that the League found itself antagonized by the worst elements of professional base ball playing. At first downright crookedness raised its hideous head, then came that other phase of professional dishonesty—contract-breaking—the door to which was opened by the rivalry with the opposition American Association; while drunkenness prevailed in the ranks to an extent which made it an obstacle to financial success. All these elements of opposition to playing the game in its integrity were, of necessity, obliged to be met and conquered by arbitrary enactments and strong coercive measures, which would naturally be objectionable under a better condition of things. Experience, in fact, taught the League that nothing short of the ungloved hand would be able to cope successfully against the evils that that organization had to encounter during the era of the rule of the "rough" element in the professional fraternity.

That the combination of individual club interests—which resulted from the reconstruction of the League on the basis of a twelve-club membership in 1892—has proved to be of the greatest advantage to the welfare of the professional fraternity at large, goes without saying. Its marked success as a governmental power during the past six years prove, beyond all doubt, that the existence of one great major league, to govern the professional class, is the only possible method by which that *honesty in the sport* and *honorable conduct in running its business*, so essential for financial success in professionalism, can be preserved, and the only policy of governmental power that can be pursued with any degree of creditable success.

The Rise and Progress of Professional Base Ball

IT may be justly said that five distinct eras have marked professional base ball history during the past thirty years of its existence, and the first era began with the organization of the old Professional Association in 1871. The second era was commenced with the reform movement which started in the fall of 1875 and culminated in the organization of the National League in 1876. The attempt at rebellion against League authority made by the old Union Association in 1884 may be called the third era; while the fourth began with the costly Players' revolt in 1890. Second in importance only to the advent of the National League was the era which began in 1892, which completed the evolution of professional base ball from its crude government of the early '70s to the complete system which now controls the whole professional class of the country at large. These five eras in the annals of professionalism in base ball were all marked by results which advanced the evolution of the professional system toward the goal of thorough honesty in the full development of the sport.

Professionalism in base ball, though introduced, in a measure, as early as 1860—in which year the Excelsior club of Brooklyn remunerated (*sub rosa*) its noted pitcher, Creighton, for his services—was not openly adopted until 1864, when the prominent clubs of Brooklyn and New York began playing for a share of the gate money, taken in on match days, at the Union and Capitoline grounds, the charge for admission then being ten cents. It was not until 1869, however, that a regular professional team was organized, and the first salaried base ball nine known to the game was the team of the Cincinnati club of that year, which, from its first match in April, 1869, to its celebrated contest with the Atlantics of Brooklyn in June, 1870, did not lose a single game, an achievement as yet unequaled in the annals of base ball. The Cincinnati team of 1867 was composed of amateurs under the professional management of the late Harry Wright, who also acted as their captain and pitcher, the assisting team being all amateurs, comprising Messrs. Howe, first base; Schwartz, second base; Kemper, third base; Neff, shortstop; Johnson, left field; Ellard, right field; Grant, centre field, and McLean, catcher.

The Old Cincinnati Red Stockings.

No more interesting chapter is contained in the history of base ball than that describing the series of tours made by the Cincinnatis in 1869. After opening the campaign of that year, and defeating every prominent club in Ohio, they started on their first Eastern trip, beginning with a match with the Niagara club of Buffalo and ending with the Olympics of Washington, their list of victories including the successive defeat of such noted clubs as the Haymakers of Troy, the Lowells of Boston, the champions of Harvard College, the Mutuals of New York, the Atlantic and Eckford clubs of Brooklyn, the Athletics of Philadelphia, the Marylands of Baltimore and the Nationals and Olympics of Washington. On their return home after their Eastern tour they met the Washington Olympics again, and then took the Forest City club of Rockford into camp, besides defeating some other Western clubs; and following these victories came visits from noted Eastern teams, their second game with the Haymakers of Troy, played at Cincinnati, proving to be the exceptional contest of the season, as it ended in a tie game, the only game they failed to win that year. Then came their visit to the great West, beginning at St. Louis, and, after a series of games in California, ending at Nebraska City.

RECORD OF 1869.

Cincinnati vs.	Score.	Cincinnati vs.	Score.
Great Western, at Cincinnati..	45-9	Buckeye, at Cincinnati........	71-15
Kekionga, at Fort Wayne......	83-8	Forest City, at Rockford......	15-14
Antioch, at Yellow Springs....	41-7	Cream City, at Milwaukee.....	85-7
Kekionga, at Fort Wayne......	41-7	Forest City, at Chicago........	53-32
Independent, at Mansfield.....	48-14	Forest City, at Rockford	28-7
Forest City, at Cleveland......	25-6	Central City (Syracuse), at Cin.	37-9
Niagara, at Buffalo............	42-6	Central City " "	86-2
Alert, at Rochester............	18-9	Forest City (Cleveland), "	43-20
Union, at Lansingburgh, N. Y.		Riverside, at Portsmouth......	40-7
(Haymakers)................	38-31	Eckford, at Cincinnati.........	45-18
National, at Albany...........	49-8	Southern (New Orleans), at Cin.	35-3
Mutual, at Springfield, Mass...	80-5	Union (Lansingburgh), "	17-17
Lowell, at Boston	29-9	Buckeye, "	103-8
Tri-Mountain, at Boston.......	40-12	Alert (Rochester), "	32-19
Harvard, at Cambridge........	30-11	Olympic (Pittsburg), "	54-2
Mutual, at Brooklyn...........	4-2	Union (St. Louis), at St. Louis.	70-9
Atlantic, " ...	30-11	Empire, "	31-14
Eckford, " ...	24-5	Eagle, at San Francisco	35-4
Irvington, at Irvington, N. J..	20-4	Eagle, "	58-4
Olympic, at Philadelphia......	22-11	Pacific, "	54-5
Athletic, "	27-18	Atlantic, "	76-5
Keystone, "	45-30	Omaha, at Omaha..............	65-1
Maryland, at Baltimore........	47-7	Otoes, at Nebraska City.......	50-3
National, at Washington	24-8	Occidental, at Quincy.........	51-7
Olympic, "	16-5	Marion, at Indianapolis	63-4
Olympic, at Cincinnati........	25-14	Athletic, at Cincinnati.........	17-12
Olympic, "	82-10	Kentucky, at Louisville	59-8
Forest City, at Rockford	84-13	Mutual (New York), at Cin....	17-8
Olympic, at Cincinnati........	19-7		

The foregoing record ended the Cincinnati club's season of 1869, and it left them undisputed champions of the base ball world. Their victorious career, however, was resumed in 1870, during which year, from their first game of that season in April, to the period of their second visit to the East, they kept adding victory after victory until June 14, on which day occurred their memorable eleven-inning contest with the Atlantics of Brooklyn. Here is the record of continuous victories in 1870 up to June 14:

RECORD OF 1870 TO JUNE 14.

CINCINNATI vs.	Score.	CINCINNATI vs.	Score.
Eagle, at Louisville	94-7	Riverside (Portsmouth) at Cin.	32-3
Pelican, at New Orleans	51-1	Forest City, at Cleveland	27-13
Southern, "	80-6	Flour City, at Rochester	56-18
Atlantic, "	39-6	Ontario, at Oswego	46-1
Lone Star, "	26-7	Old Elm, at Pittsfield	66-9
Robt. E. Lee, "	24-4	Harvard, at Cambridge	46-17
Oriental, at Memphis	100-2	Lowell, at Boston	18-4
Forest City (Cleveland), at Cin.	12-2	Clipper, at Lowell	32-5
Forest City " "	24-10	Tri-Mountain, at Boston	30-6
College Hill, at College Hill	72-10	Fairmount, at Worcester	77-16
Orion, at Lexington	75-0	Mutual, at Brooklyn	16-3
Union, at Urbana	108-3	Atlantic, " (11 in'gs)	7-8
Dayton, at Dayton	104-9		

This latter defeat was the first the Cincinnati club had sustained since Oct. 1, 1868, and the year-and-a-half of triumphs stands to this day as a record unequaled in the annals of base ball. The team that accomplished this most exceptionable achievement comprised the following nine players:

A. Brainard, pitcher; D. Allison, catcher; Gould, first base; Sweasy, second base; Waterman, third base; Geo. Wright, shortstop; Leonard, left field; H. Wright, centre field; McVey, right field.

After the noteworthy check to the victorious career of the Red Stockings at Brooklyn on June 14, 1870, the Cincinnatis defeated the Unions of Morrisania the next day by 14 to 0, and they followed it up by successive defeats as follows: Eckfords, by 24 to 7; Philadelphia Athletics, by 27 to 25, and, in fact, they defeated every club they played with from June 15 to July 26, inclusive. On July 27, however, the Red Stockings were defeated by the Philadelphia Athletics at Cincinnati by 11 to 7, their second defeat that year. Resuming their series of victories again, they defeated every opposing team from July 28 to Sept. 7, inclusive, and then it was that they began their first series with the Chicago team at Cincinnati, and they were defeated by the visitors by 10 to 6. From that day to Oct. 15 they added eight victories to their record, and then visiting Chicago they lost their second game with the White Stockings, and this gave the latter the series, the rule deciding the championship at that period being the winning of best two out of three games.

From Chicago the Cincinnatis went East, and though they played with the Haymakers at Troy, the Athletics at Philadelphia and the Mutuals at Brooklyn they won all of these games. But in playing off their series with the Atlantics of Brooklyn—played on neutral ground at Philadelphia—the Atlantics won the third game of the series by 11 to 7. Once more on their return home the Cincinnatis met the visiting Mutuals at Cincinnati, and defeated them for the fourth time that year. Thus, from April to November, 1870, they played a total of 74 games, of which they lost but 6, viz., 2 with the Chicagos, 2 out of 3 with the Atlantics, and 1 each with the Athletics of Philadelphia and Forest Citys of Rockford.

Going over the records of the then prominent professional clubs of the country, which included the Eastern teams of New York, Brooklyn, Philadelphia, Troy and Washington, and the Western teams of Cincinnati, Chicago, Cleveland and Rockford, we find the record of victories and defeats of those clubs, together with the percentage of each club's victories for 1870, to be as follows:

The Prominent Clubs of 1870.	Victories.	Defeats.	Per cent.	The Prominent Clubs of 1870.	Victories.	Defeats.	Per cent.
Chicago of Chicago........	65	5	.929	Forest City of Cleveland...	26	11	.708
Cincinnati of Cincinnati...	68	6	.919	Haymakers of Troy.......	32	14	.696
Mutual of New York......	68	17	.800	Olympic of Washington...	29	19	.604
Athletic of Philadelphia..	37	10	.787	Union of Morrisania......	20	18	.526
Forest City of Rockford..	44	12	.786	Eckford of Brooklyn......	12	15	.444
Atlantic of Brooklyn......	41	16	.719				

The Championship of 1870.

Prior to the organization of the "*National Association of Professional Base Ball Players,*" in the spring of 1871, there was no legal code in existence to govern championship contests, but custom sanctioned the rule of "best two out of three games" as the way to settle the question, and the playing of the first three games gave the club winning two out of the three the right to the nominal title of champions.

As we said before, the close of the campaign of 1869 saw the Cincinnati Red Stockings, under the management of the late Harry Wright, unquestioned champions of the base ball world. But in 1870 the championship question of that year became a much disputed one, and to this day it has never been satisfac-

torily settled. The contest for championship honors in 1870—
it was merely a nominal title—lay between the Cincinnati Red
Stockings, the Chicago White Stockings, the Atlantics of
Brooklyn, the Mutuals of New York and the Athletics of
Philadelphia. There were several other clubs in the field that
year, but they stood no show in the arena with the above five.
These rivals played 36 games together during 1870, some of
them playing more than the necessary quota, while all played
at least 2 games out of the regular 3. In the table giving the
figures of the victories and defeats in this total of 36 games the
Athletics had the best percentage of victories record, they
playing 18 games, the Mutuals 17, the Atlantics 15, the Cincinnatis 12 and the Chicagos but 10. Here is the table in question:

RECORD OF TOTAL GAMES PLAYED IN 1870.

Clubs.	Athletic.	Chicago.	Cincinnati.	Atlantic.	Mutual.	Victories.	Per cent.
Athletic		2	1	4	4	11	.611
Chicago	1		2	2	1	6	.600
Cincinnati	2	0		1	4	7	.583
Atlantic	1	1	2		2	6	.400
Mutual	3	1	1	2		6	.353
Defeats	7	4	5	9	11	36	

It will be seen by the above table that the Athletics took the
lead, but that fact did not give them an equitable claim to the
championship. Appended is another table showing the victories
and defeats, as also the percentage of victories figures, under
the rule of playing only three games with each other club,
leaving the extra exhibition games, played by three of the five
clubs, off the list:

RECORD OF BEST TWO OUT OF THREE GAMES PLAYED.

Clubs.	Chicago.	Cincinnati.	Athletic.	Atlantic.	Mutual.	Victories.	Per cent.
Chicago		2*	1	2	1	6	.600
Cincinnati	0		2	1	2	5	.500
Athletic	2	1		2	1	6	.500
Atlantic	1	2	1		2	6	.462
Mutual	1	0	2	2		5	.455
Defeats	4	5	6	7	6	28	

By the figures of the latter more equitable table, it will be seen that the Chicago club bore off the palm, and that club was more entitled to the championship of 1870 than any other of the five leading competitors of the season. The Athletics tied in percentage figures with the Cincinnatis, but the fact that the Reds beat the Athletics two out of three gives them the advantageous position.

The following are the names of the players of each club who took part in a majority of the games of the season of 1870:

RECORD OF THE PLAYERS' NAMES.

Chicago—Pinkham, pitcher; Hodes, catcher; Flynn, first base; J. Wood, second base; Duffy, third base; Myerle, shortstop; Cuthbert, left field; Tracey, centre field; M. King, right field.

Cincinnati—Brainard, pitcher; D. Allison, catcher; Gould, first base; Sweasy, second base; Waterman, third base; George Wright, shortstop; Leonard, left field; H. Wright, centre field; McVey, right field.

Athletic—McBride, pitcher; Malone, catcher; Fisler, first base; Reach, second base; Schaffer, third base; Radcliffe, shortstop; Bechtel, left field; Sensenderfer, centre field; Heubell, right field.

Atlantic—Zettlein, pitcher; Ferguson, catcher; Start, first base; Pike, second base; C. Smith, third base; Pearce, shortstop; Chapman, left field; Geo. Hall, centre field; McDonald, right field.

Mutual—Walters, pitcher; C. Mills, catcher; E. Mills, first base; Patterson, second base; Nelson, third base; J. Hatfield, shortstop; Swandell, left field; Eggler, centre field; Higham, right field.

It should be borne in mind, in the perusal of this chapter of professional base ball history, that from the period of the advent of the professional Red Stockings in 1869 to that of the organization of the National League in 1876, the government of the professional class of the fraternity virtually lay in the hands of the players themselves; inasmuch as from 1869 to 1871 each club was run on an individual basis. Each club, of course, had its corps of officials, but practically the players ran the business. All professional contests at that period were mere gate-money exhibition affairs, there being no schedule of championship games and no ruling governmental power to control the fraternity; and this semi-disorganized state of affairs was not long in giving birth to evils which threatened the very life of professionalism.

Betting large amounts on the result of contests had some years before had its pernicious influence in preventing games from being played in their integrity. One notable instance of the dishonesty resulting from the betting evil occurred in the metropolitan arena as early as 1865, in which three members of the old Mutual team of that year were tried and convicted of selling a game to the Eckford club in September, 1865. This sample of crookedness came solely from the betting evil, there being no gate-money influences bearing upon the question at that time, as the match in question was played on free grounds at Hoboken. The lesson of this rottenness in the ranks, and the punishment inflicted, had its due effect for a time; but, ultimately, the evil broke out again in the various phases of professional life, and by 1871 the fraternity had come to realize the fact of the necessity for the existence of a professional national association to remedy the existing condition of things, and in the spring of 1871 the "National Association of Professional Base Ball Players" was organized, which association existed up to the fall of 1875, when the demoralization which had marked its brief career, under the government of the players, reached such a point that reform measures became necessary to avoid bankruptcy. The movement to purify professionalism in base ball, which was started during the winter of 1875, culminated in 1876 in the organization of the "*National League of Professional Base Ball Clubs*," the change in the name from "Players" to "Clubs" being significant; and for the first time in the history of professional base ball the government of the class was taken out of the hands of the players and placed in those of business men of weight and influence, whose avowed purpose, as expressed in the League constitution, was "to elevate the game of base ball and to make professional ball playing respectable and honorable."

It is not our purpose, in this concise chapter on professionalism in base ball, to enter into any detailed history either of the old National Association or of the National League which succeeded it in 1876, as it would require the pages of a whole book to do this; therefore I shall confine the chapter to what I have already written on the subject, and to the interesting statistics connected with the twenty-seven annual championship campaigns which took place between 1871 and 1897, inclusive, the records given being those required to make up a complete reference record for the use of the fraternity in the future.

Record of the Old Professional Association, from 1871 to 1875, Inclusive.

The championship campaign of 1871 began with the entry of ten representative clubs for the championship of the association, viz., the Boston Red Stockings — a newly organized club—the Athletics of Philadelphia, the Chicago White Stockings, the Forest City club of Cleveland, the Haymakers of Troy, the Mutuals of New York, the Olympics of Washington and the Forest City club of Rockford, Ill. The Kekiongas of Fort Wayne were also among the entries, but their games were thrown out, as they played no legal game after the middle of July. The Eckfords of Brooklyn also entered the lists, but not until August, and consequently these games were not counted. The legal record made up at the close of the season left the eight legitimate contestants occupying the following relative positions in the pennant race of 1871:

RECORD OF 1871.

First Division Clubs.	Victories.	Defeats.	Per cent.	Second Division Clubs.	Victories.	Defeats.	Per cent.
Athletic	19	7	.731	Mutual	14	17	.452
Boston	19	9	.679	Cleveland	9	17	.346
Chicago	16	9	.640	Washington	7	14	.332
Troy	12	14	.462	Rockford	7	18	.280

Difference in percentage points between the leader and tail-ender, 451 points.
 The above record includes only the legal games counted.
 The Eckford club's figures of all games played were .895, and the Kekiongas .333.

The result of the first campaign of the Professional Association was not very satisfactory. It was plainly manifest to impartial observers that the basis of the new organization was not the one desired to conserve the best interests of the professional class. Of course the first season was largely an experimental one and improvement was looked for in 1872, but it did not come.

As a matter of old-time interest, and for reference, we give below the names of the players of the eleven clubs most prominent in the professional campaign of 1871, and who were the first contestants for championship honors under a legal code of rules. The clubs are given in the order of their position in the pennant race of that year. Those whose names are in italics are dead.

Philadelphia (Athletics)—Malone, catcher; McBride. pitcher; Fisler, first base; Reach, second base; Meyerle, third base; Radcliff, shortstop; Cuthbert, left field; Sensenderfer, centre field; Heubell, right field.
 Boston—McVey, catcher; Spalding, pitcher; Gould, first base; Barnes, second base; Shaffer, third base; Geo. Wright, shortstop; Cone left field; *H. Wright*, centre field; *Birdsall*, right field; Jackson, substitute.
 Chicago—*Hodes*, catcher; Zettlein, pitcher; McAtee, first base; Wood, second base; Pinkham, third base; *Duffy*, shortstop; Treacy, left field; M. King, centre field, Simmons, right field.
 Troy (Haymakers)—McGeary, catcher; *McMullin*, pitcher; Flynn, first base; Craver, second base; Bellan, third base; Flowers, shortstop; S. King, left field; Yorke, centre field; *Pike*, right field.
 New York (Mutuals)—C. Mills, catcher; Wolters, pitcher; Start, first base; *Ferguson*, second base; *Smith*, third base; Pearce, shortstop; Hatfield, left field; Eggler, centre field; Patterson, right field.

BASE BALL GUIDE. 13

Cleveland (Forest City)—J. White, catcher; A. Pratt, pitcher; Carleton, first base; Kimball, second base; Sutton, third base; Bass, shortstop; Faber, left field; A. Allison, centre field; E. White, right field.
Washington (Olympics)—D. Allison, catcher; *Brainard*, pitcher; E. Mil ls first base; Sweasy, second base; Waterman, third brse; Force, shortstop; Leonard, left field; Geo. Hall, centre field; Berthrong, right field.
Rockford (Forest City)—Hastings, catcher; Fisher, pitcher; Mack, first base; Addy, second base; Anson, third base; Fulmer, shortstop; Ham, left field; Bird, centre field; Stires, right field.
Brooklyn (Eckfords)—Hicks, catcher; Martin, pitcher; A. Allison, first base; Swandell, second base; Nelson, third base; Holdsworth, shortstop; Gedney, left field; Shelly, centre field; Chapman, right field; W. Allison, substitute.

The Atlantics of Brooklyn only played in 21 games in 1871, of which they lost 8, while the Eckfords played in 60, of which they won 37. The Atlantic nine of 1871 comprised the following players:

Atlantics—Noonan, catcher; Malone, pitcher; *Dehlman*, first base; Burdock, second base; Boyd, third base; *J. Hall*, shortstop; Remsen, left field; Kenny, centre field; *McDonald*, right field.

In 1872 eleven clubs entered for the Association championship, the cities represented being Boston, New York, Brooklyn, Philadelphia, Baltimore, Washington, Troy and Mansfield, Conn., in the East, and Chicago and Cleveland in the West. Two clubs entered from Washington, but one withdrew before the close of the season.

The Baltimore club entered the lists this year with a very mixed up team, its nine comprising Graves, catcher; Matthews, pitcher; E. Mills, first base; Pike, second base; Higham, third base; Radcliffe, shortstop; Yorke, left field; G. Hall, centre field, and Fisher, right field.

The following ten clubs ended with a legal record:

RECORD OF 1872.

First Division Clubs.	Won.	Lost.	Per cent.	Second Division Clubs.	Won.	Lost.	Per cent.
Boston..............	39	8	.830	Cleveland............	6	15	.286
Athletic.............	30	14	.682	Atlantic.............	8	27	.229
Baltimore...........	34	19	.642	Olympic.............	2	7	.222
Mutual..............	34	20	.630	Mansfield............	5	19	.208
Troy................	15	10	.600	Eckford.............	3	26	.103

The Boston club, which were in equity entitled to the championship of 1871, won easily in 1872, and, as will be seen by the appended records, bore off championship honors each season until the Association was succeeded by the National League in 1876.

In 1873 nine clubs entered for the Association championship, but only eight were accorded a position in the record at the close of the campaign. The Maryland club of Baltimore, after losing five games, afterwards retired from the arena. In 1873 a rival club to the Athletics of Philadelphia entered the field, it being the Philadelphias, and they not only outplayed their local opponents and would probably have won the pennant but for some questionable methods employed towards the finish. They led the Athletics in the race by a percentage of victories of .679 to .549. In that year Tim Murnane played first base and Anson shortstop for the Athletics. A new aspirant from New Jersey entered the lists in 1873, the Resolutes of Elizabeth, which nine included D. Allison, catcher; Wolters, pitcher; Mike Campbell, first base; Laughlin, second base; Swandell, third base; Jack Farrell, shortstop; Fleet, left field; Austin, centre field, and Hugh Campbell, right field. Here is the record of 1873 in full:

RECORD OF 1873.

First Division Clubs.	Victories.	Defeats.	Per cent.	Second Division Clubs.	Victories.	Defeats.	Per cent.
Boston	43	16	.729	Mutual	29	24	.547
Philadelphia	36	17	.679	Atlantic	17	37	.315
Baltimore	33	22	.600	Washington	8	31	.205
Athletic	28	23	.549	Resolute	2	21	.087

No more striking evidence of the unsatisfactory working of affairs under the old Association's management can be presented than that shown by the championship record of 1874. Eight clubs entered the lists that year, one only of which represented the West, viz., Chicago. The other cities sending teams being Boston, New York, Brooklyn, Philadelphia, Baltimore and Hartford, two clubs entering from Philadelphia. At the close of the championship season, when the Association's committee examined the records, it was found that out of 232 games scheduled to be played, only 185 legally counted in the decisive record, 96 games of the schedule being left unplayed. The official record at the finish was as follows:

RECORD OF 1874.

First Division Clubs.	Victories.	Defeats.	Per cent.	Second Division Clubs.	Victories.	Defeats.	Per cent.
Boston	43	17	.717	Chicago	19	30	.388
Mutual	34	22	.607	Atlantic	19	32	.373
Athletic	31	21	.596	Hartford	14	35	.286
Philadelphia	25	28	.472	*Baltimore	9	38	.191

Difference in percentage points between the leader and tail-ender, 626 points.   * The Maryland games were thrown out by the committee.

The professional season of 1875 saw the management of the affairs of the Professional Association culminate in a manner so damaging to the welfare of the fraternity at large as to lead to a movement for reform measures, which finally gave the death blow to the old association, and its place was taken by a new organization, the main object of which was the substitution of a professional league governed by clubs for an association controlled chiefly by players. In 1875 sundry evils in the professional system of the period had grown to such an extent that they threatened its future existence. Contract breaking, "revolving," the failure to meet engagements, and what was worse than all, pool gambling influences, led to the development of a degree of dishonesty in the ranks which brought professional ball-playing down to the level of the turf contests of the period. It was under this condition of affairs that the season of 1875 terminated, and there was commenced the reform movement which led to the establishment of the "National League of Professional Base Ball Clubs" in 1876, and this it was that saved the life of the professional system.

In 1875 thirteen clubs entered the lists for the association championship, representing seven Eastern and three Western cities—New York, Boston, Brooklyn, Washington, Hartford and New Haven each entering one club from the East, Chicago and Keokuk, Ia., one each from the West, and Philadelphia entering three clubs and St. Louis two. Such an arrangement in itself was a barrier to success in the season's campaign, and the final result proved it, as only eleven of the thirteen clubs played out their quota of games. Philadelphia entered the old Athletics, the Philadelphias and the new Centennial club, the St. Louis club and the Red Stockings of St. Louis being the two clubs from that city. We append the full record of 1875 as a matter of curiosity, and just to show how the old association managed its championship campaign the last year of its existence:

First Division Clubs.	Victories.	Defeats.	Per cent.	Second Division Clubs.	Victories.	Defeats.	Per cent.
Boston...............	71	8	.809	St. Louis Reds.........	4	14	.222
Athletic...............	55	28	.756	Washington...........	4	22	.156
Hartford..............	54	28	.639	New Haven...........	7	39	.152
St. Louis.............	29	39	.574	Centennial............	2	13	.133
Philadelphia.........	37	31	.544	Western...............	1	12	.077
Chicago..............	30	37	.448	Atlantic...............	2	42	.065
Mutual...............	29	38	.426				

Bankruptcy attended the closing up of the affairs of the majority of the above clubs in 1875. The most noteworthy contest of the old Association's last season was that played at Chicago, June 19, between the Chicago White Stockings and the Dark Blues of Hartford, in which the veteran pugilist, Billy McLean of Philadelphia, acted as umpire. For ten successive innings not a run was scored on either side, but in the eleventh the Chicagos won by 1 to 0. Zettlein pitched for Chicago and Arthur Cummings for Hartford, the late veteran, Robert Ferguson, being manager and third baseman of the Blues, with D. Allison, catcher; E. Mills, Burdock and Ferguson being on the bases, Casey as shortstop, and York, Remsen and Bond in the outfield, the nine including no less than six Brooklyn players. Besides Zettlein, the Chicago nine included Higham, catcher, Devlin, Miller and Warren on the bases; Peters as shortstop, and Glenn, Hines and Hastings in the outfield. It is interesting to note the makeup of the St. Louis club for the year that club first entered the professional association. It was as follows: Miller, catcher; Bradley, pitcher; Dehlman, first base; Battin, second base; Fleet, third base; Dick Pearce, shortstop, with Cuthbert, Pike and Chapman in the outfield. Billy Barnie was catcher of the Western team of Keokuk that year, with Golden as pitcher. Matthews and Hicks were the Mutuals' battery, McBride and Clapp that of the Athletics, Zettlein and Hastings for Chicago, Fisher and Snyder for the Philadelphias, and Spalding and White for the Bostons, it being the last year that they played together in the Boston club.

The Advent of the National League.

In finishing up this concise chapter of the history of professional base ball playing, we purpose to confine our statistics to the records of each championship season of the League from 1876 to 1897, inclusive, without going into any description of the three eras which have marked the twenty-one years of National League existence, nor the secession movement in 1884, the players' revolt in 1890, and the reconstruction of the League in 1892. The records in question are as follows, and show at a glance just how the clubs finished each season. The Boston and Chicago clubs are the only ones which have been in the League continuously since its formation. The Bostons have won the pennant seven times and the Chicagos six times during that period.

BASE BALL GUIDE.

RECORD OF 1876.

First Division Clubs.	Victories.	Defeats.	Per cent.	Second Division Clubs.	Victories.	Defeats.	Per cent.
Chicago...............	52	14	.788	Louisville............	30	36	.455
Hartford..............	47	21	.691	Mutual...............	21	35	.375
St. Louis..............	45	19	.703	Athletic	14	45	.237
Boston................	39	31	.557	Cincinnati............	9	56	.135

Difference in percentage points between the leader and tail-ender, 653 points.

RECORD OF 1877.

Boston................	31	17	.648	St. Louis.............	19	29	.396
Louisville.............	28	20	.583	Chicago..............	18	30	.375
Hartford..............	24	24	.500	Cincinnati............	15	42	.263

Difference in percentage points between the leader and tail-ender, 385 points.

RECORD OF 1878.

Boston................	41	19	.707	Chicago..............	30	30	.500
Cincinnati............	37	23	.617	Indianapolis..........	24	36	.400
Providence...........	33	27	.550	Milwaukee............	15	45	.250

Difference in percentage points between the leader and tail-ender, 457 points.

RECORD OF 1879.

Providence...........	55	23	.705	Cincinnati............	38	36	.514
Boston................	49	29	.628	Cleveland............	24	53	.312
Chicago...............	44	32	.579	Troy.................	19	56	.253
Buffalo...............	44	32	.579	Syracuse.............	15	27	.357

Difference in percentage points between the leader and tail-ender, 348 points.

RECORD OF 1880.

Chicago...............	67	17	.798	Worcester............	40	43	.482
Providence...........	52	32	.619	Boston...............	40	44	.474
Cleveland.............	47	37	.559	Buffalo...............	24	58	.293
Troy..................	41	42	.494	Cincinnati............	21	59	.263

Difference in percentage points between the leader and tail-ender, 535 points.

RECORD OF 1881.

Chicago...............	56	28	.667	Troy.................	39	45	.464
Providence...........	47	37	.559	Boston...............	38	45	.458
Buffalo...............	45	38	.542	Cleveland............	36	48	.429
Detroit................	41	43	.488	Worcester............	32	50	.390

Difference in percentage points between the leader and tail-ender, 277 points.

RECORD OF 1882.

First Division Clubs.	Victories.	Defeats.	Per cent.	Second Division Clubs.	Victories.	Defeats.	Per cent.
Chicago	55	29	.655	Cleveland	42	40	.512
Providence	52	32	.619	Detroit	42	41	.506
Buffalo	45	39	.536	Troy	35	48	.422
Boston	45	39	.536	Worcester	18	66	.214

Difference in percentage points between the leader and tail-ender, 441 points.

RECORD OF 1883.

Boston	63	35	.643	Buffalo	52	45	.536
Chicago	59	39	.602	New York	46	50	.479
Providence	58	47	.592	Detroit	40	58	.408
Cleveland	55	42	.567	Philadelphia	17	81	.173

Difference in percentage points between the leader and tail-ender, 470 points.

RECORD OF 1884.

Providence	84	28	.750	New York	62	50	.554
Boston	73	38	.658	Philadelphia	39	73	.348
Buffalo	64	47	.577	Cleveland	35	77	.313
Chicago	62	50	.554	Detroit	28	84	250

Difference in percentage points between the leader and tail-ender, 500 points.

RECORD OF 1885.

Chicago	87	25	.776	Boston	46	66	.410
New York	85	27	.758	Detroit	41	67	.379
Philadelphia	56	54	.509	Buffalo	38	74	.339
Providence	53	57	.481	St. Louis	36	72	.333

Difference in percentage points between the leader and tail-ender, 443 points.

RECORD OF 1886.

Chicago	90	34	.725	Boston	56	61	.478
Detroit	87	36	.707	St. Louis	43	79	.352
New York	75	44	.630	Kansas City	30	91	.247
Philadelphia	71	43	.622	Washington	28	92	.233

Difference in percentage points between the leader and tail-ender, 492 points.

RECORD OF 1887.

Detroit	79	45	.637	Boston	61	60	.504
Philadelphia	75	48	.610	Pittsburg	55	69	.444
Chicago	71	50	.587	Washington	46	76	.377
New York	68	55	.553	Indianapolis	37	89	.294

Difference in percentage points between the leader and tail-ender, 343 points.

BASE BALL GUIDE. 19

RECORD OF 1888.

First Division Clubs.	Victories.	Defeats.	Per cent.	Second Division Clubs.	Victories.	Defeats.	Per cent.
New York.............	84	47	.641	Detroit...............	68	63	.519
Chicago...............	77	58	.578	Pittsburg.............	66	68	.493
Philadelphia..........	69	61	.531	Indianapolis..........	50	85	.370
Boston................	70	64	.522	Washington...........	48	86	.358

Difference in percentage points between the leader and tail-ender, 283 points.

RECORD OF 1889.

New York.............	83	43	.659	Pittsburg.............	61	71	.462
Boston................	83	45	.648	Cleveland.............	61	72	.459
Chicago...............	67	65	.508	Indianapolis..........	59	75	.440
Philadelphia..........	63	64	.496	Washington...........	41	83	.331

Difference in percentage points between the leader and tail-ender, 328 points.

RECORD OF 1890.

Brooklyn..............	86	43	.667	Boston................	76	57	.571
Chicago...............	83	53	.610	New York.............	63	68	.481
Philadelphia..........	78	53	.595	Cleveland.............	44	88	.333
Cincinnati............	78	55	.586	Pittsburg.............	23	114	.168

Difference in percentage points between the leader and tail-ender, 499 points.

RECORD OF 1891.

Boston................	87	51	.630	Cleveland.............	65	74	.468
Chicago...............	82	53	.607	Brooklyn..............	61	69	.445
New York.............	71	61	.538	Cincinnati............	56	81	.409
Philadelphia..........	68	69	.496	Pittsburg.............	55	80	.407

Difference in percentage points between the leader and tail-ender, 223 points.

RECORD OF 1892—FIRST HALF.

Boston................	52	22	.703	Washington...........	35	41	.461
Brooklyn..............	51	26	.662	Chicago...............	31	39	.443
Philadelphia..........	46	30	.605	St. Louis.............	31	42	.425
Cincinnati............	44	31	.587	New York.............	31	43	.419
Cleveland.............	40	33	.548	Louisville............	30	47	.390
Pittsburg.............	37	39	.487	Baltimore.............	20	55	.267

Difference in percentage points between the leader and tail-ender, 436 points.

SECOND HALF.

Cleveland.............	53	23	.697	Chicago...............	39	37	.513
Boston................	50	26	.658	Cincinnati............	33	37	.507
Brooklyn..............	44	33	.571	Louisville............	33	42	.440
Pittsburg.............	43	34	.558	Baltimore.............	26	46	.361
Philadelphia..........	41	36	.532	St. Louis.............	25	52	.325
New York.............	40	37	.519	Washington...........	23	52	.307

Difference in percentage points between the leader and tail-ender, 390 points.

FULL SEASON'S RECORD OF 1892.

First Division Clubs.	Victories.	Defeats.	Per cent.	Second Division Clubs.	Victories.	Defeats.	Per cent.
Boston	102	48	.680	Chicago	70	76	.479
Cleveland	93	54	.624	New York	71	80	.470
Brooklyn	95	59	.617	Louisville	63	89	.414
Philadelphia	87	66	.569	Washington	58	93	.384
Cincinnati	82	68	.547	St. Louis	56	94	.373
Pittsburg	80	73	.523	Baltimore	46	101	.313

Difference in percentage points between the leader and tail-ender, 367 points.

RECORD OF 1893.

Boston	86	44	.662	Brooklyn	65	63	.508
Pittsburg	81	48	.628	Baltimore	60	70	.462
Cleveland	73	55	.570	Chicago	51	71	.445
Philadelphia	72	53	.558	St. Louis	57	75	.432
New York	68	64	.515	Louisville	50	75	.400
Cincinnati	65	63	.508	Washington	40	89	.310

Difference in percentage points between the leader and tail-ender, 352 points.

RECORD OF 1894.

Baltimore	89	39	.695	Pittsburg	65	65	.500
New York	88	44	.667	Chicago	57	75	.432
Boston	83	49	.629	St. Louis	56	76	.424
Philadelphia	71	56	.559	Cincinnati	54	75	.419
Brooklyn	70	61	.534	Washington	45	87	.341
Cleveland	68	61	.527	Louisville	36	94	.277

Difference in percentage points between the leader and tail-ender, 418 points.

RECORD OF 1895.

Baltimore	87	43	.669	Pittsburg	71	61	.538
Cleveland	84	46	.646	Cincinnati	66	64	.508
Philadelphia	78	53	.595	New York	66	65	.504
Chicago	72	58	.554	Washington	43	85	.336
Brooklyn	71	60	.542	St. Louis	39	92	.298
Boston	71	60	.542	Louisville	35	96	.267

Difference in percentage points between the leader and tail-ender, 402 points.

RECORD OF 1896.

Baltimore	90	39	.698	New York	64	67	.489
Cleveland	80	48	.625	Philadelphia	62	68	.477
Cincinnati	77	50	.606	Washington	58	73	.443
Boston	74	57	.565	Brooklyn	58	73	.443
Chicago	71	57	.555	St. Louis	40	90	.308
Pittsburg	66	63	.512	Louisville	38	92	.290

Difference in percentage points between the leader and tail-ender, 408 points.

RECORD OF 1897.

First Division Clubs.	Victories.	Defeats.	Per cent.	Second Division Clubs.	Victories.	Defeats.	Per cent.
Boston	93	39	.705	Washington	61	71	.462
Baltimore	90	40	.692	Pittsburg	60	71	.454
New York	83	48	.634	Chicago	59	73	.447
Cincinnati	76	56	.576	Philadelphia	55	77	.417
Cleveland	69	62	.527	Louisville	52	78	.400
Brooklyn	61	71	.462	St. Louis	29	102	.229

Difference in percentage between the leader and tail-ender, 476 points.

In concluding this special article on professional base ball, we want to state the important fact that it is to the National League, up to 1892, and to the great major league, now in such successful operation, that the game is largely indebted for the great popularity it has achieved. In the first place the game could never have reached its present point of excellence in field work but for the time and attention the professional clubs were enabled to devote to its thorough development, inasmuch as the amateur clubs could never have given the game the time and labor required for its evolution which the professional clubs were enabled to do; and, moreover, not one club in a thousand could have spared the money to fit up and keep in serviceable condition such finely equipped ball grounds as those now owned by the leading professional clubs of the National League. To these facts, too, are to be added the statement that to the National League's government of the professional class of the fraternity is due the lasting credit of sustaining the integrity of play in the game up to the highest standard.

That the reorganized League has become a permanent institution goes without saying, and each year of its existence will only see it more firmly established as the sole power for the government of the whole of the professional base ball fraternity. The assimilation of the old American Association element in the reorganized League is complete. Nothing would induce the magnates of the four clubs—now part and parcel of the League—to go back to the old condition of things, of a divided governmental power in the control of the fraternity, from the fact that practical experience of the most costly character proved the idea to be a fallacy; the only strength of the old dual government, depending upon its fidelity to the National Agreement compact, while its weakness—plainly proved in 1891—lay in the opportunity it afforded the class of "star" players of the fraternity to use the rival organizations for the purpose of keeping up fancy salaries, and the opportunity it afforded for contract-breaking and "revolving," two evils impossible under the government of the great major league.

 The Professional Season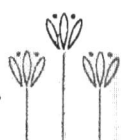
☙of 1897☙

THE professional base ball season of 1897 was entered upon under circumstances not very promising for the financial success of the clubs of the various leagues and associations which comprise the fraternity at large, inasmuch as it followed close upon the heels of an exciting Presidential election campaign, and began just as the country had emerged from a depressed condition of monetary affairs in business life; and consequently the liberal patronage of professional sports, which invariably follows upon an era of financial prosperity, was wanting last year to a considerable extent. But the professional class in base ball have for years held such a high reputation for pursuing their contests on the field with a degree of honesty unequaled by any other sport, that they have commanded a patronage under adverse circumstances which other field sports have failed to equal; hence the championship contests of 1897 were attended by larger crowds than the unpromising business outlook at the start of the campaign led the magnates of the League to expect.

Besides the grand championship campaign of the major league, which forms the stellar attraction each year in the professional base ball world, there were the lesser lights of the minor leagues, the campaigns of which were more or less attractive. Prominent among this latter class were the Eastern, New England and Atlantic Leagues in the East, and the Western League, Western Association and Interstate League in the West, together with several State leagues, among the most successful of which was that of Connecticut. The Southern League started, but broke down at the very outset, and the Texas League lost some of its members in midsummer, besides which several State leagues went under; and, in fact, but a minority of the minor leagues played their schedule out to a finish, and only the best managed leagues reaped financial success, though not one struck any Klondike veins in the way of a gate-money harvest.

A conspicuous feature of the several championship campaigns of 1897 was a continuation of the abuse known as "kicking," which, since 1894, had, year after year, been increasing; until, in 1897, it had reached the culminating point of low prize-ring tactics, and had brought positive danger to the good name of the professional base ball business at large. While, in the exciting scenes and incident to a series of close contests in a championship pennant race, there is apt to be more or less personal rivalry trenching upon the bitter; as, also, outbursts of hot temper and questionable language and actions; still there is a point, even in the most exciting contest, beyond which no well-managed team of players should be allowed to go, and that point was reached time and again this past season, when actual rowdyism on the field disgraced alike the players, the manager and the higher officials of the clubs which openly countenanced it by not promptly prohibiting it.

The papers still harp on the old, mistaken idea that because a swift pitcher intimidates young batsmen into striking out, that consequently he is a great pitcher. This is an exploded idea.

The great want of the day in the college base ball arena is a strong representative National Association of College Clubs, based upon State College Club Associations, something college base ball has never yet benefited by. When the American College Base Ball Association was organized in 1879 it practically became a sectional organization representing only the leading colleges of the Eastern States.

It should be remembered that base ball was first introduced into England by American exemplars of our national game as long ago as 1874, twenty-four years; while in Australia its advent there occurred as late as 1888, and yet the game since then has made more progress in public favor in Australia than it has in more than twenty years in England. We hope for more rapid progress each year there now, as the base ball has now got a good foothold in England, and that, of course, will help it in Australia.

It is to the introduction of base ball as a national pastime, in fact, that the growth of athletic sports in general in popularity is largely due; and the game has pointed out to the mercantile community of our large cities that "all work and no play" is the most costly policy they can pursue, both in regard to the advantages to their own health and in the improvement in the work of their employes; the combination of work and play yielding results in better work and more satisfactory service than was possible under the old rule.

Here is a record of the results of one side batting against an elastic ball sent in by poor pitchers, and of good pitching and sharp fielding against muffin batsmen on the other side. The contrast shown was presented on the occasion of the game played on May 17, 1870, between the Forest City and Atlantic clubs of Cleveland. At the end of the fifth inning the game stood at the unprecedented score of 132 to 1 in favor of the Forest Citys—101 first base hits and 180 total. In the first and third innings the Forest Citys made 52 and 53, respectively.

What can present a more attractive picture to the lover of outdoor sports than the scene presented at a base ball match between two trained professional teams competing for championship honors, in which every point of play is so well looked after in the field that it is only by some extra display of skill at the bat that a single run is obtained in a full nine-innings game? If it is considered, too, that base ball is a healthy, recreative exercise, suitable for all classes of our people, there can be no surprise that such a game should reach the unprecedented popularity it has.

 The League's Championship Campaign of 1897

THE sixth annual championship campaign of the National League, since the year of its reconstruction in 1892, occurred in 1897, and it was a season which still further proved the great advantage the governmental power of the League is to the professional class of the fraternity in promoting its general welfare, and in preserving that integrity of play in the professional arena which has marked the organization's career for the past quarter of a century. In fact, it may be aptly said that the professional machine now runs along as smoothly as a well-oiled engine, and though now and then, on exceptional occasions, certain trials occur to test the innate strength of the organization, the League never fails to be equal to the ordeal in the most trying emergency. It is a noteworthy fact in this connection that Mr. A. G. Spalding, from the period of the League's trials and tribulations during the decade of the seventies up to the time of the fiery ordeal it passed through in the year of the players' revolt in 1890, was always an ardent advocate of the existence of a strong major league to govern the entire professional fraternity; and the major organization, which began its history in 1892, has undoubtedly proved the wisdom of his views.

The championship pennant race of 1897, as a whole, was not up to the mark of those of the previous pennant campaigns since 1892; that is, looking at it in the light of an evenly contested race, such as the difference in percentage points between the leader and tail-ender of each year, this special race record for the past six years being as follows:

RECORD OF DIFFERENCE OF PERCENTAGE POINTS.

Year.	Difference in points.	Year.	Difference in points	Year.	Difference in points.
1892	367	1894	418	1896	408
1893	352	1895	402	1897	476

But the exciting finish of the race of 1897 in September last between the Boston and Baltimore clubs made the contest exceptional in that one respect. It is rather surprising, when one comes to look at the question in a true business light, that the twelve members of the League copartnership cannot see that their financial interests are best conserved when the clubs join forces in a legitimate effort to even up their respective club teams, so as to make the pennant race of each year as closely contested a one as possible, for therein unquestionably lies their greatest financial success. Let us glance at the records of the past six years of League history, just to see what the results of this existing method of making the pennant races one-sided shows are.

Here is a table showing the names of the clubs which not only occupied one or other of the three leading positions in each of the six annual pennant races, but also of those which were one or other of the three tail-enders in each race:

RECORD OF LEADERS AND TAIL-ENDERS.

Year.	First Place.	Second Place.	Third Place.	Tenth Place.	Eleventh Place.	Twelfth Place.
1892	Boston	Cleveland	Brooklyn	Wash'gt'n	St. Louis	Baltimore
1893	Boston	Pittsburg	Cleveland	St. Louis	Louisville	Wash'gt'n
1894	Baltimore	New York	Boston	Cincinnati	Wash'gt'n	St. Louis
1895	Baltimore	Cleveland	Philad'lp'a	Wash'gt'n	St. Louis	Louisville
1896	Baltimore	Cleveland	Cincinnati	Brooklyn	St. Louis	Louisville
1897	Boston	Baltimore	New York	Philad'lp'a	Louisville	St. Louis
Total Clubs	2	4	6	5	3	4

It will be seen that while only two of the twelve clubs held the leading place in the six years of championship contests, only four others occupied the last ditch during that period. In other words, while the Boston and Baltimore clubs alone shared championship honors in six years, the St. Louis and Louisville clubs alternately lay in the last ditch four years out of the six, while six other clubs were in the intermediate place.

The evenness of a pennant race is a very potent factor in promoting the financial success of each year's championship campaign; a fact which the majority of the professional club magnates do not appear to fully realize, or they would make greater efforts to even up the playing strength of their respective league club teams than they have hitherto done. Up to the time of the organization of the existing major league not the slightest effort was made by the clubs of the old League and Association to even up their teams each year with the view of insuring a closely contested pennant race; the rule then being for each club to be run on the plan of each one for itself and the devil take the hindmost. Of course, this shortsighted policy was in costly conflict with the running of the clubs on true business principles, the motto of which in all true copartnership is "*All for one and one for all.*" It may truly be said that the more closely a pennant race is contested from start to finish the greater the attraction, and, in consequence, the larger the patronage.

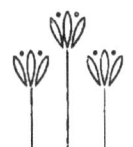 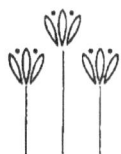

The League Pennant Race of 1897

WHEN the pennant race of 1897 began in Boston on April 19 with the defeat of the local team by the visiting Philadelphias, Boston stock did not open up very well in the League market, and it took a downward step the same week, when the Baltimores won three straight from the Bostons at Baltimore. The New York team, too, when it began the race with three straight defeats in New York at the hands of the Phillies, felt the effect of its bad start in the race. Out West the Cleveland and Chicago teams, from which better things were expected, both opened badly, while Cincinnati, and especially Louisville, began the season in lively style. When the April campaign ended and the pennant race record of May 1 appeared, the twelve clubs were found occupying the following relative positions in the race:

RECORD ON MAY 1.

First Division Clubs.	Victories.	Defeats.	Per cent.	Second Division Clubs.	Victories.	Defeats.	Per cent.
Philadelphia	8	1	.889	Washington	2	4	.333
Baltimore	7	1	.875	New York	2	5	.286
Cincinnati	6	1	.857	Cleveland	2	5	.286
Louisville	5	1	.833	St. Louis	2	5	.286
Pittsburg	3	2	.600	Chicago	2	6	.250
Brooklyn	3	6	.333	Boston	1	6	.143

On May 1 Philadelphia stock was in the ascendant and paying crowds flocked to the club's park. Baltimore paper, too, was quoted above par, and Cincinnati was the favorite in Western cities; while Louisville began to have a dark horse reputation, and Pittsburg managed to hold its own. But all the others were quoted at more or less of a discount, as no less than seven of the twelve clubs had lost more games than they had won up to the end of the April campaign; Boston occupying the last ditch on May 1, with Chicago on the ragged edge, while Cleveland, New York and St. Louis had to be content with the low percentage figures of .286 each. Washington, which club led the second division, only had .333, the same as Brooklyn, who led the Senators, owing to their having won more games from Washington in their series than the latter did.

The Race in May. April is the month of experimental contests in the pennant race campaign of each year, and the results at the end of that month have no important bearing in indicating the probable outcome in September. But in May the real work of the campaign begins to show itself, and the sifting process commences, during which the League wheat is separated from the chaff, and the coming leaders and tail-enders begin to be located in their appointed divisions. Philadelphia ended in April in the lead, while Boston was in the last ditch, but the first week of May had not ended before Philadelphia was superseded by Baltimore, and Boston had rapidly risen from the tail-end place. The surprise party of the month was the position of the Louisvilles on May 7, when they occupied second place, with the percentage figures of .700 to their credit. By May 13 Boston had got into the first division, and St. Louis had settled down to its old place at the tail end, with Chicago close by. During the latter part of May the Phillies fell off badly, while Cincinnati got into second place. When the May campaign ended the record of the race on June 1 left the twelve clubs occupying the following relative positions in the contest:

First Division Clubs.	Victories.	Defeats.	Per cent.	Second Division Clubs.	Victories.	Defeats.	Per cent.
Baltimore	23	8	.742	Philadelphia	17	17	.500
Cincinnati	23	11	.676	Brooklyn	16	16	.500
Boston	20	12	.625	Louisville	15	16	.484
Pittsburg	18	12	.600	Chicago	11	22	.333
Cleveland	17	14	.548	Washington	9	21	.300
New York	15	13	.536	St. Louis	6	28	.176

By this time the New York Giants began to wake up, and they entered the first division the first week in June, leaving Brooklyn at the head of the second division. The June campaign each year generally sees the clubs settled down to steadier work in the running, and the innate strength or weakness of the several teams begins to be developed, the teams having the advantage of competent management almost invariably getting well up in the front during June. It was in this month that the Boston management began a new point in the working of their team. Mr. Soden had noticed that the kicking habit among the League players had undoubtedly had a demoralizing effect on the players in preventing thorough team-work in the ranks; so, to put a check on it in the Boston team he gave out the notice that every fine incurred by any of his players would have to be paid out of their own pockets, and the result was beneficial in the extreme, one effect being that the Bostons got right into second place as early as June 8, thereby sending Cincinnati to third place. By June 10 four Eastern and two Western teams occupied places in the first division, viz., Baltimore, Boston, Cincinnati, New York, Cleveland and Brooklyn; and it is a noteworthy fact that the same six ended the season in the first division. Before the expiration of the month of June, Boston replaced Baltimore in the lead, the change taking place on June 21. The highest percentage point reached by Boston this month was on June 25, when their figures stood at .740 to Baltimore's .694, a lead of 46 points.

RACE RECORD ON JULY 1.

First Division Clubs.	Victories.	Defeats.	Per cent.	Second Division Clubs.	Victories.	Defeats.	Per cent.
Boston...............	41	14	.745	Pittsburg.............	26	28	.481
Baltimore.............	37	17	.685	Brooklyn	26	29	.473
Cincinnati	34	17	.667	Washington...........	22	32	.407
New York.............	33	21	.611	Louisville	21	33	.389
Cleveland.............	28	27	.509	Chicago...............	21	35	.375
Philadelphia.	28	30	.483	St. Louis......	11	45	.196

Boston won 21 games out of 23 in June, while Baltimore won but 12 out of 20. Washington did better than Baltimore, winning 14 out of 24.

July is the test month in the League race, the clubs losing or winning the most ground in July generally being found in the first or second divisions at the finish accordingly. During the whole of July the Bostons did not lessen their hold of first place in the race even for a single day; while most of the month Baltimore had to be content with third place, the former leading the latter by .682 to .657 on July 18. Before July ended, however, Baltimore had got back to second place. Here is how the twelve clubs stood in the race on August 1:

THE RACE RECORD ON AUGUST 1.

First Division Clubs.	Victories.	Defeats.	Per cent.	Second Division Clubs.	Victories.	Defeats.	Per cent.
Boston...............	56	24	.700	Pittsburg	37	43	.463
Baltimore.............	52	26	.667	Chicago...............	37	47	.440
Cincinnati............	51	27	.654	Louisville............	37	49	.430
New York.............	47	31	.603	Brooklyn	34	46	.425
Cleveland	44	36	.550	Washington...........	29	50	.367
Philadelphia	40	44	.476	St. Louis..............	22	63	.247

The month of August is the least profitable of any month, and it was especially dull last year, inasmuch as the unevenness of the pennant race was plainly shown at the end of July, when the difference between the leader and tail-ender was no less than 453 points, when anything like an even contest would have seen the difference in points not exceeding 200. The decline in interest in the race began as soon as it was practically settled that such clubs as Philadelphia, Pittsburg and Chicago would be almost certain to end in the second division, while even as early as August 1 it was certain that the Boston and Baltimore clubs would lead the first division, and Louisville and St. Louis end the second division. The Bostons maintained their vantage ground in the race through August up to the 27th, when the Baltimores led them by 4 points, .683 to .679. It was in August that Brooklyn fell down so badly, that team, which in the last week in June was in sixth place, reaching eleventh position on August 18. Chicago pulled up in August, but only for a short time; New York got into third place the last of the month, but got no higher, the Giants' victories over the Chicagos and the defeats the Cincinnatis sustained at Baltimore on August 27 sending Cincinnati to fourth place, and they failed to get higher after that. Here is the race record on September 1.

RECORD ON SEPTEMBER 1.

First Division Clubs.	Victories.	Defeats.	Per cent.	Second Division Clubs.	Victories.	Defeats.	Per cent.
Baltimore	73	32	.695	Philadelphia	49	61	.445
Boston	75	34	.688	Louisville	48	62	.436
New York	67	38	.638	Brooklyn	47	61	.435
Cincinnati	62	43	.590	Washington	46	60	.434
Cleveland	54	51	.514	Pittsburg	46	60	.434
Chicago	50	59	.439	St. Louis	26	82	.241

The only interesting feature of the race in September was the remarkably close contest between the Baltimores and Bostons for first place. On August 27 Baltimore again occupied the lead in the race for the first time since June 22, and they retained it up to September 24, when Boston led them by 7 points. On September 25 Baltimore led Boston by a single point, but on the 27th the Bostons went to the front once more and stayed there. The last week in September saw a close fight for sixth place between Washington and Brooklyn, the latter finally getting the place, though tied in percentage figures, as in their series with Washington they won by 8 games to 4, and that gave them the title to sixth place.

The end of the season—October—saw the same six clubs in the second division as were there as early as June, with one exception, Brooklyn driving Pittsburg out of the first division. The appended record is the most complete of its kind yet published in the GUIDE, as it shows at a glance the victories and defeats scored by the clubs of each division, one against the other.

THE FULL RACE RECORD OF 1897.

CLUBS.	First Division vs. First Division.							First Division vs. Second Division.							Grand Total.	Per cent. of Victories.
	Boston.	Baltimore.	New York.	Cincinnati	Cleveland.	Brooklyn.	Victories.	Washington.	Pittsburg.	Chicago.	Philadelphia.	Louisville.	St. Louis.	Victories.		
Boston...............		6	8	9	7	9	39	7	10	8	10	9	10	54	98	.705
Baltimore............	6		5	6	7	9	33	9	9	9	10	10	10	57	90	.692
New York............	4	7		5	9	9	34	9	8	7	7	6	12	49	83	.692
Cincinnati...........	3	6	7		7	5	28	8	5	7	8	9	11	48	76	.576
Cleveland............	5	4	3	5		5	22	8	6	8	9	5	11	47	69	.527
Brooklyn.............	3	3	3	7	7		23	7	7	6	6	5	7	38	61	.462
Defeats..............	21	26	26	32	37	37	179	48	45	45	50	44	61	293	472	

CLUBS.	Second Division vs. First Division.							Second Division vs. Second Division.							Grand Total.	Per cent. of Victories.
	Boston.	Baltimore.	New York.	Cincinnati.	Cleveland.	Brooklyn.	Victories.	Washington.	Pittsburg.	Chicago.	Philadelphia.	Louisville.	St. Louis.	Victories.		
Washington..........	5	3	3	4	4	5	24		7	5	8	8	9	37	61	.402
Pittsburg............	2	3	3	7	6	5	26	6		6	7	8	8	34	60	.454
Chicago..............	4	3	5	5	4	6	27	7	6		5	6	8	32	59	.447
Philadelphia.........	2	2	5	4	3	6	22	4	5	7		9	8	33	55	.417
Louisville...........	3	1	6	3	7	7	27	4	4	6	3		8	25	52	.400
St. Louis............	2	2	0	1	1	5	11	3	4	4	4	3		18	29	.229
Defeats..............	18	14	22	24	25	34	137	23	26	28	27	34	41	179	316	

A summary of the preceding table gives the following records showing how the clubs of each division stand in percentage of victories figures, in their victories and defeats, division against division.

FIRST DIVISION RECORDS.

First Division vs. First Division.	Won.	Lost.	Per cent.	First Division vs. Second Division.	Won.	Lost.	Per cent.
Boston................	39	21	.650	Boston................	54	18	.750
New York	34	26	.567	Baltimore.............	57	14	.708
Baltimore.............	33	26	.559	New York.............	49	22	.690
Cincinnati	28	32	.467	Cincinnati	48	24	.667
Brooklyn	23	37	.383	Cleveland.............	47	25	.653
Cleveland.............	22	37	.373	Brooklyn	38	34	.528
Totals	179	179		Totals	293	137	

SECOND DIVISION RECORDS.

Second Division vs. First Division.	Won.	Lost.	Per cent.	Second Division vs. Second Division.	Won.	Lost.	Per cent.
Louisville............	27	44	.380	Washington...........	37	23	.617
Chicago	27	45	.375	Pittsburg.............	34	26	.567
Pittsburg.............	26	45	.366	Philadelphia..........	33	27	.550
Washington...........	24	48	.333	Chicago...............	32	28	.533
Philadelphia..........	22	50	.306	Louisville............	25	34	.424
St. Louis.............	11	61	.153	St. Louis.............	18	41	.305
Totals	137	293		Totals	179	179	

It will be seen by the above tables that the Boston club led all the other clubs in scoring victories in each division; but New York, while leading Baltimore in scoring victories over first division clubs, was led by Baltimore in victories over second division clubs. Louisville, too, while leading all of the second division clubs in scoring victories over first division opponents, stood next to last against second division adversaries; while Washington, though but fourth against first division clubs, led all of their class against second division opponents. This is one of the anomalies of the yearly pennant races, which is somewhat similar to that which almost invariably leaves a generally successful team exceptionally weak against one particular club.

Batsmen, in order to excel in the art of handling the bat scientifically, must get out of the old rut of fungo hitting, and apply themselves to the study of the art, the aim and intent of which is to forward runners around the bases by place hitting, thereby making base hits by the least expenditure of strength, and in a manner which yields the most attractive features of the game in handsome displays of fielding and base-running.

The Sectional Campaign

AMONG the most interesting features of the championship race each year, are the sectional campaigns, during which the six Eastern clubs and their six Western rivals, respectively, tour the East and West alternately. It is a noteworthy fact, in connection alike with the home-and-home campaign and those of the East and West, that in both sections the clubs which have been leaders and tail-enders each season in the pennant race, have been the highest and lowest in the two classes of campaigns, thereby showing that the one-sided character of each season's race is due to the peculiar strength or weakness of the minority of the twelve, and not to that of their being Eastern or Western teams particularly. For instance, while the six Eastern teams have invariably led the six Western in total victories each season during the past six years, the Cleveland team has been most among the three leaders and the Washington among the tail-enders. Here is the record showing how the clubs of the two sections stand in total victories and defeats scored against each other during the period from 1892 to 1897 inclusive; from which it will be seen that the six Eastern teams have been victorious by a majority of victories ranging from 10 in 1893 to 110 in 1894, with intermediate figures during the other four years.

SIX YEARS' RECORD OF EAST VS. WEST CAMPAIGN.

Years.	Sections.	Victories.	Defeats.	Difference in Totals.	Years.	Sections.	Victories.	Defeats.	Difference in Totals.
1892	East vs. West	252	209	43	1895	East vs. West	238	188	50
1893	" " "	219	209	10	1896	" " "	233	197	36
1894	" " "	268	158	110	1897	" " "	264	169	95
						Grand Totals...	1474	1130	344

It is an an interesting problem for the League magnates to solve in the future, why it is that the six Western teams should annually lose a majority of their games in their contests with their six rivals in the League arena. Such a condition of things ought not to exist in a business copartnership like the League,

Copyright, 1897, by F. G. Selee and F. O. Woodruff.

Sullivan   Stivetts   Allen   Ganzel   Klobedanz   Lewis   Lake
Long   Nichols   Yeager   Selee (Mgr.)   Duffy (Capt.)   Tenney   Hamilton
Collins   Stahl   Lowe

BOSTON BASE BALL CLUB, 1897.

Clarke　Amole　　Hoffer　　　　Corbett　　　　Pond　　　Robinson
Reitz　 Jennings　Von Der Horst (Pres.) Hanlon (Mgr.) Kelley Doyle
Quinn　 O'Brien　 McGraw　Bowerman　Keeler　Maul　Stenzel

Stafford Beckley Doheny Wilson Houle Zeidler Souder W. Clark Sullivan Meekin
         Tiernan W. H. (Dad) Clarke Joyce (Capt.) Davis Gleason Zearfoss
         Seymour   Shea   Gettig   Van Haltren Warner Standish

NEW YORK BASE BALL CLUB, 1897.

Copyright, 1897, by Bellsmith, Cincinnati, O.
Hoy   Brown   Ritchie   Holliday   Rhines   Beckley   Miller   Peitz   Vaughn   Shriver
Dwyer   McPhee   Corcoran   Ewing (Capt.)   Irwin   Breitenstein   Ehret
           Burke   George (Mascot)   Damman

Copyright, 1897, by Gardner & Co., Brooklyn, N.Y.

Dunn A. Smith Jones Stein Schoch Hannivan
Payne Lachance Fisher Kennedy Anderson Shindle
Daub Grim Griffin Barnie (Mgr.) Burrell McMahon
Canavan G. Smith

BROOKLYN BASE BALL CLUB, 1897.

Copyright, 1897, by Rice, Washington, D. C.

Reilly Cartwright McJames Maul Swaim Farrell Ashe Brown German
  DeMontreville Kimble McGuire Schmelz (Mgr.) Mercer Lush Norton
               O'Brien   Selbach   Abbey   Wrigley

WASHINGTON BASE BALL CLUB, 1897.

Kittridge Terry Ryan
Briggs Griffith Everett
Friend Donahue Thornton
Lange Dahlen Decker

CHICAGO BASE BALL CLUB, 1897.

Dolan　Johnson　Hill　Werden　Wilson　Butler　Stafford
　　　Clark　Clingman Clark (Capt. and Mgr.) Wagner　Magee
　　　　Evans　Cunningham　Frazer　Dexter

LOUISVILLE BASE BALL CLUB, 1897.

The First East vs. West Series of 1897. The first series of games between the Eastern and Western club teams of the National League of 1897 began at Cleveland, Pittsburg, Louisville and St. Louis on May 10, and the series ended at Chicago and Cincinnati on May 31, the record in full being as follows:

FIRST EAST VS. WEST RECORD.

Eastern Clubs.	Victories.	Defeats.	Per cent.	Western Clubs.	Victories.	Defeats.	Per cent.
Boston	12	7	.632	Cincinnati	13	5	.722
Baltimore	11	7	.611	Cleveland	10	6	.625
Brooklyn	11	7	.611	Pittsburg	10	9	.526
New York	7	9	.438	Chicago	8	10	.444
Philadelphia	7	10	.412	Louisville	5	9	.357
Washington	5	12	.294	St. Louis	2	15	.118
Totals	54	52	.509	Totals	52	54	.491

Boston took the lead in this Western campaign and earned the reputation at once of being the most prominent rival the Baltimores had in the pennant race. The latter club and the Brooklyns tied on the tour in doing well against the Western clubs; but the other three lost more games than they won on the tour, Washington making a very poor record. Of the Western teams, those of Cincinnati, Cleveland and Pittsburg did the best against their Eastern rivals.

The first Eastern tour of the Western teams began at New York on May 28 and ended on June 19. The record is as follows:

FIRST WEST VS. EAST RECORD.

Eastern Clubs.	Victories.	Defeats.	Per cent.	Western Clubs.	Victories.	Defeats.	Per cent.
Boston	16	0	1.000	Chicago	6	7	.462
Baltimore	10	2	.833	Cincinnati	4	6	.400
New York	11	4	.733	Cleveland	5	11	.313
Washington	8	5	.615	St. Louis	4	13	.235
Brooklyn	9	6	.600	Pittsburg	3	13	.188
Philadelphia	9	8	.529	Louisville	3	14	.176
Totals	64	25	.719	Totals	25	64	.281

During this campaign Boston made an exceptional record. When it began they stood fourth in the race with the percentage of victories figures of .607, and when it ended that club was second with percentage of .733, their team winning every game during the series. Every one of the Western teams lost more games than they won on the tour, the Chicagos being the most successful, while Pittsburg and Louisville did very badly.

The Eastern teams won 64 games to the Western's 25; while out West the visitors from the East on the first tour won 54 to 52. The third sectional campaign began on July 4 in the West, and it being Sunday only the Baltimore and Washington clubs played, and both were defeated, the one at Cincinnati and the other at Chicago. The holiday was kept on Monday, July 5, when Cincinnati again beat Baltimore, and Washington won one game and lost one, the other clubs finishing off their respective home-and-home schedules. The tour ended on July 28, at St. Louis, Louisville, Pittsburg and Cleveland, with the following record:

Western Clubs.	Victories.	Defeats.	Per cent.	Eastern Clubs.	Victories.	Defeats.	Per cent.
Cleveland	12	5	.706	Philadelphia	11	8	.579
Chicago	13	8	.619	New York	11	9	.550
Cincinnati	12	7	.600	Baltimore	10	10	.500
Louisville	10	11	.476	Boston	9	10	.474
St. Louis	8	12	.400	Washington	8	13	.381
Pittsburg	6	12	.333	Brooklyn	6	12	.333
Totals	61	55	.530	Totals	55	62	.470

In this campaign the Western clubs had the best of it, as they won 61 games to 55 by the Eastern clubs; Cleveland, Chicago, and Cincinnati leading the Western clubs, while Louisville, St. Louis and Pittsburg lost more games than they won. Singularly enough, Philadelphia led all the Eastern clubs on the tour, Brooklyn being the tail-ender, as they lost 12 out of 18 games.

The last sectional campaign of the season began in the East on August 19 and ended on September 15, the Eastern teams winning 94 games to the Western's 35 only. Here is the record in full.

BASE BALL GUIDE. 35

LAST WEST VS. EAST RECORD.

Eastern Clubs.	Victories.	Defeats.	Per cent.	Western Clubs.	Victories.	Defeats.	Per cent.
Baltimore	21	3	.875	Cincinnati	8	17	.320
New York	18	4	.818	Cleveland	7	15	.318
Boston	16	4	.800	Pittsburg	6	14	.300
Washington	16	6	.727	Louisville	6	14	.300
Brooklyn	13	8	.619	Chicago	6	17	.261
Philadelphia	9	10	.474	St. Louis	2	17	.105
Totals	94	35	.729	Totals	35	94	.271

COMPLETE SUMMARY RECORD.

Clubs.		East.					West.						Against East.	Against West.	Totals.	Series Won, Lost and Tied.
		Boston.	Baltimore.	New York.	Brooklyn.	Washington.	Philadelphia.	Cincinnati.	Cleveland.	Pittsburg.	Chicago.	Louisville.	St. Louis.				
Boston	Won		6	8	9	7	10	9	7	10	8	9	10	40	58	98	Won, 10
	Lost		6	4	3	5	2	8	5	2	4	3	2	20	19	39	Lost, 0 / Tied, 1
Baltimore	Won	6		5	9	9	10	6	7	9	9	10	10	39	51	90	Won, 8
	Lost	6		7	3	3	2	6	4	3	3	1	2	21	19	40	Lost, 1 / Tied, 2
New York	Won	4	7		9	9	7	5	9	8	7	6	12	36	47	83	Won, 8
	Lost	8	5		3	3	5	7	3	3	5	6	0	24	24	48	Lost, 2 / Tied, 1
Brooklyn	Won	3	3	3		7	6	7	7	7	6	5	7	22	39	61	Won, 5
	Lost	9	9	9		5	6	5	5	5	6	7	5	38	33	71	Lost, 4 / Tied, 2
Washington	Won	5	3	3	5		8	4	4	7	5	8	9	24	37	61	Won, 4
	Lost	7	9	9	7		4	8	8	5	7	4	3	36	35	71	Lost, 7 / Tied, 0
Philadelphia	Won	2	2	5	6	4		4	3	5	7	9	8	19	36	55	Won, 3
	Lost	10	10	7	6	8		8	9	7	5	3	4	41	36	77	Lost, 7 / Tied, 1
Cincinnati	Won	3	6	7	5	8	8		7	5	7	9	11	37	39	76	Won, 7
	Lost	9	6	5	7	4	4		5	7	5	3	1	35	21	56	Lost, 3 / Tied, 1
Cleveland	Won	5	4	3	5	8	9	5		6	8	5	11	34	35	69	Won, 4
	Lost	7	7	9	7	4	3	7		6	4	7	1	37	25	62	Lost, 6 / Tied, 1
Pittsburg	Won	2	3	3	5	5	7	7	6		6	8	8	25	35	60	Won, 4
	Lost	10	9	8	7	7	5	5	6		6	4	4	46	25	71	Lost, 5 / Tied, 2
Chicago	Won	4	3	5	6	7	5	5	4	6		6	8	30	29	59	Won, 2
	Lost	8	9	7	6	5	7	7	8	6		6	4	42	31	73	Lost, 6 / Tied, 3
Louisville	Won	3	1	6	7	4	3	3	7	4	6		8	24	28	52	Won, 3
	Lost	9	10	6	5	8	9	9	5	8	6		3	47	31	78	Lost, 6 / Tied, 2
St. Louis	Won	2	2	0	5	3	4	1	1	4	4	3		16	13	29	Won, 0
	Lost	10	10	12	7	9	8	11	11	8	8	8		56	46	102	Lost, 11 / Tied, 0

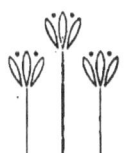 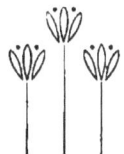

The Monthly Campaigns of 1897

ONE of the most interesting of the statistical chapters of the GUIDE each year is that describing the ups and downs of the clubs each month in the pennant race, as shown by the records of the victories and defeats scored each month of the season by each of the twelve clubs. These records include each separate month's victories and defeats, the names of the clubs being given in the order of percentage of victories scored each individual month. Here are the records in question:

THE APRIL RECORD.

First Division.	Victories.	Defeats.	Per cent.	Second Division.	Victories.	Defeats.	Per cent.
Philadelphia............	7	1	.875	Washington............	2	4	.333
Baltimore..............	7	1	.875	St. Louis..............	2	4	.333
Cincinnati.............	6	1	.857	New York.............	2	5	.286
Louisville..............	5	1	.833	Chicago...............	2	6	.250
Pittsburg..............	3	2	.600	Cleveland.............	1	5	.167
Brooklyn..............	3	5	.375	Boston................	1	6	.143

The above record is also the pennant race record as it stood on April 30.

THE MAY RECORD.

First Division.	Victories.	Defeats.	Per cent.	Second Division.	Victories.	Defeats.	Per cent.
Boston................	17	6	.789	Brooklyn..............	12	11	.522
Baltimore..............	16	7	.696	Louisville.............	10	14	.417
Cleveland..............	16	8	.667	Philadelphia...........	9	16	.360
Cincinnati	17	9	.654	Chicago...............	8	16	.333
Pittsburg..............	15	9	.628	Washington...........	7	17	.292
New York.............	12	8	.600	St. Louis.............	4	22	.154

On May 31 the three leaders in the pennant race were the Baltimore, Cincinnati and Pittsburg clubs, and the three tailenders were the Chicago, Washington and St. Louis teams.

THE JUNE RECORD.

First Division.	Victories.	Defeats.	Per cent.	Second Division.	Victories.	Defeats.	Per cent.
Boston	22	2	.917	Philadelphia	11	13	.458
New York	19	7	.731	Cleveland	10	14	.417
Cincinnati	10	6	.625	Chicago	9	13	.409
Washington	13	10	.565	Pittsburg	8	16	.333
Baltimore	13	9	.591	Louisville	6	17	.261
Brooklyn	11	12	.478	St. Louis	5	18	.217

On June 30 the Boston, Baltimore and Cincinnati clubs led in the pennant race, and the three tail-enders were Louisville, Chicago and St. Louis.

THE JULY RECORD.

Clubs.	Victories.	Defeats.	Per cent.	Clubs.	Victories.	Defeats.	Per cent.
Cleveland	17	8	.680	Philadelphia	13	14	.481
Baltimore	16	9	.640	Louisville	15	17	.469
Cincinnati	17	10	.630	Pittsburg	11	16	.407
Boston	16	10	.615	St. Louis	10	18	.357
Chicago	17	12	.586	Brooklyn	8	18	.308
New York	15	11	.577	Washington	7	19	.269

On July 31 the race record showed that the Boston, Baltimore and Cincinnati clubs were still in the van, while the Brooklyn, Washington and St. Louis clubs were the tail-enders.

THE AUGUST RECORD.

Clubs.	Victories.	Defeats.	Per cent.	Clubs.	Victories.	Defeats.	Per cent.
Baltimore	20	6	.769	Cincinnati	12	15	.444
New York	19	7	.731	Brooklyn	12	15	.444
Boston	18	10	.643	Cleveland	10	15	.406
Washington	16	10	.615	Pittsburg	9	16	.360
Chicago	13	11	.542	Philadelphia	8	17	.320
Louisville	13	13	.500	St. Louis	5	20	.200

On August 31 Baltimore, Boston and New York were the three leaders in the race, with Brooklyn, Washington and St. Louis as the three tail-enders.

The last month's record includes the games played up to October 3, the last day of the scheduled season.

THE SEPTEMBER RECORD.

Clubs.	Victories.	Defeats.	Per cent.	Clubs.	Victories.	Defeats.	Per cent.
Boston	19	5	.792	Pittsburg	14	12	.538
Baltimore	18	8	.692	Cincinnati	14	14	.500
New York	17	10	.630	Chicago	9	15	.375
Washington	16	10	.615	Philadelphia	7	16	.304
Brooklyn	15	10	.600	Louisville	4	17	.190
Cleveland	15	12	.556	St. Louis	3	22	.120

The end of the campaign on October 3 saw Boston, Baltimore and New York in the van, with Philadelphia, Louisville and St. Louis as the tail-enders, Boston winning the championship and St. Louis the leathern medal as the occupant of the last ditch, for the first time during the six annual races.

THE SUMMARY RECORD.

Appended is a full summary record of the work done by the twelve clubs during the entire championship season of 1897, the first table giving the figures of the victories, defeats, drawn games, series won, lost and tied, and the percentage-of-victories record of each individual club:

	First Division Clubs.						Second Division Clubs.					
	Boston.	Baltimore.	New York.	Cincinnati.	Cleveland.	Brooklyn.	Washington.	Pittsburg.	Chicago.	Philadelphia.	Louisville.	St. Louis.
Victories	93	90	83	76	69	61	61	60	59	55	52	29
Defeats	39	40	48	56	62	71	71	71	73	77	78	102
Drawn games	3	6	6	2	1	4	3	4	6	2	4	1
Total games	135	136	137	134	132	136	135	135	138	134	134	132
Series won	10	8	8	7	4	5	4	4	2	3	8	0
Series lost	0	1	2	3	6	4	7	5	6	7	6	11
Series tied	1	2	1	1	1	2	0	2	3	1	2	0
Per cent	.705	.692	.634	.576	.489	.462	.462	.458	.447	.417	.400	.220

In addition to the above, another record table is given, which comprises one of the most interesting statistical tables yet published:

BASE BALL GUIDE. 39

	First Division Clubs.					Second Division Clubs.					
	Boston.	Baltimore.	New York.	Cincinnati.	Cleveland.	Brooklyn.	Washington.	Pittsburg.	Chicago.	Philadelphia.	Louisville.	St. Louis.
"Chicago" victories...........	6	3	8	4	5	4	7	2	2	2	2	1
"Chicago" defeats.............	2	2	2	5	5	6	4	1	4	3	6	6
Extra-innings victories........	3	3	1	4	2	3	2	6	4	3	2	3
Extra-innings defeats..........	2	2	5	3	2	4	4	1	3	5	3	2
Won by one run................	19	13	16	29	15	16	9	21	18	21	14	13
Lost by one run...............	11	13	14	13	18	17	21	16	22	22	18	19
Single-figure victories.........	57	56	59	51	48	41	45	49	42	30	39	24
Double-figure victories.........	36	34	24	25	21	20	16	11	17	22	13	5
Single-figure defeats..........	27	31	35	44	52	43	53	44	50	57	57	59
Double-figure defeats..........	12	9	13	12	10	28	18	27	23	20	21	43
Victories at home..............	55	53	51	49	49	38	40	38	38	32	34	18
Victories abroad...............	38	37	32	27	20	23	21	22	21	23	18	11
Defeats at home...............	12	15	19	18	15	29	25	27	30	33	32	41
Defeats abroad................	27	25	29	38	47	42	46	44	43	44	46	61
Total runs scored.............	848 to 350	748 to 368	722 to 325	577 to 285	607 to 240	521 to 248	518 to 236	430 to 237	465 to 247	468 to 242	407 to 230	180 to 112

The detailed record of the games drawn during the championship campaign of 1897 is appended.

RECORD OF DRAWN GAMES.

Date.	Contesting Clubs.	Where Played	Pitchers.	In'gs.	Score.
Apr. 26	Boston vs. Philadelphia....	Philadelphia..	Lewis........Taylor	9	8-8
" 26	Washington vs. New York.	New York....	Mercer......Doheny	9	3-3
" 26	Pittsburg vs. Louisville....	Louisville....	Tannehill....Frazer	12	3-3
" 29	Cleveland vs. St. Louis....	St. Louis.....	Young........Esper	9	6-6
" 30	Boston vs. Washington....	Washington..	J.Sullivan.McJames	10	3-3
May 1	Chicago vs. Louisville.....	Louisville....	Denzer.........Hill	9	5-5
" 3	Baltimore vs. Brooklyn....	Brooklyn.....	Corbett......Payne	11	3-3
" 6	Brooklyn vs. New York....	New York....	McMahon....Clarke	10	9-9
" 31	Baltimore vs. Chicago.....	Chicago......	Corbett....Callahan	9	6-6
Aug. 4	Pittsburg vs. Cincinnati...	Cincinnati....	Gardner.....Dwyer	6	4-4
" 10	Baltimore vs. Brooklyn....	Brooklyn.....	Corbett......Payne	8	3-3
" 24	Chicago vs. Baltimore.....	Baltimore....	Friend.........Pond	8	5-5
" 28	Chicago vs. New York.....	New York....	Thornton..Seymour	8	6-6
" 31	Chicago vs. Boston........	Boston.......	Klobedanz....Briggs	11	8-8
Sept. 2	Cincinnati vs. New York...	New York....	Ehret.......Meekin	9	3-3
" 4	Louisville vs. Washington.	Washington..	Cu'ni'gh'mM'James	10	7-7
" 10	Pittsburg vs. New York....	New York....	Hastings...Seymour	9	2-2
" 11	Chicago vs. Baltimore.....	Baltimore....	Thornton....Corbett	9	3-3
" 13	New York vs. Brooklyn....	Brooklyn. ...	Gettig.....Kennedy	7	8-8
" 14	Louisville vs. Pittsburg....	Louisville....	Magee........Killen	5	2-2
" 16	Philadelphia vs. Baltimore.	Baltimore.....	Taylor........Nops	9	4-4

The record of games in which the losing side did not score a single run comprises a list of no less than 46 games, with scores ranging from 1 to 0 to 17 to 0. Of the former closely contested games there were no less than 8, while of the one-sided games marked by double figure scores for the winning side there were 7, of which the Boston defeat of the New York team by 17 to 0 was the worst defeat any club sustained in the whole list. Here is the record in full:

"CHICAGO" VICTORIES AND DEFEATS.

Date.	Contesting Clubs.	Where Played	Pitchers.	In'gs.	Score.
Apr. 28	Cincinnati vs. Cleveland..	Cincinnati....	Damman....Cuppy	9	5-0
May 7	Boston vs. Washington...	Boston.......	J.Sullivan.McJames	9	4-0
" 11	Cleveland vs. Brooklyn...	Cleveland....	Cuppy....... Payne	9	7-0
" 15	Pittsburg vs. Washington.	Pittsburg....	Tannehill...Mercer	9	2-0
" 17	Baltimore vs. Louisville..	Louisville....	Nops.....Hemming	9	5-0
" 25	New York vs. Chicago....	Chicago......	Rusie....... Denzer	9	8-0
" 27	Louisville vs. Washington	Louisville....	Hill ... .Mercer	9	5-0
June 3	St. Louis vs. Brooklyn....	Brooklyn.....	Donahue.McMahon	6	1-0
" 9	Washington vs. St. Louis.	Washington...	Mercer ... Donahue	9	6-0
" 12	Philadelphia vs. Clevel'd.	Philadelphia.	Taylor......Wilson	9	5-0
" 17	New York vs. Cleveland..	New York....	Meeker......Young	9	5-0
" 18	New York vs. Cleveland..	New York....	Seymour.McDerm't	9	5-0
" 19	Brooklyn vs. Cincinnati..	Brooklyn.....	Kennedy....Dwyer	9	1-0
" 26	Baltimore vs. Boston.....	Boston	Corbett..... Nichols	9	1-0
" 27	Cleveland vs. Chicago....	Chicago......	Powell. .. Griffith	9	5-0
" 30	Cincinnati vs. St. Louis...	St. Louis....	Breitenst'n.Donah'e	9	8-0
July 3	Cincinnati vs. Louisville..	Louisville....	Breitenstein..Frazer	9	12-0
" 5	New York vs. Brooklyn...	New York....	Rusie....... Payne	9	10-0
" 5	Washington vs. Chicago..	Chicago......	McJames....Friend	9	4-0
" 8	Brooklyn vs. St. Louis ...	St. Louis....	Payne....Donahue	9	1-0
" 15	New York vs. Louisville..	Louisville....	Rusie........ Miller	9	10-0
" 15	Philadelphia vs. St. Louis	St. Louis....	Orth......Donahue	9	2-0
" 20	Pittsburg vs. Brooklyn...	Pittsburg....	Killen....... Payne	9	3-0
" 25	Chicago vs. Louisville....	Chicago......	Callahan..Cun'gh'm	7	1-0
" 25	Washington vs. St. Louis.	St. Louis....	Mercer ......Lucid	9	8-0
Aug. 7	Cincinnati vs. Brooklyn..	Cincinnati....	Rhines........Hill	9	5-0
" 10	Boston vs. New York.....	Boston	Klobedanz.Seymour	9	1-0
" 11	Washington vs. Philad'p'a	Washington ..	Mercer.....Wheeler	9	6-0
" 12	Washington vs. Brooklyn	Washington..	McJames..Kennedy	9	3-0
" 13	Chicago vs. Cincinnati ...	Cincinnati...	Griffiths .... Rhines	9	2-0
" 18	Boston vs. Washington...	Boston	Lewis....... Mercer	9	8-0
" 19	Cleveland vs. Baltimore..	Baltimore	Young......Amale	9	8-0
" 19	New York vs. Louisville..	New York....	Meekin W.H.Clarke	9	1-0
" 20	Cleveland vs. Baltimore..	Baltimore	Powell........Pond	9	5-0
" 23	Brooklyn vs. Pittsburg...	Brooklyn.....	Kennedy ... Hughey	7	1-0
" 25	New York vs. Cleveland..	New York....	Seymour .... Young	9	5-0
" 25	Washington vs. Cincinnati	Washington..	McJames .... Ehret	9	4-0
" 25	Louisville vs. Boston.....	Boston	Magee...J.Sullivan	9	11-0
" 27	Baltimore vs. Cincinnati..	Baltimore....	Hoffer......Rhines	9	5-0
" 27	New York vs. Chicago....	New York....	M. Sullivan..Briggs	9	6-0
" 27	Washington vs. St. Louis.	Washington..	Monahan....Sudhoff	9	3-0
Sept. 11	Boston vs. Philadelphia..	Boston...:...	Klobedanz.....Orth	9	11-0
" 17	Boston vs. New York.....	Boston	Nichols.... Sullivan	9	17-0
" 18	Cleveland vs. Cincinnati..	Cleveland....	Young...... Rhines	9	6-0
" 22	Boston vs. Brooklyn	Boston	Stivetts.......Payne	7	12-0
" 25	Brooklyn vs. Philadelphia	Brooklyn.....	Fisher......Wheeler	9	3-0

The list of games requiring extra innings to be played before the game was over numbers 36, ranging from games of 10 innings each up to contests requiring from 11 to 14 innings to be played to settle the contest. Of these there were twenty-one of 10 innings each, eight of 11 innings, four of 12 innings, and one each of 13 and 14 innings. The smallest score was 2 to 1, and the highest score 13 to 12. Pittsburg won the most games in the extra innings record, and New York and Philadelphia lost the most extra innings games. August was the most prolific month for extra innings games, whilst the fewest were played in June. Here is the record in full:

RECORD OF EXTRA INNINGS GAMES FOR 1897.

Date.	Contesting Clubs.	Where Played	Pitchers.	In'gs.	Score.
Apr. 22	Cleveland vs. Chicago...	Cincinnati....	Rhines......Griffith	10	8-7
" 26	Brooklyn vs. Baltimore..	Baltimore....	Payne........Hoffer	10	4-3
" 26	Pittsburg vs. Louisville...	Louisville....	Tannehill....Frazer	12	3-7
" 30	Boston vs. Washington..	Washington..	J. Sulliv'n.McJames	10	3-3
May 1	Philadelphia vs. B'klyn..	Philadelphia..	Taylor....Kennedy	10	3-2
" 3	Baltimore vs. Brooklyn..	Brooklyn.....	Corbett......Payne	11	3-3
" 6	Brooklyn vs. New York.	New York...	McMahon....Clarke	10	9-9
" 18	Philad'p'a vs. Louisville.	Louisville....	McMahon......Hill	12	3-2
" 14	Cincinnati vs. New York.	Cincinnati....	Ehret........Meekin	11	6-5
" 19	Cincinnati vs. Philad'p'a.	Cincinnati...	Dwyer......Taylor	10	7-6
" 19	Boston vs. Chicago......	Chicago......	Klobedanz..Griffith	10	7-6
" 20	Louisville vs. Brooklyn..	Louisville....	Cun'ham..Kennedy	13	13-12
" 22	Cleveland vs. New York.	Cleveland...	Cuppy........Rusie	10	4-3
June 22	Wash'ton vs. Philad'p'a..	Washington..	German......Fifield	10	12-11
" 23	Pittsburg vs. Chicago....	Pittsburg.....	Killen......Griffith	11	6-5
" 24	St. Louis vs. Pittsburg...	Pittsburg	Hart......Tannehill	12	7-6
July 3	Cleveland vs. St. Louis..	Cleveland....	Powell.....Donahue	10	8-4
" 8	Chicago vs. Boston......	Chicago......	Griffith......Nichols	10	2-1
" 18	Cincinnati vs. Wash'ton.	Cincinnati....	Br'tenstein..Mercer	10	4-3
" 25	Baltimore vs. Cleveland..	Cleveland....	Corbett......Wilson	10	6-5
" 26	New York vs. Cleveland.	Cleveland....	Rusie ....Powell	11	6-5
" 27	Chicago vs. Cincinnati..	Chicago......	Callahan....Rhines	10	4-3
Aug 4	B'klyn vs. Washington..	Brooklyn.....	Dunn........Mercer	11	2-1
" 5	Philad'p'a vs. New York.	Philadelphia..	Taylor......Meekin	12	5-4
" 6	Pittsburg vs. St. Louis...	St. Louis.....	Hawley...Donahue	14	5-4
" 9	Pittsburg vs. Cin'nati....	Cincinnati....	Gardner..Br'tenst'n	10	7-5
" 10	Wash'ton vs. Philad'p'a.	Washington..	King ....Fifield	10	7-6
" 12	Boston vs. New York....	New York....	J. Sullivan..Meekin	12	5-4
" 14	Baltimore vs. Philad'p'a.	Philadelphia..	Hoffer.........Orth	10	11-10
" 14	Chicago vs. Cincinnati..	Cincinnati....	Thornton......Ehret	10	10-9
" 21	St. Louis vs. Brooklyn...	Brooklyn.....	Donahue..Kennedy	11	4-3
" 26	Pittsburg vs. Philad'a....	Philadelphia..	Hughey.....Taylor	11	4-3
" 31	Chicago vs. Boston......	Boston.......	Briggs...Klobedanz	11	8-8
Sept. 2	St. Louis vs. Baltimore..	Baltimore....	Sudhoff........Pond	10	4-3
" 4	Louisville vs. Wash'ton	Washington..	C'n'gham.McJames	10	7-5
" 11	Pittsburg vs. Louisville..	Pittsburg.....	Killen..Cunningh'm	10	6-7

During the League championship campaign of 1897 an aggregate of 807 games were played, of which 788 were victories and defeats—one of which was forfeited without being played—and 20 games were drawn. There were seven games forfeited, all of which were marked by runs scored except one. The list of these forfeited games is as follows:

May 3—New York vs. Washington, at Washington; forfeited for refusing to put players out.
June 1—New York vs. Pittsburg, at New York; declared forfeited for disputing decisions by umpire.
June 3—New York vs. Louisville, at New York; declared illegal by President Young.
July 24—Cleveland vs. Philadelphia, at Cleveland; declared forfeited for disputing decisions of umpire.
August 1—Louisville vs. St. Louis, at St. Louis; declared forfeited for violation of playing rules.
August 4—Louisville vs. Cleveland, at Louisville; declared forfeited for violation of playing rules.
Sept. 8—Washington vs. Cleveland, at Washington; declared forfeited for leaving the field.
Sept. 10—Baltimore vs. Louisville, at Baltimore; declared forfeited for refusing to play.

Defeat is tough at any stage, but when the tail-enders come along and smash the leaders, then the agony of the moment is exquisite.—*Chicago Post*.

The pitcher who kicks on called balls and strikes is simply a fool for his pains. No matter how impartial the umpire who is the judge behind the bat may desire or intend to be, he would not be human if he gave the doubt in favor of the kicker and against the player who silently acquiesces in the decision he cannot possibly have reversed by his kicking.

How many players are there in the League teams who realize the fact that when they play poor ball they cut down the gate receipts hundreds of dollars at a time? All they seem to realize is that whether they play well or badly, they draw their salaries each pay day regularly, and for this are they ball players, or rather, they think that is what they are solely in the club for.

To hit from the shoulder at swift pitching is weak play at the bat. To pop up the ball in the air in the fungo style of the batting practice in vogue, is still worse. The more the chances given the field for catches by the batting side, the weaker the batting. The acme of scientific batting is the placing of balls from skilful, strategic pitching. It is very difficult to do it, but it can be done. John Ward was one of the players who did it finely. Another feature of scientific batting is the tapping of the ball safely to short outfield for single hits off swift pitching. Then, too, the "bunting" of the ball for base-hits is another feature, and I know of no prettier hit when done properly. But to bunt the ball successfully requires great skill. Not one batsman in twenty can do this bunting properly. It is laughable to see a batsman, who is used to the old time slugging, try to do it. They think it's so easy, whereas it is far easier to hit out for a home run than to earn a base by a good "bunt."

 The Individual Club Records of 1897

IN making up the tables giving the individual club records of 1897 we present two separate records, the first one recording the victories and defeats, drawn games, series won, lost and tied, and the peicentage of victories with each opposing team. The second record presents additional statistics, such as the "Chicago" victories and defeats with each club, the number of games won and lost by a single run, the single and double figure scores in victories and defeats scored by each club with each opposing team on the home fields, as well as on fields abroad. The two tables combine all the essential points in an individual club's season's record.

In the case of the championship team of the season, however, an exception is made to the extent of giving the pennant winner a special chapter to itself.

The National League's Champion Club of 1897.

The Boston club, which won the League championship in 1897, stands to-day as the only professional club, known to National League annals, which has presented a team in each year's championship campaign, from the inaugural year of the old Professional National Association in 1871, up to the closing League year of 1897, a period of twenty-seven years of professional club history. Moreover, the Boston club leads every other professional club in the country in holding the record of having won eleven annual pennant races in the professional arena, four of which were won consecutively, from 1872 to 1875 inclusive, under the regime of the old Professional Association; while the other seven pennants were won in the National League arena, viz., in 1877 and '78, in 1883, and in 1891, '92, '93 and '97. In all these twenty-seven years of Boston club history, the club's teams have been under the control of but four managers, viz., the late veteran, Harry Wright, from 1871 to 1881, inclusive; John Morrill, from 1882 to 1888, inclusive; James Hart in 1889; and Mr. Selee from 1890 to 1897, inclusive. The appended table—specially prepared by the editor, who has seen the Boston teams play each year from 1871 to 1897, inclusive—gives the full record of the club in all of the pennant races its teams have taken part in since the club was organized during the winter of 1870 and '71.

THE HISTORICAL RECORD OF THE BOSTON CLUB FROM 1871 TO 1897, INCLUSIVE.

Year.	Organization.	Victories.	Defeats.	Per cent.	Race Position.	Manager.	Number of Clubs.
1871	National Associa'n	22	10	.688	Second	Harry Wright	8
1872	" "	39	8	.830	First	Harry Wright	10
1873	" "	43	16	.729	First	Harry Wright	8
1874	" "	52	18	.743	First	Harry Wright	8
1875	" "	71	8	.899	First	Harry Wright	10
1876	National League	39	31	.557	Fourth	Harry Wright	8
1877	" "	31	17	.648	First	Harry Wright	6
1878	" "	41	19	.707	First	Harry Wright	6
1879	" "	49	29	.628	Second	Harry Wright	8
1880	" "	40	44	.474	Sixth	Harry Wright	8
1881	" "	38	45	.458	Sixth	Harry Wright	8
1882	" "	45	39	.536	Fourth	Morrill	8
1883	" "	63	35	.643	First	Morrill	8
1884	" "	73	38	.658	Second	Morrill	8
1885	" "	46	66	.410	Fifth	Morrill	8
1886	" "	56	61	.478	Fifth	Morrill	8
1887	" "	61	60	.504	Fifth	Morrill	8
1888	" "	70	64	.522	Fourth	Morrill	8
1889	" "	83	45	.648	Second	Hart	8
1890	" "	76	57	.571	Fifth	Selee	8
1891	" "	87	51	.630	First	Selee	8
1892	" "	102	48	.680	First	Selee	12
1893	" "	86	44	.662	First	Selee	12
1894	" "	83	49	.629	Third	Selee	12
1895	" "	71	60	.542	Sixth	Selee	12
1896	" "	74	57	.565	Fourth	Selee	12
1897	" "	93	39	.705	First	Selee	12

It will be seen by the above complete record that the Boston club stands credited with the highest percentage of victories figures known in the annals of the League, viz., that of 1875, when their percentage reached .899. Again, in no one single pennant race of the twenty-seven the club participated in did their team fall lower down in any annual race than sixth place, and then only three times in the twenty-six years; while they occupied first place eleven times; second position, four times; third place, once; fourth place, three times, and fifth position, four times. The lowest percentage figures recorded in a race was in 1885, when they occupied fifth position that year with a percentage of but .410. But the club has ranged from the percentage of .500 and over up to over .800 in no less than twenty-three of the twenty-seven pennant races. Their total victories in the twenty-seven annual campaigns reached 1,634, against 1,005 defeats. Another "best on record" which the Boston club holds is that of the highest total of victories in a single pennant race, viz., in 1892, when the club won 102 games and only sustained 48 defeats.

The Boston Club's Championship Record in 1897.

The Boston club won the League pennant of 1897 under a measure of difficulties which was overcome with commendable pluck, perseverance and good management. The team opened the race in April very inauspiciously, inasmuch as at the close of the April campaign they had only won a single game out of 9 played, 2 having been drawn, their solitary victory being scored in Philadelphia. They closed their May campaign with a record of 17 victories to but 6 defeats, and on May 31 the team stood fourth in the race.

The Bostons, in June, won 22 games and lost but 2, the race record on June 30 leaving the club first in the race, with the percentage figures at .741 to Baltimore's .679; the latter team having 9 defeats in June, out of 22 games won and lost.

On July 31 the Bostons occupied first place with the percentage figures of .700 to Baltimore's .667. They did well during August, too, but during the last week of that month Baltimore rallied on their home grounds, and on August 31 they stood in the van with the percentage of .695 to their credit to Boston's .685. Then came the September nip-and-tuck fight between the two teams up to September 24, during which period the Baltimores retained their position in the van, but only by a few points. On September 26 Baltimore led Boston by .704 to .703, and the next day saw the Bostons leading with .705 to Baltimore's .698, the Bostons' victory in Brooklyn, and Washington's defeat of Baltimore at Baltimore on September 30, giving the pennant to Boston finally by .705 to .692.

THE FIRST RECORD.

BOSTON vs.	First Division.						Second Division.						Grand Totals.
	Baltimore.	New York.	Cincinnati.	Cleveland.	Brooklyn.	Totals.	Washington.	Pittsburg.	Chicago.	Philadelphia.	Louisville.	St. Louis.	Totals.	
Victories.....................	6	8	9	7	9	39	7	10	8	10	9	10	54	93
Defeats.......................	6	4	3	5	3	21	5	2	4	2	3	2	18	39
Drawn games..................	0	0	0	0	0	0	1	0	1	1	0	0	3	3
Total games...................	12	12	12	12	12	60	13	12	13	13	12	12	75	135
Series won....................	0	1	1	1	1	4	1	1	1	1	1	1	6	10
Series lost....................	0	0	0	0	0	0	0	0	0	0	0	0	0	0
Series tied....................	1	0	0	0	0	1	0	0	0	0	0	0	0	1

Per cent. of victories—Against Baltimore, .500; New York, .667; Cincinnati, .750; Cleveland, .583; Brooklyn, .750; total, first division clubs, .650. Washington, .583; Pittsburg, .833; Chicago, .667; Philadelphia, .833; Louisville, .750; St. Louis, .833; total, second division clubs, .750. Grand total, .705.

The record showing the additional statistics of the championship season contains the "Chicago" victories and defeats scored, the record of the games marked by single and double figures scores—the former showing the best kind of play—the record of games won and lost by a single run, the extra innings victories and defeats, together with that of games won and lost on grounds at home and abroad; also the total of extra innings games played, the whole forming a complete record of the team's play during the entire championship season.

THE SECOND RECORD.

Boston vs.	First Division.					Second Division.						Grand Totals.
	Baltimore.	New York.	Cincinnati.	Cleveland.	Brooklyn.	Totals.	Washington.	Pittsburg.	Chicago.	Philadelphia.	Louisville.	St. Louis.	Totals.	
"Chicago" victories............	0	2	0	0	1	3	2	2	0	1	0	0	5	8
"Chicago" defeats.............	1	0	0	0	0	1	0	0	0	0	1	0	1	2
Single-figure victories.........	3	6	5	5	4	23	6	7	5	9	6	1	34	57
Single-figure defeats...........	5	2	2	3	1	13	4	2	3	1	2	2	15	28
Double-figure victories.........	3	2	4	2	5	16	1	3	3	1	3	9	20	36
Double-figure defeats...........	1	2	1	2	2	8	1	0	1	1	1	0	4	12
Won by one run.................	2	4	1	1	3	11	1	2	1	2	1	1	8	19
Lost by one run................	1	0	1	0	0	2	1	1	3	1	2	1	9	11
Extra-innings victories.........	0	1	0	0	0	1	0	0	1	0	0	0	1	2
Extra-innings defeats...........	0	0	0	0	0	0	0	0	1	0	0	0	1	1
Home victories..................	4	4	5	4	5	22	4	6	6	5	5	7	33	55
Home defeats....................	2	2	1	2	1	8	2	0	0	1	1	0	4	12
Victories abroad................	2	4	4	3	4	17	3	4	2	5	4	3	21	38
Defeats abroad..................	4	2	2	3	2	13	3	2	4	1	2	2	14	27
Extra inning games..............	0	1	0	0	1	1	1	0	3	0	0	0	4	5

The Baltimore club, in the opening championship campaign of the reorganized National League in 1892, came out of the fight in a badly knocked-out condition, inasmuch as at the close of the pennant race of that year they lay in the last ditch, with the percentage figures of only .313 to their credit, or 367 points behind the Boston champions of that year. In 1893 the Baltimores improved their position by finishing eighth in the pennant race, only 200 points behind the Bostons, who for the third successive year won the League pennant. In 1894 the Baltimores got together a team which landed them winners in the race, the Bostons this time having to be content with third place. In 1895, too, the Baltimores again went to the front, as they did in 1896, but in 1897 Boston once more led them in the pennant race. Each club, therefore, stands credited with three pennant victories, won during the first six years' history of the reconstructed League. Here is the Baltimore's six years record:

PENNANT RACE RECORD.

Years.	Victories.	Defeats.	Per cent.	Position.	Years.	Victories.	Defeats.	Per cent.	Position.
1892	46	101	.313	Twelfth.	1895	87	43	.669	First.
1893	60	70	.462	Eighth.	1896	90	39	.698	First.
1894	89	39	.695	First.	1897	90	40	.692	Second.

The Baltimores' Season of 1897.

The Baltimore team opened the pennant race in 1897 with three straight victories over the Bostons at Baltimore, and they closed the April campaign with a decided lead in the race over Boston, Philadelphia tieing in percentage figures with .875 each, while Boston was last in the race with but .143, the difference in points between the first two clubs and the Bostons being no less than 732. The Baltimores kept in the van nearly the whole of May. In the meantime Boston had jumped up from the last ditch to fourth place, and on May 31 while Baltimore led with the percentage figures of .742, Boston stood fourth with .600. Baltimore kept in the van through the best part of June, but on June 30 the record showed Boston in the lead with the percentage of .741 to Baltimore's .679. Boston led Baltimore all through July, and on July 31 led the race with the percentage figures of .700 to Baltimore's .667. In August the Baltimores allowed the Cincinnatis to force them down to third place, the record on August 11 leaving Boston with .682, Cincinnati with .659 and Baltimore with .655.

After that, however, the Baltimores got back to second place in the race, and as the time for the finish approached it began to be quite a nip-and-tuck fight for the lead. Before the end of August the Baltimores resumed the lead in the race, the percentage record on August 31 showing them to be in the van with .692 to Boston's .685. They retained the lead up to September 24, and then lost it, Boston then leading with .709 to Baltimore's .702. The lead again alternated before the close, but Boston finally went to the front on September 27, and at the finish on October 2 Boston led with .705 to Baltimore's .692.

THE FULL SEASON'S RECORD OF 1897.

BALTIMORE VS	First Division.					Second Division.						Grand Totals.
	Boston.	New York.	Cincinnati.	Cleveland.	Brooklyn.	Totals.	Washington.	Pittsburg.	Chicago.	Philadelphia.	Louisville.	St. Louis.	Totals.	
Victories	6	5	6	7	9	33	9	9	9	10	10	10	57	90
Defeats	6	7	6	4	3	26	3	3	?	2	1	2	14	40
Drawn games	0	0	0	0	2	2	0	0	3	1	0	0	4	6
Total games	12	12	12	11	14	61	12	12	15	13	11	12	75	186
Series won	0	0	0	1	1	2	1	1	1	1	1	1	6	8
Series lost	0	1	0	0	0	1	0	0	0	0	0	0	0	1
Series tied	1	0	1	0	0	2	0	0	0	0	0	0	0	2

Per cent. of victories—Against Boston, .500; New York, .417; Cincinnati, .500; Cleveland, .636; Brooklyn, .750; total, first division clubs, .559. Washington, .750; Pittsburg, .750; Chicago, .750; Philadelphia, .833; Louisville, .969; St. Louis, .833; total, second division clubs, .803. Grand total, .692.

The Baltimores' percentage of victories figures against the five first division clubs opposed to them was .559, while against the six second division clubs they were no less than .803. The Baltimores only lost one series, and that one was with New York, they tieing with Boston and Cincinnati. They played no less than 15 games with the Chicagos, 3 being drawn. They had to play 14, too, with the Brooklyns. Their highest percentage of victories against any one club was .969 against the Louisvilles, while their lowest was .417, against New York. The record of additional statistics of the club is as follows:

BALTIMORE VS.	First Division.					Second Division.						Grand Totals.
	Boston.	New York.	Cincinnati.	Cleveland.	Brooklyn.	Totals.	Washington.	Pittsburg.	Chicago.	Philadelphia.	Louisville.	St. Louis.	Totals.	
"Chicago" victories	1	0	1	0	0	2	0	0	0	0	0	0	0	2
"Chicago" defeats	0	0	0	2	0	2	0	0	0	0	1	0	1	3
Single-figure victories	5	4	5	5	3	22	7	6	5	6	8	2	34	56
Single-figure defeats	3	6	3	4	2	18	2	2	3	2	1	2	12	30
Double-figure victories	1	1	1	2	6	11	2	3	4	4	2	8	23	34
Double-figure defeats	3	1	3	0	1	8	1	1	0	0	0	0	2	10
Won by one run	1	0	1	2	1	5	1	2	2	1	2	0	8	13
Lost by one run	2	2	4	1	1	10	0	1	0	1	0	1	3	13
Extra-innings victories	0	0	1	0	1	0	0	0	1	0	0	1	2
Extra-innings defeats	0	0	0	1	1	0	0	0	0	1	1	2
Home victories	4	3	6	4	5	22	4	5	6	4	6	4	29	51
Home defeats	2	3	0	2	1	8	2	1	0	2	0	2	7	15
Victories abroad	2	2	0	3	4	11	5	4	3	6	4	6	28	39
Defeats abroad	4	4	6	2	2	18	1	2	3	0	1	0	7	25

The New Yorks' Season of 1897.

The New York club began its campaign as one of the League twelve in 1892 with a comparatively poor record. The season was a divided one, and in the first half the club got no higher than tenth place. In the second half, however, they ended in sixth position. In the full season's record they were left in eighth place. Even at that they beat out the Eastern teams of Washington and Baltimore, together with Louisville and St. Louis, they ending the season with the percentage figures of .470. Ward, that year, was manager of the Brooklyns, which team ended in third place, 147 points ahead of New York. In 1893 New York managed to end the race in fifth place, leading Brooklyn by .515 to .508. In 1894 Ward returned to New York, and by his good management of the team he closed the season in second place with the percentage figures of .667 to Baltimore's .695. Moreover, he won the Temple Cup series, and considerably lessened the eclat attached to the championship victory. In 1895 the New Yorks ended the race in ninth position. In 1896 they did very little better, though they had a stronger team than in 1895, but the best it could do was to end in seventh place. There was the consolation left of seeing Brooklyn finish still lower—tenth position—there being a bitter rivalry between these metropolitan teams each year. In 1897 the make-up of the team was improved to a considerable extent, and they managed to pull up to third place in September, after ending May in sixth position. But for the engagement of Pitcher Rusie the team would not have ended higher than fifth. Here is the club's record in the pennant race from 1892 to 1897, inclusive :

PENNANT RACE RECORD.

Years.	Victories.	Defeats.	Per cent.	Position.	Years.	Victories.	Defeats.	Per cent.	Position.
1892	71	80	.470	Eighth.	1895	66	65	.504	Ninth.
1893	68	64	.515	Fifth.	1896	64	67	.489	Seventh.
1894	88	44	.667	Second.	1897	83	48	.634	Third.

THE FULL SEASON'S RECORD OF 1897.

The following is the record of total victories and defeats, with the drawn games, played by the New Yorks with each club, as also the series won, lost and tied with each, and the percentage of victories figures in the championship race of 1897 :

50   SPALDING'S OFFICIAL

NEW YORK VS.	FIRST DIVISION.						SECOND DIVISION.							Grand Totals.
	Boston.	Baltimore.	Cincinnati.	Cleveland.	Brooklyn.	Totals.	Washington.	Pittsburg.	Chicago.	Philadelphia.	Louisville.	St. Louis.	Totals.	
Victories..........................	4	7	5	9	9	34	9	8	7	7	6	12	49	83
Defeats............................	8	5	7	3	3	26	3	3	5	5	6	0	22	48
Drawn games...................	0	0	1	0	2	3	1	1	1	0	0	0	3	6
Total games.....................	12	12	13	12	14	63	8	12	13	12	12	12	74	137
Series won.......................	0	1	0	1	1	3	1	1	1	1	0	1	5	8
Series lost.......................	1	0	1	0	0	2	0	0	0	0	0	0	0	2
Series tied.......................	0	0	0	0	0	0	0	0	0	0	1	0	1	1

Per cent. of victories—Against Boston, .333; Baltimore, .583; Cincinnati, .417; Cleveland, .750; Brooklyn, .750; total, first division clubs, .567. Washington, .750; Pittsburg, .727; Chicago, .583; Philadelphia, .583; Louisville, .500; St. Louis, 1.000; total, second division clubs, .690. Grand total, .634.

The New York team's percentage of victories against their first division opponents was .567; while against the six second division clubs it was .690. They scored a percentage of 1.000 against St. Louis, and only .333 against Boston. They lost their series with Boston, Baltimore and Cincinnati, and tied with Louisville. The record of additional statistics of the club is as follows:

NEW YORK VS.	FIRST DIVISION.						SECOND DIVISION.							Grand Totals.
	Boston.	Baltimore.	Cincinnati.	Cleveland.	Brooklyn.	Totals.	Washington.	Pittsburg.	Chicago.	Philadelphia.	Louisville.	St. Louis.	Totals.	
"Chicago" victories...............	0	0	0	3	1	4	1	0	2	0	2	0	5	9
"Chicago" defeats................	2	0	0	0	0	2	0	0	0	0	0	0	2	2
Single-figure victories..................	2	6	4	8	6	26	5	5	5	5	4	9	33	59
Single-figure defeats......	6	4	5	2	3	20	3	2	3	2	5	0	15	35
Double-figure victories..........	2	1	1	1	3	8	4	2	2	2	2	3	15	23
Double-figure defeats..................	2	1	2	1	0	6	0	1	2	3	1	0	7	13
Won by one run......	0	2	2	2	2	8	2	2	0	1	3	2	8	16
Lost by one run..........	4	0	3	1	1	9	0	2	1	1	1	0	5	14
Victories at home.....................	2	4	4	7	4	21	4	4	4	5	4	9	30	51
Defeats at home.	4	2	2	1	2	11	2	1	2	1	2	0	8	19
Victories abroad......................	2	3	1	2	5	13	5	4	3	2	2	3	18	32
Defeats abroad......	4	3	5	2	1	15	1	2	3	4	4	0	14	29

The Cincinnatis' Season of 1897.

The Cincinnati club went through the first season of the reconstructed League in 1892 with a fairly good record, their team ending fourth in the first half, but only eighth in the second. In the full season's record, however, they ended fifth, leading all the Western clubs except Cleveland. In 1893 they were not so successful, as they had to be content with seventh place in the race at the finish. In 1894 they had a bad season of it, they finishing behind all of the clubs except Washington and Louisville, their team ending in tenth place that year. They did a little better in 1895, when they finished in eighth position. Their best race record in the League, however, was made in 1896, when they closed the season in third position, leading all the clubs except Baltimore and Cleveland. In 1897 they lost ground again and had to finish in fourth place, but that was the best any Western club did that year. Here is the club's race record for the six years in full:

PENNANT RACE RECORD.

Years.	Victories.	Defeats.	Per cent.	Position.	Years.	Victories.	Defeats.	Per cent.	Position.
1892	82	68	.547	Fifth.	1895	66	64	.508	Eighth.
1893	65	63	.508	Seventh.	1896	77	50	.606	Third.
1894	54	75	.419	Tenth	1897	76	56	.576	Fourth.

THE FULL SEASON'S RECORD OF 1897.

CINCINNATI vs	First Division.						Second Division.						Grand Totals.
	Boston.	Baltimore.	New York.	Cleveland.	Brooklyn.	Totals.	Washington.	Pittsburg.	Chicago.	Philadelphia.	Louisville.	St. Louis.	Totals.	
Victories..................	3	6	7	7	5	28	8	5	7	8	9	11	48	76
Defeats...................	9	6	5	5	7	32	4	7	5	4	3	1	24	56
Drawn games..............	0	0	1	0	0	1	0	1	0	0	0	0	1	2
Total games...............	12	12	13	12	12	61	12	13	12	12	12	12	73	134
Series won................	0	0	1	1	0	2	1	0	1	1	1	1	5	7
Series lost................	1	0	0	0	1	2	0	1	0	0	0	0	1	3
Series tied................	0	1	0	0	0	1	0	0	0	0	0	0	0	1

Per cent. of victories—Against Boston, .250; Baltimore, .500; New York, .583; Cleveland, .583; Brooklyn, .417; total, first division clubs, .467. Washington, .667; Pittsburg, .417; Chicago, .583; Philadelphia, .667; Louisville, .750; St. Louis, .917; total, second division clubs, .667. Grand total, .576.

The Cincinnati club's team in 1897 lost three series of games, two with first division clubs and one with a second division team, Boston, Brooklyn and Pittsburg getting the best of them. But they tied Baltimore and won from New York and Cleveland in the first division. Their percentage figures against their first division opponents were .467, and against the six of the second division .667. Their highest figures against a single club were .917, and their smallest .250. The record of additional statistics is appended:

CINCINNATI vs	FIRST DIVISION.					SECOND DIVISION.							Grand Totals.
	Boston.	Baltimore.	New York.	Cleveland.	Brooklyn.	Totals.	Washington.	Pittsburg.	Chicago.	Philadelphia.	Louisville.	St. Louis.	Totals.	
"Chicago" victories	0	0	0	1	0	1	0	0	0	0	2	1	3	4
"Chicago" defeats	0	1	0	1	1	3	1	0	1	1	0	0	3	6
Single-figure victories	2	3	5	6	3	19	6	2	7	7	7	10	39	58
Single-figure defeats	5	5	4	4	6	24	2	7	4	3	3	1	20	44
Double-figure victories	1	3	2	1	2	9	2	3	0	1	2	1	9	18
Double-figure defeats	4	1	1	1	1	8	2	0	1	1	0	0	4	12
Won by one run	1	4	3	2	0	10	5	0	5	4	2	3	19	29
Lost by one run	1	1	2	1	1	6	1	3	2	0	0	1	7	13
Extra-innings victories	0	0	1	0	0	1	1	0	1	0	0	0	2	3
Extra-innings defeats	0	0	0	0	0	0	0	1	2	0	0	0	3	3
Home victories	2	6	5	6	2	21	5	3	4	6	4	6	28	49
Home defeats	4	0	1	1	4	10	1	3	2	1	1	0	8	18
Victories abroad	1	0	2	1	3	7	3	2	3	2	5	5	20	27
Defeats abroad	5	6	4	4	3	22	3	4	3	3	2	1	16	38

The Clevelands' Season of 1897.

The Cleveland club during the first six years of the reorganized League had a good playing record, except in 1894 and 1897. In 1892 they came in second in the race, after leading in the first half of the season. In 1893, too, they finished a good third. But in 1894 they had to be content with sixth place, and then they led all of the Western clubs, they being the only Western team in the first division that year. In 1895 and 1896 they finished second, and, moreover, defeated Baltimore in one of the Temple Cup series. But in 1897 they fell off badly, and were close behind Cincinnati in fifth position. Here is the club's race record for the past six years:

PENNANT RACE RECORD.

Years.	Victories.	Defeats.	Per cent.	Position.	Years.	Victories.	Defeats.	Per cent.	Position.
1892	93	56	.624	Second.	1895	84	46	.646	Second.
1893	73	55	.570	Third.	1896	80	48	.625	Second.
1894	68	61	.527	Sixth.	1897	69	62	.527	Fifth.

THE FULL SEASON'S RECORD.

CLEVELAND vs.	First Division.						Second Division.						Grand Totals.
	Boston.	Baltimore.	New York.	Cincinnati.	Brooklyn.	Totals.	Washington.	Pittsburg.	Chicago.	Philadelphia.	Louisville.	St. Louis.	Totals.	
Victories	5	4	3	5	5	22	8	6	8	9	5	11	47	69
Defeats	7	7	9	7	7	37	4	6	4	3	7	1	25	62
Drawn games	0	0	0	0	0	0	0	0	0	0	0	1	1	1
Total games	12	11	12	12	12	59	12	12	12	12	12	13	73	132
Series won	0	0	0	0	0	0	1	1	1	0	1	4	4
Series lost	1	1	1	1	1	5	0	0	0	0	1	0	1	6
Series tied	0	0	0	0	0	0	1	0	0	0	0	0	1	1

Per cent. of victories—Against Boston, .417; Baltimore, .364; New York, .250; Cincinnati, .417; Brooklyn, .417; total, first division clubs, .373. Washington, .667; Pittsburg, .500; Chicago, .667; Philadelphia, .750; Louisville, .417; St. Louis, .917; total, second division clubs, .653. Grand total, .489.

The Clevelands lost no less than six series of games in 1897, something that had not occurred before in the whole six seasons of the major league. Not only did they lose every series with the first division clubs, but also with the tail-end Louisvilles, besides having a tie with the Pittsburgs, and yet they managed to retain fifth place in the race. Their percentage figures against their first division opponents were only .373, but against the six second division clubs they were .653. Their smallest figures were .250 and their highest .917. Here is their additional statistics record:

CLEVELAND vs.	First Division.						Second Division.						Grand Totals.
	Boston.	Baltimore.	New York.	Cincinnati.	Brooklyn.	Totals.	Washington.	Pittsburg.	Chicago.	Philadelphia.	Louisville.	St. Louis.	Totals.	
"Chicago" victories	0	2	0	1	1	4	1	0	1	0	0	0	2	6
"Chicago" defeats	0	0	3	1	0	4	0	0	0	0	1	0	1	5
Single-figure victories	8	4	2	4	5	18	5	3	7	6	2	7	30	48
Single-figure defeats	5	5	8	6	7	31	4	5	4	2	6	0	21	52
Double-figure victories	2	0	1	1	0	4	3	3	1	3	3	4	17	21
Double-figure defeats	2	2	1	1	0	6	0	1	0	1	1	1	4	10
Won by one run	0	1	1	1	1	4	1	2	3	2	0	2	10	14
Lost by one run	1	2	1	2	2	8	2	2	2	1	2	0	9	17
Extra-innings victories	0	0	1	0	0	1	0	0	0	0	0	1	1	2
Extra-innings defeats	0	1	1	0	0	2	0	0	0	0	0	0	0	2
Victories at home	3	2	2	4	4	15	6	5	6	5	4	8	34	49
Defeats at home	3	3	2	1	2	11	0	1	0	1	2	1	5	16
Victories abroad	2	2	1	1	1	7	2	1	2	4	1	11	21	28
Defeats abroad	4	4	7	6	5	26	4	5	4	2	5	0	20	46

The Brooklyns' Season of 1897.

The best record made by the Brooklyn club in the major league's six years of history was in 1892, when, under Ward's management, they ended second in the first half of the season and third in the second half, and also third in the whole season's race, beating New York that season, alike in series won and in percentage figures, the latter by .617 to .470. In 1893 they were tied for sixth place with Cincinnati—each at .508 —five other clubs, including New York, leading them. In 1894 and 1895 they managed to reach fifth position at the end of the season, but in 1896 their worst-on-record in a League pennant race marked the close of their season, as they ended tenth, with the percentage figures of .443, every other club except St. Louis and Louisville leading them. Last year they did better, as they closed the season of 1897 tied with Washington for sixth place. Here is their six years' race record:

PENNANT RACE RECORD.

Years.	Victories.	Defeats.	Per cent.	Position.	Years.	Victories.	Defeats.	Per cent.	Position.
1892	95	59	.617	Third.	1895	71	60	.542	Fifth.
1893	68	63	.515	Sixth.	1896	58	73	.443	Tenth.
1894	70	61	.534	Fifth.	1897	61	71	.462	Sixth.

THE FULL SEASON'S RECORD.

| Brooklyn vs. | First Division. | | | | | | Second Division. | | | | | | Grand Totals. |
	Boston.	Baltimore.	New York.	Cincinnati.	Cleveland.	Totals.	Washington.	Pittsburg.	Chicago.	Philadelphia.	Louisville.	St. Louis.	Totals.	
Victories...................	3	3	3	7	7	23	7	7	6	6	5	7	38	61
Defeats....................	9	9	9	5	5	37	5	5	6	6	7	5	34	71
Drawn games............	0	2	2	0	0	4	0	0	0	0	0	0	0	4
Total games.............	12	14	14	12	12	64	12	12	12	12	12	12	72	136
Series won................	0	0	0	1	1	2	1	1	0	0	0	1	3	5
Series lost.................	1	1	1	0	0	3	0	0	0	0	1	0	1	4
Series tied.................	0	0	0	0	0	0	0	0	1	1	0	0	2	2

Per cent. of victories—Against Boston, .250; Baltimore, .250; New York, .250; Cincinnati, .583; Cleveland, .583; total, first division clubs, .383. Washington, .583; Pittsburg, .583; Chicago, .500; Philadelphia, .500; Louisville, .417; St. Louis, .583; total, second division clubs, .528. Grand total, .462.

The Brooklyn team lost a majority of their series with the first division clubs, their percentage of victories figures in that division being but .383, while they won but three series in the second division ranks, their percentage figures being but .528. Their smallest percentage figures were .250, and their highest .583. Here is their additional statistics record:

BROOKLYN VS.	First Division.					Second Division.						Grand Totals.
	Boston.	Baltimore.	New York.	Cincinnati.	Cleveland.	Totals.	Washington.	Pittsburg.	Chicago.	Philadelphia.	Louisville.	St. Louis.	Totals.	
"Chicago" victories	0	0	0	1	0	1	0	1	0	1	0	1	3	4
"Chicago" defeats	1	0	0	0	1	2	1	1	0	0	0	1	3	5
Single-figure victories	1	2	3	6	7	19	6	4	3	4	2	3	22	41
Single-figure defeats	4	3	6	3	5	21	4	5	3	3	3	5	23	44
Double-figure victories	2	1	0	1	0	4	1	3	3	2	3	4	16	20
Double-figure defeats	5	6	3	2	0	16	1	0	2	3	4	0	10	26
Won by one run	0	1	1	1	2	5	5	3	1	1	0	1	11	16
Lost by one run	3	1	2	0	1	7	1	1	1	2	2	3	10	17
Victories at home	2	2	1	3	5	13	5	6	3	5	2	4	25	38
Defeats at home	4	6	5	3	1	17	1	1	2	1	4	2	11	28
Victories abroad	1	1	2	4	2	10	2	1	3	1	3	3	13	23
Defeats abroad	5	5	4	2	4	20	4	4	3	5	3	3	22	42

The Washingtons' Season of 1897.

The Washington club has been among the three tail-end clubs of the League during every one of the six years of the major league's races except in 1897. The Senators ended tenth in 1892, though they were seventh in the first half of that season, and they fell into the last ditch in 1893, when their lowest percentage figures was the record, .310. In 1894 they began to mount up by degrees in the race record, ending that year in eleventh place, tenth in 1895 and ninth in 1896. In 1897, however, they made a good rally for a higher place than usual, and they "astonished the Browns" that season by tieing Brooklyn for sixth place, scoring the highest percentage figures for the six years, viz., .462 Here is their record:

PENNANT RACE RECORD.

Years.	Victories.	Defeats.	Per cent.	Position.	Years.	Victories.	Defeats.	Per cent.	Position.
1892	58	93	.384	Tenth.	1895	43	85	.336	Tenth.
1893	40	89	.310	Twelfth.	1806	58	68	.448	Ninth.
1894	45	87	.341	Eleventh.	1897	61	71	.462	Seventh.

THE FULL SEASON'S RECORD OF 1897.

The Washington's record of total victories, defeats, drawn games, series won, lost and tied, as also their percentage of victories figures with each club, is as follows:

WASHINGTON VS.	First Division.							Second Divis'n					Grand Totals.
	Boston.	Baltimore.	New York.	Cincinnati.	Cleveland.	Brooklyn.	Totals.	Pittsburg.	Chicago.	Philadelphia.	Louisville.	St. Louis.	Totals.	
Victories............................	5	3	3	4	4	5	24	7	5	8	8	9	37	61
Defeats.............................	7	9	9	8	8	7	48	5	7	4	4	3	23	71
Drawn games......................	1	0	1	0	0	0	2	0	0	0	1	0	1	3
Total games........................	13	12	13	12	12	12	74	12	12	12	13	12	61	135
Series won.........................	0	0	0	0	0	0	0	1	0	1	1	1	4	4
Series lost.........................	1	1	1	1	1	1	6	0	1	0	0	0	1	7
Series tied.........................	0	0	0	0	0	0	0	0	0	0	0	0	0	0

Per cent. of victories—Against Boston, .417; Baltimore, .250; New York, .250; Cincinnati, .333; Cleveland, .333; Brooklyn, .417; total, first division clubs, .333. Pittsburg, .583; Chicago, .417; Philadelphia, .667; Louisville, .667; St. Louis, .750; total, second division clubs, .617. Grand total, .462.

The feature of the Washington club's season of 1897 was the close fight they had with the champion Bostons and their signal triumph over the Philadelphias. They almost did as well against the first division clubs as Brooklyn, and beat them out against the second division by .617 to Brooklyn's .528. Their lowest percentage figures were .250 and their highest .750.

Here is their additional statistics record for 1897:

WASHINGTON VS.	First Division.							Second Divis'n					Grand Totals.
	Boston.	Baltimore.	New York.	Cincinnati.	Cleveland.	Brooklyn.	Totals.	Pittsburg.	Chicago.	Philadelphia.	Louisville.	St. Louis.	Totals.	
"Chicago" victories...............	0	0	0	1	0	1	2	0	1	1	0	3	5	7
"Chicago" defeats................	2	0	1	0	1	0	4	0	0	0	1	0	1	5
Single-figure victories.............	4	2	3	2	4	4	19	4	2	6	7	7	26	45
Single-figure defeats..............	6	7	5	6	5	6	35	3	5	3	4	3	18	53
Double-figure victories............	1	1	0	2	0	1	5	3	3	3	1	2	11	16
Double-figure defeats.............	1	2	4	2	3	1	13	2	2	1	0	0	5	18
Won by one run..................	1	0	0	1	2	1	5	0	0	3	0	1	4	9
Lost by one run...................	1	1	0	5	2	4	13	1	1	4	0	1	7	20
Victories at home.................	3	1	1	3	4	4	16	4	2	6	6	6	24	40
Defeats at home..................	3	5	5	3	2	2	20	2	4	0	0	0	6	26
Victories abroad..................	2	2	2	1	0	1	8	3	3	2	2	3	13	21
Defeats abroad...................	4	4	4	5	6	5	28	3	3	4	4	3	17	45

The Pittsburgs' Season of 1897.

The poorest race record made by the Pittsburg club during the past six years was that of 1897. In the first half of 1892 they ended sixth, and in the second half fourth, and at the end of the full season they stood sixth. In 1893 they made a good fight for the lead in the race, and ended as high as second position. In 1894 and 1895, however, the best they could do was to lead the second division clubs. They did better in 1896, when they ended in the first division; but last year they had to be content with eighth place. Even at this, they beat Chicago. Here is their race record for the past six years:

PENNANT RACE RECORD.

Years.	Victories.	Defeats.	Per cent.	Position.	Years.	Victories.	Defeats.	Per cent.	Position.
1892	80	73	.523	Sixth.	1895	71	61	.538	Seventh.
1893	81	48	.628	Second.	1896	66	63	.572	Sixth.
1894	65	65	.500	Seventh.	1897	60	71	.454	Eighth.

THE FULL SEASON'S RECORD.

The Pittsburg's record of total victories, defeats, drawn games, series won, lost and tied, and percentage of victories with each club for 1897, is as follows:

PITTSBURG VS.	First Division.							Second Divis'n						Grand totals.
	Boston.	Baltimore.	New York.	Cincinnati.	Cleveland.	Brooklyn.	Totals.	Washington.	Chicago.	Philadelphia.	Louisville.	St. Louis.	Totals.	
Victories	2	3	3	7	6	5	26	5	6	7	8	8	34	60
Defeats	10	9	8	5	6	7	45	7	6	5	4	4	26	70
Drawn games	0	0	1	1	0	0	2	0	0	0	2	0	2	4
Total games	12	12	12	13	12	12	73	12	12	12	14	12	62	135
Series won	0	0	0	1	0	0	1	0	0	1	1	1	3	4
Series lost	1	1	1	0	0	1	4	1	0	0	0	0	1	5
Series tied	0	0	0	0	1	0	1	0	1	0	0	0	1	2

Per cent. of victories—Against Boston, .167; Baltimore, .250; New York, .273; Cincinnati, .583; Cleveland, .500; Brooklyn, .417; total first division clubs, .366. Washington, .417; Chicago, 500; Philadelphia, .583; Louisville, .667; St. Louis, .667; total, second division clubs,.567. Grand total, .458.

The only first division club the Pittsburgs won a series from was the Cincinnati, their percentage of victories figures against the clubs of that division being only .366, and against the second division clubs .567. The lowest percentage record the team made was .167 and the highest .667. The additional statistics record of the club is as follows:

PITTSBURG VS.	FIRST DIVISION.						SECOND DIVIS'N					Grand Totals.
	Boston.	Baltimore.	New York.	Cincinnati.	Cleveland.	Brooklyn.	Totals.	Washington.	Chicago.	Philadelphia.	Louisville.	St. Louis.	Totals.	
"Chicago" victories............	0	0	0	0	0	1	1	0	0	0	0	0	0	1
"Chicago" defeats.............	2	0	0	0	0	1	3	0	0	1	0	0	1	4
Single-figure victories........	2	2	2	7	5	5	23	3	5	6	7	5	26	49
Single-figure defeats..........	7	6	5	2	3	4	27	4	4	2	3	4	17	44
Double-figure victories.......	0	1	1	0	1	0	3	2	1	1	1	3	8	11
Double-figure defeats........	3	3	3	3	3	3	18	8	2	3	1	0	9	27
Won by one run..............	1	1	2	3	2	1	10	1	2	4	4	1	12	22
Lost by one run..............	2	2	2	0	2	3	11	0	2	1	0	2	5	16
Victories at home.............	2	2	2	4	5	4	19	3	3	5	5	19	38
Defeats at home..............	4	4	4	2	1	1	16	3	3	3	1	1	11	27
Victories abroad..............	0	1	1	3	1	1	7	2	3	4	3	3	15	22
Defeats abroad...............	6	5	4	3	5	6	29	4	3	2	18	3	15	44

✼

The Chicagos' Season of 1897.

The most unsuccessful season, with one exception, known in the annals of the Chicago club was that of 1897. From 1876 to 1892, inclusive, the lowest position the Chicago club occupied in a League pennant race was fifth, and that was in 1877. From that year up to the '90s there was but two years that the club was not among the first three, and that was in 1878 and 1884, when they stood fourth. In 1893, however, they got down to ninth place, and in 1897 they did the same. Here is the club's race record during the twelve club regime, from 1892 to 1897, inclusive:

PENNANT RACE RECORD.

Years.	Victories.	Defeats.	Position.	Per cent.	Years.	Victories.	Defeats.	Position.	Per cent.
1892	70	76	Seventh.	.479	1895	72	58	Fourth.	.554
1893	51	71	Ninth.	.445	1896	71	57	Fifth.	.555
1894	57	75	Eighth.	.432	1897	59	73	Ninth.	.447

The close of the season of 1897 completed Manager Anson's twenty-first year of his career as manager and captain of the Chicagos, an unequaled record as a base ball manager. During this period Manager Anson bore off the League pennant

BASE BALL GUIDE. 59

with his team five times, was second in four seasons, and third in four years, and fourth in three years; twice his team was fifth, and only four times in twenty-one years did the Chicago team end lower than fifth.

THE FULL SEASON'S RECORD OF 1897.

CHICAGO VS.	First Division.						Second Divis'n					Grand Totals.
	Boston.	Baltimore.	New York.	Cincinnati.	Cleveland.	Brooklyn.	Totals.	Washington.	Pittsburg.	Philadelphia.	Louisville.	St. Louis.	Totals.	
Victories...........................	4	3	5	5	4	6	27	7	6	5	6	8	32	59
Defeats.............................	8	9	7	7	8	6	45	5	6	7	6	4	28	73
Drawn games........................	1	3	1	0	0	0	5	0	0	0	1	0	1	6
Total games........................	13	15	13	12	12	12	77	12	12	12	13	12	61	138
Series won..........................	0	0	0	0	0	0	0	1	0	0	0	1	2	2
Series lost.........................	1	1	1	1	1	0	5	0	0	1	0	0	1	6
Series tied.........................	0	0	0	0	0	1	1	0	1	0	1	0	2	3

Per cent. of victories—Against Boston, .333; Baltimore, .250; New York, .417; Cincinnati, .417; Cleveland, .333; Brooklyn, .500; total, first division clubs, .375. Washington, .583; Pittsburg, .500; Philadelphia, .417; Louisville, .500; St. Louis, .667; total, second division clubs, .533. Grand total, .447.

Against the six first division clubs the Chicago team's percentage of victories figures were but .250, and against the five second division clubs opposed to them their figures were .533. They lost their series with all of the first division teams, they tieing with Brooklyn, and they only won two of their series with the second division clubs. The record of additional statistics is appended:

CHICAGO VS.	First Division.							Second Divis'n					Grand Totals.
	Boston.	Baltimore.	New York.	Cincinnati.	Cleveland.	Brooklyn.	Totals.	Washington.	Pittsburg.	Philadelphia.	Louisville.	St. Louis.	Totals.	
"Chicago" victories................	0	0	0	1	0	0	1	0	0	0	1	0	1	2
"Chicago" defeats	0	0	2	0	1	0	3	1	0	0	0	0	1	4
Single-figure victories.............	3	3	3	4	4	3	20	5	4	4	4	7	24	44
Single-figure defeats...............	5	5	5	7	7	3	32	2	5	3	6	2	18	50
Double-figure victories.............	1	0	2	1	0	2	6	2	2	1	2	1	8	14
Double-figure defeats...............	3	4	2	0	1	3	13	3	1	4	0	2	10	23
Won by one run.....................	3	0	1	2	2	1	9	1	2	2	2	2	9	18
Lost by one run.....................	1	2	0	5	3	1	12	0	2	2	5	1	10	22
Victories at home...................	4	3	3	3	4	3	20	3	3	2	4	4	16	36
Defeats at home.....................	2	3	3	3	2	3	16	3	3	4	2	2	14	30
Victories abroad....................	0	0	2	2	0	3	7	3	3	3	2	4	15	22
Defeats abroad......................	6	6	3	4	6	3	28	2	3	3	4	2	14	42

The Philadelphias' Season of 1897.

The Philadelphias in 1897 reached the lowest position the club had ever occupied in a pennant race since it became a League club. The Philadelphias began its career in the League in 1883 under poor management, and ended eighth in that season's race, occupying the last ditch. In 1884 it ended sixth, and at the close of the season the late Harry Wright became the team manager, and from that year until he was superceded, the team never ended a race lower than fourth, besides being second in 1887 and third three times. From 1892 to 1897, while in the twelve-club League, it did fairly well up to 1896, when it ended eighth. But in 1897 it reached its lowest point—tenth place—every Eastern club surpassing it. Here is the club's past six years race record:

PENNANT RACE RECORD.

Years.	Victories.	Defeats.	Per cent.	Position.	Years.	Victories	Defeats.	Per cent.	Position.
1892	87	66	.569	Fourth.	1895	78	53	.595	Third.
1893	72	57	.558	Fourth.	1896	62	68	.477	Eighth.
1894	71	56	.559	Fourth.	1897	55	77	.417	Tenth.

THE FULL SEASON'S RECORD OF 1897.

The record of the Philadelphia club in total victories, defeats, drawn games and series won, lost and tied for 1897, together with the percentage of victories against every opposing club, is as follows:

PHILADELPHIA VS.	First Division.							Second Divis'n						Grand Totals.
	Boston.	Baltimore.	New York.	Cincinnati.	Cleveland.	Brooklyn.	Totals.	Washington.	Pittsburg.	Chicago.	Louisville.	St. Louis.	Totals.	
Victories	2	2	5	4	3	6	22	4	5	7	9	8	33	55
Defeats	10	10	7	8	9	6	50	8	7	5	3	4	27	77
Drawn games	1	1	0	0	0	0	2	0	0	0	0	0	0	2
Total games	13	13	12	12	12	12	74	12	12	12	12	12	60	134
Series won	0	0	0	0	0	0	0	0	0	1	1	1	3	3
Series lost	1	1	1	1	1	0	5	1	1	0	0	0	2	7
Series tied	0	0	0	0	0	1	1	0	0	0	0	0	0	1

Per cent. of victories—Against Boston, .167; Baltimore, .167; New York, .417; Cincinnati, .333; Cleveland, .250; Brooklyn, .500; total, first division clubs, .306. Washington, .333; Pittsburg, .417; Chicago, .583; Louisville, .750; St. Louis, .667; total, second division clubs, .550. Grand total, .417.

The Phillies percentage of victories against the first division clubs was the lowest of any other club except St. Louis, viz., .306, while against the second division clubs their figures were .550. Their lowest percentage figures against a single club were .167, and their highest .750. The additional statistic records are appended :

PHILADELPHIA vs.	First Division.						Second Divis'n					
	Boston.	Baltimore.	New York.	Cincinnati.	Cleveland.	Brooklyn.	Totals.	Washington.	Pittsburg.	Chicago.	Louisville.	St. Louis.	Totals.	Grand Totals.
"Chicago" victories	0	0	0	1	0	0	1	0	1	0	1	1	3	4
"Chicago" defeats	1	0	0	0	0	1	2	1	0	0	0	0	1	3
Single-figure victories	1	2	2	2	2	3	12	3	2	3	7	6	21	33
Single-figure defeats	9	6	5	7	6	4	37	6	6	4	2	2	20	57
Double-figure victories	1	0	3	1	1	3	9	1	3	4	2	2	12	21
Double-figure defeats	1	4	2	1	3	2	13	2	1	1	1	2	7	20
Won by one run	1	1	1	0	1	2	6	4	1	2	4	4	15	21
Lost by one run	2	1	1	4	2	1	11	3	4	2	0	2	11	22
Victories at home	1	0	4	3	2	5	15	4	2	3	4	4	17	32
Defeats at home	5	6	2	2	4	1	20	2	4	3	2	2	13	33
Victories abroad	1	2	1	1	1	1	7	0	3	4	5	4	16	23
Defeats abroad	5	4	5	6	5	5	30	6	3	2	1	2	14	44

✳

The Louisvilles' Season of 1897. During the past six years the Louisville club has not been able to close a pennant race higher than ninth position. In fact, in three successive years out of the six pennant races, they monopolized the last ditch. In 1897, during the early part of the season, the club raised the hopes of its friends considerably by closing the May campaign at the head of the second division; but after that they fell back into the old rut, and ended the race no higher than eleventh position. Here is their race record from 1892 to 1897, inclusive :

PENNANT RACE RECORD.

Years.	Victories.	Defeats.	Per cent.	Position.	Years.	Victories.	Defeats.	Per cent.	Position.
1892	63	89	.414	Ninth.	1895	35	96	.267	Twelfth.
1893	50	75	.400	Eleventh.	1896	38	93	.290	Twelfth.
1894	30	94	.277	Twelfth.	1897	52	78	.400	Eleventh.

THE FULL SEASON'S RECORD FOR 1897.

LOUISVILLE VS.	First Division.							Second Divis'n					Grand Totals.
	Boston.	Baltimore.	New York.	Cincinnati.	Cleveland.	Brooklyn.	Totals.	Washington.	Pittsburg.	Chicago.	Philadelphia.	St. Louis.	Totals.	
Victories	3	1	6	3	7	7	27	4	4	6	3	8	25	52
Defeats	9	10	6	9	5	5	44	8	8	6	9	3	34	78
Drawn games	0	0	0	0	0	0	0	1	2	1	0	0	4	4
Total games	12	11	12	12	12	12	71	13	14	13	12	11	63	134
Series won	0	0	0	0	1	1	2	0	0	0	0	1	1	3
Series lost	1	1	0	1	0	0	3	1	1	0	1	0	3	6
Series tied	0	0	1	0	0	0	1	0	0	1	0	0	1	2

Per cent. of victories—Against Boston, .250; Baltimore, .091; New York, .500; Cincinnati, .250; Cleveland, .583; Brooklyn, .583; total, first division clubs, .380. Washington, .333; Pittsburg, .333; Chicago, .500; Philadelphia, .250; St. Louis, .727; total, second division clubs, .424. Grand total, .400.

The 1897 record, it will be seen, is not one to be proud of. The club had the material, but not the required ability to direct it properly—hence its low position in the race. Its lowest percentage of victories figures "beat the record," viz., .091, and yet in one instance its figures reached .727, the highest. Against the first division clubs the club had a better record than Philadelphia, .380; but against the second division clubs their figures were but .424. Here is the additional statistics record for 1897:

LOUISVILLE VS.	First Division.							Second Divis'n					Grand Totals.
	Boston.	Baltimore.	New York.	Cincinnati.	Cleveland.	Brooklyn.	Totals.	Washington.	Pittsburg.	Chicago.	Philadelphia.	St. Louis.	Totals.	
"Chicago" victories	1	0	0	0	0	0	1	1	0	0	0	1	2
"Chicago" defeats	0	1	2	2	0	0	5	0	0	1	1	0	2	7
Single-figure victories	2	1	5	3	6	3	20	4	3	6	2	5	20	40
Single-figure defeats	6	8	4	7	2	2	29	7	7	4	7	3	28	57
Double-figure victories	1	0	1	0	1	4	7	0	1	0	1	4	6	13
Double-figure defeats	3	2	2	2	3	3	15	1	1	2	2	0	6	21
Won by one run	2	0	1	0	2	2	7	0	0	5	0	2	7	14
Lost by one run	1	2	3	2	0	0	8	0	4	2	4	1	11	19
Home victories	2	1	4	2	5	3	17	4	3	4	1	5	17	34
Home defeats	4	4	2	5	1	3	19	6	3	2	4	1	16	35
Victories abroad	1	0	2	1	2	4	10	0	1	2	2	3	8	18
Defeats abroad	5	6	4	4	4	2	25	2	5	4	4	2	17	42

BASE BALL GUIDE. 63

The St. Louis' Season of 1897. For the first time in the past six years the St. Louis club occupied the last ditch in the pennant race of the major league. It had been on the ragged edge three times before, but last year the team tumbled in head over heels, with the lowest score—29 victories to 102 defeats—known to the major league's annals. Here is the club's race record for the past six years:

PENNANT RACE RECORD.

Years.	Victories.	Defeats.	Per cent.	Position.	Years.	Victories.	Defeats.	Per cent.	Position.
1892	56	94	.373	Eleventh.	1895	39	92	.298	Eleventh.
1893	57	75	.432	Tenth.	1896	40	90	.308	Eleventh.
1894	56	76	.424	Ninth.	1897	29	102	.229	Twelfth.

THE FULL SEASON'S RECORD FOR 1897.

The club's record of victories, defeats and drawn games for 1897, as also that of series won, lost and tied, together with the percentage of victories figures against each opposing club, is as follows:

| St. Louis vs. | First Division. | | | | | | Second Divis'n | | | | | Grand Totals. |
	Boston.	Baltimore.	New York.	Cincinnati.	Cleveland.	Brooklyn.	Totals.	Washington.	Pittsburg.	Chicago.	Philadelphia.	Louisville.	Totals.	
Victories	2	2	0	1	1	5	11	3	4	4	4	3	18	29
Defeats	10	10	12	11	11	7	61	9	8	8	8	8	41	102
Drawn games	0	0	0	0	1	0	1	0	0	0	0	0	0	1
Total games	12	12	12	12	13	12	73	12	12	12	12	11	59	132
Series won	0	0	0	0	0	0	0	0	0	0	0	0	0	0
Series lost	1	1	1	1	1	1	6	1	1	1	1	1	5	11
Series tied	0	0	0	0	0	0	0	0	0	0	0	0	0	0

Per cent. of victories—Against Boston, .167; Baltimore, .167; New York, .000; Cincinnati, .083; Cleveland, .083; Brooklyn, .417; total, first division clubs, .153. Washington, .250; Pittsburg, .333; Chicago, .333; Philadelphia, .333; Louisville, .273; total, second division clubs, .305 Grand total, .229.

Their percentage figures against the first division clubs were only .153, and but .305 against those of the second division. Their lowest club percentage was .000—they losing every game with New York—and their highest was but .417. In fact, their season was the "worst on record." Here is the additional statistics record for 1897:

| ST. LOUIS VS. | First Division. ||||||| Second Divis'n ||||| Grand Totals. |
	Boston.	Baltimore.	New York.	Cincinnati.	Cleveland.	Brooklyn.	Totals.	Washington.	Pittsburg.	Chicago.	Philadelphia.	Louisville.	Totals.	
"Chicago" victories	0	0	0	0	0	1	1	0	0	0	0	0	0	1
"Chicago" defeats	0	0	0	1	0	1	2	3	0	0	1	0	4	6
Single-figure victories	2	2	0	1	0	5	10	3	4	2	2	3	14	24
Single-figure defeats	1	2	9	10	7	3	32	7	5	6	6	4	28	60
Double-figure victories	0	0	0	0	1	0	1	0	0	2	2	0	4	5
Double-figure defeats	9	8	3	1	4	4	29	2	3	2	2	4	13	42
Won by one run	1	1	0	1	0	3	6	1	2	1	1	1	6	12
Lost by one run	1	0	2	3	2	1	9	1	1	2	4	1	9	18
Victories at home	2	0	0	1	0	3	6	3	3	2	2	2	12	18
Defeats at home	3	6	3	5	3	3	23	3	3	4	4	3	17	40
Victories abroad	0	2	0	0	1	2	5	0	1	2	2	1	6	11
Defeats abroad	7	4	9	6	8	4	38	6	5	4	4	5	24	62

A Twenty-Two Years' Record.

As a matter of reference we append a table which shows the victories and defeats, games played and the percentage of victories of each pennant-winning club from 1876 to 1897:

Year.	Pennant Winners.	Won.	Lost.	Played.	Per cent. of Victories.	Grand Total Games Played Each Year.	Managers.	No. of Clubs Playing.
1876	Chicago	52	14	66	.788	257	Spalding	8
1877	Boston	31	17	48	.646	120	Harry Wright	6
1878	Boston	41	19	60	.680	180	Harry Wright	6
1879	Providence	55	23	78	.705	288	George Wright	8
1880	Chicago	67	17	84	.798	332	Anson	8
1881	Chicago	56	28	84	.667	334	Anson	8
1882	Chicago	55	29	84	.655	334	Anson	8
1883	Boston	63	35	98	.643	390	Morrill	8
1884	Providence	84	28	112	.750	447	Bancroft	8
1885	Chicago	87	25	112	.776	442	Anson	8
1886	Chicago	90	34	124	.725	480	Anson	8
1887	Detroit	79	45	124	.637	492	Watkins	8
1888	New York	84	47	131	.641	532	Mutrie	8
1889	New York	83	43	126	.659	518	Mutrie	8
1890	Brooklyn	86	43	129	.667	531	McGunnigle	8
1891	Boston	87	51	138	.630	545	Selee	12
1892	Boston	102	48	150	.680	913	Selee	12
1893	Boston	86	43	129	.667	774	Selee	12
1894	Baltimore	89	39	128	.695	782	Hanlon	12
1895	Baltimore	87	43	130	.669	783	Hanlon	12
1896	Baltimore	90	39	129	.698	778	Hanlon	12
1897	Boston	93	39	132	.705	788	Selee	12

Horton Garry Schiebeck Willis Shaw Lampe Eagan Malarky Lezotte Kisinger
Smith O'Brien Buckenberger (Mgr.) Ryan Earl

SYRACUSE STARS—CHAMPIONS EASTERN LEAGUE, 1897.

Nadeau　Henry　McKenna　Moynihan　Gochnaur　Magoon
Sharrott　Pettinger　Burnham (Mgr.)　Birmingham　Wich
　　　　　　　Shea　Sheckard

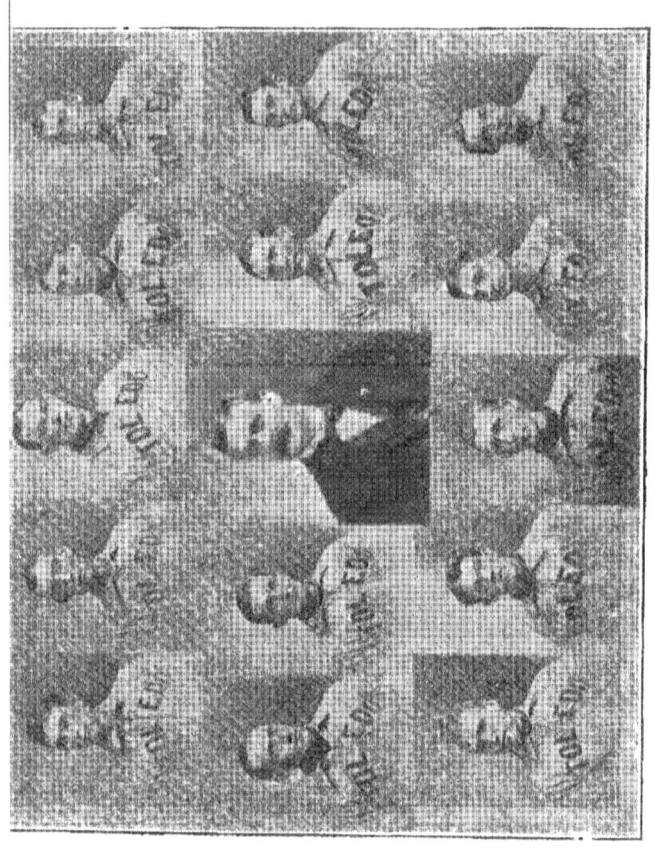

Smith   Hasamaer   Gilks (Capt.)   Beck   Hartman
Myers   Arthur   Strobel (Mgr.) Langsford McDonough
Ferguson Ewing   Blue   Darby   Kelb

TOLEDO BASE BALL CLUB—CHAMPIONS INTER-STATE LEAGUE, 1897.

INDIANAPOLIS BASE BALL CLUB—CHAMPIONS WESTERN LEAGUE, 1897.

LANCASTER BASE BALL CLUB—CHAMPIONS ATLANTIC LEAGUE, 1897.

Hickey   McCann   Dean   Lauer   Phillips   Andrews
Hoffner   Ripley (Mgr.)   Wm. Stroud (Pres.)   G. Stroud (Treas.)   McDonald
   McGinnis   Baker   Conwell   Cockran
HAMILTON BASE BALL CLUB—CHAMPIONS CANADIAN LEAGUE, 1897.

MacFarland Van Buren Hutchinson
Kennedy Cole Hill (Mgr.) McDougal Flood
Fuller Mahaffy Fisher Donnelly
CEDAR RAPIDS BASE BALL CLUB—CHAMPIONS WESTERN ASSOCIATION, 1897.

Clements Gardner Corcoran Theisen
Dietrich Bone Chapman (Mgr.) Buckley Pfenninger
Dwyer Donovan (Capt.) Courtney
MERIDEN BASE BALL TEAM, 1897.

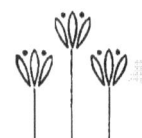The Pitching of 1897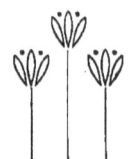

OF the four departments of the game of base ball, viz., *Pitching, Batting, Fielding* and *Base-Running*, the delivery of the ball to the bat is the most important. Indeed, the "battery" of a club's team—the pitcher and catcher—is the main reliance of the attacking force in a contest, and it is chiefly on the excellence of the "battery" work in a match that success in the contest depends. Of course, effective support behind the bat greatly contributes to a pitcher's success; but the best of catchers would be of comparatively little use unless he was faced by a first-class occupant of the pitcher's "box." The pitcher of a team, therefore, is regarded as the principal player of the base ball field.

The true art of pitching has of late years been practiced to a greater extent than ever before, and especially by the leading pitchers of the National League. In fact, it has come to be generally recognized that the possession of great speed in delivery is not alone sufficient to insure success, for without thorough command of the ball in pitching, mere speed is worse than useless. Then, too, strategic skill—technically termed "head-work"—is an important requirement. This latter essential was practically brought into play last season with more telling effect than ever before. The brainy class of pitchers, who excel in strategy in the box, were successful not only in deceiving the eye of the batsman in judging the speed of the delivery, as to the ball being sent in fast or slow; but also in puzzling his judgment in regard to the direction the ball is sent to him, as to its being sent in higher or lower than he wants it. Then, too, there is the strong point of a pitcher being prompt to take sudden advantage of the batsmen being temporarily "out of form" for effective batting; to which may be added that other point of strategic skill in pitching—tempting the batsman to hit high balls for outfield catches. All of these features of strategic pitching insure a degree of success in the box unknown to the pitcher who relies solely on mere intimidating speed in pitching, such as is characteristic of mere "cyclone" pitchers.

Of course, the use of the "curves" in pitching is essential to success, but to insure the best effects of the curves, command of the ball, so as to curve it over the plate, is absolutely necessary. Many of the pitchers of 1897 seemed to think that the sole aim of a pitcher should be to strike out opposing batsmen by mere intimidating speed, whereas where one such pitcher succeeds, a dozen strategists will win games by their head-work in the box. As we said before, great speed in delivery, without the essential requirement of thorough command of the ball, is worse than useless, if only from its great cost in "battery" errors.

Masterly skill in disguising the change of pace in delivery was a marked feature of the work of the leading pitchers in 1897; the successful working of the curved "drop" ball, too, was also noteworthy. But the season of 1897 was one in which exhibitions of uncontrolled temper by pitchers, and of the utter folly of disputing the umpire's decisions on called strikes and called balls, were far too frequent, not only for successful pitching, but for the good name of the professional fraternity at large. No player can succeed in strategic pitching who cannot control a hot temper. A quick temper is at constant war with the cool judgment and nerve so essential in strategic pitching; and in regard to disputing decisions on strikes and balls, the stupidity of such a course is so plainly apparent that it is surprising that any pitcher of intelligence will so far forget himself as to indulge in it. All kinds of kicking against decisions by umpires is, to a more or less extent, downright stupid work; but the most senseless of all is the kicking by pitchers, for not a solitary point can be gained by it, while its costly nature is very apparent.

The Individual Club Pitching of 1897.

The utter failure of any enforcement of an intelligent rule descriptive of runs earned solely off the pitching—and no such rule was at command in 1897—has left the GUIDE'S rule of percentage of victories pitched in to become the established criterion of effective work in the pitcher's box; and in this edition of the GUIDE for 1898 we present a series of tables showing the work of every pitcher in each individual club of the League for 1897, which is a more complete statistical pitching record than any yet published. The official pitching records still fail to give the data for an intelligent analysis of each pitcher's work, though they are better this year than before. The headings for a complete analysis record of the pitcher's work in the box, at the bat and in the field during a season's campaign should be as follows:

BASE BALL GUIDE. 67

Pitcher.	Games pitched in.	Innings pitched in.	Times struck out opponents.	Average of strike-outs per inning.	Bases on balls.	Average of bases on balls per game.	Wild pitches per game.	Hit batsman per game.	Base-hits off the pitching.	Average of base-hits per game.	Runs scored off the pitching.	Average of runs scored per game.	Bases on balks.	Catches made off pitching.	Pitcher's batting average.	Pitcher's fielding average.	Pitcher's stolen bases.
Totals ...												.					

To obtain such data material changes would have to be made in the scoring rules of the game.

While it is true that the success or failure on the part of a pitcher to win victories largely depends upon the excellence or weakness of the field support given him, nevertheless the percentage of victories pitched in present figures more reliable, as a criterion of good work, than any of the crude and incomplete earned-run figures hitherto used.

The Boston Club's Pitching Record.

The Boston club's champion team of 1897 contained but five pitchers, and out of the 132 games pitched in by the corps which were either victories or defeats three of the five pitchers were occupants of the box in no less than 109 games, viz., Klobedanz, Nichols and Lewis, Stivetts pitching in but 15 and Sullivan in only 8, drawn games not being included. The percentage figures show Klobedanz to have been the most successful throughout the campaign, as Nichols did not get well into his usual fine work until the middle of May. Nichols was, however, the most effective against four of the five first division clubs opposed to him; but failing to pitch in a victory against Brooklyn, Klobedanz was able to lead him in percentage figures against the first division clubs, the latter pitching in three straight victories against Brooklyn, while Nichols did not win a game from them. This left Klobedanz with the percentage of .667 to Nichols' 632 against the five first division clubs, though Nichols won more games from Baltimore, Cincinnati and Cleveland than Klobedanz, and did better against New York. He was very effective against Cleveland, he winning four out of five games with that team. Lewis led the trio against Brooklyn, while Stivetts' best work was done against New York and Cincinnati. Sullivan only pitched in one victory, and that was against New York.

Against the second division clubs Klobedanz took a decided lead, his percentage figures against the six clubs in question being .882 to Nichols' .792, Lewis' figures being .706. The full season's pitching record for 1897 is as follows:

BOSTON vs.		Baltimore.	New York.	Cincinnati.	Cleveland.	Brooklyn.	Totals.	Washington.	Pittsburg.	Chicago.	Philadelphia.	Louisville.	St. Louis.	Totals.	Grand Totals.	Per cent. of Victories.
		\multicolumn{6}{c}{First Division.}	\multicolumn{7}{c}{Second Division.}		
Klobedanz	Won	2	2	2	3	3	12	0	4	3	4	2	2	15	27	.771
	Lost	2	2	1	1	0	6	2	0	0	0	0	0	2	8	
Nichols	Won	3	2	3	4	0	12	3	3	4	2	4	3	19	31	.738
	Lost	3	1	1	1	1	7	1	1	1	2	0	0	5	12	
Lewis	Won	1	1	2	0	5	9	2	3	1	2	2	2	12	21	.667
	Lost	0	1	1	2	1	5	1	1	1	0	1	1	5	10	
Stivetts	Won	0	2	2	0	1	5	0	0	0	2	1	2	5	10	.667
	Lost	1	0	0	0	1	2	0	0	2	0	0	1	3	5	
Sullivan	Won	0	1	0	0	0	1	2	0	0	0	0	1	3	4	.500
	Lost	0	0	0	1	0	1	1	0	0	0	2	0	3	4	
Totals		12	12	12	12	12	60	12	12	12	12	12	12	72	132	

The pitching record of the Boston club's pitching corps against the clubs of the two divisions, respectively, is appended, in order to show which excelled in percentage figures against the clubs of each of the two divisions. Here is the table:

AGAINST FIRST DIVISION.

Pitchers.	Victories.	Defeats.	Per cent.
Stivetts	5	2	.714
Klobedanz	12	6	.667
Lewis	9	5	.643
Nichols	12	7	.632
Sullivan	1	1	.500

AGAINST SECOND DIVISION.

Pitchers.	Victories.	Defeats.	Per cent.
Klobedanz	15	2	.882
Nichols	19	5	.792
Lewis	12	5	.706
Stivetts	5	3	.628
Sullivan	3	3	.500

The Baltimore Club's Pitching Record.

Taking his work in the box as a whole, Corbett was Baltimore's most successful pitcher in the box in 1897, he excelling all of the six pitchers of the club in percentage of victories

BASE BALL GUIDE.

figures against the five first division clubs opposed to him, Pond being second in this respect and Nops third. Hoffer failed to equal his good record of 1896, while Amole, Blackburn and Maul failed to exceed the average percentage figures of .500. In the campaign against the second division clubs Nops took the lead with the highest percentage figures on record for so many games played, as he won 14 out of 15 played, giving a percentage of .933. Corbett, however, was close to him with .867. Corbett troubled the Bostons greatly, he winning three out of the four games he pitched against the champions. Blackburn was next to useless, while Maul only pitched in a single game, and that was a defeat. Here is the record in full.

Baltimore vs.		First Division.						Second Division.							Grand Totals.	Per cent. of Victories.
		Boston.	New York.	Cincinnati.	Cleveland.	Brooklyn.	Totals.	Washington.	Pittsburg.	Chicago.	Philadelphia.	Louisville.	St. Louis.	Totals.		
Nops	Won	0	2	1	2	0	5	2	3	1	3	3	2	14	19	.792
	Lost	2	2	0	0	0	4	1	0	0	0	0	0	1	5	
Corbett	Won	3	2	2	2	2	11	2	2	2	2	2	3	13	24	.727
	Lost	1	1	2	1	1	6	0	1	0	0	1	0	2	8	
Pond	Won	1	0	1	2	4	8	3	1	3	2	1	1	11	19	.679
	Lost	1	1	1	1	1	5	1	0	1	0	0	1	3	8	
Hoffer	Won	2	1	1	3	8	2	2	2	3	2	3	14	22	.667	
	Lost	2	2	2	0	1	7	0	1	2	1	0	0	4	11	
Amole	Won	0	0	1	0	0	1	0	1	0	0	1	1	3	4	.500
	Lost	0	1	0	1	0	2	1	0	0	1	0	0	2	4	
Blackburn	Won	0	0	0	0	0	0	0	0	1	0	1	0	2	2	.400
	Lost	0	0	1	1	0	2	0	1	0	0	0	0	1	3	
Maul	Won	0	0	0	0	0	0	0	0	0	0	0	0	0	0	.000
	Lost	0	0	0	0	0	0	0	0	0	0	0	1	1	1	
Totals		12	12	12	11	12	59	12	12	12	12	11	12	71	130	

The division record, showing which pitchers excelled against the clubs of the two divisions, is appended :

AGAINST FIRST DIVISION.

Pitchers.	Victories.	Defeats.	Per cent.
Corbett	11	6	.647
Pond	8	5	.615
Nops	5	4	.556
Hoffer	8	7	.533
Amole	1	2	.333
Blackburn	0	2	.000

AGAINST SECOND DIVISION.

Pitchers.	Victories.	Defeats.	Per cent.
Nops	14	1	.933
Corbett	13	2	.867
Pond	11	3	.786
Hoffer	14	4	.778
Blackburn	2	1	.667
Amole	3	2	.600

It will be seen that practically the Baltimore club had but four pitchers in the campaign, as Corbett, Pond, Nops and Hoffer pitched in 116 of the 130 victories and defeats of the season, Maul's one game not being included in the above table.

The New York Club's Pitching Record.

The brunt of the work done by New Yorks' pitching corps fell upon three of the seven pitchers they employed in 1897, the three in question being the veterans Rusie and Meekin, and the colt Seymour, the two former pitching in 69 of the 131 victories and defeats of the club last season. Rusie took a decided lead over all the others alike against the first division clubs and those of the second, Meekin being second against the former, and Seymour second against the latter. M. Sullivan led both Seymour and Doheny against the first division clubs; but like Meekin he fell down before those of the second division. Rusie knocked spots out of his old rivals of Brooklyn, he winning five of the six games he pitched against Barnie's team. Meekin, too, did not pitch in a defeat against Brooklyn. Seymour was most successful against Cleveland in the first division. Clarke had the third best percentage figures, but his victories were won against the tail-ender, St. Louis, and his defeat at the hands of Louisvile. Here is the full record for 1897:

NEW YORK vs.		Boston.	Baltimore.	Cincinnati.	Cleveland.	Brooklyn.	Totals.	Washington.	Pittsburg.	Chicago.	Philadelphia.	Louisville.	St. Louis.	Totals.	Grand Totals.	Per cent. of Victories.
Rusie	Won	1	3	3	2	5	14	3	2	2	3	2	2	14	28	.757
	Lost	2	0	1	2	1	6	0	1	2	0	0	0	3	9	
Meekin	Won	2	2	1	2	3	10	0	1	2	1	2	4	10	20	.625
	Lost	2	1	2	0	0	5	2	2	0	2	1	0	7	12	
Seymour	Won	0	1	1	3	1	6	4	2	1	3	1	2	13	19	.594
	Lost	3	2	2	1	2	10	0	0	0	0	3	0	3	13	
Doheny	Won	0	0	0	1	0	1	1	2	0	0	1	0	4	5	.556
	Lost	0	1	1	0	0	2	0	0	1	1	0	0	2	4	
M. Sullivan	Won	1	1	0	1	0	3	1	0	2	0	0	2	5	8	.500
	Lost	1	1	1	0	0	3	1	0	2	1	1	0	5	8	
Clark	Won	0	0	0	0	0	0	0	0	0	0	0	2	2	2	.067
	Lost	0	0	0	0	0	0	0	0	0	1	0	1	1		
Gettig	Won	0	0	0	0	0	0	1	0	0	0	0	1	1	1	.500
	Lost	0	0	0	0	0	0	0	0	1	0	0	1	1		
Totals		12	12	12	12	12	60	12	11	12	12	12	12	71	131	

But for the telling work of four out of New York's seven pitchers in 1897 the club would scarcely have occupied sixth position at the end of the season. Rusie was just as effective against the first division clubs as he was against the second division ones. Meekin did better against the first division than he did against the second, while Seymour found the second division much easier than the strong teams of the first division. Sullivan only pitched in 16 games, breaking even with games won and lost.

Here is the division record of the season:

AGAINST FIRST DIVISION.   AGAINST SECOND DIVISION.

Pitchers.	Victories.	Defeats.	Per cent.	Pitchers.	Victories.	Defeats.	Per cent.
Rusie	14	6	.700	Rusie	14	3	.824
Meekin	10	5	.667	Seymour	13	3	.813
M. Sullivan	3	3	.500	Doheny	4	2	.667
Seymour	6	10	.375	Clarke	2	1	.667
Doheny	1	2	.333	Meekin	10	7	.588
Clarke	0	0	.000	M. Sullivan	5	5	.500
Gettig	0	0	.000	Gettig	1	1	.500

The Cincinnati Club's Pitching Record.

The Cincinnati club's pitching corps in 1897 comprised seven players, and of these only three took part in a majority of the games played, Rhines pitching in 37, Breitenstein in 36 and Dwyer in 29, making a total of 102 games these three pitched in out of 132 won and lost. Ehret pitched in 19 and Damman in 9 only, the other two of the full corps pitching in a single defeat each. The most effective pitcher against the first division clubs was Damman, while Dwyer led against those of the second division, Breitenstein being second against both divisions. Rhines was third against the first division, but Breitenstein led the whole corps in effective box-work against Boston, Baltimore and New York, though second to Damman in total percentage figures. Only four of the seven pitchers exceeded the percentage figures of .500, while Ehret did not reach that average.

Here is the record of the corps in full for 1897:

CINCINNATI vs.		First Division.						Second Division.						Grand Totals.	Per cent. of Victories.
		Boston.	Baltimore.	New York.	Cleveland.	Brooklyn.	Totals.	Washington.	Pittsburg.	Chicago.	Philadelphia.	Louisville.	St. Louis.	Totals.		
Damman........	Won	0	0	2	2	0	4	0	0	1	1	0	0	2	6	.667
	Lost	1	0	1	0	0	2	0	1	0	0	0	0	1	3	
Breitenstein........	Won	1	2	3	2	2	10	2	1	1	3	2	4	13	23	.030
	Lost	1	2	1	2	1	7	1	3	0	0	1	1	6	13	
Dwyer........	Won	0	2	0	0	2	4	1	2	1	3	4	3	14	18	.621
	Lost	3	2	0	1	2	8	1	1	0	1	0	0	3	11	
Rhines........	Won	1	2	1	2	1	7	3	2	3	1	2	2	13	20	.526
	Lost	2	1	3	2	2	10	1	1	2	2	1	0	7	17	
Ehret........	Won	1	0	1	1	0	3	2	0	1	0	1	2	6	9	.474
	Lost	2	1	0	0	2	5	1	0	3	0	1	0	5	10	
Brown........	Won	0	0	0	0	0	0	0	0	0	0	0	0	0	0	.000
	Lost	0	0	0	0	0	0	0	0	0	1	0	0	1	1	
Pietz........	Won	0	0	0	0	0	0	0	0	0	0	0	0	0	0	.000
	Lost	0	0	0	0	0	0	0	1	0	0	0	0	1	1	
Totals........		12	12	12	12	12	60	12	12	12	12	12	12	72	132	

The division record of the season is appended:

AGAINST FIRST DIVISION.   AGAINST SECOND DIVISION.

Pitchers.	Victories.	Defeats.	Per cent.	Pitchers.	Victories.	Defeats.	Per cent.
Damman.............	4	2	.667	Dwyer................	14	3	.824
Breitenstein.........	10	7	.588	Breitenstein.........	13	6	.684
Rhines...............	7	10	.412	Damman.............	2	1	.667
Ehret................	3	5	.375	Rhines...............	13	7	.650
Dwyer...............	4	8	.333	Ehret................	6	5	.545
Brown...............	0	0	.000	Brown...............	0	1	.000
Pietz................	0	0	.000	Pietz................	0	1	.000

As a rule, the more pitchers a club uses in a season the lower their pennant race record. In 1897 the Bostons mainly depended on three pitchers and won the race. The tail-end St. Louis club, on the other hand, employed eleven pitchers, and were left in the last ditch, while the Louisvilles, with thirteen pitchers, hardly fared any better, they having te be content with eleventh place. It is simply a case of "too many cooks spoiling the broth."

The Cleveland Club's Pitching Record.

The Cleveland club employed nine pitchers in their corps of 1897, and yet the four leaders pitched in no less than 122 games out of the 130 won and lost. Cuppy lead in total percentage figures, with Wilson second, Young third and Powell fourth. Cuppy did the best of the four against the first division clubs, and stood next to Young against those of the second division—if we except McDermott, who only pitched in two games against the latter, while Young pitched in 14 victories out of 15 games. Cuppy was the only pitcher who had a percentage of .500 and over against the first division clubs. Young was badly punished by the Bostons, while Cuppy did not lose a game against them. Pappalau, McAllister and Clarke were useless to the team, neither of them pitching in a single victory, and Brown only in one; McDermott pitching in but three victories. Here is the record in full:

CLEVELAND vs		Boston.	Baltimore.	New York.	Cincinnati.	Brooklyn.	Totals.	Washington.	Pittsburg.	Chicago.	Philadelphia.	Louisville.	St. Louis.	Totals.	Grand Totals.	Per cent. of Victories.
Cuppy	Won	3	0	1	0	2	6	1	0	1	2	0	1	5	11	.647
	Lost	0	3	1	1	0	5	0	0	0	0	1	0	1	6	
Wilson	Won	0	0	1	1	1	3	3	1	2	3	2	4	15	18	.581
	Lost	1	2	1	3	2	9	1	1	1	1	0	0	4	13	
Young	Won	0	2	1	3	1	7	2	2	3	3	2	2	14	21	.568
	Lost	5	1	3	0	3	12	2	0	0	2	0	4	16		
Powell	Won	2	1	0	1	1	5	1	2	2	1	1	3	10	15	.556
	Lost	1	0	2	2	1	6	1	2	1	2	0	0	6	12	
McDermott	Won	0	1	0	0	0	1	1	0	0	0	0	0	1	2	.429
	Lost	0	1	1	1	1	4	0	0	0	0	0	0	0	4	
Brown	Won	0	0	0	0	0	0	1	0	0	0	0	1	1	1	.250
	Lost	0	0	0	0	0	0	0	0	1	0	1	1	3	3	
Pappalau	Won	0	0	0	0	0	0	0	0	0	0	0	0	0	0	.000
	Lost	0	0	0	0	0	0	0	0	0	1	0	1	1		
McAllister	Won	0	0	0	0	0	0	0	0	0	0	0	0	0	0	.000
	Lost	0	0	1	0	0	1	0	1	0	0	0	0	1	2	
Clarke	Won	0	0	0	0	0	0	0	0	0	0	0	0	0	0	.000
	Lost	0	0	0	0	0	0	2	1	0	1	0	4	4		
Totals		12	11	12	12	12	59	12	12	12	12	11	12	71	130	

Appended is the division record, by which it will be seen that but one pitcher of the nine used during the season reached the average percentage figures of .500 against the first division clubs. Against those of the second division, Young, Cuppy and Wilson were very successful.

PITCHERS.	AGAINST FIRST DIVISION.			PITCHERS.	AGAINST SECOND DIVISION.		
	Victories.	Defeats.	Per cent.		Victories.	Defeats.	Per cent.
Cuppy	6	5	.545	McDermott	2	0	1.000
Powell	5	6	.455	Young	14	1	.933
Young	7	12	.368	Cuppy	5	1	.833
Wilson	3	9	.250	Wilson	15	4	.789
McDermott	1	4	.200	Powell	10	6	.625
Brown	0	0	.000	Brown	1	3	.250
Pappalau	0	0	.000	Pappalau	0	1	.000
Clark	0	0	.000	McAllister	0	1	.000
McAllister	0	0	.000	Clarke	0	4	.000

The Brooklyn Club's Pitching Record.

Of the 132 victories and defeats record for the Brooklyn club in 1897, in which their corps of seven pitchers took part, three of them pitched in 94 of the games and the other four in the remaining 38 games ; so it will be seen that much of the season was wasted in experimental pitching. Of the seven pitchers the club only two reached the average percentage figures of .500 against the first division clubs, while four of them did not do as well as that against the clubs of the second division. Kennedy led the first division, with Fischer close to him. Dunn was the most effective against the second division. Here is the record in full :

BROOKLYN VS.		FIRST DIVISION.						SECOND DIVISION.							Grand Totals.	Per cent. of Victories.
		Boston.	Baltimore.	New York.	Cincinnati.	Cleveland.	Totals.	Washington.	Pittsburg.	Chicago.	Philadelphia.	Louisville.	St. Louis.	Totals.		
Dunn	Won	1	1	1	1	1	5	2	0	3	2	1	1	9	14	.686
	Lost	1	2	1	2	1	7	1	0	0	0	0	1	8		
Fischer	Won	1	0	0	2	0	3	2	1	0	1	1	1	6	9	.563
	Lost	1	1	0	0	1	3	1	0	1	1	1	0	4	7	
Kennedy	Won	1	1	1	3	3	9	1	3	2	1	1	1	9	18	.474
	Lost	2	2	3	1	1	9	2	2	1	1	2	3	11	20	
Payne	Won	0	1	1	0	2	4	2	3	0	2	1	2	10	14	.412
	Lost	3	1	5	1	2	12	1	2	1	1	3	0	8	20	
Daub	Won	0	0	0	1	1	2	0	0	1	0	1	2	4	6	.375
	Lost	2	2	0	1	0	5	0	1	2	1	0	1	5	10	
Brown	Won	0	0	0	0	0	0	0	0	0	0	0	0	0	0	.000
	Lost	0	1	0	0	0	1	0	0	0	0	0	0	0	1	
McMahon	Won	0	0	0	0	0	0	0	0	0	0	0	0	0	0	.000
	Lost	0	0	0	0	0	0	0	1	2	1	1	4	4		
Totals		12	12	12	12	12	60	12	12	12	12	12	12	72	132	

McMahon and Brown did not win a single game, while Daub and Payne had more defeats than victories to their record. The record shows just how each pitcher fared against the other teams:

Pitchers.	Victories.	Defeats.	Per cent.	Pitchers.	Victories.	Defeats.	Per cent.
\multicolumn{4}{l}{AGAINST FIRST DIVISION.}	\multicolumn{4}{l}{AGAINST SECOND DIVISION.}
Kennedy	9	9	.500	Dunn	9	1	.900
Fischer	3	3	.500	Fischer	6	4	.600
Dunn	5	7	.417	Payne	10	8	.550
Daub	2	5	.286	Kennedy	9	11	.450
Payne	4	12	.250	Daub	4	5	.444
McMahon	0	0	.000	Brown	0	0	.000
Brown	0	1	.000	McMahon	0	4	.000

The Washington Club's Pitching Record.

The Washington club had a pitching corps of eight players in 1897, and yet but two of them reached average percentage figures against the first division clubs, and only three against those of the second division. Bresnahan was the most effective against both divisions, while Swain stood second against the first division and Mercer against the second. The veteran King was third against both divisions. Mercer did not do better than fourth against the first division clubs, while McJames, an excellent pitcher, failed badly against both divisions. Maul, Norton and German were practically useless to the club, though all three rating as effective men in other clubs. Bresnahan, who led the corps in total percentage figures, did not pitch against the three leaders in the race, but he won his games against Cincinnati, Cleveland and Brooklyn. On the other hand, Mercer beat all the others against the three leaders, while McJames was handled roughly by Boston and Baltimore, as was Mercer by New York and Brooklyn.

The complete record of each pitcher's work is appended:

| | First Division. | | | | | | | Second Divis'n | | | | | | |
WASHINGTON VS.	Boston.	Baltimore.	New York.	Cincinnati.	Cleveland.	Brooklyn.	Totals.	Pittsburg.	Chicago.	Philadelphia.	Louisville.	St. Louis.	Totals.	Grand Totals.	Per cent. of Victories.
Bresnahan Won	0	0	0	1	1	1	3	0	0	0	1	1	2	5	.833
Lost	0	0	0	0	0	0	0	1	0	0	0	0	1	1	
Mercer Won	2	1	1	1	1	1	7	4	2	4	1	4	15	22	.537
Lost	2	2	4	2	2	4	16	1	1	0	1	0	3	19	
King Won	1	1	0	1	0	0	3	0	0	1	3	2	6	9	.500
Lost	0	2	2	1	1	0	6	1	1	0	0	1	3	9	
German Won	0	0	0	0	0	0	0	0	1	1	0	1	3	3	.429
Lost	1	0	0	0	1	0	2	1	0	0	1	0	2	4	
Swain Won	2	1	0	0	0	2	1	6	0	1	1	0	0	2	8	.421
Lost	0	0	1	3	0	1	5	0	3	2	0	1	6	11	
McJames Won	0	0	2	1	0	1	4	3	1	1	3	1	9	13	.342
Lost	4	4	1	2	4	2	17	1	2	2	2	1	8	25	
Maul Won	0	0	0	0	0	0	0	0	0	0	0	0	0	0	.000
Lost	0	1	0	0	0	0	1	0	0	0	0	0	1	
Norton Won	0	0	0	0	0	0	0	0	0	0	0	0	0	0	.000
Lost	0	0	1	0	0	0	1	0	0	0	0	0	1	
Totals	12	12	12	12	12	11	71	12	12	12	12	12	60	131	

Here is the division record. Norton and Maul took part in a few innings in one game, but are not on record as winning or losing a game:

AGAINST FIRST DIVISION. AGAINST SECOND DIVISION.

Pitchers.	Victories.	Defeats.	Per cent.	Pitchers.	Victories.	Defeats.	Per cent.
Bresnahan	3	0	1.000	Bresnahan	5	1	.833
Swain	6	5	.545	Mercer	22	19	.537
King	3	6	.333	King	9	9	.500
Mercer	7	16	.304	Swain	8	11	.421
McJames	4	17	.190	McJames	13	25	.342
Maul	0	0	.000	German	2	4	.333
Norton	0	0	.000	Maul	0	0	.000
German	0	2	.000	Norton	0	0	.000

The Pittsburg Club's Pitching Record.

The Pittsburg club had but six pitchers in their corps in 1897, and out of the 131 victories and defeats recorded, Hawley and Killen alone pitched in 77, thereby doing the brunt of the box-work of the season, as the other four aggregated the balance of the games—37. Hastings led the pitching against the first division clubs, Hawley being second. But the latter led Hastings against the clubs of the second division. Hastings was the only pitcher who reached the percentage average of .500 against the first division clubs, Killen and Hughey tieing at .375 each. The former, however, did poorly against those of the second division, while Hughey held the tail-end position in total percentages. Here is the record:

PITTSBURG VS.		Boston.	Baltimore.	New York.	Cincinnati.	Cleveland.	Brooklyn.	Totals.	Washington.	Chicago.	Philadelphia.	Louisville.	St. Louis.	Totals.	Grand Totals.	Per cent. of Victories.
		\multicolumn{6}{c}{First Division.}		\multicolumn{5}{c}{Second Divis'n}			
Hastings	Won	0	0	0	1	1	1	3	0	1	1	0	1	3	6	.545
	Lost	1	1	0	0	1	0	3	1	0	0	1	0	2	5	
Hawley	Won	0	1	1	3	3	0	8	2	3	1	2	2	10	18	.500
	Lost	5	1	2	2	1	2	13	1	1	1	1	5	18	
Tannehill	Won	0	0	1	0	1	0	2	2	0	2	1	1	6	8	.500
	Lost	1	1	2	0	1	0	5	0	1	1	0	1	3	8	
Gardner	Won	0	0	0	1	0	0	1	0	1	0	2	1	4	5	.455
	Lost	1	1	0	0	0	2	4	1	1	0	0	0	2	6	
Killen	Won	2	1	1	2	1	2	9	0	1	1	3	3	8	17	.415
	Lost	2	4	3	2	3	1	15	3	3	2	0	1	9	24	
Hughey	Won	0	1	0	0	0	2	3	1	0	2	0	0	3	6	.375
	Lost	0	1	1	1	0	2	5	1	0	1	2	1	5	10	
Totals								12 12 11 12 12 12 71 12 12 12 12 12 60							131	

Here is the division record:

	AGAINST FIRST DIVISION.				AGAINST SECOND DIVISION.		
PITCHERS.	Victories.	Defeats.	Per cent.	PITCHERS.	Victories.	Defeats.	Per cent.
Hastings	3	3	.500	Hawley	10	5	.667
Hawley	8	13	.381	Tannehill	6	3	.667
Killen	9	15	.375	Gardner	4	2	.667
Hughey	3	5	.375	Hastings	3	2	.600
Tannehill	2	5	.286	Killen	8	9	.471
Gardner	1	4	.200	Hughey	3	5	.375

The Chicago Club's Pitching Record.

No less than nine pitchers were tried during the campaign, and of these not one reached the percentage average of .500 against the first division clubs, and only three of the nine pitchers against those of the second division. In aggregate percentage figures, too, only three exceeded .500; viz., Callahan, Griffith and Friend. Callahan did the best work of the club's season, Griffith—who had such a fine record in 1896—falling off considerably in 1897. Griffith excelled against the three leaders, Callahan not pitching in a single victory against Boston, Baltimore and New York. Korwan was a bad failure, and Briggs even worse. Griffith, Friend and Callahan won a total of 21 victories against the six first division clubs, while the other six pitchers of the corps only aggregated a total of 6 victories against the same division. Here is the record in full:

Chicago vs.		First Division.						Second Divis'n					Grand Totals.	Per cent. of Victories.
		Boston.	Baltimore.	New York.	Cincinnati.	Cleveland.	Brooklyn.	Totals.	Washington.	Pittsburg.	Philadelphia.	Louisville.	St. Louis.	Totals.		
Callahan	Won	0	0	0	2	0	2	4	1	1	2	2	2	8	12	.600
	Lost	1	1	0	0	2	1	5	0	1	1	0	3	8	
Griffith	Won	1	3	3	2	1	2	12	4	1	0	2	3	10	22	.564
	Lost	3	2	3	1	2	2	13	0	2	1	0	1	4	17	
Friend	Won	1	0	1	0	2	1	5	1	2	2	1	1	7	12	.545
	Lost	1	1	2	1	1	0	6	1	0	1	2	0	4	10	
Thornton	Won	0	0	0	1	0	1	2	0	1	0	1	1	3	5	.357
	Lost	1	2	0	0	1	0	4	1	1	1	0	2	5	9	
Korwan	Won	0	0	0	0	0	0	0	0	0	0	0	1	1	1	.250
	Lost	0	1	0	0	0	0	1	0	1	0	1	0	2	3	
Denzer	Won	1	0	1	0	0	0	2	0	0	0	0	0	0	2	.200
	Lost	1	0	1	3	1	1	7	0	0	1	0	0	1	8	
Briggs	Won	1	0	0	0	1	0	2	0	0	1	0	1	2	4	.190
	Lost	1	2	1	3	1	1	9	3	1	2	2	0	8	17	
Wright	Won	0	0	0	0	0	0	0	0	0	1	0	0	1	1	1.000
	Lost	0	0	0	0	0	0	0	0	0	0	0	0	0	0	
Terry	Won	0	0	0	0	0	0	0	0	0	0	0	0	0	0	.000
	Lost	0	0	0	0	0	0	0	0	0	0	0	1	1	1	
Totals		12	12	12	13	12	11	72	12	12	12	12	12	60	132	

Against First Division.				Against Second Division.			
Pitchers.	Victories.	Defeats.	Per cent.	Pitchers.	Victories.	Defeats.	Per cent.
Griffith	12	13	.480	Callahan	8	3	.727
Friend	5	6	.455	Griffith	10	4	.714
Callahan	4	5	.444	Friend	7	4	.636
Thornton	2	4	.333	Thornton	3	5	.375
Denzer	2	7	.222	Korwan	1	2	.332
Briggs	2	9	.182	Briggs	2	8	.200
Wright	0	0	.000	Wright	1	0	1.000
Terry	0	0	.000	Denzer	0	1	.000
Korwan	0	1	.000	Terry	0	1	.000

The Philadelphia Club's Pitching Record.

Out of a corps of no less than ten pitchers employed by the Philadelphia club in 1897 but one solitary pitcher reached the percentage average against the six first division clubs, that one only pitching in three games against the first division. Four of the corps did not pitch in a single victory against either division, and only one of the ten had more victories than defeats. Dunkle led not only in total percentage of victories figures, but also in percentage against the first division clubs. Both Orth and Taylor were away off against the leaders, Orth losing 8 games to Boston, Baltimore and New York, and winning but 4; while Taylor did not win a game from Boston and Baltimore and lost 7 games to the three clubs. Fifield was the deadest failure of the entire corps, he losing 12 games out of 13 with the first division clubs, and 18 out of 22 with the whole twelve clubs. Johnson won and lost a game, while Lipp, Sparks and Becker did not win a single game. Here is the record in full:

PHILADELPHIA vs.		Boston.	Baltimore.	New York.	Cincinnati.	Cleveland.	Brooklyn.	Totals.	Washington.	Pittsburg.	Chicago.	Louisville.	St. Louis.	Totals.	Grand Totals.	Per cent. of Victories.
Dunkle	Won	0	1	0	0	1	0	2	1	0	1	1	0	3	5	.714
	Lost	0	0	0	0	0	1	1	0	1	0	0	0	1	2	
Wheeler	Won	0	0	0	1	0	1	2	1	0	3	2	3	9	11	.458
	Lost	0	0	2	1	1	3	7	1	2	0	1	2	6	13	
Orth	Won	2	1	1	3	0	1	8	1	2	0	1	3	7	15	.455
	Lost	4	3	1	2	2	0	12	2	2	2	0	0	6	18	
Taylor	Won	0	0	3	0	2	2	7	1	2	2	3	1	9	16	.444
	Lost	2	3	2	4	3	1	15	1	1	1	1	5	20		
Fifield	Won	0	0	0	0	0	1	1	0	1	1	2	0	4	5	.217
	Lost	3	3	2	1	2	1	12	3	1	0	1	1	6	18	
Carsey	Won	0	0	1	0	0	0	1	0	0	0	0	1	1	2	.667
	Lost	0	0	0	0	1	0	1	0	0	0	0	0	0	1	
Johnson	Won	0	0	0	0	0	1	1	0	0	0	0	0	0	1	.500
	Lost	0	0	0	0	0	0	0	0	0	1	0	0	1	1	
Lipp	Won	0	0	0	0	0	0	0	0	0	0	0	0	0	0	.000
	Lost	0	1	0	0	0	0	1	0	0	0	0	0	0	1	
Sparks	Won	0	0	0	0	0	0	0	0	0	0	0	0	0	0	.000
	Lost	1	0	0	0	0	0	1	0	0	0	0	0	0	1	
Becker	Won	0	0	0	0	0	0	0	0	0	0	0	0	0	0	.000
	Lost	0	0	0	0	0	0	0	1	0	1	0	0	2	2	
Totals		12	12	12	12	12	12	72	12	12	12	12	12	60	132	

Pitchers.	Victories.	Defeats.	Per cent.	Pitchers.	Victories.	Defeats.	Per cent.
AGAINST FIRST DIVISION.				**AGAINST SECOND DIVISION.**			
Dunkle	2	1	.667	Dunkle	3	1	.750
Orth	8	12	.400	Taylor	9	5	.643
Taylor	7	15	.318	Wheeler	9	6	.600
Wheeler	2	7	.222	Orth	7	6	.538
Fifield	1	12	.077	Fifield	4	6	.400
Johnson	1	0	1.000	Carsey	1	0	1.000
Carsey	1	1	.500	Lipp	0	0	.000
Becker	0	0	.000	Sparks	0	0	.000
Lipp	0	1	.000	Johnson	0	1	.000
Sparks	0	1	.000	Becker	0	2	.000

The Louisville Club's Pitching Record.

The Louisville club, out of a pitching corps of no less than thirteen men, had only two pitchers whose percentage figures reached the average of .500. Even St. Louis' record was better, in proportion to the number of their pitchers. Five of the Louisville corps did not win a single victory against the clubs of either division, and there were only two of the thirteen that did not have more defeats pitched in charged to them than they were credited with victories. The club had excellent material at command, both in "battery" force and field support, to have maintained the vantage ground they had obtained prior to the June campaign; but from some cause or other the promise of the early part of the season was lost by the failure of the latter part of the campaign, and the weakness of the pitching corps had much to do with it. Evans was the most effective pitcher of the corps against the first division clubs, but he did not pitch against the three leaders, Cunningham taking the lead in this latter respect. In fact, taking the latter's work in the box as a whole, he was the best pitcher of the whole corps, as he pitched in three times as many games as Evans did and excelled the latter against the second division clubs. Frazer took the lead against the second division clubs, but stood third against those of the first division. Three of the corps pitched in 43 games out of 129 won and lost, the other ten pitchers playing in the box in the remaining 86 games. No less than five of the thirteen pitched in but one game each, all defeats, while three others averaged but 7 games each. Here is the record in full:

BASE BALL GUIDE.   81

LOUISVILLE VS.		First Division.						Second Divis'n						Grand Totals.	Per cent. of Victories.
		Boston.	Baltimore.	New York.	Cincinnati.	Cleveland.	Brooklyn.	Totals.	Washington.	Pittsburg.	Chicago.	Philadelphia.	St. Louis.	Totals.		
Evans...................	Won	0	0	0	1	1	1	3	0	0	1	0	1	2	5	.625
	Lost	0	0	0	0	0	0	0	0	0	1	2	0	3	3	
Cunningham............	Won	1	1	1	1	1	3	8	1	3	0	0	2	6	14	.500
	Lost	1	0	3	3	0	0	7	1	2	2	1	1	7	14	
Frazer..................	Won	0	0	2	1	3	1	7	2	1	3	1	1	8	15	.455
	Lost	3	2	0	3	0	2	10	2	1	1	3	1	8	18	
Hemming..............	Won	0	0	2	0	0	0	2	0	0	1	0	0	1	3	.429
	Lost	1	1	0	0	0	1	3	1	0	0	0	0	1	4	
Clarke	Won	0	0	0	0	0	1	1	0	0	1	0	0	1	2	.333
	Lost	1	0	1	0	1	0	3	0	0	1	0	0	1	4	
Dowling................	Won	0	0	1	0	0	0	1	0	0	0	0	0	0	1	.333
	Lost	1	0	0	0	1	0	2	0	0	0	0	0	0	2	
Magee	Won	2	0	0	0	0	0	2	0	0	0	1	1	2	4	.286
	Lost	1	2	1	0	2	1	7	2	1	0	0	0	3	10	
Hill....................	Won	0	0	0	0	1	1	2	1	0	0	1	3	5	7	.280
	Lost	1	4	0	3	0	1	9	2	4	0	3	0	9	18	
Herman	Won	0	0	0	0	0	0	0	0	0	0	0	0	0	0	.000
	Lost	0	0	0	0	0	0	0	0	0	0	0	1	1	1	
Jones..................	Won	0	0	0	0	0	0	0	0	0	0	0	0	0	0	.000
	Lost	0	0	0	0	0	0	0	0	0	1	0	0	1	1	
Hart	Won	0	0	0	0	0	0	0	0	0	0	0	0	0	0	.000
	Lost	0	0	0	0	1	0	1	0	0	0	0	0	0	1	
Waddell................	Won	0	0	0	0	0	0	0	0	0	0	0	0	0	0	.000
	Lost	0	1	0	0	0	0	1	0	0	0	0	0	0	1	
Miller..................	Won	0	0	0	0	0	0	0	0	0	0	0	0	0	0	.000
	Lost	0	0	1	0	0	0	1	0	0	0	0	0	0	1	
Totals.................		12	11	12	12	11	12	70	12	12	12	12	11	59	129	

Here is the division record:

AGAINST FIRST DIVISION.

Pitchers.	Victories.	Defeats.	Per cent.
Evans................	3	0	1.000
Cunningham.........	8	7	.583
Frazer...............	7	10	.412
Hemming............	2	3	.400
Dowling.............	1	2	.333
Clarke...............	1	3	.250
Magee...............	2	7	.222
Hill..................	2	9	.182
Waddell.............	0	1	.000
Miller................	0	1	.000
Hart.................	0	1	.000
Jones................	0	0	.000
Herman	0	0	.000

AGAINST SECOND DIVISION.

Pitchers.	Victories.	Defeats.	Per cent.
Frazer...............	8	8	.500
Hemming............	1	1	.500
Clarke	1	1	.500
Cunningham.........	6	7	462
Evans................	2	3	.400
Magee...............	2	3	.400
Hill..................	5	9	.351
Dowling.............	1	2	.333
Waddell.............	0	0	.000
Miller................	0	0	.000
Hart.................	0	0	.000
Jones................	0	1	.000
Herman.............	0	1	.000

The St. Louis Club's Pitching Record.

Not one of the whole St. Louis pitching corps of 1897 reached a higher total percentage than .400, and eight of the eleven did not reach .300. Out of the ten who pitched against the six first division clubs there were five who did not win a single victory, and three who only pitched in a single victory each. There were four also who did not pitch in a single victory against the second division clubs. The brunt of the pitching work of the St. Louis team in 1897 fell upon Hart and Donahue, the former pitching in 38 games and the latter in 40 of the 131 games won and lost during the campaign. Donahue excelled Hart against the first division clubs, but Hart led him against those of the second division. Coleman, who led in total percentage figures, only pitched in a single victory in each division, and McDermott did not win a game against the first division clubs.

Here is the full record for 1897:

St. Louis vs.		Boston.	Baltimore.	New York.	Cincinnati.	Cleveland.	Brooklyn.	Totals.	Washington.	Pittsburg.	Chicago.	Philadelphia.	Louisville.	Totals.	Grand Totals.	Per cent. of Victories.
		\multicolumn{7}{c}{First Division.}									
Coleman	Won	0	0	0	0	1	0	1	0	1	0	0	0	1	2	
	Lost	0	0	0	2	0	0	2	0	1	0	0	0	1	3	.400
Esper	Won	1	0	0	0	0	0	1	0	0	0	0	0	0	1	
	Lost	1	0	1	0	0	1	3	0	1	1	1	1	3	6	.333
McDermott	Won	0	0	0	0	0	0	0	1	0	0	0	0	1	1	
	Lost	0	0	2	0	0	0	2	0	0	0	0	0	0	2	.333
Hart	Won	0	1	0	0	0	2	3	1	3	1	1	1	7	10	
	Lost	1	4	4	2	4	2	17	2	1	2	3	3	11	28	.263
Carsey	Won	0	0	0	0	0	1	1	0	0	0	2	0	2	3	
	Lost	0	2	1	1	1	0	5	0	1	0	2	1	4	9	.250
Donahue	Won	0	1	0	1	0	2	4	1	0	2	1	1	5	9	
	Lost	3	3	3	3	3	3	18	4	4	2	2	1	13	31	.225
Hutchison	Won	0	0	0	0	0	0	0	0	0	0	1	1	1		
	Lost	1	1	0	0	1	0	3	0	0	1	0	0	1	4	.200
Lucid	Won	0	0	0	0	0	0	0	1	0	0	0	1	1		
	Lost	1	0	0	1	1	0	3	1	0	0	0	1	2	5	.167
Sudhoff	Won	1	0	0	0	0	0	1	0	0	0	0	0	0	1	
	Lost	1	0	1	2	1	0	5	1	1	1	0	0	3	8	.111
Grimes	Won	0	0	0	0	0	0	0	0	0	0	0	0	0		
	Lost	0	0	0	0	0	0	0	0	0	1	0	1	2	2	.000
Kissenger	Won	0	0	0	0	0	0	0	0	0	0	0	0	0		
	Lost	2	0	0	0	0	1	3	1	0	0	0	0	1	4	.000
Totals		12	12	12	12	12	12	72	12	12	12	12	11	59	131	

Pitchers.	Victories.	Defeats.	Per cent.	Pitchers.	Victories.	Defeats.	Per cent.
\multicolumn{4}{c}{AGAINST FIRST DIVISION.}	\multicolumn{4}{c}{AGAINST SECOND DIVISION.}
Coleman	1	2	.333	McDermott	1	0	1.000
Esper	1	3	.250	Coleman	1	1	.500
Donahue	4	18	.182	Hutchison	1	1	.500
Sudhoff	1	5	.167	Hart	7	11	.389
Carsey	1	5	.167	Lucid	1	2	.339
Hart	3	17	.150	Carsey	2	4	.332
McDermott	0	2	.000	Donahue	5	13	.278
Hutchison	0	3	.000	Esper	1	6	.143
Lucid	0	3	.000	Sudhoff	0	3	.000
Grimes	0	0	.000	Grimes	0	2	.000
Kissenger	0	3	.000	Kissenger	0	1	.000

The summary record showing the leading pitcher of each of the twelve clubs who had pitched in five games and over, as shown by the total percentage figures, is as follows. The names are given in the order of the clubs as the latter stand in the pennant race record of the season:

Pitchers.	Clubs.	Victories.	Defeats.	Per cent.	Pitchers.	Clubs.	Victories.	Defeats.	Per cent.
Klobedanz	Boston	27	8	.771	Bresnahan	Washington	5	1	.833
Nops	Baltimore	19	5	.792	Hastings	Pittsburg	6	5	.545
Rusie	New York	28	9	.757	Callahan	Chicago	12	8	.600
Damman	Cincinnati	6	3	.667	Dunkle	Philadelphia	5	2	.714
Cuppy	Cleveland	11	6	.647	Evans	Louisville	5	3	.625
Dunn	Brooklyn	14	8	.636	Coleman	St. Louis	2	3	.400

The record showing the order of the percentage figures is as follows :

Pitchers.	Victories.	Defeats.	Per cent.	Pitchers.	Victories.	Defeats.	Per cent.
Bresnahan	5	1	.833	Cuppy	11	6	.647
Nops	19	5	.792	Dunn	14	8	.636
Klobedanz	27	8	.791	Evans	5	3	.625
Rusie	28	9	.751	Callahan	8	3	.600
Dunkle	5	2	.714	Hastings	6	5	.545
Damman	6	3	.667	Coleman	2	3	.400

The summary which presents the best data for showing the most effective work done in the box is the appended record, giving the names of the pitchers who pitched in 10 games and over against the first division clubs in 1897. The names are given in the order of the pitcher's percentage of victories figures:

Pitchers.	Clubs.	Games.	Per cent.	Pitchers.	Clubs.	Games.	Per cent.
Rusie	New York	20	.700	Cunningham	Louisville	15	.533
Klobedanz	Boston	18	.667	Kennedy	Brooklyn	18	.500
Corbett	Baltimore	17	.647	Griffith	Chicago	25	.480
Breitenstein	Cincinnati	17	.588	Orth	Philadelphia	20	.400
Cuppy	Cleveland	11	.545	Hawley	Pittsburg	21	.381
Swain	Washington	11	.545	Donahue	St. Louis	22	.182

It will be seen that, with a few exceptions, the order of names follow those of the order of club names in the final pennant race record, a pretty good test of the value of the pitching.

The Pitching Lessons of the Campaign of 1897.

The lessons to be derived from the pitching experience of the championship campaign of 1897 may be summed up as follows: First, as to the nature of first-class box-work. And the lesson taught is that the primary essentials of success are *thorough command of the ball* in delivery, especially as regards controlling the direction of curved balls; familiarity with the strategic points of play, as shown in the use of *change of pace in delivery;* the intelligent use of the slow drop balls, and the skilful point of pitching for catches; the constant study of the strong and weak points of opposing batsmen, and the entire avoidance of the utter folly of disputing the umpire's decisions on called balls and strikes, not forgetting the important matter of entirely controlling a bad and quick temper, for without this latter important essential the use of "head-work" and of sound judgment in the position is impossible. All of these essentials of success in pitching can only be made available by players who are of strictly temperate habits and who are possessed of more than ordinary intelligence, for no weak-brained fellow can ever excel as a pitcher, though he may have the physique to stand the pressure of box-work and the power to throw a ball swiftly to the bat.

There is no questioning the fact that indulgence in hot temper, and in the stupidity of "kicking" against the umpire's decisions on strikes and balls, had more to do with the non-success of the majority of the pitchers in 1897 than all other causes combined.

The League's Veteran Pitchers.

On looking over the records of the pitchers of the League as found in the League GUIDES of each year from 1890 to 1897, inclusive—a compilation of which was kindly sent us by Mr. H. G. McFarland of Chicago—we find that, out of the hundreds of pitchers employed by the League clubs during that period, there were but nineteen who are entitled to be ranked with the class of veteran pitchers of the League for the decade of the '90s, the limit of the class being a record of five years of continuous service in League clubs. This list of veterans includes three who have been in the League as pitchers for eight years of continuous service; five who have served seven years; nine who have been pitchers for the past six years, and two who have a credit of five years in the League as pitchers. Of these nineteen, Nichols, Young and Terry served the whole eight years, with a total percentage of victories pitched in of .665, .650 and .544, respectively. Next to these are five who have served in the League as pitchers for seven years, these being Rusie, with the percentage figures of .592; Killen, with .564; Hutchison and Esper, with .541 each, and Rhines with .530. Then come nine others who have been in the position in the League since it was reconstructed in 1892, and two others who have only served five years continuously. The complete record is as follows:

VETERAN PITCHERS' RECORD.

	1890.	1891.	1892.	1893.	1894.	1895.	1896.	1897.	Total Victories.	Total Defeats.	Total Games.	Total per cent.
Nichols	.587	.612	.686	.696	.733	.628	.667	.738	245	123	368	.665
Young	.588	.583	.783	.667	.543	.767	.674	.568	216	116	332	.650
Terry	.634	.286	.741	.632	.278	.600	.483	.000	104	87	191	.544
Rusie		.459	.630	.525	.611	.735	.511		.757	214	147	361	.592
Killen			.000	.500	.702	.583	.538	.620	.415	130	102	232	.564
Hutchison	.618	.694	.529	.400	.471	.419		.200	168	142	310	.541
Esper			.606	.700	.816	.512	.455	.787	.333	92	78	170	.541
Rhines	.622	.372	.429	.250		.625	.588	.526	98	87	185	.530
Cuppy			.648	.607	.568	.667	.625	.647	127	76	203	.625
Stivetts			.702	.636	.650	.500	.629	.667	128	74	202	.625
Dwyer			.595	.563	.486	.581	.714	.621	119	82	201	.596
Taylor			1.000	.500	.706	.667	.512	.444	97	71	168	.577
McMahon			.404	.590	.758	.714	.600	.000	89	68	157	.567
Carsey			.556	.647	.533	.585	.458	.333	98	82	180	.544
Kennedy			.600	.581	.545	.594	.405	.474	113	101	214	.527
Meekin			.855	.370	.783	.593	.667	.625	119	83	202	.488
Daub			.500	.500	.400	.500	.560	.375	47	53	100	.470
Griffiths				.500	.645	.641	.676	.564	91	54	145	.628
Hawley				.227	.419	.580	.500	.500	92	102	194	.474

Rusie pitched in a League club in 1889, but only the records of the nineties are given in the table on the preceding page.

The summary of the above table, with the names of the pitchers given in the order of percentage figures instead of that of years of service, as the previous table is, is appended:

Pitchers.	Years of Service.	Per cent.	Pitchers.	Years of Service.	Per cent.
Nichols	8	.665	Terry	8	.544
Young	8	.650	Carsey	6	.544
Griffith	5	.628	Hutchison	7	.541
Cuppy	6	.625	Esper	7	.541
Stivetts	6	.625	Rhines	7	.530
Dwyer	6	.596	Kennedy	6	.527
Rusie	7	.592	Meekin	6	.488
Taylor	6	.577	Hawley	5	.474
McMahon	6	.567	Daub	6	.470
Killen	7	.564			

The following record shows how the pitchers of Mr. Young's official record stand relatively in their percentage figures, showing their skill in fielding in that position. The names are given in the order of the best percentage figures:

Pitcher.	Club.	Per cent.	Pitcher.	Club.	Per cent.
Fisher	Brooklyn	.964	Hoffer	Baltimore	.868
Stivetts	Boston	.953	Briggs	Chicago	.865
Friend	Chicago	.945	Daub	Brooklyn	.864
Cuppy	Cleveland	.943	Callahan	Chicago	.842
Breitenstein	Cincinnati	.932	Hart	St. Louis	.837
Ehret	Cincinnati	.917	Rhines	Cincinnati	.836
Kennedy	Brooklyn	.916	Powell	Cleveland	.833
Donahue	St. Louis	.913	Young	Cleveland	.829
Tannehill	Pittsburg	.912	Klobedanz	Boston	.828
Hawley	Pittsburg	.905	Dunn	Brooklyn	.827
Wheeler	Philadelphia	.905	Keller	Pittsburg	.818
Orth	Philadelphia	.908	Lewis	Boston	.806
Carsey	Philadelphia	.900	Hill	Louisville	.805
Nops	Baltimore	.894	Taylor	Philadelphia	.783
Wilson	Chicago	.886	Mercer	Washington	.775
Fifield	Philadelphia	.884	Sullivan	New York	.773
Cunningham	Louisville	.884	Hughey	Pittsburg	.771
King	Washington	.884	Seymour	New York	.769
Griffith	Chicago	.881	Frazer	Louisville	.765
Dwyer	Cincinnati	.877	Meekin	New York	.758
Payne	Brooklyn	.876	Corbett	Baltimore	.744
Thornton	Chicago	.875	Swain	Washington	.735
Nichols	Boston	.872	McJames	Washington	.734
Rusie	New York	.871	Magee	Louisville	.705
Pond	Baltimore	.870			

Secretary Young's official table of pitching statistics—made up from the scores of the official scorers of each club—differ in many respects from the published scores of the newspaper scorers, and always will while the existing code of scoring rules last. We have gone over Mr. Young's table, and glean from it sundry interesting facts, which we give below. In the first place, in comparing the records of those who excel in smallest average of runs earned off the pitching—an unreliable record, by the way—with their individual records of percentage of victories pitched in, we find the result to be as follows:

PITCHERS.	CLUBS.	Percentage.	Average of earned runs per game.	PITCHERS.	CLUBS.	Percentage.	Average of earned runs per game.
Rusie	New York	.784	1-27	Dwyer	Cincinnati	.562	1-79
Seymour	New York	.600	1-28	Nops	Baltimore	.769	1-81
McJames	Washington	.375	1-48	Frazer	Louisville	.444	1-84
Cuppy	Cleveland	.588	1-53	Powell	Cleveland	.577	1-88
Mercer	Washington	.547	1-56	Tannehill	Pittsburg	.562	1-88
Hill	Louisville	.291	1-64	Rhines	Cincinnati	.543	1-91
Nichols	Boston	.732	1-68	Pond	Baltimore	.680	1-92
Corbett	Baltimore	.774	1-71				

The names are given in the order of the earned runs average. It will be seen that but one of the pitchers who has an average of runs per game earned off his pitching, which do not reach 2 to a game, stands in the same order as that of the percentage of victories pitched in, and that one is Rusie. Seymour is second in earned runs average, but Corbett, Nops, Nichols and Pond, excel him in percentage of victories figures. McJames, too, is third in earned runs average, and yet in percentage of victories figures fourteenth on the list. The fact is, the earned runs record has ceased to be useful, as it cannot be relied upon as data, because of the varied opinion of official scorers as to the proper definition of an earned run, not an earned run in reality, but simply a run plainly earned off the pitching, and that only. Here is a record showing who the pitchers are who struck out at least 100 batting opponents during 1897:

PITCHERS.	CLUBS.	Struck out oppon'nts.	PITCHERS.	CLUBS.	Struck out oppon'nts.
McJames	Washington	161	Rusie	New York	140
Seymour	New York	157	Griffith	Chicago	105
Corbett	Baltimore	151			

Here is another, showing who were the weakest in giving batting adversaries bases on balls, the list being limited to those who gave at least 100 during the season:

Pitchers.	Clubs.	Bases on balls.	Pitchers.	Clubs.	Bases on balls.
Seymour.	New York	165	Klobedanz	Boston	123
Hart	St. Louis	149	Lewis	Boston	123
Kennedy	Brooklyn	146	Corbett	Baltimore	106
Frazer	Louisville	141	Donahue	St. Louis	101
McJames	Washington	136			

And lastly, here is a third, showing who were so wild in their delivery as to hit batsmen:

Pitchers.	Clubs.	Hit Batsmen.	Pitchers.	Clubs.	Hit Batsmen.
Mercer	Washington	27	Frazer	Louisville	24
Taylor	Philadelphia	25	Klobedanz	Boston	24
Hawley	Pittsburg	25	Hill	Louisville	20
Corbett	Baltimore	24			

Mr. Young's pitchers' record gives only the names of those who pitched in at least 15 games, and the list contains only 49 pitchers of the total of 99 who took part as pitchers in the League championship games of 1897. Looking over the pitching record we find that Orth of the Philadelphias leads the pitchers in highest percentage of base hits, .347, and McGuire of Washington the catchers, .338. Breitenstein of Cincinnati leads the pitchers in highest fielding percentage of chances accepted, .952, and Pietz of the same club leads the catchers with .956. Callahan of Chicago leads the pitchers in total runs scored, 57, and also in total bases stolen, 13. Douglas of St. Louis leads the catchers in total runs scored with 12, and A. Smith of Brooklyn the catchers in stolen bases with 14.

It will be seen by the preceding records that the pitchers are, as a rule, poor in run getting and in stealing bases. Nine of the list did not steal a single base during the season of 1897 and eight of them did not exceed single figures in run-getting.

We present a new series of statistical tables this year designed to give a better idea of the relative playing strength of the twelve club teams of the National League as they stood at the close of 1897. There are teams and teams; in other words, while the playing corps of a club is known as "the team of the club," it really comprises three teams when in active operation in the field, viz., the "battery" team, which includes the pitchers and catchers; the infield team, which comprises the three basemen and shortstop, and the outfield team, which includes the left, centre and right fielders.

Of course, if one wants to know what an individual player's batting or fielding average is, there are the regular official League tables at command to tell you; but if it be desired to know what was the general strength of a battery team, or that of an infield or outfield, one would have to go through a tiresome analysis of each table. To avoid this we have made up a table of team figures showing how each club stands in the relative strength of its three branch teams. The first we give are the tables of battery teams, the names of the players of each club comprising the teams being given in the order of the pennant race record, and the individual pitchers' names in the order of their percentage of victories pitched in, while the catchers' names are in the order of games played in as catchers.

FIRST DIVISION CLUBS.

Player and Position.	Club.	Per cent. base-hits.	Per cent. fielding.	Runs.	Stolen bases.
Klobedanz, pitcher	Boston	.316	.828	27	1
Nichols, pitcher	Boston	.264	.872	21	4
Lewis, pitcher	Boston	.254	.806	15	3
Bergen, catcher	Boston	.247	.928	45	5
Ganzell, catcher	Boston	.274	.908	14	1
Nops, pitcher	Baltimore	.217	.894	7	0
Corbett, pitcher	Baltimore	.257	.744	27	6
Pond, pitcher	Baltimore	.244	.820	15	3
Robinson, catcher	Baltimore	.313	.925	25	1
Clarke, catcher	Baltimore	.274	.923	32	7
Rusie, pitcher	New York	.288	.871	25	1
Meekin, pitcher	New York	.280	.758	22	4
Seymour, pitcher	New York	.248	.769	13	2
Warner, catcher	New York	.274	.930	48	9
Wilson, catcher	New York	.310	.880	29	7
Breitenstein, pitcher	Cincinnati	.270	.952	4	0
Dwyer, pitcher	Cincinnati	.285	.877	15	4
Rhines, pitcher	Cincinnati	.172	.836	13	0
Peitz, catcher	Cincinnati	.297	.956	34	5
Schriver, catcher	Cincinnati	.310	.935	26	3
Cuppy, pitcher	Cleveland	.148	.943	5	0
Wilson, pitcher	Cleveland	.222	.886	16	3
Young, pitcher	Cleveland	.218	.829	16	3
Zimmer, catcher	Cleveland	.314	.950	52	7
Crieger, catcher	Cleveland	.230	.924	15	4
Dunn, pitcher	Brooklyn	.228	.827	19	2
Fisher, pitcher	Brooklyn	.200	.964	6	0
Kennedy, pitcher	Brooklyn	.269	.916	10	0
Grim, catcher	Brooklyn	.261	.904	25	3
A. Smith, catcher	Brooklyn	.309	.844	36	14

SECOND DIVISION CLUBS.

Player and Position.	Club.	Per cent. base-hits.	Per cent. fielding.	Runs.	Stolen bases.
Mercer, pitcher	Washington	.333	.775	22	7
King, pitcher	Washington	.193	.884	8	0
Swain, pitcher	Washington	.222	.735	7	3
Farrell, catcher	Washington	.327	.934	52	11
McGuire, catcher	Washington	.338	.926	30	9
Killen, pitcher	Pittsburg	.257	.818	16	2
Hawley, pitcher	Pittsburg	.216	.905	10	0
Tannehill, pitcher	Pittsburg	.266	.912	24	4
Sugden, catcher	Pittsburg	.219	.917	30	9
Merritt, catcher	Pittsburg	.270	.917	21	3
Callahan, pitcher	Chicago	.308	.842	57	13
Griffith, pitcher	Chicago	.236	.881	29	1
Friend, pitcher	Chicago	.274	.945	13	1
Kittridge, catcher	Chicago	.198	.954	20	9
Donahue, catcher	Chicago	.234	.914	29	4
Wheeler, pitcher	Philadelphia	.205	.905	11	2
Orth, pitcher	Philadelphia	.347	.903	26	7
Taylor, pitcher	Philadelphia	.252	.783	12	0
Clements, catcher	Philadelphia	.239	.940	18	2
Boyle, catcher	Philadelphia	.259	.929	36	2
Cunningham, pitcher	Louisville	.289	.884	13	1
Frazer, pitcher	Louisville	.168	.765	10	2
Hill, pitcher	Louisville	.100	.805	5	1
Wilson, catcher	Louisville	.216	.889	45	9
Dexter, catcher	Louisville	.291	.829	39	11
Hart, pitcher	St. Louis	.245	.837	14	5
Carsey, pitcher	St. Louis	.269	.900	3	0
Donahue, pitcher	St. Louis	.216	.913	11	1
Murphy, catcher	St. Louis	.177	.948	12	2
Douglas, catcher	St. Louis	.327	.901	72	12

FIRST DIVISION CLUBS.

Player and Position.	Club.	Per cent. base-hits.	Per cent. fielding.	Runs.	Stolen bases.
Tenney, first base	Boston	.325	.988	125	38
Lowe, second base	Boston	.314	.953	87	18
Collins, third base	Boston	.346	.931	102	16
Long, shortstop	Boston	.327	.908	88	26
Doyle, first base	Baltimore	.356	.979	93	62
Reitz, second base	Baltimore	.289	.964	76	26
McGraw, third base	Baltimore	.326	.892	89	42
Jennings, shortstop	Baltimore	.353	.933	131	60
Clarke, first base	New York	.282	.987	62	17
Gleason, second base	New York	.311	.927	88	40
Joyce, third base	New York	.305	.861	110	30
G. Davis, shortstop	New York	.358	.932	114	64
Beckley, first base	Cincinnati	.325	.977	84	22
McPhee, second base	Cincinnati	.307	.965	45	10
Irwin, third base	Cincinnati	.293	.939	88	35
Corcoran, shortstop	Cincinnati	.288	.923	76	16
Tebeau, first base	Cleveland	.267	.994	62	10
Childs, second base	Cleveland	.386	.944	105	25
Wallace, third base	Cleveland	.339	.935	99	17
McKean, shortstop	Cleveland	.273	.924	86	18
LaChance, first base	Brooklyn	.308	.981	86	30
Shoch, second base	Brooklyn	.290	.939	39	9
Shindle, third base	Brooklyn	.289	.905	82	25
G. Smith, shortstop	Brooklyn	.207	.914	47	3

SECOND DIVISION CLUBS.

Infielder and Position.	Clubs.	Per cent. of base hits.	Per cent. of fielding.	Total runs.	Total stolen bases.
Tucker, first base	Washington	.329	.982	52	18
O'Brien, second base	Washington	.242	.935	37	5
Reilly, third base	Washington	.275	.914	66	16
DeMontreville, shortstop	Washington	.349	.887	92	33
H. Davis, first base	Pittsburg	.309	.967	69	23
Padden, second base	Pittsburg	.281	.942	84	18
Donnelly, third base	Pittsburg	.187	.909	40	58
Ely, shortstop	Pittsburg	.282	.927	65	12
Anson, first base	Chicago	.302	.987	66	16
Connor, second base	Chicago	.296	.942	40	12
Everitt, third base	Chicago	.314	.879	63	27
Dahlen, shortstop	Chicago	.296	.929	67	16
Lajoie, first base	Philadelphia	.363	.984	107	22
Geier, second base	Philadelphia	.285	.954	51	19
Nash, third base	Philadelphia	.258	.919	45	4
Gillen, shortstop	Philadelphia	.258	.894	32	2
Werden, first base	Louisville	.303	.985	76	16
Rogers, second base	Louisville	.148	.919	21	4
Clingman, third base	Louisville	.230	.949	59	10
Stafford, shortstop	Louisville	.270	.888	69	10
Grady, first base	St. Louis	.276	.975	51	7
Hallman, second base	St. Louis	.250	.941	49	17
Hartman, third base	St. Louis	.301	.866	67	18
Cross, shortstop	St. Louis	.288	.921	60	20

FIRST DIVISION CLUBS.

Outfielder and Position.	Clubs.	Per cent. of base hits.	Per cent. of fielding.	Total runs.	Total stolen bases.
Duffy, left field	Boston	.341	.958	131	45
Hamilton, centre field	Boston	.344	.953	153	70
Stahl, right field	Boston	.359	.935	111	14
Kelley, left field	Baltimore	.389	.954	113	50
Stenzel, centre field	Baltimore	.351	.981	113	77
Keeler, right field	Baltimore	.432	.970	147	63
Holmes, left field	New York	.284	.902	51	32
Van Haltren, centre field	New York	.332	.934	122	45
Tiernan, right field	New York	.331	.941	123	34
Burke, left field	Cincinnati	.269	.940	71	32
Hoy, centre field	Cincinnati	.290	.938	88	40
Miller, right field	Cincinnati	.317	.932	83	32
Burkett, left field	Cleveland	.383	.943	128	27
McAleer, centre field	Cleveland	.224	.947	5	5
Sockalexis, right field	Cleveland	.331	.887	43	17
Anderson, left field	Brooklyn	.332	.926	93	42
Griffin, centre field	Brooklyn	.320	.955	137	23
Jones, right field	Brooklyn	.322	.948	133	62

SECOND DIVISION CLUBS.

Outfielder and Position.	Club.	Per cent. of base hits.	Per cent. of fielding.	Total runs.	Total stolen bases.
Selbach, left field	Washington	.317	.955	144	58
Brown, centre field	Washington	.287	.927	93	27
Abbey, right field	Washington	.264	.953	54	10
E. Smith, left field	Pittsburg	.311	.908	101	28
Brodie, centre field	Pittsburg	.298	.983	47	17
Donovan, right field	Pittsburg	.326	.948	83	39
Decker, left field	Chicago	.307	.917	71	12
Lange, centre field	Chicago	.352	.952	119	83
Ryan, right field	Chicago	.309	.940	104	35
Delehanty, left field	Philadelphia	.377	.966	110	28
Dowd, centre field	Philadelphia	.284	.908	93	41
Cooley, right field	Philadelphia	.327	.960	124	30
Clarke, left field	Louisville	.406	.921	122	60
Pickering, centre field	Louisville	.296	.983	67	40
Wagner, right field	Louisville	.344	.917	38	22
Lally, left field	St. Louis	.273	.892	57	11
Harley, centre field	St. Louis	.288	.912	43	20
Turner, right field	St. Louis	.289	.940	58	10

It is now plainly evident that the efforts of A. G. Spalding & Bros. to introduce our American national game in England and to popularize it as one of England's future field games, to rank side by side with cricket, lacrosse and foot ball, is likely to be successful in the near future.

No player, captain or subordinate has a right, under the rules, to argue with the umpire on any decision in which an error of judgment only, and not one of misinterpretation of the rules, is concerned. He not only has not the right to so argue, but it is a piece of stupid blundering to do it, as he thereby uselessly prejudices the umpire against him.

It has come to be a fixed rule, in the business of managing a professional club team, that the manager should be given full power to sign and release any player of his team at will. Without this power a manager is one in name only, and his position is a useless one; as only under the rule of having arbitrary control of his men can he enforce disciplinary regulations, or get thorough team-work out of his men.

One of the most absurd statements made relative to the success of the Boston team in winning the pennant race in 1897 is that of their having "played in great luck." On the same basis, we suppose, the Louisvilles were brought down from second place in the race on May 12 to eleventh position in September by "hard luck." It was "great luck," we presume, that took Boston from the tail-end position on May 8 up to second place on June 8. For "great luck" in the one case, read plucky, uphill fighting, with team-work in all of the departments of the game; and in the other for "hard luck" substitute poor support of the pitching, a lack of unity of effort and inferior management. Players who fail to bat, to field or to run bases well, or who lack head-work in their "battery" positions, find fruitful excuse in the plea of "hard luck" and "rotten umpiring." There are, of course, occasions when Dame Fortune will "help the brave to win the fair," but "great luck" never won a pennant yet, nor has "hard luck" ever lost one.

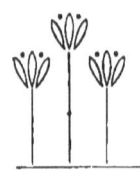 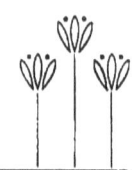

The Batting of 1897

THE experience of the season of 1897 in batting was such as to show comparatively little gain in the way of improvement in really skilful scientific batting; though, as a whole, there was better work done in this line in 1897 than in 1896. But the majority of the batsmen—especially in the ranks of the minor league clubs—still stick to the old rutty method of batting, in which striving for home runs and little else is regarded as the very acme of skill in handling the ash. The only criterion of batting which the existing scoring rules admit of, is that of the column of base-hit averages, and the batsmen who rate high in this column of League statistics are set down as among "the best batsmen in the League," though they may have dozens of superiors who lead them in the skilful point of forwarding runners around the bases by their base-hits; there being no data at command in the scoring code which presents a reliable criterion of skilful scientific batting, such as the record of "runs forwarded by base-hits" presents, and until the means for arriving at this special data is given in the rules, team-work at the bat will still be retarded as it hitherto has been.

The worthlessness of the column of base-hit averages as a criterion of skilful batting is shown in several instances in the official batting averages for 1897, sent in by Secretary Young. For instance, Stivetts of Boston is placed fourth on the list of League batsmen who excel in base-hit averages, and consequently—according to the only data of the kind—he is one of the four best batsmen in the League, while George Davis of the New York club is rated as ninth on the list. And yet look at the record of the two in games played in, runs scored, base-hit averages, sacrifice hits, stolen bases and fielding averages:

Player.	Pos.	Games.	Runs.	Base-hit ave.	Sacrifice hits.	Stolen bases.	Fielding ave.
Stivetts	Pitcher	26	43	.388	1	2	.953
Davis	Shortstop	131	114	.358	5	64	.932

What is the trifling lead in base-hit averages compared with the manifest superiority in base-stealing and in team-work at the bat shown by Davis?

We append a record showing the three players who lead each club in base-hit averages, to which are added the total runs scored, the sacrifice hits, stolen bases, and also the fielding average of each of the three players of each club; by this record it can be seen at a glance how valuable or otherwise a player may be to a club outside of his base-hit averages; the latter affording no true criterion of a player's value to a club as a batsman playing solely for his side, and not for a mere base-hit average record as most of them do. The names are given in the order of the pennant race record of the twelve clubs.

RECORD OF THREE LEADING BATSMEN IN BASE-HIT AVERAGES.

Player and Position.	Clubs.	Games.	Base-hit average.	Total runs.	Sacrifice hits.	Stolen bases.	Fielding average.
Stivetts, left field	Boston	49	.388	43	1	2	.940
Stahl, right field	Boston	111	.359	111	5	14	.935
Collins, third base	Boston	133	.346	102	8	16	.931
Keeler, right field	Baltimore	128	.432	147	12	63	.970
Kelley, left field	Baltimore	129	.389	113	9	50	.954
Jennings, shortstop	Baltimore	115	.353	130	17	60	.933
G. Davis, shortstop	New York	131	.358	114	5	64	.932
Van Haltren, centre field	New York	131	.332	122	6	45	.934
Tiernan, right field	New York	129	.381	123	1	34	.941
Holliday, left field	Cincinnati	58	.328	49	2	4	.933
Beckley, first base	Cincinnati	114	.325	84	4	22	.977
Schriver, catcher	Cincinnati	52	.310	26	4	3	.985
Burkett, left field	Cleveland	128	.383	128	10	27	.943
Wallace, third base	Cleveland	131	.339	99	14	17	.935
Childs, second base	Cleveland	114	.336	105	17	25	.944
Anderson, left field	Brooklyn	116	.332	93	11	42	.926
Jones, right field	Brooklyn	135	.322	133	13	62	.948
Griffin, centre field	Brooklyn	134	.320	137	12	23	.955
DeMontreville, second base	Washington	132	.349	92	14	33	.947
McGuire, catcher	Washington	82	.338	52	1	11	.926
Mercer, pitcher	Washington	42	.333	22	4	7	....
Rothfuss, first base	Pittsburg	31	.348	19	1	3	.979
Donovan, right field	Pittsburg	120	.326	83	9	39	.948
Elmer Smith, left field	Pittsburg	122	.311	101	6	28	.908
Lange, centre field	Chicago	117	.352	119	9	83	.952
Thornton, right field	Chicago	71	.329	40	4	14	.755
Everett, third base	Chicago	90	.314	63	11	27	.879
Delehanty, centre field	Philadelphia	120	.377	110	5	28	.966
Lajoie, first base	Philadelphia	126	.363	107	5	22	.984
Orth, pitcher	Philadelphia	42	.347	26	2	7	....
Clark, left field	Louisville	129	.406	122	3	60	.927
Wagner, centre field	Louisville	61	.344	38	5	22	.917
Werden, fitst base	Louisville	134	.301	76	5	16	.985
Douglas, first base	St. Louis	127	.327	77	3	12	.993
Hartman, third base	St. Louis	126	.301	67	4	18	.866
Turner, left field	St. Louis	102	.289	58	7	10	.940

Taking the combined records of the trios of the three leading clubs in the pennant race, it will be seen that while the Balti-

more trio lead in the totals of base-hit averages, with Boston
second and New York third, they also lead in total runs scored,
in sacrifice hits and in stolen bases; but in total fielding averages the Boston trio lead. The Baltimore trio who led their
club in base-hit averages made 173 stolen bases, to but 32 by
the three Boston players who led their club in base-hit averages.
They also led both the Boston and New York trios in sacrifice
hits. This is only a mere straw to show which way the wind
blows, but it also shows very plainly how little the mere basehit averages count in comparison with the other records which
go to make up team-work play at the bat.

It will be seen that of the twelve trios, while Keeler led in
base-hit average, as also in total runs, he stood second in total
stolen bases; but he had the best fielding average of any player
outside of the first basemen, the latter of whom always lead in
that respect, owing to the greater number of chances offered in
that position.

The official batting statistics of the League for 1897 show
that Keeler of Baltimore led in base-hit averages, Hamilton in
total runs scored, McCreery of St. Louis in sacrifice hits, and
Lange of Chicago in stolen bases. Those who were second
and third in these essentials were Clark of Louisville and Kelley
of Baltimore in base-hit averages, Keeler and Jennings of
Baltimore in total runs scored, Tenney of Boston and Hoy of
Cincinnati in sacrifice hits, and Hamilton of Boston and Davis
of New York in stolen bases. Though there was nothing in
the scoring rules of 1897 to show how effective the base-hit
batting of the season was in forwarding runners around the
bases, what little there was goes to show that Keeler of Baltimore did the most effective team work at the bat in 1897 of all
the players in the League. The essentials of team-work at the
bat are "place hitting," "sacrifice hitting," "bunting and
forwarding runners by base hits," the latter being the acme of
skilful batting. Another feature is that of safe hits over the
heads of infielders, but too short of the outfield positions to
admit of catches. Home runs, while obliging the batsman to
do 120-yard sprint running, at exhaustive cost of physical
strength, entirely puts a stop to chances for fine fielding,
inasmuch as six or seven of the nine men in the field in such
case merely have to watch the runner do his 120-yard run,
while the solitary outfielder does his running in going after
the batted ball. The veriest tyro in a knowledge of the best
points of the game frequently equals the professional expert in
hitting for home runs, and yet that same novice could no more
make a "bunt hit," a good "sacrifice hit," or "place a ball"
to forward a runner than he could fly. This plain fact shows
what folly it is to rank home-run hitting as the acme of batting.

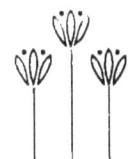 # The Fielding of 1897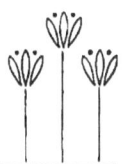

AS hitherto in the annals of the game, since the organization of the National League, fielding takes precedence, year in and year out, over every other department of the game of base ball, simply because it monopolizes the time devoted to practice. From the hour that the two contesting teams enter a field to compete in a match game to the time the umpire calls "Play Ball" and the contest begins, fielding alone is the marked feature of the preliminary practice, batting and base-running being "not in it" in comparison. The pitchers engage a little in what they call practice, but it is comparatively useless for training purposes. But the fielders get all the practice they want, and far more than their due share; and the result is that while fielding has reached a point of excellence in the game unequalled by that of any other of its departments, batting in base ball gets little, if any, and consequently is behind the times, as it will be until it receives its due share of proper training practice.

The fielding statistics still continue to fall short of data on which any reliable criterion of the comparative excellence of a player in his home position can be arrived at. The averages tell us that Jones, Brown and Robinson stand first, second and third as first base players, judged by their relative percentage figures of chances for putting players out which are offered and accepted. But there is really nothing else in the way of data by means of which one can judge the relative playing strength of a team in fielding. Each position differs in the amount of chances offered for put-outs in the game; but this difference is not brought to bear on the averages under the existing rules. The official statistics showing the fielding figures present column after column of useless figures, all that is really requisite being the number of games played in each position and the percentage of chances for outs offered and accepted, the details of put outs, assists and errors being unnecessary and useless.

The number of games a player takes part in should be taken into consideration in making up the relative positions of players in the fielding statistics. Take for instance the table showing the fielding percentages of the infield and outfield teams of the League for 1897, and we find that Douglas of the St. Louis club stands second on the list in fielding percentage as a first

Fincke   Bartlett   DeForest   Ferry   Camp   Hazen
  Hamlin   Greenway   Keator   Letton   Read
Wallace   Goodwin   Wear   Hecker
YALE UNIVERSITY BASE BALL TEAM, 1897.

Rand   Lynch   Stevenson   Haughton   Curtis (Mgr.)   Norton   Davis
Litchfield   Paine   Dean (Capt.)   Scannell   Chandler   Fitz
Loughlin   Beale   Burgess
Sears

Altman Smith Kafer Bradley McMasters Thompson Butler Geer Suter
Kelley Easton Barrett Wilson (Capt.) Jayne
Sankey

PRINCETON UNIVERSITY BASE BALL TEAM, 1897.

Haskell Brown Bassford Fuller (Mgr.) Kingsley Murtaugh Beacham Hackett Bole
Young Stratton Affell Cook
Blair
Miller

UNIVERSITY OF PENNSYLVANIA BASE BALL TEAM, 1897.

Stagg   Adkinson   Herschberger   Abells   'Brown   Sawyer
  Leighton   Gardner   Clark (Capt.)   Merrifield   Vernon
UNIVERSITY OF CHICAGO BASE BALL TEAM, 1897.

UNIVERSITY OF ILLINOIS BASE BALL TEAM, 1897.

T. Gannon　Fugitt　Shepp (Asst. Mgr.)　W. Gannon　J. Grace　Senior　G. White (Mgr.)　Pomeroy
　　　　　　　E. Grace　Reed　W. White　"Chimmie" (Mascot)　Carman (Capt.)

baseman, while Beckley is nineteenth on the list, the former having a percentage of chances accepted of .993 while the latter has .977, just 16 points less; and yet Douglas played in only 17 games at first base while Beckley played in 114. The fact is, the averages, both in the batting and fielding records each year, afford no criterion of the true batting and fielding strength of the three teams comprising base ball nines, viz., the battery team, the infield team and the outfield team, each of which have had no data hitherto on which to base a reliable opinion of their relative strength as teams. This essential we have endeavored to present in this year's GUIDE by a series of team tables which, though not as complete as desired, still give a better idea of the relative strength of opposing teams than has hitherto been at command.

In making out our fielding table we use the totals of the games each fielder participated in as a fielder in his home position. We have selected the fielders in each position who played in at least 100 games for all the infielders and outfielders, while for the battery players' table we select the pitchers who have played in at least 30 games, and the catchers who have played in at least 50 games.

THE BATTERY FIELDERS' RECORD FOR 1897.

PITCHERS.

Player.	Club.	Games.	Fielding Average.	Batting Average.	Runs.	Stolen Bases.
Breitenstein	Cincinnati	34	.982	.270	15	4
Kennedy	Brooklyn	40	.916	.269	10	0
Donahue	St. Louis	42	.913	.216	11	1
Hawley	Pittsburg	34	.905	.216	10	0
Orth	Philadelphia	32	.903	.347	26	7
Cunningham	Louisville	30	.884	.239	13	1
Griffith	Chicago	40	.881	.236	29	1
Dwyer	Cincinnati	33	.877	.285	13	0
Payne	Brooklyn	33	.876	.252	13	0
Nichols	Boston	41	.872	.264	21	4
Rusie	New York	37	.871	.288	25	1
Hoffer	Baltimore	33	.868	.238	20	2
Hart	St. Louis	37	.837	.245	14	5
Rhines	Cincinnati	35	.836	.168	4	0
Young	Cleveland	40	.829	.218	16	3
Klobedanz	Boston	38	.828	.316	27	1
Killen	Pittsburg	40	.818	.257	16	2
Lewis	Boston	32	.806	.254	15	3
Taylor	Philadelphia	36	.783	.252	12	0
Mercer	Washington	43	.775	.333	22	7
Seymour	New York	32	.769	.248	13	2
Frazer	Louisville	37	.765	.1~2	10	2
Meekin	New York	35	.758	.280	22	4
Corbett	Baltimore	35	.744	.257	27	6

CATCHERS.

Player.	Club.	Games.	Fielding Average.	Batting Average.	Runs.	Stolen Bases.
Pietz	Cincinnati	72	.956	.297	34	5
Kittridge	Chicago	77	.954	.198	26	9
Zimmer	Cleveland	81	.950	.314	52	7
Murphy	St. Louis.	51	.948	.177	12	2
Schriver	Cincinnati	52	.935	.310	20	3
Farrell	Washington	64	.934	.327	40	8
Warner	New York	110	.930	.274	48	9
Bergen	Boston	82	.928	.247	45	5
McGuire	Washington	76	.926	.338	52	11
Clarke	Baltimore	59	.923	.274	32	7
Sugden	Pittsburg	81	.917	.219	30	9
Merritt	Pittsburg.	53	.917	.270	21	3
Donohue	Chicago.	53	.914	.234	29	4
Grim	Brooklyn	76	.904	.261	25	3
Douglas	St. Louis	61	.901	.327	77	12
Wilson	Louisville	105	.889	.218	46	9
McFarland	Philadelphia	64	.886	.267	32	3

It will be seen that while Breitenstein has the best fielding average in his position as pitcher, Orth has the best batting figures; while Griffith is credited with scoring the most runs, and Orth in getting the best record in stolen bases, the latter showing the pitchers as very poor base-runners as a rule. Among the catchers Pietz has the best fielding figures; while McGuire excels in base-hit averages, Douglas in total runs, and also in stolen bases.

THE INFIELDERS' FIELDING RECORD.

The fielding record of the infield players who have played in their positions in 100 games and over for 1897 is as follows:

FIRST BASEMEN.

Player.	Club.	Games.	Fielding Average.	Batting Average.	Runs.	Stolen Bases.
Tenney	Boston	128	.988	.325	125	38
Clarke	New York	110	.987	.282	62	17
Anson	Chicago	101	.987	.302	66	16
Werden	Louisville	134	.985	.301	77	16
Lajoie	Philadelphia	106	.984	.363	107	22
LaChance	Brooklyn	125	.981	.308	86	30
Doyle	Baltimore	114	.979	.356	93	62
Beckley	Cincinnati	114	.977	.325	84	22

SECOND BASEMEN.

Player.	Club.	Games.	Fielding Average.	Batting Average.	Runs.	Stolen Bases.
Reitz	Baltimore	127	.964	.289	76	26
Lowe	Boston	121	.953	.314	87	18
Childs	Cleveland	114	.944	.336	105	25
Padden	Pittsburg	135	.942	.281	84	18
Hallman	St. Louis	110	.941	.250	49	17
Gleason	New York	131	.927	.311	88	40

THIRD BASEMEN.

Player	Club	Games	FA	BA	Runs	SB
Clingman	Louisville	115	.949	.232	60	11
Irwin	Cincinnati	134	.939	.293	88	35
Wallace	Cleveland	130	.935	.339	99	17
Collins	Boston	133	.931	.346	102	16
Reilly	Washington	101	.914	.275	66	16
Shindle	Brooklyn	134	.905	.289	82	25
McGraw	Baltimore	105	.892	.326	89	42
Hartman	St. Louis	126	.866	.301	67	18
Joyce	New York	108	.861	.305	110	30

SHORTSTOPS.

Player	Club	Games	FA	BA	Runs	SB
Jennings	Baltimore	115	.938	.353	131	60
Davis	New York	131	.932	.358	114	64
Ely	Pittsburg	133	.927	.282	65	12
McKean	Cleveland	127	.924	.273	86	18
Cross	St. Louis	130	.921	.288	60	36
G. Smith	Brooklyn	113	.914	.207	47	3
Long	Boston	106	.908	.327	88	26
DeMontreville	Washington	101	.887	.349	92	33
Stafford	Louisville	109	.883	.270	69	12

The record shows Tenney as having the best fielding average among the first basemen while Lajoie has the best batting average, Tenney leading in total runs, and Doyle in base-stealing. Among the second basemen Reitz leads in fielding, Childs in batting and total runs scored, and Gleason in stolen bases. Among the third basemen Clingman bears off the fielding honors, Collins in batting and in total runs scored, and Irwin in stolen bases. Among the shortstops Jennings has the best fielding record and made the most runs; Geo. Davis had the best batting average and stole the most bases.

THE OUTFIELDERS' FIELDING RECORD.

The record of the outfielders who have played in their positions in at least 100 games in 1897 is as follows:

OUTFIELDERS.

Player.	Club.	Games.	Fielding Average.	Batting Average.	Runs.	Stolen Bases.
Brodie	Pittsburg	100	.983	.298	47	17
Keeler	Baltimore	128	.970	.432	147	63
Delehanty	Philadelphia	128	.966	.377	110	28
Cooley	Philadelphia	129	.960	.327	124	80
Duffy	Boston	127	.958	.341	181	45
Griffin	Brooklyn	134	.955	.320	137	23
Selbach	Washington	126	.955	.317	114	58
Kelley	Baltimore	128	.954	.389	113	50
Hamilton	Boston	125	.953	.344	153	70
Lange	Chicago	117	.952	.352	119	83
Donovan	Pittsburg	120	.948	.326	83	39
Jones	Brooklyn	135	.948	.322	133	62
Burkett	Cleveland	128	.943	.383	128	27
Tiernan	New York	129	.941	.331	123	34
Ryan	Chicago	135	.940	.309	104	35
Turner	St. Louis	102	.940	.289	58	10
Hoy	Cincinnati	128	.938	.290	48	22
Stahl	Boston	111	.935	.359	111	14
Van Haltren	New York	131	.934	.332	122	45
Pickering	Louisville	109	.933	.296	67	40
Miller	Cincinnati	119	.932	.317	83	32
Stenzel	Baltimore	131	.931	.351	113	77
Clark	Louisville	129	.927	.406	127	60
Brown	Washington	116	.927	.287	98	27
Anderson	Brooklyn	114	.926	.332	98	42
E. Smith	Pittsburg	121	.908	.311	101	28
Dowd	Philadelphia	102	.908	.284	98	41
McCreery	Louisville and New York	136	.873	.285	91	25

Delehanty leads the left fielders in fielding average, Brodie the centre fielders and Keeler the right fielders, besides which Keeler leads all the outfielders in batting averages and in total runs scored, while Lange leads all in stolen bases.

It is worth while to state at the end of this chapter that there are two classes of fielders in the ranks of the professional base ball fraternity who become conspicuous during a season's campaign, and they are the head-work players and the mere machine fielders. The former are known by their earnest method of doing their work in their respective home positions, while the latter are players who only do their work perfunctorily—that is, as mere human machines. The former go for a ball with their minds bent on making the play, even at the risk of a chargeable error, while the latter avoid all risks they can which involve the chance of a misplay. The former class are the team-workers of the club, the latter mere record players, who seek to avoid an increase in their error-column figures, even if it is at the cost of poor support of the battery force in the field.

There may be said, too, to be a third class of fielders, men who are apt to weaken their general play by fits of the sulks, occasioned by some just criticism of their play which they have been amenable to. These sulky players are a hard lot to get along with when they indulge in these ugly moods. Generally this latter class belong to the hot-tempered players in the ranks, fellows who are constantly allowing nerve and judgment to be ruined by their ill temper. Such fielders can no more "play for the side" or do regular team-work in the field than they can fly.

A great essential of success in fielding, as in all other of the departments of the game, is this endeavoring on the part of the fielder to always *play for the side*—that is, to use his most earnest efforts to aid his club to win, no matter at what cost to his individual record. In selecting fielders for their teams managers should bear in mind this important fact and not trust to a player's fielding average.

The Run-Getting of 1897.

The main effort of the players on each side in a match game should be devoted to run-getting. It is that which wins games. There are two methods of getting runs in a game of ball, viz., by batting and base-running. Of course, the object of pitching and fielding is to prevent runs being made, while the batsmen and base-runners devote their best efforts to make runs. On both sides these opposite results are only attainable by combined effort. The batsmen send runners to the bases, and the base-runners help themselves around by base-stealing. The pitcher tries to strike out the batsman and the fielders to throw out the runners. The battle in the game, therefore, is to get the most runs, and that either by your own skilful work or by the errors of your opponents.

Though skilful run-getting is an art in itself, material aid is derived from the batting; but he must be a rather poor ball player who depends upon players on his side to bat him around the bases. Unluckily, there is no data to be had in the scoring rules on which to base a criticism of skill in run-getting except that of base-stealing. But, as a general rule, the player who scores the best average of runs to a game while equalling his opponent in base hit figures, deserves the precedence. Here is a record showing the leading run-getters of 1897, the list including those who made at least 100 runs during the season:

Player.	Club.	Games.	Runs.	Player.	Club.	Games.	Runs.
Hamilton	Boston	125	153	Selbach	Washington	126	114
Keeler	Baltimore	128	147	G. Davis	New York	131	114
Griffin	Brooklyn	134	137	Kelley	Baltimore	129	113
Jones	Brooklyn	135	133	Stenzel	Baltimore	131	113
Jennings	Baltimore	115	131	Stahl	Boston	111	111
Duffy	Boston	134	131	Joyce	New York	110	110
Burkett	Cleveland	128	128	Delehanty	Philadelphia	129	110
Cooley	Philadelphia	131	124	Lajoie	Philadelphia	126	107
Tiernan	New York	129	123	Childs	Cleveland	114	105
Clark	Louisville	129	122	Ryan	Chicago	135	104
Van Haltren	New York	131	122	Collins	Boston	133	102
Lange	Chicago	117	119	E. Smith	Pittsburg	122	101

Of course, the best run-getters in a game are the successful base-stealers, and next to them are the team-workers at the bat who make the most base-hits when runners are on the bases, the third class being those who, in striving for base-hits, hit the ball so that, in case of failure to make the hit, at least make a sacrifice hit.

The Base=Stealing of 1897.

Equal justice was not done in recording stolen bases in 1897, owing to the ridiculous wording of the stolen-base rule in the scoring code of the game. For instance, here is one clause in the rule which illustrates this fact very plainly. Section 8 of the Scoring Rules says:

"Any attempt to steal a base must go to the credit of the base-runner, whether the ball is thrown wild or muffed by the fielder."

This simply credits a runner with having stolen a base, though but for the wild throw of the catcher, or the muff of the thrown ball by the base-player, the runner would have been put out. No base can be fairly said to be stolen which is made through any kind of a fielding or battery error.

Each season's experience only shows more and more the fact that good base-running is one of the most important essentials of success in winning games. Effective pitching is a great aid; so is skilful batting; but it is equally as necessary, after a base has been obtained by a good hit, that other bases should be secured by skilful running of bases. It is a difficult task to get to first base safely in the face of the effectual fire from a first-class "battery," backed up by good support in the field; but it is still more difficult when the base is safely reached to secure the other three bases. The fact is, a greater degree of intelligence is required in the player who would excel in base-running than is needed either in fielding or in batting. Any softbrained heavyweight can occasionally hit a ball for a home run; but it requires a shrewd, intelligent player, with his wits about him, to make a successful base-runner. Presence of mind, prompt action on the spur of the moment, quickness of perception, and coolness and nerve, are among the requisites of a successful base-runner. Players habitually accustomed to hesitate to do this, that or the other, in attending to the varied points of a game, can never become good base-runners. There is so little time allowed to judge of the situation that prompt action becomes a necessity with the base-runner. He must "hurry up" all the time. Then, too, he must be daring in taking risks, while at the same time avoiding recklessness in his running. Though fast running is an important aid in base-running, a fast runner who lacks judgment, coolness, and, in fact, "head-work," in his running, will not equal a poor runner who possesses the nerve and intelligence required for the work.

Here is a stolen base record of 1897 which gives not only the total bases stolen during the season by players who took part in at least 60 games, and who scored at least 20 stolen bases, but also the average stolen bases per game:

RECORD OF STOLEN BASES.

Player.	Club.	Games.	Stolen bases.	Average per game.	Player.	Club.	Games.	Stolen bases.	Average per game.
Lange	Chicago	117	88	0-71	Cross	St. Louis	130	36	0-28
Stenzel	Baltimore	131	77	0-59	Joyce	New York	110	30	0-27
Hamilton	Boston	125	70	0-56	Miller	Cincinnati	119	32	0-27
Doyle	Baltimore	114	62	0-54	Tiernan	New York	129	34	0-27
Jennings	"	115	60	0-52	E. Smith	Pittsburg	122	28	0-26
Keeler	"	128	63	0-49	Irwin	Cincinnati	134	35	0-26
G. Davis	New York	131	64	0-49	Harley	St. Louis	39	20	0-25
Selbach	Washington	126	58	0-46	Ryan	Chicago	135	35	0-25
Clark	Louisville	129	60	0-46	DeMontrev'e	Washington	132	38	0-25
Jones	Brooklyn	135	62	0-46	Long	Boston	106	26	0-24
McCormick	Chicago	100	44	0-44	LaChance	Brooklyn	125	30	0-24
Kelley	Baltimore	129	50	0-43	Brown	Washington	116	27	0-23
Holmes	Louisville	80	32	0-40	Cooley	Philadelphia	131	30	0-23
Pickering		109	40	0-37	O'Connor	Cleveland	100	22	0-23
Wagner	"	61	22	0-36	Childs	"	114	25	0-22
Anderson	Brooklyn	116	42	0-36	H. Davis	Pittsburg	107	23	0-21
Van Haltren	New York	131	45	0-35	Burkett	Cleveland	128	27	0-21
Burke	Cincinnati	94	30	0-34	Reitz	Baltimore	127	26	0-20
Donovan	Pittsburg	120	39	0-33	Beckley	Cincinnati	114	22	0-19
Dowd	St. Louis	125	41	0-33	Shindle	Brooklyn	134	25	0-19
Hoy	Cincinnati	128	40	0-31	McCreery	New York	138	25	0-18
Everett	Chicago	90	27	0-30	Lajoie	Philadelphia	26	22	0-17
Gleason	New York	134	40	0-30	Griffin	Brooklyn	13½	23	0-17
Tenney	Boston	131	38	0-29					

Official League Statistics

COMPILED BY N. E. YOUNG, PRESIDENT OF THE NATIONAL LEAGUE.

BATTING RECORD

Of Players Who Have Taken Part in Fifteen or More Championship Games—Season of 1897.

Rank.	Name.	Club.	Games.	At Bat.	Runs.	1st Bases.	Per cent.	T. B.	S. H.	S. B.
1	Keeler	Baltimore	128	562	147	243	.432	304	12	63
2	Clark	Louisville	129	525	122	213	.406	287	3	60
3	Kelley	Baltimore	129	503	113	196	.389	250	9	50
4	Stivetts	Boston	49	196	43	76	.388	113	1	2
5	Burkett	Cleveland	128	519	128	199	.383	246	10	27
6	Delehanty	Philadelphia	129	530	110	200	.377	281	5	28
7	Lajoie	Philadelphia	126	545	107	198	.363	309	5	22
8	Stahl	Boston	111	468	111	168	.359	240	5	14
9	G. Davis	New York	131	525	114	188	.358	263	5	64
10	Doyle	Baltimore	114	463	93	165	.356	211	2	62
11	Jennings	Baltimore	115	436	131	154	.353	204	17	60
12	Lange	Chicago	117	482	119	170	.352	235	9	83
13	Stenzel	Baltimore	131	538	113	189	.351	258	3	77
14	DeMontreville	Washington	132	563	92	197	.349	245	14	33
15	Rothfuss	Pittsburg	31	112	19	39	.348	50	1	3
16	Orth	Philadelphia	42	147	26	51	.347	69	2	7
17	Collins	Boston	133	529	102	183	.346	255	8	16
18	Wagner	Louisville	61	241	38	83	.344	114	5	22
18	Hamilton	Boston	125	506	153	174	.344	212	4	70
19	Duffy	Boston	134	554	131	189	.341	264	13	45
20	Wallace	Cleveland	131	522	99	177	.339	264	14	17
21	McGuire	Washington	82	328	52	111	.338	152	1	11
22	Childs	Cleveland	114	443	105	149	.336	187	17	25
23	Mercer	Washington	42	135	22	45	.333	57	4	7
24	Van Haltren	New York	131	571	122	190	.332	237	6	45
24	Anderson	Brooklyn	116	488	93	162	.332	228	11	42
25	Tiernan	New York	129	534	123	177	.331	242	1	34
25	Sockalexis	Cleveland	66	281	43	93	.331	127	4	17
26	Thornton	Chicago	71	258	40	85	.329	106	4	14
26	Tucker	Boston and Washington	98	370	52	122	.329	167	3	18
27	Holliday	Cincinnati	53	189	49	62	.328	87	2	4
28	Long	Boston	106	452	88	148	.327	201	17	26
28	Cooley	Philadelphia	131	566	124	185	.327	239	10	30
28	Douglas	St. Louis	127	522	77	171	.327	209	3	12

BASE BALL GUIDE. 105

BATTING RECORDS—*Continued*.

Rank.	Name.	Club.	Games.	At Bat.	Runs.	1st Bases.	Per cent.	T. B.	S. H.	S. B.
28	Farrell.........	Washington...............	65	257	40	84	.327	102	5	8
29	Donovan......	Pittsburg.................	120	475	83	155	.326	185	9	39
	McGraw......	Baltimore.................	105	389	89	127	.326	146	8	42
30	Tenney.......	Boston...................	131	566	125	184	.325	216	27	88
	Beckley......	New York and Cincinnati	114	437	84	142	.325	207	4	22
31	Bowerman......	Baltimore.................	33	127	17	41	.323	48	1	3
32	Jones..........	Brooklyn.................	135	553	133	178	.322	218	13	62
33	Griffin.........	Brooklyn.................	134	530	137	170	.320	227	12	23
34	Selbach.......	Washington...............	126	486	114	154	.317	229	6	58
	Miller.........	Cincinnati................	119	439	83	139	.317	186	21	32
35	Klobedanz.....	Boston...................	38	136	27	43	.316	57	3	1
36	Gettman	Washington...............	37	146	29	46	.315	64	1	8
37	Lowe..........	Boston...................	121	500	87	157	.314	217	13	18
	Zimmer.......	Cleveland................	81	296	52	93	.314	122	5	7
	Everett........	Chicago.................	90	379	63	119	.314	154	11	27
38	Robinson.......	Baltimore................	47	182	25	57	.313	65	1	0
39	Hoffmeister...	Pittsburg................	47	189	33	59	.312	91	1	4
40	Smith..........	Pittsburg................	122	463	101	145	.311	214	6	28
	Gleason.......	New York................	134	555	88	173	.311	198	5	40
41	Wilson........	New York................	44	158	29	49	.310	65	0	7
	Schriver.......	Cincinnati...............	52	174	26	54	.310	76	4	3
	Leahy.........	Washington and Pittsburg..	43	145	23	45	.310	60	1	9
42	Allen..........	Boston...................	33	123	31	38	.309	45	3	3
	Davis.........	Pittsburg................	107	427	69	132	.309	206	10	28
	Ryan..........	Chicago.................	135	518	104	160	.309	240	10	35
	A. Smith......	Brooklyn.................	61	233	36	72	.309	90	6	14
43	LaChance.....	Brooklyn.................	125	523	86	161	.308	235	8	30
	Callahan......	Chicago.................	90	354	57	109	.308	149	8	13
44	McPhee.......	Cincinnati...............	80	277	45	85	.307	113	16	10
	Decker........	Chicago.................	109	423	71	130	.307	171	9	12
45	Vaughn........	Cincinnati...............	50	193	21	59	.305	82	4	4
	Joyce.........	New York................	110	306	110	121	.305	163	5	30
46	Anson.........	Chicago.................	112	423	66	128	.302	157	9	16
47	Werden.......	Louisville................	134	512	77	154	.301	218	5	16
	Hartman......	St. Louis.................	126	522	67	157	.301	197	4	18
48	Brodie.........	Pittsburg................	100	372	47	111	.298	147	8	17
49	Peitz..........	Cincinnati...............	73	256	34	76	.297	102	7	5
50	Connor........	Chicago.................	77	287	40	85	.296	120	5	12
	Dahlen........	Chicago.................	75	277	67	82	.296	130	13	16
	Pickering.....	Louisville and Cleveland...	109	426	67	126	.296	151	8	40
51	Irwin..........	Cincinnati...............	134	505	88	143	.293	186	10	25
52	Dexter.........	Louisville................	68	246	41	72	.292	100	2	11
53	Hoy...........	Cincinnati...............	128	493	88	144	.290	185	23	40
	O'Connor.....	Cleveland...............	100	399	48	116	.290	151	6	22
	Shoch.........	Brooklyn.................	79	272	39	79	.290	93	12	9
	Turner........	St. Louis.................	102	415	58	120	.289	163	7	10
54	Shindle........	Brooklyn.................	134	540	82	156	.289	215	21	25
	Reitz..........	Baltimore.................	127	476	76	138	.289	172	6	26
	Corcoran.....	Cincinnati...............	108	444	76	128	.288	176	12	16
	Rusie..	New York................	37	142	25	41	.288	48	0	1
55	Cross..........	St. Louis.................	130	462	60	133	.288	185	13	36
	Harley........	St. Louis.................	89	333	48	96	.288	119	6	20
	Ritchie........	Cincinnati...............	100	337	58	97	.288	116	13	8

BATTING RECORDS—Continued.

Rank.	Name.	Club.	Games.	At Bat.	Runs.	1st Bases.	Per cent.	T. B.	S. H.	S. B.
56	Brown.........	Washington.................	116	473	93	136	.287	168	8	27
57	{ Dwyer........	Cincinnati..................	35	91	13	26	.285	29	7	0
	{ McCreery....	Louisville and New York...	138	522	91	149	.285	201	30	25
	{ Geier........	Philadelphia................	88	316	51	90	.285	103	5	19
58	{ Dowd,.......	St. Louis and Philadelphia.	125	539	93	153	.284	185	14	41
	{ Holmes.......	Louisville and New York...	80	306	51	87	.284	111	6	32
	{ Wrigley.....	Washington.................	102	391	65	111	.284	150	13	8
59	{ Clarke.......	New York...................	118	440	62	124	.282	167	4	17
	{ Ely..........	Pittsburg...................	133	520	65	147	.282	186	15	12
60	Padden........	Pittsburg...................	135	515	84	145	.281	186	20	18
61	{ Smith........	Louisville..................	21	75	8	21	.280	27	1	2
	{ Meekin.......	New York...................	88	139	22	39	.280	45	0	4
62	Lally.........	St. Louis...................	87	367	57	102	.278	134	6	11
63	Sullivan.......	New York...................	21	65	6	18	.277	18	0	0
64	Grady.........	St. Louis and Philadelphia.	87	337	51	93	.276	136	5	7
65	Riley..........	Washington.................	101	352	66	97	.275	128	9	16
66	{ Ganzel.......	Boston......................	27	102	15	28	.274	37	3	1
	{ Warner.......	New York...................	110	397	48	109	.274	128	4	9
	{ Clarke.......	Baltimore...................	63	241	32	66	.274	78	3	7
	{ Friend.......	Chicago.....................	24	91	13	25	.274	30	1	1
67	{ McKean.......	Cleveland...................	127	527	86	144	.273	201	6	18
	{ McCormick...	Chicago.....................	100	413	88	113	.273	148	4	44
	{ Merritt......	Pittsburg...................	56	207	21	56	.270	66	6	3
68	{ Breitenstein..	Cincinnati..................	39	122	15	33	.270	44	4	4
	{ Stafford......	New York and Louisville...	119	465	69	126	.270	173	11	12
	{ Burke........	Cincinnati..................	94	386	71	104	.269	125	4	30
69	{ Kennedy.....	Brooklyn...................	42	145	10	39	.269	52	2	0
	{ Carsey.......	Philadelphia and St. Louis.	15	52	3	14	.269	18	1	0
70	O'Brien........	Baltimore...................	38	138	22	37	.268	42	2	10
71	{ McFarland...	St. Louis and Philadelphia.	67	239	32	64	.267	95	14	3
	{ Tebeau.......	Cleveland...................	111	415	62	111	.267	145	9	10
72	Tannehill.....	Pittsburg...................	53	184	24	49	.266	62	0	4
73	{ Abbey........	Washington.................	78	306	54	81	.264	103	3	10
	{ Nichols.......	Boston......................	42	144	21	38	.264	51	2	4
	{ Quinn........	Baltimore...................	71	284	34	75	.264	97	3	14
74	{ Cross........	Philadelphia................	88	345	37	90	.261	128	11	11
	{ Grim.........	Brooklyn...................	76	283	25	74	.261	83	8	3
75	Boyle.........	Philadelphia................	73	282	36	73	.259	94	5	2
76	{ Nash.........	Philadelphia................	102	337	45	87	.258	113	11	4
	{ Gillen........	Philadelphia................	74	271	32	70	.258	86	10	2
77	{ Killen........	Pittsburg...................	41	132	16	34	.257	42	0	2
	{ Corbett......	Baltimore...................	36	140	27	36	.257	46	1	6
78	Blake..........	Cleveland...................	31	117	18	30	.256	39	2	4
79	Lewis.........	Boston......................	35	110	15	28	.254	31	7	3
80	{ Payne........	Brooklyn...................	39	111	13	28	.252	30	3	0
	{ Taylor........	Philadelphia................	37	135	12	34	.252	45	2	0
81	{ Shugart......	Philadelphia................	40	163	20	41	.251	67	1	6
	{ Johnson......	Louisville..................	44	168	16	41	.251	48	1	2
82	{ Cartwright...	Washington.................	33	124	19	31	.250	35	0	9
	{ Hallman......	Philadelphia and St. Louis.	112	431	49	108	.250	124	12	17
83	Seymour.......	New York...................	41	141	13	35	.248	49	1	2
84	Bergen........	Boston......................	83	324	45	80	.247	104	2	5
85	Lake..........	Boston......................	16	61	2	15	.246	19	2	2

BASE BALL GUIDE. 107

BATTING RECORDS—*Continued.*

Rank.	Name.	Club.	Games.	At Bat.	Runs.	1st Bases.	Per cent.	T. B.	S. H.	S. B.
86	Hart	St. Louis	43	155	14	38	.245	49	0	5
87	{ Daub	Brooklyn	18	45	11	11	.244	14	2	2
	{ Pond	Baltimore	31	90	15	22	.244	25	3	3
88	O'Brien	Washington	84	318	87	77	.242	104	3	5
89	Nance	Louisville	34	120	25	29	.241	46	3	3
90	{ Cunningham	Louisville	30	96	13	23	.239	31	5	1
	{ Clements	Philadelphia	49	184	18	44	.239	71	4	2
	{ Yeager	Boston	26	92	20	22	.239	36	3	2
91	{ Burrill	Brooklyn	31	105	15	25	.238	32	2	1
	{ Hoffer	Baltimore	41	143	20	34	.238	47	2	2
92	Griffith	Chicago	46	161	29	38	.236	53	3	1
93	{ Fifield	Philadelphia	24	77	11	18	.234	28	2	0
	{ Donahue	Chicago	53	188	29	44	.234	56	4	4
94	Magee	Louisville	20	60	4	14	.233	15	1	0
95	{ Houseman	St. Louis	76	267	32	62	.232	77	4	12
	{ Clingman	Louisville	115	406	60	94	.232	130	8	11
96	{ Pfeffer	Chicago	32	113	10	26	.230	27	2	5
	{ Creiger	Cleveland	38	139	15	32	.230	37	3	4
97	Connor	St. Louis	22	83	13	19	.229	26	1	3
98	Dunn	Brooklyn	34	127	19	29	.228	32	4	2
99	Swain	Washington	24	71	7	16	.225	17	1	3
100	McAleer	Cleveland	23	89	5	20	.224	22	1	5
101	{ Wilson	Cleveland	35	117	16	26	.222	28	3	3
	{ Canavan	Brooklyn	63	239	25	53	.222	78	1	10
102	Sugden	Pittsburg	83	288	30	63	.219	77	13	9
103	{ Young	Cleveland	45	156	16	34	.218	43	3	3
	{ Wilson	Louisville	106	385	46	84	.218	107	11	9
104	Nops	Baltimore	28	92	7	20	.217	26	2	0
105	{ Donohue	St. Louis	44	152	11	32	.216	47	4	1
	{ Hawley	Pittsburg	36	125	10	27	.216	31	0	0
106	Ehret	Cincinnati	27	66	6	14	.212	16	2	2
107	McAllister	Cleveland	40	137	20	29	.211	36	4	4
108	Dolan	Louisville	35	133	10	28	.210	34	0	7
109	G. Smith	Brooklyn	113	430	47	89	.207	111	7	8
110	Lyons	Pittsburg	36	131	22	27	.206	47	1	5
111	Wheeler	Philadelphia	25	78	11	16	.205	23	1	2
112	Gettig	New York	20	74	8	15	.203	21	0	3
113	Powell	Cleveland	28	99	10	20	.202	21	4	1
114	Fisher	Brooklyn	18	60	6	12	.200	14	1	0
115	Kittridge	Chicago	77	263	26	52	.198	71	7	9
116	King	Washington	18	57	8	11	.193	12	0	0
117	Briggs	Chicago	21	79	5	15	.190	18	2	2
118	Donnelly	Pittsburg and New York	66	246	40	46	.187	53	4	18
119	Murphy	St. Louis	55	203	12	36	.177	38	4	2
120	Frazer	Louisville	36	116	10	20	.172	24	2	2
121	Rhines	Cincinnati	36	101	4	17	.168	20	2	0
122	Hoek	Louisville	15	49	5	8	.163	10	2	0
123	McJames	Washington	41	125	12	20	.160	25	0	1
124	Gardner	Pittsburg	28	78	13	12	.153	19	2	2
125	{ Cuppy	Cleveland	17	54	5	8	.148	10	1	0
	{ Rogers	Louisville	40	148	21	22	.148	36	3	4
126	Hughey	Pittsburg	20	61	4	8	.115	9	1	0
127	Hill	Louisville	26	73	5	7	.095	9	2	1

FIELDING RECORD, 1897.

FIRST BASEMEN.

Rank.	Name.	Club.	Games.	Put Outs.	Assists.	Errors.	Total Chances.	Per cent.
1	Tebeau	Cleveland	91	912	42	5	959	.994
2	Douglas	St. Louis	17	146	7	1	154	.993
3	Vaughn	Cincinnati	85	842	17	4	863	.989
4	Decker	Chicago	38	398	28	5	431	.988
4	Tenney	Boston	128	1239	79	16	1334	.988
	W. Clarke	New York	110	1065	66	15	1146	.987
5	Boyle	Philadelphia	25	217	6	3	226	.987
	Anson	Chicago	101	940	23	13	976	.987
6	Lyons	Pittsburg	34	326	17	5	348	.985
	Werden	Louisville	134	1339	121	23	1483	.985
7	Lajoie	Philadelphia	106	1070	37	18	1125	.984
	Connor	St. Louis	22	237	11	4	252	.984
8	O'Conner	Cleveland	38	340	9	6	355	.983
9	Tucker	Boston and Washington	98	904	46	17	967	.982
10	LaChance	Brooklyn	125	1280	62	26	1368	.981
11	Rothfuss	Pittsburg	30	231	11	5	247	.979
	Doyle	Baltimore	114	1102	75	25	1202	.979
12	O'Brien	Baltimore	25	203	9	5	217	.977
	Beckley	Cincinnati and New York	114	994	58	23	1075	.977
13	Grady	Philadelphia and St. Louis	84	805	50	22	877	.975
14	Davis	Pittsburg	62	564	27	20	611	.967
15	Cartwright	Washington	33	291	25	11	327	.966

SECOND BASEMEN.

Rank.	Name.	Club.	Games.	Put Outs.	Assists.	Errors.	Total Chances.	Per cent.
1	McPhee	Cincinnati	80	205	269	17	491	.965
	Cross	Philadelphia	41	71	125	7	203	.965
2	Reitz	Baltimore	127	282	448	27	757	.964
3	Smith	Louisville	21	47	59	4	110	.963
4	Tebeau	Cleveland	17	34	53	4	91	.956
5	Corcoran	Cincinnati	44	125	143	12	280	.955
6	Geier	Philadelphia	37	89	120	10	219	.954
7	Lowe	Boston	121	272	404	33	709	.953
8	DeMontreville	Washington	31	80	98	10	188	.947
9	Childs	Cleveland	114	322	386	42	750	.944
10	Connor	Chicago	77	179	295	29	503	.942
	Padden	Pittsburg	135	372	399	47	818	.942
11	Hallman	Phila. and St. Louis	110	283	337	39	659	.941
12	Shoch	Brooklyn	65	185	232	27	444	.939
13	O'Brien	Washington	84	229	250	33	512	.935
14	Houseman	St. Louis	36	93	117	16	226	.929
15	Gleason	New York	131	306	403	56	765	.927
16	Callahan	Chicago	30	68	96	14	178	.921
17	Rogers	Louisville	37	83	122	18	223	.919
18	Canavan	Brooklyn	63	154	165	33	352	.906
19	Dolan	Brooklyn	18	43	68	12	123	.902
20	Dowd	St. Louis and Phila	23	57	72	15	144	.895
21	Pfeffer	Chicago	82	72	94	21	187	.888
22	Johnson	Louisville	33	72	93	22	187	.882

THIRD BASEMEN.

Rank	Name	Club	Games	Put Outs	Assists	Errors	Total Chances	Per cent.
1	Quinn	Baltimore	34	40	82	6	128	.952
2	Clingman	Louisville	115	175	275	24	474	.949
3	Irwin	Cincinnati	134	189	231	27	447	.939
4	Wallace	Cleveland	130	194	255	31	480	.935
5	Collins	Boston	138	213	303	38	554	.931
6	Nash	Philadelphia	77	115	145	23	283	.919
7	Riley	Washington	101	147	228	35	410	.914
8	Donnelly	Pittsburg and New York	66	70	121	19	210	.909
9	Shindle	Brooklyn	134	179	248	45	472	.905
10	McGraw	Baltimore	105	116	182	36	334	.892
11	Cross	Philadelphia	44	65	87	19	171	.888
12	Everett	Chicago	83	125	146	37	308	.879
13	McCormick	Chicago	53	56	118	26	200	.870
14	Hartman	St. Louis	126	162	253	64	479	.866
15	Davis	Pittsburg	32	55	59	18	132	.863
16	Joyce	New York	108	167	200	60	427	.861
17	Wrigley	Washington	29	37	67	18	122	.852
18	Hoffmeister	Pittsburg	47	50	68	28	146	.808

SHORTSTOPS.

Rank	Name	Club	Games	Put Outs	Assists	Errors	Total Chances	Per cent.
1	Quinn	Baltimore	21	61	58	4	123	.967
2	Jennings	Baltimore	115	336	417	54	807	.933
3	G. Davis	New York	131	346	436	57	839	.932
4	Dahlen	Chicago	75	215	297	39	551	.929
5	Ely	Pittsburg	133	306	460	60	826	.927
6	McKean	Cleveland	127	231	381	50	662	.924
7	Corcoran	Cincinnati	64	164	211	31	406	.923
8	Cross	St. Louis	130	330	514	72	916	.921
9	G. Smith	Brooklyn	113	216	399	58	673	.914
10	Allen	Boston	82	80	115	18	213	.910
10	Nash	Philadelphia	19	51	51	10	112	.910
11	Long	Boston	106	276	347	63	686	.908
12	McCormick	Chicago	45	110	152	30	292	.897
12	Ritchie	Cincinnati	69	146	204	40	390	.897
13	Gillen	Philadelphia	69	131	198	39	368	.894
14	DeMontreville	Washington	101	262	359	79	700	.887
15	Wrigley	Washington	31	70	112	24	206	.883
15	Stafford	Louisville and New York	109	210	364	76	650	.883
16	Shugart	Philadelphia	40	103	130	33	266	.875
17	Dolan	Louisville	18	40	50	16	106	.849
18	Callahan	Chicago	16	24	54	15	93	.838

OUTFIELDERS.

Rank	Name	Club	Games	Put Outs	Assists	Errors	Total Chances	Per cent.
1	Nance	Louisville	34	60	8	0	68	1.000
2	Blake	Cleveland	31	86	3	1	90	.988
3	Brodie	Pittsburg	100	216	11	4	231	.983
4	Keeler	Baltimore	128	218	14	7	229	.970
5	Delehanty	Philadelphia	128	262	22	10	294	.966
6	Gettman	Washington	37	49	3	2	54	.963
7	Lajoie	Philadelphia	18	42	6	2	50	.960
7	Cooley	Philadelphia	129	325	15	14	354	.960
8	Duffy	Boston	127	263	12	12	287	.958

OUTFIELDERS—*Continued.*

Rank.	Name.	Club.	Games.	Put Outs.	Assists.	Errors.	Total Chances.	Per cent.
	Houseman	St. Louis	33	60	5	3	68	.955
9	Griffin	Brooklyn	134	352	13	17	382	.955
	Selbach	Washington	126	304	14	15	333	.955
10	Kelley	Baltimore	128	238	15	12	265	.954
11	Hamilton	Boston	125	299	9	15	323	.953
	Abbey	Washington	78	128	14	7	149	.953
12	Lange	Chicago	117	262	17	14	293	.952
13	Donovan	Pittsburg	120	185	16	11	212	.948
	Jones	Brooklyn	135	233	21	14	268	.948
14	McAleer	Cleveland	23	51	3	3	57	.947
15	Douglas	St. Louis	43	79	7	5	91	.945
16	Burkett	Cleveland	128	220	14	14	248	.943
17	O'Conner	Cleveland	54	95	3	6	104	.942
18	Tiernan	New York	129	180	14	12	206	.941
	Burke	Cincinnati	94	225	11	15	251	.940
19	Ryan	Chicago	135	211	28	14	253	.940
	Turner	St. Louis	102	147	10	10	167	.940
	Stivetts	Boston	26	43	4	3	50	.940
20	Hoy	Cincinnati	128	352	11	24	387	.938
21	Stahl	Boston	111	169	18	13	200	.935
22	Van Haltren	New York	131	268	31	21	320	.934
	Geier	Philadelphia	43	73	12	6	91	.934
23	Pickering	Cleveland and Louisville	109	245	19	19	283	.933
	Holliday	Cincinnati	43	67	4	5	76	.933
24	Miller	Cincinnati	119	203	18	16	237	.932
25	Stenzel	Baltimore	131	259	13	20	292	.931
26	Wrigley	Washington	33	42	10	4	56	.929
27	Clark	Louisville	129	283	23	24	330	.927
	Brown	Washington	116	252	18	21	291	.927
28	Anderson	Brooklyn	114	256	7	21	284	.926
29	Decker	Chicago	72	113	9	11	133	.917
	Wagner	Louisville	52	105	17	11	133	.917
30	McAllister	Cleveland	27	40	2	4	46	.913
31	Harley	St. Louis	89	189	19	20	228	.912
32	E. E. Smith	Pittsburg	121	240	17	26	283	.908
	Dowd	St. Louis and Philadelphia	102	179	9	19	207	.908
33	Tannehill	Pittsburg	32	80	7	9	96	.906
34	Leahy	W'hington and Pittsburg	24	35	3	4	42	.905
35	Holmes	New York and Louisville	79	120	9	14	143	.902
36	Ritchie	Cincinnati	20	29	5	4	87	.895
37	Lally	St. Louis	85	198	9	25	232	.892
38	Sockalexis	Cleveland	66	117	9	16	142	.887
39	McCreery	Louisville and New York	136	193	22	31	246	.873
40	A. Smith	Brooklyn	17	31	3	5	39	.872
41	Dexter	Louisville	26	37	7	7	51	.863
42	Callahan	Chicago	20	39	5	9	53	.830
43	Thornton	Chicago	58	70	7	25	102	.755

BASE BALL GUIDE.

CATCHERS' RECORDS.

Rank.	Name.	Club.	Games Played.	Put Outs.	Assists.	Errors.	Passed Balls.	Total Chances.	Percentage Accepted.
1	Peitz...............	Cincinnati............	72	258	67	8	7	340	.956
2	Kittridge............	Chicago...............	77	314	79	13	6	412	.954
3	Zimmer.............	Cleveland............	81	276	88	11	6	381	.950
4	Murphy.............	St. Louis.............	51	157	63	9	3	232	.948
5	Clements...........	Philadelphia..........	48	164	40	8	5	217	.940
6	Schriver............	Cincinnati............	52	147	40	8	5	200	.935
7	Farrell..............	Washington..........	64	222	91	16	6	335	.934
8	Warner.............	New York............	110	521	130	33	16	700	.930
9	Boyle...............	Philadelphia..........	48	151	45	9	6	211	.929
10	Bergen..............	Boston...............	82	352	62	15	17	446	.928
11	McGuire............	Washington..........	76	289	88	19	11	407	.926
12	Robinson............	Baltimore............	47	185	36	8	10	239	.925
13	Creiger.............	Cleveland............	38	124	46	12	2	184	.924
14	Clarke..............	Baltimore............	59	191	38	15	4	248	.923
15	{ Sugden	Pittsburg.............	81	307	80	22	13	422	.917
	{ Merritt	Pittsburg.............	53	201	43	14	8	266	.917
16	Donohue............	Chicago..............	53	217	72	18	9	316	.914
17	Ganzel..............	Boston...............	26	102	26	10	3	141	.908
18	Grim................	Brooklyn.............	76	237	100	18	18	373	.904
19	Douglas.............	St. Louis.............	61	169	69	15	11	264	.901
20	Lake................	Boston...............	16	49	13	2	5	69	.898
21	Wilson..............	Louisville............	105	338	120	27	30	515	.889
22	McFarland..........	St. Louis and Philadelphia	64	206	74	16	20	316	.886
23	Wilson..............	New York............	29	125	22	12	8	167	.880
24	Bowerman..........	Baltimore............	33	154	27	10	20	211	.858
25	Burrill..............	Brooklyn.............	27	75	23	16	1	115	.852
26	A. Smith............	Brooklyn.............	38	103	43	18	9	173	.844
27	Dexter..............	Louisville............	24	63	29	9	10	111	.829

PITCHERS' RECORDS IN ALPHABETICAL ORDER.

Name.	Club.	Games Played.	Per cent. of Victories.*	Per cent. of Base Hits off Pitcher.	Av. Runs Scored Per Game.	Av. Runs Earned Per Game.	Hit Batsmen.	Bases Given on Called Balls.	No. Struck Out.	Per cent. Fielding Chances Accepted.
Breitenstein......	Cincinnati..........	34	.708	.271	4.76	2.03	8	85	91	.932
Briggs.	Chicago............	20	.210	.324	8.20	3.10	9	87	62	.865
Callahan..........	Chicago............	21	.571	.309	5.05	2.14	8	56	52	.842
Cunningham......	Louisville..........	30	.517	.300	5.07	2.03	14	72	52	.884
Cuppy	Cleveland..........	17	.588	.279	4.06	1.53	5	25	23	.943
Corbett	Baltimore..........	35	.774	.262	4.86	1.71	24	106	151	.744
Carsey............	Phila. and St.Louis.	15	.400	.318	6.86	3.33	7	53	13	.900

*Exclusive of tie games.

PITCHERS' RECORDS—*Continued.*

Name.	Club.	Games Played.	Per cent. of Victories.*	Per cent. of Base Hits off Pitcher.	Av. Runs Scored Per Game.	Av. Runs Earned Per Game.	Hit Batsmen.	Bases Given on Called Balls.	No. Struck Out.	Per cent. Fielding Chances Accepted.
Donohue	St. Louis	42	.238	.334	7.07	3.40	18	100	59	.913
Dwyer	Cincinnati	33	.562	.302	4.28	1.79	11	47	40	.877
Dunn	Brooklyn	23	.636	.283	6.35	2.65	10	63	25	.827
Daub	Brooklyn	17	.353	.319	6.82	3.18	9	47	19	.864
Ehret	Cincinnati	22	.428	.313	6.04	2.91	12	37	39	.917
Fisher	Brooklyn	15	.600	.287	6.00	3.87	1	46	31	.964
Frazer	Louisville	37	.444	.283	6.05	1.84	24	141	74	.765
Fifield	Philadelphia	23	.174	.310	6.04	2.61	8	68	32	.884
Friend	Chicago	28	.545	.289	6.35	2.30	19	84	59	.945
Griffith	Chicago	40	.525	.296	5.95	2.65	18	86	105	.881
Hawley	Pittsburg	34	.500	.282	6.11	2.73	25	88	84	.905
Hughey	Pittsburg	20	.450	.311	6.15	2.50	7	46	43	.771
Hart	St. Louis	37	.243	.320	7.70	3.51	17	149	67	.837
Hill	Louisville	25	.291	.265	5.12	1.64	20	70	57	.805
Hoffer	Baltimore	33	.697	.290	5.85	2.54	15	99	62	.868
Killen	Pittsburg	40	.461	.291	5.80	2.70	9	72	99	.818
King	Washington	17	.412	.308	6.64	2.88	9	42	30	.884
Kennedy	Brooklyn	40	.487	.284	5.12	2.10	8	146	80	.916
Klobedanz	Boston	38	.729	.291	5.34	2.84	24	123	93	.828
Lewis	Boston	32	.645	.278	5.37	2.37	10	123	62	.806
Meekin	New York	35	.606	.281	5.23	2.17	8	100	84	.758
Magee	Louisville	17	.250	.296	7.53	2.70	11	95	38	.705
Mercer	Washington	43	.547	.290	4.97	1.56	27	98	93	.775
McJames	Washington	42	.375	.272	5.12	1.48	19	136	161	.734
Nops	Baltimore	27	.769	.271	3.85	1.81	9	50	66	.894
Nichols	Boston	41	.732	.253	3.80	1.68	3	72	136	.872
Orth	Philadelphia	32	.406	.309	6.03	3.31	5	76	67	.903
Powell	Cleveland	26	.577	.272	4.23	1.88	9	55	61	.833
Pond	Baltimore	26	.680	.271	4.96	1.92	13	72	58	.870
Payne	Brooklyn	33	.419	.291	6.48	2.79	19	70	87	.876
Rhines	Cincinnati	35	.548	.277	4.80	1.91	18	83	69	.836
Rusie	New York	37	.784	.253	3.89	1.27	10	86	140	.871
Seymour	New York	32	.600	.241	4.34	1.28	19	165	157	.769
Sullivan	New York	19	.555	.312	6.47	2.95	14	71	47	.773
Swain	Washington	20	.350	.311	6.10	3.25	10	54	46	.735
Stivetts	Boston	16	.625	.283	4.56	2.12	5	41	27	.953
Tannehill	Pittsburg	17	.562	.281	5.70	1.88	8	21	33	.912
Thornton	Chicago	16	.429	.294	5.69	2.31	5	50	57	.875
Taylor	Philadelphia	36	.470	.298	5.55	2.69	25	73	85	.783
Wheeler	Philadelphia	25	.520	.292	5.36	3.04	6	76	67	.905
Wilson	Cleveland	29	.586	.298	6.07	2.89	9	82	66	.886
Young	Cleveland	40	.538	.290	4.85	2.25	8	51	90	.829

* Exclusive of tie games.

 Minor League Arena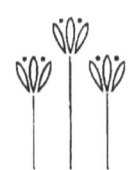

THE branch organizations of the National League, known as the "minor" leagues, did not flourish financially in 1897 to the extent they might have done had they all been run on the plan of true business principles, as a small minority of them were. Unfortunately, the club rivalry among the leagues was such as to lead them to violate one of the most essential of their business rules, and that was their failure to strictly observe the salary limit law agreed upon by all of the minor leagues. This law is one that cannot be violated except at the cost of financial loss to the league of which the offending club is a member. This fact is plainly acknowledged by all, and all start out each season with the intention of carrying the rule out to the letter of the law. But half the season is not over before one or more of the clubs of the various minor leagues are found to be secretly violating the rule. While this evil is allowed to exist, entire financial success in the minor league arena is out of the question. One or two clubs in a league may make money by it, but only at the cost of the majority. The fact is, the failure to strictly observe the salary limit rule in the minor league arena is an act of club dishonesty which reflects discredit on the minor league clubs which are guilty of it.

To promote the permanency of a league it is essential to have men of high character, as well as of sufficient wealth, at the head of each club, as far as possible—men who enter a club to promote the popularity of their favorite game, as well as to advance the welfare of the club financially; and it is to this exceptional class of minor league club magnates that this class of leagues have mainly to look for permanent success in each individual organization.

The system of organizing minor leagues in the professional base ball arena in connection with the existing great major league—the latter of which very properly governs the whole of the professional fraternity at large—is one which it has taken many years of costly experience to fully develop and to place on a permanent basis; and the major league very properly looks to the minor branches to help them perfect the system; but this help is lacking when a minor league violates one of its own primary rules, as it does in the case of paying a higher salary list than the League laws allow.

In regard to the thoughtless charges made at times by minor league officials that the major league is taking advantage of them, it would be well to bear in mind the important fact that *the National League cannot antagonize minor league interests in any way except at the cost of the welfare of their own league.* The business interests of both the great major league and the minor organizations should be identical; the one as the governmental power of the whole professional fraternity, the other as the governed class. It is folly to suppose that the ruling league would ignore their own best business interests by any selfish action looking to the self-aggrandizement of their own individual clubs at the cost of a loss to any minor league. However appearances may lead the minor league people to think that the major organization is unduly regardless of the former's interests, depend upon it that ultimately the best course for the welfare of both will be found to have been taken. The majority of the National League magnates comprise too many men of integrity, judgment, intelligence and experience, not to mention their wealth, not to use their ruling power to the best advantage of the professional clubs of the country at large. It is very certain that but for the existence of the National League, with its present governmental power, the minor leagues could not do a paying business, even if they could live at all.

The minor leagues in 1897 met with considerable financial success, compared with what they did in 1896, the best managed of the leagues, of course, paying the best. It was not a favorable year for professional base ball, and yet the majority of the clubs did fairly well. In the East the excellently managed Eastern League had a good season, only one change in its circuit being made, and that was largely due to a fire at the Rochester club's grounds, Montreal replacing the former city in the League. The well-managed New England League went through the season creditably, and the Atlantic League did better than in 1896. Out West some improvement was manifested in 1897, for though the Western Association, the Southern and Texas Leagues all got into difficulty, the Western and Inter-State Leagues were fairly successful, and the Texas League would have been so but for the violation of the salary limit rule by their clubs.

In a game at Toronto on June 8 between the Toronto and Scranton teams, the game at the end of the tenth inning stood at 0 to 0, the only game of the kind played by any of the minor league teams in 1897. In the eleventh inning Toronto won by 3 to 1. Dinneen pitched for Toronto and Gillon for Scranton. Toronto only scored four hits, while Scranton made six.

The Minor League Records.

The following tables show the pennant race records of each of the minor leagues of 1897 which closed the season without any serious loss of membership. The strongest and best managed of the minor leagues was the Eastern League, of which the able and experienced veteran, Mr. P. T. Powers, is President. It was the League's seventh season, and the pennant race proved to be a closely contested one, five of the eight clubs exceeding the percentage figures of .500, there only being 384 points in difference between the percentages of the leader and tail-ender. Here is the League's race record for 1897:

EASTERN LEAGUE RACE RECORD.

	Victories.	Defeats.	Per cent.		Victories.	Defeats.	Per cent.
Syracuse	86	50	.632	Buffalo	72	60	.545
Toronto	75	52	.591	Scranton	54	61	.452
Springfield	70	56	.556	Montreal	49	75	.395
Providence	71	58	.550	Wilkesbarre	30	91	.248

The fourth season of the Western League—the next in the strength of its clubs to the Eastern—ended in 1897, and from some cause or other it was not a financial success, and its pennant race was far from being evenly contested, no less than 487 points marking the difference in percentage figures between the leader and tail-ender. Here is the pennant race record for 1897, in which it will be seen that the Indianapolis club had its own way after the first half of the season:

WESTERN LEAGUE RACE RECORD.

	Victories.	Defeats.	Per cent.		Victories.	Defeats.	Per cent.
Indianapolis	100	34	.746	Detroit	71	67	.514
Columbus	88	48	.647	Minneapolis	48	94	.314
Milwaukee	84	51	.622	Kansas City	41	100	.291
St. Paul	84	52	.618	Grand Rapids	35	100	.259

One of the most evenly contested pennant races of all the professional leagues of 1897 was that which marked the second campaign of the Inter-State League, only 147 points dividing the percentage figures of the leader and fifth club at its finish, as will be seen by the following race record of the League:

INTER-STATE LEAGUE RACE RECORD.

	Victories.	Defeats.	Per cent.		Victories.	Defeats.	Per cent.
Toledo	86	47	.647	Mansfield	64	64	.500
Dayton	83	53	.610	Youngstown	61	69	.469
New Castle	74	54	.578	Springfield	50	83	.376
Fort Wayne	69	59	.539	Wheeling	38	96	.256

The Western Association's season of 1897 was not a financial success, the "hard times" out West last year materially affecting the patronage of its clubs, as it did most of the clubs of the minor leagues in the West. The pennant race record given below shows that the championship campaign was a fairly good one. The difference in percentage points between the leader and tail-ender was 355 points.

WESTERN ASSOCIATION RACE RECORD.

Cedar Rapids	85	41	.675	Quincy	60	68	.469
St. Joseph	80	46	.635	Peoria	57	68	.456
Des Moines	67	57	.540	Dubuque	47	81	.367
Rockford	68	58	.540	Burlington	40	85	.320

The last on the list of the eight-club leagues was the Atlantic League, and its pennant race record showed a difference in percentage points between the leader and tail-ender of .381, showing a less even contest than that of the Western Association. Here is the race record for 1897:

ATLANTIC LEAGUE RACE RECORD.

Lancaster	90	45	.667	Norfolk	66	72	.478
Newark	89	52	.631	Paterson	68	79	.463
Hartford	78	55	.586	Athletic	49	89	.355
Richmond	71	59	.546	Reading	40	100	.286

One of the best managed of the six minor leagues in 1897 was that of the New England League, under Messrs. Murnane and Morse, and its pennant race was so closely contested that no club was able to win its pennant. There were only 292 points difference between the leader and tail-ender in percentage figures, and at the fall meeting the League's delegates were unable to make out a winner, the teams of Brockton and Newport being so evenly matched that a tie had to be declared. The pennant race record was as follows:

NEW ENGLAND LEAGUE RACE RECORD.

Brockton	70	37	.654	Fall River	47	59	.443
Newport	70	37	.654	Taunton	40	68	.370
Pawtucket	54	51	.514	New Bedford	38	67	.362

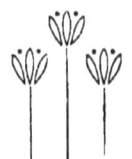 # The Eastern League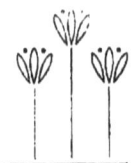

THE Eastern League averages in base-hits, runs, stolen bases and sacrifice hits for 1897 present a long list of players, as will be seen by the appended record, in which Brouthers stands at the head of the list in base-hit percentages; Lush stole the most bases, Green led in run-getting, and Cooney in sacrifice hits. Here is the record:

Player.	Club.	Games.	Runs.	S. H.	S. B.	Per cent.
Brouthers	Springfield	126	112	5	21	.415
J. Bannon	Springfield	55	64	1	36	.366
Woods	Springfield	70	50	1	10	.366
Bonner	Scranton	118	83	8	14	.360
Freeman	Toronto	124	107	5	37	.357
McGann	Toronto	128	128	6	32	.354
Griffin	Scranton	48	28	2	1	.352
Gilboy	Buffalo	132	110	6	26	.350
Walters	Scranton	83	67	6	3	.341
Snyder	Toronto	39	35	1	9	.340
Wise	Buffalo	122	94	8	22	.338
Knight	Providence	128	27	6	12	.335
Goeckel	Wilkesbarre	118	71	13	22	.330
W. McFarland	Rochester, Montreal	19	7	1	0	.328
Atherton	Wilkesbarre	53	28	1	7	.327
Beard	Scranton, Syracuse	84	59	5	11	.326
Wagner	Toronto	101	77	2	20	.325
Henry	Rochester, Montreal	72	39	3	9	.324
Lezotte	Syracuse	136	90	2	21	.323
Lush	Toronto	91	128	6	70	.319
Taylor	Toronto	116	65	10	6	.319
Baker	Montreal, Toronto	35	18	1	0	.319
D. McFarlan	Rochester, Montreal	32	24	1	0	.315
Jud Smith	Syracuse	134	120	9	28	.313
O'Brien	Syracuse, Scranton	110	93	6	31	.313
Massey	Scranton	114	69	4	14	.313
White	Toronto	118	103	4	50	.312
Meaney	Wilkesbarre, Scranton	94	60	3	18	.312
R. C. Grey	Buffalo	133	118	4	19	.309
Richter	Rochester, Montreal	121	78	4	21	.308
W. Eagan	Syracuse	135	128	2	50	.306
Gilbert	Springfield	127	79	5	15	.305
Lyons	Providence	131	91	17	33	.304
McHale	Toronto	118	108	10	50	.302
P. Eagan	Scranton	98	77	0	14	.302
D. Smith	Toronto	85	74	15	16	.301
Green	Springfield	124	134	5	45	.301
Lynch	Rochester, Montreal	94	87	9	31	.301

BATTING AVERAGES—*Continued.*

Player.	Club.	Games.	Runs.	S. H.	S. B.	Per cent.
Mains	Springfield, Toronto	43	19	1	0	.301
F. Shannon	Rochester, Montreal	124	114	3	31	.301
Urquhart	Buffalo	70	31	1	8	.300
Gaston	Toronto	23	11	3	1	.299
Dixon	Providence	120	77	6	17	.299
Dooley	Rochester, Montreal	122	80	5	14	.299
Sullivan	Buffalo, Scranton	112	74	3	12	.298
Daly	Scranton, Wilkesbarre	41	21	3	5	.298
Ryan	Syracuse	87	51	5	11	.296
Scheffler	Springfield	78	69	4	42	.294
Drauby	Providence	104	71	5	7	.293
Betts	Wilkesbarre	120	83	10	11	.293
Garry	Syracuse	135	94	19	19	.292
Harry Smith	Buffalo	25	13	0	7	.292
Fearey	Rochester	28	19	1	1	.291
Mills	Wilkesbarre	26	13	5	7	.289
Odwell	Wilkesbarre	72	39	0	16	.287
Greminger	Buffalo	133	92	8	13	.286
Casey	Toronto	108	84	3	41	.285
Shearon	Rochester, Montr'l, Syrac'e	110	89	12	15	.285
Butler	Montreal	16	15	0	2	.284
Diggins	Wilkesbarre	81	30	2	3	.284
Weigand	Providence	134	32	5	40	.283
Braun	Providence	57	21	2	2	.283
Dolan	Springfield	18	14	0	1	.283
Earle	Syracuse	113	59	12	21	.282
Lampe	Syracuse	43	21	4	1	.280
Field	Buffalo	130	100	9	17	.275
Abbey	Providence	30	25	3	9	.274
T. Bannon	Syracuse, Montreal	106	78	8	39	.274
Lytle	Rochester	17	12	2	2	.271
Williams	Toronto	37	30	1	2	.269
Clymer	Buffalo	130	104	8	26	.269
Cooney	Providence	126	70	22	14	.269
Mulvey	Rochester	58	29	5	9	.269
Rogers	Springfield	69	52	5	9	.267
Zahner	Buffalo, Rochester	60	26	7	5	.266
Barry	Buffalo, Scranton	82	47	1	21	.264
O'Brien	Providence	25	18	1	9	.264
Bottemus	Rochester, Wilkesbarre	115	87	7	14	.263
Dan Shannon	Rochester, Wilkesbarre	104	66	3	5	.261
Wellner	Wilkesbarre, Scranton	23	5	1	1	.260
G. Gray	Buffalo	40	14	1	0	.259
Shaw	Syracuse	63	24	2	4	.257
Ollie Smith	Springfield	81	51	7	18	.257
Duncan	Springfield	106	48	7	8	.255
Bassett	Providence	129	63	8	6	.255
C. Smith	Wilkesbarre, Montreal	70	25	3	6	.255
McNamara	Montreal	35	19	1	4	.254
Fuller	Springfield	120	106	5	26	.252
Nichols	Springfield	40	29	0	14	.252
Murray	Providence	65	33	2	14	.251
Sharrott	Wilkesbarre	29	29	2	14	.248

BATTING AVERAGES—*Continued.*

Player.	Club.	Games.	Runs.	S. H.	S. B.	Per cent.
Staley	Toronto	20	7	2	0	.246
McMahon	Wilkesbarre	79	24	6	12	.243
O'Neill	Providence	15	4	0	2	.241
Gonding	Wilkesbarre	63	27	5	8	.241
Scheibeck	Syracuse	122	61	12	13	.238
R. Moore	Springfield	58	24	3	1	.234
Prowse	Wilkesbarre	31	9	1	1	.230
Gunson	Scranton	57	20	3	9	.229
Berger	Montreal	33	14	3	1	.224
Coogan	Providence	50	23	1	4	.222
Norton	Toronto	27	9	1	3	.222
Mallarkey	Syracuse	46	17	5	3	.221
Sholta	Wilkesbarre	21	13	4	2	.220
Maguire	Scranton	118	48	7	4	.219
Powell	Wilkesbarre	27	17	1	5	.218
Brown	Buffalo	42	18	1	0	.213
Coughlin	Springfield, Wilkesbarre	15	7	1	2	.213
Boyd	Scranton	81	26	2	10	.204
Harper	Scranton	31	13	3	2	.200
McPartlin	Buffalo, Toronto	23	7	0	0	.197
Hodson	Providence	41	16	4	1	.195
Willis	Syracuse	40	11	4	0	.192
Becker	Rochester, Montreal	16	3	0	1	.185
Korwan	Springfield	27	8	0	1	.185
Dinneen	Toronto	34	11	3	1	.183
Rudderham	Providence	23	6	1	0	.172
Gannon	Rochester, Montreal	33	9	1	0	.172
Kissinger	Syracuse	19	5	1	0	.167
Morse	Scranton	25	7	2	0	.165
Souders	Buffalo	27	6	0	0	.157
Keenan	Wilkesbarre	38	7	3	5	.154
Gillon	Scranton	34	15	7	2	.148
Egan	Providence	34	11	4	4	.119
Yerrick	Rochester, Montreal	35	13	3	0	.100

FIELDING AVERAGES—CATCHERS.

Name and Club.	Games.	Per cent.	Name and Club.	Games.	Per cent.
Shaw, Syracuse	62	.976	Zahner, Buffalo and Roch.	57	.938
Ryan, Syracuse	80	.974	McNamara, Montreal	32	.938
Boyd, Scranton	75	.970	Snyder, Toronto	37	.934
Gunson, Scranton	48	.961	Urquhart, Buffalo	67	.932
Dixon, Providence	108	.960	Baker, Toronto and M'ntr'l	27	.931
Coogan, Providence	25	.951	Nichols, Springfield	27	.929
Diggins, Wilkesbarre	84	.944	Harry Smith, Buffalo	25	.925
Duncan, Springfield	105	.940	Gonding, Wilkesbarre	49	.917
Fearey, Rochester	28	.940	O'Neill, Rochester	15	.910
Casey, Toronto	90	.939			

FIRST BASEMEN.

Name and Club.	Games.	Per cent.	Name and Club.	Games.	Per cent.
Field, Buffalo	130	.984	Goeckel, Wilkesbarre	118	.976
Brouthers, Springfield	126	.983	McGann, Toronto	128	.973
Earle, Syracuse	113	.982	Massey, Scranton	114	.971
Drauby, Providence	101	.982	Dooley, Roch'r and Mont'l.	122	.971
Bassett, Providence	25	.976			

SECOND BASEMEN.

Name and Club.	Games.	Per cent.	Name and Club.	Games.	Per cent.
W. Eagan, Syracuse	135	.958	Rogers, Springfield	69	.934
O'Brien, Providence	25	.955	Bonner, Scranton	118	.931
Wise, Buffalo	122	.951	Mills, Wilkesbarre	26	.915
Moore, Springfield	58	.948	Shannon, Roch'r, Wilk'b're.	104	.904
Taylor, Toronto	116	.947	Weigand, Providence	108	.878
Henry, Roch'r and Montr'l.	33	.935	Sholta, Wilkesbarre	21	.843

THIRD BASEMEN.

Name and Club.	Games.	Per cent.	Name and Club.	Games.	Per cent.
Bassett, Providence	104	.926	D. Smith, Toronto	85	.889
Greminger, Buffalo	133	.919	Maguire, Scranton	118	.881
Jud Smith, Syracuse	134	.904	Atherton, Wilkesbarre	58	.866
Gilbert, Springfield	119	.901	C. Smith, Wilk'b're, Mont'l.	70	.865
Mulvey, Rochester	58	.897	Weigand, Providence	26	.839
Henry, Rochester	39	.895	Lush, Toronto	22	.823

SHORTSTOPS.

Name and Club.	Games.	Per cent.	Name and Club.	Games.	Per cent.
Beard, Sc'nton and Syracuse	84	.940	Barry, Buffalo and Sc'nton.	59	.884
Cooney, Providence	126	.921	Prowse, Wilkesbarre	31	.877
Scheibeck, Syracuse	121	.901	F. Shannon, Roch., Montreal.	124	.875
Sullivan, Buffalo and Sc'nton	112	.899	Wagner, Toronto	88	.874
Fuller, Springfield	119	.892	Lush, Toronto	33	.845
McMahon, Wilkesbarre	79	.889			

OUTFIELDERS.

Name and Club.	Games.	Per cent.	Name and Club.	Games.	Per cent.
Knight, Providence	128	.959	Betts, Wilkesbarre	119	.923
Murray, Providence	65	.959	White, Toronto	113	.918
Clymer, Buffalo	130	.959	T. Bannon, Syracuse, Mont.	105	.917
Walters, Scranton	83	.958	Meaney, Wil'b're, Scranton.	88	.916
Garry, Syracuse	135	.956	R. C. Grey, Buffalo	133	.915
Lezotte, Syracuse	130	.956	Gilboy, Buffalo	132	.912
Griffin, Scranton	41	.958	Ollie Smith, Springfield	81	.909
McHale, Toronto	118	.949	Freeman, Toronto	124	.904
Lynch, Roch'r and Montr'l.	83	.948	Daly, Scranton, Wilkesb're.	41	.900
J. Bannon, Springfield	55	.947	P. Eagan, Scranton	98	.895
Bottemus, Roch'r, Wilk'b're	115	.946	Richter, Roch., Montreal	101	.894
Lyons, Providence	131	.945	Lush, Toronto	29	.892
Shearon, Roch., Mont., Syr.	110	.941	O'Brien, Syracuse, Scranton.	108	.890
Woods, Springfield	31	.940	Berger, Montreal	16	.889
Sharrott, Wilkesbarre	29	.930	Powell, Wilkesbarre	27	.889
Green, Springfield	124	.925	Abbey, Providence	30	.864
Scheffler, Springfield	78	.923	Lytle, Rochester	17	.861

The following table is that giving the full record of the pitchers of the Eastern League who pitched in 10 games and over in 1897. It shows their relative strength in batting, base-stealing and run-getting, as well as their percentage of victories in pitching:

PITCHER.	CLUB.	Victories.	Defeats.	Per cent.	Batting Average	Fielding Average	Runs Scored.	Stolen Bases.
Norton...............	Toronto...............	15	5	.756	.222	.967	9	3
Kissenger...........	Syracuse...............	11	4	.733	.167	.952	5	0
Dolan...............	Springfield............	9	4	.692	.283	.918	14	1
Dineen...............	Toronto...............	19	9	.679	.183	.866	11	1
Mallarkey...........	Syracuse...............	27	14	.659	.221	.886	17	3
Staley...............	Toronto...............	9	5	.643	.246	.848	7	0
Lampe...............	Syracuse...............	22	13	.629	.280	.843	21	1
Gray.................	Buffalo...............	22	13	.629	.259	.945	14	0
Hodson..............	Providence...........	23	14	.622	.195	.842	16	1
Souders.............	Buffalo...............	16	10	.615	.157	.945	6	0
McPartlin...........	Toronto...............	11	7	.611	.197	.967	7	0
Gaston..............	Toronto...............	12	8	.600	.299	.869	11	1
Goeckel.............	Wilkesbarre..........	6	4	.600	.330	....	71	22
Wood................	Springfield............	16	11	.593	.366	.983	50	10
Mains................	Toronto...............	20	14	.588	.301	.927	19	0
Willis................	Syracuse...............	21	16	.568	.192	.897	11	0
Korwan..............	Springfield............	14	11	.560	.185	.965	8	1
Braun................	Providence...........	22	18	.550	.283	.933	21	2
Eagan................	Providence...........	17	14	.548	.119	....	11	4
Williams.............	Toronto...............	17	15	.531	.269	.977	30	2
Brown...............	Buffalo...............	19	17	.528	.213	.920	18	0
Yerrick..............	Montreal.............	16	16	.500	.100	.929	13	0
McFarland...........	Montreal.............	12	12	.500	.328	.810	7	0
Gillon...............	Scranton.............	15	16	.484	.143	.886	15	2
Harper..............	Scranton.............	13	14	.481	.200	.947	13	2
Inks..................	Buffalo...............	6	7	.462	....	....	....	....
Johnson.............	Scranton.............	5	6	.454	....	....	....	....
McFarlan...........	Montreal.............	6	8	.429	.315	.912	24	0
Rudderham........	Providence...........	8	13	.381	.172	.947	6	0
Coughlin............	Wilkesbarre.........	3	7	.300	.213	.945	7	2
Keenan..............	Wilkesbarre..........	10	26	.278	.154	.902	7	5
Gannon..............	Montreal.............	8	21	.276	.172	.878	9	0
Wellner.............	Scranton.............	6	16	.273	.260	.885	5	1
Becker..............	Montreal.............	4	12	.250	.185	.885	2	1
Odwell...............	Wilkesbarre..........	7	22	.241	.287	.900	39	16

After twenty-one successive victories by the Lancaster club of the Atlantic League up to August 27, the team had to submit to defeat at Richmond, Va., at the hands of the Richmond team.

On May 20 the Providence and Scranton teams of the Easern League played a thirteen-inning game, which ended with a score of 1 to 1 at the end of the thirteenth inning. Eagan pitched for Providence and Gillon for Scranton.

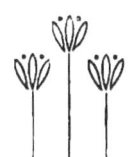 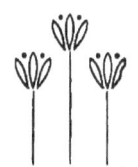

The Western League

THE Western League averages for 1897, as given out officially by President Johnson, are very complete, but on account of lack of room we are obliged to abridge most of the tables. The following are the important figures of the batting, running and stolen-base records:

Player and Club.	Games.	Runs.	S. B.	Per cent.	Player and Club.	Games.	Runs.	S. B.	Per cent.
McBride, St. Paul...	123	170	44	.387	Campau, G. Rapids.	132	109	25	.303
Dungan, Detroit....	137	143	20	.378	Crooks, Columbus...	131	87	23	.302
Wood, Indianapolis.	88	62	21	.375	Pickett, Kansas City	127	81	25	.298
Deady, Min, Ind, Det	72	57	22	.369	Smith, Milwaukee...	15	12	2	.298
Carney, Kansas City	49	34	9	.358	Nicholson, K.C'y, D.	111	95	31	.296
McFarland, Indian's	131	136	47	.357	J. Bannon, K. City..	76	62	30	.295
Frank, Columbus ...	130	126	29	.357	Tebeau, Columbus..	135	99	35	.293
Gray, Indianapolis..	125	131	13	.351	Hulen, Columbus...	130	140	34	.293
Isbell, St. Paul......	50	44	13	.351	Blake, Milwaukee...	85	63	29	.293
McCarthy, Indian's.	85	83	23	.350	Parrott, St.P., Minn.	128	92	21	.290
Stafford, Milwaukee.	134	118	28	.348	J. Foreman, K.C,Col	30	14	1	.289
Glasscock, St. Paul..	132	137	56	.347	Speer, Milwaukee...	132	70	29	.289
Weaver, Milwaukee	138	102	28	.343	Hogriever, Indian's.	140	158	72	.288
Dillard, Detroit.....	92	84	4	.343	Burnett, Detroit....	82	71	20	.288
Motz, Indianapolis..	136	121	38	.347	Mack, Milwaukee...	27	12	4	.288
George, St. Paul....	139	141	49	.340	Whistler, Detroit...	46	40	6	.287
Nicholl, Detroit.....	127	99	20	.340	Goar, Indianapolis..	39	27	3	.286
Butler, Columbus...	105	94	27	.338	Baker, Minneapolis.	21	10	2	.285
Mertes, Columbus ..	134	155	97	.337	Gillen, St. Paul.....	41	40	12	.285
Miller, Minneapolis.	134	107	45	.336	Stewart, Indian's ...	132	105	27	.282
Newell, Grand Rap's	42	41	9	.335	Myers, Milwaukee...	115	91	15	.282
Nyce, St. Paul......	111	109	20	.324	Lake, Kansas City..	47	29	7	.282
Daly, Milwaukee...	137	106	46	.333	Hatfield, G. Rapids.	45	23	11	.280
Slagle, Grand Rap's.	132	136	40	.328	Letcher, Minneapo's	104	76	23	.280
Buckley, Columbus.	86	52	7	.327	Phillips, Indian's...	48	34	2	.279
Hines, Detroit......	124	129	20	.326	Truby, Kansas City.	18	10	1	.278
Lewee, Milwaukee..	126	91	11	.325	Twincham, G. Rap's	112	62	16	.277
Ganzel, Grand Rap's	125	87	5	.324	Meeks, Kansas City.	19	11	1	.277
Beard, Detroit......	23	35	4	.324	Dowling, Milwaukee	12	7	0	.276
Fear, Grand Rapids.	19	14	3	.323	Pappalau, G. Rapids	24	7	1	.275
Steinfeldt, Detroit..	136	112	26	.322	Phill'pi, Minneapo's.	28	6	0	.275
McGarr, Columbus..	78	55	14	.321	Glenalvin,G.R,St.P.	111	101	25	.274
McKinney, G. Rap's	54	34	7	.318	Griffin, St. Paul.....	75	39	10	.273
McVicker, Kan. City	140	114	21	.315	Flynn, Indianapolis.	121	129	36	.272
Shugart, St. Paul....	88	82	31	.314	Kahoe, Indianapolis.	88	59	15	.272
Genins, Columbus...	132	117	24	.309	Jones, Milwaukee...	15	8	0	.267
Delehanty, Mil.,Det	92	91	25	.308	Hagerman, G. Rap's	11	7	0	.265
Davis, Detroit......	51	32	12	.307	Mullane, St. Paul...	53	31	6	.264
Trost, Detroit	93	54	7	.306	Gettinger, Kan. City	97	50	10	.262
Wadsworth, Detroit.	20	13	2	.305	Ball, Minneapolis...	120	96	41	.261

BATTING AVERAGES—Continued.

Player and Club.	Games.	Runs.	S. B.	Per cent.	Player and Club.	Games.	Runs.	S. B.	Per cent.
Nicol, Milwaukee...	136	114	28	.259	McKibben, G. Rap..	77	42	15	.220
Terry, Milwaukee...	35	11	1	.257	Menefee, Kan. City.	131	66	37	.229
Wright, Milwaukee.	56	48	12	.256	F. Foreman, Ind....	46	18	2	.228
McCauley, Detroit..	72	40	13	.253	Keener, Columbus..	25	10	1	.225
Blanford, Kan. City.	92	44	5	.253	Hutchison, Minn...	44	19	1	.224
Strauss, G. Rapids..	52	32	4	.252	Barnes, Milwaukee..	39	18	1	.216
Thomas, Detroit....	48	20	2	.252	Ganzel, Minneapolis.	22	10	3	.208
Kuehne, Minneapo's	84	39	11	.250	T. Bannon, K. City..	21	16	12	.200
Fisher, Columbus...	76	46	5	.250	Driscoll, G. Rapids..	35	11	1	.199
Hollingsworth, St.P.	95	65	33	.245	Rettger, Columbus..	37	19	0	.191
McGill, St. Paul....	15	8	0	.245	B. Jones, Columbus.	32	11	4	.189
O'Rourke, Kan.City	99	79	37	.243	Cross, St. P., G. R..	44	14	6	.186
Cassidy, Minneap'lis	30	23	15	.243	Fricken, St. Paul...	33	12	3	.181
Friend, Kansas City.	16	10	1	.241	Clarkson, Mil., Det.	21	7	0	.180
Eustace, Ind., Minn.	122	77	4	.241	Carney, Minneapolis	26	7	0	.178
Roat, G. R., Minn..	118	66	19	.241	Eagan, Detroit......	30	7	0	.172
Wolters, Ind., Col..	28	9	3	.240	Moran, Minneapolis.	15	3	1	.161
Taylor, Milwaukee..	17	9	0	.240	Hahn, Detroit......	39	13	1	.157
Cartwright, Minn...	24	14	5	.239	Brady, G. Rapids...	27	9	0	.131
Allen, Detroit......	61	40	4	.237	Figgemier, Minn. ..	41	13	2	.120
Daniels, Columbus..	19	9	1	.232	Scott, Grand Rapids	28	6	2	.120
Spies, St. Paul......	112	69	23	.229	Reidy, Milwaukee.	38	10	0	.104
Boyle, Minneapolis..	89	43	8	.229					

The fielding averages—only the games played in and the per cent. of chances accepted are necessary—are given below:

FIRST BASEMEN.

Name and Club.	Games.	Per cent.	Name and Club.	Games.	Per cent.
Mack, Milwaukee............	11	.990	Cassidy, Minneapolis.......	31	.972
Ganzel, Grand Rapids......	125	.983	Stafford, Milwaukee........	127	.965
Tebeau, Columbus..........	133	.981	Pickett, Kansas City.......	70	.965
Carney, Kansas City.......	49	.981	Cartwright, Minneapolis....	24	.963
Dillard, Detroit............	78	.979	Menefee, Kansas City......	15	.959
J. Ganzel, Minneapolis.....	22	.977	Meeks, Kansas City........	19	.597
Motz, Indianapolis..........	136	.975	Parrott, Minneapolis........	28	.956
Glasscock, St. Paul.........	127	.973	Trost, Detroit..............	11	.944
Whistler, Detroit...........	44	.972			

SECOND BASEMEN.

	Games.	Per cent.		Games.	Per cent.
Pickett, Kansas City.......	39	.968	Driscoll, Grand Rapids.....	35	.902
Crooks, Columbus..........	131	.951	Delehanty, Mil., Detroit...	81	.900
Beard, Detroit.............	20	.941	Roat, Minneapolis.........	70	.898
Hollingsworth, St. Paul....	59	.935	Steinfeldt, Detroit..........	11	.897
Nicholson,Det.,St.P., K.C.	111	.934	Hines, Detroit.............	41	.888
Stewart, Indianapolis.......	132	.931	Truby, Kansas City........	18	.885
Glenalvin, G. Rap., St.Paul.	111	.925	Nyce, St. Paul	27	.781
Daly, Milwaukee...........	137	.914			

THIRD BASEMEN.

Name and Club.	Games.	Per cent.	Name and Club.	Games.	Per cent.
Hollingsworth, St. Paul	14	.956	Kahoe, Indianapolis	12	.868
Kuehne, Minneapolis	54	.936	Myers, Milwaukee	115	.849
Eustace, Minn. and Ind	81	.911	Smith, Milwaukee	15	.848
Gray, Indianapolis	125	.908	Nyce, St. Paul	84	.885
Hatfield, Grand Rapids	45	.904	Gillen, St. Paul	13	.828
McGarr, Columbus	78	.902	McKinney, Grand Rapids	44	.824
Genins, Columbus	54	.883	Newell, Grand Rapids	30	.816
Pickett, Kansas City	18	.882	Reilly, Kansas City	39	.762
O'Rourke, Kansas City	99	.879	Preston, St. Paul	18	.750
Steinfeldt, Detroit	125	.869			

SHORTSTOPS.

Name and Club.	Games.	Per cent.	Name and Club.	Games.	Per cent.
Kuehne, Minneapolis	25	.966	Kahoe, Indianapolis	12	.868
Lewee, Milwaukee	126	.928	Griffin, Grand Rapids	72	.869
Allen, Detroit	61	.895	Ball, Minneapolis	112	.867
Hulen, Columbus	130	.883	Flynn, Indianapolis	79	.849
Connaughton, Kansas City	135	.878	Eustace, Ind. and Minn	41	.848
Wheelock, Grand Rapids	13	.875	Hollingsworth, St. Paul	20	.834
Shugart, St. Paul	88	.871	Gillen, St. Paul	27	.830
Hines, Detroit	83	.871	Delehanty, Mil. and Det	11	.823

OUTFIELDERS.

Name and Club.	Games.	Per cent.	Name and Club.	Games.	Per cent.
McCarthy, Indianapolis	85	.955	Mertes, Columbus	123	.907
Wright, Milwaukee	56	.955	Hogriever, Indianapolis	140	.904
Genins, Columbus	66	.954	Dungan, Detroit	137	.901
Weaver, Milwaukee	138	.948	Letcher, Minneapolis	104	.897
Nicoll, Detroit	127	.945	Gettinger, Kansas City	97	.897
McBride, St. Paul	133	.933	Slagel, Grand Rapids	132	.896
Flynn, Indianapolis	40	.925	George, St. Paul	139	.896
Nichol, Milwaukee	136	.923	Davis, Detroit	51	.896
McFarland, Indianapolis	131	.919	Menefee, Kansas City	106	.876
Tom Bannon, Kansas City	21	.916	Campau, Grand Rapids	120	.875
Parrott, Minneapolis	100	.915	Strauss, Grand Rapids	21	.873
Frank, Columbus	130	.915	Burnett, Detroit	58	.871
McVicker, Kansas City	140	.914	Gear, Kansas City	76	.870
Butler, Columbus	105	.913	McKibben, Grand Rapids	69	.857
Blake, Milwaukee	84	.912	James Bannon, Kansas City	76	.850
Miller, Minneapolis	79	.909	Isbell, Indianapolis	72	.839
Preston, St. Paul	33	.908	Deady, St. Paul	33	.844

CATCHERS.

Name and Club.	Games.	Per cent.	Name and Club.	Games.	Per cent.
Twineham, Grand Rapids	96	.970	Moran, Minneapolis	15	.925
Spies, St. Paul	134	.962	Fisher, Columbus	72	.922
Lake, Kansas City	44	.955	Miller, Minneapolis	24	.920
Wood, Indianapolis	88	.952	Trost, Detroit	52	.916
Speer, Milwaukee	132	.950	Kline, St. Paul	17	.911
Buckley, G. Rap., Col'bus	84	.948	Mack, Milwaukee	13	.906
Boyle, Minneapolis	87	.936	Dugdale, Kansas City	10	.902
Kahoe, Indianapolis	60	.929	McCauley, Detroit	72	.881
Blanford, Kansas City	88	.928	Fear, Grand Rapids	16	.855

We have prepared a special record of the pitcher's averages from the official figures in which our record is limited to those pitchers who reached a percentage of victories pitched in of over .500 and who pitched in 10 games and over.

Pitcher.	Club.	Games.	Per cent. of Victories.	Batting Average.	Fielding Average.	Stolen Bases.	Wild Pitches.	Average of E'ned runs.
Terry	Milwaukee	27	.815	.257	.911	1	4	1.90
Jones	Milwaukee	14	.786	.267	.897	0	2	1.88
Goar	Indianapolis	36	.778	.286	.971	3	8	1.30
Phillips	Indianapolis	40	.750	.279	.920	2	9	1.89
F. Foreman	Indianapolis	36	.750	.228	.969	2	5	1.51
Rettger	Columbus	32	.750	.191	.858	0	3	2.00
Jones	Columbus	23	.739	.189	.927	4	7	1.45
Keener	Columbus	19	.737	.225	.943	1	5	1.96
Daniels	Columbus	18	.722	.232	.962	1	1	1.65
Phyle, St. Paul	St. Paul	27	.704	*	.928	....	3	1.83
Thomas	Detroit	40	.650	.252	.869	2	11	2.06
Taylor	Milwaukee	15	.600	.240	.951	0	6	2.27
McGill	St. Paul	15	.600	.245	.920	0	12	2.41
Mullane	St. Paul	25	.560	.264	.919	6	11	1.73
Reidy	Milwaukee	34	.559	.104	.805	0	3	1.92
Fricken	St. Paul	27	.556	.181	.908	3	5	1.64
Isbell	St. Paul	11	.545	.351	.884	13	4	1.76
Eagan	Detroit	24	.542	.172	.889	0	10	2.44
Wadsworth	Detroit	13	.538	.305	.926	2	4	2.55
Denzer	St. Paul	17	.529	*	*	....	....	1.50
Barnes	Milwaukee	36	.528	.216	.951	1	6	2.07

*Neither Denzer's nor Phyle's names are in the batting record of the Western League sent us by President Johnson, and Denzer is not in the fielding record.

The percentage figures of the pitchers who pitched in not less than 10 games, and whose percentage did not reach over .500, are as follows:

Pitcher.	Victories.	Defeats.	Per cent.	Pitcher.	Victories.	Defeats.	Per cent.
Hahn	17	17	.500	A. Clarkson	6	11	.353
Hutchison	16	20	.444	Figgemier	13	25	.342
J. Foreman	11	19	.440	Burnett	7	14	.333
Cross	15	20	.429	McFarland	4	8	.333
Papalau	8	11	.421	Brady	5	15	.250
Scott	10	16	.385	Carney	4	12	.250
Phillipi	8	13	.381	Friend	4	10	.286
Abbey	15	26	.366	Pardee	3	13	.188
Welter	9	16	.360	Herman	1	8	.111

 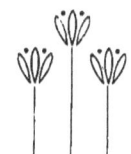

New England League

THE best compilation of statistics emanating from the minor leagues is that sent to the GUIDE by Secretary J. C. Morse of the New England League, which we give below. The first table given is that of the batting and base-running statistics. In his introduction Mr. Morse says: "While the batting averages of the first ten men are not up to those of last year, when seven of the leading batsmen stood above the .370 mark, there are, however, thirty of this season's flock who have records above .300."

Player.	Club.	Games.	Runs.	S. H.	S. B.	Per cent.
Hickey	Brockton	25	20	0	16	.379
Sheckard	Brockton	107	117	18	52	.370
Irwin	Taunton	88	60	1	17	.364
Kreig	Brockton	75	64	2	3	.364
Simon	Taunton	77	71	1	19	.361
Rollins	Brockton	37	19	4	5	.349
News	Pawtucket	82	73	2	13	.346
Delehanty	Fall River	25	18	0	5	.344
Stouch	Pawtucket	100	70	1	14	.340
Smith	Pawtucket	68	51	3	8	.339
Pickett	Newport	95	75	0	20	.336
Beaumont	Pawtucket	107	100	10	32	.333
Magoon	Brockton	107	85	5	27	.332
Ladd	Fall River	103	83	10	19	.331
G. Moore	Taunton	102	65	1	20	.329
Stephenson	Newport	47	37	0	2	.325
Todd	Pawtucket	37	18	1	5	.325
Buelow	Pawtucket	84	55	1	18	.324
McKenna	Brockton	47	31	2	5	.324
Hernon	New Bedford	101	87	8	37	.322
Kelley	Fall River	42	36	5	13	.320
Crisham	Newport	108	63	1	10	.318
Kelley	Newport	108	87	2	24	.312
Bean	Newport	97	70	4	27	.308
Henry	Brockton	107	86	9	40	.305
Whiting	Pawtucket	100	84	9	29	.305
J. Connor	Fall River	58	39	1	31	.304
Hill	Fall River	68	48	1	9	.302
Johnson	Taunton	75	42	0	5	.302
Wise	Pawt'k't Taunt'n, Fall R.	59	40	0	10	.301
Moss	Pawtucket	76	54	2	12	.300
Weisbecker	Pawtucket	95	96	4	32	.295
Rupert	Fall River	27	21	1	7	.295

Player.	Club.	Games.	Runs.	S. H.	S. B.	Per cent.
Nadeau	Brockton	106	96	4	15	.293
Davis	New Bedford, Taunton	63	36	8	10	.292
Mills	Newport	75	35	4	14	.290
Fitzmaurice	Taunton, New Bedford	73	45	2	24	.289
Shea	Brockton	74	39	3	5	.288
R. Connor	Fall River	47	32	2	9	.287
Kuhns	Fall River	21	14	0	4	.287
Sharrott	Brockton	53	39	4	28	.283
Tighe	New Bedford	97	57	1	13	.283
Burke	Taunton	70	31	0	0	.282
Birmingham	Fall River, Brockton	52	24	3	10	.281
Cavanaugh	Brockton, Fall River	87	48	5	6	.278
Gilbert	Newport	104	72	4	40	.275
Long	New Bedford	100	69	7	44	.274
Leighton	Taunton	36	17	0	8	.271
Wiley	Taunton	28	13	2	3	.270
Hawley	Newport	51	33	2	6	.266
Ellis	New Bedford, Newport	86	53	3	25	.265
Gallagher	Newport	38	18	0	7	.264
Glen	New Bedford	39	13	2	13	.264
McDougall	Taunton	49	24	2	3	.259
Coughlin	Pawtucket	107	70	1	16	.258
Murphy	New Bedford	75	44	7	24	.258
Moynihan	Fall River, Brockton	32	12	3	0	.255
Stanhope	Taunton, New Bedford	77	36	2	5	.254
Sexton	New Bedford	70	36	4	9	.253
W. Delaney	Taunton	57	38	3	9	.252
Norcom	Fall River	32	19	0	4	.250
Anderson	New Bedford	30	12	1	0	.247
Harrington	Taunton	100	38	4	12	.247
Smith	Fall River	41	13	3	6	.237
Reilley	Fall River	102	58	1	17	.234
Grant	Newport	98	47	8	20	.234
Hall	New Bedford	35	13	1	4	.229
Miller	Fall River	23	9	0	4	.226
McCafferty	Pawtucket	34	16	0	0	.224
Gochnaur	Brockton	91	63	12	14	.221
McManus	Fall River	96	69	1	30	.217
Flanagan	Fall River, New Bedford	41	10	1	1	.214
Counihan	New Bedford	54	25	1	6	.211
Callopy	New Bedford	46	26	4	6	.205
Gilbert	Fall River	50	20	4	10	.205
R. Moore	Taunton	46	28	1	1	.204
Day	New Bedford	53	17	2	4	.197
Cronin	Fall River	17	8	0	1	.188
Doe	Fall River	15	5	0	2	.188
Foley	Newport	33	10	0	0	.188
Dinsmore	Newport	73	24	2	4	.184
Sechrist	New Bedford	33	12	1	1	.183
Herwig	Taunton	27	15	3	7	.182
McDermott	New Bedford	28	8	0	3	.175
Weithoff	Taunton	25	13	0	0	.167
Pettinger	Brockton	22	7	2	0	.148
Wich	Brockton, Pawtucket	23	6	0	1	.134
Knorr	Pawtucket	27	7	0	1	.108
McGamwell	Taunton	15	4	1	0	.070

The percentage figures of the fielding statistics of the league—the put outs, assists and errors being superfluous—are given below:

CATCHERS.

Name and Club.	Games.	Per cent.	Name and Club.	Games.	Per cent.
Crisham, Newport	102	.961	J. Connor, Fall River	15	.941
Murphy, New Bedford	74	.951	Buelow, Pawtucket	84	.938
Shea, Brockton	74	.949	Burke, Taunton	60	.934
Rollins, Brockton	84	.946	McManus, Fall River	59	.934
Stanhope, Taunton, N. Bed.	58	.943	Rupert, Fall River	24	.898

PITCHERS.

Name and Club.	Games.	Per cent.	Name and Club.	Games.	Per cent.
Sechrist, New Bedford	33	.997	McKenna, Brockton	40	.926
Weithoff, Taunton	22	.976	Hawley, Newport	38	.925
Pettinger, Brockton	22	.969	Cronin, Fall River	17	.923
Knorr, Pawtucket	27	.965	Gerry, Fall River	14	.917
Foley, Newport	33	.959	Miller, Fall River	19	.900
McCafferty, Pawtucket	28	.958	McDougall, Taunton	38	.895
Todd, Pawtucket	36	.951	McGamwell, Taunton	15	.870
Gallagher, Newport	35	.950	Anderson, New Bedford	28	.833
Flanagan, F. River, N. Bed.	40	.948	Norcom, Fall River	15	.828
Day, New Bedford	39	.929	Cook, Fall River	11	.762

FIRST BASEMEN.

Name and Club.	Games.	Per cent.	Name and Club.	Games.	Per cent.
Beaumont, Pawtucket	107	.989	Wise, Fall River	33	.974
R. Connor, Fall River	47	.982	Tighe, Pawtucket	97	.973
Birmingham, F.R., Brock.	52	.977	Kreig, Brockton	75	.968
Kelley, Newport	108	.977	Wiley, Taunton	15	.955
Irwin, Taunton	88	.976			

SECOND BASEMEN.

Name and Club.	Games.	Per cent.	Name and Club.	Games.	Per cent.
Grant, Newport	21	.968	R. Moore, Taunton	46	.927
Stouch, Pawtucket	99	.958	W Delaney, Taunton	57	.917
Smith, Fall River	41	.940	Gochnaur, Brockton	79	.903
Mills, Newport	75	.939	McDermott, New Bedford	28	.902
Davis, New Bedford	52	.937	Hickey, Brockton	25	.898
Gilbert, Fall River	50	.935	Doe, Fall River	15	.845

THIRD BASEMEN.

Name and Club.	Games.	Per cent.	Name and Club.	Games.	Per cent.
Coughlin, Pawtucket	106	.942	Magoon, Brockton	107	.881
Ellis, N. Bedford, Newport	83	.908	G. Moore, Taunton	102	.876
Callopy, New Bedford	46	.888	Dinsmore, Newport	69	.862
Kuhns, Fall River	21	.884	Cavanaugh, Fall River	48	.848
Delehanty, Fall River	25	.882			

SHORTSTOPS.

Name and Club.	Games.	Per cent.	Name and Club.	Games.	Per cent.
Hall, New Bedford	35	.919	Glenn, New Bedford	39	.854
Bean, Newport	97	.905	Sheckard, Brockton	59	.853
Reilly, Fall River	102	.900	Harrington, Taunton	97	.815
Moss, Pawtucket	76	.894	Cavanaugh, Brockton	33	.792

A. L. C. Atkinson Ludlow McGee   Anderson Sheehan Heard
Lunn   Condon Watkins (Coach) Wehrle McMurray Keith
                  Sullivan   Cooley   Miller   Butler Cartwright

UNIVERSITY OF MICHIGAN BASE BALL TEAM, 1897.

Hall Cohen (Coach) Krug Nott (Coach) Hennessey Chesebrough Sims
McLaren Kuster Kaarsburg Elston (Capt.) Wheeler Hoag Foster
Sykes Mascot

UNIVERSITY OF CALIFORNIA TEAM—INTERCOLLEGIATE CHAMPIONS, 1897.

STANFORD UNIVERSITY BASE BALL TEAM, 1897.

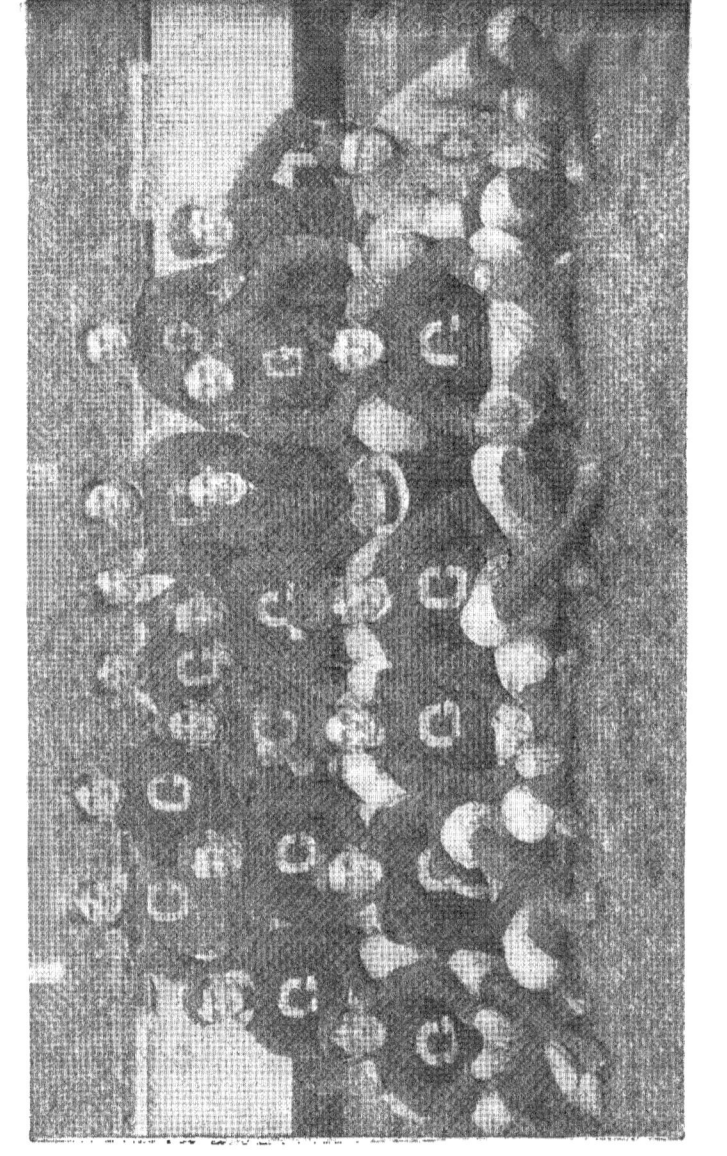

WILLIAMS COLLEGE BASE BALL TEAM—CHAMPIONS INTERCOLLEGIATE ASSOCIATION OF NEW ENGLAND.

Peirce   W. Fauver   Clancy   G. Fauver   Winter   Angus
         Sherrill   C. Fauver   Woodworth   Miller
              Meriam
OBERLIN COLLEGE BASE BALL TEAM, 1897.

Cleaves (Scorer) Baxter (Mgr.) Libby Greenlaw
Stanwood Bodge Haines (Capt.) Hull Wilson (Sub.)
Bacon Smith (Sub.) Clarke Gould (Sub.)
BOWDOIN COLLEGE BASE BALL TEAM, 1897.

Nelson (Asst. Mgr.) Steptoe Trinkle (Mgr.) White Coogan (Coach) Huger
O'Brien Collier Mellor Bonney (Capt.) McNair Martin
Nalle Hoxton Hunt O'Keffe Brock

UNIVERSITY OF VIRGINIA BASE BALL TEAM

BASE BALL GUIDE.

LEFT FIELDERS.

Name and Club.	Games.	Per cent.	Name and Club.	Games.	Per cent.
Weisbecker, Pawtucket	95	.934	Ladd, Fall River	103	.919
Long, New Bedford	77	.933	Herwig, Taunton	27	.914
Simon, Taunton	77	.929	Pickett, Newport	95	.892
Nadeau, Brockton	102	.920	Sexton, New Bedford	23	.826

CENTRE FIELDERS.

Name and Club.	Games.	Per cent.	Name and Club.	Games.	Per cent.
Johnson, Taunton	33	.972	Henry, Brockton	105	.919
Sexton, New Bedford	35	.959	Long, New Bedford	22	.912
Hill, Fall River	61	.946	Leighton, Taunton	19	.875
Gilbert, Newport	104	.926	Hernon, New Bedford	34	.873
Whiting, Pawtucket	93	.924	Kelley, Fall River	36	.830

RIGHT FIELDERS.

Name and Club.	Games.	Per cent.	Name and Club.	Games.	Per cent.
News, Pawtucket	46	.969	Sheckard, Brockton	38	.897
J. Connor, Fall River	33	.949	Counihan, New Bedford	35	.882
Hernon, New Bedford	62	.946	Stephenson, Newport	47	.859
Sharrott, Brockton	53	.946	Fitzmaurice, Taunton	57	.857
Grant, Newport	49	.923	Leighton, Taunton	17	.857
Smith, Pawtucket	62	.905	Johnson, Taunton	42	.853
McManus, Fall River	37	.899			

The dividing of the fielding statistics into left, centre and right fielders is an improvement over the National League outfielding record table.

RECORD OF THE "CENTURY" PLAYERS.

Player and Position.	Club.	Games.	Batting average.	Fielding average.	Runs.	Stolen bases.	Sacrifice hits.	Times took bases on balls.	Times each struck out.
Sheckard, r. f.	Brockton	107	.370	.897	117	52	13	35	20
Stouch, 2b	Pawtucket	100	.340	.953	70	14	1	37	30
Beaumont, 1b	Pawtucket	107	.333	.989	100	32	10	25	10
Magoon, 3b	Brockton	107	.332	.881	85	27	5	50	22
Ladd, l. f.	Fall River	103	.331	.919	83	19	10	29	29
G. Moore, 3b	Taunton	102	.329	.876	65	20	1	28	23
Hernon, c. f.	New Bedford	101	.322	.873	87	37	8	79	17
Crisham, c.	Newport	103	.318	.961	63	10	1	15	31
Kelley, 1b	Newport	108	.312	.977	87	24	2	17	28
Henry, c. f.	Brockton	107	.305	.919	86	40	9	36	23
Whiting, c. f.	Pawtucket	100	.305	.924	84	20	9	32	28
Nadeau, l. f.	Brockton	106	.293	.920	96	15	4	32	24
Gilbert, c. f.	Newport	104	.275	.926	72	40	4	44	19
Long, c. f.	New Bedford	100	.274	.912	69	44	7	25	25
Coughlin, 3b	Pawtucket	107	.258	.942	70	16	2	26	17
Harrington, s. s.	Taunton	100	.247	.812	38	12	4	22	11
Reilly, s. s.	Fall River	102	.234	.900	58	17	1	41	25

The appended table is another special record showing what those pitchers did not only in pitching, but in batting, base-running and run-getting, some of which the official League tables do not show. Only pitchers who have pitched in at least ten games are included in the record:

PITCHERS' SPECIAL RECORD.

Pitcher.	Club.	Victories.	Defeats.	Per cent. of victories.	Batting average.	Fielding average.	Runs.	Stolen bases.
Pettinger	Brockton	16	6	.727	.143	.969	7	0
McCafferty	Pawtucket	20	8	.714	.224	.958	16	0
Hawley	Newport	26	11	.676	.266	.925	33	6
McKenna	Brockton	24	13	.648	.324	.926	31	5
Foley	Newport	21	12	.636	.688	.959	10	0
Miller	Fall River	12	7	.632	.226	.900	9	4
Moynahan	Fall River	19	13	.594	.255	....	12	0
Gallagher	Newport	20	14	.588	.134	.950	6	1
Wick	Brockton	13	10	.565	.108	.883	7	1
Knorr	Pawtucket	14	13	.519	.108	.965	7	1
Todd	Pawtucket	17	16	.515	.325	.951	18	5
Weithoff	Taunton	11	11	.500	.167	.976	13	3
Cronin	Fall River	9	9	.500	.188	.923	8	1
McDougal	Taunton	17	19	.472	.259	.896	24	3
Sechrist	New Bedford	15	18	.455	.183	.977	12	1
Flanagan	New Bedford	17	23	.425	.214	.948	10	1
Norcom	New Bedford	5	10	.333	.250	.828	19	4
Anderson	New Bedford	9	10	.321	.247	.833	12	0
Gallagher	Pawtucket	3	7	.300	.264	.853	18	7
McGamwell	Taunton	4	10	.286	.070	.870	4	0
Wilder	Pawtucket	3	8	.273	.344	.931	5	1
Gerry	Fall River	3	11	.214	.237	.917	2	0
Ashe	Newport	1	10	.000	.353	.913	7	0

The New Jersey State League, which began early in May, was disbanded on June 1, owing to the failure of the Bridgeton and Milville people to fulfil their promises.

The Buffalo team of the Eastern League on August 18 defeated the National League team of Cleveland at Buffalo in handsome style by 5 to 1, McPartlin pitching against the Cleveland pitcher, Wilson.

The Maine League ended its season prematurely on July 6, at which date Portland led with a percentage of .724, followed by Lewiston with .548, Bangor with .394 and Belfast with .293. The disbandment of the Augusta and Rockland teams in June broke up the League's circuit.

The longest game in the minor league arena in 1897 was that played in the Atlantic League between the Newark and Norfolk nines. At the close of the sixteenth inning the score stood at 3 to 3. In the next inning Newark scored five more runs to Norfolk's one, thereby winning by 8 to 4.

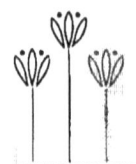 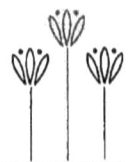

Western Association

THE batting, base-running and run-getting record of the Western Association for 1897, as made out by President Hickey—with unnecessary figures left out—is as follows:

Player and Club.	Games.	Runs.	S. B.	Per cent.	Player and Club.	Games.	Runs.	S. B.	Per cent.
Waldron, St. Joseph.	112	117	51	.353	Fisher, Cedar Rapids	124	102	21	.276
Lippert, Burlington.	87	92	76	.349	Seisler, Peoria	120	73	35	.272
Klusman, St. Joseph	118	95	10	.345	Wheelock, Des M's..	68	48	25	.272
Phillips, Quincy	106	95	40	.345	Purvis, Des Moines.	47	21	6	.272
Hill, Cedar Rapids..	120	89	87	.327	Donnelly, Ced. Rap's	57	29	14	.271
Dillon, Rockford	106	102	27	.327	Donovan, St. Joseph	119	80	13	.269
Kitson, Burlington..	58	42	20	.325	Quinn, Rock., Peoria.	99	57	19	.269
Wright, Peoria	121	90	36	.324	Roach, Peoria	44	24	1	.269
Anderson, Rockford	38	25	4	.328	Kreig, Des Moines..	25	21	2	.269
Visner, Rock., DesM.	60	56	11	.320	Burke, Peoria	116	100	41	.267
Mohler, Des Moines.	121	121	75	.318	Streit, Dubuque	58	25	7	.267
Pace, Des Moines. ..	68	59	22	.312	Sullivan, Dubuque..	124	69	27	.262
Lohman, Des Moines	120	91	48	.311	Flaherty, Pe., Rock.	105	78	38	.262
VanBuren, Ced. Rap.	126	123	52	.310	Ferguson, Rock., Q'y	114	85	44	.261
Frisbie, Quincy	122	114	40	.308	McGreevy, Quincy .	87	41	14	.261
Gallagher, Pe., Rock.	82	70	34	.307	Huff, Rockford	87	64	12	.260
Flood, Cedar Rapids.	119	102	38	.306	Smith, Dubuque	33	23	10	.260
Fuller, Cedar Rapids	124	100	82	.305	Francis, Peoria	21	18	7	.260
W. King, Rockford.	94	68	19	.305	Graver, Quincy	57	80	8	.259
Viox, St. Joseph.	115	130	46	.308	Dundon, Dubuque.	123	74	43	.258
Connors, Peoria	114	110	62	.303	McQuaid, Dubuque.	114	76	44	.258
Healy, Burlington	92	79	31	.299	Long, Peoria	15	7	3	.258
Esterquest, Rockf'd.	124	103	49	.298	J. O'Connell, Quincy.	124	70	26	.256
Kennedy, Ced. Rap's	122	119	43	.296	D. Williams, Bur'ton.	80	54	21	.256
Newman, Rockford.	110	113	55	.295	T. O'Connell, Du'que	46	18	5	.255
Kinlock, St. Joseph.	71	50	48	.295	McDougal, Ced. Rap.	37	22	1	.250
Wolverton, Dubuque	112	85	22	.294	McCready, Des M's.	120	74	25	.248
Sweeney Du., Qu'cy.	94	82	15	.290	Berryhill, Bur'gton..	98	52	24	.248
J. Williams, St. Joe.	121	109	25	.286	Underwood, Rockf'd	79	43	6	.248
Dugdale, Pe., Bur'n.	46	17	6	.286	Hickey, Des Moines.	119	87	41	.247
Hutchison, Ced. Rap.	126	102	37	.285	Mahaffy, Ced. Raps..	43	26	3	.244
Warner, Rockford...	95	72	86	.285	Violet, Rock., Bur..	121	87	55	.243
Truby, Rock., Pe'ia.	63	50	11	.284	Wilson, Des Moines.	40	18	5	.243
Hartsell, Burlington	20	16	3	.282	Collins, St. Joseph..	89	37	6	.242
Baer, Dubuque	117	104	26	.281	Hanson, Peoria	19	4	1	.240
Morrissey, Dubuque.	79	43	5	.278	McCarthy, Des M's.	46	87	12	.289
McKibben, Des M's.	46	50	82	.278	Risley, St. Joseph...	88	50	29	.237
Letcher, Des Moines	23	19	9	.278	Lutenburg, Quincy..	98	59	25	.236
Kane, Bur., St. J'ph.	101	69	29	.277	Cantillon, Dubuque.	89	52	10	.236
Andrews, Des M's...	95	74	28	.277	Sharp, Dubuque	28	22	2	.235
Cole, Cedar Rapids .	125	78	26	.276	White, Burlington...	84	46	25	.234

BATTING AVERAGES—*Continued.*

Player and Club.	Games.	Runs.	S. B.	Per cent.	Player and Club.	Games.	Runs.	S. B.	Per cent.
McCann, Burlington.	55	33	17	.234	Nonomaker, Du., Q'y	44	22	5	.207
Jackson, Quincy....	33	23	6	.234	Bubser, Rockford. .	22	7	0	.206
Oswald, St. J., Peoria.	107	95	34	.232	Sawyer, St. Joseph..	123	80	52	.203
Berte, Quincy.......	99	51	14	.230	Mesmer, Burlington.	45	19	4	.200
Meredith, St. Joseph	56	27	9	.230	Samuels, Burlington	31	7	4	.200
Coons, Burlington...	54	16	3	.226	Mauck, Des Moines.	50	12	4	.197
Butler, Dubuque....	38	18	4	.226	Babbitt, Rockford...	94	54	25	.193
Neville, Peoria......	21	15	5	.223	Pardee, St. Joseph..	27	11	2	.191
McCauley, Rockford	20	11	2	.223	Burris, Peoria.......	33	22	3	.189
Breen Burlington....	111	66	24	.218	Talbot, Peoria......	41	14	1	.186
Bradley, Burlington.	18	9	24	.218	Cooper, Des Moines.	54	17	4	.185
Freck, Peoria.......	15	14	5	.218	Monroe, Quincy	19	7	0	.171
Dixon, Dubuque....	46	19	14	.214	Bey, Peoria....... .	20	15	13	.166
Ebright, Peoria.....	17	4	2	.213	Sonier, Des M., Bur.	33	8	1	.161
Parrott, Dubuque...	15	6	2	.213	Carisch, Ced. Rapids.	25	11	10	.154
Hausen, St. Joseph..	27	24	4	.211	Rafferty, Bur., Qu., P.	26	5	0	.153
McCormick, Quincy	58	33	12	.210	Groves, Peoria.....	18	7	2	.147
Traffley, Quincy....	57	27	5	.210					

Waldron led in best per cent. of base-hits, Viox in total runs scored and Lippert in total stolen bases.

The performances of all players who took part in fifteen or more games during the season are recorded. The averages follow:

FIELDING AVERAGES—CATCHERS.

Name and Club.	Games.	Per cent.	Name and Club.	Games.	Per cent.
Dugdale, Peoria, Burlingt'n	43	.973	Lohman, Des Moines	111	.902
Fuller, Cedar Rapids.......	124	.957	Hausen, St. Joseph	27	.896
Sullivan, Dubuque	122	.952	D. Williams, Burlington....	66	.895
Traffley, Quincy...........	45	.934	Seisler, Peoria	28	.889
Collins, St. Joseph.........	86	.930	Raffert, Bu'l't'n, Qu'cy, Pe'a	25	.879
Quinn, Rockford, Peoria...	95	.920	Berryhill, Burlington	19	.866
Graver, Quincy............	57	.907	Messmer, Burlington.......	15	.823
Huff, Rockford............	72	.904			

FIRST BASEMEN.

	Games	Per cent		Games	Per cent
Kreig, Des Moines...., ...	16	.992	Berryhill, Burlington	28	.964
Klusman, St. Joseph........	118	.984	Purvis, Des Moines	47	.961
Lutenburg, Quincy.........	98	.984	Kane, Burlington	73	.959
Pace, Des Moines...........	23	.982	Kling, Rockford	75	.954
Morrissey, Dubuque	79	.978	Dixon, Dubuque...........	31	.951
McCauley, Rockford	20	.976	Wilson, Des Moines........	38	.950
Hutchison, Cedar Rapids...	126	.971	Huff, Rockford	15	.934
Wright, Peoria.............	117	.966			

SECOND BASEMEN.

Name and Club.	Games.	Per cent.	Name and Club.	Games.	Per cent.
Fisher, Cedar Rapids	124	.948	Wolverton, Dubuque	17	.891
Viox, St. Joseph	114	.946	Warner, Rockford	95	.884
J. O'Connell, Quincy	124	.936	Long, Peoria	15	.880
Mohler, Des Moines	121	.933	Ebright, Peoria	17	.878
Cantillon, Dubuque	71	.933	Neville, Peoria	20	.874
Truby, Rockford, Peoria	52	.904	Violet, Burlington	30	.868
Healy, Burlington	92	.902	Freck, Peoria	15	.838
T. O'Connell, Dubuque	30	.897			

THIRD BASEMEN.

Name and Club.	Games.	Per cent.	Name and Club.	Games.	Per cent.
McCormick, Quincy	54	.949	Dundon, Dubuque	42	.877
Esterquest, Rockford	46	.929	Flaherty, Rockford	105	.859
Hill, Cedar Rapids	120	.898	Sawyer, St. Joseph	123	.850
Wolverton, Dubuque	81	.880	Bradley, Burlington	18	.839
Ferguson, Quincy	50	.879	Hickey, Des Moines	118	.838
Burke, Peoria	102	.878	Mesmer, Burlington	20	.782
Berryhill, Burlington	45	.878	Violet, Burlington	20	.734

SHORTSTOPS.

Name and Club.	Games.	Per cent.	Name and Club.	Games.	Per cent.
Berte, Quincy	99	.925	J. Williams, St. Joseph	118	.865
Esterquest, Rockford	69	.920	Wheelock, Des Moines	63	.864
Breen, Burlington	111	.894	Kennedy, Cedar Rapids	121	.855
Francis, Peoria	15	.890	Babbitt, Rockford	55	.853
Parrott, Dubuque	15	.886	McCready, Des Moines	57	.843
Dundon, Dubuque	74	.877	Sharp, Dubuque	24	.827
Oswald, Peoria	97	.866	Samuels, Burlington	18	.808

OUTFIELDERS.

Name and Club.	Games.	Per cent.	Name and Club.	Games.	Per cent.
Newman, Rockf'd, St. Joe	110	.978	Baer, Dubuque	116	.901
Kitson, Burlington	25	.969	Babbit, Rockford	25	.894
Jackson, Quincy	33	.950	White, Burlington	84	.893
Cole, Cedar Rap's, St. Joe	125	.949	McCann, Burlington	55	.892
McCready, Des Moines	54	.937	Bey, Peoria	20	.892
Kinlock, St. Joseph	69	.936	Frisbie, Quincy	114	.891
Connors, Peoria	114	.933	McKibben, Des Moines	46	.890
Risley, St. Joseph	40	.927	T. O'Connell, Dubuque	15	.884
Van Buren, Cedar Rapids	122	.926	Phillips, Quincy	106	.883
Donovan, Rockford, Quincy	116	.923	Violet, Burlington, Rockf'd	69	.870
Ferguson, Rockf'd, Des M's	52	.921	Andrews, Des Moines	80	.869
Visner, Rockford, Des M's	69	.920	Donnelly, Cedar Rapids	22	.869
Flood, Cedar Rapids	105	.917	Letcher, Des Moines	23	.862
Groves, Peoria	18	.916	Lippert, Burlington	87	.858
Waldron, St. Joseph	112	.915	Pace, Des Moines	31	.857
McCarthy, Des Moines	46	.908	Dillon, Rockford	86	.853
McQuaid, Dubuque	114	.906	Hartsell, Burlington	20	.849
McGreevey, Quincy	27	.905	Seisler, Peoria	36	.846
Sweeney, Dubuque, Quincy	94	.902	Streit, Dubuque	20	.818
Gallagher, Peoria, Rockf'd	80	.902			

President Hickey sent in the best pitching table of any of the minor league officials from the West. Here it is in full:

PITCHERS' AVERAGES.

Player and Club.	No. of games.	Per cent.	Ave. games won per game.	Ave. runs earned per game.	Ave. bases on balls per game.	Ave. strike-outs per game.	Total hits by pitched ball.	Total wild pitches.	Per cent.	Stolen bases.
Pardee, St. Joseph	25	.640	1.74	2.81	4.76	11	1	.915	2	
McDougal, Cedar Rapids	35	.628	1.44	2.83	3.64	18	3	.955	1	
Streit, Dubuque	30	.433	1.42	3.79	4.27	29	7	.892	....	
Roach, Peoria	44	.568	1.44	1.58	3.04	16	2	.869	1	
Meredith, St. Joseph	41	.682	1.73	2.13	3.47	13	8	.884	9	
Carisch, Cedar Rapids	25	.600	1.19	3.67	3.31	17	13	.944	10	
Mahaffy, Cedar Rapids	40	.750	1.54	2.89	2.72	37	3	.905	3	
Mauck, Des Moines	44	.545	1.84	3.00	2.58	17	17	.942	4	
Kane, St. Joseph	18	.444	2.22	3.95	2.26	10	4	.914	....	
Sonier, Des Moines, Burlington	30	.583	2.12	3.01	2.62	28	1	.911	1	
Anderson, Rockford	27	.629	1.56	2.12	2.92	19	5	.908	4	
Burris, Peoria	23	.434	2.29	3.81	2.39	16	3	.935	....	
Underwood, Rockford	42	.547	1.74	3.20	2.97	22	10	921	6	
Butler, Dubuque	31	.419	2.21	3.33	2.58	7	6	.941	....	
Talbot, Peoria	33	.454	2.07	2.93	2.21	15	5	.901	....	
Risley, St. Joseph	33	.666	1.96	2.90	1.73	20	4	.966	29	
Smith, Dubuque	18	.333	1.80	3.87	3.74	14	4	.925	....	
Bubser, Rockford	16	.500	2.15	3.63	3.63	16	2	.921	6	
Cooper, Des Moines	50	.500	2.25	3.22	2.91	42	2	.918	4	
Kitson, Burlington	32	.437	2.04	2.59	4.81	25	12	.932	....	
McGreevey, Quincy	42	.523	2.38	2.78	2.52	20	1	.917	14	
Hackett, Quincy	39	.538	2.37	2.49	2.26	29	3	.902	....	
Coons, Burlington	38	.315	2.55	2.36	2.22	34	11	.933	....	
Hanson, Peoria	15	.333	2.00	1.84	1.84	3	2	.900	....	
Donnelly, Cedar Rapids	25	.480	2.21	3.36	1.89	12	8	.926	....	
Monroe, Quincy	19	.473	3.10	1.94	2.31	2	5	.948	....	
Nonomaker, Dubuque, Quincy	42	.547	2.66	2.72	3.63	12	3	.923	5	

The Connecticut State League.

One of the most successful of the State leagues in 1897 was that of Connecticut, and the six-club race ended with the success of Manager Jack Chapman's team, though he had the veteran League manager, James O'Rourke of Bridgeport, as one of his rivals. Manager Connor, another League veteran, being in the race with his Waterbury team. The race record is as follows:

Clubs.	Won.	Lost.	P.C.	Clubs.	Won.	Lost.	P.C.
Meriden	52	24	.684	Torrington	31	39	.456
Derby	40	31	.563	Waterbury	34	43	.442
Bridgeport	33	37	.471	Bristol	29	46	.378

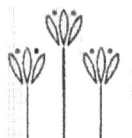 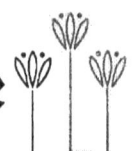

The Inter-State League

THE Inter-State League in 1897 was the only eight-club minor league organization, with one exception, that went through the season without a break in its organization. Moreover, its pennant race was the most evenly contested of any in the whole professional arena last season, only 147 points dividing the leader from the fifth club in percentage of victories. The League's statistics, as sent in by President Powers, are appended:

Player and Club.	Games.	Runs.	Per cent.	Player and Club.	Games.	Runs.	Per cent.
Platt, Dayton	11	10	.439	Paterson, Youngstown.	90	47	.305
Hoffmeister, Springf'd.	61	55	.413	Grafflus, New Castle...	85	61	.304
Myers, Toledo	126	114	.411	O'Brien, Wheeling	81	46	.303
Flick, Dayton	126	135	.386	Youngman, Dayton....	10	3	.303
McKevitt, Fort Wayne	103	108	.351	Welsh, Ft. Wayne, M..	19	15	.303
Lytle, Wheel'g, N. C..	90	46	.350	Cargo, Dayton	66	40	.302
Kihm, Fort Wayne	124	129	.350	Woodruff, N. C.,M	15	16	.302
Katz, Mansfield	98	127	.348	Torreyson, S'd,N.C,W.	85	69	.301
Beck, Toledo	119	122	.343	Brown, Dayton	23	17	.300
Burke, Mansfield	45	50	.338	Taylor, Wheeling	111	67	.300
Hartman, Toledo	126	152	.336	Reisling, Wheeling, Y.	29	10	.300
Frank, Dayton	41	45	.335	Rhinehart, Spr'd, N.C.	71	44	.298
J. Reiman, Dayton	126	124	.335	B. Miller, New Castle.	125	119	.298
Sharp, Fort Wayne	84	58	.335	W. Campbell, Wheel'g.	53	24	.298
Gilks, Toledo	126	109	.333	Wetzel, Dayton	67	69	.298
Hickman, New Castle.	26	10	.333	Smith, Toledo	127	123	.297
Lynch, Mansfield	85	104	.331	Whaley, Wheeling	35	28	.297
Cooke, Fort Wayne	112	105	.328	Outcalt, Mansfield	18	13	.294
Werrick, Mansfield	93	97	.328	McDonough, Toledo...	29	22	.292
Babb, Fort Wayne	109	101	.322	Farrell, Springfield	113	102	.291
Morrissey, Fort Wayne	12	12	.322	O'Meara, Fort Wayne..	74	76	.291
Van Geisen, Mansfield.	24	11	.318	Sipler, Mansfield	48	48	.290
Langsford, Toledo	80	62	.318	Ashenback, Springfield	67	50	.289
T. Campbell, Ft.Wayne	99	72	.318	Fitch, Fort Wayne	92	58	.289
Rosebraugh, Dayton	33	6	.317	Ross, New Castle	126	87	.288
Parker, Fort Wayne	26	23	.316	G. Reiman, Dayton	47	35	.288
Whistler, Springfield..	67	53	.313	Nattress, New Castle..	125	108	.287
Martin, Sprinf'd, Day.	98	82	.312	Coggswell, Springfield.	35	21	.286
Fleming, New Castle..	124	78	.312	Curran, Springfield	56	48	.286
A. Robinson, Wheel'g.	43	31	.311	Greenwald, Dayton	99	69	.284
Steen, Youngstown	121	76	.309	Brodie, Youngstown	62	24	.284
Rickert, Youngstown .	103	83	.308	Ferguson, Toledo	33	30	.280
Somers, Mansf'ld, N.C.	106	62	.308	Bullock, Wheeling	12	6	.279
Latham, Mansfield	91	115	.305	La Rotf, Dayton	34	23	.278
Mangan, Mansfield, D.	105	104	.305	Musser, Youngstown .	107	76	.278

BATTING AVERAGES—Continued.

Player and Club.	Games.	Runs.	Per cent.	Player and Club.	Games.	Runs.	Per cent.
Shay, Wheeling	85	24	.278	Williams, Springfield	17	5	.230
Cooper, Youngstown	123	100	.277	McGinniss, Wheeling	55	36	.228
Tate, New Castle	70	39	.274	Kimball, N. C., Y	20	9	.222
J. Robinson, F.W,Sp,M	111	73	.273	Deisel, Wheeling	28	8	.222
Curtis, Wheeling	43	29	.273	Whitridge, Springfield	15	9	.218
Coyle, Wheeling	65	33	.272	Beadle, Mansfield	13	3	.216
Grant, Dayton, Mans	34	23	.271	Rupert, Springfield	36	13	.216
Kuhn, Springfield	104	55	.271	Strouthers, Mansfield	27	15	.216
Zinrain, Youngstown	117	49	.270	Blue, Toledo	26	22	.213
Miles, Springfield	61	47	.268	Berry, Youngstown	126	53	.212
Hogan, Dayton	103	95	.267	Cavanaugh, Springfield	14	6	.211
Royce, Youngstown	32	11	.265	Toft, Wheeling	39	17	.211
Poole, Springfield	25	10	.263	Armor, Dayton	19	14	.211
Bradley, Wheeling	57	38	.261	Smith, New Castle	44	13	.209
Donohue, Wheeling	27	14	.260	Weand, Dayton	53	34	.209
Messett, Wheeling	97	47	.260	Stoltz, Mansfield	15	8	.204
Reilly, Springfield	59	45	.259	Garvey, Wheeling, Y	47	14	.203
Lyons, W., Youngst'n	125	100	.258	Jordan, Youngstown	54	23	.203
Vetters, Wheeling	97	51	.257	Darby, Ft.Wayne, Tol.	26	16	.200
Hollowell, N. C. & W	18	1	.255	Stivick, Springfield	85	29	.200
Eggert, Toledo, Mans.	87	17	.255	Keenan, Toledo	40	31	.198
Hewitt, New Castle	36	14	.252	Kelb, Toledo	27	21	.197
A. Miller, Wheeling	34	13	.252	Carroll, Mansfield, W	58	61	.183
Arthur, Toledo	118	74	.252	Wolover, Springfield	12	6	.178
Russell, New Castle	155	65	.250	McNichol, Toledo	18	8	.176
Francis, Mansfield	48	42	.246	Easton, Wheeling	21	12	.169
McShan, Dayton	42	24	.242	Allowell, Fort Wayne	12	8	.167
Herr, Fort Wayne	36	16	.240	Brown, Youngstown	10	2	.167
Haggerty, Fort Wayne	37	32	.240	Madden, Springfield	16	6	.162
Kelner, Dayton	31	22	.239	Woodlock, Springfield	56	26	.158
Hassamaer, Toledo	98	70	.236	Minnehan, Fort Wayne	32	16	.156
Daly, Mansfield, Wh'g.	12	7	.234	Severs, Fort Wayne	20	4	.107
Ely, Mansfield	51	25	.233	Dolan, Springfield	12	1	.098
Donovan, Toledo	52	26	.233	Hughes, Mansfield	10	2	.086
Beam, Mansfield	10	6	.232				

The fielding statistics are as follows:

FIRST BASEMEN.

Name.	Games.	Per cent.	Name.	Games.	Per cent.
Royce	30	.980	J. Reiman	126	.980
O'Brien	81	.984	Curran	56	.965
Myers	116	.981	Patterson	90	.956
Kihm	124	.981	Latham	91	.958
Russell	126	.981	Strouthers	27	.934
Whistler	57	.980			

SECOND BASEMEN.

Name.	Games.	Per cent.	Name.	Games.	Per cent.
Werrick	92	.939	Woodlock	56	.913
Miller	126	.928	Grant	34	.901
Wetzel	67	.926	Miles	61	.898
Sharp	84	.922	Bradley	47	.893
Kuhn	45	.919	Coyle	16	.886
Reiman	51	.917	Whaley	85	.879
Beck	100	.917	Haggerty	87	.877
Musser	107	.916			

THIRD BASEMEN.

Name.	Games.	Per cent.	Name.	Games.	Per cent.
Werrick	22	.921	Hoffmeister	61	.862
Hassamaer	88	.911	Reilly	21	.856
Cargo	66	.909	McDonough	29	.853
Lyons	125	.902	Shay	35	.821
McShan	42	.882	Taylor	17	.817
Babb	109	.881	Carroll	28	.810
Ross	126	.864	Eggert	26	.776
Burke	45	.862			

SHORTSTOPS.

Name.	Games.	Per cent.	Name.	Games.	Per cent.
Kuhn	59	.950	Berry	126	.868
Fitch	92	.922	Mangan	92	.866
Francis	48	.893	Farrell	16	.884
Langsford	80	.890	Taylor	94	.817
Cook	30	.879	La Rott	34	.776
Nattress	125	.872	Deisel	28	.750

OUTFIELDERS.

Name.	Games.	Per cent.	Name.	Games.	Per cent.
A. Miller	34	.965	Cook	77	.907
W. Campbell	26	.958	Cooper	123	.902
T. Campbell	29	.957	Katz	98	.902
Gilks	126	.955	Robinson	43	.900
Brodie	20	.952	McGinnis	55	.898
Hogan	103	.944	Gill	42	.889
Steen	121	.944	Robinson	111	.889
Vetters	126	.929	Fleming	124	.886
Farrell	68	.927	Rickert	103	.879
Smith	126	.927	Hartman	126	.878
Aschenback	67	.926	Lytle	90	.871
Armor	19	.925	Tate	70	.870
Flick	124	.921	Brady	68	.854
Somers	106	.919	Sipler	48	.850
Curtis	43	.917	Coyle	29	.830
McKevitt	123	.911	Martin	87	.802
Frank	44	.911			

CATCHERS.

Name.	Games.	Per cent.	Name.	Games.	Per cent.
Arthur	118	.900	O'Meara	32	.945
Weand	53	.974	Greenwood	99	.943
Kelner	31	.974	Welsh	19	.925
Grafflus	85	.969	Rupert	86	.924
Donovan	52	.967	Williams	17	.920
Zinram	117	.954	Campbell	70	.920
Lynch	107	.954	Stivick	85	.884
Messett	97	.952	Toft	39	.856

The pitching records as sent in were rather meagre, the percentage of earned runs table being as follows:

PITCHERS' AVERAGES.

Pitcher.	No. of games.	Average of Earned runs.	Pitcher.	No. of games.	Average of Earned runs.
Alloway	13	1.00	Garvey	33	1.91
Platt	11	1.09	Bates	11	1.91
Emig	25	1.24	Coyle	12	2.00
Von Geisen	14	1.29	Jordan	42	2.05
Hickman	24	1.33	Keenan	33	2.15
Rosebrough	29	1.34	Madden	13	2.15
Brown	27	1.40	Campbell	32	2.25
Blue	54	1.60	Herr	28	2.32
Martin	11	1.64	Darby	34	2.55
Smith	38	1.71	Reiman	33	2.40
Brodie	42	1.74	Poole	24	2.47
Beam	16	1.74	Severs	15	2.47
Kelb	32	1.75	Ely	43	2.56
Whitridge	11	1.82	Ferguson	22	2.69
Cogswell	22	1.82	Beadle	10	3.00
Kimball	17	1.88	Wayne	10	3.00
Hewitt	34	1.88	Hollowell	10	3.50
Minnahan	34	1.89	Easton	10	6.00

The Arkansas League managed to get along up to the last of August, at which time its four-club record stood as follows:

	Won.	Lost.	Per cent.		Won.	Lost.	Per cent.
Little Rock	30	6	.833	Fort Smith	13	23	.361
Hot Springs	16	14	.533	Texarkana	8	22	.265

The Michigan League record on August 16 ended as follows:

	Won.	Lost.	Per cent.		Won.	Lost.	Per cent.
Saginaw	9	4	.692	Flint	5	6	.455
Bay City	6	5	.545	Port Huron	4	9	.308

The Ohio-West Virginia League disbanded on July 4 with the following four-club record:

	Won.	Lost.	Per cent.		Won.	Lost.	Per cent.
Zanesville	28	13	.683	Marietta	18	23	.439
Parkersburg	22	21	.512	Four Cities	16	27	.372

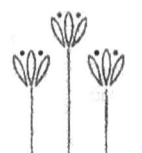 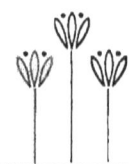

The Atlantic League

PRESIDENT BARROWS of the Atlantic League sent in a big array of figures in the way of Atlantic League averages for 1897, from which we have gleaned data for the appended tables, the first of which are those showing the batting averages, the run-getting, stolen base, and sacrifice hit records, as follows:

Name.	Club.	Games.	Runs.	Sacrifice Hits.	Stolen Bases.	Per cent.
Wagner	Paterson	74	61	0	19	.379
Gilroy	Norfolk	18	14	0	8	.373
Wright	Newark	130	144	2	20	.372
Cassidy	Newark	98	85	13	26	.372
Holmes	Newark	30	34	3	31	.361
Carey	Athletic, Reading	131	83	4	5	.351
Stratton	Reading	84	82	2	14	.338
Elberfeld	Richmond	136	107	6	45	.335
Yeager	Lancaster	66	39	1	4	.335
Burns	Hartford	126	82	1	32	.333
Hannivan	Lancaster	77	72	23	10	.333
Leidy	Lancaster	130	129	11	37	.330
Heidrick	Paterson	118	102	12	50	.327
Weddige	Norfolk	135	79	9	29	.326
Seybold	Lancaster	133	129	2	18	.323
O'Hagan	Newark	131	150	14	59	.322
Vickery	Hartford	71	34	3	5	.322
Delehanty	Newark	22	20	4	8	.321
Minnehan	Reading	104	59	6	14	.321
Sheehan	Newark	128	92	14	44	.320
Stocksdale	Richmond	32	16	3	3	.319
Keister	Paterson	132	110	2	34	.318
J. Rothfuss	Newark	90	85	2	4	.316
C. McFarlan	Norfolk	130	89	3	26	.310
Laroque	Lancaster	120	128	0	37	.310
Cogan	Newark	48	16	2	6	.309
Thornton	Hartford	131	82	8	27	.307
Ward	Lancaster	129	104	8	45	.306
West	Lancaster	35	14	2	0	.305
Cavelle	Hartford	120	86	10	71	.304
Robinson	Paterson	27	14	2	0	.301
Elsey	Richmond	132	108	8	27	.300
Hargrove	Richmond	129	96	6	43	.298
Dougherty	Hartford	134	97	5	45	.298
Kelley	Norfolk	74	48	5	22	.295
Weihl	Norfolk	134	88	11	43	.293
McVey	Athletic	134	94	4	26	.287

BATTING AVERAGES—*Continued.*

Name.	Club.	Games.	Runs.	Sacrifice Hits.	Stolen Bases.	Per cent.
Hardesty	Paterson	120	73	10	18	.284
Buttermore	Lancaster	133	146	4	39	.284
Hamburg	Athletic, Paterson	126	65	4	11	.280
R. Schaub	Athletic	142	81	6	13	.279
Lucid	Reading	12	7	1	1	.278
Leahy	Norfolk	132	72	22	19	.277
McIntyre	Reading	141	70	12	22	.277
Marr	Richmond	92	65	15	18	.277
Leighton	Reading	38	21	3	6	.276
Johnson	Paterson	23	17	0	4	.276
Haller	Paterson	34	26	3	5	.273
Smink	Newark, Hartford, Pat'n.	78	43	3	19	.271
Gettig	Newark	66	35	5	15	.270
Cargo	Newark	45	25	2	11	.270
Amole	Reading	38	10	0	0	.268
W. McFarland	Norfolk	36	10	0	2	.267
Madison	Lancaster	121	69	1	15	.266
Stuart	Newark, Richmond	126	75	21	37	.266
Wells	Richmond	100	31	11	24	.265
Raymond	Reading	74	32	1	8	.264
Henry	Lancaster	35	24	0	4	.264
Slater	Reading	130	86	7	44	.263
F. Schaub	Athletic	89	41	3	7	.263
Foster	Richmond	108	55	10	35	.261
Schmidt	Richmond	39	12	1	1	.260
Radford	Hartford	127	113	12	68	.260
Kain	Richmond	127	82	10	53	.259
Pfanmiller	Norfolk	49	25	2	6	.256
Wentz	Norfolk	135	68	16	16	.255
Spratt	Reading	134	88	7	18	.254
Gallagher	Paterson	16	6	1	6	.254
Wente	Lancaster	85	52	1	8	.254
Newell	Reading, Paterson, H'tf'd.	70	48	4	11	.253
Mack	Hartford	114	83	8	24	.252
Cote	Newark	26	8	1	1	.250
Snyder	Norfolk	111	44	7	10	.249
Schaffer	Norfolk, Paterson	71	43	4	21	.249
Ulrich	Athletic, Lanc., Richm'd.	84	49	6	12	.249
Roach	Hartford	132	62	8	16	.247
Daley	Newark	150	79	6	26	.246
Gastright	Hartford	38	8	1	1	.246
Smith	Norfolk	103	36	6	14	.245
Chesbro	Richmond	37	13	1	2	.242
Osborne	Athletic	36	15	0	0	.241
Hatfield	Newark	90	52	2	20	.240
Zearfoss	Newark	43	21	3	2	.237
Boyle	Athletic, Paterson, Rich.	30	15	2	5	.236
Flaherty	Paterson	45	22	2	2	.236
Heine	Newark, Hartford	47	38	0	17	.234
Fox	Athletic	116	45	1	13	.234
Clausen	Norfolk, Lanc., Reading.	37	15	1	1	.233
McDonald	Richmond	109	68	8	24	.233
Coleman	Athletic	28	8	0	1	.233

BATTING AVERAGES—*Continued.*

Name.	Club.	Games.	Runs.	Sacrifice Hits.	Stolen Bases.	Per cent.
Heydon	Norfolk, Reading	83	31	0	2	.232
Moran	Athletic, Newark, H'tf'd.	121	90	6	36	.232
Viau	Paterson	39	17	0	3	.231
Stimmel	Richmond	18	5	0	1	.229
Childs	Athletic	129	66	14	8	.229
Conroy	Paterson	36	18	0	2	.229
Hodge	Newark	27	17	1	5	.228
Jones	Paterson	39	19	3	2	.228
Hill	Reading	19	12	2	3	.227
Touhey	Paterson	81	36	13	3	.225
Steelman	Richmond	42	14	2	1	.221
Ames	Athletic	57	19	0	1	.219
Carrick	Newark	51	27	5	4	.217
Gallagher	Reading	49	20	10	11	.216
Smith	Paterson	92	51	5	12	.214
Roth	Lancaster	82	39	7	3	.213
Battam	Athletic, Reading	87	43	9	17	.211
Harley	Athletic	23	....	0	4	.211
Westlake	Paterson	89	53	4	8	.209
Leever	Richmond	43	21	4	1	.206
Gilman	Newark, Paterson	84	40	12	11	.205
A. Rothfuss	Newark	91	40	11	5	.201
Grove	Paterson	71	30	1	7	.201
Rainey	Reading	38	18	0	2	.200
Jordan	Athletic	20	7	1	0	.194
Barkley	Reading, Norfolk	65	24	6	10	.188
McMackin	Reading, Hartford	60	9	4	2	.186
Bowen	Hartford	39	9	8	5	.182
Newton	Norfolk	43	15	0	4	.180
Simon	Hartford	18	11	3	6	.178
Kinsella	Reading	37	10	2	0	.177
Garvin	Athletic, Reading	56	14	2	1	.177
Sprogel	Paterson, Lancaster	35	13	3	1	.172
Johnstone	Newark	37	15	2	0	.165
Cain	Athletic	33	9	1	2	.164
Turner	Reading	18	11	1	0	.150
Davis	Athletic	29	12	1	1	.146
Herndon	Reading	27	4	1	0	.128
Fry	Hartford	36	8	3	1	.125
Bishop	Norfolk	20	3	2	1	.121
Hepting	Lancaster	12	2	0	2	.106

From the above record it will be seen that while Wagner led in base-hit percentage, O'Hagan had the best run getting record. Moran led in stealing bases, and Childs in total sacrifice hits.

The fielding percentages of the League are as shown on the following page.

FIELDING AVERAGES—FIRST BASEMEN.

Name and Club.	Games.	Per cent.	Name and Club.	Games.	Per cent.
Wells, Richmond	83	.988	Laroque, Lancaster	112	.975
Carey, Athletic, Reading	127	.986	Slater, Reading	85	.974
Cote, Norfolk	15	.985	Cassidy, Newark	20	.973
Hamburg, Ath., Paterson	41	.982	Touhey, Paterson	47	.970
Haller, Paterson	34	.982	Smink, New.,Har.,Paterson	24	.966
O'Hagan, Newark	106	.977	Kelley, Norfolk	51	.961
J. Rothfuss, Newark	84	.977	Wente, Lancaster	26	.960
Thornton, Hartford	128	.975	Coleman, Athletic	20	.955
Shaffer, Norfolk, Paterson	70	.975	Newell, Read., Pat., Har	16	.952

SECOND BASEMEN.

Name and Club.	Games.	Per cent.	Name and Club.	Games.	Per cent.
Johnson, Paterson	23	.967	Gilman, Newark, Paterson	83	.930
Delehanty, Newark	22	.949	Cassidy, Newark	78	.928
Radford, Hartford	18	.941	Smith, Paterson	60	.927
Ward, Lancaster	129	.941	Childs, Athletic	124	.924
Wentz, Norfolk	135	.935	Stuart, Richmond	115	.922
McIntyre, Reading	134	.933	Gettig, Newark	18	.921
Mack, Hartford	114	.933	McDonald, Richmond	70	.908

THIRD BASEMEN.

Name and Club.	Games.	Per cent.	Name and Club.	Games.	Per cent.
Dougherty, Hartford	134	.900	Hannivan, Lancaster	75	.884
R. Schaub, Athletic	142	.895	Daley, Newark	150	.882
Wagner, Paterson	61	.898	Conroy, Paterson	17	.879
Weddige, Norfolk	135	.893	Spratt, Reading	29	.875
Minnehan, Reading	27	.889	Raymond, Reading	58	.860
Newell, Read., Pater'n, Har.	53	.886	Henry, Lancaster	35	.854
Elberfield, Richmond	134	.884			

SHORTSTOPS.

Name and Club.	Games.	Per cent.	Name and Club.	Games.	Per cent.
Leahy, Norfolk	132	.926	Conroy, Paterson	19	.888
Hatfield, Newark	91	.921	Spratt, Reading	22	.883
Radford, Hartford	119	.917	Gallagher, Reading	47	.873
Heine, Newark, Hartford	36	.917	Cargo, Newark	42	.867
Ulrich, Ath., Lan., Rich'd	53	.906	McDonald, Richmond	39	.851
Keister, Paterson	124	.899	Battam, Athletic	87	.847
Raymond, Reading	16	.898	Rainey, Reading	15	.854
Madison, Lancaster	120	.898			

OUTFIELDERS.

Name and Club.	Games.	Per cent.	Name and Club.	Games.	Per cent.
Smith, Norfolk	101	.986	Hamburg, Ath., Paterson	83	.943
Simon, Hartford	18	.973	Marr, Hartford, Richmond	92	.941
C. McFarland, Norfolk	129	.954	Leidy, Lancaster	130	.937
Hargrove, Richmond	129	.953	Holmes, Newark	30	.937
O'Hagan, Newark	44	.951	Smith, Paterson	19	.936
Harley, Athletic	23	.950	Sheehan, Newark	128	.935
Wright, Newark	130	.950	Heidrick, Paterson	116	.934
Stratton, Reading	81	.949	Cavelle, Hartford	120	.933
Hill, Reading	19	.947	Seybold, Lancaster	133	.933

BASE BALL GUIDE. 143

OUTFIELDERS—*Continued.*

Name and Club.	Games.	Per cent.	Name and Club.	Games.	Per cent.
Hardesty, Paterson	118	.932	Kain, Richmond	117	.906
McVey, Athletic	134	.929	Weihl, Norfolk	134	.900
Burns, Hartford.,	108	.924	F. Schaub, Athletic	48	.895
Grove, Paterson	71	.923	Elsey, Richmond	132	.898
Buttermore, Lancaster	131	.923	Slater, Reading	38	.892
Spratt, Reading	83	.919	Osborne, Athletic	18	.889
Moran, Ath., New., Har	121	.919	Kelley, Norfolk	23	.857
Gallagher, Paterson	16	.913	McMackin, Read., Har	18	.857
Gettig, Newark	15	.913	Minnehan, Reading	76	.852
Leighton, Reading	38	.911	Robinson, Paterson	27	.846

PITCHERS.

Osborne, Athletic	18	1.000	Vickery, Hartford	50	.920
Jordan, Athletic	18	1.000	Cain, Athletic	20	.919
Herndon, Reading	23	.976	Viau, Paterson	39	.918
Chesbro, Richmond	37	.965	Bowen, Hartford	36	.911
Gastright, Hartford	26	.951	Ames, Athletic	43	.911
Amole, Reading	36	.946	Leever, Richmond	40	.909
Yeager, Lancaster	47	.943	Cogan, Newark	34	.908
West, Lancaster	35	.940	Clausen, N'flk, Lan., Read.,	37	.904
Stimmel, Richmond	18	.938	Gettig, Newark	31	.904
Pfanmiller, Norfolk	37	.936	Johnstone, Newark	37	.898
Jones, Paterson	28	.936	Sprogel, Paterson, Lan.	35	.893
Garvin, Athletic, Reading	48	.936	Schmidt, Richmond	38	.890
Fry, Hartford	36	.934	McMackin, Read., Har	39	.886
Flaherty, Paterson	45	.923	Newton, Norfolk	40	.854
Bishop, Norfolk	20	.922	W. McFarlan, Norfolk	24	.851
Carrick, Newark	50	.920			

CATCHERS.

Barckley, Read., Norfolk	56	.983	Heydon, Norfolk, Read	76	.942
Westlake, Paterson	86	.975	Roth, Lancaster	81	.941
Wente, Lancaster	59	.974	Fox, Athletic	100	.941
Foster, Richmond	72	.965	Zearfoss, Newark	37	.938
Steelman, Richmond	29	.965	Touhey, Paterson	28	.938
Snyder, Norfolk	102	.961	Smink, New., Har., Pat	35	.936
Roach, Hartford	132	.957	Hodge, Newark	26	.904
A. Rothfuss, Newark	91	.953	F. Schaub, Athletic	36	.874
Wells, Richmond	17	.942	Kinsella, Reading	22	.860

The New York State League closed its season of 1897 on Sept. 11 with the appended record:

	Won.	Lost.	Per cent.		Won.	Lost.	Per cent.
Canandaigua	53	35	.602	Lyons	45	45	.500
Palmyra	51	35	.593	Cortland	29	36	.446
Auburn	50	41	.549	Geneva	25	60	.294

The pitching percentages of those who pitched in ten games and over are appended:

NAME.	CLUB.	Games.	Victories.	Defeats.	Per cent.
Yeager	Lancaster	37	28	9	.758
Carrick	Newark	42	31	11	.738
Vickery	Hartford	44	30	14	.682
Bowen	Hartford	31	20	11	.645
West	Lancaster	31	20	11	.645
Gastright	Hartford	22	14	8	.636
Cogan	Newark	32	20	12	.625
Jordan	Athletic	16	10	6	.625
Jones	Paterson	38	23	15	.605
Sprogell	Paterson, Lancaster	33	19	14	.576
Leever	Richmond	35	20	15	.571
Schmidt	Richmond	35	20	15	.571
Clausen	Norfolk, Reading, Lancaster	37	21	16	.568
Hepting	Lancaster	11	6	5	.545
Gettig	Newark	24	13	11	.542
Pfanmiller	Norfolk	34	18	16	.529
W. McFarland	Norfolk	21	11	10	.524
Johnstone	Newark	33	17	16	.515
Chesbro	Richmond	35	18	17	.514
Flaherty	Paterson	38	19	19	.500
Herndon	Reading	20	10	10	.500
Stimmell	Richmond	16	8	8	.500
J. Dolan	Lancaster, Athletic	10	5	5	.500
Viau	Paterson	37	18	19	.487
Newton	Norfolk	36	15	21	.417
Weeks	Paterson	11	5	7	.417
Garvin	Athletic, Reading	44	18	26	.409
Bishop	Norfolk	20	8	12	.400
Frye	Hartford	31	12	19	.388
Amole	Reading	33	12	21	.364
Osborne	Athletic	21	6	15	.286
Ames	Athletic	39	11	28	.282
Cain	Athletic, Paterson, Reading	18	5	13	.278
McMackin	Newark, Hartford, Reading	30	6	24	.200
Lucid	Reading	10	2	8	.200

Up to July 4, 1897, the Washington Territory League had roused up quite a reaction in favor of the game at Spokane. A paragraph in a Spokane paper of July 4 said: "Spokane is once more enjoying professional base ball. Not since the days of the old Pacific Northwest League has base ball been in such a healthy condition in this section as at the present time. We have a three-team league, known as the Kootenay and Washington League, comprising the cities of Spokane, Kaslo and Rossland. The season opened on May 24, and up to the present time everything has been moving along swimmingly. Spokane leads in the race at the present time with a percentage of .666, with Kaslo a close second."

 # New York State League

BATTING AVERAGES.

Name.	Games.	Runs.	Per cent.	Name.	Games.	Runs.	Per cent.
Householder	11	9	.428	Cronin	24	14	.284
Ryan	41	38	.383	Kanaley	18	10	.282
Duggleby	71	53	.365	Heine	23	21	.280
Genegal	86	88	.364	Frary	38	19	.279
Rhuland	81	86	.363	Meara	42	36	.278
E. Murphy	65	41	.354	Shinnick	84	81	.276
Twaddle	91	72	.349	Northwang	76	46	.275
Bernhard	39	37	.343	Stout	54	42	.275
Nelson	61	44	.340	Ketchum	49	35	.275
Ross	61	46	.336	Luby	18	15	.274
Croft	59	51	.333	W. Friel	37	20	.273
McNamara	39	35	.330	Vought	50	30	.270
McQuade	86	80	.329	M. Friel	26	16	.269
Frick	86	51	.327	Vorhis	10	6	.264
McFall	47	29	.347	Hart	20	14	.259
Shea	91	77	.323	Harris	72	72	.258
Larkin	22	15	.323	Dennis	70	45	.254
Ashe	16	14	.323	White	72	44	.250
McManus	68	52	.320	Ball	21	11	.250
Toman	91	102	.319	Young	25	7	.247
Gorman	83	63	.319	Berger	16	12	.246
Barber	88	78	.319	Mosier	17	8	.246
Carey	56	52	.315	Halbriter	44	23	.244
Keenan	17	17	.312	Moore	22	16	.235
Lever	83	88	.312	McBride	10	3	.235
Wittrock	49	34	.308	Dextraze	18	8	.233
Gannon	79	74	.306	Faatz	13	5	.229
Hayward	77	85	.304	Tull	54	30	.228
Moran	10	6	.303	McNary	80	54	.227
Cargo	66	55	.302	Russell	14	9	.226
Case	68	56	.302	Dannehower	34	8	.224
Cohn	81	73	.300	Roney	10	7	.222
Villman	37	21	.299	Wagner	29	11	.221
Mullens	20	13	.297	Sweeney	67	45	.218
Houlihan	31	25	.296	Miller	36	14	.196
Mitchell	20	11	.295	Dailey	58	27	.190
Connor	59	71	.294	W. Benner	23	8	.185
Freck	57	59	.293	Nugent	60	23	.185
J. Benner	12	10	.293	Milligan	33	17	.179
Sorber	83	69	.290	Sheehan	17	6	.172
S. Murphy	75	51	.290	Yerkes	31	10	.171
Townsend	61	41	.290	Pfrom	31	12	.170
Case	72	52	.289	Van Alstine	11	7	.161
Moran	76	56	.288	Moriarty	15	5	.138
O'Neill	50	28	.284	Heberling	11	5	.135

FIELDING AVERAGES—CATCHERS.

Name.	Games.	Per cent.	Name.	Games.	Per cent.
Berger	16	.990	Nothwang	76	.950
Young	25	.989	Frary	38	.945
Nelson	61	.985	White	72	.933
O'Neil	52	.960	McNamara	39	.908
Moran	76	.954	Moore	22	.907
J. Benner	12	.950	Case	72	.874

FIRST BASEMEN.

Name.	Games.	Per cent.	Name.	Games.	Per cent.
Luby	18	.983	S. Murphy	75	.963
Householder	11	.981	Ryan	41	.952
Townsend	61	.969	Genegal	86	.950
Sweeney	67	.965	Dailey	58	.950
Faatz	13	.954	Vorhis	10	.921

SECOND BASEMEN.

Name.	Games.	Per cent.	Name.	Games.	Per cent.
Shinnick	84	.929	Roney	10	.885
Stout	54	.910	Cohen	81	.864
McManus	68	.897	Ball	21	.862
Connors	59	.895	W. Benner	23	.839
McQuade	86	.888			

THIRD BASEMEN.

Name.	Games.	Per cent.	Name.	Games.	Per cent.
M. Friel	26	.900	Gorman	83	.853
Heberling	11	.892	Nugent	60	.817
Hayward	77	.883	Van Alstine	11	.780
Shea	91	.865	Halbritter	44	.772
McNary	80	.864	Mosier	17	.762

SHORTSTOPS.

Name.	Games.	Per cent.	Name.	Games.	Per cent.
Toman	91	.902	Freck	57	.860
Heine	23	.882	Ross	61	.859
Houlihan	31	.872	Cronin	24	.845
Cargo	66	.869	Keenan	17	800
Vought	50	.860			

OUTFIELDERS.

Name.	Games.	Per cent.	Name.	Games.	Per cent.
Carey	56	.947	Meara	42	.887
Twaddle	91	.940	Dennis	70	.884
Ketchum	49	.932	Frick	86	.879
Gannon	79	.930	Croft	59	.872
Case	68	.920	Dextraze	18	.868
Ruhland	81	.921	Ashe	16	.857
Harris	72	.919	Kanaley	18	.842
Wagner	29	.917	Sorber	83	.829
Lever	83	.914	Moran	10	.800
Barber	88	.914	Russell	14	.763
Hart	29	.890			

PITCHERS.

Name.	Games.	Per cent.	Name.	Games.	Per cent.
Villman	37	.964	Yerkes	31	.887
E. Murphy	65	.956	Miller	36	.887
Friel	37	.943	Larkin	22	.866
Tull	54	.940	Wittrock	40	.862
Bernhard	30	.937	Moriarty	15	.862
Duggleby	71	.919	Mitchell	20	.846
Milligan	33	.918	Pfrom	41	.837
Dannehower	34	.910	McBride	10	.825
McFall	47	.908	Sheehan	17	.781
Mullens	20	.902			

The only record of the pitching in the New York State League which has been published is the following earned-run averages:

PITCHERS' RECORDS.

Name.	Number of games.	Average runs per game.	Name.	Number of games.	Average runs per game.
Duggleby	32	1.31	Villman	21	1.95
Mitchell	15	1.46	Pfrom	27	1.96
Murphy	29	1.48	Moriarty	13	2.07
Larkin	18	1.55	Yerkes	25	2.07
Bernhard	34	1.61	Miller	33	2.09
Tull	24	1.70	Dannehower	30	2.40
Mullen	20	1.80	Milligan	27	2.55
Friel	27	1.88	McFall	37	2.56
Sheehan	17	1.88			

The Central League.

The Central League, which started well in 1897 with six clubs, including Henderson, Evansville, Washington, Ind., Cairo, Paducah and Terre Haute, closed its brief season on July 20 owing to the disbandment of the Washington club, when the other clubs, being all behind financially, concluded it was best to close up. The record at the end was as follows:

	Won.	Lost.	Per cent.		Won.	Lost.	Per cent.
Henderson	39	29	.574	Paducah	31	35	.470
Evansville	39	31	.557	Cairo	29	35	.453
Washington	32	31	.508	Terre Haute	29	36	.446

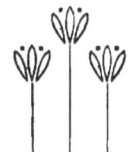 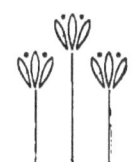

Maine State League

THE statistics sent in by the Maine State League officials for 1897 differ in their fielding records from those of any of the other minor leagues, as will be seen by the appended tables, inasmuch as they give the records by club teams instead of by the several positions. Here are the two records. No pitching records were sent in.

BATTING AVERAGES.

Player and Club.	Games.	Runs.	Per cent.	Player and Club.	Games.	Runs.	Per cent.
Hill, Belfast	18	23	.408	Fitzpatrick, Rockland	20	17	.278
Roussey, Portland	14	22	.408	Sheehan, Rockland	20	17	.277
Stevens, Portland	6	2	.400	Fogarty, Augusta	15	13	.277
Conroy, Lewiston	9	10	.400	Burns, Portland	14	12	.269
Callopy, Belfast	18	21	.383	Coburn, Rockland	14	11	.265
Delaney, Augusta	17	17	.379	Houle, Portland	14	22	.264
Nichols, Portland	14	24	.378	Sullivan, Lewiston	19	17	.260
Hayes, Bangor	13	6	.375	Carriveau, Belfast	3	5	.250
Dolan, Lewiston	19	27	.373	Deisel, Portland	14	11	.250
Polhemus, Portland	14	18	.361	Lezotte, Lewiston	15	12	.250
Veith, Augusta	17	20	.351	Mackey, Bangor	19	9	.239
Pulsifer, Lewiston	12	15	.346	Handiboe, Augusta	17	9	.235
Gilbert, Lewiston	19	24	.345	Viau, Rockland	8	4	.222
Murphy, Rockland	20	18	.345	Thorne, Lewiston	10	10	.220
Webster, Belfast	17	17	.342	Killeen, Lewiston	9	4	.219
Wiley, Rockland	19	19	.342	Quinn, Rockland	20	15	.219
McCarthy, Augusta	7	1	.333	Connor, Augusta	17	11	.215
McGuirk, Portland	14	18	.328	Gaston, Belfast	18	10	.211
Regan, Belfast	15	20	.327	Flack, Bangor	20	6	.209
Birmingham, Bangor	9	9	.321	McBride, Belfast	6	2	.208
Mazena, Belfast	18	25	.320	Mahoney, Rockland	11	5	.205
Chestnet, Rockland	20	15	.319	Kane, Belfast	13	11	.197
Coughlin, Portland	14	23	.318	Engel, Portland	6	3	.189
Edgar, Lewiston	16	13	.315	Dilworth, Belfast	3	0	.182
Burrill, Lewiston	7	9	.312	Butnam, Augusta	17	8	.181
France, Lewiston	18	21	.311	McKenzie, Bangor	17	11	.175
Bass, Rockland	6	8	.310	Gildea, Augusta	8	5	.172
Trainer, Bangor	17	6	.309	Casey, Bangor	15	5	.164
Dorsey, Rockland	20	20	.309	Cronin, Bangor	10	5	.147
Meagher, Bangor	20	14	.308	Kearns, Bangor	10	3	.146
Schrecongost, Augusta	17	16	.308	Donahue, Belfast	5	3	.143
Miller, Portland	8	5	.304	J. Kelley, Lewiston	5	2	.142
McDermott, Belfast	18	17	.295	Connors, Bangor	17	3	.115
Wise, Bangor	9	8	.289	C. Kelley, Lewiston	4	3	.083
Newell, Bangor	8	7	.286	Weeks, Augusta	3	1	.000
Hanscom, Augusta	17	19	.282				

FIELDING AVERAGES — PORTLAND.

	Per cent.		Per cent.
Coughlin, r. f.	.950	Miller, p.	1.000
Nichols, c.	.979	Burns, 3b.	.860
Houle, l. f.	.892	Deisel, s. s.	.881
McGuirk, 1b.	1.000	Stevens, p.	.900
Polhemus, c. f.	.969	Engel, p.	1.000
Roussey, 2b.	.900		

AUGUSTA.

Schrecongost, c.	.980	Fogarty, r. f.	.906
Butnam, 1b.	.972	Veith, s. s.	.863
Handiboe, 2b.	.934	Gildea, p.	.952
Connor, r. f.	.935	McCarthy, p.	1.000
Delaney, 3b.	.904	Weeks, p.	.167
Hanscom, l. f.	.905		

BELFAST.

Kane, c. f.	.909	Gaston, c.	.915
McDermott, 2b.	.967	Carriveau, p.	.788
Mazena, s. s.	.878	McBride, p.	.895
Callopy, 3b.	.863	Dilworth, p.	.889
Hill, l. f.	.833	Reagan, 1b., s. s.	.889
Webster, r. f.	.862	Donahue, 1b.	1.000

LEWISTON.

Gilbert, 2b.	.863	Burrill, l. f.	.894
France, c. f.	.878	Killeen, p.	1.000
Sullivan, 3b.	.843	Conroy, p.	.944
Pulsifer, l. f., r. f.	.897	Kelley, p.	.909
Thorne, c. f., 1b.	.908	C. Kelley, c.	.894
Dolan, s. s.	.877	Lezotte, 1b.	.970
Edgar, c.	.959		

BANGOR.

Casey, r. f., p.	.966	McKenzie, s. s.	.866
Mackay, c.	.955	Trainer, 3b.	.873
Connor, s. s., r. f.	.760	Cronin, p.	.833
Hayes, c.	.789	Newell, p.	.914
Flack, l. f.	.838	Birmingham, 1b.	.965
Meagher, 2b.	.911	Wise, r. f.	1.000
Kearns, r. f.	.881		

ROCKLAND.

Sheehan, s. s.	.827	Murphy, s. s.	.785
Dorsey, c. f.	.906	Wiley, c., 1b.	.944
Fitzpatrick, 2b.	.925	Viau, p.	.931
Quinn, l. f.	.926	Bass, p.	1.000
Coburn, 1b.	.925	Black, p.	.500
Chestnet, r. f.	.979	Mahoney, c.	.849

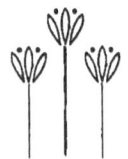 # The Texas League

THE Texas League in 1897 started in for a very successful season, apparently, their eight clubs opening the campaign earlier than any other of the minor leagues, as they played their first games on April 17, the National League not beginning until April 19. At the end of the first week the clubs stood in the pennant race in the following order: Denison, Houston, Dallas, Fort Worth, Austin, Galveston, San Antonio and Paris, the difference in points between the leader and tail-ender being 525. Between April 24 and August 11 quite a change of base occurred, the Houston club not only dropping from first to fifth place, but it dropped out of the league altogether, and this had a demoralizing effect, as on August 4 the Austin club disbanded. The Texas League had a double season in 1897, its first season ending on June 27 with the appended record:

Clubs.	Victories.	Defeats.	Per cent.	Clubs.	Victories.	Defeats.	Per cent.
San Antonio	44	23	.657	Denison	34	35	.493
Houston	39	27	.591	Fort Worth	32	35	.478
Galveston	38	30	.559	Dallas	28	39	.418
Austin	35	32	.522	Paris	20	47	.299

The Waco club took the place of the Denison club in July, the latter's franchise being transferred to Waco. Shortly after this change an incident occurred worthy of special note. While the Waco team was playing in Dallas the last of July, players Chiles, Kimerer, Bristow, Hardy and Alexander of Manager Drake's Waco team, "jumped" their contracts and left for the Arkansas League. These contract breakers should be left out of every minor league club team they try to get into in 1898.

The statistics of the Texas League for 1897 only cover the first half of the season, which lasted from April 17 to June 27, and the tables of averages in batting and fielding only include those of players who took part in 15 games and over, no player taking part in more than 73 games. The batting, base-stealing and run-getting figures are as follows:

BATTING AVERAGES.

Player and Club.	Games.	Runs.	S. B.	Per cent.	Player and Club.	Games.	Runs.	S. B.	Per cent.
Nance, Galveston....	73	69	17	.405	Jacobs, Paris........	49	37	13	.284
Chiles, Denison.....	64	56	18	.386	Alexander, Denison,.	63	47	20	.283
Weikart, Austin.....	66	55	10	.371	Kimmerer, Houston.	59	48	11	.283
Klopf, Galveston....	68	64	20	.369	McColley, Ft. Worth.	54	32	5	.283
Knox, Houston......	17	12	8	.359	Parvin, Houston.....	26	12	1	.277
Badger, Austin.	63	56	24	.352	Bammert, Denison..	71	66	16	.275
Cote, Houston.......	70	67	26	.341	Hill, Paris..........	48	26	8	.266
J. Hess, Galveston..	73	60	12	.340	Mulkey, Ft. Worth...	34	14	3	.265
Keefe, San Antonio..	71	66	6	.338	Pequinney, Ft. Worth	69	39	5	.265
Kemmer, Denison...	71	51	14	.335	Dowie, Denison.....	71	63	31	.264
Bailey, San Antonio.	71	55	9	.324	Pettijohn, Austin....	71	60	15	.264
Kohnle, San Antonio	71	75	10	.324	J. Partridge, P., A'n	33	20	2	.263
Martin, Austin......	66	69	18	.324	McCloskey, Dallas...	37	12	11	.261
T. Hess, Galveston..	69	65	4	.321	Boland, Paris........	62	37	6	.261
Isaacs, Fort Worth..	21	8	1	.319	Burns, Paris........	69	57	15	.260
Devinney, Houston.	68	68	37	.316	Dillon, Paris........	44	17	1	.260
Knau, San Antonio..	71	60	10	.316	Hayes, Houston.....	20	8	..	.258
Clark, San Antonio..	71	53	45	.313	Weyhing, Dallas....	35	12	1	.256
Weber, San Antonio.	65	53	15	.313	Sullivan, Austin.....	70	52	9	.256
Blackburn, Dallas...	57	40	8	.311	Aschenback, H'ton..	61	48	16	.254
O'Connor, San Ant..	70	64	22	.310	Reynolds, Ft. Worth.	70	60	11	.253
Stein, Paris.........	64	34	6	.307	McGann, Galveston.	50	28	2	.252
Goodell, Fort Worth.	26	15	2	.304	Page, Denison.......	71	39	18	.251
Nie, Paris....	36	23	6	.303	B. Partridge, Austin.	22	22	6	.248
Meyers, Houston....	70	47	11	.302	Chamberlain, F, W...	39	16	3	.247
Bristow, Denison....	39	27	6	.302	Nolan, Paris........	33	13	2	.245
Hobright, Paris......	62	44	13	.300	Becker, Houston....	63	35	20	.245
Cooley, Dallas......	67	52	15	.299	Beckwith, Dallas....	15	4	2	.245
Herbert, S. Antonio.	37	23	..	.299	Gilpatrick, S. Ant'io.	23	16	1	.244
Drinkwater, Austin.	25	15	..	.299	Reed, Houston......	66	42	22	.242
Morrison, Austin....	49	37	7	.298	Wolover, Ft. Worth.	62	38	6	.240
Turner, Galveston...	62	46	9	.298	Welch, Dallas.......	59	39	4	.239
Stanley, San Antonio	71	44	6	.298	Lawrence, Dallas....	70	45	14	.238
Hall, Dallas	69	43	9	.297	Miller, Denison.....	42	29	7	.237
Spencer, Austin.....	67	46	11	.295	Rose, Denison.......	17	6	8	.227
Hoover, Dallas......	69	60	26	.293	Mesmer, Austin.....	66	41	16	.225
Colliflower, Austin..	26	15	3	.293	Cope, Galveston.....	19	5	3	.219
Gettleman, F. Worth.	68	66	35	.292	McGinnis, Denison..	22	7	..	.217
Huston, Galveston..	73	57	18	.291	Underwood, Ft. W....	15	5	..	.208
Hill, Fort Worth....	70	30	3	.289	Peeples, Paris.......	47	23	9	.202
Weisbecker, Ft.W'th	53	30	16	.288	Beecher, Denison....	57	23	4	.197
Tackaberry, Ft. W'th	16	8	2	.288	Menefee, Dallas.....	69	50	5	.197
Pender, Houston....	54	34	15	.287	Sparks, Galveston...	33	15	..	.186
Mullaney, Dallas....	56	39	2	.286	Crowell, Houston....	28	7	1	.174
Pabst, Fort Worth...	47	36	6	.284					

The Central Pennsylvania League started in May, 1897, with six clubs, located at Demorest, Shamokin, Milton, Pottsville, Bloomsburg and Sunbury, and at the outset the former club on May 24 led with 1.000 percentage of victories, while the Sunbury's had not won a game. Of course, such a one-sided race could not last long, and eventually the League disbanded.

CATCHERS.

Name and Club.	Games.	Per cent.	Name and Club.	Games.	Per cent.
Welch, Dallas	54	.979	Weckbecker, Fort Worth	47	.958
Cote, Houston	70	.979	Miller, Denison	23	.938
Stanley, San Antonio	71	.978	Menefee, Dallas	22	.937
Sullivan, Austin	70	.969	Alexander, Denison	16	.928
T. Hess, Galveston	56	.968	Wolover, Fort Worth	52	.904
Boland, Paris	61	.965	J. Hess, Galveston	18	.903

FIRST BASEMEN.

Name and Club.	Games.	Per cent.	Name and Club.	Games.	Per cent.
Myers, Houston	70	.988	Kemmer, Denison	52	.971
Turner, Galveston	20	.983	Parks, Fort Worth	47	.970
O'Connor, San Antonio	66	.981	McColley, Fort Worth	54	.967
Mullaney, Dallas	56	.977	Huston, Galveston	37	.954
Weikart, Austin	66	.974			

SECOND BASEMEN.

Name and Club.	Games.	Per cent.	Name and Club.	Games.	Per cent.
Reed, Houston	49	.945	Dowie, Denison	31	.931
McGann, Galveston	24	.943	Weber, San Antonio	52	.922
Morrison, Austin	45	.937	Stein, Paris	21	.867
Hill, Fort Worth	70	.935			

THIRD BASEMEN.

Name and Club.	Games.	Per cent.	Name and Club.	Games.	Per cent.
Pender, Houston	40	.929	Clark, San Antonio	59	.868
Mesmer, Austin	64	.911	Devinney, Houston	30	.864
Dowie, Denison	40	.905	Klopf, Galveston	26	.861
Hall, Dallas	39	.900	Hoover, Paris	54	.833
Jacobs, Paris	25	.897	Cope, Galveston	19	.829
Pequinney, Fort Worth	69	.880	Kemmer, Denison	19	.824

SHORTSTOPS.

Name and Club.	Games.	Per cent.	Name and Club.	Games.	Per cent.
Klopf, Galveston	20	.966	Peeples, Paris	34	.863
Bammert, Denison	71	.926	Reynolds, Fort Worth	70	.858
Knau, San Antonio	71	.887	Spencer, Austin	67	.856
Hall, Dallas	60	.883	Devinney, Houston	39	.854
Burns, Paris	69	.865	Beecher, Denison	45	.845

OUTFIELDERS.

Name and Club.	Games.	Per cent.	Name and Club.	Games.	Per cent.
Blackburn, Dallas	23	.976	Gettleman, Fort Worth	65	.927
B. Partridge, Austin	16	.963	Hobright, Dallas	62	.919
J. Hess, Galveston	42	.961	Miller, Denison	19	.912
Klopf, Galveston	19	.961	Becker, Houston	63	.909
Lawrence, Dallas	51	.953	Page, Denison	68	.908
Chamberlain, Fort Worth	24	.951	Stein, Paris	39	.904
Bailey, San Antonio	71	.949	Cooley, Dallas	65	.903
Kohnle, San Antonio	71	.947	Turner, Galveston	43	.900
Pettijohn, Austin	71	.943	Underwood, Fort Worth	15	.897
McCloskey, Dallas	32	.941	Tackaberry, Fort Worth	15	.897
Kimmerer, Houston	33	.939	McGann, Galveston	26	.893
Hill, Paris	47	.939	Martin, Austin	66	.885
Nance, Galveston	73	.938	Badger, Austin	46	.880
Aschenback, Houston	61	.936	Alexander, Denison	47	.851
Dillon, Paris	20	.933	Nic, Paris	22	.801
Chiles, Denison	41	.932	Keefe, San Antonio	59	.883
Huston, Galveston	24	.929	Menefee, Dallas	37	.786

The following are the pitching averages sent us by President Ward of the Texas League. They give the list of pitchers who pitched in at least 8 games in the first completed series of the League's season of 1897. The percentage of victories figures were not sent.

PITCHERS' AVERAGES.

Pitcher.	Club.	No. of games.	Earned runs per game.	Per cent.
Hays	Houston	21	1.10	.919
McGinnis	Denison	17	1.12	.911
Herbert	San Antonio	24	1.17	.951
Drinkwater	Austin	23	1.22	.957
Chamberlain	Fort Worth	25	1.24	....
J. Partridge	Austin	24	1.25	.948
Huston	Galveston	17	1.35	....
Weber	San Antonio	8	1.38	....
Gilpatrick	San Antonio	22	1.41	.947
Stultz	Houston	12	1.42	....
Parvin	Galveston	22	1.45	.849
Nolan	Paris	26	1.50	.833
Sparks	Galveston	20	1.55	.951
Mulkey	Fort Worth	22	1.64	.971
Blackburn	Dallas	23	1.70	.970
Burris	Denison	8	1.75	....
Goodell	Fort Worth	25	1.76	.932
Crowell	Houston	24	1.79	.905
Kimmerer	Houston	12	1.83	....
Hardy	Denison	9	1.89	....
Isaacs	Paris	15	1.93	.847
Colliflower	Austin	22	2.00	.911
Hill	Houston	10	2.00	....
Weyhing	Dallas	29	2.07	.875
Brigance	Dallas	10	2.10	....
Bristow	Denison	26	2.12	.942
McCormick	Denison	12	2.25	....
Dillon	Paris	22	2.45	.900
Quigg	Denison	11	2.73	....

The Steinert Cup series for the championship of the Eastern League for 1897 was battled for by Toronto and Syracuse. Each club had won three games when a disagreement arose as to where the next game should be played, each one wanting to play in its own city. As neither side would yield, the series ended abruptly. After investigation, however, the Eastern League officials upheld Toronto and abolished all future contests of this description.

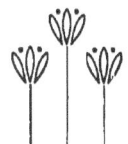 

The Canadian League

THE records of the Canadian League for 1897 present two interesting facts for the consideration of the club managers, and the first is that the club which won the championship had a team which excelled in base-running, in sacrifice hits, in run-getting, in fielding and in base-hits, while the tail-ender in the race excelled only in home run hits and in three-baggers. They were called a crack team of hard hitters, but in team-work at the bat they were nowhere.

RECORD OF 1897.

Clubs.	Victories.	Defeats.	Per cent.
Hamilton	34	22	.607
London	26	27	.491
Guelph	21	32	.396
Totals	81	81	

BATTING AVERAGES.

Name and Club.	Games.	Runs.	Per cent.	Name and Club.	Games.	Runs.	Per cent.
Conn, London	8	8	.471	McDonald, Hamilton	61	45	.272
Cockman, London	32	35	.413	Rodden, Toronto	12	9	.271
Busse, Guelph	28	25	.374	Lowney, Guelph	9	7	.270
Lauer, Hamilton	56	55	.355	Sechrist, London	56	35	.269
Phillips, Hamilton	58	51	.351	Bradford, Guelph	23	13	.269
Conwell, Hamilton	40	28	.345	McIlroy, Guelph	51	31	.265
Brown, Guelph	8	9	.344	Green, Guelph	24	22	.259
Gunther, London	51	44	.335	McDermott,Tor.,G.,H.	9	5	.259
McAndrews, Hamilton	35	19	.333	Moore, Guelph	17	8	.258
Jordan, Guelph	11	10	.333	Hardy, Toronto	10	3	.258
Snyder, London	19	19	.333	Crowe, Guelph, Lon	24	4	.257
Congalton, Guelph	46	35	.318	Dean, Hamilton	61	59	.252
Vigneux, Guelph	17	16	.317	Ward, London	51	41	.251
Thorp, Guelph	13	13	.311	Sippi, London	58	48	.250
Johnson, London	36	21	.306	Boyle, Guelph	21	11	.250
Reed, Toronto, Lon	43	26	.299	Blakey, Toronto	9	2	.250
Fischer, Guelph	22	20	.299	Roberts, Ham., Gue.	28	21	.247
Strowger, Tor,Lon,Gue	36	29	.297	Hickey, Tor., Lon., H.	53	42	.244
Connolly, London	13	11	.297	McDade, Hamilton	13	8	.242
Baker, Hamilton	24	15	.289	Cochran, Hamilton	33	17	.239
McCann, Hamilton	28	23	.286	Seifert, Hamilton	15	10	.222
Keenan, London	44	39	.285	McGinnis, Hamilton	9	6	.217
Mallot, Hamilton	34	18	.284	O'Connor, Guelph	20	9	.178
Sheppard, Tor., Gue	25	14	.280	Kershaw, London	23	11	.148
O'Brien, Guelph	42	28	.278	Murphy, Guelph	22	9	.141
Dark, Guelph	47	35	.276	Doty, Guelph	12	2	.135
Hoffner, Hamilton	59	36	.273	Carney, London, Ham.	8	6	.095

FIELDING AVERAGES—PITCHERS.

Name.	Club.	Per cent.	Name.	Club.	Per cent.
McGinnis	Hamilton	.933	Doty	Guelph	.853
Johnson	London	.930	Crowe	Guelph, Lon.	.825
Kershaw	London	.910	Hardy	Toronto	.821
Bradford	Guelph	.904	Cochran	Hamilton	.820
McDermott	Tor, Gue, Ham.	.892	Jordan	Guelph	.808
Carney	London, Ham.	.889			

CATCHERS.

Conwell	Hamilton	.951	Baker	Hamilton	.917
Snyder	London	.924	Vigneux	Guelph	.900
Reid	London	.923	Roberts	Hamilton, Gue.	.897
Moore	Guelph	.919			

INFIELDERS.

Lauer	Hamilton	.986	Phillips	Hamilton	.880
Busse	Guelph	.970	Ward	London	.876
Blakey	Toronto	.965	O'Brien	Guelph	.875
Gunther	London	.968	Green	Guelph	.872
O'Connor	Guelph	.944	Keenan	London	.858
Sheppard	Guelph	.935	Lowney	Guelph	.831
Dean	Hamilton	.925	Rodden	Toronto	.827
McDade	Hamilton	.922	McAndrews	Hamilton	.823
Boyle	Guelph	.921	Hickey	Tor., Lon., H.	.805
Connolly	London	.911	Murphy	Guelph	.805
Sippi	London	.902	Thorp	London	.797
Brown	Guelph	.900			

OUTFIELDERS.

Sheppard	Guelph	.935	Mallot	Hamilton	.857
McCann	Hamilton	.934	Seifert	London	.846
Congalton	Guelph	.917	Dark	Guelph	.835
Hoffner	Hamilton	.897	Scrowger	Tor., Lon., G.	.828
Sechrist	London	.893	Cockman	London	.806
McDonald	Hamilton	.881	Conn	London	.800
Fischer	Guelph	.862			

PITCHERS.

Name.	Club.	Games.	Per cent. of victories.	Average of earned runs.	Batting average.	Fielding average.
McGinnis	Hamilton	7	.714	1.42	.217	.933
Cochran	Hamilton	31	.709	1.12	.239	.820
Bradford	Guelph	14	.500	1.21	.269	.904
Doty	Guelph	10	.500	1.10	.135	.853
Kershaw	London	19	.473	1.68	.148	.910
Johnson	London	24	.458	1.08	.306	.930
McDermott	Hamilton	9	.444	1.11	.259	.892
Jordan	Guelph	10	.400	1.40	.333	.808
Crowe	London	19	.368	1.31	.257	.825
McGamwell	Toronto	6	.333	1.50	....	..
Hardy	Toronto	8	.250	0.87	.258	...

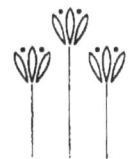 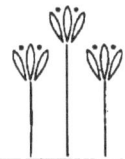

The College Arena

OF course the great attraction of the college season each year is the series of championship games between the nines of Harvard, Yale and Princeton; and the season of 1897 was made specially noteworthy by the reunion of Yale and Harvard on the ball field after a suspension of meetings on the field which should never have occurred. The triangular series of games began on May 15 at Princeton, and ended on June 29 at New Haven. Princeton had to play three games with both Harvard and Yale to win its series with each, while Harvard won two straight from Yale. Here is the record of the series for 1897:

Date.	Contesting Clubs.	Where Played.	Pitchers.	Score.
May 15	Princeton vs. Harvard...	Princeton.......	Wilson........Paine	6-3
" 29	Harvard vs. Princeton...	Cambridge......	Paine........Wilson	7-4
June 1	Princeton vs. Harvard,..	New Haven.....	Jayne.........Paine	2-0
" 5	Yale vs. Princeton	New Haven.....	Greenway..Wilson*	10-9
" 12	Princeton vs. Yale	Princeton.......	Jayne........Hamlin	16-8
" 19	Princeton vs. Yale	New York......	Jayne.........Feary	22-8
" 23	Harvard vs. Yale,.......	Cambridge......	Paine........Hecker	7-5
" 29	Harvard vs. Yale........	New Haven.....	Paine........Fincke	10-8

* Ten innings.

The summary record of the series is appended:

Club.	Princeton.	Harvard.	Yale.	Victories.	Per cent. of Victories.
Princeton...............		6-3, 2-0	16-8, 22-8	4	.800
Harvard................	7-4		7-5, 10-8	3	.600
Yale...................	10-9			1	.200
Defeats...............	2	2	4	8	

The full and complete record of the whole eight games of the season is as follows:

THE FIRST MATCH—PRINCETON VS. HARVARD.

The first game of the series between Princeton and Harvard for 1897 was played at Princeton on May 15. But for a wild

BASE BALL GUIDE. 157

infield throw and a passed ball in the ninth inning, the Harvards would not have scored a run in the game. The score:

PRINCETON.	R.	1B.	P.O.	A.	E.	HARVARD.	R.	1B.	P.O.	A.	E.
Bradley, c. f.......	2	0	2	0	0	Rand, l. f........	1	0	1	0	0
Easton, l. f........	1	0	2	0	0	Haughton, 1b.....	1	1	13	2	0
Altman, r. f.......	1	1	2	0	0	Beale, c. f	0	0	3	0	0
Butler, s. s........	2	2	2	6	3	Scannell, c........	0	0	9	0	0
Kelley, 1b.........	0	1	12	1	0	Stevenson, 3b.....	0	1	0	4	1
Smith, 2b.........	0	1	3	8	1	Burgess, r. f......	0	1	0	0	0
Kafer, c...........	0	1	3	1	0	Dean, 2b..........	0	0	0	1	0
Hillebrand, 3b.....	0	0	1	3	0	Chandler, s. s.....	0	0	1	5	0
Wilson, p..........	0	0	0	1	0	Paine, p	1	1	0	4	2
Totals...........	6	6	27	15	4	Totals...........	3	4	27	16	3

Princeton............................. 1 0 0 1 4 0 0 0 ..—6
Harvard.............................. 0 0 0 0 0 0 0 0 3—3

Earned runs—Princeton, 5. Stolen bases—Butler, Easton. Double plays—Hillebrand, Smith and Kelley; Chandler, Dean and Scannell. First base on balls—Off Paine, 4. Struck out—By Wilson, 3; by Paine, 8. Hit by pitcher—By Paine, 2; by Wilson, 1. Passed balls—Kafer, Scannell. Umpire—Mr. Campbell. Time of game, 1:50.

THE SECOND MATCH—HARVARD VS. PRINCETON.

The second game of the series—Princeton vs. Harvard—was played at Holmes field, Cambridge, on May 29. The score:

PRINCETON.	R.	1B.	P.O.	A.	E.	HARVARD.	R.	1B.	P.O.	A.	E.
Bradley, c. f.......	1	1	1	1	0	Rand, l. f........	1	2	3	0	0
Wilson, p..........	1	1	0	0	1	Haughton, 1b.....	1	1	14	0	0
Altman, r. f.......	0	0	3	1	0	Lynch, c. f........	1	0	0	0	0
Butler, s. s........	0	1	2	5	3	Scannell, c........	2	3	6	1	0
Kelley, 1b.........	0	2	6	0	0	Stevenson, 3b.....	0	0	1	3	0
Smith, 2b..........	1	0	2	3	2	Burgess, r. f......	0	0	1	0	0
Kafer, c...........	1	1	5	3	0	Dean, 2b..........	1	1	2	5	0
Hillebrand, 3b.....	0	2	4	0	2	Chandler, s. s.....	1	0	0	3	3
Sankey, l. f.......	0	1	1	0	0	Paine, p..........	0	1	0	3	0
Totals...........	4	9	24	13	8	Totals...........	7	8	27	15	3

Harvard....................... 0 0 1 0 4 0 0 2 ..—7
Princeton .. .. 0 0 0 0 0 2 2 0 0—4

Stolen bases—Burgess, Rand, Smith, Kafer. Double plays—Butler and Kelley; Altman and Kafer. First base on balls—Off Paine, 2; off Wilson, 2. Hit by pitched ball—Bradley. Struck out—Wilson, Altman, Butler, Kelley, Sankey, Rand, Lynch, Stevenson and Dean. Passed balls—Scannell, 1; Kafer, 2. Time of game—1:50. Umpire—Mr. Miah Murray.

THE THIRD MATCH — PRINCETON VS. HARVARD.

The third game of the series was played on neutral ground, the Yales placing their fine field at New Haven at the disposal of the contesting clubs. Despite the rain of the morning, nearly 4,000 people were present, and they had a base ball treat afforded them, as the contest proved to be close and exciting throughout, and replete with fine plays. The score:

PRINCETON.	R.	1B.	P.O.	A.	E.	HARVARD.	R.	1B.	P.O.	A.	E.
Bradley, c. f	1	1	3	0	0	Rand, l. f	0	1	1	0	0
Wilson, l. f	0	2	2	0	0	Haughton, 1b	0	4	15	0	0
Altman, r. f	0	0	1	0	0	Beale, c. f	0	1	1	0	1
Butler, s. s	0	1	1	0	0	Scannell, c	0	2	4	1	0
Kelley, 1b	1	2	13	0	1	Stevenson, 3b	0	0	1	3	0
Smith, 2b	0	3	2	2	1	Burgess, r. f	0	0	1	0	0
Kafer, c	0	4	4	2	0	Dean, 2b	0	1	2	4	0
Hillebrand, 3b	0	0	1	1	1	Chandler, s.s	0	0	2	2	1
Jayne, p	0	1	0	7	0	Paine, p	0	1	0	2	0
Totals	2	14	27	12	3	Totals	0	10	27	12	2

Princeton..................1 0 0 0 0 1 0 0 0—2
Harvard...................0 0 0 0 0 0 0 0 0—0

Struck out—By Jayne, 3; by Paine, 4. Hit by pitched ball—Rand. Bases on balls—By Jayne, 2; by Paine, 6. Wild pitch—Paine. Passed balls, Kafer, 1; Scannell, 1. Double plays—Jayne and Kelley. Time—2:00. Umpire—Mr. Miah Murray.

THE FOURTH MATCH—YALE VS. PRINCETON.

The first meeting of the Yale and Princeton University nines took place at New Haven on June 5, and lasted 10 innings, Yale finally winning after a most exciting contest. The score:

YALE.	R.	1B.	P.O.	A.	E.	PRINCETON.	R.	1B.	P.O.	A.	E.
Keator, c. f	1	2	2	0	1	Bradley, c. f	3	3	3	0	0
Farnham, l. f	1	1	0	1	0	Easton, l. f	0	2	2	0	1
Letton, 1b	1	3	13	0	0	Kafer, c	1	1	6	0	0
Greenway, p	1	1	0	2	1	Kelley, 1b	2	2	11	1	0
Fincke, 3b	2	1	2	4	1	Smith, 2b	1	1	4	5	0
Camp, s. s	2	2	6	4	2	Altman, r f	0	3	0	1	0
Wallace, r f	1	0	1	0	0	Butler, s. s	1	1	1	2	2
Hazen, 2b	1	3	1	5	0	Hillebrand, 3b	0	0	1	5	0
Murphy, c	1	1	5	1	0	Wilson, p	0	0	0	0	0
						Jayne, p	1	1	1	2	1
Totals	10	14	30	17	5	Totals	9	14	*29	16	4

*Two out when winning run was made.

Yale......................4 1 0 0 2 0 0 0 2 1—10
Princeton.................1 0 0 0 3 1 1 1 2 0— 9

Earned runs—Yale, 6; Princeton, 4. Stolen bases—Yale, 3; Princeton, 5. Double plays—Fincke, Hazen and Letton; Butler, Smith and Kelley. Bases on balls—Off Jayne, 3; off Greenway, 6. Hit by pitcher—By Jayne, 1. Struck out—By Greenway, 5; by Jayne, 5. Passed ball—Murphy. Umpire—Mr. James O'Rourke. Time of game, 2:50.

THE FIFTH MATCH—YALE VS. PRINCETON.

The second game of the Yale-Princeton series was played at Princeton on June 12, on which occasion the Princeton nine won. The score:

PRINCETON.	R.	1B.	P.O.	A.	E.	YALE.	R.	1B.	P.O.	A.	E.
Bradley, c. f.......	3	0	2	0	0	Keator, c. f.	1	3	2	0	0
Easton, l. f........	3	2	1	0	2	Farnham, l. f......	0	0	0	0	0
Kafer, c...........	1	2	10	3	0	Letton, 1b.........	1	1	9	0	0
Kelley, 1b.........	2	0	9	1	0	Greenway, l. f.....	2	2	2	1	0
Smith, 2b.........	5	3	1	2	1	Fincke, 3b.........	1	3	1	2	0
Altman, r. f., p....	0	1	1	1	0	Camp, s. s.........	0	0	2	4	0
Butler, s. s........	1	4	0	3	1	Hazen, 2b.........	1	1	1	3	0
Wilson, 3b........	0	0	2	3	3	Goodwin, c........	1	1	9	2	1
Jayne, p..........	1	0	0	2	0	Hamlin, p.........	0	0	0	3	0
Suter, r. f........	0	1	1	0	0	Fearey, p..........	0	0	1	0	1
						Wallace, r. f......	1	0	0	0	0
Totals 16		13	27	15	7	Totals.......... 8		11	27	15	2

```
Princeton.......................... 4  0  1  5  0  0  1  1  4—16
Yale............................... 0  2  0  1  0  0  2  3  0— 8
```

Earned runs—Princeton, 10; Yale, 5. Stolen bases—Butler (2), Smith (2), Bradley, Easton, Keator. First base on balls—Off Jayne, 3; off Altman, 2; off Hamlin, 7; off Fearey, 5; Hit by pitcher—Easton (3), Keator. Struck out—By Jayne, 3; by Altman, 4; by Fearey, 4. Left on bases—Princeton, 8; Yale, 9. Passed ball—Kafer. Wild pitch—Fearey. Time—2:50. Umpire—Mr. Campbell.

THE SIXTH MATCH—PRINCETON VS. YALE.

The sixth match of the entire series was played on the neutral ground at Manhattan Field, New York, on June 19. It was the third game between Princeton and Yale, each having won a game, and of course, it attracted a large assemblage of spectators. The contest, however, proved to be a one-sided affair, Princeton virtually winning the game in the third inning. The score:

PRINCETON.	R.	1B.	P.O.	A.	E.	YALE.	R.	1B.	P.O.	A.	E.
Bradley, c. f......	2	0	1	1	1	Keator, c. f......	3	2	3	0	1
Easton, l. f........	2	2	2	0	0	Hazen, 2b.........	2	1	1	1	0
Kafer, c...........	1	2	10	1	2	Letton, 1b........	1	2	9	0	0
Kelley, 1b	2	2	10	0	1	Greenway, l. f.....	0	0	1	1	0
Smith, 2b..........	4	0	2	5	0	Fincke, 3b.........	0	2	1	3	1
Altman, r. f.......	4	3	1	0	0	Camp, s. s.........	1	2	1	2	1
Butler, s. s........	2	4	0	3	1	Wallace, r. f.......	0	0	2	0	0
Hillebrand, 3b....	3	3	0	0	0	Goodwin, c........	1	0	8	0	3
Jayne, p..........	2	3	1	3	2	Feary, p....	0	0	1	4	0
Totals.........22		19	27	13	7	Totals.......... 8		9	27	11	6

```
Princeton......................... 4  1  7  2  6  1  1  0  0—22
Yale.............................. 2  0  1  3  1  0  0  0  1— 8
```

Earned runs—Princeton, 3; Yale, 1. First base on balls—Off Feary, 10; off Jayne, 6. Struck out—By Jayne, 7; by Feary, 2; by Hecker, 1. Stolen bases—Kelley, Butler, Smith (2). Double plays—Princeton, 1; Yale, 1. Wild pitch—Feary, 1. Passed balls—Goodwin, 4; Kafer, 2. Hit by pitcher—Bradley, Easton, Smith. Umpire—Mr. Campbell. Time of game—3:00.

THE SEVENTH MATCH—YALE VS. HARVARD.

The first contest for several years past between the Yale and Harvard nines took place on Holmes field, Cambridge, on June 23, the contest proving most exciting. The score:

YALE.	R.	1B.	P.O.	A.	E.	HARVARD.	R.	1B.	P.O.	A.	E.
Keator, c. f.	2	0	4	1	0	Rand, l. f.	2	1	0	0	0
Hazen, 2b.	0	0	3	2	0	Haughton, 1b.	0	1	8	0	0
Letton, 1b.	1	2	11	0	0	Beale, c. f.	0	1	1	0	0
Greenway, l. f.	0	2	1	0	1	Scannell, c.	0	1	12	0	0
Fincke, 3b., p.	0	0	0	4	1	Stevenson, 3b.	1	1	0	0	2
Camp, s. s.	1	1	1	2	1	Burgess, r. f.	1	1	2	0	1
Wallace, r. f.	1	2	1	0	0	Dean, 2b.	0	2	3	2	1
Goodwin, c.	0	0	2	2	4	Chandler, s. s.	1	0	0	0	1
Hecker, p.	0	0	0	1	0	Paine, p.	2	0	1	5	0
Reed, 3b.	0	0	1	0	0						
Totals	5	7	24	12	7	Totals	7	8	27	7	5

Harvard..................... 0 1 3 0 0 0 2 1 ..—7
Yale......................... 0 0 1 3 0 0 0 0 1—5

First base by errors—Yale, 4; Harvard, 2. Left on bases—Yale, 9; Harvard, 5. Stolen bases—Yale, 2; Harvard, 6. Sacrifice hits—Harvard, 2. Struck out—By Fincke, 2; by Paine, 12. Hit by pitcher—By Fincke, 1; by Paine, 1. Wild pitches—Hecker, 1: Fincke, 1. Bases on balls—Off Hecker, 3; off Fincke, 1; off Paine, 2. Umpire—Mr. Miah Murray. Time of game—1:55.

The last game of the Tri-University series of 1897 was played at New Haven, on June 29, in the presence of over 8,000 people, Harvard being the victor. The score:

HARVARD.	R.	1B.	P.O.	A.	E.	YALE.	R.	1B.	P.O.	A.	E.
Rand, l. f.	2	1	3	0	0	Keator, c. f.	2	2	3	0	1
Haughton, 1b.	0	0	8	0	2	Hazen, 2b.	0	0	3	3	0
Beale, c. f.	0	0	1	0	0	Letton, 1b.	3	1	10	0	1
Scannell, c.	0	0	14	0	1	Greenway, l. f.	3	3	4	1	0
Stevenson, 3b.	0	0	0	1	0	Reed, 3b.	0	0	0	0	1
Burgess, r. f.	2	1	0	0	0	Camp, s. s.	0	2	1	8	0
Dean, 2b.	2	0	0	4	2	Wallace, r. f.	0	0	1	0	0
Chandler, s. s.	2	1	1	2	1	Fincke, p.	0	0	3	2	2
Paine, p.	2	1	0	0	0	Goodwin, c.	0	0	2	1	1
						Sullivan, r. f.	0	0	0	0	0
Totals	10	4	27	7	6	Totals	8	8	27	10	6

Harvard..................... 1 3 0 4 0 0 2 0—10
Yale......................... 0 1 0 2 2 0 3 0 0— 8

Earned runs—Harvard, 1; Yale, 2. Sacrifice hit—Dean. First base on balls—By Paine, 3; by Fincke, 7. Struck out—By Paine, Hazen (3), Reed, Camp, Wallace (2), Fincke (3), Goodwin (2), Sullivan; by Fincke, Stevenson. Double play—Camp to Hazen to Letton. Passed balls—Scannell, 1; Goodwin, 1. Wild pitch—By Fincke, 1. Hit by pitched ball—Dean (2). Time of game—2:40. Umpire—Mr. Campbell.

ADRIAN C. ANSON

Copyright, 1897, by John Betz, Jr., Baltimore, Md.

E. F.   C.   Edw.   F. De Hass   H. R.   Jas. A.   J. W.   H. M.   Dr. T. Hunt   Col. J. I.
Becker   Von Der Ahe   Hanlon   Robison   Von Der Horst   Hart   Spalding   Pulliam   Stucky   Rogers
Jno. T. Brush   A. J. Reach   F. A. Abell   N. E. Young   J. E. Wagner   Stanley Robison   C. H. Byrne

DELEGATES TO THE SCHEDULE MEETING OF THE NATIONAL LEAGUE AND AMERICAN ASSOCIATION OF BASE BALL CLUBS,

Held at the Hotel Rennert, Baltimore, February 25-27, 1897.

WM. KEELER,
Champion Batsman, 1897.
JOHN A. MCPHEE,
Second Base, Cincinnati.

LAVE CROSS,
Second Base, Philadelphia.
OLIVER TEBEAU,
First Base, Cleveland.

THE LEADING PLAYERS OF THE LEAGUE, 1897.

PEITZ, Catcher, Cincinnati.

AMOS RUSIE, Pitcher, New York.

JOS. QUINN, Third Base, Baltimore.

BASE BALL GUIDE. 161

THE PRINCETON'S GAME RECORD.

Date.	Contesting Clubs.	Where Played.	Pitchers.	Score.
Mar. 31	Princeton vs. Rutgers	Princeton	Wilson....Deshler*	24-4
April 3	Princeton vs. Union	Princeton	Jayne.....Matcher*	46-1
" 7	Princeton vs. Vermont U.	Princeton	Jayne.......Miner	11-0
" 10	Princeton vs. Elizabeth (P.)	Elizabeth	Wilson...Higginst	14-5
" 12	Boston (P) vs. Princeton	Princeton	Stivetts......Jayne	8-2
" 14	New York (P) vs. Princeton	New York	Clark.......Wilson	18-6
" 16	Baltimore (P) vs. Princeton	Baltimore	Pond....Hillebrand	10-1
" 17	Princeton vs. Georgetown	Washington	Jayne.......Clancy	10-1
" 19	Princeton vs. Georgetown	Washington	Wilson......Walsh	15-7
"	Princeton vs. Virginia U.	Charlottesv'e		9-3
"	Princeton vs. N. Carolina U	Charlottesv'e		9-2
" 24	Princeton vs. Pa. State Col.	Princeton	Hillebrand..Nesbitt	11-1
" 28	Princeton vs. Lehigh	Bethlehem	Jayne.......Senior	14-1
May 1	Princeton vs. Cornell	Ithaca	Wilson.......Bole	6-2
" 4	Princeton vs. Lawrenceville	Princeton	Hillebrand....Arnit	15-1
" 5	Princeton vs. Lehigh	Princeton	Altman.....Carman	11-4
" 8	Pri'eton (1900) vs. Yale (1900)	New Haven	Hillebrand ... Dunn	5-2
" 8	Princeton vs. Brown	Providence	Jayne......, Brady	11-4
" 10	Princeton vs. Virginia U.	Princeton	Altman......Miller†	17-4
" 12	Princeton vs. Lafayette	Easton	Jayne.......Nevin	6-3
" 19	Princeton vs. Frank.-Marsh	Princeton	Jayne.......Brown	21-0
" 22	Princeton vs. Georgetown	Princeton		18-2
" 26	Princeton vs. Cornell	Princeton	Jayne........Bole	15-4
" 28	Princton vs. Andover	Andover	Altman....Hawkins	11-0
" 29	Prince. (1900) vs. Br'wn(1900)	Princeton	Angle........Brown‡	14-13
June 2	Princeton vs. Brown	Princeton	Wilson.Summersgill	23-10
" 5	Prince. (1900) vs. Yale (1900)	Princeton	Angle...Whittlesey	11-10

*Six innings.   †Seven innings.   ‡Eleven innings.

THE HARVARD'S GAME RECORD.

Date	Contesting Clubs	Where Played	Pitchers	Score
April 10	Harvard vs. Tufts	Cambridge	Paine.....Sanborne	20-0
" 12	Harvard vs. College Nine	Cambridge		6-3
" 14	Harvard vs. Pawtucket (P.)	Cambridge	Paine.....Donovan	13-6
" 19	Harvard vs. Brockton	Brockton	Paine........Hall	7-5
" 21	N. Bedford(P.) vs. Harvard	New Bedford	Flan'gan.Haughton	7-4
" 24	Dartmouth vs. Harvard	Hanover	Tabor........Paine	4-3
" 27	Brown vs. Harvard	Providence	Summersgill..Paine	8-2
" 28	College Nine vs. Harvard	Cambridge		7-3
" 29	Harvard vs. Dartmouth	Cambridge	Paine........Tabor	7-6
May 1	Harvard vs. Williams	Williamstown		17-15
" 5	Brown vs. Harvard	Cambridge	Brady.......Paine	4-0
" 7	Harvard vs. Cornell	Cambridge	Paine.........Bole	10-4
" 12	Harvard vs. Va. University	Cambridge	Fitz........O'Brien	9-3
" 15	Harv'd(1900) vs. Br'wn(1900)	Cambridge	McCormick ..Crane	7-3
" 19	Harvard vs. Williams	Cambridge	Paine......Plunkett	4-2
" 21	Harv'd (1900) vs. Yale (1900)	Cambridge	Cozzens...Simmons	7-4
" 22	Harvard vs. Pa. Univer'ty	Philadelphia	Paine......Dickson	6-2
" 26	Harvard vs. Amherst	Amherst	Scannell ..Johnston	6-0
" 31	Yale (1900) vs. Harv'd (1900)	New Haven	Whittl'y.McCorm'k	9-5
June 2	Harvard vs. Vt. University	Cambridge	Fitz........Miner	5-3
" 5	Harvard vs. Georgetown	Cambridge	Paine.......Clancy	9-0
" 8	Holy Cross vs. Harvard	Worcester	Linnehan....Paine	3-2
" 12	Harvard vs. Pa. Univer'ty	Cambridge	Paine.......Brown	8-0
" 16	Brown vs. Harvard	Providence	Summersgill..Paine	13-7
" 19	Holy Cross vs. Harvard	Cambridge	Linnehan......Fitz	6-2

YALE'S GAME RECORD.

Date.	Contesting Clubs.	Where Played.	Pitchers.	Score.
April 3	Yale vs. Johns Hopkins..	New Haven..	Wallace...Goodrich*	27-0
" 7	Wesleyan vs. Yale........	New Haven..	Townsend....Feary	4-3
" 10	New York (P.) vs. Yale...	New York....	Doheny......Wallace	11-3
" 14	Yale vs. Manhattan Col..	New York....	Hecker....Donovan	9-8
" 15	Yale vs. Georgetown......	Washington..	Feary.........Walsh	8-7
" 16	Yale vs. Hampton.........	Newport, Va.	Wallace.....Enright	10-4
" 17	U. of Virginia vs. Yale...	Charlottesv'e.	Collier.......Hecker	13-5
" 24	Yale vs. U. of Virginia...	New Haven..	Greenway..Plunkett	10-1
" 28	Yale vs. Amherst.........	Amherst......	Hecker...Johnston*	9-2
May 1	Yale vs. Brown...........	New Haven..	Greenway....Brady	6-2
" 5	Lafayette vs. Yale........	New Haven..	Nevins........Feary	11-8
" 8	Yale vs. Wesleyan........	Middletown..	Hecker...Townsend	10-3
" 11	Yale vs. U. of Virginia...	New Haven..	Hamlin ......Collier	5-4
" 14	Yale vs. Andover.........	Andover......	Hamlin..Stephenson	7-6
" 15	Yale vs. Brown...........	Providence...	Gr'nway.Sum'ersgill	6-5
" 19	Yale vs. Amherst.........	New Haven..	Hecker......Boyden	15-2
" 21	Harv'd (1900)vs.Yale(1900)	Cambridge...	Cozzens....Simmons	7-4
" 22	Yale vs. Orange...........	Orange.......	Hecker ..Westervelt	5-4
" 26	Yale vs. Lehigh..........	New Haven..	Greenway......White	22-3
" 29	Brown vs. Yale...........	Providence...	Sedgwick....Hecker	19-9
" 31	Yale vs. Edgewood.......	New Haven..	Hamlin.....Hinman	21-3
June 2	Yale vs. Holy Cross......	Springfield...	Linnehan......Ferry	11-5
" 5	Prince.(1900) vs.Yale(1900)	Princeton....	Angle....Whittlesey	11-10

* Eight innings.

CORNELL UNIVERSITY RECORD.

Date.	Contesting Clubs.	Where Played.	Pitchers.	Score.
April 22	Cornell vs. Rochester U..	Ithaca........	Stratton......Oatley	34-1
" 24	Cornell vs. Union........	Ithaca	Bole ......Thatcher	44-5
" 27	Cornell vs. Syracuse......	Ithaca	Bole.......Voorhees	7-2
May 1	Princeton vs. Cornell.....	Ithaca	Wilson.........Bole	6-2
" 7	Harvard vs. Cornell......	Cambridge...	Paine..........Bole	10-4
" 8	Newton A. C. vs. Cornell.	Newton......	Dowd......Stratton	6-5
" 10	Holy Cross vs. Cornell...	Worcester....	McKenna ......Bole	5-0
" 13	U. of Virginia vs. Cornell.	Ithaca	...............Bole	7-4
" 18	Cornell vs. Pennsylvania.	Ithaca	Bole........Dickson	6-2
" 22	Cornell vs. Michigan.....	Ithaca	Bole.........Miller	14-2
" 26	Princeton vs. Cornell.....	Princeton	Jayne..........Bole	15-4
" 27	Cornell vs. Fordham......	Fordham.....	Stratton......Kelly	13-8
" 28	N. Y. Univ. vs. Cornell...	New York....	Foster.........Bole	6-5
" 29	Pennsylvania vs. Cornell.	Philadelphia..	Dickson........Bole	8-3
" 31	Cornell vs. Williams......	Williamstown	Blair.......Plunkett	11-6
June 5	Lafayette vs. Cornell.....	Ithaca	Nevins.........Blair	5-1
" 11	Oberlin vs. Cornell.......	Oberlin	Faurer.........Bole	7-2
" 12	Cornell vs. Michigan.....	Ann Arbor...	Blair..... ....Miller	6-4

The Intercollegiate Association's Statistics.

The championship honors of the Intercollegiate Association of New England, which comprises the college clubs of Williams, Dartmouth and Amherst, were won by the Williams College nine in 1897, with Dartmouth second and Amherst third in the pennant race, as will be seen by the appended race record:

Clubs.	Williams.	Dartmouth.	Amherst.	Victories.	Per cent. of Victories.	Drawn Games.
Williams...........................		1	4	5	.714	1
Dartmouth.........................	2		2	4	.571	1
Amherst............................	0	2		2	.250	0
Defeats.............................	2	3	6	11		

BATTING AVERAGES.

Player and Position.	College.	Games.	Runs.	Sacrifice Hits.	Stolen Bases.	Base-hit Average.
Drew, catcher...................................	D	8	6	0	3	.419
Folsom, second base.........................	D	8	9	0	7	.350
McCornack, left field........................	D	8	11	0	10	.325
Crolius, shortstop.............................	D	8	5	0	6	.316
Tabor, pitcher..................................	D	8	8	0	5	.313
Heffernan, shortstop.........................	W	8	3	2	3	.294
Sullivan, catcher..............................	A	8	3	0	0	.282
Dewey, centre field...........................	W	8	3	1	2	.278
Rowe, centre field and first base........	D	4	0	0	0	.267
Goodrich, first base..........................	W	8	5	0	3	.257
Doughty, left field............................	W	8	4	0	0	.250
Ross, catcher...................................	W	8	6	0	6	.222
Tinker, right field.............................	A	8	2	0	2	.214
L. Hodgkins, third base.....................	D	8	4	2	1	.212
Johnston, pitcher..............................	A	6	2	1	1	.208
Drysdale, third base..........................	W	8	5	0	7	.206
Ashton, second base.........................	W	8	3	0	6	.194
Fletcher, third base...........................	A	7	6	0	2	.194
Seaver, right field.............................	W	8	3	0	2	.188
W. Hodgkins, centre field..................	D	6	3	0	4	.167
Gregory, centre field and shortstop.....	A	8	5	1	6	.158
Foster, left field...............................	A	8	6	1	3	.143
Plunkett, pitcher...............................	W	8	2	0	0	.133
Kellogg, second base........................	A	8	7	1	5	.118
Thompson, third base and shortstop...	A	7	2	0	1	.111
Adams, right field............................	D	8	2	2	1	.094
Putnam, right field, centre field and first base...	D	6	3	0	3	.077
Otterson, first base...........................	A	5	3	0	0	.063

FIELDING AVERAGES—PITCHERS.

Name.	College.	Games.	Put Outs.	Assists.	Errors.	Per cent.
Johnston	Amherst	6	0	20	0	1.000
Tabor	Dartmouth	8	4	21	1	.962
Plunkett	Williams	8	1	20	4	.840
Boyden	Amherst	2	1	2	1	.750
Blake	Amherst	1	0	0	0	.000

CATCHERS.

Ross	Williams	8	65	11	1	.987
Sullivan	Amherst	8	42	18	2	.968
Drew	Dartmouth	8	65	14	6	.929
Davis	Williams	1	0	0	0	.000

FIRST BASEMEN.

Boyden	Amherst	1	9	0	0	1.000
Putnam	Dartmouth	3	24	1	0	1.000
Tyler	Amherst	3	27	1	0	1.000
Watson	Dartmouth	2	18	1	1	.950
Goodrich	Williams	8	74	0	5	.937
Otterson	Amherst	5	52	2	4	.931
Rowe	Dartmouth	3	21	0	3	.875

SECOND BASEMEN.

Ashton	Williams	8	19	21	3	.930
Kellogg	Amherst	8	31	20	10	.835
Folsom	Dartmouth	8	32	12	9	.830

THIRD BASEMEN.

Thompson	Amherst	1	2	3	0	1.000
DeWitt	Amherst	1	0	1	0	1.000
L. Hodgkins	Dartmouth	8	13	17	4	.882
Drysdale	Williams	8	23	12	6	.854
Fletcher	Amherst	7	6	9	7	.682
Morse	Amherst	1	0	0	1	.000

SHORTSTOPS.

Gregory	Amherst	2	1	7	1	.889
Thompson	Amherst	7	18	26	7	.848
Heffernan	Williams	8	14	18	8	.800
Crolius	Dartmouth	8	18	23	14	.745

LEFT FIELDERS.

McCornack	Dartmouth	8	11	1	2	.857
Foster	Amherst	8	13	4	3	.850
Doughty	Williams	8	17	0	3	.850

BASE BALL GUIDE. 165

CENTRE FIELDERS.

Name.	College.	Games.	Put Outs.	Assists.	Errors.	Per cent.
Rowe	Dartmouth	1	1	0	0	1.000
Dewey	Williams	8	17	5	3	.880
Gregory	Amherst	6	22	3	7	.781
W. Hodgkins	Dartmouth	6	10	0	3	.769
DeWitt	Amherst	2	1	0	1	.500
Putnam	Dartmouth	2	0	0	5	.000

RIGHT FIELDERS.

Name.	College.	Games.	Put Outs.	Assists.	Errors.	Per cent.
Tinker	Amherst	8	9	1	0	1.000
Seaver	Williams	8	8	1	0	1.000
Putnam	Dartmouth	1	1	0	0	1.000
Adams	Dartmouth	8	7	3	1	.909
Davis	Williams	2	1	0	1	.500

TEAM BATTING. TEAM FIELDING.

College.	Runs.	S. H.	S. B.	Per cent.	College.	Put Outs.	Assists.	Errors.	Per cent.
Dartmouth	52	4	40	.263	Williams	239	88	34	.906
Williams	35	8	30	.222	Amherst	229	117	44	.887
Amherst	39	4	20	.168	Dartmouth	225	93	44	.878

PITCHERS' AVERAGES.

Name.	Won.	Lost.	Per cent.
Plunkett	5	2	.714
Tabor	4	3	.625
Johnston	2	4	.333
Boyden	0	2	.000
Totals	11	11	

Brown College, of Providence, R. I., had a formidable team in 1897. Of 28 games played they won 20. They defeated Harvard three times and Yale once. They were defeated twice by Yale, twice by Princeton, twice by the professional Providence team and once each by Holy Cross and University of Pennsylvania.

Lafayette College had 15 victories to 6 defeats in 1897. Among the more prominent teams over whom they scored were Yale, Wesleyan, University of Pennsylvania, Cornell, University of Virginia, Fordham and West Point. They sustained defeat at the hands of Princeton, University of North Carolina (twice), Georgetown, Fordham and Oritani Field Club.

CORRECT DIAGRAM OF A BALL FIELD.

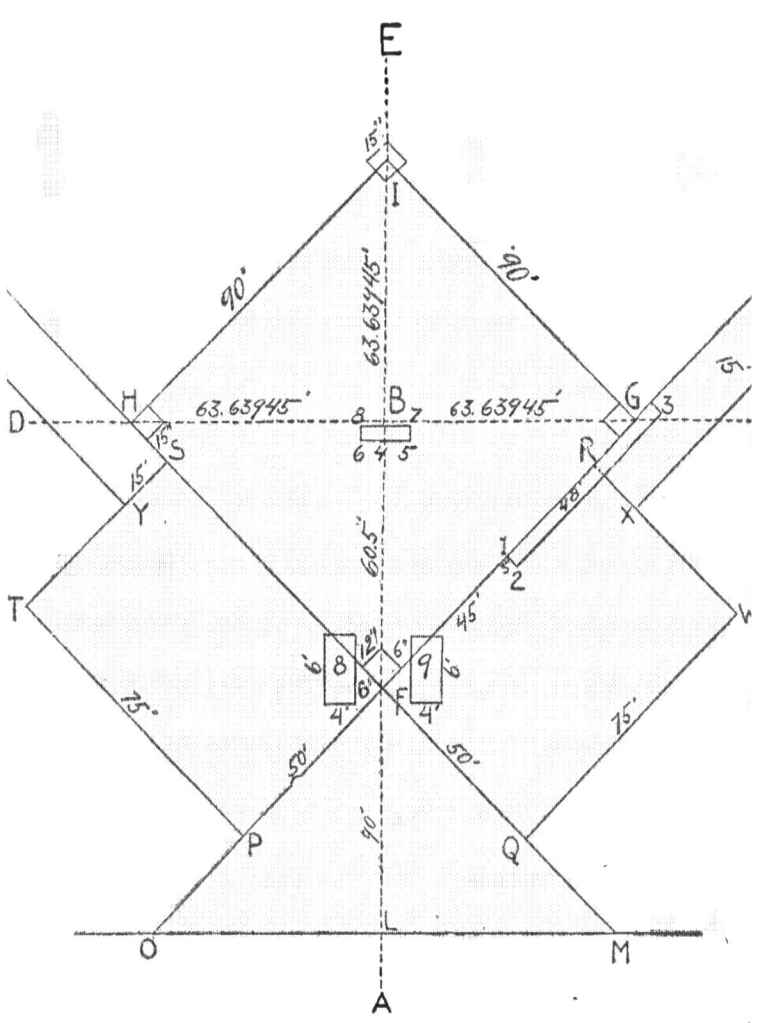

NOTE.—For Specifications See Rules From No. 2 to No. 12.

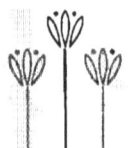 # The Playing Rules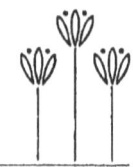

OF PROFESSIONAL BASE BALL CLUBS

As Adopted by the National League and American Association of Professional Base Ball Clubs.

Alterations and additions to the rules are indicated by *Italics*.

RULE 1.—THE BALL GROUND.

The Ground must be an inclosed field, sufficient in size to enable each player to play in his position as required by these rules.

RULE 2.

To lay off the lines governing the positions and the play of the game known as Base Ball, proceed as follows:

From a point, A, within the grounds, project a right line out into the field, and at a point, B, 154 feet from point A, lay off lines B C and B D at right angles to the line A B; then, with B as centre and 63.63945 feet as radius, describe arcs cutting the lines B A at F and B C at G, B D at H and B E at I. Draw lines F G, G E, E H and H F, and said lines will be the containing lines of the Diamond or Infield.

RULE 3.—THE CATCHER'S LINES.

With F as centre and 90 feet radius, an arc cutting line F A at L, and draw lines L M and L O at right angles to F A; and continue same out from F A not less than 90 feet.

RULE 4.—THE FOUL LINE.

From the intersection point, F, continue the straight lines F G and F H until they intersect with the lines L M and L O, and then from the points G and H in the opposite direction until they reach the boundary lines of the grounds.

RULE 5.—THE PLAYERS' LINES.

With F as centre and 50 feet radius, describe arcs cutting lines F O and F M at P and Q; then, with F as centre again and 75 feet radius, describe arcs cutting F G and F H at R and

S; then from the points P, Q, R and S draw lines at right angles to the lines F O, F M, F G and F H, and continue same until they intersect at the points T and W.

Rule 6.—The Captain and Coacher's Line.

With R and S as centres and 15 feet radius, describe arcs cutting lines R W and S T at X and Y, and from the points X and Y draw lines parallel with lines F H and F G, and continue same out to the boundary lines of the ground.

Rule 7.—The Three Foot Line.

With F as centre and 45 feet radius, describe an arc cutting line F G at 1, and from 1 out to the distance of 3 feet draw a line at right angles to F G, and marked point 2; then from point 2, draw a line parallel with the line F G to a point 3 feet beyond the point G, and marked 3; then from the point 3 draw a line at right angles to line 2, 3, back to and intersecting with line F G, and from thence back along line G F to point 1.

Rule 8.—The Pitcher's Plate.

With point F as centre and 60.5 feet as radius, describe an arc cutting the line F B at a point 4, and draw a line 5, 6, passing through point 4 and extending 12 inches on either side of line F B; then with line 5, 6, as a side, describe a **parallelogram** 24 inches by 6 inches.

Rule 9.—The Bases.

Within the angle F, describe a square the sides of which shall be 12 inches, two of its sides lying upon the lines F G and F H, and within the angles G and H describe squares the sides of which shall be 15 inches, the two outer sides of said square lying upon the lines F G and G I and F H and H I, and at the angle E describe a square whose sides shall be 15 inches and so described that its sides shall be parallel with G I and I H and its centre immediately over the angular point E.

Rule 10.—The Batsman's Line.

On either side of the line A F B describe two parallelograms 6 feet long and 4 feet wide (marked 8 and 9), their length being parallel with the line A F B, their distance apart being 6 inches added to each end of the length of the diagonal of the square within the angle F, and the centre of their length being upon said diagonal.

Rule 11.

The Home Base at F and the Pitcher's Plate at 4 must be of whitened rubber, and so fixed in the ground as to be even with the surface.

PLAYING RULES.

RULE 12.

The First Base at G, the Second Base at E, and the Third Base at H must be of white canvas bags, filled with soft material and securely fastened in their positions described in Rule 9.

RULE 13.

The lines described in Rules 3, 4, 5, 6, 7 and 10 must be marked with lime, chalk or other suitable material, so as to be distinctly seen by the umpire.

NOTE.—For a simple way to lay off a ball field see addenda to playing rules on page 189.

RULE 14.—THE BALL.*

SECTION 1. Must not weigh less than five nor more than five and one-quarter ounces avoirdupois, and it must measure not less than nine nor more than nine and one-quarter inches in circumference. The Spalding League Ball, or the Reach American Association Ball, must be used in all games played under these rules.

SEC. 2. For each championship game two regulation balls shall be furnished by the home club to the umpire for use. When the ball in play is batted to foul ground and out of sight of the umpire, the other ball shall be immediately brought into play. As often as one of the two in use shall be lost a new one must be substituted, so that the umpire shall at all times after the game begins have two balls in his possession and ready for use. The moment the umpire delivers an alternate ball to the pitcher, it comes into play, and shall not be exchanged until it, in turn, passes out of sight to foul ground. At no time shall the ball be intentionally discolored by rubbing it with the soil or otherwise. In the event of a new ball being intentionally discolored, or otherwise injured by a player, the umpire shall, upon appeal from the captain of the opposite side, forthwith demand the return of that ball, and shall substitute another new ball and impose a fine of $5.00 upon the offending player.

SEC. 3. In all games the balls played with shall be furnished by the home club, and the last ball in play shall become the property of the winning club. Each ball to be used in championship games shall be examined, measured and weighed by the Secretary of the League, inclosed in a paper box, and sealed

---

* The Spalding League Ball has been adopted by the National League for the past twenty-one years, and is used in all League contests.

For junior clubs (clubs composed of boys under 16 years of age) we recommend them to use the Spalding Boys' League Ball, and that games played by junior clubs with this ball will count as legal games the same as if played with the Official League Ball.

with the seal of the Secretary, which seal shall not be broken, except by the umpire, in the presence of the captains of the two contesting nines after play has been called.

The home club shall have, at least, a dozen regulation balls on the field ready for use on the call of the umpire during each championship game.

SEC. 4. Should the ball become cut or ripped so as to expose the interior, or in any way so injured as to be, in the opinion of the umpire, unfit for fair use, he shall, upon appeal by either captain, at once put the alternate ball into play and call for a new ball.

RULE 15.—THE BAT.

Must be entirely of hard wood, except that the handle may be wound with twine or a granulated substance supplied, not to exceed eighteen inches from the end.

It must be round, and it must not exceed two and three-quarter inches in diameter in the thickest part, nor exceed forty-two inches in length,

RULE 16.—THE PLAYERS AND THEIR POSITIONS.

The players of each club in a game shall be nine in number, one of whom shall act as captain, and in no case shall less than nine men be allowed to play on each side.

RULE 17.

The players' positions shall be such as may be assigned them by their captain, except that the pitcher, while in the act of delivering the ball to the bat, must take the position as defined in Rules 8 and 29.

RULE 18.

Players in uniform shall not be permitted to occupy seats *on the stands*, or to stand among the spectators.

RULE 19.

SECTION 1. Every club shall adopt uniforms for its players, but no player shall attach anything to the sole or heel of his shoes other than the ordinary base ball shoe plate.

SEC. 2. The catcher and first baseman are permitted to wear a glove or mitt of any size, shape or weight. All other players are restricted to the use of a glove or mitt weighing not over ten ounces, and measuring in circumference, around the palm of the hand, not over fourteen inches.

RULE 20.—PLAYERS' BENCHES.

SECTION 1. The players' benches must be furnished by the home club and placed upon a portion of the ground outside of and not nearer than 25 feet to the players' lines. One such bench must be for the exclusive use of the visiting club, and one for the exclusive use of the home club. All players of the side at the bat must be seated on their bench, except such as are legally assigned to coach base-runners, and also the batsman *except* when called to the bat by the umpire, and under no circumstances shall the umpire permit any person, except the club president, managers and players in uniform to occupy seats on the benches.

SEC. 2. To enforce this rule the captain of the opposite side may call the attention of the umpire to a violation, whereupon the umpire shall immediately order such player or players to be seated. If the order is not obeyed within one minute the offending player or players shall be debarred from further participation in the game, and shall be obliged to leave the playing field forthwith.

RULE 21.—THE GAME.

SECTION 1. Every championship game must be commenced not later than two hours before sunset.

SEC. 2. A game shall consist of nine innings to each contesting nine, except that

(*a.*) If the side first at bat scores less runs in nine innings than the other side has scored in eight innings, the game shall then terminate.

(*b.*) If the side last at bat in the ninth innings scores the winning run before the third man is out, the game shall terminate.

RULE 22.—A TIE GAME.

If the score be a tie at the end of the nine innings, play shall be continued until one side has scored more runs than the other in an equal number of innings, provided, that the side last at bat scores the winning run before the third man is out, the game shall terminate.

RULE 23.—A DRAWN GAME.

A drawn game shall be declared by the umpire when he terminates a game on account of darkness or rain, after five equal innings have been played, if the score at the time is equal on the last even innings played; except when the side that went second to bat is then at the bat, and has scored the same number of runs as the other side, in which case the umpire shall declare the game drawn without regard to the score of the last equal innings.

RULE 24.—A CALLED GAME.

If the umpire calls "Game" on account of darkness or rain at any time after five innings have been completed, the score shall be that of the last equal innings played, except, that the side second at bat shall have scored one or more runs than the side first at bat, in which case the score of the game shall be the total number of runs made.

Rule 25.—A Forfeited Game.

A forfeited game shall be declared by the umpire in favor of the club not in fault, at the request of such club, in the following cases:

Section 1. If the nine of a club fail to appear upon the field, or being upon the field, fail to begin the game within five minutes after the umpire has called "Play" at the hour appointed for the beginning of the game, unless such delay in appearing, or in commencing the game, be unavoidable.

Sec. 2. If, after the game has begun, one side refuses or fails to continue playing, unless such game has been suspended or terminated by the umpire.

Sec. 3. If, after play has been suspended by the umpire, one side fails to resume playing within one minute after the umpire has called "Play."

Sec. 4. If a team resorts to dilatory movements to delay the game.

Sec. 5. If, in the opinion of the umpire, any one of the rules of the games is wilfully violated.

Sec. 6. If, after ordering the removal of a player, as authorized by Rules 20, 52 *and* 61, said order is not obeyed within one minute.

Sec. 7. *If, because of removal of players from the game by the umpire, there be less than nine players in either team.*

Sec. 8. *If, when two games are scheduled to be played on the same afternoon, the second game be not commenced within ten minutes of the time of completion of the first game. The umpire of the first game shall be the timekeeper.*

Sec. 9. In case the umpire declares the game forfeited, he shall transmit a written notice thereof to the president of the League within twenty-four hours thereafter. However, a failure on the part of the umpire to so notify the president shall not affect his decision declaring the game forfeited.

Rule 26.—No Game.

"No game" shall be declared by the umpire if he shall terminate play on account of rain or darkness before five innings on each side are completed. Except in a case when the game is called, and the club second at bat shall have more runs at the end of its fourth innings than the club first at bat has made in its five completed innings; in such case the umpire shall award the game to the club having made the greatest number of runs, and it shall be a legal game and be so counted in the championship record.

RULE 27.—SUBSTITUTES.

SECTION 1. In every championship game each side shall be required to have present on the field, in uniform, a sufficient number of substitute players to carry out the provision which requires that not less than nine players shall occupy the field in any innings of a game.

SEC. 2. Any such player may be substituted at any time by either club, but a player thereby retired shall not thereafter participate in the game.

SEC. 3. The base-runner shall not have a substitute run for him except by the consent of the captains of the contesting teams.

RULE 28.—CHOICE OF INNINGS—CONDITION OF GROUND.

The choice of innings shall be given to the captain of the home club, who shall also be the sole judge of the fitness of the ground for beginning a game after rain, but, after play has been called by the umpire, he alone shall be the judge as to the fitness of the ground for resuming play after the game has been suspended on account of rain.

RULE 29.—THE PITCHER'S POSITION.

The pitcher shall take his position facing the batsman with both feet square on the ground, and in front of the pitcher's plate; but in the act of delivering the ball to the bat, one foot must be in contact with the pitcher's plate, defined in Rule 8. He shall not raise either foot, unless in the act of delivering the ball to the bat, nor make more than one step in *such delivery*.

RULE 30.—A FAIRLY DELIVERED BALL.

A Fairly Delivered Ball to the bat is a ball pitched or thrown to the bat by the pitcher while standing in his position and facing the batsman, the ball so delivered to pass over any portion of the home base not lower than the batsman's knee nor higher than his shoulder.

RULE 31.—AN UNFAIRLY DELIVERED BALL.

An Unfairly Delivered Ball is a ball delivered by the pitcher, as in Rule 30, except that the ball does not pass over any portion of the home base, or does pass over the home base, above the batsman's shoulder or below the *line of his* knee.

RULE 32.—BALKING.

A Balk shall be:

SECTION 1. Any motion made by the pitcher to deliver the ball to the bat without delivering it.

SEC. 2. Any delivery of the ball to the bat while his (pivot) foot is not in contact with the pitcher's plate, as defined in Rule 29.

SEC. 3. Any motion in delivering the ball to the bat by the pitcher while not in the position defined in Rule 29.

SEC. 4. The holding of the ball by the pitcher so long as, in the opinion of the umpire, to delay the game unnecessarily.

SEC. 5. Standing in position *and making any motion* to pitch without having the ball in his possession, except in the case of a "block-ball," as provided by Rule 35, section 2.

When the pitcher feigns to throw the ball to a base he must resume the above position and pause momentarily before delivering the ball to the bat.

If the pitcher fails to comply with the requirements of this rule the umpire must call "A balk."

SEC. 6. *The making of any motion the pitcher habitually makes in his method of delivery, without his immediately delivering the ball to the bat.*

SEC. 7. *If the pitcher feigns to throw the ball to a base and does not resume his legal position and pause momentarily before delivering the ball to the bat.*

RULE 33.—DEAD BALLS.

A Dead Ball is a ball delivered to the bat by the pitcher that touches any part of the batsman's person or clothing while standing in his position without being struck at, or that touches any part of the umpire's person or clothing while he is standing on foul ground without first passing the catcher.

RULE 34.

In case of a foul strike, foul hit ball not legally caught out, dead ball, or base-runner put out for being struck by a fair-hit ball, the ball shall not be considered in play until it is held by the pitcher standing in his position and the umpire shall have called play.

RULE 35.—BLOCK BALLS.

SECTION 1. A Block is a batted or thrown ball that is touched, stopped or handled by any person not engaged in the game.

SEC. 2. Whenever a block occurs the umpire shall declare it and the base-runners may run the bases without being put out until the ball has been returned to and held by the pitcher standing in his position.

SEC. 3. In the case of a block, if the person not engaged in the game should retain possession of the ball, or throw or kick it beyond the reach of the fielders, the umpire should call "Time" and require each base-runner to stop at the last base touched by him until the ball be returned to the pitcher standing in his position and the umpire shall have called "Play."

RULE 36.—THE BATSMAN'S POSITION—ORDER OF BATTING.

The batsmen must take their position within the batsman's lines, as defined in Rule 10, in the order in which they are named in the batting order, which batting order must be submitted by the captains of the opposing teams to the umpire before the game, and this batting order must be followed except in the case of a substitute player, in which case the substitute must take the place of the original player in the batting order. After the first inning the first striker in each inning shall be the batsman whose name follows that of the last man who has completed his turn—time at bat—in the preceding inning.

RULE 37.

SECTION 1. When their side goes to the bat the players must immediately return to the players' bench, as defined in Rule 20, and remain there until the side is put out, except when called to the bat or they become *coachers or* substitute base-runners; provided, that the captain or one player only, except that if two or more base-runners are occupying the bases then the captain and one player, or two players, may occupy the space between the player's lines and the captain's lines to coach base-runners.

SEC. 2. No player of the side "at bat," except when batsman, shall occupy any portion of the space within the catcher's lines, as defined in Rule 3. The triangular space behind the home base is reserved for the exclusive use of umpire, catcher and batsman, and the umpire must prohibit any player of the side "at bat" from crossing the same at any time while the ball is in the hands of, or passing between, the pitcher and catcher, while standing in their positions.

SEC. 3. The players of the side "at bat" must occupy the portion of the field allotted them, but must speedily vacate any portion thereof that may be in the way of the ball, or any fielder attempting to catch or field it.

RULE 38.—THE BATTING RULES.

SECTION 1. A Fair Hit is a ball batted by the batsman—while he is standing within the lines of his position—that first touches "fair" ground, or the person of a player, or the umpire, while standing on fair ground, and then settles on fair ground before passing the line of first or third base.

SEC. 2. A Foul Hit is a similarly batted ball that first touches "foul" ground, or the person of a player, or the umpire, while standing on "foul" ground.

SEC. 3. Should such "fair hit" ball bound or roll to foul ground, before passing the line of first or third base, and settle on foul ground, it shall be declared by the umpire a foul ball.

SEC. 4. Should such "foul hit" ball bound or roll to fair ground and settle there before passing the line of first or third base, it shall be declared by the umpire a fair ball.

RULE 39.

A foul tip is a ball batted by the batsman while standing within the lines of his position that goes foul sharp from the bat to the catcher's hands.

RULE 40.

A bunt hit is a ball delivered by the pitcher to the batsman who, while standing within the lines of his position, makes a deliberate attempt to hit the ball so slowly within the infield that it cannot be fielded in time to retire the batsman. If such a "bunt hit" goes to foul ground a strike shall be called by the umpire.

RULE 41.—BALLS BATTED OUTSIDE THE GROUNDS.

When a batted ball passes outside the grounds, the umpire shall decide it Fair should it disappear within, or Foul should it disappear outside of the range of the foul lines, and Rule 38 is to be construed accordingly.

RULE 42.

A fair batted ball that goes over the fence shall entitle the batsman to a home run, except, that should it go over the fence at a less distance than two hundred and thirty-five (235) feet from the home base, when he shall be entitled to two bases only, and a distinctive line shall be marked on the fence at this point.

RULE 43.—STRIKES.

A Strike is:

SECTION 1. A ball struck at by the batsman without its touching his bat; or,

SEC. 2. A fair ball legally delivered by the pitcher, but not struck at by the batsman.

SEC. 3. Any intentional effort to hit the ball to foul ground, also in the case of a "bunt hit," which sends the ball to foul ground, either directly, or by bounding or rolling from fair ground to foul ground, and which settles on foul ground.

SEC. 4. A ball struck at, if the ball touches any part of the batsman's person.

SEC. 5. A ball tipped by the batsman, and caught by the catcher, within ten feet from home base.

RULE 44.

A Foul Strike is a ball batted by the batsman when any part of his person is upon ground outside the lines of the batsman's position.

RULE 45.—THE BATSMAN IS OUT.

The Batsman is Out:

SECTION 1. If he fails to take his position at the bat in his order of batting, unless the error be discovered and the proper batsman takes his position before a time "at bat" is recorded, and, in such case, the balls and strikes called must be counted in the time "at bat" of the proper batsman, and only the proper batsman shall be declared out, *and no runs shall be scored or bases run because of any act of the improper batsman,* provided, this rule shall not take effect unless the out is declared before the ball is delivered to the succeeding batsman. *Should batsman declared out by this rule be sufficient to retire the side, the proper batsman the next innings is the player who would have come to bat had the players been out by ordinary play.*

SEC. 2. If he fails to take his position within one minute after the umpire has called for the batsman.

SEC. 3. If he makes a foul hit other than a foul tip, as defined in Rule 39, and the ball be momentarily held by a fielder before touching the ground; provided, it be not caught in a fielder's hat or cap, or touched by some object other than a fielder before being caught.

SEC. 4. If he makes a foul strike.

SEC. 5. If he attempts to hinder the catcher from fielding or throwing the ball by stepping outside the lines of his position, or otherwise obstructing or interfering with the player.

SEC. 6. If, while the first base be occupied by a base-runner, three strikes be called on him by the umpire, except when two men are already out.

SEC. 7. If, after two strikes have been called, the batsman obviously attempts to make a foul hit, as in Rule 43, section 3.

SEC. 8. If, while attempting a third strike, the ball touches any part of the batsman's person, in which case base-runners occupying bases shall return as prescribed in Rule 49, section 5.

SEC. 9. If he hits a fly ball that can be handled by an

infielder while first and second bases are occupied, or first, second and third with only one out. In such case the umpire shall, as soon as the ball is hit, declare infield or outfield hit.

SEC. 10. If the third strike is called in accordance with section 4, Rule 43.

SEC. 11. The moment a batsman is declared out by the umpire, he (the umpire) shall call for the batsman next in order to leave his seat on the bench and take his position at the bat, and such player of the batting side shall not leave his seat on the bench until so called to bat, except as provided by Rule 37, section 1, and Rule 52.

BASE-RUNNING RULES.

RULE 46.—WHEN THE BATSMAN BECOMES A BASE-RUNNER.

The Batsman becomes a Base-Runner:

SECTION 1. Instantly after he makes a fair hit.

SEC. 2. Instantly after four balls have been called by the umpire.

SEC. 3. Instantly after three strikes have been declared by the umpire.

SEC. 4. If, while he be a batsman, without making any attempt to strike at the ball, his person or clothing be hit by a ball from the pitcher; unless, in the opinion of the umpire, he plainly avoids making any effort to get out of the way of the ball from the pitcher, and thereby permits himself to be so hit.

SEC. 5. Instantly after an illegal delivery of a ball by the pitcher.

An illegal delivery of the ball is made if the pitcher's pivot foot be not in contact with the rubber plate at the time of the delivery of the ball, or if he takes more than one step in delivery, or if, after feigning to throw to a base, he fails to pause momentarily before delivering the ball to the bat.

RULE 47.—BASES TO BE TOUCHED.

The base-runner must touch each base in regular order, viz., first, second, third and home bases, and when obliged to return (except on a foul hit) must retouch the base or bases in reverse order. He shall only be considered as holding a base after touching it, and shall then be entitled to hold such base until he has legally touched the next base in order or has been legally forced to vacate it for a succeeding base-runner. However, no base-runner shall score a run to count in the game until the base-runner preceding him in the batting list (provided there has been such a base-runner who has not been put out in that inning) shall have first touched home base without being put out.

Rule 48.—Entitled to Bases.

The base-runner shall be entitled, without being put out, to take the base in the following cases:

Section 1. If, while he was batsman, the umpire called four balls.

Sec. 2. If the umpire awards a succeeding batsman a base on four balls, or for being hit with a pitched ball, or in case of an illegal delivery—as in Rule 46, section 5—and the base-runner is thereby forced to vacate the base held by him.

Sec. 3. If the umpire calls a "Balk."

Sec. 4. If a ball, delivered by the pitcher, pass the catcher, and touch the umpire, or any fence or building within ninety feet of the home base.

Sec. 5. If, upon a fair hit, the ball strikes the person or clothing of the umpire on fair ground.

Sec. 6. If he be prevented from making a base by the obstruction of an adversary, unless the latter be a fielder having the ball in his hand ready to meet the base-runner.

Sec. 7. If the fielder stop or catch a batted ball with his hat or any part of his uniform except his gloved hand.

Rule 49.—Returning to Bases.

The base-runner shall return to his base, and shall be entitled to so return without being put out:

Section 1. If the umpire declares a foul tip (as defined in Rule 39), or any other foul hit not legally caught by a fielder.

Sec. 2. If the umpire declares a foul strike.

Sec. 3. If the umpire declares a dead ball, unless it be also the fourth unfair ball and he be thereby forced to take the next base, as provided in Rule 48, section 2.

Sec. 4. If the person or clothing of the umpire interferes with the catcher, or he is struck by a ball thrown by the catcher to intercept a base-runner.

Sec. 5. The base-runner shall return to his base if, while attempting a strike, the ball touches any part of the batsman's person.

Rule 50.—When Base-Runners Are Out.

The Base-Runner is Out:

Section 1. If, after three strikes have been declared against him while batsman and the catcher fail to catch the third strike ball, he plainly attempts to hinder the catcher from fielding the ball.

Sec. 2. If, having made a fair hit while batsman, such fair hit ball be momentarily held by a fielder before touching the ground, or any object other than a fielder; Provided, it be not caught in a fielder's hat or cap.

PLAYING RULES.

SEC. 3. If, when the umpire has declared three strikes on him while batsman, the third strike ball be momentarily held by a fielder before touching the ground; PROVIDED, it be not caught in a fielder's hat or cap, or touch some object other than a fielder before being caught.

SEC. 4. If, after three strikes or a fair hit, he be touched with the ball in the hand of a fielder before he shall have touched first base.

SEC. 5. If, after three strikes or a fair hit, the ball be securely held by a fielder while touching first base with any part of his person before such base-runner touches first base.

SEC. 6. If, in running the last half of the distance from home base to first base, while the ball is being fielded to first base, he runs outside the three-foot lines, as defined in Rule 7, unless to avoid a fielder attempting to field a batted ball.

SEC. 7. If, in running from first to second base, from second to third base, or from third to home base, he runs more than three feet from a direct line between such bases to avoid being touched by the ball in the hands of a fielder; but in case a fielder be occupying the base-runner's proper path in attempting to field a batted ball, then the base-runner shall run out of the path, and behind said fielder, and shall not be declared out for so doing.

SEC. 8. If he fails to avoid a fielder attempting to field a batted ball, in the manner described in sections 6 and 7 of this rule, or if he, in any way, obstructs a fielder attempting to field a batted ball, or intentionally interferes with a thrown ball; PROVIDED, that if two or more fielders attempt to field a batted ball, and the base-runner comes in contact with one or more of them, the umpire shall determine which fielder is entitled to the benefit of this rule, and shall not decide the base-runner out for coming in contact with any other fielder.

SEC. 9. If, at any time while the ball is in play, he be touched by the ball in the hands of a fielder, unless some part of his person is touching a base he is entitled to occupy; PROVIDED, the ball be held by the fielder after touching him.

SEC. 10. *The base-runner in running to first base may* overrun said base, without being put out for being off said base, after first touching it, provided he returns at once and retouches the base, after which he may be put out as at any other base. If, in over-running first base, he also attempts to run to second base, or after passing the base he turns to his left from the foul line, he shall forfeit such exemption from being put out.

SEC. 11. If, when a fair or foul hit ball (other than a foul tip as referred to in Rule 39) is legally caught by a fielder, such ball is legally held by a fielder on the base occupied by the base-runner when such ball was struck (or the base-runner be touched with the ball in the hands of a fielder), before he retouches said base after such fair or foul hit ball was so caught; PROVIDED, that the base-runner shall not be out, in such case, if, after the ball was legally caught as above, it be delivered to the bat by the pitcher before the fielder holds it on said base, or touches the base-runner with it; but if the base-runner in attempting to reach a base, detaches it before being touched or forced out, he shall be declared safe.

SEC. 12. If, when a batsman becomes a base-runner, the first base, or the first and second bases, or the first, second and third bases, be occupied, any base-runner so occupying a base shall cease to be entitled to hold it, until any following base-runner is put out, and may be put out at the next base, or by being touched by the ball in the hands of a fielder in the same manner as in running to first base at any time before any following base-runner is put out.

SEC. 13. If a fair hit ball strike him before touching the fielder, and, in such case, no base shall be run unless forced by the batsman becoming a base-runner, and no run shall be scored or any other base-runner put out.

SEC. 14. If, when running to a base, or forced to return to a base, he fail to touch the intervening base, or bases, if any, in the order prescribed in Rule 47, he may be put out at the base he fails to touch, or being touched by the ball in the hands of the fielder in the same manner as in running to first base; PROVIDED, that the base-runner shall not be out in such case if the ball be delivered to the bat by the pitcher before the fielder holds it on said base, or touches the base-runner with it.

SEC. 15. If, when the umpire calls "Play," after any suspension of a game, he fails to return to and touch the base he occupied when "Time" was called before touching the next base; PROVIDED, the base-runner shall not be out, in such case, if the ball be delivered to the bat by the pitcher before the fielder holds it on said base or touches the base-runner with it.

RULE 51.—WHEN BATSMAN OR BASE-RUNNER IS OUT.

The umpire shall declare the batsman or base-runner out, without waiting for an appeal for such decision, in all cases where such player is put out in accordance with these rules, except as provided in Rule 50, sections 10 and 14.

RULE 52.—COACHING RULES.

The Coacher shall be restricted to coaching the base-runner only, and shall not be allowed to address any remarks except to the base-runner, and then only in words of necessary direction;

and shall not use language which will in any manner refer to, or reflect upon a player of the opposing club, the umpire or the spectators, and not more than one coacher, who may be a player participating in the game, or any other player under contract to it, in the uniform of either club, shall be allowed at any one time, except, that if base-runners are occupying two or more of the bases, then the captain and one player, or two players in the uniform of either club, may occupy the space between the players' lines and the captains' lines to coach base-runners. To enforce the above the captain of the opposite side may call the attention of the umpire to the offence, and, upon a repetition of the same, the offending player shall be debarred from further participation in the game, and shall leave the playing field forthwith.

RULE 53.—THE SCORING OF RUNS.

One run shall be scored every time a base-runner, after having legally touched the first three bases, shall touch the home base before three men are put out. (Exception)—If the third man is forced out, or is put out before reaching first base, a run shall not be scored.

THE UMPIRE OR UMPIRES AND THEIR RESPECTIVE DUTIES.

RULE 54.

When two umpires are assigned to duty each shall serve in his regularly appointed position and discharge the duties of the same as provided for by this code of rules.

RULE 55.

No umpire shall be changed during the progress of a championship game, except by reason of personal illness or injury incapacitating him for the discharge of his duties.

RULE 56.

When two umpires are assigned, one shall be known as the "Umpire" and the other as the "Assistant Umpire." The former's regular position in the game shall be behind that of the batsman, and the latter's position in the field near either first, second or third bases; and the umpires shall not exchange duties during the progress of a game, except by consent of the captains of the opposing teams.

RULE 57.

The umpire shall perform all the duties devolving upon a single umpire, except giving decisions on first, second

PLAYING RULES.

and third bases and deciding points of play in running such bases, which shall devolve upon the assistant umpire, except as regards third base when any other base is occupied by a base-runner, in which event the umpire shall decide all points of play arising at third base. It shall be the duty of the umpires to assist or advise each other in rendering any decision when requested by the other umpire.

RULE 58.

The umpire shall act as the government representative of the League, and as such shall have the power to enforce every section of the code of playing rules of the game, and he shall have the power to order any player, or captain, or club manager, to do or to omit to do, any action that he may deem necessary to give force or effect to the laws of the game.

RULE 59.

There shall be no appeal from any legal decision of either the umpire or the assistant umpire.

RULE 60.

Under no circumstances shall any player be allowed to dispute a decision by either umpire, in which only an error of judgment is involved; and no decision rendered by either umpire shall be reversed, except it be plainly shown by the code of rules to have been illegal; and in such case the captain alone shall be allowed to make the appeal for reversal.

RULE 61.

SECTION 1. In all cases of violation of these rules, either by a player or a manager, the penalty shall be a prompt removal of the offender from the grounds, followed by such period af suspension from actual service in the club as the umpire or the President of the League may elect; providing the term of suspension by the umpire shall not exceed three days, including date of removal.

SEC. 2. The umpire shall immediately after the suspension of a player forward to the President a report of the suspension and the causes therefor. In flagrant cases he shall make such report by telegraph.

RULE 62.

Before the commencement of a game the umpire shall see that the rules governing all the materials of the game are strictly observed. He shall ask the captain of the home club whether there are any special ground rules to be enforced, and if there are, he shall see that they are duly enforced, provided they do not conflict with any of these rules.

Rule 63.

The umpire shall not only call "*play*" at the hour appointed for the beginning of the game, but also announce "*game called*" at its legal conclusion.

Rule 64.

The umpire shall suspend play for the following causes: First, if rain is falling so heavily as to oblige the spectators on the open field and open stands to seek shelter, in which case he shall note the time of suspension; and should rain fall continuously for thirty minutes thereafter he shall terminate the game.

Rule 65.

The umpire shall suspend play in case of an accident to himself or to the assistant umpire, or to a player which incapacitates him or them from service in the field, or in order to remove from the grounds any player or spectator who has violated the rules.

Rule 66.

In suspending play from any legal cause, the umpire shall call "*time;*" when he calls "*time*" the play shall be suspended until he calls "*play*" again, and during the interim no player shall be put out, base be run, or run be scored. "*Time*" shall not be called by the umpire until the ball is held by the pitcher standing in his position.

Rule 67.

The umpire shall call and count as a "*ball*" any unfair ball delivered by the pitcher to the batsman, but not before such ball has passed the line of the home base. He shall also call and count as a "*strike*" every fairly delivered ball which passes over any portion of the home base, and within the batsman's legal range, as defined in Rule 43, which is not struck at by the batsman, or a foul tip which is caught by the catcher, standing close up behind the batsmrn, or which after being struck at and not hit, strikes the person of the batsman; or when the ball is purposely hit foul by the batsman, or when the ball is bunted foul by the batsman.

Rule 68.

If but one umpire is assigned, his duties and powers shall be that of both the umpire and the assistant umpire, and he shall be permitted to occupy such positions on the field as will best enable him to discharge his duties.

RULE 69.—FIELD RULES.

No club shall allow open betting or pool-selling upon its ground, nor in any building owned or occupied by it.

RULE 70.

No person shall be allowed upon any part of the field during the progress of a game in addition to the players in uniform, the manager of each side and the umpire, except such officers of the law as may be present in uniform, and such officials of the home club as may be necessary to preserve the peace.

RULE 71.

No manager, captain or player shall address the spectators during the progress of the game, except in case of necessary explanation.

RULE 72.

Every club shall furnish sufficient police force upon its own grounds to preserve order, and in the event of a crowd entering the field during the progress of a game and interfering with the play in any manner, the visiting club may refuse to play further until the field be cleared. If the ground be not cleared within fifteen minutes thereafter, the visiting club may claim, and shall be entitled to the game, by a score of nine runs to none (no matter what number of innings has been played).

RULE 73.—GENERAL DEFINITIONS.

"Play" is the order of the umpire to begin the game, or to resume play after its suspension.

RULE 74.

"Time" is the order of the umpire to suspend play. Such suspension must not extend beyond the day of the game.

RULE 75.

"Game" is the announcement by the umpire that the game is terminated.

RULE 76.

An "Inning" is the term at bat of the nine players representing a club in a game, and is completed when three of such players have been put out, as provided in these rules.

RULE 77.

A "Time at Bat" is the term at bat of a batsman. It begins when he takes his position and continues until he is put out or becomes a base-runner; except when, because of being hit by a pitched ball, or in case of an illegal delivery by the pitcher, or in case of a sacrifice hit purposely made to the infield which, not being a base-hit, advances a base-runner without resulting in a put-out, except to the batsman, as in Rule 45.

RULE 78.

"Legal" or "Legally" signifies as required by these rules.

SCORING.

RULE 79.

In order to promote uniformity in scoring championship games the following instructions, suggestions and definitions are made for the benefit of scorers, and they are required to make all scores in accordance therewith.

BATTING.

SECTION 1. The first item in the tabulated score, after the player's name and position, shall be the number of times he has been at bat during the game. *No time at bat shall be scored if the batsman be hit by a pitched ball while standing in his position, and after trying to avoid being so hit, or in case of the pitcher's illegal delivery of the ball to the bat which gives the batsman his base, or when he intentionally hits the ball to the field, purposely to be put out, or if he is given first base on called balls.*

SEC. 2. In the second column should be set down the runs made by each player.

SEC. 3. In the third column should be placed the first-base hits made by each player. A base-hit should be scored in the following cases:

When the ball from the bat strikes the ground within the foul lines and out of reach of the fielders.

When a hit ball is partially or wholly stopped by a fielder in motion, but such player cannot recover himself in time to handle the ball before the striker reaches first base.

When a ball is hit *with such force* to an infielder that he cannot handle it in time to put out the batsman. (In case of doubt over this class of hits, score a base-hit and exempt the fielder from the charge of an error.)

When a ball is hit so slowly towards a fielder that he cannot handle it in time to put out the batsman.

That in all cases where a base-runner is retired by being hit by a batted ball, the batsman should be credited with a base-hit.

When a batted ball hits the person or clothing of the umpire, as defined in Rule 48, section 5. *In no case shall a base-hit be scored when a base-runner has been forced out by the play.*

Sec. 4. In the fourth column shall be placed the sacrifice hits, which shall be credited to the batsman who, when no one is out or when but one man is out, advances a runner a base by a bunt hit, which results in putting out the batsman, or would so result if the ball were handled without error.

Fielding.

Sec. 5. The number of opponents put out by each player shall be set down in the fifth column. Where a batsman is given out by the umpire for a foul strike, or where the batsman fails to bat in proper order, the put-out shall be scored to the catcher. *In all cases of "out" for interference, running out of line, or infield fly dropped, the "out" should be credited to the player who would have made the play, but for the action of the base-runner or batsman.*

Sec. 6. The number of times the player assists shall be set down in the sixth column. An assist should be given to each player who handles the ball in assisting a run-out or other play of the kind.

An assist should be given to a player who makes a play in time to put a runner out, even if the player who could complete the play fails through no fault of the player assisting.

And generally an assist should be given to each player who handles or assists in any manner in handling the ball from the time it leaves the bat until it reaches the player who makes the put-out, or in case of a thrown ball, to each player who throws or handles it cleanly and in such a way that a put-out results, or would result if no error were made by the receiver.

Assists should be credited to every player who handles the ball in the play which results in a base-runner being called out for interference or for running out of line.

Errors.

Sec. 7. An error shall be given in the seventh column for each misplay which allows the striker or base-runner to make one or more bases when perfect play would have insured his being put out, except that "wild pitches," "bases on balls," bases on the batsman being struck by a "pitched ball," or in case of illegal pitched balls, balks and passed balls, *all of which comprise battery errors,* shall not be included in said column. In scoring errors of batted balls see section 3 of this rule.

An error shall not be scored against the catcher for a wild throw to prevent a stolen base, unless the base-runner advances an extra base because of the error.

No error shall be scored against an infielder who attempts to complete a double play, unless the throw is so wild that an additional base is gained.

STOLEN BASES.

A stolen base shall be credited to the base-runner whenever he reaches the base he attempts to steal unaided by a fielding or by a battery error or a hit by the batsman.

RULE 80.

The Summary shall contain:

SECTION 1. *The score made in each innings of the game.*

SEC. 2. The number of bases stolen by each player.

SEC. 3. The number of two-base hits made by each player.

SEC. 4. The number of three-base hits made by each player.

SEC. 5. The number of home runs made by each player.

SEC. 6. The number of double and triple plays made by each side and the names of the players assisting in the same.

SEC. 7. The number of innings each pitcher pitched in.

SEC. 8. The number of base-hits made off each pitcher.

SEC. 9. The number of times the pitcher strikes out the opposing batsmen.

SEC. 10. The number of times the pitcher gives bases on balls.

SEC. 11. The number of wild pitches charged to the pitcher.

SEC. 12. The number of times the pitcher hits batsmen with pitched ball.

SEC. 13. The number of passed balls by each catcher.

SEC. 14. The time of the game.

SEC. 15. *The names and positions of each umpire.*

A SIMPLE WAY FOR LAYING OFF A BALL FIELD.

Lay a tape-line from centre of backstop out into the field 217 feet 3½ inches to second base. At 90 feet from backstop place home plate, with the tape-line dividing it diagonally. Between 150 feet 6 inches and 150 feet 10 inches from the backstop place the pitcher's plate, with the tape-line dividing it at the centre; 153 feet 7¾ inches from backstop drive a stake. At right angles to the tape-line, and 63 feet 7¾ inches from the stake and 90 feet from both home plate and second base, place first base on one side and third base on the other. This done remove the stake. Lay lines connecting the bases thus laid, forming the diamond, extending the lines from home base and first base and home base and third base in each direction to the fence, thus forming the foul lines and the catcher's position. Parallel with these lines and 50 feet away lay the player's lines, extending from intersection with lines already laid 75 feet. From this point lay lines at right angles to lines just described, extending to the base lines. At right angles to these and parallel with the base lines, 15 feet distant, lay the coacher's lines, extending, say, 30 feet towards the outfield. Parallel with and 3 feet distant from the base line from home base to first base lay a line beginning 45 feet from home plate and extending just past first base.

On each side of home plate, parallel with line from centre of backstop to second base and 6 inches distant from home plate, lay lines 6 feet long, running three feet each way from a line through the centre of home plate, also lay other lines parallel with and 4 feet distant from the ones just described. Form these into parallelograms 4 feet by 6 feet in dimension, thus forming the batsman's position.

Observe Rules 11, 12 and 13.

ADVICE TO UMPIRES.

You are the absolute master of the field from the beginning to the termination of a game. You are by these rules given full authority to order any player, captain or manager to do or omit to do any act which you may deem necessary to maintain your dignity and compel respect from players and spectators. (Rule 58.)

The rules are created to be enforced to the letter. If they are poor rules the fault is not yours. If they are disobeyed you are to blame.

Before "play" is called satisfy yourself that the field is correctly laid off with lines, bases and plates in proper places, and that the materials supplied for the game are as required by the rules. (Rule 62.)

Notify each captain that the rules will be enforced exactly as they are written, and that for each violation the prescribed penalty will follow. Do not in any case temporize with a rule breaker.

Make all decisions as you see them. Never attempt to "even up" after having made a mistake.

Be strict in what may seem to be trivial matters, thereby "nipping in the bud" trouble before it fully develops.

Specially observe Rules 20 and 37, which require players to occupy their respective benches; also section 6 of Rule 25, which specifies that a player ordered from the field shall go within one minute from the time you order his removal from the game.

Do not allow a player (not even a captain) to leave his position (which is the bench or coacher's box, for the captain whose side is at bat, or the regular fielding position of the captain whose side is not at bat) to argue with you. The captain only is allowed to appeal to you (and he only from his proper position) on a legal misinterpretation of the rules. If he claims that you have erred, it is proper that the spectators should know what the claim is. (Rule 60.)

Coachers have heretofore been a disturbing element to the umpire. Rule 52 provides just what his and what your duties are. These rules are mandatory, not discretionary. If you allow them to be violated you become the chief culprit and do not properly perform the duties of your position. Bear in mind that you are not responsible for the creation of the rules or the penalties prescribed by them.

The umpire who enforces the rules, maintains his dignity and compels respect, gives the fullest satisfaction to both teams and to the spectators.

Compel respect from all and your task will be an easy one.

INDEX TO RULES AND REGULATIONS.

	Sec.	Rule.
The Ground		1
The Field		2
Catcher's Lines		3
Foul Lines		4
Players' Lines		5
The Captain and Coacher's Line		6
Three-foot Line		7
Pitcher's Plate		8
The Bases		9
The Batsman's Line		10
The Home Base		11
First, Second and Third Bases		12
Lines Must Be Marked		13
The Ball		14
Weight and Size	(1)	14
Number of Balls Furnished	(2)	14
Fining Player for Discoloring New Ball	(2)	14
Furnished by Home Club	(3)	14
Replaced if Injured	(4)	14
The Bat		15
Material of	(1)	15
Shape of	(2)	15

THE PLAYERS AND THEIR POSITIONS.

	Sec.	Rule.
Number of Players in the Game		16
Players' Positions		17
Players not to Sit with Spectators		18
Club Uniforms	(1)	19
Gloves	(2)	19
Players' Benches	(1)	20
Players Debarred from Game for Not Occupying Benches	(2)	20

THE GAME.

	Sec.	Rule.
Time of Championship Game	(1)	21
Number of Innings	(2)	21
Termination of Game	(a)	21
The Winning Run	(b)	21
A Tie Game		22
A Drawn Game		23
A Called Game		24
A Forfeited Game		25
Failure of the Nine to Appear	(1)	25
Refusal of One Side to Play	(2)	25
Failure to Resume Playing	(3)	25
If a Team Resorts to Dilatory Practice	(4)	25
Wilful Violation	(5)	25
Disobeying Order to Remove Player	(6)	25
Less than Nine Players	(7)	25
Second Game to be Commenced Within Ten Minutes	(8)	25
Written Notice to President	(9)	25

	Sec.	Rule.
No Game		26
Substitutes		27
Sufficient Number of Substitute Players	(1)	27
When Player May Be Substituted	(2)	27
Base-Runner	(3)	27
Choice of Innings—Condition of Ground		28
The Pitcher's Position		29
Delivery of the Ball—Fair Ball		30
Unfair Ball		31
Balking		32
Motion to Deceive	(1)	32
Foot Not in Contact with Pitcher's Plate	(2)	32
Pitcher Outside of Lines	(3)	32
Delay by Holding Ball	(4)	32
Standing in Position to Pitch Without Having Ball	(5)	32
Any Motion Made Without Immediately Delivering Ball	(6)	32
If the Pitcher Feigns to Throw Ball and Does Not Resume Legal Position	(7)	32
A Dead Ball		33
A Foul Strike		34
Block Balls		35
Stopped by Person Not in Game	(1)	35
Ball Returned	(2)	35
Base-Runner Must Stop	(3)	35
The Batsman's Position—Order of Batting		36
Where Players Must Remain	(1)	37
Space Reserved for Umpire	(2)	37
Space Allotted Players "At Bat"	(3)	37
Batting Rules—Fair Hit		38
Foul Hit	(2)	38
Fair Hit Which Rolls to Foul Ground	(3)	38
Foul Hit Which Rolls to Fair Ground	(4)	38
A Foul Tip		39
A Bunt Hit		40
Balls Batted Outside the Grounds		41
A Fair Batted Ball Over the Fence		42
Strikes		43
Ball Struck at by Batsman	(1)	43
Fair Ball, Delivered by Pitcher	(2)	43
Intentional Effort to Hit Ball to Foul Ground	(3)	43
Foul Hit While Attempting a Bunt Hit	(3)	43
Ball Struck at after Touching Batsman's Person	(4)	43
Ball Tipped by Batsman	(5)	43
A Foul Strike		44
The Batsman is Out		45
Failing to Take Position at Bat in Order	(1)	45
Failure to Take Position within One Minute after being Called	(2)	45
If he Makes a Foul Hit	(3)	45
If he Makes a Foul Strike	(4)	45
Attempt to Hinder Catcher	(5)	45
Three Strikes Called by Umpire	(6)	45
Attempt to Make a Foul Hit after Two Strikes have been Called	(7)	45
If Ball Hits Him While Making Third Strike	(8)	45
If He Hits a Fly Ball that can Be Handled by Infielder while Bases are Occupied with only One Out	(9)	45
If Third Strike is Called	(10)	45
Batsman Must Not Leave Bench Until Called by Umpire	(11)	45

JAMES O'ROURKE,   HORACE A. KEITH,
Mgr. Bridgeport Club.   Pres. Brockton Club.
CAL. DAVIS,
Pres. and Sec'y Canadian Base Ball League, 1897.
JAS. T. SHECKARD,   STURGES WHITLOCK,
Leading Batsman N. E. League.   Pres. Connecticut State League.

INDEX TO RULES AND REGULATIONS. 193

BASE-RUNNING RULES.

	SEC.	RULE.
The Batsman Becomes a Base-Runner............................		46
After a Fair Hit...	(1)	46
After Four Balls are Called..	(2)	46
After Three Strikes are Declared...............................	(3)	46
If Hit by Ball While at Bat...	(4)	46
After Illegal Delivery of Ball.......................................	(5)	46
Bases to be Touched..		47
Base-Runner Shall Not Pass Another Base-Runner to Reach Home Base		47
Entitled to Bases...		48
If Umpire Calls Four Balls...	(1)	48
If Umpire Awards Succeeding Batsman Base...............	(2)	48
If Umpire Calls Balk...	(3)	48
If Pitched Ball by Pitcher Passes Catcher...................	(4)	48
Ball Strikes Umpire...	(5)	48
Prevented from Making Base..	(6)	48
Fielder Stops Ball with Any Part of His Dress............	(7)	48
Returning to Bases..		49
If Foul Tip..	(1)	49
If Foul Strike..	(2)	49
If Dead Ball..	(3)	49
If Person of Umpire Interferes with Catcher...............	(4)	49
If the Ball Touches the Batsman's Person...................	(5)	49
Base-Runner Out...		50
Attempt to Hinder Catcher from Fielding Ball.............	(1)	50
If Fielder Hold Fair Hit Ball..	(2)	50
Third Strike Ball Held by Fielder................................	(3)	50
Touched with Ball After Three Strikes.......................	(4)	50
Touching First Base..	(5)	50
Running from Home Base to First Base......................	(6)	50
Running from First to Second Base............................	(7)	50
Failure to Avoid Fielder...	(8)	50
Touched by Ball While In Play....................................	(9)	50
Base-Runner May Overrun First Base.........................	(10)	50
Fair or Foul Hit Caught by Fielder..............................	(11)	50
Batsman Becomes a Base-Runner................................	(12)	50
Touched by Hit Ball Before Touching Fielder.............	(13)	50
Running to Base..	(14)	50
Umpire Calls Play...	(15)	50
When Batsman or Runner is Out...		51
Coaching Rules...		52
Scoring of Runs..		53

THE UMPIRES.

	RULE.
Each Shall Serve in His Regularly Appointed Position...........	54
Umpires Shall Not Be Changed...	55
Titles and Positions...	56
Duties...	57
Powers...	58
No Appeal from Legal Decisions...	59
Disputed Decisions...	60
Penalties for Violation of Rules.................................... (1)	61
Report of Suspension.. (2)	61
Shall See that the Rules are Strictly Observed.........................	62
Shall Call Play...	63
Suspend Play.. 64, 65,	66
Shall Call Balls and Strikes...	67
When Only One Umpire is Assigned.......................................	68

INDEX TO RULES AND REGULATIONS.

FIELD RULES.

	SEC. RULE.
No Club Shall Allow Open Betting	69
Who Shall Be Allowed on the Field	70
Spectators Shall Not Be Addressed	71
Every Club Shall Furnish Police Force	72

GENERAL DEFINITIONS.

		SEC. RULE.
Play		73
Time		74
Game		75
An Inning		76
A Time at Bat		77
Legal		78
Scoring		79
Batting	(1)	79
Runs Made	(2)	79
Base Hits	(3)	79
Sacrifice Hits	(4)	79
Fielding	(5)	79
Assists	(6)	79
Errors	(7)	79
Stolen Bases		79
The Summary		80
Score Made in Each Inning	(1)	80
Number of Bases Stolen	(2)	80
Number of Two-Base Hits	(3)	80
Number of Three-Base Hits	(4)	80
Number of Home Runs	(5)	80
Number of Double and Triple Plays	(6)	80
Number of Innings Each Pitcher Pitched In	(7)	80
Number of Base-Hits Off Each Pitcher	(8)	80
Number of Batsmen Struck Out by Each Pitcher	(9)	80
Number of Bases on Balls by Each Pitcher	(10)	80
Wild Pitches	(11)	80
Number of Batsmen Hit by Each Pitcher	(12)	80
Passed Balls	(13)	80
Time of Game	(14)	80
Name and Position of Each Umpire	(15)	80

THE "BRUSH RESOLUTION."

The following is the text of the measure for the suppression of rowdyism on the ball field introduced by Mr. John T. Brush, and adopted by the National League at the St. Louis meeting, March 1, 1898:

A measure entitled a measure for the suppression of obscene, indecent and vulgar language upon the ball field by players engaged in playing a game of ball during the championship season, while under contract to a club, member of the National League and American Association of Professional Ball Clubs, to the end that the game may retain its high position as respectable and worthy of confidence and support of the refined and cultured classes of American citizenship.

In pursuance of this measure of reform and to define and carry into effect its intent and purposes, be it resolved as follows:

First—It shall be the duty of each club president or chief officer to furnish to the manager or captain of his team a printed or typewritten copy of this enactment, together with a copy of offences and evils which are sought to be remedied by this measure, all of which shall be read and fully explained to all of the players and employees of the club at the beginning of the contract season and to all others who may thereafter join the club during the playing season, and a copy thereof shall also be delivered to such players and employees, and the captain and manager of each club shall obtain for and deliver to the president of said club, who shall within five days thereafter forward the same to the President of the League, the signatures of all the players and employees of said club, acknowledging that this legislation with all of its provisions has been brought to each and every player's and employee's attention.

Second—To perpetuate base ball as the national game of the United States, preserve its respectability, surround it with such additional safeguards as to warrant absolute public confidence in its methods and purposes, to reform and promote the mutual interests of professional base ball clubs and professional base ball players, it shall be competent for any person or persons, whether player, manager, umpire or club official of any club, member of this League, or spectator, to submit information and testimony in writing under oath concerning obscene, indecent or vulgar language (other than profanity, that being otherwise and especially provided for in the playing rules) during the progress of a game upon the ball field by a player or employee of a National League club of which they have personal knowledge. The information and corroborative evidence under oath may be submitted to the President of the League, who shall have the right to suspend the offender pending investigation by the tribunal hereinafter created, or not, as he may elect, being governed in judgment by the circumstances and gravity of the offence and character of the evidence.

Third—All charges of offence under this measure with the supporting evidence shall be submitted to the President of the League under oath within forty-eight hours of its alleged commission, and the President shall immediately furnish a copy of the same to the accused for his defence, with written notice of the suspension, if any.

Fourth—Any one under contract to a National League club who may be charged with using offensive language within the intent and meaning of this measure, shall be furnished with a copy of the charges, which, to receive consideration, must be substantiated by corroborative evidence, and after the receipt thereof by the accused five days shall be allowed the one charged with the offence for transmitting by some express company to the President of the League, under oath, of the defence, and the case when thus prepared shall be submitted by the President to a tribunal of three judges selected by this League, to be called the "Board of Discipline," who shall have absolute authority to acquit or convict upon the evidence submitted, according to the rules adopted for its government, and from which there shall be no appeal, except to the Board of Directors of the League, as hereinafter provided.

Fifth—When a case is thus submitted to said board the President of the tribunal shall carefully consider it from the evidence submitted, taking into account the nature and gravity of the offence, its importance as affecting the welfare of the national game, the provocation for its commission, and such other circumstances as may be submitted that are entitled to be considered. He shall report in writing his opinion and finding in the premises, and if the offence be proven he shall affix the penalty that in his judgment should be imposed, and forward the same, together with his opinion and conclusions and all the papers, to his associate nearest in territory, who shall attach thereto his opinion and conclusions and judgment, and forward the same to the remaining member of the tribunal, who shall forward his opinion, conclusions and finding, and all the papers in the case to the president of the tribunal. He in turn shall return the papers and opinions, conclusions and findings to the President of the League, who shall carry into effect the judgment of said board or a majority thereof, by suspending the player from his club for the period determined by the tribunal or a majority, or acquit him, as the case may be.

Sixth—When the members of the tribunal or a majority thereof do not agree upon a judgment, the President of the League shall select some one of the opinions as the one to be followed (providing it be not the extreme penalty), and that shall be considered the judgment and be enforced according to the provisions of section 5.

Seventh—The penalty for using obscene, indecent, and vulgar language, within the meaning and intent of this measure, is entirely within the discretion of the tribunal, and may be suspension for days, for months, for the unexpired season, for a year, or for life, according to the conditions, circumstances and nature of the offence, it being the sentiment of the League that creates this law that an unwarranted, unprovoked, and brutal use of vulgarity to a spectator, or within the presence of spectators and within the hearing of ladies, should debar the offender forever from service with his club, or any other club, member of this League or subject to its jurisdiction.

Eighth—The extreme penalty proposed in this measure, namely, "life expulsion," shall require the unanimous approval of the three members of the tribunal, and provided also, before imposing such a penalty, the accused shall be notified, that he can defend in person and by counsel, if he elects, in which event the President of the tribunal shall call a meeting of said board at some city to be selected by him most convenient to the members and the accused, the traveling expenses and hotel bills of the board to be paid by the League.

Ninth—When two members concur in the penalty to be imposed, that shall be considered as the judgment of the tribunal, except as provided in rules 6 and 8.

Tenth—That justice may be done and no wrong committed, it shall be competent for either parties to a case submitted to the tribunal to show under oath the character and standing of those who make the charges and give evidence, and before the "life expulsion" can be imposed the accused may, if he elect, receive the opportunity of cross-examining the witnesses against him by depositions.

Eleventh—There shall be no appeal from a decision by the tribunal or a majority for a hearing or a reopening of the case, except by unanimous vote of the Board of Directors, based upon new evidence.

Twelfth—The tribunal shall be selected by the National League with due regard for fitness, integrity, knowledge of and interest in the national game of base ball. One of its members shall be designated President of the tribunal, and no one shall be a member who is financially interested in a club member of this League. Whenever a case is submitted under the provisions of this enactment, each member of the tribunal shall carefully examine all evidence submitted, and render his decision according to the same; and no hearing shall be secret, unless so requested by both parties to the controversy.

Thirteenth—The first tribunal under this provision shall be composed of L. C. Krauthoff, who shall be elected to serve three years or until his successor is elected; Louis Kramer, who shall serve two years or until his successor is elected, and Frederick K. Stearns, who shall serve one year or until his successor is elected; and beginning with 1899 and each year thereafter there shall be one member elected to serve three years.

Fourteenth—If a player under suspension pending investigation should be acquitted by the tribunal, his salary shall be paid by the President of the League for the time he was under suspension.

Fifteenth—To compensate in part for the loss to a club of a player who has been suspended under these provisions for a period longer than one year, the club may select one member of the League to represent it, and the President of the League shall select some member of the League to represent the League, and the two, if unable to agree, shall select the third member of the League, and they or a majority of them shall place a fair estimate of value upon the release of the player so disciplined, and the League shall pay to the club one-half of such award, and in case said persons or a majority do not arrive at an award, said Board of Discipline or a majority thereof shall make the award.

Sixteenth—All elections to fill vacancies in the tribunal shall be by ballot upon nominations, and it shall require a majority vote to elect.

Seventeenth—All vacancies in the tribunal caused by death or resignation shall be temporarily filled by the President of the League, until the next meeting at which an annual election occurs, when it shall be filled by ballot for the unexpired term.

Eighteenth—The compensation to be allowed to the members of the tribunal shall be fixed by the President of the League according to the circumstances of each case, and be paid by the League, together with traveling expenses and hotel bills, if they meet together as provided in section 8.

Nineteenth—For all communications with this tribunal the express companies shall be used in lieu of the United States mail.

Twentieth—The annual meeting for the election of members to fill vacancies upon the tribunal shall be the annual schedule meeting of the League.

Twenty-first—This enactment for government of the players may be altered or amended at any annual or schedule meeting of the League by a majority vote.

Twenty-second—The President of the League is authorized to publish this measure in the official records of the League book, and to provide a sufficient number of copies of the same to supply all requirements of a thorough distribution among players and employees of the clubs, members of the National League.

Twenty-third—The members of said board shall meet at some convenient point within thirty days from its creation and establish rules and regulations for its government not inconsistent with this " measure," and shall have the right to employ a stenographer at the expense of the League in the cases mentioned in section 8 at any joint meeting of the members of said board.

ADDRESS TO PLAYERS.

At a meeting of the National League and American Association of Professional Base Ball Clubs, held in St. Louis, February 28, 1898, a measure was adopted for the suppression of the use of obscene and vulgar language by ball players upon the ball field. The enormity of this evil and the extent to which it has grown, as shown by the vast amount of evidence that was submitted by those having knowledge of the facts, has made it imperative on the part of the League to adopt drastic measures for its suppression.

This committee is instructed by the League to serve all players under contract to a club member of the National League and American Association of Professional Base Ball Clubs with a copy of the law above referred to, which will be in force this season. You are requested to carefully read the same and become acquainted with all of its provisions and its intents and purposes. We say to you frankly and emphatically that vulgarity and obscenity upon the ball field must be stopped, regardless of results to the player who gives offence.

This adress, the law, and the private instructions will be furnished and read to you, and you are each required to sign acknowledgement, to be filed with the President of the League, that this measure is fully understood. The Board of Discipline is composed of men who have had large experience in matters pertaining to base ball. They are men of national reputation and all selected to serve upon this tribunal because of fitness, high character and interest in the future of the game. No member of the tribunal has a financial interest in the National League nor in any of its clubs; therefore they may be expected to act impartially and for what may be deemed to be for the best interest of all.

If any player suffers because of this law of reform and its penalties, it will be his own fault. There is nothing in the game that calls for the use of vile language, and the League is positively determined that ungentlemanly language in a gentleman's game shall no longer be permitted. In the future let it be understood that no player need ever again submit tamely and without redress to the filthy and insulting language of an opposing player. In the future let it be understood that the umpire is not without redress and is not to be driven into resigning because of the vile insults which will not permit him to serve longer without entire loss of self respect.

Let it be distinctly understood that in the future we propose to protect the patrons from the villainously filthy language that is used by a very limited number of players. Let it be fully understood by club official, umpire and player that this measure results from a cry of alarm from the press and the public, and in response to the universal demand for reformation the League pledges itself to the press and public to suppress the evils hereby sought to be remedied at any or whatever cost.

JOHN T. BRUSH,
JAMES A. HART, } Committee.
A. H. SODEN,

THE RETIREMENT OF A. C. ANSON.

Professional base ball history records the development of many an original character in the ranks alike of its press writers, its club magnates, and its most noteworthy players; but it can be safely said that the most unique figure can be found in the person of the League's greatest representative on the field, Adrian Constantine Anson, who to-day stands forth as one of the most sturdy, fearless and honest exemplars of professional base ball known to the game. The bright particular attribute of Anson's character is his sterling integrity, combined with which is his thorough independence. The former was strikingly illustrated at the very outset of his career as a member of the Chicago club team in 1876, when he kept true to his agreement with that club, though under the base ball law as it then existed, the club could not enforce its contract; and his independence was plainly exhibited in the act of his refusing this year to accept a money testimonial at the hands of his base ball friends, he preferring to depend upon his existing physical powers for his maintenance rather than upon the proffered financial aid.

In some respects Anson resembles a rough diamond, his brusque manner and impulsive temper needing the keen polish of the refining wheel of the conventional amenities of life to make his inherent worth shine forth in its full brilliancy. Anson too, reminds one somewhat of that old Western pioneer, Davy Crockett, inasmuch as his practical motto is "when you know you're right, go ahead." This latter trait was conspicuously shown in the year of the players' revolt in 1890, when, almost alone as a minority man, he stood by the National League in its greatest hour of need, in opposition to the desertion of hundreds of his confreres in the League ranks. In these prominent characteristics, we say, Anson stands as the most unique player known in the annals of the professional fraternity.

We regret that the GUIDE has not space enough at command to give even a brief sketch of the twenty-two years of Anson's career while a member of the Chicago team—from 1876 to 1897 inclusive. Indeed, a very interesting compilation could be made to fill a book in itself with a detailed biography of Anson since he first handled a ball in a match game in 1867 up to the close of the past year. But we have only room for a brief chapter, the feature of which is the particulars of the movement made to give him a special testimonial, which we now proceed officially to report. First, as to his record:

Anson was the third baseman of the Forest City nine of Rockford, Ill., in 1871, and he began his professional career that year. In 1872 he was third baseman of the Athletic Club of Philadelphia. He played in the shortstop's position in the same club in 1873, and in 1874 began playing in the same club in his home position of first baseman, which position he retained in 1875. At that period, before the introduction of the League rules, the base-hit averages were made up on the basis of the average of base-hits per game, and Anson's figures were as follows:

	1871	1872	1873	1874	1875
Anson	1—64	1—91	2—02	1—78	1—48

In England in 1874 Anson played at right field, as Fisler was the Athletic's first baseman on the trip.

In 1876 Anson began his noted career as a member of the Chicago Club, and he covered third base and occasionally went behind the bat, as he did in 1878, in which year he was catcher in 41 games, Start playing first base the latter year. It was in 1879 that Anson took up his home position at first base, and he led the League first basemen. We give, as a reference table, Anson's batting and fielding averages for the period of twenty-three years, twenty-two of which were in the service of the Chicago Club, of which team he became manager and captain in 1880.

ANSON'S TWENTY-THREE YEARS' RECORD OF BATTING AND FIELDING.

The appended figures—with the exception of 1875 and 1876—are from the National League's official records, the GUIDE of 1876 not containing any League statistics:

Years.	Games.	Per cent. base hits.	Per cent. fielding.	Years.	Games.	Per cent. base hits.	Per cent. fielding.
1875	69	.318	.820	1887	122	.421	.947
1876	66	.342	.826	1888	134	.343	.985
1877	67	.335	.868	1889	134	.341	.982
1878	59	.336	.818	1890	139	.311	.978
1879	49	.407	.974	1891	136	.294	.981
1880	84	.338	.977	1892	147	.274	.971
1881	84	.399	.975	1893	101	.322	.981
1882	82	.367	.948	1894	83	.394	.988
1883	98	.307	.964	1895	122	.338	.990
1884	111	.337	.954	1896	106	.335	.982
1885	112	.322	.971	1897	112	.302	.987
1886	125	.371	.949				

As we said before, it would take a volume to give in full the statistics, incidents and noteworthy events connected with Anson's unequalled career on the diamond field. Suffice it to say, that when it was ascertained that the veteran manager of the Chicago club was destined to sever his connection with that club as a player or official, his old friend, the ex-President of the Chicago club, Mr. A. G. Spalding, set to work to get up just such a testimonial as was last year presented to the champion batsman of the English cricket world, Dr. W. G. Grace, as a complimentary recognition of Anson's great record as the veteran batting champion of the American base ball world. It was a voluntary movement on Mr. Spalding's part, and it met with pronounced success in the form of endorsement of the testimonial; but, strange to say, when Anson heard of it, in his peculiar brusque way he said: "I refuse to accept anything in the shape of a money gift. The public owes me nothing, and I am neither old nor a pauper. I can earn my own living as hitherto, and, moreover, I am by no means out of base ball." This characteristic declaration only increased the respect in which the veteran was generally held. Afterwards he gave forth the following card of thanks for the intended compliment:

CHICAGO, Feb. 5, 1898.

To My Friends:

The kind offer to raise a large public subscription for me, the first notice of which I received by a chance meeting with Mr. Spalding late in the afternoon preceding the publication in the daily papers, is an honor and compliment I duly appreciate; implying, as i does, the hearty good will and the close fellowship of the originator of th movement, A. G. Spalding, causes me to regard it the higher. There are times when one hesitates to receive favors even from friends, and at this hour I deem it both unwise and inexpedient to accept the generosity so considerately offered.

A. C. ANSON.

Among the most important signatures endorsing the movement started by Mr. Spalding were those of ex-President A. G. Mills of the New York Athletic Club, P. T. Powers, President of the Eastern League, and E. B. Talcott and J. Walter Spalding of the New York club of 1892.

The prominent base ball scribes of the country who followed Mr. Spalding's lead in this respect included Messrs. F. C. Richter, of the Philadelphia *Sporting Life;* C. C. Spink, of the St. Louis *Sporting News;* H. Chadwick, of the New York *Sporting Review;* J. C. Morse, T. Murnane and W. S. Barnes, of the Boston *Herald*, *Globe* and *Journal;* F. Hough, D. Mills and H. S. Fogel, of the Philadelphia *Inquirer*, *Times* and *Ledger;* Ren Mulford, C. H. Zuber, H. Weldon and J. Ed Grillo, of the Cincinnati *Post*, *Times-Star*, *Enquirer* and *Commercial Tribune;* G. H. Dickinson and G. E. Stackhouse, of the New York *Journal* and *Tribune;* A. Yeager, of the Brooklyn *Eagle;* F. B. Patterson and J. H. Anderson, of the Baltimore *Sun* and *Herald;* W. M. Robison and N. Rose, of the Cleveland *Plaindealer* and *Leader;* J. D. Pringle and C. D. Powers, of the Pittsburg *Dispatch* and *Leader*, and W. W. Douglas, of the Louisville *Courier-Journal*.

Of the League magnates who promptly answered Mr. Spalding's call within a few days there were Messrs. John T. Brush of Cincinnati, C. H. Ebbetts of Brooklyn, W. H. Watkins of Pittsburg, H. C. Pulliam of Louisville, and Chris Von Der Ahe of St. Louis. But it would require more space than the GUIDE can give to publish the host of letters which were received later on by Mr. Spalding favoring the testimonial, but one of which objected to the money contribution, the latter preferring a different form for the offering to the veteran.

As a sample of the replies sent to the above-named gentlemen, we append the only letter we have at command, viz., that sent to the Editor of the GUIDE, which is as follows:

CHICAGO, February 9, 1898.
Henry Chadwick, Brooklyn, N. Y.

DEAR SIR: Your kind telegram relative to the proposed testimonial has just been handed me by Mr. Spalding, along with several others. I feel under many obligations for the kindly sentiment expressed, and cannot too heartily express my sincere thanks for the generous motive which prompted it. There was a strong inclination on my part to accept the testimonial, as it would have facilitated the achievement of an end I have long wished for, but under the circumstances I do not see my way clear to accept it.

I have not as yet made any definite plans for the future, but hope to be actively connected with base ball.

Please be assured that I am extremely grateful and thoroughly appreciate the compliment shown. Sincerely yours, A. C. ANSON.

Had Mr. Spalding's projected testimonial been fully carried out it would have resulted in a compliment that any American might have been proud of, and one entirely devoid of any form of charitable gift whatever.

EDITOR LEAGUE GUIDE.

THE LATE CHARLES H. BYRNE.

In the death of Chas. H. Byrne the professional base ball fraternity lost one of the truest and best friends they have ever had among the League club magnates and the game at large its most efficient advocate and supporter. From the year Mr. Byrne made his advent in the base ball arena up to the year of his last illness, he was foremost in every movement that was calculated to benefit the national game. Speaking individually, I have to state that I first became acquainted with Chas. H. Byrne in the spring of 1883. He was then in the real estate business and had an office in Liberty street, near Broadway, New York. At my first interview with him I was impressed with the natural courtesy of his manner and the educated intelligence of his conversation. As I came to know him more intimately, traits of character were brought out which raised him greatly in my esteem; and from that time to the day of his death, not a single favorable impression has been removed from my mind concerning the high opinion I had formed of him during the first year of our acquaintance.

Mr. Byrne was not only a man of remarkable executive ability, but he possessed the rare qualification of quick perception in grasping the salient points of every business transaction he entered upon. And with this he had a methodical way of preserving documentary evidence calculated to bear with telling effect on anything he undertook to accomplish. It was this peculiar habit of his that made him so effective in supporting any measure he deemed advantageous to the game, and which enabled him to be so strong in opposition to those who sought to achieve mere individual club aggrandizement rather than the interests of the League at large.

Personally, Mr. Byrne was Chesterfieldian in his manners, especially to the fair sex, with whom he was the most popular of the League magnates. He was full of geniality, and that, too, despite his suffering from that most trying of all diseases to one's disposition, dyspepsia. Kind-heated and liberal to a high degree, Mr. Byrne did more for his players than any of his confreres, either in the old Association or the League; so much so, indeed, that it became a most desirable position for a player to hold to be one of the Brooklyn club's team. His sole reward for this, in too many instances, however, was an ingratitude that made him at times heartsore.

HENRY CHADWICK.

The Tour of the Australian Ball Players.

A noteworthy event of the base ball season of 1897 was the tour of the United States made by the team of Australian base ball players, under the management of Mr. Harry Musgrave, who, a year before, so successfully piloted the Australian cricketers through the United States and Canada, after their triumphant tour of England. The visit of the Australians was simply an experimental one ; that is, it was partly a pleasure trip and partly a tour made by a picked team of Australian base ball players to see how the strongest nine they could get together for the purpose would compare with the representative base ball teams of America. The result proved to be eminently satisfactory to the visitors from a social point of view, but in ball playing, compared with those of our leading amateur nines, the Australians practically realized that they had yet much to learn of the scientific points of the game ; while in contrast with strong teams of the professional arena, they were simply "not in it."

RECORD OF THE AUSTRALIANS' GAMES IN AMERICA IN 1897.

Date:	Contesting Clubs.	Where Played.	Pitchers.	Score.
April 20	Australians vs. Santa Clara.	San Jose.....	Kemp.....Steffani	18-10
May 10	Australians vs. Santa Cruz..	Santa Cruz...	Laver....Devereau	12-7
" 20	Australians vs. Ogden......	Ogden........	Kemp.....Emmett	9-8
" 21	Australians vs. Ogden......	Ogden........	Kemp.....Emmett	6-4
" 28	Australians vs. Denver.....	Denver	Laver....Gerhardt	18-17
June 14	Australians vs. Ch. & Br. Subs	Brooklyn.....	Kemp....Korwan	11-8
" 21	Australians vs. Veterans....	Boston.......	Kemp....Spalding	27-13
" 25	Australians vs. N. Attleboro	N. Attleboro.	Over......Bannon	12-11
July 5	Australians vs. W. N. Y....	Weehawken..	Over........Baldt	30-20
April 19	Olympic vs. Australians....	San Francisco	Weldon......Kemp	20-9
" 20	Stockton vs. Australians....	Stockton.....	Lockhead...Laver	12-7
" 24	Reliance vs. Australians....	San Francisco	McKinnon..Laver	21-19
" 25	San Francisco A.C. vs. Aus.	San Francisco	Raymond....Laver	26-25
May 2	Suisin vs. Australians.......	Suisin........	Tillman.....Kemp	10-7
" 9	Santa Cruz vs. Australians..	Santa Cruz...	Dauhenbis...Kemp	11-6
" 15	San Francisco A.C. vs. Aus.	San Francisco	Krug........Laver	19-11
" 26	Omaha vs. Australians.....	Omaha	Jellin.......Laver	13-9
June 6	Illinois C. C. vs. Australians	Chicago......	Smith.......Kemp	9-7
" 10	Duquesne vs. Australians...	Pittsburg	McNeil......Laver	9-7
" 22	Brockton vs. Australians...	Brockton.....	Wick........Kemp	18-8
" 26	Newton A.C. vs. Australians	N'wt'n C'ntre	Dowd........Kemp	14-6
" 27	Pawtucket vs. Australians..	Providence...	Leith.........Over	12-9
July 1	Orange A.C. vs. Australians	Orange.......	Westervelt....Over	21-5
" 3	Atlantic C. vs. Australians.	Atlantic City.	Voorhees....Laver	18-0
" 7	Phila. Ama. vs. Australians.	Philadelphia.	McFetridge..Kemp	9-3

THE TEMPLE CUP SERIES.

The post-season series of games between the first and second clubs in contest for the championship of the National League, and known as the "Temple Cup Series," was played for the last time in 1897, the League officials, for the best interests of the game, having abolished all future contests and returned the cup to its liberal donor, Mr. Temple, of Pittsburg. The complete record since the inception of the series is given below:

RECORD OF 1894.

Date.	Contesting Clubs.	Where Played.	Pitchers.	Score.
Oct. 4	New York vs. Baltimore....	Baltimore .	Rusie........Esper	4-1
" 5	New York vs. Baltimore....	Baltimore ...	Meekin.....Gleason	9-6
" 6	New York vs. Baltimore....	Baltimore ...	Rusie....Hemming	4-1
" 8	New York vs Baltimore....	New York...	Meekin... Hawke *	16-3

*Eight innings.

RECORD OF 1895.

Date.	Contesting Clubs.	Where Played.	Pitchers.	Score.
Oct. 2	Cleveland vs. Baltimore....	Cleveland....	Young....McMahon	5-4
" 3	Cleveland vs. Baltimore....	Cleveland....	Cuppy ......Hoffer	7-2
" 5	Cleveland vs. Baltimore....	Cleveland....	Young ...McMahon	7-1
" 7	Baltimore vs. Cleveland....	Baltimore ...	Esper ... . Cuppy	5-0
" 8	Cleveland vs. Baltimore....	Cleveland....	Young...... Hoffer	5-2

RECORD OF 1896.

Date.	Contesting Clubs.	Where Played.	Pitchers.	Score.
Oct. 2	Baltimore vs. Cleveland....	Baltimore....	Hoffer.......Young	7-1
" 3	Baltimore vs. Cleveland....	Baltimore....	Corbett.....Wallace	7-2
" 5	Baltimore vs. Cleveland....	Baltimore....	Hoffer.......Cuppy	6-2
" 8	Baltimore vs. Cleveland....	Cleveland....	Corbett......Cuppy	5-0

RECORD OF 1897.

Date.	Contesting Clubs.	Where Played.	Pitchers.	Score.
Oct. 4	Boston vs. Baltimore........	Boston	Nichols....... Nops	13-12
" 5	Baltimore vs. Boston........	Boston	Corbett..Klobedanz	13-11
" 6	Baltimore vs. Boston........	Boston	Hoffer...Klobedanz	8-3
" 9	Baltimore vs. Boston........	Baltimore. .	Nops.......Stivetts	12-11
" 11	Baltimore vs. Boston........	Baltimore. ..	Hoffer.... Hickman	9-3

OFFICE OF PRESIDENT

[N]ATIONAL LEAGUE AND AMERICAN ASSOCIATION
OF
PROFESSIONAL BASE BALL CLUBS.

N. E. YOUNG, PRESIDENT &
            SECRETARY

Washington, DC Dec. 28 1891.

I take special pleasure in bearing testimony to the superior quality of the "Spalding League Ball." It has been in constant use by the National League for the past fifteen (15) years, and has been unanimously adopted by by the new National League and American Association of Professional B.B. Clubs for the coming five years. During the long time that it has been in exclusive use by League Clubs, scarcely a word of complaint as to its quality has been received from Club officials, manager or player. I have no hesitation in recommending it as the perfection of a League Ball.

N. E. Young

NATIONAL LEAGUE AND AMERICAN ASSOCIATION SCHEDULE.
SEASON OF 1898.

CLUBS.	In Boston.	In Brooklyn.	In New York	In Philadel'a	In Baltimore	In Wash'ton.	In Pittsburg.	In Cleveland	In Chicago	In Cincinn'ti	In Louisville.	In St. Louis
Boston	......	July 6, 23, 25, 26 Oct. 6, 7, 8	Apr. 15,16, 18, May 4, J'ly 4 a.m. p.m. Sep. 3	April 25, 26, 27, 28 July 7, 8, 9	April 20, 21, 22, 23 Oct. 13, 14, 15	Apr. 29, 30 May 2, 3 Oct. 10, 11, 12	June 24, 25, 27, 28 Aug. 27, 29, 30	June 29,30 July 1, 2 Aug. 31 Sept. 1, 2	June 20, 21, 22, 23 Aug. 24, 25, 26	May 19, 20, 21 Aug. 6, 8, 9, 10	May 26, 27, 28 Aug. 2, 3, 4, 5	May 23, 24, 25 J'ly 28, 29, 30, Au. 1
Brooklyn	May 13, 14, 16, 17 Sept. 24, 26, 27	......	May 9, 10 June 11,13 July 7, 8 Sept. 6	April 15, 16, 18, 19 Oct. 13, 14, 15	April 25, 26, 27, 28 Sept. 29,30 Oct. 1	April 20, 21, 22, 23 July 4, a.m., p.m., 5	June 29,30 July 1, 2 Aug. 24, 25, 26	June 20, 21, 22, 23 Aug. 27, 28, 29	June 24, 25, 26, 27 Aug. 31 Sept. 1, 3	May 23, 24, 25 July 28, 29, 30, 31	May 19, 20, 21, 22 Aug. 6, 7, 8	May 26, 27, 28 Aug. 2, 3, 4, 5
New York	Apr. 19 May 5, 6, 7 Sept. 8, 9, 10	May 11, 12 June 14,15 J'ly 9, S't 5, a.m., p.m.	......	April 20, 21, 22, 23 June 18 Oct. 3, 4.	Apr. 29,30 May 2 J'ly 26, Oct. 10, 11, 12	April 25, 26, 27, 28 Sept. 29,30 Oct. 1	June 20, 21, 22, 23 Aug. Sept. 1, 2	June 24, 25, 26, 27 Aug. 24, 25, 26	J'e 29, 30 July 1, 2 Aug. 27, 28, 29	May 26, 27, 28 Aug. 2, 3, 4, 5	May 23, 24, 25 July 28, 29, 30, 31	May 19, 20, 21, 22 Aug. 6, 7, 8
Philadelphia	June 11, 13, 14, 15 Sept. 29, 30 Oct. 1	April 29, 30 May 2, 3 Oct. 10, 11, 12	June 16, 17 Sept. 24, 26, 27, 28 Oct. 5	......	May 4, 5, 6, 7 July 4, a.m., p.m., 5	May 9, 10, 11, 12 Sept. 8, 9, 10	May 23, 24, 25 J'ly 28,29, 30, Aug. 1	May 19, 20, 21 Aug. 2 3, 4, 5	May 26, 27, 28 Aug. 6, 8, 9, 10	June 29,30 July 1, 2 Aug. 27, 29, 30	June 24, 25, 27, 28 Aug. 24, 25, 26	June 20, 21, 22, 23 Aug. 31 Sept. 1, 2
Baltimore	May 9, 10, 11, 12 Oct. 3, 4, 5	May 16, 17, 18 Sept. 7, 8, 9, 10	May 3 July 23, 25 Sept. 13, Oct. 6, 7, 8	May 13, 14, 16, 17 Sept. 5, a. m., p. m., 6	......	Apr. 15, 18 June 13, 14 July 7, 9 Sept. 26	May 21, 30, 30, 31 Aug. 6, 8 Sept. 3	May 22, 26, 27, 28 July 30, 31 Aug. 1	May 23, 24, 25 Aug. 2, 3, 4, 5	June 20, 21, 22, 23 Aug. 7, 24, 25	June 29, 30 July 1, 2 Au 30, 31 Sept. 1	June 24, 25, 26, 27 Aug. 27, 28, 29
Washington	June 16,17 18, Sept. 5, a.m., p.m. 6, 7	May 4, 5, 6, 7 Oct. 3, 4, 5	May 13, 14, 16, 17 Oct. 13, 14, 15	July 23, 25, 26, 27 Oct. 6, 7, 8	Apr. 16, 19 F'e 11, J'y 8 Sept. 12, 24, 27	......	May 26, 27, 28 Aug. 2, 3, 4, 5	May 23, 24, 25 Aug. 6, 7, 8, 9	May 19, 20, 21, 22 July 29, 30, 31	June 24, 25, 26, 27 Aug. 31 Sept. 1, 3	June 20, 21, 22, 23 Aug. 27, 28, 29	J'e 29, 30 July 1, 2 Aug. 24, 25, 26

CLUBS.	In Boston.	In Brooklyn.	In New York	In Philadel'a	In Baltimore.	In Wash'ton.	In Pittsburg.	In Cleveland	In Chicago	In Cincinnati	In Louisville.	In St. Louis
Pittsburg.	July 15, 16, 18, 19 Sept. 21, 22, 23	July 11, 12, 13, 14 Sept. 17, 19, 20	July 20, 21, 21, 22 Sept. 14, 15, 16	June 2, 3, 4, 6 Aug. 16, 17, 18	May 18, 19, 20 Aug. 12, 13, 15	June 7, 8, 9, 10 Aug. 19, 20, 22	....	May 8, J'e 12, 13, 19 J'y3,Sept. 11, Oct. 2	Aug. 7, Sept. 4, 5, 5, 25, 26, 27	Apr. 20,21, 23 May1,22 July 24 Aug. 28	Apr. 15, 16, 17,18 Oct. 6, 7, 8	Apr. 24, 25, 26, 27 Oct. 4, 5, 5
Cleveland	June 2, 3, 4, 6 Aug. 12, 13, 15	June 7, 8, 9, 10 Aug. 16, 17, 18	May 30, a. m.p.m.,31 J'el,Aug. 19, 20, 22	July 11, 12, 13, 14 Sept. 21, 22, 23	July 20, 21, 21, 22 Sept. 17, 19, 20	July 15, 16,18, 19 Sept. 14, 15, 16	June 11,18 Sept. 10 Oct. 1, 10, 11, 12	....	May 9, 10, 11, 12 July 4, 4, 5	Apr. 15, 16, 17 Se. 4, 5, 5 Oct. 9	Apr. 24, 25, 26, 27 Oct. 13, 14, 15	Apr. 20, 21, 22, 23 Oct. 6, 7, 8
Chicago	May 30, a. m.p.m.,31 J'el,Aug. 16, 17, 18	June 2, 3, 4, 6 Aug. 19, 20, 22	June 7, 8, 9, 10 Aug. 12, 13, 15	July 20, 21, 21, 22 Sept. 14, 15, 16	July 15, 16, 18, 19 Sept. 21, 22, 23	July 11, 12, 13, 14 Sept. 17, 19, 20	May 4, 5, 6, 7 Oct. 13, 14, 15	May 13, 14, 15, 16 July 23, 24 Sept. 12	....	Apr. 24, 25, 26 July 10 S't. 6,7,8	Apr. 20, 21, 22,23 Sept. 28, 29, 30	Apr 15,16,17, 18, 19 Oct. 9,10
Cincinnati.	June 7, 8, 9, 10 Aug. 19, 20, 22	May 30, a. m.,p.m.,31 J'el,Aug. 12, 13, 15	June 2, 3, 4, 6 Aug. 16, 17, 18	July 15, 16, 18, 19 Sept. 17, 19, 20	July 11, 12, 13, 14 Sept. 14, 15, 16	July 20, 21, 21, 22 Sept. 21, 22, 23	Apr. 29,30 May 2, 3 July 23, 25, 26	Sept. 24, 25, 26, 27 Oct. 3, 4, 5	June 16, 17, 18, 19 July 7, 8, 9	....	June 12, 13, 14, 15 Oct. 10, 11, 12	May 9, 10, 11, 12 13, 14, 15
Louisville	July 11, 12, 13, 14 Sept. 17, 19, 20	July 20, 21, 21, 22 Sept. 14, 15, 16	July 15, 16, 18, 19 Sept. 21, 22, 23	May 30, a, m.p.m.,31 7, J'el,Aug. 19, 20, 22	June 2, 3, 4, 6 Aug. 16, 17, 18	June 2, 3, 4, 6 Aug. 12, 13, 15	May 9, 10, 11, 12 July 7, 8, 9	May 4, 5, 6, 7 Sept. 7, 8, 9	Apr. 29, 30 May 1, 2 July 3 Oct. 1, 2	May 8, 14, 15 July 4,4 Se. 10,11	....	June 16, 17, 18,19 Sept. 25, 26,27
St. Louis.	July 20, 21, 21, 22 Sept. 14, 15, 16	July 15, 16, 18, 19 Sept. 21, 22, 23	July 11, 12, 13, 14 Sept. 17, 19, 20	June 7, 8, 9, 10 Aug. 12, 13, 15	June 2, 3, 4, 6 Aug. 19, 20, 22	May 30, a. m.p.m.,31 J'el,Aug. 16, 17, 18	May 13, 14, 15, 16 July 4, 4, 5	Apr. 29,30 May 1, 2 July 7, 8, 9	May 8 June 12, 13, 14, 15 Sept.10,11	May4,5, 6,7 J'y3 Sept. 9 Oct 2	July 24, 25, 26 Sept. 2, 4, 5, 5	....

Spalding's Trade = Mark Base Balls.

The Spalding League Ball adopted by the National League and American Association of Professional Base Ball Clubs. Warranted to last a full game without ripping or losing its elasticity or shape.

Each.

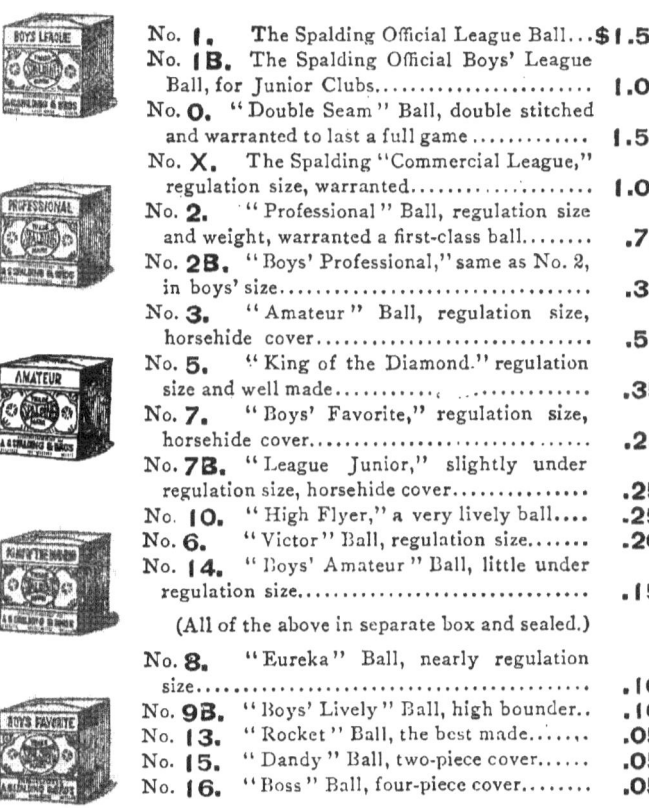

No. 1.	The Spalding Official League Ball...	$1.50
No. 1B.	The Spalding Official Boys' League Ball, for Junior Clubs..................	1.00
No. 0.	"Double Seam" Ball, double stitched and warranted to last a full game............	1.50
No. X.	The Spalding "Commercial League," regulation size, warranted.................	1.00
No. 2.	"Professional" Ball, regulation size and weight, warranted a first-class ball........	.75
No. 2B.	"Boys' Professional," same as No. 2, in boys' size............................	.35
No. 3.	"Amateur" Ball, regulation size, horsehide cover............................	.50
No. 5.	"King of the Diamond." regulation size and well made.....................	.35
No. 7.	"Boys' Favorite," regulation size, horsehide cover............................	.25
No. 7B.	"League Junior," slightly under regulation size, horsehide cover..............	.25
No. 10.	"High Flyer," a very lively ball....	.25
No. 6.	"Victor" Ball, regulation size.......	.20
No. 14.	"Boys' Amateur" Ball, little under regulation size..............................	.15

(All of the above in separate box and sealed.)

No. 8.	"Eureka" Ball, nearly regulation size...	.10
No. 9B.	"Boys' Lively" Ball, high bounder..	.10
No. 13.	"Rocket" Ball, the best made......	.05
No. 15.	"Dandy" Ball, two-piece cover......	.05
No. 16.	"Boss" Ball, four-piece cover........	.05

NEW YORK   **A. G. SPALDING & BROS.**   CHICAGO

Spalding's Trade=Mark Bats.

No. **A1.** League Model, made of finest selected timber, oil finish, and in various models. Each bat in separate bag. Lengths, 32, 33, 34, 35 and 36 inches. Highest quality. Each..................................**75c.**

No. **3-0.** Spalding's Black End Wagon Tongue Ash Bat, League quality. Handle roughened by our patented process for better grip. Each, **50c.**

No. **OX.** Spalding's Black End "Axletree" Bat, finest straight grained ash, improved models....................................Each, **25c.**

No. 2X.

No. **2X.** Spalding's Black End "Antique" Finish Bat, extra quality ash...Each, **20c.**

No. **4.** Spalding's Black End Willow Bat, highly finished and polished and the strongest light wood bat made...................Each, **25c.**

Spalding's Trade=Mark Boys' Bats.

No. **3X.** Spalding Junior, extra quality ash; lengths, 30 and 32 inches. Each, **25c.**

No. **2XB.** Spalding's Black End Antique Bat, selected ash; length, 31 inches..Each, **10c.**

No. **10.** Spalding's Black End Boys' Ash Bat; length, 26 inches. Each, **5c.**

NEW YORK **A. G. SPALDING & BROS.** CHICAGO

Spalding's Masks.

Black Enameled Sun Protecting Mask.
Patented.

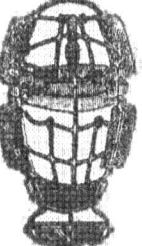

No. 0/4.

No. 4/0. This is not only the "Highest Quality" Mask made by us, but has also our patent sunshade which is formed by a piece of molded leather securely fastened to top, forming a perfect shade to the eye without obstructing the view or materially increasing the weight of the mask. Made of best soft annealed steel wire, extra heavy and black enameled, thus further preventing the reflection of light. The mask throughout is constructed of the very best material and has been highly endorsed by the leading catchers.................Each, **$5.00**

Spalding's Black Enameled Masks.

No. 3/0.

No. 3/0. Our Patent Neck Protecting Mask has an extension at bottom giving absolute protection to the neck, without interfering in the least with the movements of the head. The wire is of best annealed steel, is extra heavy and covered with black enamel to prevent the reflection of light. The padding is filled with goat hair and faced with finest imported dogskin, which, being impervious to perspiration, always remains soft and pleasant to the face......Each, **$4.00**

No. 2/0. Special League Mask, made of extra heavy and best soft annealed steel wire, black enameled, the padding filled with goat hair and covered with finest imported dogskin.....................Each, **$3.00**

No. 0X.

No. 0/X. Regulation League Mask, made of heavy soft annealed steel wire, black enameled, the padding well stuffed and faced with specially tanned horsehide. Warranted first-class and reliable in every particular. Each, **$2.50**

Regulation League Masks.

No. 0. This mask is of same style and quality as our No. 0X mask, except that the soft annealed steel wire is bright finished. The padding is well stuffed and faced with specially tanned horsehide..Each, **$2.00**

Spalding's Amateur Masks.

No. 0.

No. A. Spalding's Amateur Mask, made in same size and general style as our League masks, but of lighter soft annealed steel wire, well padded, strongly constructed and warranted perfectly safe...Each, **$1.50**

No. B. Spalding's Amateur Boys' Mask, made in same style and quality as our No. A mask, only smaller in size, for boys.........................Each, **$1.00**

No. L. Spalding's Men's Mask, heavy wire, well padded..............................Each, **$1.00**

No. C. Spalding's Youths' Masks, heavy wire and well padded, without head or chin piece......Each, **75c.**

No. D. Spalding's Youths' Masks, light wire and padded, without head or chin piece.........Each, **50c.**

No. C.

No. E. Spalding's Boys' Masks, light wire and padded, without head or chin piece..............Each, **25c.**

NEW YORK   **A. G. SPALDING & BROS.**   CHICAGO

Spalding's Catchers' Mits.

All of our Mits are furnished for either the Right or Left Hand. The Left Hand Mit always sent unless otherwise ordered. **No Throwing Glove** furnished with any of our Mits.

No. 7/0.

No. **7/0.** Baseman's Mit. This Mit, bearing the Trade-Mark of our "Highest Quality" goods, is sufficient guarantee that it is the most perfect glove in all its details that our past experience enables us to produce. The leather is of the finest quality, specially tanned for that purpose, the padding and workmanship of the very best, and the additional feature of lace back make it—as we intend it shall be—the "PERFECTION" of Catchers' Mits. Made in Rights and Lefts..................................Each, **$7.50**

No. **5/0.** Spalding's League Mit is made throughout of specially tanned and selected buckskin, making it an extra strong and durable mit, at the same time being very soft and pliable. It has our patent Lace Back and heavily padded. Made in Rights and Lefts. Each, **$5.00**

No. 0X.

No. **O.** The Spalding Mit, face, sides and fingerpiece are made of velvet tanned deerskin, and the back of selected asbestos buck, making an exceedingly easy-fitting and durable mit. It has our patent Lace Back and well padded. Made in Rights and Lefts......Each, **$2.50**

No. **OX.** Spalding's "Decker Patent" Mit is made exactly the same as our No. 0 Mit, soft tanned deerskin, with the addition of a heavy piece of sole leather on back for extra protection to the hand and fingers, as shown in cut. It has as well the patent Lace Back, and is extremely well padded. Made in Rights and Lefts..........................Each, **$3.00**

No. A.

No. **A.** Spalding's Amateur Mit is made of extra quality asbestos buck, perspiration proof and extremely tough and durable. It has our patent Lace Back, reinforced at thumb and well made and padded. Made in Rights and Lefts. Each, **$2.00**

No. **3.** The Spalding Practice Mit is made of soft tanned leather, well finished throughout and substantially padded. Made in Rights and Lefts......................Each, **$1.00**

NEW YORK **A. G. SPALDING & BROS.** CHICAGO

Spalding's Boys' Catchers' Mits.

No. 2.

No. **OXB.** Spalding's "Decker Patent" Boys' League Mit, face, edge strip and finger-piece made of velvet tanned deerskin, very soft and perspiration proof. The heavy piece of sole leather on back affords extra protection to hand and fingers. It has the patent Lace Back and is extra well padded. Made in Rights and Lefts....Each, **$2.00**

No. **2.** Spalding's Boys' Mit, face and finger-piece of mit made of drab tanned buckskin, the back of lighter and the edge-strip of darker tanned leather. It has our patent Lace Back, well padded and finished and reinforced at thumb. Made in Rights and Lefts, and little larger in size than our regular Boys' Mits......Each, **$1.50**

No. **4.** Spalding's Boys' Mit is made of soft tanned suede leather. It is extremely well padded and nicely finished throughout. Made in Rights and Lefts......Each, **50c.**

No. 5.

No. **5.** Spalding's Boys' Mit, all leather, soft and durable. Well made throughout, heavily padded and superior to any Boys' Mit ever offered at the price......Each, **25c.**

No. **6.** Boys' Mit, leather face, canvas back, well padded......Each, **15c.**

No. **7.** Boys' Mit, all canvas......Each, **10c.**

Spalding's Basemen's Mit.

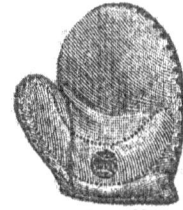

No. BX.

No. **BX.** 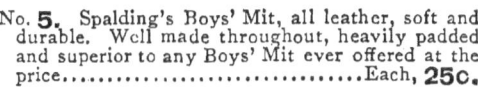 Basemen's Mit, made of fine selected and specially tanned calfskin, extremely well made throughout, and padded to meet the special requirements of a Baseman's Mit. It adapts itself nicely to the conformation of the hand without undue straining, and the addition of our patent Lace Back and "Highest Quality" Trade Mark is a sufficient guarantee of its quality and merits. Made in Rights and Lefts. Each, **$4.00**

Spalding's Basemen's and Infielders' Mits.

No. 3X.

No. **3X.** Mit, made of the very best and softest light tanned buckskin, the thumb and at wrist is extra well padded with the highest quality felt, making it a very safe and easy fitting mit, combined with strength and durability. The mit throughout is of the best workmanship, as indicated by our "Highest Quality" Trade Mark. Made in Rights and Lefts..**$3.00**

NEW YORK **A. G. SPALDING & BROS.** CHICAGO

Spalding's Basemen's and Infielders' Mits.

No. 4X.

No. 4X. Spalding's Basemen's and Infielders' Mit is made throughout of velvet tanned deerskin and edges nicely bound. It is well padded with fine felt and carefully sewed and finished. Made in Rights and Lefts................Each, **$2.00**

No. 5X. Spalding's Basemen's and Infielders' Mit, made of good quality leather, extra well padded and constructed throughout in a most substantial manner; an exceedingly good mit at a popular price. Made in Rights and Lefts...Each, **$1.00**

Boys' Basemen's and Infielders' Mits.

No. 6X.

No. 6X. Spalding's Boys' Basemen's Mit is made throughout of a good quality leather. It is well padded and makes a good and substantial mit for boys. Made in Rights and Lefts....Each, **50c.**

Infielders' Gloves.

No. 2X.  Infielders' Glove is made throughout of specially tanned buckskin, lined and correctly padded with finest felt. It fits the hand perfectly and our Trade Mark "Highest Quality" is a guarantee that the glove is perfect in all its details. Made in Rights and Lefts......................Each, **$3.00**

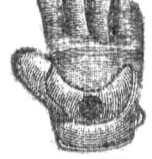

No. 2X.

No. X. Spalding's Infielders' Glove, made of selected leather, best felt padding and carefully put together. Made in Rights and Lefts. **$1.50**

No. 15. Spalding's Men's Infielders' Glove, all leather; a substantial glove at a popular price. Each, **$1.00**

No. 16. Spalding's Men's Infielders' Glove, all leather.................................Each, **50c.**

Boys' Infielders' Gloves.

No. X.

No. 13. Spalding's Boys' Infielders' Glove, selected leather, felt padded, quality and style as our No. X, in boys' sizes..................Each, **$1.00**

No. 17. Spalding's Boys' Infielders' Glove, all leather.................................Each, **25c.**

Pitchers' Toe Plates.

Worn on toe of shoe and made for left or right foot. A valuable assistant in pitching.

No. **A.** Aluminum Toe Plate..........Each, **50c.**
No. **B.** Brass Toe Plate............. " **25c.**

NEW YORK **A. G. SPALDING & BROS.** CHICAGO

Spalding's Bases.

Three Bases to a Set.   Per Set.

No. 0. League Club Bases, extra quality canvas and quilted, straps and spikes, complete... **$8.00**
No. 1. Canvas Bases, good quality canvas, not quilted, straps and spikes, complete............ **6.00**
No. 2. Canvas Bases, ordinary quality, with straps and spikes, complete................. **4.00**

Home Plates not included in above sets.

Spalding's Home Plates.   Each.

No. 1. Rubber Home Plate, complete.......... **$7.50**
No. 2. Marble Home Plate, best quality....... **2.00**

Spalding's Pitcher's Box Plates.

Made in accordance with National League regulations and of extra quality white rubber. Complete with pins.

No. 3. Spalding's Pitcher's Box Plates. Each, **$6.00**

Spalding's Club Bags.

Each.

No. 1. Canvas Club Bag, leather ends, for 24 bats............. **$5.00**
No. 2. Canvas Club Bag, leather ends, for 12 bats............. **4.00**

Individual Bags.

No. 02.   Each.

No. 01. Sole Leather Bag, for two bats..................... **$4.00**
No. 02. Heavy Canvas Bag, leather reinforce at both ends.... **1.50**
No. 03. Canvas Bag, leather reinforce at one end............ **1.00**

Score Books.

CLUB SIZES.   Each.

No. 4. Board cover, 30 games..... **$1.00**
No. 5. Cloth   "   60   " **1.75**
No. 6. Cloth   "   90   " **2.50**
No. 7. Cloth   " 120   " **3.00**

POCKET SIZES.

No. 1. Paper cover, 7 games...... **.10**
No. 2. Board   " 22   " ...... **.25**
No. 3. Cloth   " 46   " ...... **.50**

NEW YORK   **A. G. SPALDING & BROS.**   CHICAGO

Base Ball Caps.

Chicago, College, Boston and University styles.

Chicago Style.

Boston Style.

EACH.
No. 0 quality, best flannel.........$1.00
No. 1 quality, lighter flannel....... .85
No. 2 quality, good flannel......... .75
No. 3 quality, ordinary flannel.... .50
No. 4 quality, light flannel......... .40

Chicago Style, made in 0, 1st, 2d and 3d qualities.
College Style, made in all qualities.
Boston Style, made in 0, 1st, 2d and 3d qualities.
University Style, made in 0 and 1st qualities only.

Base Ball Belts.

Worsted Web Belts.

No. 3/0.

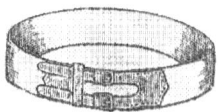
No. 2.

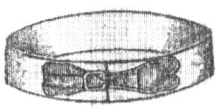
No. 47.

No. 3-0. Special League Belt, Worsted Web, 2½ inches wide, leather lined, large nickel-plated buckle.........Each, 75c.

No. 2-0. League Belt, Worsted Web, 2½ inches wide, large nickel-plated buckle,
Each, 50c.

No. 2. Worsted Web Belt, 2½ inches wide, double strap, leather covered buckles,
Each, 50c.

No. 47. Worsted Web Belt, 2½ inches wide, single strap, leather covered buckle,
Each, 50c.

Cotton Web Belts.

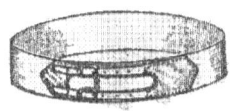
No. 23.

Colors: Red, Navy, White, Maroon and Stripes.

No. 23. Cotton Web Belt, 2½ inches wide, double strap, nickel buckles,
Each, 25c.

No. 4. Cotton Web Belt, 2½ inches, leather mounted, single strap and buckle,
Each, 20c.

Athletes' Uniform Bag.

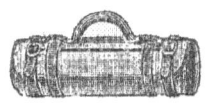

For carrying Base Ball and other uniforms. Made to roll and will not wrinkle or soil same. Separate compartments for shoes.
No. 1. Canvas............Each, $2.50
No. 2. Fine Bag Leather 5.00

NEW YORK   A. G. SPALDING & BROS.   CHICAGO

The Chicago, Milwaukee & St. Paul Railway

Runs Electric Lighted and Steam Heated Vestibuled Trains between Chicago, Milwaukee, St. Paul and Minneapolis, daily.

Through Parlor Cars on day trains between Chicago, St. Paul and Minneapolis.

Electric Lighted and Steam Heated Vestibuled Trains between Chicago and Omaha and Sioux City, daily.

Only two hours from Chicago to Milwaukee. Seven fast trains each way daily, with Parlor Car Service.

Solid trains between Chicago and principal points in Northern Wisconsin and the Peninsula of Michigan.

Through trains with Palace Sleeping Cars, Free Chair Cars and Coaches between Chicago and points in Iowa, Minnesota, Southern and Central Dakota.

The finest Dining Cars in the World.

The best Sleeping Cars. Electric Reading Lamps in Berths.

The best and latest type of Private Compartment Cars, Free Reclining Chair Cars, and buffet Library Smoking Cars.

6,155 miles of road in Illinois, Wisconsin, Northern Michigan, Iowa, Minnesota, Missouri, South Dakota and North Dakota.

Everything First-Class.

First-Class People patronize First-Class Lines.

Ticket Agents everywhere sell tickets over the Chicago, Milwaukee & St. Paul Railway.

Spalding's Inflated Body Protector.

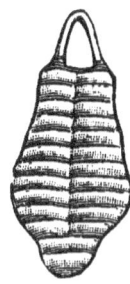

We are now the sole manufacturers of the Gray Patent Protectors, the only practical device for the protection of catchers and umpires. They are made of the best rubber, inflated with air, light and pliable, and do not interfere with the movements of the wearer under any conditions. When not in use the air may be let out and the Protector rolled in a very small space. We have added this season a Boys' Protector to the line, which is equal in quality to the other styles, only smaller in size.

Each.
No. 0. League Catchers' Protector.......... $10.00
No. 1. Amateur Catchers' Protector........ 6.00
No. 2. Boys' Catchers' Protector........... 5.00

No. 0.

Spalding's Special League Shoe Plates.

Patented.

Our Special League Plates are made of the finest tempered steel and the strength increased almost fourfold without increasing weight by our patent reinforced brace, which is formed, as shown in cut, by splitting the metal at each corner and depressing the centre, thus forming a brace at each side.

No. 0. Spalding's Special Hand Forged Steel Pair.
Toe Plates.................................$ .50
No. 2-0. Spalding's Special Hand Forged Steel
Heel Plates................................... .50
Per dozen pairs, $5.00

Professional Shoe Plates.

No. 1. Spalding's Professional Toe Plates, best
quality steel.................................. .25
No. 1H. Spalding's Professional Heel Plates,
best quality steel............................. .25
Per dozen pairs, $2.50

Amateur Shoe Plates.

No. 2. Spalding's Amateur Shoe Plates, fine
steel.. .10

Spalding's Umpire Indicator.

No. 0. Made of celluloid, exact size, 3x1½ inches. It is intended for keeping tally of balls and strikes. Endorsed and used by all League umpires..................Each, .50

No. 0.

Spalding's Scoring Tablet.

No. 1. A simple, convenient and accurate device for the record of runs and outs. It is made of celluloid and can be easily carried in any vest pocket........ .Each, .35

NEW YORK **A. G. SPALDING & BROS.** CHICAGO

The "Monon Nine"

Chicago, Lafayette, West Baden Springs,
Louisville, Indianapolis, Cincinnati,
Chillicothe, Washington
and Baltimore

THROUGH SLEEPERS DAILY

VIA

ONLY LINE TO THE FAMOUS
HEALTH RESORT

...West Baden Springs...

The Best Training Grounds in America

Big Double Deck One-Third Mile Bicycle
Track, Swimming Tank,
Gymnasium, etc.

FRANK J. REED, Gen. Pass. Agt.,
CHICAGO

CITY TICKET OFFICE, 232 SOUTH CLARK STREET

Spalding's Base Ball Shirts.

In Lace or Button Front.

		Each.
No. 0.	*Spalding* Shirt, any style.........	$5.50
No. 1.	The "University" Shirt, any style.....	4.50
No. 2.	"Interscholastic" Shirt, any style....	3.75
No. 3.	"Club Special" Shirt, any style.......	2.50
No. 4.	"Amateur Special" Shirt, any style...	1.85

Price includes Lettering on Shirts.

Spalding's Base Ball Pants.

In Tape or Elastic Bottom.

All Padded.   Pair.

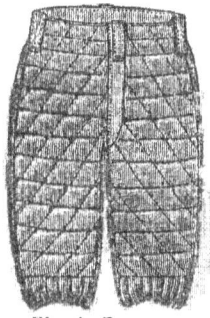

No. 0.	*Spalding* Pants..........	$6.00
No. 1.	"University" Pants.........	4.50
No. 2.	"Interscholastic" Pants.....	3.50
No. 3.	"Club Special" Pants........	2.50
No. 4.	"Amateur Special" Pants.....	1.75

Elastic Bottom.

Spalding's Base Ball Uniforms.

COMPLETE.

Including Shirt, Padded Pants, Cap, Belt and Stockings.

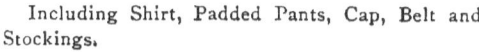

No. 0.	*Spalding* Uniform............	$14.75
No. 1.	"University" Uniform..........	11.25
No. 2.	"Interscholastic" Uniform......	9.00
No. 3.	"Club Special" Uniform.	6.25
No. 4.	"Amateur Special" Uniform....	4.50

Our line of flannels for Base Ball Uniforms consists of the best qualities in their respective grades and the most desirable colors for Base Ball Uniforms. Each grade is kept up to the highest point of excellence and quality improved wherever possible every season. Owing to the heavy weight flannels used in our Nos. 0 and 1 Uniforms, we have found it desirable, after many years of experience, to use a little lighter weight material for the shirts; this makes them more comfortable, much cooler, and wear just as well as the heavier weight.

NEW YORK   **A. G. SPALDING & BROS.**   CHICAGO

THE REACH BALL

When *merit* is the *best*, it stands pre-eminently alone as

The Best

It keeps its shape
It gives satisfaction
It is guaranteed

MAKERS

A. J. REACH CO.
PHILADELPHIA, PA.

Supporters and Bandages

Spalding's Improved Morton Supporters

Morton Supporter.

Made of Canton flannel, lace front. Each supporter in separate box.

No. 1. Improved Morton....Each, **35c.**
No. 2. Elastic on sides and back, " **50c.**
No. 3. The Orange Universal.....**50c.**

Elastic Bandages

Elastic Bandage.

This bandage is light, porous and easily applied. The pressure can be applied wherever necessary and quickly secured by inserting end under last fold.

No. 25. Width 2½ inches, 5 yards long (stretched).................. Each, **75c.**
No. 30. Width 3 inches, 5 yards long (stretched)..................Each, **$1.00**

Leather Wrist Supporter

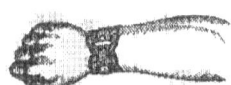
Wrist Supporter.

A perfect support and protection to the wrist. Invaluable to base ball, tennis and cricket players, or in any game where the strain is on the wrist.

No. 100. In Domestic Grain Leather— Tan, Orange or Black.......Each, **25c.**

The Hackey Ankle Supporter

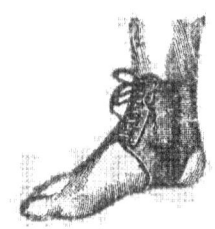
Hackey Ankle Supporter.

Patented May 24, 1887.

A. G. SPALDING & BROS., Sole Licensees.

Relieves pain immediately, cures a sprain in a short time, and prevents turning of the ankle. Make of fine, soft leather, and is worn over the stocking, lacing very tight in centre, loose at top and bottom. The shoe usually worn can be used.

No. H. Hackey Supporter...Pair, **$1.00**

Suspensories

Each.

No. 70. Non-elastic bands, knitted sack..... **$ .25**
No. 71. Non-elastic waist bands, full elastic buttock band, knitted sack................... **.35**
No. 72. Elastic Bands, fine English knitted sack.. **.50**
No. 73½. Elastic bands, all silk sack, warranted not to chafe....................... **.75**
No. 75. Elastic bands, fine Swiss bolting silk sack, satin top piece... **1.00**
No. 76. Silk elastic bands, finest Swiss bolting silk sack, satin trimmings.. **1.25**

Old Point Comfort Suspensories

Each.

No. 2. Elastic bands, adjusting buckles, lisle thread sack.....**$1.00**
No. 3. Elastic bands, adjusting buckles, satin trimmings, fine knitted silk sack................................... **1.25**
No. 4. Silk elastic bands, adjusting buckles, satin trimmings, fine knitted silk sack................................... **1.50**

NEW YORK A. G. SPALDING & BROS. CHICAGO

Sporting Life

SIXTEENTH YEAR OF ISSUE

5 CENTS **5 CENTS**

Contains everything worth knowing about
BASEBALL, CYCLING GUNS and GUNNING
Is read by men all over the United States every Saturday

SAMPLE COPIES
Sent free by mail on application

Annual Subscription, $2.00   Half-Yearly Subscription, $1.25

SPORTING LIFE PUBLISHING CO.
34 SOUTH THIRD ST.   PHILADELPHIA, PA.

Elastic Bandages

Shoulder.

Shoulder Cap Bandage

In ordering, give circumference around arm and chest separately.

No. 1.   Cotton thread........Each, $3.50
No. 1A.   Silk thread........... "   5.00

Elbow.

Elbow Bandage

In ordering, give circumference above and below elbow, and state whether intended for light or strong pressure.

No. 2.   Cotton thread........Each, $1.50
No. 2A.   Silk thread........... "   2.00

Knee.

Knee Cap Bandage

In ordering, give circumference below knee, at knee, and just above knee, and state if light or strong pressure is desired.

No. 4.   Cotton thread........Each, $1.50
No. 4A.   Silk thread........... "   2.00

Ankle.

Ankle Bandage

In ordering, give circumference around ankle and over instep and state if light or strong pressure is desired.

No. 5.   Cotton thread........Each, $1.50
No. 5A.   Silk thread........... "   2.00

Wrist.

Wrist Bandages

In ordering, give circumference around smallest part of wrist, and state whether for light or strong pressure.

No. 6.   Cotton thread........Each, $ .75
No. 6A.   Silk thread........... "   1.00

NEW YORK **A. G. SPALDING & BROS.** CHICAGO

...The...
Sporting News

C. C. SPINK, Publisher

THE BASE BALL PAPER OF THE WORLD ♣♣♣♣

INVALUABLE to players, indispensable to managers, and intensely interesting to enthusiasts in all parts of the country. Its columns teem with the live news of the game, collected by a carefully selected corps of over 500 Correspondents, and attractively presented. All professional leagues and associations receive due recognition. Departments containing contributions direct from the **Magnates, Managers** and **Players** of the game enliven THE SPORTING NEWS during the off season. The standard of excellence is so well maintained at all times that there is never a dull issue, and the casual reader invariably becomes a regular subscriber.

* * *

SUBSCRIPTION PRICE:
One year, $2.00; Six months, $1.00; Single Copies, 5 cents.

Sample copies mailed free on application. Send in your address on a postal card and receive a copy by return mail.

* * *

The Sporting News

Broadway and Olive St.   ST. LOUIS, MO.

SPALDING'S
BASE BALL SHOES.

No. 2/0.

Our "Highest Quality" Base Ball Shoe is hand-made throughout, and of specially selected kangaroo leather. Extreme care will be taken in their general construction, and no pains or expense will be spared in making this shoe not only of the very highest in quality but a perfect shoe in every detail. The plates, made exclusively for this shoe, are of the finest hand-forged steel, and firmly riveted to heel and sole.

No. **2/0.** Per Pair, **$7.50.**

SPRINTING...

Same quality as our No. 2/0 shoe, but built on our famous running shoe last. Weigh about 18 ounces to the pair, and made with extra care throughout.

No. **30 S.** Per Pair, **$10.00.**

CLUB SPECIAL...

Made of carefully selected satin calfskin, machine sewed, very substantially constructed and a first-class shoe in every particular. Steel plates riveted to heel and sole.

No. **3** Per Pair, **$5.00.**

AMATEUR SPECIAL...

Made of good quality calfskin, machine sewed. A serviceable and durable shoe and one we can specially recommend. Plates riveted to heel and sole.

No. **35.** Per Pair, **$3.50.**

COMPLETE CATALOGUE OF ALL SPORTS FREE.

A. G. SPALDING & BROS.,
New York and Chicago.

Good Sport

IN KANSAS
PRAIRIE CHICKENS, quail, jack-rabbits and ducks abound. The Arkansas Valley and its tributaries afford most satisfactory hunting grounds.

IN COLORADO
HERE the fishing rod should be unpacked. Enough trout to keep your rod and line busy may be found in hundreds of mountain streams, while away from the railroad larger game exists.

IN INDIAN TERRITORY
WILD TURKEYS, prairie chickens, quails and deer are the favorite game in Oklahoma and Indian Territory. A party of three to ten, with guide, will find great sport thirty miles or so from railroad lines.

IN TEXAS
ANYWHERE on the Gulf Coast several days can be enjoyably spent angling for the deep-sea fish that swarm the Gulf waters. Wild fowl are also prevalent in the marshes.

IN NEW MEXICO
UP in the mountains are clear streams where the possible catch of trout may exceed your biggest story—which is saying a good deal. Enough wild game in the wooded wilderness to satisfy the most ardent hunter.

Address W. J. BLACK, G. P. A., A., T. & S. F. Ry., Topeka, Kan., or C. A. HIGGINS, A. G. P. A., Chicago, for detailed information respecting any one or more of the above localities.

All Along the Santa Fe Route

Spalding's Home Library

Published Monthly and devoted to all Games and Pastimes of Interest to the Home Circle.

PER COPY, 10 CENTS.

No. 1. CHESS.	No. 13. LOTO.	No. 23. CHILDREN'S GAMES.
No. 2. WHIST.	No. 14. HEARTS.	
No. 3. DOMINOES and DICE.	No. 15. REVERSI.	No. 24. GROUP OF CARD GAMES.
No. 4. POKER.	No. 16. PIQUET.	
No. 5. BACKGAMMON.	No. 17. GO-BANG.	No. 25. DRAWING ROOM GAMES.
	No. 18. GAMES OF PATIENCE.	No. 26. GROUP OF CARD GAMES.
No. 6. EUCHRE.	No. 19. CHILDREN'S GAMES.	
No. 7. BILLIARDS.		No. 27. CHILDREN'S GAMES.
No. 8. ECARTE.	No. 20. CRIBBAGE.	
No. 9. CHECKERS.	No. 21. DRAWING ROOM GAMES.	No. 28. SKAT.
No.10. BEZIQUE.		No. 29. DRAWING ROOM GAMES.
No.11. POOL.	No. 22. GROUP OF CARD GAMES.	
No.12. PINOCHLE.		No. 30. BACCARAT.

BOOKS EVERY BOY SHOULD READ.

BASE BALL, by Walter Camp. Specially adapted for colleges and preparatory schools. Interesting chapters are devoted to the batter, catcher, pitcher, basemen, shortstop, outfielders; also chapters on batting and baserunning. Fully illustrated.

Price, 10c. postpaid.

PRACTICAL BALL PLAYING, by Arthur A. Irwin. Containing interesting chapters on individual and team batting; essentials of a good batsman, position, bunting, fielding, etc.; with instructive hints to the pitcher, catcher, basemen, shortstop and fielders. Fully illustrated.   Price, 10c. postpaid.

TECHNICAL TERMS OF BASE BALL, by Henry Chadwick, editor of Spalding's Base Ball Guide. Gives definitions of all the terms used on the ball field.

Price, 10c. postpaid.

American Sports Publishing Co. 241 Broadway New York.

SPALDING'S BASE BALL SCORE BOOKS.

No.	CLUB SIZES.			Each.	No.	POCKET SIZES.			Each.
4.	Board Cover, 80 games,			$1.00	1.	Paper Cover, 7 games,			10c.
5.	Cloth	"	60	"	1.75	2.	Board	"	22	"	25c.
6.	"	"	90	"	2.50	3.	"	"	46	"	50c.
7.	"	"	120	"	3.00		Score Cards, per doz.,			25c.

New York.   A. G. SPALDING & BROS.   Chicago.

www.ingramcontent.com/pod-product-compliance
Lightning Source LLC
Chambersburg PA
CBHW031944290426
44108CB00011B/673